Case Studies

Classroom Observations

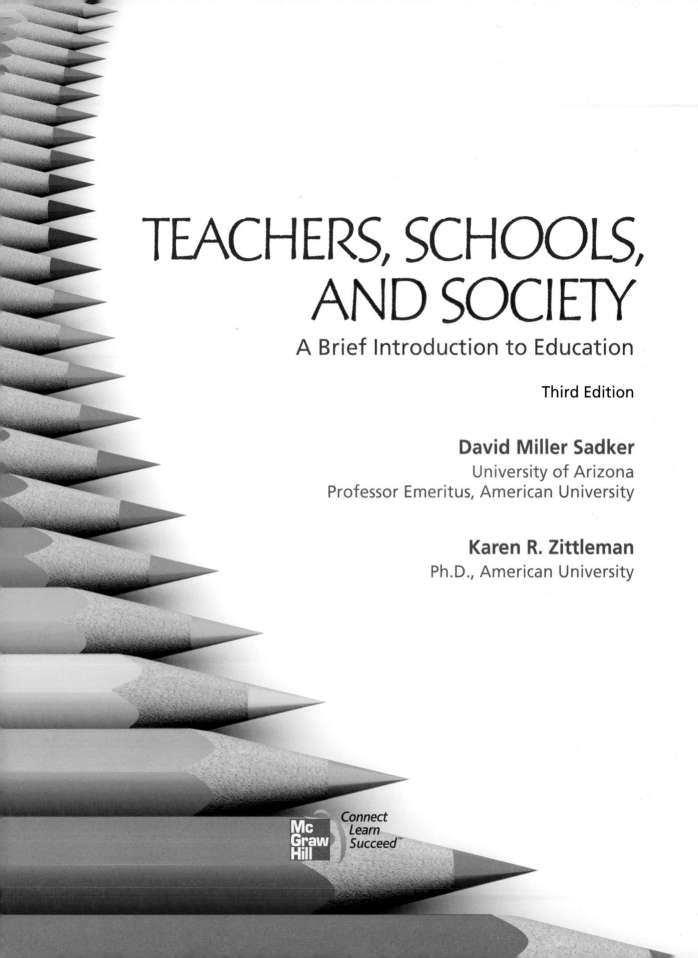

TEACHERS, SCHOOLS, AND SOCIETY

A Brief Introduction to Education

Third Edition

David Miller Sadker
University of Arizona
Professor Emeritus, American University

Karen R. Zittleman
Ph.D., American University

McGraw Hill

Connect
Learn
Succeed™

The McGraw-Hill Companies

Connect
Learn
Succeed™

Published by McGraw-Hill, an imprint of The McGraw-Hill Companies, Inc., 1221 Avenue of the Americas, New York, NY 10020. Copyright © 2012, 2009, 2007. All rights reserved. No part of this publication may be reproduced or distributed in any form or by any means, or stored in a database or retrieval system, without the prior written consent of The McGraw-Hill Companies, Inc., including, but not limited to, in any network or other electronic storage or transmission, or broadcast for distance learning.

This book is printed on acid-free paper.

3 4 5 6 7 8 9 0 RJE/RJE 1 0 9 8 7 6 5 4 3

ISBN: 978-0-07-802433-7
MHID: 0-07-802433-1

Sponsoring Editor: *Allison McNamara*
Executive Marketing Manager: *Julia Flohr Larkin*
Developmental Editor: *Maureen Spada*
Production Editor: *Ruth Sakata Corley*
Production Service: *Matrix Productions Inc.*
Text and Cover Designer: *Laurie Entringer*
Photo Research: *Robin Samper*
Buyer: *Louis Swaim*
Media Project Manager: *Jennifer Barrick*
Composition: *10/12 Melior by Laserwords*
Printing: *45# New Era Matte Plus, R. R. Donnelley & Sons/Jefferson City, MO*
Vice President Editorial: *Michael Ryan*
Publisher: *Michael Sugarman*
Editorial Director: *William Glass*
Senior Director of Development: *Dawn Groundwater*

Cover: © 3d world; fotolia

Credits: The credits section for this book begins on page C-1 and is considered an extension of the copyright page.

Library of Congress Cataloging-in-Publication Data

Sadker, David Miller, 1942–
    Teachers schools and society: a brief introduction to education / David M. Sadker, Karen R. Zittleman. — 3rd ed.
        p. cm.
    ISBN 978-0-07-802433-7 (pbk.) — ISBN 978-0-07-737837-0 ()
    1. Teaching. 2. Education—Study and teaching—United States. 3. Teachers—Training of—United States. I. Zittleman, Karen R. II. Title.
    LB1775.2S229 2011
    370.973—dc23

                                                                    2011035781

The Internet addresses listed in the text were accurate at the time of publication. The inclusion of a website does not indicate an endorsement by the authors or McGraw-Hill, and McGraw-Hill does not guarantee the accuracy of the information presented at these sites.

www.mhhe.com

About the Authors & Dedication

To those who help and inspire others

DAVID SADKER

Dr. Sadker is professor emeritus at American University (Washington, DC) and now teaches and writes in Tucson, Arizona. Along with his late wife Myra Sadker, he gained a national reputation for work in confronting gender bias and sexual harassment. The Sadkers' book, *Failing at Fairness: How Our Schools Cheat Girls,* was published by Charles Scribner in 1994 and, with Karen Zittleman, was updated in 2009, retitled *Still Failing at Fairness: How Gender Bias Cheats Girls and Boys and What We Can Do About It.* David Sadker co-edited *Gender in the Classroom: Foundations, Skills, Methods and Strategies Across the Curriculum* (Lawrence Erlbaum, 2007) as well as this textbook. David Sadker has directed more than a dozen federal education grants, and has written seven books and more than seventy-five articles in journals such as *Phi Delta Kappan, Harvard Educational Review,* and *Psychology Today.* The Sadkers' work has been reported in hundreds of newspapers and magazines, including *USA Today, USA Weekend, Parade Magazine, Business Week, The Washington Post, The London Times, The New York Times, Time,* and *Newsweek.* The Sadkers appeared on local and national television and radio shows such as *The Today Show, Good Morning America, The Oprah Winfrey Show,* Phil Donahue's *The Human Animal,* National Public Radio's *All Things Considered,* and *Dateline: NBC* with Jane Pauley. The American Educational Research Association (AERA) honored the Sadkers for the best review of research published in the United States in 1991, for their professional service in 1995, and for "scholarship, activism, and community building on behalf of women and education" in 2004. The American Association of University Women awarded the Sadkers their Eleanor Roosevelt Award in 1995, and the American Association of Colleges of Teacher Education recognized their work with the Gender Architect Award in 2001. David Sadker has received two honorary doctorates and was selected as a Torchbearer by the U.S. Olympic Committee in 2002. He facilitates *Courage and Renewal* retreats and is excited about exploring new frontiers of teaching.

KAREN R. ZITTLEMAN

Dr. Zittleman attended the University of Wisconsin for her bachelor's degree, and American University for her master's degree and doctorate. She has taught in elementary and middle schools and at American University, and has been a virtual teacher for several courses offered online through the Women's Educational Equity Act. Her articles about gender, Title IX, and teacher education appear in the *Journal of Teacher Education, Educational Leadership, Phi Delta Kappan, Principal,* and other professional journals. Dr. Zittleman is the co-author of *Still Failing at Fairness* (2009). The book documents gender bias against girls and boys in school. She is a contributing author to *Gender in the Classroom: Foundations, Skills, Methods and Strategies Across the Curriculum* and has created several equity websites. Karen Zittleman is also the author of *Making Public Schools Great for Every Girl and Boy,* an instructional guide on promoting equity in math and science instruction published by the National Educational Association, and educational film guides for *A Hero for Daisy* and *Apple Pie: Raising Champions.* She is Foundation Manager for the Myra Sadker Foundation. Her research interests have focused on educational equity, foundations of education, teacher preparation, and contemplative practices in education. Dr. Zittleman teaches and writes in Tucson, Arizona.

Brief Table of Contents

www.mhhe.com/
sadkerbrief3e   **ONLINE APPENDICES**

Table of Contents

Preface

If you think that *Teachers, Schools, and Society: A Brief Introduction to Education* was written to introduce you to the world of teaching, you are only half right. This book also reflects our excitement about a life in the classroom and is intended to spark your own fascination about working with children. We wrote this book to share with you the joys and the challenges we feel about teaching, as well as the importance of fairness and justice in school and society. With this third edition, our goals are unchanged. We work hard to provide you with information that is both current and concise, and we work even harder to create an engaging book—one that will give you a sense of the wonderful possibilities found in a career in the classroom.

The primary intent of *Teachers, Schools, and Society: A Brief Introduction to Education* is to provide a broad yet precise exposure to the realities of teaching and the role of education in our society. The text will help you answer important questions such as: Do I want to become a teacher? How do I become the best teacher possible? What should a professional in the field of education know? How are schools and teaching changing? To help you answer those questions, we offer a panoramic, diverse, and (we hope) stimulating view of education.

The text views education from several vantage points. In Part I, *Teachers and Students,* we present the world of schools, teachers, and students from the teacher's side of the desk. Part II, *Foundations,* examines the broad forces—historical, philosophical, financial and legal—that shape the underpinning of our educational system. In Part III, *Schools and Classrooms,* we explore the purposes of schools, daily life in and beyond school, and the obvious, and not so obvious, curriculum taught in school. In this last section, we also provide an overview and analysis of the reform movement and the many curricular changes now so much a part of America's schools. We conclude the text with a variety of effective teaching strategies and practical suggestions to make your first year in the classroom a success.

The third edition of Sadker/Zittleman's brief *Teachers, Schools, and Society* retains and builds upon the hallmark characteristics that made the second edition a best seller.

- **Brevity of a Streamlined Introduction to Education.** The eleven essential chapters are organized for balanced coverage of foundational, curricular, and professional topics; the brief edition provides maximum teaching flexibility while assuring coverage of crucial content areas.

- **Contemporary Focus.** Current issues and topics are presented in a balanced and exciting reading style. A few of the contemporary topics in this edition include cyberbullying, poverty, obesity, role of business in schools, and reform. *Contemporary Issues* provides a chapter focus on a specific issue in today's schools, from the notion of merit pay to the reintroduction of single-sex public schools. Students are also given practical, current instructional strategies in the new feature, *Teaching Tips.* We view this text as a living and changing narrative of today's educational issues.

- **Social Justice and Equity.** The text stresses the importance of fairness and justice in school and society, focuses on the most crucial topic areas, and integrates the most current issues in education.

  - **Focus on Fairness:** Issues of social justice and equity are at the core of this text. These pages examine the racial, economic, social, and gender issues that too often erect barriers to equal opportunity.

  - **Diverse Voices and Experiences:** Issues of multicultural education and diversity in learning are treated as fundamental and are infused from the very first chapter ("The Teaching Profession and

You") to the very last one ("Becoming an Effective Teacher"). The authors argue that only through recognizing and appreciating diversity can teaching be both effective and joyful.

Classroom Observation

5. High School Students Discuss Issues They Face as Immigrants

A growing number of students in today's schools are immigrants. In this observation, you will hear several high school students talk about their experiences in school as immigrants. You will also hear a teacher who works with them discuss her role in helping them to adapt to their new community and achieve academic and social success.

Classroom Observation videos are available on the CD Reader and at the Online Learning Center.

www.mhhe.com/sadker/brief3e

- **Standards and Testing.** Important legislation and policies are thoroughly addressed, including the arrival of national standards, the proponents and critics of the testing culture, and the new federal programs of the Obama administration. There is also a section analyzing the problems of high-stakes testing and discussing some of the alternatives to high-stakes testing.

- **Connections to INTASC Principles and PRAXIS Content.** Online INTASC Reflective Activities and Your Portfolio (RAPs) activities offer readers ways to apply text content and develop portfolio artifacts that demonstrate their understanding of INTASC principles. Study tools to aid preparation for exams of text material as well as the *PRAXIS* are available in the text and on the Online Learning Center.

- **Research Updated and Expanded to Reflect Education in America Today.** As with previous editions, the goal of the third edition is to expose you to the issues facing education today; to ensure its currency, hundreds of new references have been added. This new edition also provides updated discussions of school reform, national standards, classroom management, poverty, eating disorders and obesity, sex education, social networking, and special education. Readers will also note the revised discussions of teachers' liability in the classroom, cyberbullying, technology, and the Obama administration's educational initiatives.

- **The Reader CD-ROM.** Inside every new copy of the text is a free book. Well, we like to think of it as a free book. We call it *The Reader,* and it is published on a CD-ROM. *The Reader* offers greater depth on topics, different points of view, case studies, and video clips that allow you to apply your skills and concepts in

Obesity and Eating Disorders

What does more than 50 hours a week watching television, playing video and computer games, and eating junk food get you? Pounds, lots of extra pounds. Nine million American children ages 6 to 19—one in three—are overweight or obese. (See Figure 4.6). The trends start early: Nearly one in five 4-year-olds is obese. At special risk are children from low socioeconomic backgrounds, as well as Hispanic, black, and Native American youth whose obesity rates are often 50 percent greater than those of their peers. The consequences of obesity are staggering. Besides potential health problems such as diabetes, arthritis, and heart disease, overweight children are more likely to have low self-esteem and be absent from school. Overweight students, particularly girls, are more likely to engage in sexual activity earlier and without protection and are less likely to attend college.[81]

Schools often make the problem worse. Faced with pressures to improve test scores, school leaders often try to increase academic classroom time by eliminating recess or physical education (despite evidence showing that exercise improves academic performance). Only 4 percent of elementary schools, 8 percent of middle schools, and 2 percent of high schools provide daily physical education.[82] School meals fail, too. The National School Lunch Program, signed into law by President Truman in 1946, was designed to feed hungry

the text to specific situations. *The Reader* includes 48 readings (more than half are new in this third edition), 23 case studies, and 17 classroom videos. Each chapter ends with a page listing corresponding readings, case studies, and videos from *The Reader*.

The readings offer greater depth and a range of viewpoints on a variety of educational topics. The case studies are focused on real-life, practical problems facing a teacher. They bring a reality test to the ideas in the text. You can explore them individually, in small groups, or in class discussions. The classroom observation videos share short clips of classrooms, teachers, and students in action. They are designed to provide you with additional views of what teaching looks like. Just like the readings and the case studies, the classroom videos include analysis questions to help you explore the issues raised. To assist adopters, the inside cover of the text includes a complete table of contents for the Reader CD. We hope you enjoy and grow from the opinions and ideas that emerge from *The Reader*.

New in the Third Edition

In response to users' feedback, we're adding two new-boxed features: one titled **A Closer Look** and the other **Teaching Tips.** *A Closer Look* offers current research on school and classroom life. It includes topics such as the Development *of American Schools, Education*

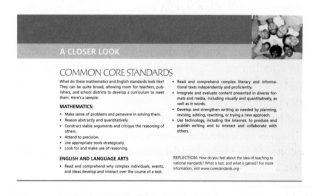

A CLOSER LOOK

COMMON CORE STANDARDS

What do these mathematics and English standards look like? They can be quite broad, allowing room for teachers, publishers, and school districts to develop a curriculum to meet them. Here's a sample:

MATHEMATICS:
- Make sense of problems and persevere in solving them.
- Reason abstractly and quantitatively.
- Construct viable arguments and critique the reasoning of others.
- Attend to precision.
- Use appropriate tools strategically.
- Look for and make use of reasoning.

ENGLISH AND LANGUAGE ARTS
- Read and comprehend why complex individuals, events, and ideas develop and interact over the course of a text.

- Read and comprehend complex literary and informational texts independently and proficiently.
- Integrate and evaluate content presented in diverse formats and media, including visually and quantitatively, as well as in words.
- Develop and strengthen writing as needed by planning, revising, editing, rewriting, or trying a new approach.
- Use technology, including the Internet, to produce and publish writing and to interact and collaborate with others.

REFLECTION: How do you feel about the idea of teaching to national standards? What is lost, and what is gained? For more information, visit www.corestandards.org

Milestones, Teachers' and Students' Rights, and *How Private is Your Personal Life? Teaching Tips* provide practical teaching ideas for the reader's first year in the classroom. A few examples of *Teaching Tips* boxes are *Social Networking Guidelines, Finance Lessons,* and *Elusive History.*

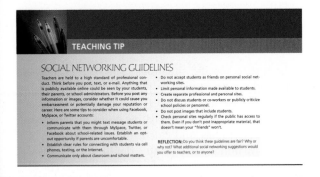

Chapter by Chapter Changes

Chapter 1: The Teaching Profession and You. The introduction about teaching becomes more personal (and positive), asking the reader to consider his/her personal and professional needs and desires regarding a career in the classroom. Is merit pay or pay-for-performance a good idea? We expand our discussion of the pros and cons of this controversial approach. We've also expanded the discussion of paths to alternative teacher certification and included a section detailing practical steps students can take starting in this course on the road to becoming a teacher.

Chapter 2: Different Ways of Learning. There is now new research on whether gender is—or is not—a learning style, as well as fresh research on male-female brain differences. Howard Gardner's Five New Minds theory is also explored. The material on special education, gifted and talented, and the Individuals with Disabilities Education Act (IDEA) has been updated.

Chapter 3: Teaching Your Diverse Students. The Invisible Knapsack concept advanced by Peggy McIntosh is now included, as well as additional coverage of multiracial children, gay, lesbian, bisexual, and transgender students, and updated demographics, statistics, figures, and charts.

Chapter 4: Student Life in School and at Home. This chapter has updated research and statistics throughout, including the sections on tracking, cyberbullying, family patterns, poverty, and obesity/eating disorders.

There is a revision of the elementary and middle school peer groups section, titled "The Gendered World of Elementary and Middle School."

Chapter 5: The Multicultural History of American Education. There is now an updated discussion on the resegregation of the nation's students, including the U.S. Supreme Court ruling that struck down plans for desegregation in Seattle and Louisville. A new Teaching Tip discusses the use of primary sources, and updated research is included on the Cherokee syllabary.

Chapter 6: Philosophy of Education. A new Teaching Tip discusses writing your philosophy statement.

Chapter 7: Financing and Governing America's Schools. We've included a new section question and new section, "Schools, Children, and Commercialism" which explores the role of business in schools. We have updated and shortened the section on adequacy in educational finance and updated the section on the federal role in education.

Chapter 8: School Law and Ethics. We've updated the section on ethical issues in the classroom, including cheating, texting, and social networking, and offer some suggestions for teachers to avoid liability in the classroom.

Chapter 9: Reforming America's Schools. This revised title reflects some of the new content in this chapter. One focus in this chapter is the central role of trust in school reform. We've expanded the discussion on the growth of choice, especially charter schools and the Race to the Top. Green schools, the "value added" concept, and Geoffrey Canada and the Harlem Children's Zone are also now included.

Chapter 10: Curriculum, Standards, and Testing. There is a fresh discussion of the Common Core State Standards, recently adopted by 48 states, as well as the recent Texas Board of Education textbook controversy. There is also a discussion of the legacy of No Child Left Behind and an updated section on technology, including hybrid courses.

Chapter 11: Becoming an Effective Teacher. We have added a section on the first year, including discussions on mentors, induction, and specific steps to make the first year teaching meaningful and effective. The chapter now includes an expanded section on classroom management, differentiated instruction, and reflective teaching.

Student Resources

The student supplements package is designed to allow students to extend their learning.

The *Teachers, Schools, and Society* Reader

The reader includes 48 contemporary, thought-provoking readings as well as historically significant excerpts, each related to specific chapter content. Each reading includes an introduction and analysis questions. In addition, 23 case studies based on actual school events help students confront significant and relevant educational questions and dilemmas. Finally, the Reader includes 17 Classroom Observation Video Clips designed to allow students to see in action the issues they are reading about. For a listing of the readings, cases, studies, and classroom observations, see the inside front cover of the book. *The Reader is packaged for free with new copies of the text or can be purchased separately.*

Online Learning Center—Study Guide and Interactive Resources

The Student Online Learning Center contains an online student Study Guide (including quizzes and study tools), Interactive Exercises (the *What Do You Think?* poll, *Interactive Activities, You Be the Judge* questions, and *Web-tivities,* questions referenced in the text), and additional resources such as Web Links, the online appendices, and *RAP* forms.

Teaching Portfolios

Teaching Portfolios is a practical guide to creating a portfolio. In additional to concise information about how to create a portfolio and what goes into one, the book includes a wealth of sample artifacts as well as discussion about creating artifacts to reflect your classroom management skills and ability to differentiate instruction. *Teaching Portfolios* can be packaged with *Teachers, Schools, and Society* for free. Contact your sales representative to add this resource to your students' text package.

Resources to Prepare for the Praxis™ Exam

An overview of the Praxis™ Exam is presented in the book's appendix.

For further study, *McGraw-Hill's Praxis I & II Exam* can be packaged with the text at a reduced price. Contact your sales representative for more information.

Acknowledgments

We are grateful for the contributions and insights of our colleagues. Professor John White of the University of North Florida reviewed and offered useful suggestions concerning the treatment of class and poverty in this edition. Professor Karen Arnold at Boston College shared some of her recent research on poverty and college students, and we are appreciative. Professor Ian Macgillivray of James Madison University provided materials and insights for the discussion of gay, lesbian, bisexual, and transgendered students. We extend a special thanks to Dr. Carl Grant, University of Wisconsin, and Louise Wilkinson. Their insightful critiques and recommendations made Chapter 3, "Teaching Your Diverse Students" a stronger, more relevant chapter.

Joe Kelly did a great job summarizing the many new readings in *The Reader,* as well as creating new questions. Dan Otter used his years of practical school experience to develop the online INTASC Reflective Activities and Your Portfolio (*RAPs*). Sean Miller of Earth Day Network offered valuable insights and suggestions concerning green schools. Ray Rose helped us update the sections describing technology in today's schools. We want to extend our thanks to our *Courage to Teach* contributors, Diane Petteway and Eric Baylin, and to all the teachers and students who shared their insights with us. We greatly appreciate the hard work and assistance of Alfred Longo from Ocean County College, Scott T. Grubbs from Valdosta State College, and Nicole Reiber from Coastal Carolina Community College in preparing supplements for this edition. S. J. especially was a constant source of inspiration and insight, and reminded us every day that this book is ultimately about touching the lives of children.

Teachers, Schools, and Society was originally inspired by a wonderful woman and bright academic star—Myra Pollack Sadker. Myra was always a major force behind providing a student-friendly introduction to teaching. In March 1995, Myra died undergoing treatment for breast cancer. Yet her insights and passion for teaching still guide our efforts: her heart and mind shine through the book. To learn more about Myra and her work, visit the Myra Sadker Foundation at www.sadker.org.

Our editor, Maureen Spada, has done an amazing job. Maureen is a skilled, hardworking, and sensitive editor, and we are lucky to have her services on the text, and her support and sensitivity beyond the book. Senior Sponsoring Editor Allison McNamara is a force of nature and a great supporter. She works with us to sort out changes in content and the features, and we owe her a great debt of gratitude. We appreciate the efforts, insights and support of Dawn Groundwater, the Director of Development. Sarah Kiefer and Zachary Norton are Editorial Coordinators on this project, and they both have worked on coordinating manuscript and information as it passes from one set of hands to another. Our thanks to Aaron Downey, our production manager, for skillfully and smoothly moving the manuscript into a published book. The McGraw-Hill team continually makes us feel that this text could not have better colleagues and friends, and we are proud to have them as our publishers.

We also thank the following reviewers of *Teachers, Schools, and Society* for generously sharing with us their experiences in teaching the book:

Susan Sheffield, Manatee Community College

Brian K. Leavell, Texas Woman's University

Theresa Stahler, Kutztown University

Beth Marks, Kennesaw State University

Dixie Denton, Ball State University

Pamela Chibucos, Owens Community College

Alfred Longo, Ocean County College

Nicole Reiber, Coastal Carolina Community College

Jeremy Wendt, Tennessee Tech University

Deron Boyles, Georgia State University

Haroldo Fontaine, Florida State University

Beth Ackerman, Liberty University

Ellen Burkhouse, Marywood University

Gwendolyn Durham, Shippensburg University

Heather Merrill, Glendale Community College

Mara Jane Cawein, University of Central Arkansas

Tony Latiker, Jackson State University

Debbie Hall Grady, Wayne Community College

Anna Kochan, University of Central Florida

Colleen Fawcett, Palm Beach State College–Lake Worth

Frederick Hammond, University of Central Oklahoma

Janis Murphy, Murray State University

Kathleen Lazarus, Daytona State College

Elizabeth, DeGiorgio, Mercer County Community College

Joan Cook, Columbia State Community College

Sherry Forrest, Craven Community College

Melissa Marks, University of Pittsburgh

Rochonda Nenonene, University of Dayton

Linda Gordon, Missouri Valley College

Julie Samuels, Pittsburgh State University

Patty Phelps, University of Central Arkansas

Judy Payne, Murray State University

Nakia Pope, Winthrop University

Christine Waugh, Purdue University Calumet

Carmen Wakefield, University of Cincinnati

Finally, we thank our students for keeping us honest, on track, and motivated. They are our inspiration.

David M. Sadker

Karen R. Zittleman

Tucson, Arizona

THE TEACHING PROFESSION AND YOU

chapter **1**

Focus Questions

1. What are the advantages and disadvantages of being a teacher?
2. What are the satisfactions—and complaints—of today's teachers?
3. Is teaching a "good fit" for you?
4. Can we consider teaching to be a profession?
5. How has teacher preparation changed over the years?
6. What are the differences between the National Education Association and the American Federation of Teachers?
7. What steps can I take now on the road to becoming a teacher?
8. Are America's schools a secret success story, doing better than the press and public believe?

WHAT DO YOU THINK? Why do you want to be a teacher? Rate the factors influencing your decision whether to become a teacher, and see how other students have rated these factors.

For inspirational stories about people who have had a powerful impact on the lives of others, go to the Online Learning Center and read the "Class Acts."

www.mhhe.com/sadkerbrief3e

Chapter Preview

This chapter looks at classroom life through the teacher's eyes. You may be thinking: I have spent years in a classroom, watching teachers and what they do. If there is one thing I know, it is teachers and teaching! But during your years in the classroom, you have looked at teaching through "student-colored glasses," a unique but somewhat distorted view, like looking through a telescope from the lens that makes everything tiny instead of large. In this chapter, we will view the classroom from the teacher's side of the desk, a very different way of looking at school.

Some of you are taking this course because you want to learn more about schools and teaching. This text will answer many of your questions and offer useful information. We know that many of you taking this course are considering a major decision: Do I want to be a teacher? This first chapter is especially designed to help you answer that question. The chapter is also about "us." Yes, us. We are now a team, this textbook, the authors, and you. When your authors were students, we did not like our textbooks. They were boring. By extension, we feared that we might not like teaching, either. Guess what—we loved teaching! We want this textbook to reflect that love—to be not only informative but also exciting and fun. This first chapter offers us the opportunity to introduce the textbook and, in a sense, to introduce ourselves. Welcome to our classroom.

A Teaching Career—Is It Right for You?

In this text, we will try mightily to include relevant information, witty insights, useful studies, and engaging chapters about teaching, school law, student diversity, educational history, and all kinds of topics that offer you a balanced view of teaching. We want you to understand the fundamentals of teaching and schooling in the United States, and we will present the information in as exciting a way as we can. To do this, we have created several features that encourage you to reflect and focus on key points. You will learn about both the positive and the negative aspects of many educational issues as you consider a possible career in teaching.

At some point, you will need to figure out if teaching is right for you. (Here's the hard part: Only you can do that.) Consider your friends' and relatives' advice, but realize that in the final analysis, it is your life, not theirs. You undoubtedly have met people who are doing work they love, and they are joyful and fulfilled. You have also met people who have made an unhappy choice, followed someone's bad advice, or given too little thought to planning their future. For them, every day is "a grind." Your goal is to find a career that puts you in that first group, a career that brings you joy and meaning. As you read through this text, stop every now and then and ask yourself: "Does this speak to my heart? Am I enjoying what I am reading? Does teaching feel right?" We know, this heart talk is not what you typically read about in textbooks, but this is not a typical textbook. In our materialistic world, talking about your inner world is not always honored. But we will work to have you consider all aspects of teaching, and nothing is more important than your personal feelings.

In a *Peanuts* cartoon, Linus comments that "no problem is so big or complicated that it can't be run away from." Charles Schulz succinctly highlighted a human frailty shared by most of us—the tendency to put aside our problems or critical questions in favor of day-to-day routine. In fact, it is amazing how little care and consideration many of us give to choosing a career. It is always easier to catch a movie, surf the Net, or even study for the next exam than it is to reflect on and plan for the future. That may be one reason why questions such as "What are you going to be when you grow up?" and "What's your next career move?" make so many of us uneasy. The big question facing many of you: Is teaching right for me? Some of you are in college or university programs and will be teaching in the next few years. Others of you may already be in a classroom, teaching as you work toward your license in one of several alternative teacher certification programs. For some of you, teaching may become a decades-long career filled with joy and satisfaction. For others, teaching time may be limited, one of several careers you explore during your working years. And still others may reach an equally useful and important realization: Teaching is not the ideal match for your interests or skills. We'd like to help you decide whether you and teaching are a good fit.

Like this perspective? In this chapter you will look at classrooms from the teachers' side of the desk.

Throughout this text, we pose a variety of questions for you to consider. We have devised a feature called You Be the Judge, which presents several sides of an issue and encourages you to sort out where you stand. When the authors have a strong opinion about these or any of the issues in the text, we will not hide it from you. But our opinion is just our opinion, and we want you to form your own ideas. To that end, we will work hard to be fair, to present more than one side of the issue, and to help you form an independent point of view. You Be the Judge is one way that we hope to spark your interest and thinking on critical issues.

In the first You Be the Judge, we highlight the joys and the concerns of a career in the classroom (see pp. 6–8), and we include comments by teachers themselves that reveal their perceptions and feelings about their work. A more structured attempt to assess teachers' views on their careers was carried out by the National Education Association (NEA). Teachers from around the nation were asked why they decided to become teachers and why they choose to stay in teaching.[1] Teachers explain that the intrinsic rewards make teaching unique, including a desire to work with young people, the importance of education, and even the love of a particular subject. Put another way, teaching touches the heart. This is not a bad bunch to have as colleagues. (See Figure 1.1.)

Metropolitan Life has been surveying American teachers for a quarter of a century and reports that many teachers are more positive than they have been in decades. Their 2008 survey indicated that two-thirds of teachers feel that they are well prepared for their profession and better prepared for classroom challenges such as poverty, limited English proficiency, and lack of parental support. Nine out of ten teachers believe that their school curriculum is

FIGURE 1.1

Why teach?

SOURCE: National Education Association, *Status of the American Public School Teacher,* 2006.

REFLECTION: Which of these reasons for teaching speak to you? Can you suggest others?

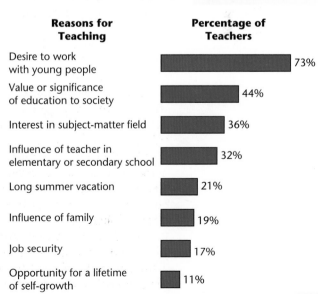

Reasons for Teaching	Percentage of Teachers
Desire to work with young people	73%
Value or significance of education to society	44%
Interest in subject-matter field	36%
Influence of teacher in elementary or secondary school	32%
Long summer vacation	21%
Influence of family	19%
Job security	17%
Opportunity for a lifetime of self-growth	11%

Focus Question 1
What are the advantages
and the disadvantages of
being a teacher?

excellent or good. And while salaries remain a problem for many teachers, especially during times of tight budgets, about two out of three teachers felt they were paid a decent salary.

But while most teachers feel better about their jobs than they did in the past, not all do. A Public Agenda survey (2009) described four in ten teachers as "disheartened," and almost the same ratio as "content." One reason for this mixed picture is the economic downturn that began in 2008 and impacted many school budgets. Another has been the direction of the education reform movement. As people work to improve schools, some have decided that ineffective teachers may be the problem with American education. Teachers in too many communities feel the pressure of both struggling school budgets and the criticism directed at them. But even under these pressures, it is helpful to remember that almost one in four reported feeling great satisfaction in their work. They were described as "idealists,"[2] whose dedication makes a difference in people's lives; perhaps this is one reason why Americans respect teachers more than they do scientists, judges, or television newscasters. Only doctors are more respected. And that is quite a compliment. (See Figure 1.2.)

Focus Question 2
What are the satisfactions—
and the complaints—of
today's teachers?

Many believe that the path to improving education is rewarding good teachers and removing weak ones, so it is not surprising that pay-for-performance has gained popularity. **Pay-for-performance,** sometimes called **merit pay,** attempts to make teaching more accountable by linking teacher and student performance to teacher salary. Simply put: better teachers earn more money. While this sounds like a pretty good idea, it has its problems.

Focus Question 3
Is teaching a "good fit" for
you?

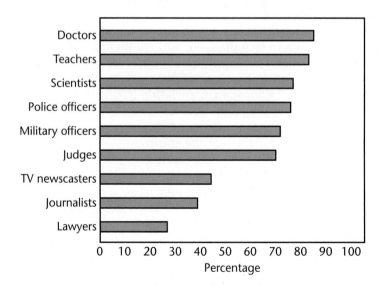

FIGURE 1.2

Public trust in various professions. "Would you generally trust each of the following types of people to tell the truth, or not?"

SOURCE: Statistics from *The Harris Poll* #61, August 8, 2006.

REFLECTION: Why do you think doctors and teachers garner so much trust? Why is there a significant drop in trust for TV newscasters, journalists, and lawyers?

A VIEW FROM THE FIELD: MERIT PAY

Danielle Price, 23, is finishing her first year of teaching seventh- and eighth-grade math at Merrill Middle School in Denver, Colorado. As a new teacher in the Denver Public School (DPS) system, Danielle was automatically enrolled in a merit pay program called Professional Compensation, or ProComp. In the ProComp program, a teacher's starting salary is based on years of experience. Teachers can add to their base salary by meeting Student Growth Objectives, completing Professional Development Units (PDU), and receiving a satisfactory evaluation. "I'm used to putting together evidence for my supervisor, having just completed my degree not long ago," Danielle says, "The PDU is a lot less work than I did in college; however, it's very time consuming collecting the evidence needed to pass the final evaluation." Teachers can earn bonuses if they fill Hard to Staff positions, such as math/science teachers, or teach in Hard to Serve Schools. As a math teacher at a Hard to Serve School, Danielle currently receives both of those bonuses, but that can change.

> It has been decided that next year we are no longer going to be classified as a Hard to Serve School, which will remove a part of my bonus. As a first-year teacher, I'm disappointed in the merit system because it adds more stress and pressure to first-year teachers in earning their bonuses. We have to meet the induction process requirements to obtain the professional license, meet ProComp requirements to get a raise, and worry about raising test scores as an inner city school district. I have worked intensely as a first-year teacher, and the compensation isn't nearly what it should be. However, I'm making more money at the end of my first year teaching in ProComp than a few of my friends who are in their fourth and fifth years of teaching and not enrolled in ProComp. I don't think they are being rewarded fairly either on the traditional step-pay scale.

Before becoming a teacher, Danielle voted to implement ProComp in the Denver Public School system.

> As a voter, I didn't know how much work it would be for teachers. ProComp didn't change my decision about applying for and accepting a position with DPS, but it is starting to influence my decision about whether to stay in the school system or not. It is difficult to work this hard for such small rewards. I know that merit pay doesn't change the way I teach; I want to set obtainable goals that challenge me as a teacher and person and my students. If I don't meet my objectives, I don't meet them; I will try again the following year, and continue to challenge myself. I don't think that teachers work harder in their classrooms to get the pay raises, but I do think we do a lot more busy work outside of class in order to earn the raises in ProComp. ProComp doesn't make better teachers, it challenges us to meet our goals we set and then be rewarded a little more than typical pay scales do for our work and dedication.

Danielle Price graduated with a BS in Mathematics and a double minor in Secondary Mathematics Education and Linguistically Diverse Learners Education from Regis University.

Although many of us feel we know a good teacher when we see one, being objective can be difficult. For example, several approaches use student test scores to decide which teachers are most effective. Is this measuring teaching, or student attendance, or family situations? Perhaps teachers who teach challenging subjects like physics or math should earn more money than first-grade teachers? (Or do we have that backward?) Perhaps teachers who work with difficult students or in high poverty areas should be paid more. (Does that mean we pay less to those who teach the gifted?) It is not unusual for school politics and personality issues to influence people's judgment. And schools can be very political places. (See Contemporary Issues: A View from the Field.) Sometimes a plan that sounds fairly easy can be fairly difficult. Pay-for-performance has its challenges, but it is popular among many, and it is part of the current reform movement that we will talk more about later.[3]

In addition to identifying and rewarding superior teachers, the recent reform effort focuses on identifying and removing weak teachers, even

A Teaching Career

THE GOOD NEWS . . .

YOU ARE NOT WORKING ALONE, STARING AT A COMPUTER SCREEN OR SHUFFLING PAPERS

If you enjoy being in contact with others, particularly young people, teaching could be the right job for you. Almost the entire working day is spent in human interaction. Young people are so often funny, fresh, and spontaneous. Your discussions may range from adding fractions to feeding pet snakes, from an analysis of *The Catcher in the Rye* to advice on applying to colleges. As America's students become increasingly diverse, you will find yourself learning about different cultures and different life experiences. Your life will be enriched by the varied worlds of different children—black, white, Hispanic, Asian, blended—all kinds of children. The children will make you laugh and make you cry, but always they will make you feel needed. "I still can't get used to how much my heart soars with every student's success, and how a piece of my heart is plucked away when any student slips away."[4]

THE SMELL OF THE CHALKBOARD, THE ROAR OF THE CROWD

You spend several days researching and planning your lesson on social protest literature for your eleventh-grade English class. You collect many fine poems and statements to share; you bring your favorite CDs and DVDs of social protest songs into the classroom; you prepare an excellent PowerPoint presentation to highlight the key labor figures and issues of the time; and you punctuate your lesson with thoughtful discussion questions and creative follow-up activities. Wow, what a lesson! The students are spellbound. They ask many questions and make plans for doing their own research on social protest. One group even decides to meet after school to create an MTV-type video of a social protest song about the destruction of the natural environment. Their animated discussion continues as the bell signals their passage to the next classroom.

When you have taught well, your students will let you know it. On special occasions, they will come up to you after class or at the end of the year to tell you, "This class is awesome." At younger grade levels, they may write you notes (often anonymous), thanking you for a good class or a good year.

I'M PROUD TO BE A TEACHER

Although teachers are sometimes battered in the media, most people continue to acknowledge the importance of teachers. Nine out of ten students give their teachers a passing grade.[6] When you become a teacher, many people will accord you respect because they admire

THE BAD NEWS . . .

STOP THE CROWD—I WANT TO GET AWAY

Right in the middle of a language arts lesson, when fifteen kids have their hands in the air, you may feel like saying, "Stop, everybody. I feel like being alone for the next fifteen minutes. I'm going to Starbucks." For the major part of each day, your job demands that you be involved with people in a fast-paced and intense way—whether you feel like it or not. Researchers report that you will be involved in as many as 1,000 verbal exchanges in a single day, almost all of them with children, which could affect behavior beyond school. One kindergarten teacher warned her 40-year-old brother "to be sure and put on his galoshes. Wow! Did he give me a strange look."[5] And as America's classrooms become more multicultural, teacher interactions will become more challenging, as teachers stretch beyond their own background to connect with a diverse student population.

IS ANYBODY THERE?

After teaching your fantastic lesson on social protest literature, you want to share your elation with your colleagues, so you head for the teachers' room and begin to talk about the lesson. But it is hard to capture the magic of what went on in the classroom. You can sense that your description is falling flat. Besides, people are beginning to give you that "What kind of superstar do you think you are?" look. You decide you had better cut your description short and talk about CDF (Casual Dress Friday).

It is rare to have another adult spend even 10 minutes observing you at work in your classroom. After you have obtained tenure, classroom observation becomes incredibly infrequent. Often, the evaluation is little more than perfunctory. Some teachers feel they and their students share a "secret life," off-limits to others. Most of your colleagues will have only a general impression of your teaching competence. The word may leak out—through students, parents, or even the custodian—if you are doing a really fine job; however, on the whole, when you call out, "Hello, I'm here, I'm a teacher. How am I doing?" there will be little cheering from anyone outside your classroom.

I DON'T GET NO RESPECT

Although many Americans value teaching, many others don't. One reason for this inconsistency is sexism in our culture. Occupations with large numbers of women generally face prestige problems, and teaching is no exception. (There may come a day when we will not have to mention

The Good News...

teachers. You will be someone whose specialized training and skills are used to benefit others. Mark Twain once wrote, "To be good is noble, but to teach others how to be good is nobler." Which would have summed up this point perfectly, except, being Mark Twain, he added: "—and less trouble."

AS A TEACHER, YOU ARE CONSTANTLY INVOLVED IN INTELLECTUAL MATTERS

You may have become very interested in a particular subject. Perhaps you love a foreign language or mathematics, or maybe you are intrigued by contemporary social issues. If you decide you want to share that excitement and stimulation with others, teaching offers a natural channel for doing so. As one teacher put it: "I want them to be exposed to what I love and what I teach. I want them to know somebody, even if they think I'm crazy, who's genuinely excited about history."[7]

Using your extended vacation times to continue your education can further advance your intellectual stimulation and growth. The Internet is a great source for finding creative teaching ideas and staying on top of emerging developments in your field. Other helpful sources are journals, weekly educational newspapers, conferences, and meetings sponsored by school districts and professional education associations. You have ready access to the intellectual community.

PORTRAIT OF THE TEACHER AS AN ARTIST

You can construct everything from original simulation games to videotapes, from multimedia programs to educational software. Even the development of a superb lesson plan is an exercise in creativity, as you strive to meet the needs of the diverse children who come into your classroom each day. Some people draw clear parallels between teachers and artists and highlight the creativity that is essential to both:

> I love to teach as a painter loves to paint, as a musician loves to play, as a singer loves to sing, as a strong man rejoices to run a race. Teaching is an art—an art so great and so difficult to master that a man [or woman] can spend a long life at it without realizing much more than his [or her] limitations and mistakes, and his [or her] distance from the ideal. But the main aim of my happy days has been to become a good teacher. Just as every architect wishes to be a good architect and every professional poet strives toward perfection.[8]

TO TOUCH A LIFE, TO MAKE A DIFFERENCE

Teaching is more than helping a child master phonics or discover meaning in seemingly lifeless history facts. Each classroom is a composite of the anguish and the joy of all its students. You can feel the pain of the child in the fourth seat who always knows the answer but is too shy to speak. Then there is the rambunctious one who spills all over the classroom in a million random ways, unable to focus on any

The Bad News...

this issue, but, for the time being, prejudice still exists.) Unfortunately, in our materialistic society, people's work is frequently measured by the size of the paycheck—and most teachers' wallets are modestly endowed. Despite the resurgence of support for teachers, when it comes to the game of impressing people, teachers are still not collecting a large pile of status chips.

THE SAME MATTERS YEAR AFTER YEAR AFTER YEAR

Yes, you will be continually involved in academic subject matter—but the word continually is a double-edged sword. Teaching, like most other jobs, entails a lot of repetition. You may tire of teaching the same subject matter to a new crop of students every September. If this happens, boredom and a feeling that you are getting intellectually stale may replace excitement. For some, working with students who seem unmoved by the ideas that excite you can be frustrating and disillusioning. You may turn to your colleagues for intellectual stimulation, only to find that they are more concerned about the cost of auto repair and TV shows than the latest genetic decoding breakthrough or the intricacies of current government policy.

Because you are just embarking on your teaching career, you may find it difficult to imagine yourself becoming bored with the world of education. However, as you teach class after class on the same subject, interest can wane.

THE BOG OF MINDLESS ROUTINE

Much is said about the creativity of teaching, but, under close inspection, the job breaks down into a lot of mindless routine as well. A large percentage of the day is consumed by clerical work, child control, housekeeping, announcements, and participation in ceremonies. Although opportunity exists for ingenuity and inventiveness, most of the day is spent in the three Rs of ritual, repetition, and routine. As one disgruntled sixth-grade teacher in Los Angeles said:

> Paper work, paper work. The nurse wants the health cards, so you have to stop and get them. Another teacher wants one of your report cards. The principal wants to know how many social science books you have. Somebody else wants to know if you can come to a meeting on such and such a day. Forms to fill out, those crazy forms: Would you please give a breakdown of boys and girls in the class; would you please say how many children you have in reading grade such and such. Forms, messengers—all day long.[9]

THE TARNISHED IDEALIST

We all hope to be that special teacher, the one students remember and talk about long after they graduate. But too often, idealistic goals give way to survival—simply making it through from one day to the next. New teachers find themselves judged on their ability to maintain a quiet, orderly room. Idealistic young teachers find the worship of control incompatible with their humanistic goals. Likewise, they

continued

The Good News...   # The Bad News...

one task or project. Or that physically unattractive victim, who inspires taunts and abuse from usually well-mannered classmates. You can be the one who makes a difference in their lives:

> I am happy that I found a profession that combines my belief in social justice with my zeal for intellectual excellence. My career choice has meant much anxiety, anger, and disappointment. But it has also produced profound joy. I have spent my work life committed to a just cause: the education of Boston high school students. Welcome to our noble teaching profession and our enduring cause.[10]

SALARIES AND TIME FLEXIBILITY

Two-thirds of teachers feel they earn a "decent salary," a figure that has doubled since 1984, although where you teach determines whether salaries are good, fair, or disappointing, and nowadays even the length of vacations can vary from community to community. The average teacher in the Dakotas or Utah earns only $30,000 to $40,000 for 10 months of teaching, yet the average teacher pay in California and parts of the northeast is about $70,000. Additional income comes through summer employment or accepting extra faculty responsibilities. Occupational benefits, such as health and retirement, are generally excellent, and working in a wealthier community brings teacher salaries into the six figures. Of course, the cost of living in these communities determines how far any salary really goes. Often (but not always) there are long vacations, and a few school districts offer opportunities to study, travel, or enjoy an extended leave or sabbatical. All these considerations make for a more relaxed and varied lifestyle—in fact, a healthy one that gives you time for yourself as well as your family.[12] Whether you use your "free time" to be with your family, to travel, or to make extra money, time flexibility is a definite plus.

feel betrayed if a student naively mistakes their offer of friendship as a sign of weakness or vulnerability. As a result, many learn the trade secret—"don't smile until Christmas" (or Chanukah, Kwanzaa, or Ramadan, depending on your community)—and adopt it quickly. Even veteran teachers throw up their hands in despair and too often leave teaching. Teacher–student conflict can lead to lost idealism, and worse. Some teachers are concerned with the increase in discipline problems and a decrease in support from parents and others. How can teachers stay inspired when their classrooms lack basic supplies?[11] Trying to make a difference may result in more frustration than satisfaction.

BUT SALARIES STILL HAVE A LONG WAY TO GO

Although teachers' salaries have improved, they still lag behind what most people would call fair, a concern made even more intense by tying student performance to teacher evaluations. Teachers would need a 30 percent pay increase to become competitive with other college-educated careers. Compared with teachers in other countries, U.S. teachers work longer hours for less pay. A history teacher says, "It's really difficult to maintain a family . . . I'm not sure I could have done it then except for a wife who's not demanding or pushy. She's completely comfortable with the things we have, and we don't have a great deal."[13] And the following comment comes from a well-to-do suburban community: "You can always tell the difference between the teachers' and the students' parking lots. The students' lot is the one with all the new cars in it."[14] The long vacations are nice—but they are also long periods without income.

www.mhhe.com/ sadkerbrief3e **YOU DECIDE . . .**

Which of these arguments and issues are most influential in determining if teaching is a good fit for you? Is there a particular point that is most persuasive, pro or con? What does that tell you about yourself? On a scale from 1 to 10, where 10 is "really committed" to

teaching, and 1 is "I want no part of that job," what number are you? Remember that number as you read the text and go through this course—and see if you change that rating in the pages and weeks ahead.

teachers with tenure. What is tenure? After teaching satisfactorily during a probationary period (usually two to four years), teachers typically receive **tenure**, an expectancy of continued employment. In the past, tenure has protected teachers from arbitrary dismissal, but it also has had the unintended impact of insulating some weak teachers from dismissal. (Did you ever have a teacher who you wished was not protected by tenure? Not much fun.) But many teachers worry that without tenure, it may not be just the weak

Classroom Observation

1. Teachers Discuss the Pros and Cons of Teaching

Deciding whether to enter the teaching profession is an important decision. As you've read in this chapter, there are many things to take into consideration when exploring teaching as a career. In this observation, you will observe experienced and new teachers as they discuss both the joys of teaching and their concerns with the profession, some of the surprises they discovered, and the advice they have for those considering a career in the classroom.

   Classroom Observation videos are available on the CD Reader and at the Online Learning Center.

www.mhhe.com/
   sadkerbrief3e

teachers who are removed. Teachers may be fired because of personality conflicts, disputes with administrators, or other reasons unrelated to teaching skills. So although tenure protections are still in place in most school districts, much consideration is being given to the best ways to identify and remove incompetent teachers, and possibly eliminating tenure entirely.[15] How do you feel about these possible tenure changes and the introduction of pay-for-performance? Both these modifications may well influence your life in the classroom.

Professionalism at the Crossroads

What noble employment is more valuable to the state than that of the man who instructs the rising generation?

—**Cicero**

Education makes a people easy to lead, but difficult to drive; easy to govern, but impossible to enslave.

—**Lord Brougham**

I shou'd think it as glorius [*sic*] employment to instruct poor children as to teach the children of the greatest monarch.

—**Elizabeth Elstob**

We must view young people not as empty bottles to be filled, but as candles to be lit.

—**Robert Schaffer**

I touch the future; I teach.

—**Christa McAuliffe**

Literature, philosophy, and history are replete with such flowery tributes to teaching. In many minds, in some of our greatest minds, teaching is considered the noblest of professions. But the realities of the job do not always mesh with such admirable appraisals, resulting in a painful clash between noble ideals and practical realities.

Focus Question 4
Can we consider teaching to be a profession?

Many teachers feel that the satisfaction they realize inside the classroom is too often jeopardized by forces beyond the classroom: politicians mandating numerous standardized tests, demanding parents offering little support, and school boards that mandate course content based on political ideology. Teachers desire more autonomy and control over their careers and, like all of us, want to be treated with more respect. Teachers increasingly see themselves as reflective decision makers, selecting objectives and teaching procedures to meet the needs of different learners.[16] They must know their subject matter, learning theory, research on various teaching methodologies, and techniques for curriculum development.[17] Some believe that the problems confronting teachers stem from the more pervasive issue of professional status and competence, and too many find it too easy to blame teachers for the problems students confront in school and in society. But the discussion does raise an interesting question: Are teachers professionals? What does it take to be a professional, anyway? *Educating a Profession,* a publication of the American Association of Colleges for Teacher Education (AACTE), lists twelve criteria for a *profession.* We have shortened these criteria below, and ask you to consider each one and decide if you believe that teaching meets these criteria. After marking your reactions in the appropriate column, compare your reactions with those of your classmates.

Do not be surprised if you find some criteria that do not apply to teaching. In fact, even the occupations that spring to mind when you hear the word *professional*—doctor, lawyer, clergy, college professor—do not completely measure up to all these criteria.

www.mhhe.com/
sadkerbrief3e
INTERACTIVE ACTIVITY
Is teaching a profession?
Do this exercise online.
See how other students
responded to each
statement.

Collectively, teachers struggle to empower their profession; individually, they struggle to empower their students.

Criteria for a Profession	True for Teaching	Not True for Teaching	Don't Know
1. Professions provide essential services to the individual and society.	_____	_____	_____
2. Each profession is concerned with an identified area of need or function (e.g., maintenance of physical and emotional health).	_____	_____	_____
3. The profession possesses a unique body of knowledge and skills (professional culture).	_____	_____	_____
4. Professional decisions are made in accordance with valid knowledge, principles, and theories.	_____	_____	_____
5. The profession is based on undergirding disciplines from which it builds its own applied knowledge and skills.	_____	_____	_____
6. Professional associations control the actual work and conditions of the profession (e.g., admissions, standards, licensing).	_____	_____	_____
7. There are performance standards for admission to and continuance in the profession.	_____	_____	_____
8. Preparation for and induction into the profession require a protracted preparation program, usually in a college or university professional school.	_____	_____	_____
9. There is a high level of public trust and confidence in the profession and in the skills and competence of its members.	_____	_____	_____
10. Individual practitioners are characterized by a strong service motivation and lifetime commitment to competence.	_____	_____	_____
11. The profession itself determines individual competence.	_____	_____	_____
12. There is relative freedom from direct or public job supervision of the individual practitioner. The professional accepts this responsibility and is accountable through his or her profession to the society.[18]	_____	_____	_____

Where do you place teaching? If you had a tough time deciding, you are not alone. Many people feel that teaching falls somewhere between professional and semiprofessional in status. Perhaps we should think of it as an "emerging" profession. Or perhaps teaching is, and will remain, a "submerged" profession. Either way, teachers find themselves in a career with both potential and frustration.

Why does all this "profession talk" matter? You may be more concerned with *real* questions: Will I be good at teaching? Do I want to work with children? What age level is best for me? Will the salary be enough to give me the quality of life that I want for myself and my family? You may be thinking, Why should I split hairs over whether I belong to a profession? Who cares? The issue of professionalism may not matter to you now or even during your first year or two of teaching, when classroom survival and performance have top priority. But if you stay in teaching, this idea of professionalism will grow in significance, perhaps becoming one of the most important issues you face. Even now, as a student, you can become more reflective in your views of teaching and learning; you can begin to refine your own professional behaviors and outlooks.

But let's keep all this in some perspective. Americans like to call themselves "professionals" because the term brings some status. But there are issues far more important than status. For example, few would argue that a lawyer is not a professional, but whereas some lawyers work to ensure that the environment is protected, others work for those who pollute. Some lawyers work to protect the rights of the disenfranchised, while others work to keep the powerful powerful. All these lawyers are professionals, but some of them make us proud, while the work of others saddens us. There is no reservation about the value of teachers' work. Teachers move the world forward, which is a meaningful way to spend one's life, and more relevant than the word *professional*.

From Normal Schools to Board-Certified Teachers

Focus Question 5
How has teacher preparation changed over the years?

Many of today's noted universities began as normal schools a century ago and were established to prepare teachers.

As you read this brief history of teacher preparation, think about whether teachers are prepared in a way commensurate with belonging to a profession.

From colonial America into the twentieth century, teacher education scarcely existed. More often than not, teachers in colonial America received no formal preparation at all. Most elementary teachers never even attended a secondary school. Some learned their craft by serving as apprentices to master teachers, a continuation of the medieval guild system. Others were indentured servants paying for their passage to America by teaching for a fixed number of years. Many belonged to the "sink-or-swim" school of teaching, accounting for the educational drowning of countless students.

MICHIGAN STATE NORMAL SCHOOL.

The smaller number of teachers working at the secondary level—in academies or Latin grammar schools and as private tutors—had usually received some college education, often in Europe. Some knowledge of the subject matter was considered desirable, but no particular aptitude for teaching or knowledge of teaching skills was considered necessary. Teaching was viewed not as a career but as temporary employment. Many of those who entered elementary teaching were teenagers who taught for only a year or two. Others were of dubious character, and early records reveal a number of teachers fired for drinking or stealing.

From this humble beginning there slowly emerged a more professional program for teacher education. In 1823, the **Reverend Samuel Hall** established a **normal school** (derived from the French *école normale,* a school that establishes model standards) in Concord, Vermont. This private school provided elementary school graduates with formal training in teaching skills. Reverend Hall's modest normal school marked the beginning of teacher education in America. Sixteen years later, in 1839, **Horace Mann** was instrumental in establishing the first state-supported normal school in Lexington, Massachusetts. Normal schools typically provided a two-year teacher training program, consisting of academic subjects as well as teaching methodology. Some students came directly from elementary school; others had completed a secondary education. Into the 1900s, the normal school was the backbone of teacher education. The lack of rigorous professional training contributed to the less-than-professional treatment afforded teachers. The following is an abbreviated teacher contract from the 1920s, a contract that offers a poignant insight into how teachers were seen . . . and treated.

Teaching Contract

Miss _____ agrees:

1. Not to get married. This contract becomes null and void immediately if the teacher marries.

2. Not to keep company with men.

3. To be home between the hours of 8 P.M. and 6 A.M. unless in attendance at a school function.

4. Not to loiter downtown in ice-cream parlors.

5. Not to smoke cigarettes. This contract becomes null and void immediately if the teacher is found smoking.

6. Not to drink beer, wine, or whiskey. This contract becomes null and void immediately if the teacher is found drinking beer, wine, or whiskey.

7. To keep the schoolroom clean:

   a. To sweep the classroom floor at least once daily.

   b. To scrub the classroom floor at least once weekly with soap and hot water.

   c. To clean the blackboard at least once daily.

   d. To start the fire at 7 A.M. so that the room will be warm by 8 A.M. when the children arrive.

8. Not to wear face powder, mascara, or to paint the lips.

SOURCE: Reprinted courtesy of the *Chicago Tribune,* September 28, 1975, Section 1.

As the contract indicates, by the 1900s, teaching was becoming a female occupation. Because both female workers and teaching were held in low regard, the reward for the austere dedication detailed in this contract was an unimpressive $75 a month. But as the twentieth century progressed, professional teacher training gained wider acceptance. Enrollments in elementary schools climbed, and secondary education gained in popularity, and so did the demand for more and better-trained teachers. Many private colleges and universities initiated teacher education programs, and normal schools expanded to three- and four-year programs, gradually evolving into state teachers' colleges. Interestingly, as attendance grew, these teachers' colleges expanded their programs and began offering courses and career preparation in fields other than teaching. By the 1950s, many of the state teachers' colleges had evolved into state colleges. In fact, some of today's leading universities were originally chartered as normal schools.

The 1980s marked the beginning of the modern effort to reshape education. A number of education reform reports fanned the flames of controversy regarding professionalism and teacher preparation, including one written by a group of prominent education deans. The Holmes Group, named for former Harvard Education Dean Henry H. Holmes, debated the teacher preparation issue for several years before releasing its report, titled *Tomorrow's Teachers* (1986).[19] The same year, the Carnegie Forum also issued a highly publicized report, *A Nation Prepared.*[20] Both reports called for higher standards and increased professionalism for the nation's teachers. The Carnegie report also called for an end to the undergraduate teaching major, to be replaced by master's-level degrees in teaching. While some universities followed this recommendation and created fifth-year teacher education programs (bachelor's and master's degrees required for teacher education candidates), other colleges continued their undergraduate education programs. Teacher education remains a hodgepodge of approaches. Some critics place much of the blame on universities themselves, for failing to adequately fund and support schools of education.[21]

But not all of the attention has been on initial teacher education. In the 1990s, the Carnegie Forum was influential in creating the **National Board for Professional Teaching Standards (NBPTS).** The goal of the NBPTS is to award *board certification* to experienced teachers whose skills and knowledge indicate their high level of achievement. Imagine yourself as a newly appointed NBPTS board member responsible for determining what skills and behaviors identify truly excellent teachers, teachers who will be known as board certified. How would you begin? The board identified five criteria: mastery of subject area, commitment to students, ability to effectively manage a classroom, continuous analysis of teaching performance, and a commitment to learning and self-improvement. (See *A CLOSER LOOK:* What Teachers Should Know and Be Able to Do).[22]

To demonstrate expertise to the NBPTS, teachers must complete a series of performance-based assessments, including written exercises that reflect mastery of their subject and understanding of the most effective teaching methods. Board candidates must also submit student work samples and videotapes of their teaching, and participate in simulations and interviews held at special assessment centers. As you might imagine, the board assessment is not inexpensive, with a price tag of several thousand dollars. Fewer than half the states and a handful of school districts now pay for their teachers to prepare for board certification.

As the NBPTS evolves, the teaching profession faces new questions. What does board certification mean? Clearly, being recognized as exceptional is psychologically rewarding. Considering that there are literally millions of teachers in the United States, to be among a selected few is a major boost. To date, less than 3 percent of teachers are board certified.[23]

Many teachers who become board certified receive stipends or are placed on a higher salary scale. Others are given release time to work with new teachers. However, such recognition is not universal. When funds are in short supply or a school district's organizational structure is inflexible, board-certified teachers may receive few tangible rewards or new responsibilities,

WHAT TEACHERS SHOULD KNOW AND BE ABLE TO DO

Whether you one day apply to become board certified, or want to give some thought to what it takes to be a successful teacher, consider the five core components of effective teaching according to the National Board for Professional Teaching Standards.

1. TEACHERS ARE COMMITTED TO STUDENTS AND THEIR LEARNING

Accomplished teachers are dedicated to making knowledge accessible to all students. They act on the belief that all students can learn. They treat students equitably, recognizing the individual differences that distinguish one student from another and take account of these differences in their practice. They adjust their practice based on observation and knowledge of their students' interests, abilities, skills, knowledge, family circumstances, and peer relationships. Equally important, they foster students' self-esteem, motivation, character, civic responsibility, and respect for individual, cultural, religious, and racial differences.

2. TEACHERS KNOW THE SUBJECTS THEY TEACH AND HOW TO TEACH THOSE SUBJECTS TO STUDENTS

Accomplished teachers have a rich understanding of the subject(s) they teach and appreciate how knowledge in their subject is created, organized, linked to other disciplines, and applied to real-world settings. Their instructional repertoire allows them to create multiple paths to the subjects they teach, and they are adept at teaching students how to pose and solve their own problems.

3. TEACHERS ARE RESPONSIBLE FOR MANAGING AND MONITORING STUDENT LEARNING

Accomplished teachers create, enrich, maintain, and alter instructional settings to capture and sustain the interest of their students and to make the most effective use of time.

They are as aware of ineffectual or damaging practice as they are devoted to elegant practice. They know how to engage groups of students to ensure a disciplined learning environment, and how to organize instruction to allow the schools' goals for students to be met. They are adept at setting norms for social interaction among students and between students and teachers. Accomplished teachers can assess the progress of individual students as well as that of the class as a whole.

4. TEACHERS THINK SYSTEMATICALLY ABOUT THEIR PRACTICE AND LEARN FROM EXPERIENCE

Accomplished teachers are models of educated persons, exemplifying the virtues they seek to inspire in students—curiosity, tolerance, honesty, fairness, respect for diversity, and appreciation of cultural differences. They draw on their knowledge of human development, subject matter and instruction, and their understanding of their students to make principled judgments about sound practice. Their decisions are grounded not only in the literature, but also in their experience.

5. TEACHERS ARE MEMBERS OF LEARNING COMMUNITIES

Accomplished teachers contribute to the effectiveness of the school by working collaboratively with other professionals on instructional policy, curriculum development, and staff development. They can evaluate school progress and the allocation of school resources in light of their understanding of state and local educational objectives. Accomplished teachers find ways to work collaboratively and creatively with parents, engaging them productively in the work of the school.

SOURCE: http://www.nbpts.org/standards/help-and-fags/standards 1901. Adapted from © 2007, National Board for Professional Teaching Standards.

REFLECTION: Can you demonstrate your understanding of each proposition with a classroom example from your past? If your schooling offers little to brag about (or your memories are faded), let your imagination give credence to the task. Envision an example from the five areas to confirm you comprehend each concept.

Teachers who aspire to be board certified go through a series of assessments, including an evaluation of their teaching skills.

despite their excellence. As you enter the teaching profession, you will want to stay abreast of the activities concerning the national board and determine if you want to work toward board certification.[24] (For a current update of NBPTS activities, visit www.nbpts.org.)

How Teachers Are Prepared Today

Even as educators strive toward professional status, there is no consensus on how best to prepare teachers. The two teacher-education approaches that currently dominate the landscape can be categorized as traditional and alternative. The traditional teacher-education path is found in more than 1,000 colleges where students study teaching and subject matter, and then do a student teaching experience. These programs lead to either a bachelor's or master's degree, or may involve a fifth year of study for those who want to obtain a teacher's license. The vast majority of teachers are prepared through traditional programs.

Alternative teacher preparation focuses on learning how to teach through a structured apprenticeship, a sort of on-the-job training. Alternative teacher education programs assume that college graduates already know their subject matter and, with some time in the classroom, can acquire and refine teaching skills. For example, a candidate might go through a summer course on the fundamentals of teaching, and then start teaching in the fall. During the year and the following summer, the candidate might be enrolled in several university-level education courses to further develop teaching skills. At the end of the year—more likely two years—the individual is licensed to teach. Of course, requirements differ (sometimes dramatically) among the hundreds of alternative programs. Most, but not all, states offer some form of alternative teacher preparation. (Visit www.teach-now.org for details.) In fact, there have always been some teachers who entered teaching after graduating from college without taking education courses. (See TEACHING TIP: First, You Get Their Attention.)

Is on-the-job teacher training a good idea? Supporters argue that these programs attract much-needed teachers, especially in underserved poor communities. And after all, learning by doing is an age-old way of preparing for a career. It was not very long ago that doctors and lawyers as well as teachers were prepared through very similar apprenticeships. There is no question about the growing popularity of these programs. In 2002–2003, more than 21,000 teachers graduated from alternative teacher-preparation programs;

FIRST, YOU GET THEIR ATTENTION

I entered teaching through the back door and did not have the advantage of an effective classroom management mentor. What I would have loved in retrospect was to have someone say to me: One of the first things you need to establish is a simple and effective method of getting your students' attention. For example, in working with elementary age children, I experimented with holding up an object. "Hey, look at this magic marker," I would say. All eyes would automatically look up because I had given them a task to perform. And with a note of wonder in my voice perhaps there was a good reason to look up. "Hey, look at this remarkable paper clip I just found and look what I can do with it."

This method was less effective as I started to work with middle schoolers. Some colleagues used the counting down method with this age group. "By the time I get to one, starting from five, everyone should be quiet." It didn't work as well for me. Then I was attending an adult workshop one weekend and the facilitator said right at the start, "When you hear me say 'Focus up!' please repeat it and stop what you are doing." Well, it worked for a roomful of two hundred adults and it worked wonders with middle schoolers as well. To repeat the words required that they interrupt what they were doing, whether it was deep engagement with their work or more likely chatting with a neighbor. Sometimes I would have to repeat it again but rarely did it take three times to quiet them down.

Most recently, I learned from a colleague who teaches kindergarten that a few simple rhythmic claps that in turn needed to be repeated by the class would achieve the same effect—simpler and easier on the voice, and a little less militaristic than the abrupt "focus up."

It is the nature of children's minds to wander, and it is the task of the teacher to gather and hold their attention when necessary instructions or other words are being spoken. What I gleaned from these experiments over the years was that the response that I needed from them was best achieved by having them perform a simple concrete action.

SOURCE: Eric Baylin, an art teacher for more than 40 years, currently teaches high school art at Packer Collegiate Institute in Brooklyn, NY.

> **REFLECTION:** Do any of Eric Baylin's techniques appeal to you? Are there other techniques that you are considering to encourage your students to focus and stay on task?

---

today, it is several times greater. Even more interesting, the vast majority of these new teachers are over 30 (almost half over 40 years of age), and about a third are male or nonwhites, creating a more diverse teacher force than graduates from traditional college-based teacher education programs. Alternative teacher preparation may graduate teachers better able to relate to today's more diverse students.[25]

Perhaps the best known of these alternative programs is Teach for America (TFA). TFA recruits, called corps members, teach for two years in under-resourced urban and rural schools. Although relatively small in size, TFA more than most has captured the imagination of many college students. In fact, TFA was created by a college student. Wendy Kopp conceptualized this program back in 1990 in her undergraduate thesis at Princeton. (That could be a motivator for you to see a class paper less as a task and more as an opportunity!) Why has TFA attracted so much attention? This

Alternative teacher education programs attract more males and minorities into teaching than traditional programs do.

program taps into the desire of recent college graduates who want to make a positive difference in the world by helping poor students succeed in school. And TFA has made itself into a very selective, elite organization, accepting only a small percentage of those who apply. Perhaps that is one reason why TFA works so well—or does it?

Not according to the critics who ask, How would you like to be enrolled in an all-too-brief summer teacher training program and then sent to teach in a difficult inner-city or rural classroom? (Or perhaps you need not imagine this if you are currently in a TFA-like program.) It would be sink or swim for you—and your students. Critics such as Stanford professor Linda Darling-Hammond argue that TFA does not adequately prepare teachers, and they and their students pay the price. In fact, many TFA corps members leave teaching after just two years in the classroom.[26] Some former TFA teachers suggest improvements, including more preteaching training, more support while in the classroom, and incentives to encourage corps members to stay in teaching. Those changes would be costly, but if more corps members stayed in teaching for more than just a few years, it would save money in the long run.[27]

These suggestions to improve TFA mirror the approach of a new and emerging teacher-preparation program called a *teaching residency.* Based on successful programs in Chicago, Denver, and Boston, this alternative teaching approach recruits talented teacher candidates ready to commit to a career in the classroom that is longer than two years. It differs from many alternative programs because it does not rush candidates into teaching. Candidates are paid to spend the entire first year observing a master teacher while taking coursework. It is not until the second and third years that candidates assume the responsibility for their own classrooms, but even then they are under the supervision of a master teacher. Teachers trained in a residency program are expected to teach for at least five years, and early reports indicate that the majority stay in teaching. As one teacher described the program, "I had an insider's perspective on how to apply what I learned in the university classroom. The first year teaching, I hit the ground running."[28]

Research is not yet conclusive on the relative effectiveness of many of these alternative programs, and it would not be a stretch to conclude that strong and weak programs can be found within each model.[29] In fact, comparing models may not be as productive as finding the answers to some critical questions—questions that can be asked of any teacher education program: Do the candidates have a strong background in their subject matter? Have they received effective pedagogical training? Has there been a carefully planned and implemented clinical experience?[30] As you begin your own teacher education program, whatever type it is, you may want to consider these questions and think about the specific content and skills you would find most useful.

Views of Teacher Education

As you begin to consider your ideal teacher-education program, you may want to pick the brains of those whose job it is to prepare teachers. Education professors have some clear ideas on what kind of teachers they want in the classroom.[31] (Although there is no guarantee that your instructor in this course agrees with his or her colleagues, it may be fun to ask and find out.) Education professors want to prepare:

- Teachers who are themselves lifelong learners and are constantly updating their skills.
- Teachers committed to teaching children to be active learners.
- Teachers who have high expectations of all their students.
- Teachers who are deeply knowledgeable about the content of the specific subjects they will be teaching.

Are these goals similar to the ones you hold? Or do you agree more with the general public who worry less about teacher knowledge of subject matter and instead prefer teachers who focus on discipline and control; emphasize traditional values such as punctuality, honesty, and politeness; and create learning experiences that inspire children, including competitive teaching strategies?[32] What do first-year teachers consider most beneficial from their teacher training programs? Preparation in lesson planning, using a range of instructional methods, practical classroom management techniques, and student assessment top the list. Importantly, and not too surprising, teachers who feel significantly prepared plan to stay in teaching longer than those who do not.[33] Whichever views are more to your liking, it is time to think of yourself as a consumer of teacher education—because in a very real sense, you are.

REFLECTION: If you were to design a teacher education program, what would it look like?

Urban Legends about Teaching

Although sensible people may disagree about how best to prepare teachers, not all views are sensible. In fact, several bizarre ideas are so popular that they qualify as urban legends: "Teachers are born, not made," or "To be a good teacher, all you really need to know is the subject you are teaching." Like the urban legend of alligators cavorting in the New York City sewer system, these teaching myths have taken on a life of their own. We should take a moment of our time to clear the air and dispel the myths.

Teachers are born, not made: It is certainly true that some students enter a teacher education program with impressive instructional skills, yet training and practice are what is needed to transform a strong teacher into a gifted one. Teaching is far from unique in this. When a group of Olympians and their coaches were asked what it takes to become a champion, none of the answers suggested that they were "born" champions. On the contrary, the athletes credited well-designed practices and good coaching. Accomplished musicians attribute their performance to hours of focused practice, as do master chess players. So, too, superior teachers are trained, not born.

All you really need to know is the subject you are teaching: Though it is true that subject mastery is critical in effective teaching, research reveals that teachers skilled in **pedagogy,** the art and science of teaching, especially teaching methods and strategies, outperform teachers with superior subject area knowledge. Clearly, the most successful teachers do not view this as an either/or proposition. Effective teaching requires both knowledge of the subject and instructional skills.[34]

Teacher education students are less talented than other college majors: (We never liked this one, either!) It is true that education majors are less likely to score in the top 25 percent on the SATs than the general college population,

PROFILE IN EDUCATION

Rafe Esquith

Rafe Esquith teaches Shakespeare to his fifth-grade students from Central Los Angeles, most of whom do not speak English as a first language. His students arrive early and leave late in order to work through a rigorous core curriculum, take part in a real-world environment, and, by the end of the year, perform Shakespeare. To read a full profile of Rafe Esquith, go to the Chapter 1 Profile in Education at www.mhhe.com/sadkerbrief3e.

so if your value system is the SAT test world, this is disappointing. But leaving the SATs, adult literacy surveys show that teachers attain scores similar to those of physicians, writers, engineers, and social workers, which is much more encouraging.[35] It saddens us that no one seems to compare education majors with others in areas such as creativity, social consciousness, and honesty, for example. We wonder why such important human qualities get overlooked.

These urban legends aside, it is certainly true that many teacher education programs are stronger today than they have been in years. And the public holds high expectations for such programs. More than two-thirds of the public believe that good teachers are best prepared through an accredited teacher training program, and four out of five Americans want these programs to prepare teachers to pass a national competency exam.[36] Some teacher preparation programs emphasize current research as well as practical classroom skills, often working in close collaboration with local schools. Many teacher education students are studying at the graduate level, bringing more of life's experiences to the classroom than did their predecessors—all signs of positive changes in teacher preparation. Yet far more can be done. Universities typically spend less on teacher education students than those enrolled in other professional schools. Some alternative licensure programs place new and relatively untrained teachers immediately in the classroom, devaluing what it takes to be a teacher in some people's minds.[37]

Quality professional preparation attracts and prepares strong teachers—teachers like Andy Baumgartner, National Teacher of the Year in 2000. But when Andy spoke truth to power and complained about the lack of significant teacher representation on a commission to reform education in his home state of Georgia, he encountered strong criticism.[38] Teachers like Andy find support in their professional organizations, groups such as the NEA and the AFT. When you take your first teaching position, you may want to join the NEA or the AFT. What's the difference? Glad you asked.

Educational Organizations

Today, teaching is one of the most organized occupations in the nation, and teachers typically belong to one of two major teacher organizations, the **National Education Association (NEA),** created in 1857, or the **American Federation of Teachers (AFT),** created in 1916 and affiliated with the American labor movement. The NEA and the AFT work to improve the salaries and the working conditions of teachers through **collective bargaining** (that is, all the teachers in a school system bargaining as one group through a chosen representative), organized actions (including strikes), and influencing education policy. In your first few years as a teacher, you will find yourself in a new environment and without the protection of tenure. Teacher associations, such as the NEA and the AFT, can help alleviate that sense of vulnerability by providing you with collegial support, opportunities for professional growth, and the security that one derives from participating in a large and influential group. Nine out of 10 teachers belong to either the NEA or AFT, and 6 out of 10 teachers are represented by one or the other in collective bargaining. It is not too early for you to start thinking about which may best represent you. So let's attend a faculty meeting here in Mediumtown and find out.

The NEA and the AFT

You have been a teacher in Mediumtown for all of two weeks, and you know about five faces and three names of other faculty members. You have just learned that there will be a teachers' meeting about the services provided by the National Education Association (NEA) and the American Federation of Teachers (AFT). Although you hear about these two organizations all the time, you know next to nothing about either. So to get to meet some of your new colleagues, and to find out about these organizations, you decide to attend.

At the meeting, you flip through the NEA brochure. You learn that the NEA is the largest professional and employee organization in the nation, with nearly 3 million members. If you join the NEA, you will benefit from publications like *NEA Today,* free legal services, and training opportunities on issues from technology to academic freedom. The NEA is a political force as well, and it works to elect pro-education candidates and to promote legislation beneficial to teachers and students. (See www.nea.org.) You like political involvement, and the NEA seems like a perfect fit. But then a speaker from the AFT takes the floor.

> When John Dewey became our first member back in 1916, he recognized that teachers need their own organization. That is why the AFT will continue to be exclusively of teachers, by teachers, and for teachers.
>
> It was the AFT that backed school desegregation years before the 1954 Supreme Court decision that established the principle that separate is not equal. We ran freedom schools for Southern black students, and we have a strong record on academic freedom and civil rights.
>
> It was the AFT that demanded and fought for the teacher's right to bargain collectively. It was the AFT leaders who went to jail to show the nation their determination that teachers would no longer stand for second-class status.
>
> And, as part of the great labor movement, the AFL-CIO, the AFT continues to show the nation that through the power of the union the voice of America's teachers will be heard.

You take a look at the AFT brochure. With over a million members, the AFT has significant influence. The AFT's image as a streetwise, scrappy union has shifted since the 1970s, and today the AFT takes a leadership role in education reform. The AFT supported national standards for teachers, charter schools, and induction programs that enable new teachers to work with master teachers and the active recruitment of people of color into the teaching profession.[39] The AFT provides services similar to the NEA, although on a smaller scale. (See www.aft.org.)

As you weigh the relative merits of the two organizations, you overhear some teachers muttering that the NEA and AFT put the salaries of teachers above the needs of children, and have pitted administrators against teachers,

Focus Question 6
What are the differences between the National Education Association and the American Federation of Teachers?

Often marked by acrimony and bitterness, strikes changed the traditional image of teachers as meek and passive public servants.

and teachers against the public, creating needless hostility. Even worse, these critics charge, unions too often protect incompetent teachers who should be removed from the classroom. (We will go into greater depth about these arguments in Chapter 9, "Reforming America's Schools".)

Still, you are intrigued by the promise of collective action and the possibilities of teacher organization.

Professional Associations and Resources

In addition to the NEA and the AFT, you will find many resources that can help you in your professional development. Publications such as *Education Week* and *Teacher Magazine* keep teachers abreast of educational developments. (The online versions are available at www.edweek.org and www.teachermagazine.org.) Journals, professional training, university courses, and professional associations can help you not only in those critical first few years, but throughout your teaching career as you refine your teaching techniques and adapt curricular resources. The Internet is a great source of classroom ideas and practical advice. For example, Inspiring Teachers (www.inspiringteachers.com) is typical of the online resources available. And sometimes, just talking to others and learning about techniques for stress reduction can make all the difference in that first job, which is the idea behind Education World (www.education-world.com).

Here are a few organizations that you may find helpful:

- *The Association for Supervision and Curriculum Development* is an international, nonprofit, nonpartisan association of professional educators whose jobs cross all grade levels and subject areas. (www.ascd.org)
- *National Middle School Association* works to improve the educational experiences afforded young adolescents, ages 10–15 years. (www.nmsa.org)
- *National Association for the Education of Young Children* pulls together preschools, child care, primary schools, cooperatives, and kindergarten educators and parents in projects to improve the quality and certification of these schools. (www.naeyc.org)
- *National Association for Gifted Children* advances the opportunities and school programs for gifted students. (www.nagc.org)
- *The Council for Exceptional Children* is the largest international professional organization dedicated to improving educational outcomes for individuals with exceptionalities, students with disabilities, and the gifted. (www.cec.sped.org)

If you are interested in subject matter specialties, many organizations, journals, and websites can meet your needs. Here is a brief sample:

- *American Alliance for Health, Physical Education, Recreation and Dance* (www.aahperd.org)
- *National Council of Teachers of English* (www.ncte.org)
- *National Council for the Social Studies* (www.ncss.org)
- *National Science Teachers Association* (www.nsta.org)
- *Teachers of English to Speakers of Other Languages* (www.tesol.org)
- *National Council of Teachers of Mathematics* (www.nctm.org)

As a teacher, you will find yourself in a learning community, not only teaching students, but also continually improving your own knowledge and skills. We hope that these resources and others in this text will set you on that path of continuous learning and growth.

Your Teacher's License, Portfolio, and Other First Steps

As you think about teaching, you might have some practical questions, such as: How do I get a teacher's license? (And while we are thinking about it, how do I get a job?!) As you read the book and continue with your teacher education program, many of these answers will emerge. But let's look at a few of the basic questions right now.

Project yourself a few years into the future. You have just completed your teacher preparation program. You stop by your local public school office and make a belated inquiry into teacher openings. The school secretary looks up from a cluttered desk, smiles kindly, and says, "We may have an opening this fall. Do you have a license?"

Oops! License? Now I remember. It's that paperwork thing. . . . I should have filled out that application back at school. I should have gone to that teacher licensure meeting. And I definitely should have read that Sadker and Zittleman textbook more carefully. I knew I forgot something. Now I'm in trouble. All that work and I will not be allowed to teach. What a nightmare! And then you wake up.

Let's consider some of the things you can do right now to avoid this nightmare and prepare yourself for a career in teaching. Let's start with that teacher's license.

A **teacher's license** is issued by the state government that grants the legal right to teach, not unlike a driver's license, which grants the legal right to drive. Teaching licenses are awarded by each of the 50 states and the District of Columbia. You should not assume that your teacher's license will automatically be issued to you when you graduate from your teacher education program, because state departments of education, not colleges and universities, issue teacher's licenses. Some colleges will apply to a designated state department in your name and request a license; others will not. Each state has its own requirements for teacher licensure. You may meet the standards in one state, but not in another. When you have questions about obtaining a license, consult your college instructor, adviser, or teacher education placement office, or contact the appropriate state department of education. Do not depend on friends, whose well-intentioned advice may not be accurate. (See the text website online Appendix A, "State Departments of Education," for the contact information.)

You can take some other steps between now and graduation to make yourself an attractive teaching candidate. Here are a few suggestions:

1. *Plan your coursework carefully.* Your first concern should be to enroll in courses that fulfill your licensure requirements. A second consideration is to make yourself more marketable by going beyond minimum course requirements. For example, technology and special education skills are often in demand by schools, as are elementary teachers with special competence in math or any teacher with a proficiency in a second language.

Focus Question 7

What steps can I take now on the road to becoming a teacher?

2. ***Do not underestimate the importance of extracurricular activities.*** Employers are likely looking for candidates whose background reflects interest and experience in working with children. A day care center or summer camp job may pay less than the local car wash, bank, or restaurant, but these career-related jobs may offer bigger dividends later on.

3. ***Develop a résumé and portfolio.*** Traditionally, a résumé has been a central document considered during job applications, but today, many colleges and school districts are moving beyond résumés and toward portfolios—a more comprehensive reflection of your skills. The term *portfolio* has traditionally been associated with artists and investors. Most artists maintain a showcase or portfolio of their best work to woo potential clients. Today, many educators have embraced portfolios. For the teacher in training, portfolios can showcase your best work, as well as demonstrate your professional growth over time. Portfolios serve many purposes. They may be used by states for licensure and licensure renewal, by school districts for merit pay increases, and by individual schools for hiring new staff. At the classroom level, teachers are using portfolios as an alternative evaluation method. Many teachers, students, and parents have found portfolios to be an authentic way to assess achievement. As a teacher in training, you'll find that your portfolio will be a valuable asset in your teacher education program and in your eventual search for a teaching position. Questions to keep in mind as you assemble this showcase include the following:

1. What do I want my portfolio to say about me as a teacher?
2. What do I want my portfolio to say about me as a student?
3. What do I want my portfolio to say about my relationship with students?
4. How can my portfolio demonstrate my growth as an educator and a learner?
5. How can my portfolio demonstrate that I will be successful as a teacher?

Consider making your portfolio:

- *Purposeful*—based on a sound foundation, such as the INTASC Standards for Licensing Beginning Teachers included in this text.
- *Selective*—choosing only the appropriate materials for a specific purpose or circumstance, such as a job application.
- *Diverse*—going beyond your transcript, student teaching critiques, and letters of recommendation to represent a broad array of teaching talent.
- *Ongoing*—relaying your growth and development over time.
- *Reflective*—both in process and in product, demonstrating your thoughtfulness.
- *Collaborative*—resulting from conversations and interactions with others (peers, students, parents, professors, teachers, and administrators).

We have included Reflective Activities and Your Portfolio, RAPs for short, online. These activities will help you through the process of creating your portfolio. RAP activities are based on the widely accepted teaching standards (INTASC) and provide a springboard for your own creative portfolio artifacts. So visit the website and benefit from the many suggestions you find there.

Building your portfolio is a three-step process: *collect, select,* and *reflect.*

1. *Collect* items for inclusion in your portfolio by completing RAPs and similar activities of your choosing.

2. *Select* items for inclusion in your portfolio from this pool of artifacts. You are encouraged to select at least one item from each of the 10 INTASC Standards for Licensing Beginning Teachers.

3. *Reflect* on what was learned from each activity. This self-assessment should serve as a powerful learning tool, one you will be able to return to again and again.

   The choices of where and how to store your portfolio can be as diverse as the contents of the portfolio itself. Many teachers use portable plastic filing cases or crates. Others turn their portfolios into books for easy toting. Increasingly, teachers are employing a myriad of electronic tools to reach students. These can include video, the Internet, and PowerPoint presentations. Perhaps the best way to include these artifacts is through something called the *Electronic Portfolio,* or *e-Portfolio.* Many software products exist to help in this process.

4. *Begin collecting recommendations.* Recommendations can greatly influence employment decisions, but you need not wait until you are student teaching to begin collecting them. Extracurricular activities, coursework, part-time employment, and volunteer work can all provide you with valuable recommendations. Collecting letters of recommendation should be a continual process, not one that begins in the last semester of your teacher education program.

Whether or not you have decided if teaching is right for you, we trust that the following chapters will offer you new perspectives on teaching and education. But before we leave this chapter, we want to address one central question now: Are America's schools failing? It is discouraging for teachers to invest their talent and energy only to be told by politicians, journalists, and even the general public that our schools are doing poorly. We would like to offer another side of the story, presenting a perspective we rarely hear.

Focus Question 8
Are America's schools a secret success story, doing better than the press and public believe?

American Schools: Better Than We Think?

School bashing is nothing new; it is as American as apple pie. In fact, some educators believe not only that the current wave of criticism is old hat, but also that it is terribly misguided, because today's schools are doing as well as they ever have—maybe, just maybe, they are doing better.

Critics decry the low performance by U.S. students on international tests. But school advocates point out that test results may reflect cultural and curricular differences, not a failing educational system. Consider that Japanese middle school students score significantly higher than U.S. students on algebra tests, but most Japanese students take algebra a year or two earlier than U.S. students do. Moreover, most Japanese children attend private academies, called *Juku* schools, after school and on weekends. By 16 years of age, the typical Japanese student has attended at least two more years of classes than has a U.S. student. Yet because of the greater comparative effectiveness of U.S. colleges in relation to Japanese colleges, many of these differences evaporate on later tests. Perhaps there are two lessons here: (1) U.S. students should spend more time in school, and (2) the Japanese need to improve the quality of their colleges.

Student selection also affects test scores. In other countries, students who do not speak the dominant language are routinely excluded. In some nations, only a small percentage of the most talented students are selected or encouraged to continue their education and go on to high school. As one might imagine, a highly selective population does quite well on international tests. In the United States, the full range of students is tested: strong and weak, English-speaking and non-English-speaking students. A larger number of U.S. test-takers are likely to be poor. Comparing all of the United States' students with another nation's best is an unfair comparison.

Americans value a comprehensive education, one in which students are involved in a wide array of activities, from theater to sports to community service. The U.S. public typically values spontaneity, social responsibility, and independence in their children, values that are not assessed in international tests. Consider the way a South Korean teacher identifies the students selected for the International Assessment of Education Progress (IAEP).

> The math teacher . . . calls the names of the 13-year-olds in the room who have been selected as part of the IAEP sample. As each name is called, the student stands at attention at his or her desk until the list is complete. Then, to the supportive and encouraging applause of their colleagues, the chosen ones leave to [take the assessment test.][40]

U.S. students taking international exams do not engender cheers from their classmates and do not view such tests as a matter of national honor, as do the South Korean students. Too often, our culture belittles intellectuals and mocks gifted students.

Despite these obstacles, our nation's students are doing quite well on several key tests. Today, the proportion of students scoring above 650 on the SAT mathematics tests had reached an all-time high. The number of students taking Advanced Placement (AP) tests soared, a sign that far more students are in the race for advanced college standing. Improvements have been documented on the California Achievement Test, the Iowa Test of Basic Skills, and the Metropolitan Achievement Test, tests used across the nation to measure student learning. One of the most encouraging signs has been the performance of students of color, whose scores have risen dramatically. Among African American students, average reading scores on the National Assessment of Educational Progress (NAEP) tests rose dramatically.[41] Decades ago, many of these students probably would not have even been in school, much less taking tests. U.S. schools are teaching more students, students are staying in school longer, and children are studying more challenging courses than ever before. According to the 2006 Lemelson-MIT

Invention Index, teenagers reported that they are pleased with the problem-solving and leadership skills, teamwork, and creativity they learned in school (see Figure 1.3).

Then why is there a national upheaval about education—why all the furor about our failing schools and why the demands for radical school reform? Educators have advanced a number of possible explanations:[42]

- Adults tend to romanticize what schools were like when they attended as children, because they always studied harder and learned more than their children do (and when they went to school, they had to walk through four feet of snow, uphill, in both directions!).

- Americans hold unrealistic expectations. They want schools to conquer all sorts of social and academic ills, from illiteracy to teenage pregnancy, and to accomplish everything, from teaching advanced math to preventing AIDS.

- Schools today work with tremendous numbers of poor students, non-English-speaking children, and special education students who just a few years ago would not be attending school as long or, in some cases, would not be attending school at all.

- In *The Manufactured Crisis,* David Berliner and Bruce Biddle put much of the blame on the press, which has been all too willing to publish negative stories about schools—stories based on questionable sources. Sloppy, biased reporting has damaged the public's perception of schools.

It is helpful to remember two points. First, criticism can be fruitful. If additional attention and even criticism help shape stronger schools, the current furor will have at least some positive impact. Second, countless students in all parts of the country work diligently every day and perform with excellence. The United States continues to produce leaders in fields as diverse as medicine and sports, business and entertainment. To a great extent, these success stories are also the stories of talented and dedicated teachers. Although their quiet daily contributions rarely reach the headlines, teachers do make a difference. You represent the next generation of teachers who will, no doubt, weather difficult times and sometimes adverse circumstances to touch the lives of students and to shape a better America.

This first chapter tells you something about us, the authors of this book: We love teaching, but want to love it more. We believe that although teaching is a wonderful career, teachers deserve more than they get, both in money and psychic rewards. We have taught in many different settings, from the military to overseas, from elementary school to the university, and while each position gave us joy, we always thought of ways to make those teaching positions better. Like so many careers, teaching has both assets and liabilities, and you would do well to consider both as you look to your own future.

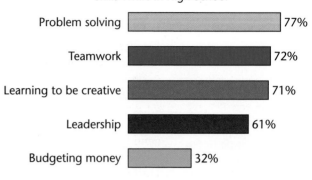

Percentage of Teens Who Feel They Have Learned Critical Skills While in High School

Problem solving	77%
Teamwork	72%
Learning to be creative	71%
Leadership	61%
Budgeting money	32%

FIGURE 1.3
Critical skills.

SOURCE: The Lemelson-MIT Invention Index 2006, http://web.mit.edu/newsoffice/2006/lemelson-teens.html.

REFLECTION: Why do so few reports about U.S. schooling examine topics like these?

www.mhhe.com/sadkerbrief3e

INTERACTIVE ACTIVITY
What job is this? Match job titles to education-related job descriptions.

www.mhhe.com/sadkerbrief3e

INTERACTIVE ACTIVITY
Edspeak. Do you know what these education-related terms mean?

SUMMARY

CHAPTER REVIEW

Go to the Online Learning Center to take a chapter self-quiz, practice with key terms, and review concepts from the chapter.

www.mhhe.com/
    sadkerbrief3e

1. **What are the advantages and disadvantages of being a teacher?**

   In the You Be the Judge feature and throughout this chapter, we consider both advantages and disadvantages of teaching. Routine, lack of respect, student apathy, and bureaucracy can wear teachers down, while the joy of working with children, caring colleagues, and intellectual stimulation motivate teachers.

2. **What are the satisfactions—and complaints—of today's teachers?**

   Although the majority of teachers are satisfied with their careers, many feel that better pay and more reasonable workloads are in order. In some cases, teachers are concerned about student discipline problems and a lack of parental and administrative support. But teaching experiences vary enormously. Some communities pay quite well and offer pleasant working conditions and strong parent support.

3. **Is teaching a "good fit" for you?**

   The most important career consideration about teaching is whether it is right for you. Salaries and free time are certainly considerations, but the answer lies as much in your heart as in any objective calculations. Your authors love teaching, but it isn't for everyone. Perhaps you will need to try it out to before you can tell if it speaks to you. If it does, you will love your work, and what is better than that? If it is not for you, it is good to find out early on. It is a big world, and there are many ways to make your contribution.

4. **Can we consider teaching to be a profession?**

   There are trends to make teaching more "professional" (five years of training, growing research base, qualifying exams, and the recognition of board-certified teachers) and counter-trends that question the status of teachers (alternative certification and lack of teacher influence over licensure and curricular standards). Some claim teaching is best described as a semiprofession. We think a better way to think about it is that teaching moves the world forward.

5. **How has teacher preparation changed over the years?**

   In the early nineteenth century, normal schools were established to prepare teachers; this was a move to create a profession. Today, the picture is mixed. Some schools require years of higher education, and superior performance is recognized through board certification. Other programs emphasize alternative certification, a type of apprenticeship not unlike what was practiced in colonial America.

6. **What are the differences between the National Education Association and the American Federation of Teachers?**

   The National Education Association (NEA) is the largest and one of the oldest professional and employee associations in the nation. The American Federation of Teachers (AFT) is smaller, more urban, and affiliated with the labor movement. Today, the NEA and the AFT are only two of the professional organizations that offer a range of services, including magazines, journals, and other professional communications; legal assistance; workshops and conferences; assistance in collective bargaining; and political activism.

7. **What steps can I take now on the road to becoming a teacher?**

   You can take actions right now to prepare yourself for a career in the classroom. Finding out your state's teacher licensure requirements, preparing your portfolio, and acquiring recommendations can begin now and help you forge a path to the teaching position you desire.

8. **Are America's schools a secret success story, doing better than the press and the public believe?**

The lower performance of U.S. students on international tests may be attributed to curricular and cultural differences, not necessarily to educational deficiencies. Many indicators, from SAT scores to AP enrollments, reflect an improvement in U.S. schools. School bashing often reflects an old tradition of journalists and a popular activity of today's politicians. Despite all this, America's schools may be doing far better than we realize.

KEY TERMS AND PEOPLE

American Federation of
  Teachers (AFT), 20

collective bargaining, 20

Reverend Samuel
  Hall, 12

Horace Mann, 13

merit pay, 4

National Board for
  Professional Teaching
  Standards (NBPTS), 14

National Education
  Association (NEA), 20

normal school, 12

pay-for-performance, 4

pedagogy, 19

teachers license, 23

tenure, 8

DISCUSSION QUESTIONS AND ACTIVITIES

1. This chapter introduces you to the importance of well-thought-out career decision making. You can read further on this decision-making process in one of the many career books now available. For example, Richard N. Bolles's *What Color Is Your Parachute?* contains many exercises that should help you clarify your commitment to teaching. Or you may want to visit Bolles's website at www.jobhuntersbible.com. These resources, or a visit to your career center, can help you determine what other careers present viable options for you.

2. Interview teachers and students at different grade levels to determine what they think are the positive and negative aspects of teaching. Share those interview responses with your classmates.

3. Suppose you could write an open letter to students, telling them about yourself and why you want to teach. What would you want them to know? When you attempt to explain yourself to others, you often gain greater self-knowledge. You might want to share your letter with classmates and to hear what they have to say in their letters. Perhaps your instructor could also try this exercise and share his or her open letter with you.

4. Check out teacher-related websites on the Internet. Schools and school districts, professional teacher organizations, and all sorts of interest groups sponsor not only websites but also listservs, chat groups, and other Internet activities. Seek out opportunities to interview practicing classroom teachers about their own classroom experiences. (Check out the Online Learning Center for related web links.)

5. Imagine that you are taking part in a career fair. Someone asks why you are exploring teaching. Briefly frame your answer.

WEB-*TIVITIES*

Go to the Online Learning Center to do the following activities:

1. The Advantages and Disadvantages of Being a Teacher
2. A Closer Look at Teach for America
3. Why Become a Teacher?
4. Teacher Tenure
5. The National Board for Professional Teaching Standards
6. Teacher Recognition: Merit Pay
7. Teacher Association: The NEA and the AFT

Articles, Case Studies, and Videos correspond to chapter content and are not always in numeric order. Go to your *Teachers, Schools, and Society Reader* CD-ROM to:

Read Current and Historical Articles

1. "Metaphors of Hope," Mimi Brodsky Chenfeld, *Phi Delta Kappan*, December 2004.
2. "A New Professional: The Aims of Education Revisited," Parker J. Palmer, *Change* magazine, November/December 2007.
3. "Closing the Teacher Quality Gap," Kati Haycock and Candace Crawford, *Educational Leadership*, April 2008.
46. "All Teachers Are Not the Same: A Multiple Approach to Teacher Compensation," Julia E. Koppich, *Education Next*, Winter 2005.
48. "Lina's Letter: A 9-Year-Old's Perspective on What Matters Most in the Classroom," David Pratt, *Phi Delta Kappan*, March 2008.

Analyze Case Studies

1. **Megan Brownlee:** A parent visits her children's favorite elementary school teacher and is surprised to discover that the teacher does not encourage her to enter the teaching profession.
2. **Jennifer Gordon:** A mature woman beginning a second career as an elementary school teacher struggles during her student teaching experience with how to deal with her cooperating teacher, who treats her very badly and corrects her in front of the class.
22. **Christie Raymond:** A mature woman in the first month of her first full-time position teaching music in an elementary school loves the work as long as the children are singing, but dislikes the school's emphasis on and her part in disciplining the students. The case describes Christie's classroom teaching in detail as well as her after-school bus duty.

Observe Teachers, Students, and Classrooms in Action

1. Classroom Observation: Teachers Discuss the Pros and Cons of Teaching
See page 9 of this text for a description of this video. You'll find the video on the CD Reader and at the Online Learning Center.

www.mhhe.com/
sadkerbrief3e

DIFFERENT WAYS OF LEARNING

Focus Questions

1. How do cognitive, affective, and physiological factors impact learning?
2. How can teachers respond to different learning styles?
3. Is gender a learning style?
4. What are the classroom implications of Howard Gardner's theory of multiple intelligences?

5. How does emotional intelligence influence teaching and learning?
6. How are the needs of learners with exceptionalities met in today's classrooms?

WHAT DO YOU THINK? Different Ways of Learning. Vote on the eight-point proposal presented on page 33 and see what the Teachers, Schools, and Society results are.

www.mhhe.com/
sadkerbrief3e

Chapter Preview

At the dawn of the twenty-first century, basic educational concepts are being redefined, re-examined, and expanded. What does "intelligence" really mean? How many kinds of intelligences are there? What is EQ (emotional intelligence quotient), and is it a better predictor of success than IQ (intelligence quotient)? Do students have different learning styles? Should classrooms be organized to meet the needs of different learning styles?

Gender is an issue in schools as some argue that girls' and boys' learning differences create the need for separate schools. Are single-sex schools a good idea? Do girls and boys learn differently? We want you to begin thinking about how teachers can recognize group differences while avoiding the dangers of stereotypic thinking, and the current gender debate is a good place to begin.

Another educational transformation is the increasing numbers of schoolchildren now identified as learners with exceptionalities—students with learning disabilities, physical disabilities, developmental disabilities, and emotional or behavioral disabilities—all of whom deserve appropriate educational strategies and materials. Students with gifts and talents represent another population with special needs too often lost in the current education system.

This chapter will broaden your ideas of how students learn and how teachers can teach to the many different ways of knowing.

Learning Styles

Imagine you are on a committee of teachers that has been asked to offer recommendations to the school board regarding academic climates to increase the academic performance of the district's students. Here is the first draft of an eight-point proposal. Take a moment and indicate your reaction to each of the points.[1]

	Strongly Agree	Agree	Disagree
1. Schools and classrooms should be quiet places to promote thinking and learning.	____	____	____
2. All classrooms and libraries should be well lighted to reduce eye strain.	____	____	____
3. Difficult subjects, such as math, should be offered in the morning, when students are fresh and alert.	____	____	____
4. School thermostats should be set at 68 to 72 degrees Fahrenheit to establish a comfortable learning environment.	____	____	____
5. Instruction should encourage auditory learning and help students to listen closely to the teacher. Watching the teacher can lead to unnecessary distractions.	____	____	____
6. Classroom periods should run between 45 and 55 minutes to ensure adequate time to investigate significant issues and practice important skills.	____	____	____
7. Students must be provided with adequate work areas, including chairs and desks, where they can sit quietly for the major part of their learning and study.	____	____	____

	Strongly Agree	Agree	Disagree
8. Emphasis should be placed on reading textbooks and listening to lectures, because this is how students learn best.	_____	_____	_____

You might find that these points seem to make a lot of sense. And, for many students, these eight recommendations may lead to higher academic achievement—for many, but not all. Ironically, for a significant number of students, these recommendations can lead to poorer performance, even academic failure. Why? Many educators believe that students have different **learning styles**—diverse ways of learning, comprehending, and using information—and that teaching to these preferred styles will increase educational success.[2]

Some students do their best work late at night, and others set an early alarm because they are most alert in the morning. Many students seek a quiet place in the library to prepare for finals; others learn best in a crowd of people with a radio blaring; still others study most effectively in a state of perpetual motion, constantly walking in circles to help their concentration. Others learn best by listening and some by reading.

Intriguing new research focusing on the ways students learn suggests that learning styles may be as unique as handwriting. The challenge for educators is to diagnose these styles and to shape instruction to meet individual student needs.

At least three factors—as diagrammed in Figure 2.1—contribute to individual learning styles. Do you recognize yourself in any of these categories?

1. *Cognitive (information processing).* Individuals have different ways of perceiving, organizing, retaining, and using information, all components of the **cognitive domain**. Some students prefer to learn by reading and looking at material (visual learners), while others need to listen and hear information spoken aloud (auditory learners). Still others learn best kinesthetically, using body movement, touch, and hands-on participation (kinesthetic learners). While some students are quick to respond, others are slower,

Focus Question 1
How do cognitive, affective, and physiological factors impact learning?

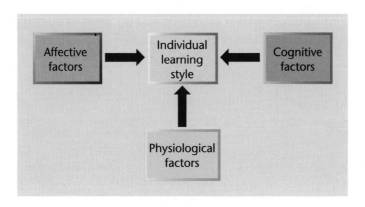

FIGURE 2.1
Factors contributing to learning styles.

REFLECTION: Describe your own learning style by identifying at least one factor under the affective, physiological, and cognitive domains.

Not all students learn best in traditional classrooms. Can teachers make reading a book in class as enjoyable as reading a book at home?

Focus Question 2

How can teachers respond to different learning styles?

preferring to observe and reflect. Some learners focus attention narrowly and with great intensity; others pay attention to many things at once. Some learners can master many concrete ideas, while others excel at abstract thinking. How would you describe your cognitive style? (See Teaching Tip: Different Learning Styles.)

2. *Affective (attitudes).* Individuals bring different levels of motivation to learning, and the intensity level of this motivation is a critical determinant of learning style. Other aspects of the **affective domain** include attitudes, values, and emotions, factors that influence curiosity, the ability to tolerate and overcome frustration, and the willingness to take risks. A fascinating aspect of the affective domain is a concept termed **locus of control**. Some learners attribute success or failure to external factors ("Those problems were confusing," "The teacher didn't review the material well," or "My score was high because I made some lucky guesses"). These learners have an external locus of control. Simply stated, they do not take responsibility for their behavior. Others attribute performance to internal factors ("I didn't study enough" or "I didn't read the directions carefully"). These students have an internal locus of control because they have the sense that they control their fate, that they can improve their performance. How would you describe your affective style?

3. *Physiology.* Clearly, a student who is hungry and tired will not learn as effectively as a well-nourished and rested child. Other physiological factors are less obvious. Different body rhythms cause some students to learn better in the day, while others are night owls. Some students can sit still for long periods of time, and others need to get up and move around. Light, sound, and temperature are yet other factors to which students respond differently based on their physiological development.[3] How would you describe your physiological style?

With this introduction to learning styles, you now know that the committee's eight recommendations will not create a productive learning climate for all students. The following section paraphrases the original recommendations, explodes myths, and provides research concerning diverse learning styles.[4]

Myth	Fact
Students learn best in quiet surroundings.	Many students learn best when studying to music or other background noise. Others need so much silence that only ear plugs will suffice.
Students learn best in well-lighted areas.	Some students are actually disturbed by bright light and become hyperactive and less focused in their thinking. For them, dimmer light is more effective.
Difficult subjects are best taught in the morning, when students are most alert.	Peak learning times differ. Some students are at their best in the morning, while others function most effectively in the afternoon or evening.

Myth	Fact
Room temperature should be maintained at a comfortable 68 to 72 degrees Fahrenheit to promote learning.	Room temperature preferences vary greatly from individual to individual, and no single range pleases all. What chills one learner may provide the perfect climate for another.
Watching the teacher can lead to unnecessary distractions.	Some students need to watch a teacher's facial expressions and body language to fully understand what is being taught. Teachers can improve student achievement by attending to both verbal and nonverbal communication.
The most appropriate length of time for a class is 45 to 55 minutes.	This period of time may be too long for some and too brief for others. The comfort time zone of the student rather than a predetermined block of hours or minutes is the factor critical to effective learning.
Students should be provided with appropriate work areas, including chairs and desks, where they spend most of their classroom time.	Many students need to move about to learn. For these learners, sitting at a desk or a computer terminal for long periods of time can actually hinder academic performance.
Reading a textbook or listening to a lecture is the best way to learn.	Diverse students learn through a variety of modes, not only through reading or listening. Although many students rely on these two perceptual modes, they are less effective for others. Some learn best through touch (for example, learning to read by tracing sandpaper letters), while others rely on kinesthetic movement, including creative drama, role-play, and field-based experiences.

As you see from these examples, teachers can better reach all students by varying their teaching and assessment methods to accommodate different learning styles. Flexibility and variety are the keys: don't assume that all students learn the way you do, and take care not to undervalue students just because their learning styles differ from yours.

Is Gender a Learning Style?

If your flying saucer arrived on earth from another world, landed in a schoolyard, and you peeked through the schoolhouse windows (using your invisible shield, of course), you might observe the following:

- In a kindergarten class, the teacher decides to put a girl between two boys in order to "calm them down."

- Throughout the school, you sense the excitement as the students talk about the championship spelling bee, the one that will decide if the girls or the boys are the better spellers.

- Outside, the boys have three basketball games in progress, while the girls are off to the side talking.

- Over the public address system, the leader of the school (called the principal) announces: "Good morning, boys and girls."

It is all so obvious. You radio back to your home base: "Planet earth dominated by two tribes: boys and girls. Will investigate further."

Focus Question 3
Is gender a learning style?

DIFFERENT LEARNING STYLES

While not all educators agree that learning styles exist, many teachers are real advocates. Using different teaching strategies helps teachers connect with all students and has the added bonus of keeping their instruction lively. Here are a few teaching tips you may want to consider:

VISUAL LEARNERS

About half of the student population learn best through their eyes, and these visual learners benefit from teachers who:

- Use textbooks, charts, course outlines, flash cards, videos, maps, and computer simulations as instructional aids.
- Ask students to highlight or color-code key points.
- Note subheadings and illustrations before students read a chapter.
- Seat visual learners away from windows and doors (to avoid distractions).
- Use overheads, PowerPoints, flip charts, and whiteboards to list key points of the lesson.
- Use guided imagery and illustrations.

KINESTHETIC LEARNERS

This style is also called tactile or haptic (Greek for "moving and doing"). These are "hands on" learners, students who learn best by doing. Teachers should consider:

- Planning student movement in class, as well as independent study time.
- Asking students to take notes and underline key points.
- Encouraging frequent but short breaks.
- Using skits and role-plays to help make instructional points.
- Integrating hands-on lessons, observations, and field explorations.
- Creating index or flash cards for students to manipulate.

AUDITORY LEARNERS

Auditory students learn best by hearing; they can remember the details of conversations and lectures, and many have strong language skills. Teachers should consider:

- Encouraging learners to recite the main points of a book or lecture or discussing the main points with others.
- Audio-taping classroom activities or reading key points onto a tape.
- Encouraging students to read the text or any new vocabulary words out loud.

REFLECTION: Choose a subject or topic that you want to teach and describe three learning activities (visual, kinesthetic, auditory) that you can use to reach students with different learning styles. How does using a variety of approaches like these influence the classroom climate?

Teachers' comments and behaviors often blindly reinforce this gender divide, yet if applied to race, religion, or ethnicity, teachers would quickly regain their vision. You will search long and hard to find a teacher who announces: "We will have a spelling bee today to see who will be the champion spellers, Jews or Christians!" Or imagine, "Good morning, blacks and whites." How about, "You two Hispanics are causing too much disruption, so I am placing a Native American between you!" Although sensitive to religious, ethnic, or racial affronts, we seem rather oblivious to gender comments. This is a situation with serious consequences.

Constant references to gender lead children to believe that teachers are intentionally signaling important distinctions between boys and girls. But are these differences significant, or are they stereotypes?

That's what Janet Hyde at the University of Wisconsin–Madison wanted to find out. Like most of us, she had heard that boys are more aggressive, better in math, science, and technology, and prefer an active and competitive learning style. Girls, on the other hand, are seen as more nurturing and intuitive, preferring to personalize knowledge; they are more successful in the arts, reading, and languages, and more compliant than boys. This cooperative and personal preference has been termed a female learning style. Hyde wanted to determine if these common gender assumptions were true.

Dr. Hyde evaluated all the studies on gender differences by using a sophisticated meta-analysis statistical procedure. What she found surprised many: there are precious few educationally relevant gender differences. So Hyde settled on a **gender similarities hypothesis**: rather than demonstrating separate learning styles and needs, males and females are actually more alike than different. According to Hyde's work, there are no important intellectual or psychological differences between females and males that require unique teaching approaches.[5] In short, more educational differences exist *within* the genders than *between* the genders. (However, some do not accept this idea and believe that boys and girls should be taught in separate schools. See Contemporary Issues: A View from the Field.)

What are the assumptions inherent in boy-versus-girl competitions? Why are gender competitions still used, while school competitions based on race, religion, or ethnicity are seen as destructive?

Hyde's work did reveal a few exceptions to the gender similarities hypothesis, such as boys were more aggressive and had a better ability to rotate objects mentally. But the reason for these few differences was not clear. Were they due to nature or nurture, or a combination of the two? After all, socialization plays a big role in our culture. The messages young girls get are that being quiet is a good idea, playing house and reading about Cinderella and Sleeping Beauty are fine, and how they look is very important. Young boys are taught to build things, read adventurous books, play sports, act tough, and never cry. Older boys are encouraged to engage in math, science, and computer-related games and to get involved in competitive sports. Girls, more than boys, are encouraged to be cooperative, to delight in reading, and to pursue the arts.

Parents play a big role in promoting such gender-related interests. Researchers at the University of Michigan followed more than 800 children and their parents for 13 years and found that traditional gender stereotypes greatly influence parental attitudes and behaviors related to children's interest in math. Parents provided more math-supportive environments for their sons than for their daughters, including buying more math and science toys. Parents, and dads especially, held more positive perceptions of their sons' math abilities than of their daughters'.[6] Socialization is powerful indeed.

Yet, our understanding of how nature and nurture influence gender roles is changing. We typically view genetics and learning styles as pretty much fixed from birth, but recent research shows that it is more complicated than that. The brain, for example, rather than being fixed, is like a muscle that can be developed and changed by our experiences. The ability of our brain to change itself and create new neural pathways is called **neuroplasticity**.[7] We are reminded of this whenever we see quiet boys who love reading or music, or girls who soar in math or on the athletic field. For teachers, this is exciting news. It means that if we offer a variety of challenging and involving activities in our classes, we not only maintain student interest, but we can help students grow and cultivate their brains. On the other hand, if we teach to a

A VIEW FROM THE FIELD: SINGLE-SEX EDUCATION

In cities all over America, educators are experimenting with single-sex education. Some schools do it to raise test scores because they believe that boys and girls learn differently. Others argue that dividing the genders removes sexual distractions and is a good behavior management strategy. If it sounds like a hodgepodge of reasons, you are correct. In fact, there is a dearth of rigorous research showing that either single-sex or coeducation is best.

A Washington, DC, middle school teacher shares his first hand experience with single-sex education:

> At first, I felt there were some real advantages to separating the girls and boys. There was certainly less teasing, which had gotten out of hand the year before. So I saw the separation as having marginal advantages. But over time, each gender developed other discipline issues. Cliques of girls began teasing each other. They replaced the boys as the discipline problem. Boys really began acting out. They actually got goofier. Then there was a second problem: boys struggling with their sexual identity really lost out. Some of these boys had girls as their best friends, and when the separate classes began, they literally lost their best friends. They were now isolated in an alpha male environment. They were treated harshly and ridiculed. The third problem was sheer numbers: there were more girls in these classes than boys. The girls' classes got much bigger. The girls got less individualized attention. So what I thought at first would be a help for girls really failed them. It was not a good idea.
>
> I pride myself in not being an ideologue. I do not like it when people get stuck in one camp or the other. Show me something that works, and I want to find out why and how we can use it. But this did not work.[*]

A report released in 2008 by the American Association of University Women confirms this teacher's concerns. The report found that the greatest challenges in educational achievement have less to do with gender and more to do with race, ethnicity, and economic status. Certainly more research is needed before we decide whether separating any of our students is the best way to educate them.

*David and Myra Sadker and Karen Zittleman, *Still Failing at Fairness* (New York: Scribners, 2009), pp. 253–288.

single learning style or use stereotypes in our teaching, we limit the brain's possibilities. So teachers are wise to encourage all their students, girls and boys, to develop their brains by exploring different learning styles, incorporating both competitive and cooperative activities, integrating both personal connections and active learning, and focusing on the arts as well as traditional subjects. There is no one-size-fits-all teaching style, and as we are about to learn, there is no one-size-fits-all intelligence either.

Multiple Intelligences

www.mhhe.com/
sadkerbrief3e

INTERACTIVE ACTIVITY
Multiple Intelligences
Label descriptions of different intelligences.

Focus Question 4
What are the classroom implications of Howard Gardner's theory of multiple intelligences?

Have you ever wondered what it really means to be a "genius"? How would you describe a genius? Have you ever met one? How would you rate your own intelligence? Above average? Average? Below average? Who decides, and what exactly is intelligence?

Traditional definitions of intelligence usually include mental capabilities, such as reasoning, problem solving, and abstract thinking. The intelligence quotient, called IQ, was developed early in the twentieth century to measure a person's innate intelligence, with a score of 100 defined as normal, or average. The higher the score, the brighter the person. Some of us grew up in communities where IQ was barely mentioned. In many cases, this lack of knowledge might have been a blessing. Others of us grew up with "IQ envy," in communities where IQ scores were a big part of our culture. Because the score was considered a fixed, permanent measure of intellect, like a person's physical height, the scores engendered strong feelings. Today we know that one's environment and well-being can greatly impact intellectual development, and we better understand that the brain and intelligence are not fixed. Rather than think of intellect as a biological given, it may be more helpful to think of the brain as a muscle to be developed.

Traditional assessments of intelligence emphasize language and mathematical-logical abilities, and this, too, is a narrow view of intelligence. Harvard psychologist **Howard Gardner** broadened the concept to define intelligence as "the capacity to solve problems or to fashion products that are valued in one or more cultural settings."[8]

Gardner identified eight kinds of intelligence, not all of which are commonly recognized in school settings, yet Gardner believes that his theory of **multiple intelligences** more accurately captures the diverse nature of human capability. Consider Gardner's eight intelligences:[9]

1. *Logical-mathematical.* Skills related to mathematical manipulations and discerning and solving logical problems ("number/reasoning smart").

2. *Linguistic.* Sensitivity to the meanings, sounds, and rhythms of words, as well as to the function of language as a whole ("word smart").

3. *Bodily kinesthetic.* Ability to excel physically and to handle objects skillfully ("body smart").

4. *Musical.* Ability to produce pitch and rhythm, as well as to appreciate various forms of musical expression ("music smart").

5. *Spatial.* Ability to form a mental model of the spatial world and to maneuver and operate using that model ("picture smart").

6. *Interpersonal.* Ability to analyze and respond to the motivations, moods, and desires of other people ("people smart").

7. *Intrapersonal.* Knowledge of one's feelings, needs, strengths, and weaknesses; ability to use this knowledge to guide behavior ("self-smart").

8. *Naturalist.* (Gardner's most recently defined intelligence) Ability to recognize and classify plants, animals, and minerals; ability to nurture animals and grow plants ("environment smart").

In regard to the last intelligence, young people spend 50 percent less time playing outside than they did in the late 1990s. Teachers and parents increasingly worry that today's children are at risk of developing "nature deficit disorder" and that the naturalist intelligence is being lost to video games, the Internet, academic pressures, and busy schedules.[10]

Gardner and his colleagues continue to conduct research. A possible ninth intelligence being explored by Gardner concerns an existential intelligence, the human inclination to formulate fundamental questions about who we are, where we come from, why we die, and the like. Gardner believes that we have yet to discover many more intelligences. (Can you think of some?)

The theory of multiple intelligences goes a long way in explaining why the quality of an individual's performance may vary greatly in different activities, rather than reflect a single standard of performance as indicated by an IQ score. Gardner also points out that what is considered intelligence may differ, depending on cultural values. Thus, in the Pacific Islands, intelligence

Physical ability and body awareness are forms of kinesthetic intelligence.

is the ability to navigate among the islands. For many Muslims, the ability to memorize the Koran is a mark of intelligence. Intelligence in Balinese social life is demonstrated by physical grace.

Gardner's theory has sparked the imaginations of many educators, some of whom are redesigning their curricula to respond to differing student intelligences. Teachers are refining their approaches in response to such questions as:[11]

- How can I promote hand and bodily movements and experiences to enhance learning?
- How can I use music to emphasize key points?
- How can I incorporate sharing and interpersonal interactions into my lessons?
- How can I encourage students to think more deeply about their feelings and memories?
- How can I use visual organizers and visual aids to promote understanding?
- How can I encourage students to classify and appreciate the world around them?

Instructional Technology

Instructional technologies can open a wide door to the multiple intelligences. For instance, authoring tools enable students to create projects that incorporate text, animation, graphics, video, and sound, integrating several intelligences. The computer and other technologies allow students to compose music or model art and science projects that enhance spatial learning. A physical education or dance teacher can videotape and then coach students on their techniques. Gardner suggests improving interpersonal intelligence by "recording tense interactions on video and having students choose the best human(e) means of reducing the tension; by involving students in blogs or Facebook that include opportunities for helpfulness or deceit; or by creating cartoon simulations or virtual reality scenarios of human dilemmas where the student has options to interact in different ways."[12] While Howard Gardner is impressed with the potential marriage of technology with his multiple intelligences approach, he has also voiced concern about teachers who get enamored with the technological wizardry and lose sight of the educational goal.

Assessment

As instruction undergoes reexamination, so does evaluation. The old pencil-and-paper tests used to assess linguistic, math, and logical intelligences seem much less appropriate for measuring these new areas identified by Gardner.[13] The **portfolio** approach (as found in the Reflective Activities and Your Portfolio section [RAPs] of the Online Learning Center for this text) is an example of

2. A Multiple Intelligences Lesson in Action

As discussed in this section, Gardner's multiple intelligences theory indicates that recognizing and appealing to their different types of intelligences can support students' learning. In this observation, you will observe an elementary teacher using Gardner's theory of multiple intelligences in her instruction through the creation of learning centers based on the different intelligences.

Classroom Observation videos are available on the CD-Reader and at the Online Learning Center.

www.mhhe.com/
sadkerbrief3e

a more comprehensive assessment, which includes student artifacts (papers, projects, DVDs, MP3 recordings, photo exhibits) that offer tangible examples of student learning. Some schools ask students to assemble portfolios that reflect progress in Gardner's various intelligences. In other cases, rather than As and Bs or 80s and 90s, schools are using descriptions to report student competence. In music, for example, such descriptions might include "The student often listens to music," "She plays the piano with technical competence," "She is able to compose scores that other students and faculty enjoy," and so on. Whether the school is exploring portfolios, descriptive assessment, or another evaluation method, Gardner's multiple intelligences theory is reshaping many current assessment practices.[14]

The Five Minds

Gardner's work on multiple intelligences has had a huge impact on how educators view teaching and learning. Along with our growing understanding of learning styles, educators today have new perspectives on what intelligence means. Now Gardner is at it again. In his book *Five Minds for the Future,* Gardner suggests new directions for schools. He points out that memorizing facts and cramming for standardized tests is not very useful in the twenty-first century. With huge amounts of information at our fingertips, with instant global communications, and with the growing intersections of cultures and countries, we have new lessons to learn. For schools to ignore these changes is self-defeating. So Gardner offers "five minds," which are really five new educational directions for the future. His five minds do not come from any sort of research (although you will see some connections to his theory of multiple intelligences); they come from what Gardner believes we will need to learn to thrive in the twenty-first century. So let go of the familiar, and let your imagination consider Gardner's five minds.[15]

The Ethical Mind Did you ever notice how often we turn away from hard truths, as though ignoring them will make them disappear? We have become inured to dishonest behavior. For example, the majority of our students cheat on exams, copy homework from others, or plagiarize term papers. Depressing as that is, we still ignore it. In adult life, these unethical behaviors lead to grievous consequences on Wall Street, in corporations, in politics, and in our personal lives. Gardner believes that we must tackle this deceit head on and teach children to think reflectively about their behavior. He would like to see more young adults choose careers that advance society, rather than focus on accruing personal wealth at the cost of leading an ethical life.

The Respectful Mind How often do you listen to misogynist rap lyrics, combative talk radio, rude television commentators; laugh (even uncomfortably) at a racist joke; or witness road rage unfold before your eyes? Disrespectful behavior in our society has become commonplace, and Gardner believes we should teach children to develop respectful minds. This means honoring people with different ideas, different cultures, and different belief systems. In fact, we have much to learn from those who have experienced different lives. In an ever-shrinking world, the lack of respectful minds can have dire consequences.

The Disciplined Mind This mind may be the most familiar to you, since it is part of today's school curriculum. The disciplined mind masters a field of study, such as literature, history, art, science, math, or even a craft. With a disciplined mind, one becomes a master of an area of work or a profession; without this mastery, one is destined to spend life simply following someone else's directions.

The Synthesizing Mind Today, we are inundated with information. Tomorrow, we will be inundated with even more information. We need to develop the ability to sort through this information, to figure out what is important and what is not so important, to see meaningful connections, and then to interpret how best we can use the data. In this information age, being able to eliminate the trivial while connecting the useful is key.

The Creating Mind Being creative is a timeless skill. A creative mind discovers new ways of looking at the world, offering new insights and a fresh way of thinking. Some believe that creativity may be America's greatest (and most underdeveloped) natural resource.

How do these five minds sound to you? Perhaps you have yet another mind that you would like added to school life. We encourage you to consider new ways of looking at teaching and learning.

Emotional Intelligence

Focus Question 5

How does emotional intelligence influence teaching and learning?

While the theories of multiple intelligences and the five minds raise fundamental questions about different ways students learn and use information, EQ, or the **emotional intelligence quotient**, offers another perspective on learning. In his book *Emotional Intelligence,* psychologist **Daniel Goleman** argues that when it comes to predicting success in life, EQ may be a better predictor than IQ. How does EQ work? The "marshmallow story" may help you understand:

www.mhhe.com/
sadkerbrief3e

> A researcher explains to a 4-year-old that he/she needs to run off to do an errand, but there is a marshmallow for the youngster to enjoy. The youngster can choose to eat the marshmallow immediately. But if the 4-year-old can wait and not eat the marshmallow right away, then an extra marshmallow will be given when the researcher returns. Eat one now, or hold off and get twice the reward.

INTERACTIVE ACTIVITY
Emotional Intelligence Quotient Quiz Take an EQ quiz to determine your own emotional intelligence quotient.

What do you think you would have done as a 4-year-old? According to the social scientists who conducted the marshmallow experiment, decisions even at this age foreshadow an emotional disposition characteristic of a successful (or less successful) adult. By the time the children in the study reached high school, the now 14-year-olds were described by teachers and parents in a way that suggested their marshmallow behaviors predicted some significant differences. Students who 10 years earlier were able to delay their gratification, to wait a while and garner a second marshmallow, were reported to be better adjusted, more popular, more adventurous, and more confident in adolescence than the group who 10 years earlier had gobbled down their marshmallows.

The children who gave in to temptation, ate the marshmallow, and abandoned their chances for a second one were more likely to be described as stubborn, easily frustrated, and lonely teenagers. In addition to the differences between the gobblers and waiters as described by parents and teachers, there was also a significant SAT scoring gap. The students who 10 years earlier could wait for the second marshmallow scored 210 points higher than did the gobblers. Reasoning and control, "the regulation of emotion in a way that enhances living,"[16] might be new, and perhaps better, measures of what we call smart, or intelligent.

Emotional intelligence "is a type of social intelligence that involves the ability to monitor one's own and others' emotions, to discriminate among them, and to use the information to guide one's thinking and actions."[17] Goleman suggests that EQ taps into the heart, as well as the head, and introduces a new gateway for measuring intelligence for children and adults.[18] By the way, how would you rate your EQ? (see A Closer Look on p. 44.)

Goleman and Gardner are toppling educational traditions, stretching our understanding of what schools are about. In a sense, they are increasing the range and diversity of educational ideas. This chapter is all about diversity. The students you will teach will learn in diverse ways, and a single IQ or even EQ score is unlikely to capture the range of their abilities and skills. But these are not the only differences students bring to school. We will end this chapter with a close look at teaching exceptional learners, from students with disabilities to gifted learners. Inclusion of these students may further broaden different learning styles and the range of skills you will need.

Exceptional Learners

In a typical classroom, a teacher faces students with a great range of abilities, from students reading years behind grade level to students reading years ahead. Both of these groups of students are described by the same broad

Focus Question 6
How are the needs of learners with exceptionalities met in today's classrooms?

SO WHAT'S YOUR EQ?

Like Daniel Goleman, Yale psychologist Peter Salovey works with emotional intelligence issues, and he identifies five elements of emotional intelligence. How would you rate yourself on each of these dimensions?

KNOWING EMOTIONS

The foundation of one's emotional intelligence is self-awareness. A person's ability to recognize a feeling as it happens is the essential first step in understanding the place and power of emotions. People who do not know when they are angry, jealous, or in love are at the mercy of their emotions.

Self-Rating on Knowing My Emotions *Always aware of my emotions_ Usually aware_ Sometimes aware_ Out of touch, clueless_*

MANAGING EMOTIONS

A person who can control and manage emotions can handle bad times as well as the good, shake off depression, bounce back from life's setbacks, and avoid irritability. In one study, up to half of the youngsters who at age 6 were disruptive and unable to get along with others were classified as delinquents by the time they were teenagers.

Self-Rating on Managing My Emotions *Always manage my emotions_ Usually manage_ Sometimes manage_ My emotions manage me_*

MOTIVATING ONESELF

Productive individuals are able to focus energy, confidence, and concentration on achieving a goal and avoid anxiety, anger, and depression. One study of 36,000 people found that "worriers" have poorer academic performance than nonworriers. (A load off your mind, no doubt!)

Self-Rating on Motivation and Focus *Always self-motivated/focused_Usually self-motivated/focused_ Sometimes self-motivated/focused_ I can't focus on when I was last focused (and I don't care)_*

RECOGNIZING EMOTIONS IN OTHERS

This skill is the core of empathy, the ability to pick up subtle signs of what other people need or want. Such a person always seems to "get it," even before the words are spoken.

Self-Rating on Empathy *Always empathetic_Usually empathetic_ Sometimes empathetic_ I rarely "get it"_*

HANDLING RELATIONSHIPS

People whose EQ is high are the kind of people you want to be around. They are popular, are good leaders, and make you feel comfortable and connected. Children who lack social skills are often distracted from learning, and the dropout rate for children who are rejected by their peers can be two to eight times higher than for children who have friends.

Self-Rating on Relationships *I am rich in friendship and am often asked to lead activities and events_ I have many friends_ I have a few friends_ Actually, I'm pretty desperate for friends_*

RATINGS

Give 4 points for each time you selected the first choice, 3 points for the "usual" or "many" second option, 2 points for the "sometimes" selection, and 1 point for the last choice.

18–20 points:	A grade—WOW! Impressive!
14–17 points:	B grade—You have considerable skills and talents.
10–13 points:	C grade—Feel free to read further on this topic.
5–9 points:	D grade—This may be a perfect subject to investigate in greater detail. Do you have a topic for your term project yet?

REFLECTION: Are you satisfied with your rating? If you earned a high rating, to what do you attribute your high EQ? If your rating was lower than you liked, how can you work on increasing your EQ? How might you develop the EQ of your students?

term: **exceptional learners**. Integrating exceptional learners into the regular classroom adds further challenge to the job of teaching diverse students.

Typically, learners with exceptionalities are categorized as students with

- learning disabilities,
- developmental disabilities/intellectual disabilities,
- emotional disturbances or behavior disorders,

- hearing impairments,
- communication disorders,
- visual impairments,
- attention deficit hyperactivity disorder,
- autism spectrum disorder,
- other health and physical impairments, or
- severe and multiple disabilities.

Although it seems a very different kind of category, gifted and talented students are also considered exceptional learners.[19]

Teaching exceptional learners—from students with disabilities to gifted and talented learners—offers teachers the opportunity to stretch their imagination and creativity. Let's begin with a group many people believe deserve little, if any, special attention. How wrong they are.

The Gifted and Talented

In Westchester County, a suburb of New York City, a 2½-year-old boy already emulates the language abilities of his parents. He speaks and reads English, French, Hebrew, Spanish, and Yiddish, and he has mastered some Danish. He is studying music theory and is conducting scientific experiments. The parents, however, are unable to find any educational facility willing and able to educate their young, gifted child. A member of their local school board told them: "It is not the responsibility or function of public schools to deal with such children." As a result, the parents considered moving to Washington state, where there was an experimental preschool program for the gifted.[20]

If you are like most Americans, you may find it difficult to consider gifted and talented children to be in any way disadvantaged. After all, gifted learners are the lucky ones who master subject matter with ease. They are the ones who shout out the solution before most of us have a chance to write down the problem. Others may have perfect musical pitch, are athletic superstars, become the class leaders who inspire us, or demonstrate insights that amaze and inform us. Many exhibit endless curiosity, creativity, and energy.

Defining **giftedness** invites controversy.[21] To some, the traditional definition of giftedness includes those with an IQ of 130 or higher; to others, the label giftedness is reserved for those with an IQ score of 160 or higher. The National Association for Gifted Children defines five elements of giftedness: artistic and creative talents, intellectual and academic abilities, and leadership skills (see Figure 2.2). Noted psychologist Robert Sternberg has suggested that a new area be included: wisdom. After years of researching what it means to be gifted, Sternberg now believes that giftedness is not just about how analytical and insightful you are, but how you use such skills. A clever business executive who uses his intelligence to earn a fortune, only to leave the company and stockholders in bankruptcy, may have been quite bright, but Sternberg argues that he should not be considered gifted. "The world is getting too dangerous. We have to train kids not just to be smart but to be wise."[22] Sternberg looks to Gandhi and Martin Luther King, Jr., as examples of wisdom too often ignored in current definitions. Although definitions of giftedness vary, only a small percentage of our population possesses this high degree of

FIGURE 2.2

Characteristics of
giftedness.

REFLECTION: Would
you include Sternberg's
concept of wisdom in this
definition? How do these
areas relate to Gardner's
multiple intelligences?

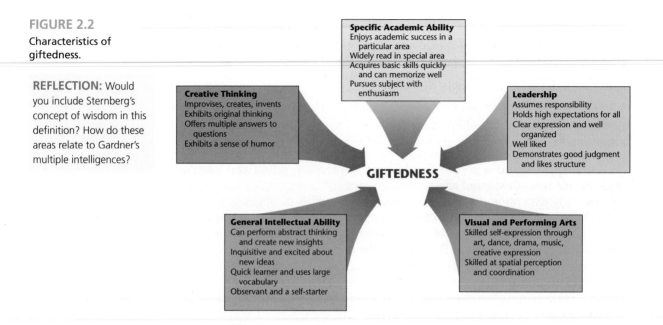

FIGURE 2.2
Characteristics of giftedness.

ability, creativity, motivation, pragmatic talent, or wisdom, making for a very exclusive club. (The National Association for Gifted Children estimates that 6 percent, or 3 million students, are academically gifted.[23])

Many gifted students do not succeed on their own. Gifted students may be haunted by a sense of isolation and loneliness, pressure to achieve, fear of failure, and negative peer pressure.[24] Gifted students talk often about their feelings of isolation and feeling different, of wanting to be "normal" and "like everyone else":[25]

> I just want to be a regular kid and not "stick out" so much all the time.
>
> I get taken advantage of. People ask to be my partner or work with me on a paper and I am stuck doing all the work. The only thing they do is make sure their name is on my paper or project. But I'm never asked to sit with them at lunch or hang out after school.
>
> I get scared for the world. Being smart allows me to see the world and what trouble we're really in.

Instead of thriving in school, too many gifted students drop out. The picture is especially dismal for gifted females, children of color, and English language learners who are more likely to drop out than gifted white males.[26] The result is that many of our nation's brightest and most competent students are lost to neglect and apathy, and some of our most talented youth do not succeed at school.

The challenges and opposition to providing special programs and educational opportunities are many. To some it seems downright undemocratic to provide special services to children who already enjoy an advantage. Moreover, struggling with shrinking revenues and federal mandates that focus on improving the test scores of lower-achieving pupils, many school districts across the country are cutting programs for their most promising students. Consequently, there is often a lack of commitment to support curriculum and teachers for extremely advanced students. And while the debate over school reform focuses on efforts to help low-performing students, no federal law offers a reward for raising the scores of high achievers and punishment if their progress lags—potentially leaving gifted students behind.[27]

Despite these challenges, many educators and parents believe that we need to do a better job of "gifted inclusion," by designing regular class activities that are more responsive to the needs of the gifted.[28] How do teachers develop an instructional plan that will be challenging, enlightening, and intriguing to students of different abilities, and still maintain a sense of community within the classroom? The regular classroom can be a major instructional resource by providing enrichment activities such as independent projects, small-group inquiry and investigations, academic competitions, and learning centers that provide in-depth and challenging content beyond regular grade-level lessons.[29] A gifted student might also spend most of the day in a regular class and be pulled out for a part of the day, perhaps an hour or so, to receive special instruction. At the secondary level, high schools have augmented their offerings with challenging courses of study, such as the **Advanced Placement** (AP) program that offers college-level courses for high-achieving high schoolers and the International Baccalaureate (IB) program, an internationally recognized degree program that includes rigorous science, math, and foreign language requirements. Special high schools, such as the Bronx High School of Science and the North Carolina School for Mathematics and Science, have long and distinguished histories of providing educational opportunities for intellectually gifted students. Other special schools have focused on programs in acting, music, and dance.

Some school districts go beyond their own resources to meet the needs of gifted students, connecting gifted high school students with the local college or community college. These students spend part of their day enrolled in college-level courses, being intellectually challenged and receiving college credit while still enrolled in high school. Still other gifted students receive additional instruction through online instruction, summer camps, or even special year-long programs that augment their regular courses. Johns Hopkins University, for example, has been sponsoring the Center for Talented Youth (CTY) in different parts of the nation for several decades. Many of these college programs are termed **accelerated programs,** for they allow gifted students to skip grades or receive college credit early. Advanced Placement courses and exams (the APs) provide similar acceleration opportunities, permitting students to graduate before their chronological peers. Many gifted students report they feel just as comfortable, both academically and socially, with their intellectual peers as they do with their chronological peers, although cases of students who found acceleration to be a disaster are also plentiful.[30]

An important characteristic of effective gifted programs is the sense of community offered, a key step in reducing student anxiety and alienation. One student was relieved to find that "there are lots of people like me and I'm not a weirdo after all."[31] Teachers are also encouraged to help gifted students understand and manage the advantages and disadvantages that can come with their high intelligence and creativity. Moreover, when gifted students are placed in appropriate programs, they are often empowered to realize their full potential. As one 12-year-old girl said:

> I enjoy being smart because I am able to accomplish many things and I feel that being smart gives me more self-esteem. I love that I have unique interests and a

place in school where I can pursue them. I enjoy challenging myself to always reach the next level.[32]

In the final analysis, it is not only the gifted who suffer from our national neglect and apathy; it is all of us. How many works of art will never be enjoyed? How many medical breakthroughs and how many inventions have been lost because of our insensitivity to the gifted?

Special Education

Perhaps you have read the book *Karen.* It is the story of a child with cerebral palsy, a child who persevered despite devastating obstacles. A formidable obstacle was an educational system that had no room for children with disabilities. The book was written by Karen's mother, who, like her daughter, refused the rejection of a hostile school and society. She wrote of her attempts to gain educational rights for her daughter and other children with disabilities:

> We constantly sought a remedy for this appalling situation which deprived so many of an education, and eventually we found a few doctors and educators who had made strides in developing valid testing methods for handicapped children. On one occasion, when I voiced a plea for the education of the handicapped, a leading state official retorted, "It would be a waste of the state's money. They'll never get jobs."
>
> We were frequently discouraged and not a little frightened as many of our "learned" men [sic] felt the same way.[33]

Such disparaging attitudes were common in our society for years and resulted in inadequate educational programs for millions of exceptional children.

Before the Revolutionary War, the most that was offered to exceptional children was protective care in asylums. The asylums made little effort to help these children develop their physical, intellectual, and social skills. Following the American Revolution, however, the ideals of democracy and the development of human potential swept the nation. Within this humanist social context, procedures were devised for teaching the blind and the deaf. Then, in the early 1800s, attempts were made to educate the "idiotic" and the "insane" children who today would be identified as having developmental disabilities or an emotional disturbance.

For many years, the legal system mirrored society's judgment that the best policy toward the disabled was "out of sight, out of mind." The courts typically saw education as a privilege rather than a right, and they ruled that children with disabilities should be excluded from schools. The notion was that the majority of children needed to be protected from those with disabilities: from the disruptions they might precipitate, from the excessive demands they might make, and from the discomfort their presence in classrooms might cause.

The years following World War II brought renewed hope and promise. Such pioneers as Grace Fernald, Marianne Frostig, and Heinz Werner—to name but a few—conducted research, developed programs, and gave new impetus to the field of **special education**. Their work was aided by the emergence of new disciplines, such as psychology, sociology, and social work. Parents also continued their struggle, individually and collectively, to obtain educational opportunities for children with disabilities. They took their cause to both the schools and the courts. Today, the educational rights of these children have been mandated by courts of law and are being put into practice in classrooms across the nation. Special education has broken away from the isolation and institutionalization so common in the late nineteenth century and has moved to mainstream exceptional children, as much as possible, into typical school settings.

Starting in the 1970s, Congress passed several landmark special education laws. In 1975, Public Law 94-142, the Education for All Handicapped Children Act, established the right of all students with disabilities to a "free and appropriate public education." Public Law 94-142 was replaced and expanded in 1991 by the **Individuals with Disabilities Education Act (IDEA)**, which not only provides a more sensitive description of the act's purpose but also extends coverage to all disabled learners between the ages of 3 and 21, including individuals with autism and traumatic brain injuries. Recognizing the importance of early intervention, special education services were extended again in 2004 to include children from birth to 2 years old. The revised 2004 IDEA further requires that only a "highly qualified" state-certified special education teacher can work with special needs learners. IDEA also provides for rehabilitation and social work services. IDEA requires that all children with disabilities "have access to the program best suited to the child's special needs which is as close as possible to a normal child's education program."[34]

Six fundamental provisions are included in IDEA:

1. ***Zero reject.*** The principle of zero reject asserts that no child with disabilities may be denied a free, appropriate public education. Representatives of the disabled have asserted that excluding children with disabilities from public schools violates the constitutional interpretation behind the Supreme Court's *Brown v. Board of Education* (1954) decision, which put an end to claims of "separate but equal" schooling. The courts have responded with landmark decisions in Pennsylvania (*Pennsylvania Association for Retarded Children v. Commonwealth*) and in Washington, DC (*Mill v. D.C. Board of Education*) that mandate public schools in those jurisdictions to provide a free education to all children with disabilities. Other federal and state decisions have followed suit.

2. ***Appropriate education.*** While the principle of zero reject ensures that children with disabilities will receive an appropriate public education, it is important to recognize that this principle goes beyond simply allowing children with disabilities to pass through the schoolhouse door. The term **appropriate education** implies that these children have the right to an education involving the accurate diagnosis of individual needs, as well as responsive programs keyed to those needs.

3. ***Nondiscriminatory education.*** The principle of nondiscriminatory education, based on the Fifth and Fourteenth Amendments of the U.S. Constitution, mandates that children with disabilities be fairly assessed so that they can be protected from inappropriate classification and tracking. Much of the court activity in this area has centered on the disproportionate number of children of color assigned to special education classes, a situation that

PROFILE IN EDUCATION

Sally Smith

Sally Smith created a "school modeled after a party" to teach her son and others with learning disabilities. Taking an approach that encourages exploration and deep learning of academic content through arts-based instruction, over 90 percent of her school's students go on to college. To read a full profile of Sally Smith, go to the Chapter 2 Profile in Education at www.mhhe.com/sadkerbrief3e.

some claim is the result of biased testing. In one case, a court ruled that IQ tests could not be used for placing or tracking students. Other courts have forbidden the use of tests that are culturally biased, and still others have ordered that testing take place in the children's native language.

4. ***Least-restrictive environment.*** Least-restrictive environment protects children with disabilities from being inappropriately segregated from their age-group peers. Court decisions have urged that students with special needs be educated in a setting that most closely resembles a regular school environment while meeting their special needs. These placements can help students develop relationships and reduce their feelings of isolation. **Mainstreaming** has traditionally referred to placing special needs students in regular classroom settings for at least part of the day. The more recent term, *inclusion,* sometimes called full **inclusion**, reflects an even stronger commitment to educate each student in a least-restrictive environment to the maximum degree possible. Separate classes and schools are to be avoided unless a child's disabilities are such that education in a regular classroom, even with the aid of special materials and supportive services, cannot be achieved. When to include and when to separate is a source of constant debate (see Figure 2.3).

5. ***Procedural due process.*** The principle of procedural due process upholds the right of those with disabilities to protest a school's decisions about their education. Due process entails the right of children with disabilities and their parents to be notified of school actions and decisions; to challenge those decisions before an impartial tribunal, using counsel and expert witnesses; to examine the school records on which a decision is based; and to appeal whatever decision is reached.

Student learning environments in the future must accommodate a variety of individual and cultural learning styles.

6. ***Individualized education program (IEP).*** Because of the diversity of disabilities, IDEA requires that a "free appropriate public education" be defined on an individual basis, using a written IEP. Each IEP must be reviewed and revised annually, ensuring that the educational goals designed for a child align with his or her learning needs and that these plans are actually delivered. Teachers shoulder the responsibilities of monitoring the needs of each child with disabilities placed in their classrooms. An IEP must include the following:

- A statement of the student's current performance, including long-term (annual) goals and short-term objectives.
- A description of the nature and duration of the instructional services designed to meet the prescribed goals.
- An overview of the methods of evaluation that will be used to monitor the child's progress and to determine whether the goals and objectives have been met.

There is no specific IEP form that must be used, as long as goals, objectives, services, and evaluation are accurately reflected. In fact, hundreds of different IEP forms are currently in use; some run as long as 20 pages; others are only 2 or 3 pages. New teachers should learn about their school district's norms

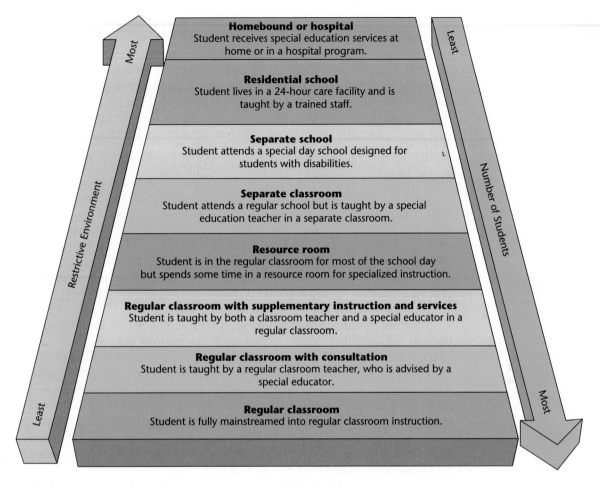

REFLECTION: Why do some believe that all teachers are special education teachers?

and procedures for writing IEPs when they begin teaching. Remember, it is not the format that is important, but whether the IEP accurately describes the educational needs and the related remedial plans. Even though writing these IEPs will undoubtedly consume a great deal of a teacher's time and energy, it often leads to better communication among the school staff, as well as between teachers and parents. Also, the practice of preparing IEPs will likely lead to more effective individualization of instruction for all children, not just those with disabilities.

IDEA has been one of the most thoroughly litigated federal laws in history. Parents whose children qualify for special education services can and do sue the school district if they believe their children's needs are not being met. Local courts agreeing with parents' views have ordered public schools to hire extra teachers or specialized personnel or to spend additional dollars to provide an appropriate education. When judges believe that a school is unable to meet the special needs of a child, even with these additional resources, they can and have ordered the public school to pay the tuition so that the student can attend a private school. However, parents will likely find it more difficult to demand better special education services for their children. The Supreme Court recently ruled that parents who disagree with a school's IEP for their child have the legal burden of proving that the plan will not provide the appropriate education. Disability advocates worry that school districts will now have little incentive to address parents' complaints, or even worse, to provide quality special education services.[35]

Today, more than 6 million students (13 percent of the total public school population) are special needs.[36] In a few areas, such as autism, growth has skyrocketed tenfold in only two decades[37] (see Figure 2.4). **Learning disabilities** constitutes the largest group of students with special needs. Students with learning disabilities have difficulties with listening, speaking, reading, writing, reasoning, or mathematical skills. A student with a learning disability might perform poorly in one area, but extremely well in another. Uneven performance, hyperactivity, disorganization, and lack of follow-through are typical problems for these students. Educational literature reflects more than 50 terms to describe students with learning disabilities.

Meeting the needs of students with special needs has strained education budgets nationwide.[38] Why the upsurge? The reasons are complex—and troubling. Some believe environmental pollutants increase children's disabilities. Others argue that special needs have always been common, but in past years went undiagnosed. Some critics wonder if today we are overdiagnosing the problem. They point to affluent communities where parents hire private psychologists to ensure that their children are identified as having learning disabilities. Why would they do this? In wealthy communities, such labels attract additional educational resources, smaller class size, and even extended time for taking high-stakes tests like the SATs.

FIGURE 2.4

Distribution of students served under IDEA.

SOURCE: U.S. Department of Education, *Condition of Education: Children and Youth with Disabilities,* Table A-6-1 (2010).

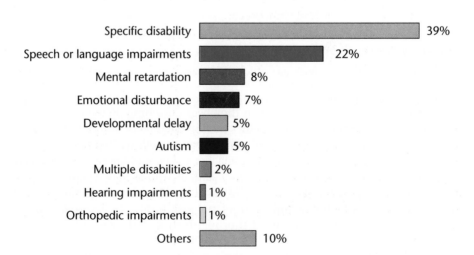

Specific disability	39%
Speech or language impairments	22%
Mental retardation	8%
Emotional disturbance	7%
Developmental delay	5%
Autism	5%
Multiple disabilities	2%
Hearing impairments	1%
Orthopedic impairments	1%
Others	10%

REFLECTION: This distribution offers an insight into which students with exceptionalities teachers are most likely to have in regular classrooms. Suggest some of the accommodations a classroom teacher might consider for each of these special needs.

But if special education means special privileges for the wealthy, the same diagnosis can mean fewer resources for the poor. Studies indicate that African American, Hispanic, and poor special education students are twice as likely to be educated in a more restrictive and separate setting than white and wealthier students. Poor parents struggle to make certain that the special education label is not attached to their children. In addition to poverty, cultural misunderstanding, low expectations, and the desire to remove "difficult" students from the classroom contribute to the high rate of African American students identified as having developmental disabilities or emotional disturbance.[39] And then there is gender. While boys' behavior gets noticed, girls are quieter in class, less likely to cause discipline concerns, and more likely to turn inward with problems and anxieties. As a result, their special education needs often go undetected and untreated.[40] So behind the growing numbers of special education students is a disturbing imbalance as boys and students of color may be overidentified.

Once identified, attention focuses on how best to educate these students.[41] Students with mild disabilities typically attend regular classrooms for part of the day and leave for a period of time to receive special instruction in a resource room. These "pull-out" programs have been criticized for stigmatizing students while failing to improve their academic performance. This concern has fueled the **regular education initiative**, which encourages schools to provide special services within the regular classroom and encourages close collaboration between classroom teachers and special educators. Today, about half of students with disabilities spend 80 percent or more of the school day in a regular classroom.[42]

Regular classroom teachers often express concerns about their ability to handle a mainstreamed classroom:

> They want us all to be super teachers, but I've got 33 kids in my class and it's really a job to take care of them without also having to deal with special needs kids too. I'm not complaining really—I wouldn't want to do anything other than what I'm doing—but it is demanding.[43]

Although classroom teachers are expected to meet many of society's obligations, including the education of students with special needs, they are not always given adequate resources for the task. Frustration is often the result. To succeed, teachers need additional planning time, appropriate curricular materials, ongoing staff development programs, and sometimes, extra classroom assistance.

Despite the criticism and problems of inclusion, one thing is certain: More students with disabilities are enjoying school life alongside their peers. Inclusion seems to thrive in schools that provide teachers with adequate planning time and resources; have open communication among teachers, administrators, and parents; promote a culture of innovation and reform; and encourage a commitment to funding the education of students with special needs.

Assistive Technology

Technology-based devices for students with special needs, called **assistive or adaptive technology**, can provide a real boost for students in and beyond the classroom. Assistive technologies include wheelchairs, switches that respond

Students with Special Needs

SHOULD BE MAINSTREAMED BECAUSE . . .

WITHOUT INCLUSION, OUR DEMOCRATIC IDEAL IS HOLLOW

Segregating the disabled mirrors the historical segregation of African Americans and other groups, a segregation already rejected by the courts. Separate can never be equal, and all students quickly learn the stigma associated with those in "special" classrooms.

SOCIETY NEEDS THE TALENTS OF ALL ITS CITIZENS

Society needs the skills and economic productivity of all our citizens. Educating the disabled in a segregated setting decreases their opportunity for full and meaningful contributions later in life.

MAINSTREAMING IMPROVES THEIR ACADEMIC AND SOCIAL RELATIONS

Studies indicate that students with special needs perform better academically when mainstreamed in regular classes. Not surprisingly, their social adjustment is also improved.

THE NONDISABLED GAIN WHEN STUDENTS WITH SPECIAL NEEDS ARE PRESENT

In our increasingly stratified society, students can spend years in school with peers just like themselves. Inclusion provides an opportunity for children to appreciate and work with people who do not necessarily reflect their own experiences and viewpoints.

SHOULD NOT BE MAINSTREAMED BECAUSE . . .

MERELY SITTING IN REGULAR CLASSROOMS DOES NOT GUARANTEE A FITTING EDUCATION

A rallying cry like "democracy" sounds impressive, but we need to ensure that students with special needs receive a quality education, and the best place for that is not necessarily in a mainstreamed classroom.

PULL-OUT PROGRAMS CAN OFFER STUDENTS WITH SPECIAL NEEDS THE RESOURCES THEY NEED TO SUCCEED

Pull-out programs for children with special needs can offer an adjusted curriculum, special instructional techniques, and smaller class size. Students with special needs can soar in classrooms designed to meet their needs, but flounder when they are inappropriately placed in regular classes.

GIFTED AND TALENTED STUDENTS ARE AT PARTICULAR RISK

Gifted and talented students fall within the special needs category, and for them, mainstreaming is a disaster. If the gifted are not challenged, they will be turned off from school, and the gifts of our most able students will be lost to society.

WHEN STUDENTS WITH SPECIAL NEEDS ARE MAINSTREAMED, NONDISABLED STUDENTS SUFFER

As teachers in regular classes adjust learning activities to accommodate students with special needs, other students lose out. The extra time, special curriculum, and attention given to students with special needs amount to time and resources taken from others in the class.

---

www.mhhe.com/
sadkerbrief3e **YOU DECIDE...**

What training would help you meet the special needs of students mainstreamed into your classroom? Can "separate" ever be "equal"? Whose needs are of most worth—those of special needs students or of "regular" students? Do their needs conflict? As a teacher, would you want children with special needs mainstreamed or pulled out? Imagine yourself the parent of a child with special needs. Would you want your child mainstreamed or pulled out?

Source: Many of these arguments are found in greater detail in Jack L. Nelson, Stuart B. Palonsky, and Kenneth Carlson, *Critical Issues in Education: Dialogue and Dialectics,* 7th edition (New York: McGraw-Hill, 2009), pp. 441–467.

Classroom Observation

3. Including Students with Special Needs

As a classroom teacher, you will most likely have at least one student with special needs and more likely several. In this observation, you will observe an elementary teacher demonstrating how he makes accommodations for his students with special needs. Teaching techniques, classroom organization, professional assistance, and multiple instructional styles enable this instructor to reach ADHD, hearing-impaired, PDD, and other students with special needs.

Classroom Observation videos are available on the CD Reader and at the Online Learning Center.

www.mhhe.com/
sadkerbrief3e

to voice commands, and computer programs that read material for blind students. For example, blind students and their teachers can use Braille software that provides easy-to-use print-to-Braille and Braille-to-print translations. Students with visual or motor problems can use voice-activated software or specialized touch screens to direct the computer's actions. ERICA (Eyegaze Response Interface Computer Aid) allows students to control a computer's keyboard and mouse through eye movement alone, allowing even the most immobile learners to interact with teachers and peers. Those with learning disabilities report that computers (especially handheld computers) are useful

Technological advances have created new and exciting learning possibilities.

for taking notes in class and keeping their schedules organized. And students with learning disabilities especially benefit from such tools as spellcheck. Students with disabilities may use a variety of innovations to help achieve successful inclusion in regular classrooms, and the list of adaptive technology devices promises to grow in the years ahead.[44] (Explore an array of assistive technology devices at Education World, www.educationworld.com/a_tech/tech/tech086.shtml.)

What are the pitfalls of such efforts, and can such "assistance" become too much? Some critics suggest that use of spelling and grammar tools for special education students (as well as others) can short-circuit learning, and that sending laptops home can lead to inappropriate use, from visiting pornography and hate group websites to unsupervised Internet shopping excursions. In fact, the entire effort to include special needs students has its critics, and

STUDENTS WITH SPECIAL NEEDS

Effective teaching of special needs students can be a challenging—and rewarding—experience. Here are a few practical suggestions to create an engaged and equitable learning environment for these students.

- Establish and frequently review classroom rules, procedures, and academic directions.

  Some students with special needs can become frustrated when they want to do the right thing, but get confused or forget. Repeating the rules keeps them—and all students—on track.

- Set fair, yet challenging expectations for all students.

  Students quickly pick up when the teacher lowers expectations. For example, a teacher should not ask easy questions just to special needs students. Asking challenging as well as simpler ones to all students is one strategy that sets a more positive tone. How challenging can the questions be? With experience you will learn how to continually challenge and not frustrate learners with special needs.

- Relate new learning to previous instruction and to the students' backgrounds and experiences.

  Seeing connections is central for learners with special needs, because words alone are not always adequate. Think of connections that tie class learning to students' lives and to previous work.

- Create high student engagement by using a variety of instructional strategies, including visual and auditory methods, hands-on activities, and shorter time segments for activities.

  The more learning channels you open, the more engaged behavior you will encourage, and the more likely that students will connect with your academic goals.

- Model skills and strategies, and always emphasize key words.

  Be mindful that what you say and what you do are not incidental, casual, or secondary. Be purposeful and clear, because your words and behaviors teach powerful lessons.

- Closely monitor independent work, and provide precise and immediate feedback.

  Unlearning a behavior is more difficult than learning it correctly the first time. Monitoring and offering clear feedback can eliminate the need to unlearn and relearn.

- Work to include joy and success in learning.

  Design activities that will give students a sense of accomplishment. Provide additional time if needed to complete assignments, and don't forget to put joy and smiles in your teaching and in your students' learning.

REFLECTION: Review these suggestions and consider how these strategies are likely to improve learning for non–special needs students as well.

---

even with technology and other resources, inclusion will not succeed unless teachers genuinely support the philosophy behind this approach. They must be committed to exploding stereotypes and able to recognize the essential value of helping all children to learn together. Their talents and commitment may be put to the test in communities like San Francisco, where students unable to feed themselves, or speak, or even go to the bathroom, are mainstreamed.[45] These students are part of a first wave of severely impaired children placed in regular classrooms. Although a difficult situation for teachers, students, and parents, the belief is that they will do far better there than in a segregated and restricted environment. Inclusion is at its heart a moral issue, one that raises the timeless principles of equality, justice, and the need for all of us to learn to live and grow together—not apart.

This chapter is all about the rich human diversity that graces our classrooms and enables all of us, teachers and students alike, to learn from one another. We will never know how many ideas, insights, inventions, and medical breakthroughs have been lost because of our inability to honor these different ways of knowing. But we can rededicate ourselves to honoring and nurturing the unique talents of each student.

SUMMARY

1. **How do cognitive, affective, and physiological factors impact learning?**

   Individuals exhibit diverse styles of learning that are affected by attitudes (such as motivation), reasoning (organization and retention of information), and physical needs. Because students exhibit a wide range of individual differences, there is no single optimal educational climate.

2. **How can teachers respond to different learning styles?**

   Teachers may need to adjust room temperature, lighting, and noise level, and plan a variety of activities to accommodate individual student needs. Teachers can work to complement various learning styles, such as visual, kinesthetic, or auditory.

3. **Is gender a learning style?**

   The jury is still out on this question. For example, a number of boys seem to prefer competitive learning, while many girls opt for cooperative learning activities. Is this due to genetics or socialization or some combination of the two? Certainly, the continued emphasis by schools on gender differences, segregating students by sex in comments, daily activities, and even in separate classrooms and schools does little to help cross-gender understanding or harmony.

4. **What are the classroom implications of Howard Gardner's theory of multiple intelligences?**

   Gardner's theory of multiple intelligences suggests that teachers plan their lessons to incorporate and develop intelligences that go beyond the traditional verbal and mathematical/logic (e.g., ask students to reenact historical events through dance). Gardner's theory of five minds further deepens our understanding of intelligences.

5. **How does emotional intelligence influence teaching and learning?**

   Daniel Goleman advocates that teachers develop students' emotional (EQ) gifts by helping them understand their emotions, "read" the emotions of others, and learn how to manage relationships.

6. **How are the needs of learners with exceptionalities met in today's classrooms?**

   The Individuals with Disabilities Education Act (IDEA) guarantees students with disabilities access to public education. Although gifted and talented students also are considered exceptional, their needs are often neglected. There continues to be much debate around the wisdom of inclusion or mainstreaming.

CHAPTER REVIEW

Go to the Online Learning Center to take a chapter self-quiz, practice with key terms, and review concepts from the chapter.

www.mhhe.com/sadkerbrief3e

KEY TERMS AND PEOPLE

accelerated programs, 47

Advanced Placement, 47

affective domain, 34

appropriate education, 49

assistive (adaptive) technology, 53

cognitive domain, 33

emotional intelligence quotient (EQ), 42

exceptional learners, 44

Howard Gardner, 39

gender similarities hypothesis, 37

giftedness, 45

Daniel Goleman, 42

inclusion, 50

individualized education program (IEP), 50

Individuals with Disabilities Education Act (IDEA), 49

learning disabilities, 52

learning styles, 33

least-restrictive environment, 50

locus of control, 34

mainstreaming (inclusion), 50

multiple intelligences, 39

neuroplasticity, 37

DISCUSSION QUESTIONS AND ACTIVITIES

WEB-*TIVITIES*

Go to the Online Learning Center to do the following activities:
1. Multiple Intelligences
2. Exceptional Learners

1. How would you characterize your own learning style? Interview other students in your class to determine how they characterize their learning styles. Based on these interviews, what recommendations could you offer your course instructor about how to meet the needs of different students in your class?

2. Do you believe that females and males have different gender learning styles? Provide some examples to support your position.

3. Interview people who graduated from single-sex schools and ask them about their experiences. Did they find single-sex schools to be an advantage or not? In what ways? Do males and females have different assessments? What was lost by not attending a coed school? What was gained?

4. Can you develop additional intelligences beyond the ones Gardner identifies? (This is often best accomplished in groups.)

5. Investigate a special education program in a local school. Describe its strengths. What suggestions do you have for improving it? What is your position on "full inclusion"?

YOUR CD-ROM: THE TEACHERS, SCHOOLS, AND SOCIETY READER WITH CLASSROOM OBSERVATION VIDEO CLIPS

Articles, Case Studies, and Videos correspond to chapter content and are not always in numeric order. Go to your *Teachers, Schools, and Society Reader* CD-ROM to:

Read Current and Historical Articles

4. "An Educator's Primer to the Gender War," David Sadker, *Phi Delta Kappan,* November 2002.

5. "Succeeding Through the Arts," Sally Smith, *Their World,* 1996/1997.

6. "The Truth About Boys and Girls," Sara Mead, *Education Sector Reports,* June 2006.

7. "Confronting Ableism," Thomas Heir, *Educational Leadership,* February 2007.

8. "Talent Development: A 'Must' for a Promising Future," Julia Link Roberts, *Phi Delta Kappan,* March 2008.

Analyze Case Studies

3. **Carol Brown:** A teacher, after socially integrating a diverse class, sees her efforts threatened when a child's pencil case disappears and is thought to have been stolen. Her students' reactions are not what she had expected.

4. **Joan Martin, Marilyn Coe, and Warren Groves:** A classroom teacher, a special education teacher, and a principal hold different views about mainstreaming a

boy with poor reading skills. The dilemma comes to a head over the method of grading him at the end of the marking period.

Observe Teachers, Students, and Classrooms in Action

2. **Classroom Observation: A Multiple Intelligences Lesson in Action**

3. **Classroom Observation: Including Students with Special Needs**

See pages 41 and 55 for descriptions of these videos. You'll find the video on the CD Reader and at the Online Learning Center.

www.mhhe.com/
sadkerbrief3e

chapter 3

TEACHING YOUR DIVERSE STUDENTS

Focus Questions

1. In what ways are U.S. schools failing culturally diverse students?
2. How do deficit, expectation, and cultural difference theories explain disparate academic performance among various racial, ethnic, and cultural groups?
3. How do phrases like "melting pot" and "tossed salad" both capture and mask American identity?
4. What are the political and instructional issues surrounding bilingual education?
5. What are the purposes and approaches of multicultural education?
6. Why is culturally responsive teaching important?
7. How can teachers use culturally responsive teaching strategies?

www.mhhe.com/
sadkerbrief3e

WHAT DO YOU THINK? Cultural Diversity of Students.
Estimate the racial, ethnic, and social class backgrounds of today's students.

Chapter Preview

The United States has just experienced the greatest immigration surge in its history. In the past few decades, newly minted Americans have arrived mainly from Latin America and Asia, but also from the Caribbean, the Middle East, Africa, and Eastern Europe. Today, about 1 in 10 Americans is foreign born, and the native language of well over 30 million Americans is a language other than English. By 2030, half of all schoolchildren will be of color. These demographics create a remarkable and formidable challenge for the nation's schools.[1] Some advocate a multicultural approach to education that recognizes and incorporates this growing student diversity into teaching and the curriculum. Others fret that disassembling our Eurocentric curriculum and traditional approaches to education may harm our U.S. culture. For many teachers, the struggle is to teach students with backgrounds different from their own. How to best do this is a tough question, and one that this chapter addresses directly, not only with breathtaking information and some astute (we hope) insights, but with practical suggestions as well.

Student Diversity

Since the 1960s, more immigrants have come to this country than at the beginning of the twentieth century, a time often thought of as the great era of immigration and Americanization. Today, about one in three Americans are of color. Demographic forecasting, the study of people and their vital statistics, predicts that by 2030 half the school population will be from non-European ethnic groups. You will teach in a nation more diverse and less Eurocentric than the one you grew up in.

So let's begin to explore our changing student population by defining some basic terms that are critical, but often used incorrectly. **Race** refers to a group of individuals sharing a common socially determined category often related to genetic attributes, physical appearance, and ancestry. Yet, racial categories can vary by society. For example, in the United States an individual with any known African ancestry is considered black. But in Caribbean and Latin American nations, race is often determined not by physical attributes, but by social class. In these countries, "money lightens": upward social mobility increases the likelihood of being classified as white. **Ethnicity** refers to shared common cultural traits such as language, religion, and dress. A sense of shared peoplehood is one of the most important characteristics of ethnicity. A Latino or Hispanic, for example, belongs to an ethnic group, but might belong to the Negro, Caucasian, or Asian race. **Culture** is a set of learned beliefs, values, symbols, and behaviors, a way of life shared by members of a society. There is not only a national culture, but also microcultures or subcultures. There are cultures related to class, religion, or sexual orientation, to offer but a few examples. These subcultures carry values and behaviors that differ from others in the same nation or the same community.[2] The willingness of people to understand and appreciate different cultures, races, and ethnicities is often at the heart of the diversity issue in the United States. The challenge for educators is to ensure that all our students achieve.

The 2000 Census added a new demographic by asking citizens to report if they were **multiracial**—that is, claiming ancestors from two or more races. Nearly 7 million Americans responded yes. Most of the respondents were under 18, and in at least 10 states, more than a quarter of school-aged children were in the multiracial category, indicating that this group will grow in the years ahead. Few studies have investigated the specific challenges facing multiracial-multiethnic children, but we see some cultural inequities already emerging. Tiger Woods is considered by many to be our first great black golfer. Few refer to him as our first great Thai golfer. President Barack Obama is called our first black president, not our first half-white president. For them and others, any black heritage becomes shorthand for race identity. Teachers and schools have much to learn in honoring the full background of multiracial children and avoiding convenient and simplistic labels.

The United States is changing. Between 1980 and 2008, the white population declined from 80 percent to 66 percent; the Hispanic population increased from 6 percent to 15 percent; the black population remained constant at about 12 percent; and the Asian/Pacific Islander population increased from less than 2 percent of the total population to 4 percent. During this period, that new category of multiracial children continued to grow as well.[3] (See Figure 3.1.)

Focus Question 1
In what ways are U.S. schools failing culturally diverse students?

Failing at Fairness

These population changes challenge our schools, as these statistics illustrate:[4]

- Hispanic, Native American, and African American students score consistently lower on standardized tests than do their Asian and white classmates.

- Almost half of the nation's historically under-resourced populations—Hispanic, African American, and Native American—are not graduating from high school.

- In Houston, Oakland, Cleveland, and New York, with large populations of poor students and students of color, between 50 and 70 percent of the students do not graduate high school.

- The percentages of children who were living in poverty were higher for blacks (34 percent), American Indians/Alaska Natives (33 percent), Hispanics (27 percent), and Native Hawaiians or other Pacific Islanders (26 percent), than for Asians (11 percent) or whites (10 percent).

- Students from low-income families are six times more likely to drop out of school than are the children of the wealthy.

- In recent years, the achievement gap between white and minority students has not narrowed, despite the focus of No Child Left Behind on increasing the test scores of African American and Hispanic students.

Most Americans do not blame schools for these achievement gaps, yet a majority (57 percent) feel it is up to the schools to close the gaps.[5] The Gallup Public Opinion poll suggests that Americans understand that issues outside of school affect what goes on in school. Even before children arrive at the schoolhouse door, poverty takes its toll. Lower birth weight, poor nutrition, and higher incidences of lead poisoning among children from low-income families contribute to academic and cognitive problems.[6] Preschool children from low-income households know fewer words, speak less, and have fewer, if any, books. And "poverty" is not a synonym for color, because most of the poor in the United States are white. Poverty affects students from all groups.

Race and ethnicity are, of course, well-publicized factors in academic performance. The test scores and graduation rates of African American and Hispanic American students lag behind those of white and Asian American students, in part because of a costly disconnect between school and home

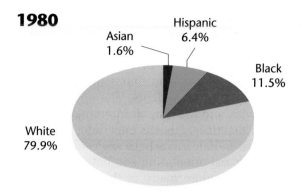

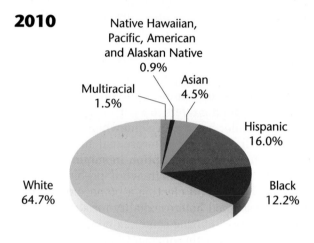

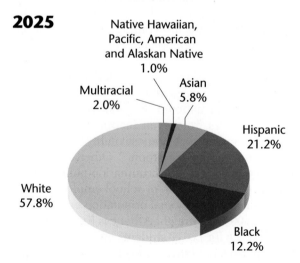

FIGURE 3.1

Resident population percentages in 1980, 2010, and projected to 2025.

SOURCE: U.S. Department of Education, National Center for Education Statistics, "Status and Trends in the Education of Racial and Ethnic Minorities," NCES 2010-015, July 2010.

REFLECTION: How can teachers best prepare to teach America's changing demographics?

cultures. African American peers sometimes mock school achievement as "acting white," suggesting academic success is racial or cultural treason. Hispanic families may encounter not only cultural barriers, but also language barriers. In truth, the failure of our society to bridge and honor differences among ethnic and racial groups contributes to the weaker test scores and lower graduation rates of many students. The home–school disconnect has other dimensions: Jewish and Muslim children may encounter school obstacles to their religious practices, atheists encounter hostility to their nonreligious beliefs, American Indian tribes have seen schools attack their cultures and values, and even sexual orientation conflicts are now part of school life. In this chapter, we will explore many of these diversity dimensions. As a teacher and as a citizen, working to eliminate social and economic injustice is as important to academic success as anything you do in the classroom.

Lesbian, Gay, Bisexual, and Transgender Students (LGBT)

Being gay, lesbian, bisexual, or straight refers to a person's sexual orientation, an innate characteristic that determines who one is attracted to sexually and romantically. Being transgender refers to a person's gender identity—a person's innate sense of being male, female, or somewhere in between. Many school practices assume that all people are heterosexual and either male or female. A typical curriculum reflects this assumption in subtle and not so subtle ways. Literature like *Romeo and Juliet,* math word problems like "David bought Karen one dozen roses . . .", and electing a homecoming king and queen are obvious examples of assumed heterosexuality for all. However, some schools are altering these practices: inviting same-sex couples to the prom, providing gender-neutral or individual bathrooms and locker rooms for transgender students, and including LGBT people and perspectives in the curriculum.[7]

This sign can be found outside classrooms and school offices to announce a safe zone for LGBT students.

The person displaying this "Safe Zone" symbol is supportive of lesbian, gay, bisexual and transgender individuals.

Safe Zone provided by:

More and more gay students are coming out of the closet earlier, often in middle school, and are finding support among peers and teachers. Others find no support and liken school to a war zone. For Lawrence King, a 15-year-old in California who was shot and killed by a 14-year-old classmate, war zone is not an exaggeration. These different responses to LGBT students reflect our national division. A number of states have laws preventing teachers from even mentioning the word "homosexual"; some states mandate that homosexuality be presented in exclusively negative terms in the classroom.[8] Other school districts recognize LGBT people in their nondiscrimination policies, sending a clear message that no student, parent, or school employee will be discriminated against because of their sexual orientation or gender identity. There are more than 3,500 Gay-Straight Alliances (GSAs), student clubs that provide a safe space for LGBT students and their allies.[9] GSAs sometimes engender controversy, but the 1984 Federal Equal Access Act states that if schools allow any noncurricular clubs, they have to allow them all.

Depending on where you teach, you may or may not be able to include LGBT issues in your teaching. But wherever you teach, you can ensure that democratic norms of equality are followed, and that all students are respected regardless of individual differences. Students do not have to agree "It's okay to be gay," but they should understand that "It's not okay to discriminate against those who are

SOME CONSIDERATIONS FOR TEACHING LGBT STUDENTS

Your visible support can help LGBT achieve in school. You can do the following:

1. Post a "Safe Zone" sign in your classroom or office.

2. Don't tolerate intolerance. Immediately respond to comments like "fag" or "dyke" and explain that such bigotry is not acceptable.

3. Integrate the contributions of LGBT figures in science, history, athletics, the arts, and other areas of the curriculum.

4. Avoid assumptions about any particular student being gay. The range of behaviors and attitudes within each sex is enormous.

5. On the other hand, honor confidences shared with you by LGBT students.

6. Work to keep the school as a safe place for LGBT students. Think about becoming an advisor to the Gay-Straight Alliance.

Adapted from "Ally Yourself with LGBT Students," *Teaching Tolerance,* Fall 2010, p. 35.

REFLECTION: Why is being sensitive to LGBT issues a good classroom strategy, even if you do not think you have any LGBT students in your class?

---

gay." By providing a safe place for all students, teachers can create nurturing classrooms where every child can learn and every family is welcome.

Putting a Price on Racism

"Welcome to class," says the professor as you take your seat. "I want you to respond to the following case study. This, of course, is fictional, but suspend disbelief, read the parable, and tell me what you think."

As a student in this class, you think this sounds kind of interesting (and a good grade in this course would be really nice). So you settle down and read the brief scenario:

> You are a white person and are visited by an official who explains that a mistake has been made. You were actually born to black parents who live far from where you grew up. The error has to be rectified. At midnight, you will become black, acquiring a darker skin, and body and facial features that reflect your African heritage. Your knowledge and ideas, your "inside," however, will remain the same.
>
> Now this is an unusual and rare problem, the official explains, but the error was not yours, and the organization that he represents is ready and able to offer you appropriate recompense. His records indicate that you are likely to live another 50 years. How much financial recompense would you request?

You look around and see your classmates, each from their own unique perspective of race and ethnicity, settle into the task. You wonder: How much money will your white classmates ask for? How will the students of color respond to this controversial, some would say offensive, class exercise? Now the *big* question: How much money would *you* ask for?

Although the parable is not true, the scenario is. Professor Andrew Hacker at Cornell put this question to white students in his class and asked them to come up with a settlement figure: How much money would they want to offset the "error"? If you are wondering what figure Hacker's students came up with, most felt that a reasonable payment for the mistake would be $50 million, $1 million for each coming black year.

That acclaimed study became the focus of a popular book, *Two Nations: Black, White, Separate, Hostile, Unequal* (1992), and while it raised some poignant questions, it left many unanswered.[10] What if Professor Hacker had continued the experiment with other groups? How much money would a Hispanic American, an African American, and an Asian American request if a mistake were made and they had to live the rest of their lives as a member of another race or culture? Would they request less compensation for the "administrative" blunder? The same $50 million? Would they want more money?

Just posing the problem underscores the U.S. tendency to look to the courts to fix any mistake, no matter how bizarre. Of course, in this story, money is the all-American panacea, a salve for any social injury. But despite these confounding issues, the parable is fascinating, and the questions it raises are intriguing.

Why did Professor Hacker construct this strange story, and how did he interpret the payment? He believed that the story unmasks America's hidden racism. Professor Hacker considers white privilege to be so commonplace that most of us are no longer able to "see" it. He uses the parable because it makes visible the hidden advantage society gives to white Americans. In Hacker's estimation, the $50 million that his students thought was "fair" compensation represents the value that white people place on the color of their own skin. When you hear the word *race,* what comes to your mind? Is it the image of a black man? Or perhaps you visualize an Asian woman? We would wager that most of you reading this text do not visualize a white person. When "race" is mentioned in America, we tend to picture people of color, the ones who are not like the majority that dominate newspapers, books, and much of the media. For example, from time to time, a news commentator might point out how many African Americans are now in Congress. But when is the last time you heard a report of the number of whites in Congress? Like Andrew Hacker, author Peggy McIntosh helps us see the hidden privileges of being in the majority. She refers to these privileges as an "invisible knapsack," because those in the majority often do not even see their advantages. Here are a few examples of the invisible race knapsack, the hidden privileges of being white. As a white person:

- When I am cited for a traffic violation, I can be sure I have not been singled out because of my race.

- I can watch television or read the front page of the paper and see my race widely represented.

- If I walk into a meeting late, people don't assume that my lateness reflects on my race.

- I do not have to educate my children to be aware of systemic racism for their own daily physical protection.

- When I ask to talk to the "person in charge," I can feel confident that I will be talking to a person of my own race.

- I can take a job with an affirmative action employer without having my colleagues believe that I was hired because of my race and not my qualifications.

- I can walk into a stationery store and find a card to send with pictures of my race.

- People don't ask me to explain how my race feels about a topic.

Can you add to the list? If you'd like to see other examples, visit www
.nymbp.org/reference/WhitePrivilege.pdf.

If you are white, or heterosexual, or Christian (and most teachers are), you
also have a knapsack of hidden privileges, whether you know it or not.[11] But
if your students come from other backgrounds, they bring fewer privileges
to school. If teachers are to connect and communicate with the growing student diversity in their classroom, they will need to learn more about students
whose backgrounds are different from their own. This chapter is intended to
help you do just that.

Theories of Why Some Groups Succeed and Others Do Not

A number of theories have emerged to explain why some groups soar in
school, while others flounder. Some of the explanations are fatalistic, others are more hopeful. Here are three—deficit theory, expectation theory, and
cultural difference theory. The argument for **deficit theory** is that certain
students do poorly in school because of their cultural, social, or linguistic
background. The values, language patterns, and behaviors learned at home
put these students at an academic disadvantage. Fewer books read, fewer
vocabulary words used by parents, and little understanding of the relationship between education and careers contribute to the cultural deficit.
A nefarious branch of this theory held that genetic and IQ deficiencies of
certain groups, especially people of color, were the root cause of academic
underachievement. Most deficit theory proponents today steer clear of such
genetic claims.

Those who subscribe to **expectation theory** believe that some children do
poorly because their teachers do not expect much of kids from certain racial
and ethnic groups. As a result, they teach these students differently, and the
students' academic performance suffers. This insight was first made popular
by a classic study done by Rosenthal and Jacobson, which is described in
greater detail later in this text. In the study, students were randomly chosen
and the teachers told these students would experience an intellectual growth
spurt during the year. Lo and behold, over the year, their grades improved.
Teacher expectations of improved performance led to improved performance.
Now imagine the opposite, teachers who expect less from certain students,
and you see how harmful this "self-fulfilling prophesy" can be.

A third explanation for student achievement argues for better cross-cultural
understanding. **Cultural difference theory** asserts that academic problems can
be overcome if educators study and mediate the cultural gap separating school
and home. Let's consider a case in point:

> Polynesian children in a Hawaiian village are performing poorly on the school
> reading tests. They seem unresponsive to the extra time and effort made by
> teachers to improve their reading performance. Why is this happening, and how
> can the situation be improved?

In this example, educators studied the Polynesian culture and discovered that older children, rather than adults, play a major role in educating the
young. Accordingly, the school established a peer-learning center to provide
the opportunity for older children to teach younger ones. By recognizing and

Focus Question 2
How do deficit, expecta-
tion, and cultural difference
theories explain different
academic performance
among various racial, ethnic, and cultural groups?

Classroom Observation

5. High School Students Discuss Issues They Face as Immigrants

A growing number of students in today's schools are immigrants. In this observation, you will hear several high school students talk about their experiences in school as immigrants. You will also hear a teacher who works with them discuss her role in helping them to adapt to their new community and achieve academic and social success.

Classroom Observation videos are available on the CD Reader and at the Online Learning Center.

www.mhhe.com/
sadkerbrief3e

adopting cultural traditions, the school was able to dramatically improve students' reading scores.[12]

What role do these theories play in the classroom? Deficit theory teaches us that groups bring different experiences and values to the classroom, and some of these differences do not mesh with mainstream school culture. Mainstream society terms this mismatch a deficit. The economic poverty of some groups contributes to such deficits, an issue that many believe should be addressed by the larger society. Expectation theory teaches us the power of teacher attitudes, that the attitudes you bring to the classroom influence your students, for better or worse. Cultural difference theory teaches us the rich nature of the human experience and how much we can teach each other. This chapter is intended to do just that: help us appreciate each other.

From the Melting Pot to Cultural Pluralism

Focus Question 3
How do phrases such as "melting pot" and "cultural pluralism" both capture and mask American identity?

Start a discussion about cultural, racial, or ethnic differences at a social gathering—or even more challenging, in a work environment—and feel the tension grow as competing theories of group differences emerge. Introduce issues like affirmative action, immigration laws, classes being taught in Spanish or Laotian, or racial profiling, and some people become unglued. More than a few people will listen politely, carefully avoiding uttering a sound. Some might stay silent but wonder if the conversation is genuine or simply an attempt at "political correctness." Others, articulating beliefs they perceive as acceptable, may voice hopeful insights, but in their heart of hearts, they themselves do not believe them. A few may say things they will later regret, words that may spark an attack, or a charge of racism:

"Why don't they learn to speak English? My grandparents had nothing, but they learned the language. Are people today too lazy or do they simply not care?"

"I am fine with racial equality. I like it as a concept. I just wonder why all my friends are my race."

"I treat all people the same, but some groups have a chip on their shoulder."

Keep Students Together or Mix Them Up?

depends on you [?]
does [?] emphasis?
accept the awareness
— embrace vs. disgrace

TEACHING KIDS IN SETTINGS SEGREGATED . . .

BY GENDER, CAN FOCUS ON ACADEMIC NEEDS

Same-gender classes help students focus on academics, not on each other. Girls can get extra encouragement in math and science; boys can get special assistance in reading and language arts.

BY COMMUNITY, PROMOTES RACIAL AND ETHNIC PRIDE

Let's eliminate the alienation caused by busing students out of their neighborhood. Students feel accepted and take pride in local schools, where they can study with friends and learn from a curriculum that reflects and honors their heritage.

BY RELIGION, ALLOWS APPROPRIATE AND SACRED OBSERVANCE

Secular American school norms and laws force all religious groups to make compromises. Some religious holidays are ignored, adult-led prayer in school is prohibited, school dress codes may conflict with religious requirements, and schools routinely ignore religious dietary law. By educating religious groups separately, different histories and beliefs can be honored and practiced. Students can pray as they like and pursue their religion without ridicule or taunting from peers, or interference from civil authorities.

BY NEED, OFFERS AN EDUCATIONAL HAVEN FOR LGBT STUDENTS

Special schools can help LGBT students cope with their unique personal and academic circumstances. Being with LGBT students protects them from comparisons and ridicule that might exist elsewhere.

TEACHING KIDS TOGETHER . . .

PROMOTES GENDER EQUALITY

Learning and succeeding together in the classroom prepares boys and girls to live and work together as adults. Equitable instruction and curriculum will teach students how to eliminate traditional gender barriers in society.

FOSTERS CULTURAL AND RACIAL UNDERSTANDING

We must not allow our nation to be fractured along racial, ethnic, and class lines. Integrating children of different backgrounds mirrors our ideal of a democratic society. Cross-cultural classrooms enrich the learning experience.

PROMOTES RESPECT AND UNDERSTANDING OF RELIGIOUS DIFFERENCES

Religious practices are the domain of religious institutions and should not become the focal point of school life. Learning about different religions can help all of us to grow. Restricting each of us to one set of beliefs will eventually divide and separate Americans. By learning together, students gain valuable lessons as they prepare to live and work together as adults in a vibrant and diverse democracy. We see all too well in other countries how religion and government can create problems.

GIVES LGBT STUDENTS HOPE FOR THE FUTURE

Attending a regular school gives all students insight into different lifestyles. Learning together as children can help us all live together as adults.

www.mhhe.com/
sadkerbrief3e **YOU DECIDE . . .**

Do you believe equal educational opportunity is best achieved in separate or integrated classrooms? Is your position consistent or does it vary, depending upon the identified group? Extend this You Be the Judge feature by developing the arguments for either integrating or separating two other groups discussed in this chapter (or identify new groups).

Start a discussion about cultural, racial, or ethnic differences at a social gathering, and you may wish you never did.

Many of us continue to live in silence about race and ethnicity. As a nation, we have yet to come to terms with our multicultural society. Many believe that the United States is a wondrous melting pot where the Statue of Liberty opens her arms to all the world's immigrants. This was the image painted by Israel Zangwill in a 1910 play that coined the term *melting pot.*

> America is God's Crucible, the Great Melting Pot where all races of Europe are melting and reforming . . . Germans and Frenchmen, Irishman and Englishmen, Jews and Russians—into the Crucible with you all! God is making the American . . . The real American has not yet arrived. He is only in the Crucible, I tell you—he will be the fusion of all races, the coming superman.[13]

For many, "melting in" became a reality. Groups incorporated into the mainstream culture are said to have gone through **assimilation** or **enculturation.** Countless immigrants today cling to this idea of being transformed into a new citizen, a new person, an American. But the melting pot image, although enticing, describes only a part of the American reality.

Picture yourself traveling in another country and a person who has never been to America asks you to describe your country—how would you do it? Would you describe our great West, its majestic Rockies and mysterious deserts? Or perhaps you would choose South Beach in Miami, a city with a 1940s art deco feel and a beach at its doorstep. Or perhaps New York City catches your fancy, with its breathtaking skyscrapers, its world-class museums, and the wonders of Broadway theaters. Some of you might paint a picture of the magnificent Maine coast, or the rich Midwest farmlands, the pristine Alaskan wilderness, or perhaps the lush Hawaiian Islands. Okay, we will stop here because suddenly we are feeling an urge to travel. You probably already appreciate our point: A fair description of our nation would include all its diverse regions, from coast to coast.

Now, let's change the question, and imagine that you are asked not to describe America but to describe an American. How would you do it? Would you resort to the melting pot image: a white European, perhaps arriving penniless and now a rich American? Or perhaps you would take the question quite literally and describe our Native Americans, our many different Indian tribes. Or better yet, we hope that you have learned the lesson from the first question. Not only is our nation geographically diverse, our people are diverse as well. Americans live in communities called Germantown and Chinatown, maintaining traditions from their land of origin. Americans have dark skins, but they also have light skins, and every shade in between. They speak Spanish and Arabic, pray to Buddha and Christ, or perhaps look for spiritual answers in their own hearts, like the Quakers. What do we call this diversity? This is **cultural pluralism,** a recognition that some groups, voluntarily or involuntarily, have maintained their culture and their language. We now recognize that there are many kinds of Americans, and like geographic diversity, they make our nation diverse and beautiful. Different groups teach us different ways of seeing and understanding the world. As we learn to appreciate one another's experiences and viewpoints, our nation grows not only stronger but also wiser.

Schools are one of the portals where diverse Americans meet. It is a place where we can learn from one another. Teachers are the gatekeepers to that learning. If they are open to other cultures and peoples, they and their students will learn and grow.

Bilingual Education

Focus Question 4
What are the political and instructional issues surrounding bilingual education?

What is going on in America? It is amazing, and disturbing, to ride on a road and see street signs that are printed not only in English but in other languages as well. What's more, even legal documents are now being written in foreign languages. How unnerving to walk down an American street and not understand what people are talking about. Maybe this isn't America. I feel like a stranger in my own land. Why don't they learn to speak English?

Sound like a stroll through today's Miami, or San Diego, or perhaps San Antonio? Good try, but you not only have the wrong city, you are also in the wrong century. Benjamin Franklin expressed this view in the 1750s.[14] He was disgruntled that Philadelphia had printed so many things, including street signs, in another language (German, in this case). Even the Articles of Confederation were published in German as well as English, and children were taught in Dutch, Italian, and Polish.

Bilingual education in the United States is hundreds of years old, hardly a "new" issue. In 1837, Pennsylvania law required that school instruction be given on an equal basis in German as well as English. In fact, that example provides us with a fairly concise definition of **bilingual education,** the use of two languages for instruction. But, almost a century later, as the United States was being pulled into World War I, foreign languages were seen as unpatriotic. Public pressure routed the German language from the curriculum, although nearly one in four high school students was studying the language at the time. Individual states went even further. Committed to a rapid assimilation of new immigrants, and suspicious of much that was foreign, these states prohibited the teaching of *any* foreign language during the first eight years of schooling. (The Supreme Court found this policy not only xenophobic but unconstitutional as well, in *Meyer v. State of Nebraska,* 1923.)[15]

Despite the long history of bilingual education in this country, many school districts never really bought into the concept. In districts without bilingual education, students with a poor command of English had to sink or swim (or perhaps, more accurately, "speak or sink"). Students either learned to speak English as they sat in class, or they failed school, an approach sometimes referred to as **language submersion.** If submersion was not to their liking, they could choose to leave school. Many did. Congress responded with the Bilingual Education Act in 1968, providing

Being a good teacher in the years ahead will almost surely mean working with a culturally diverse population.

In some bilingual education programs, English is learned as a second language while the student takes other academic work in his or her native language.

financial incentives, what some people call "a carrot approach," to encourage schools to initiate bilingual education programs. Not all districts chased the carrot.

During the early 1970s, disillusioned parents initiated lawsuits. In 1974, the Supreme Court heard the case of ***Lau v. Nichols.*** This class action lawsuit centered around Kinney Lau and 1,800 other Chinese students from the San Francisco area who were failing their courses because they could not understand English. The Court unanimously affirmed that federally funded schools must "rectify the language deficiency" of students. Teaching students in a language they did not understand was not an appropriate education. The Court's decision in *Lau v. Nichols* prompted the U.S. Department of Education Office of Civil Rights to issue the "*Lau* Remedies," guidelines for school districts that specify that "language minority students should be taught academics in their primary language until they could effectively benefit from English language instruction."[16] Under this provision, school districts must take positive steps to eliminate language barriers to learning.

Bilingual Education Models

More than 5 million **English language learners (ELLs)** are enrolled in public elementary and secondary schools (nearly 10 percent of school enrollment), and the number is steadily increasing (see Figure 3.2). About half of these

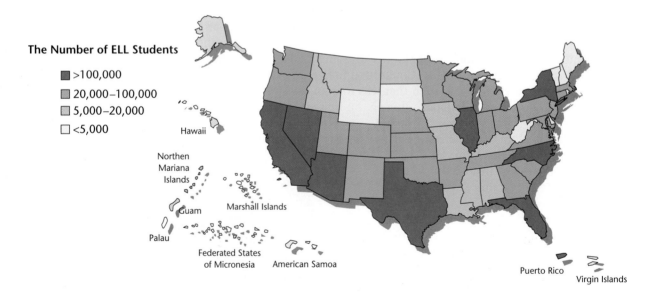

The Number of ELL Students

- >100,000
- 20,000–100,000
- 5,000–20,000
- <5,000

Hawaii

Northen Mariana Islands

Guam

Marshall Islands

Palau

Federated States of Micronesia

American Samoa

Puerto Rico

Virgin Islands

FIGURE 3.2

The distribution of ELL students.

SOURCE: U.S. Department of Education, OELA, www.ed.gov; National Clearinghouse for English Language Acquisition, Washington, DC, May 2010. http://www.ncela.gwu.edu/files/uploads/9/growingLEP_0708.pdf.

REFLECTION: What are the implications of this demographic on your life in the classroom? How can your teacher preparation help you to teach ELL students?

non-English-speaking youngsters are from families that have recently come to the United States. Surprisingly, many ELL students were born in this country but have not yet learned English at home or in their community. About one in five school-age children speak a language other than English at home, with Spanish the most common.[17] As these non-English-speaking students enter schools, most will need to make sense of a new language, a new culture, and possibly new ways of interacting with teachers and classmates. Teachers can greatly assist this transition by creating a stable classroom environment.

English language learners typically work to master English and academic content. Several models of bilingual education help students reach these goals. These models vary in ease of implementation and effectiveness, and often reflect the underlying philosophy of a local community or state. These philosophies fall along the continuum of cultural assimilation (immersion and ESL models) to cultural pluralism (maintenance and dual language methods).[18]

Typically in bilingual education programs, English language learners acquire English as a second language while taking other academic subjects in their native language. The **transitional approach** uses the native language as a bridge to English language instruction. Academic subjects are first taught using the native language, but progressively students transition to English, their new language. Cultural assimilation is often stressed. The goal is to prepare for English-only classrooms, typically within two to three years. The **maintenance** or **developmental approach** is designed to help children develop academic skills in both their native language and English. Instruction occurs in both languages to create a truly bilingual student. An ideal maintenance program provides **dual-language instruction** from kindergarten through twelfth grade, although few exist at the secondary level. Students develop cognitively in both languages, learning about the culture and history of their ethnic group as well as that of the dominant culture. This two-way bilingual education adapts the maintenance approach to develop the language abilities of ELLs *and* their English-speaking peers. For example, children who speak Spanish are placed in the same class with children who speak English, and students learn each other's languages and work academically in both languages. (See Contemporary Issues: A View from the Field.)

In the **immersion** approach, instruction is exclusively in English. Immersion cannot truly be considered bilingual but is used with ELLs nonetheless. Teachers using an immersion model often understand the students' native language but deliver lessons in a "sheltered" or simplified English vocabulary that attempts to familiarize students with English while learning academic content. **English as a Second Language (ESL)** supplements immersion programs by providing special pull-out classes for additional instruction in reading and writing English. The goal is to assimilate learners into the English language as quickly as possible. While research suggests that English-only instruction is not as cognitively effective as sound bilingual programs, ESL instruction may work well for students highly motivated to be part of a mainstreamed English-only classroom.[19]

Language submersion is an extreme example of immersion. Submersion places students in classes where only English is spoken, and instruction is not modified at all. It is fundamentally a "sink or swim" approach.

A VIEW FROM THE FIELD: TWIN CLASSROOMS

Nicole Miller, 25, is a second grade teacher at PS 108 in Brooklyn, New York, a kindergarten through fifth grade school with almost 1,000 students. Nicole teaches in a dual language program; for most of the students at PS 108, Spanish is the primary language spoken in the home. As of 2006, about 80 percent of the students were new immigrants. Although Nicole teaches in English, there are challenges to the dual language program.

> My first challenge is teaching students who are not proficient in English; my classroom is meant to be a place where only English is spoken by teachers and students. Another major challenge is the academic gap between students in my classes. For instance, I have students who only know a handful of sight words and are not able to write a complete sentence independently and I have other students who are reading books and writing five paragraph pieces. Creating lessons that don't leave anyone out is a daily challenge. It is so important to support the struggling students while still challenging the thriving students.

Picture twin classrooms across the hall from each other, one with half English dominant students and the other half ELLs. The two teachers work together, one teaching in English—that's Nicole—and one teaching primarily in Spanish—that's Ms. Lourdes Castillo. "The students alternate which class they go to each day," explains Nicole. "We are supposed to be doing the same thing at every moment throughout the day, so we plan together. However, it is tough to find the necessary read-alouds available in both languages and we are using different texts for guided reading. Then we teach phonics; again, very different in each language. My point is that it is difficult, but my partner teacher and I collaborate. The goal is to make the daily transition as seamless as possible for our students."

Though she doesn't feel any teacher preparation program can "truly prepare you for the challenges of running a classroom," Nicole believes she was given a sound philosophical basis for her teaching career. "I was taught to be progressively minded and to be an advocate for my students." After clearing the hurdles of classroom management, Nicole is an enthusiastic participant in the dual language program. "The program's purpose is to teach all children a second language, be it English or Spanish, while still pushing them academically in their native language. That is a huge benefit to all students; the thought that they will leave elementary school bilingual is pretty amazing."

Nicole Miller graduated from Roger Williams University with dual majors in Elementary Education and Anthropology and Sociology.

The Bilingual Controversy

As schools struggle to meet the needs of ELL students, bilingual education continues to spark political controversy. Millions of students speak hundreds of languages and dialects, including not only Spanish but also Mandarin, French, Hmong, Urdu, Russian, Polish, Korean, Tagalog, and Swahili. Misunderstandings are multiplied when language barriers are accompanied by racial and ethnic differences, leading to even greater isolation and segregation for many ELL students. While some struggle to make bilingual education work, others believe that it never will.

Many people worry that bilingual education threatens the status of English as the nation's primary vehicle of communication. As a result, an **English-only movement** has emerged (see Figure 3.3). Those who support this movement feel that English is a unifying national bond that preserves our common culture. They believe that English should be the only language used or spoken in public and that the purpose of bilingual education should be to quickly teach English to ELL students. It is not surprising that the Bilingual Education Act of 1968 expired in 2002 and was not renewed, and many programs today emphasize rapid transition into English.

Bilingual education advocates argue that the United States is a mosaic of diverse cultures and that diversity should be honored and nurtured. One

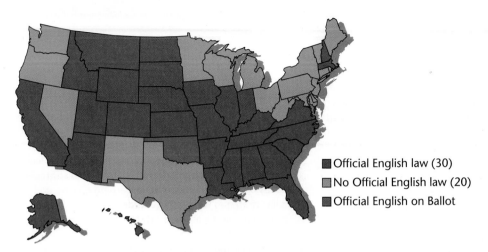

States with Official English Rule and Year Enacted

■ Official English law (30)
□ No Official English law (20)
■ Official English on Ballot

Alabama (1990)	Illinois (1969)	Nebraska (1920)
Alaska (1998)	Indiana (1984)	New Hampshire (1995)
Arizona (2006)	Iowa (2002)	North Carolina (1987)
Arkansas (1987)	Kansas (2007)	North Dakota (1987)
California (1986)	Kentucky (1984)	South Carolina (1987)
Colorado (1988)	Louisiana (1811)	South Dakota (1995)
Florida (1988)	Massachusetts (1975)	Tennessee (1984)
Georgia (1986 & 1996)	Mississippi (1987)	Utah (2000)
Hawaii* (1978)	Missouri (1998 & 2008)	Virginia (1981 & 1996)
Idaho (2007)	Montana (1995)	Wyoming (1996)

FIGURE 3.3

States with official English language.

SOURCE: U.S. English, Inc. (2010), Washington, DC.

REFLECTION: Do you see any pattern in which states have passed this law? Does this influence your decision as to where you might want to teach? Do you believe such English-only laws have any practical impact?

problem, they point out, is that we simply do not have enough competent bilingual teachers who can respond to the large numbers of ELL children now in our schools. They argue that it is unfair to blame bilingual education for the slow progress some students are making. Achieving proficiency in any second language can take years.[20] Bilingual advocates oppose the English-only movement, and they feel that it promotes intolerance, will turn back the clock, and may very well be unconstitutional. Education writer James Crawford points out, "It is certainly more respectable to discriminate by language than by race. . . . Most people are not sensitive to language discrimination in this nation, so it is easy to argue that you're doing someone a favor by making them speak English."[21]

Research on Bilingual Education

What does the research say about the effectiveness of bilingual education? Educators are just now beginning to analyze long-term data, and they are uncovering some useful findings. In one case, the researchers found that when language-minority students spend more time learning in their native language, they are more likely to achieve at comparable and even higher levels in English.[22] Another study found that the earlier a student starts learning a new language, the more effective that language becomes in an academic setting.[23] Yet another study showed that no single approach holds a monopoly on success, and different approaches to bilingual education can each be

PROFILE IN EDUCATION

Carlos Ovando

Carlos Ovando immigrated to the United States with his family as a teenager. Now a professor of education, Ovando shares his first-hand experience of learning English, and how it was not until his bilingual ability was celebrated that he was able to find confidence in his academic abilities. To read a full profile of Carlos Ovando, go to the Chapter 3 Profile in Education at www.mhhe.com/sadkerbrief3e.

ENGLISH LANGUAGE LEARNERS

Here are several strategies for teaching English language learners:

- **Get to know your students, and when possible, use their backgrounds to make connections to the material being learned.** Creating a comfortable and safe classroom climate for your students despite the language and culture differences is an important first step. By connecting to their backgrounds, you will help ELL students feel that their new classroom culture is less alien and distant.

- **Give explicit directions, emphasize key words, and offer concrete examples to enhance the understanding of ELL students.** Simple strategies such as emphasizing key words, offering examples of your main points, and using visuals such as the chalkboard, flash cards, games, graphics, and puzzles can increase the understanding of ELL students.

- **Plan for and expect the active involvement of ELL students.** It is a good idea to call on all students to keep their attention and focus. ELL students are no exception. A preferred strategy is to ask a question before calling out a specific name so that all students have time to consider their answer. Feel free to use a variety of questioning strategies, but avoid rhetorical questions, since ELL students may not understand them. Waiting a bit longer for students to respond will give ELL students more time to process the question in their new language.

- **Do not depend simply on verbal, teacher-centered learning, but incorporate a variety of instructional strategies.** Hands-on activities, cooperative learning groups, and other strategies will help ELL students develop their language skills and learn new information through avenues other than teacher talk.

- **Always provide time to check for understanding and be sure to provide precise and immediate feedback.** Unlearning the wrong word or behavior is more difficult than learning it correctly the first time. Monitoring and offering clear feedback can eliminate the need to unlearn and relearn.

REFLECTION: Although these skills are designed for ELL students, how might they enhance your teaching effectiveness for all students?

effective, suggesting that local school systems should carefully select the programs and teachers most appropriate for their communities.[24]

One major bilingual study, directed by Virginia Collier and Wayne Thomas, evaluated the experiences of 42,000 students over a 13-year period. Early findings suggested that students enrolled in well-implemented bilingual programs actually *outperform* students in monolingual programs. One successful approach assumed bilingual education to be a two-way street, one in which English speakers and ELL students would learn from each other. In this model, during the Spanish part of the day, the Spanish-speaking students explained the lessons to native-English peers, while during English instruction, the reverse took place. Collier and Thomas report that, by fourth grade, the students in these two-way classes had actually outperformed the native English speakers who attended English-only classes.[25] This study suggests that if our teachers could competently teach in two languages, academic achievement for all students might increase, along with all students becoming bilingual—now isn't that a remarkable possibility?

More than two centuries ago, Ben Franklin expressed his fears about the multiple languages heard on America's streets. His concerns have echoed through the centuries, despite a world in which national borders seem to be blurring or even disappearing. In today's global community, Russians and Americans are working together in space, such international organizations as the United Nations and NATO are expanding their membership, and corporations are crossing national boundaries to create global mergers in an international marketplace.

Moreover, technological breakthroughs, such as the Internet, have made international communications not just possible but commonplace. However, for most Americans, these international conversations are viable only if the other side speaks English. In this new international era, Americans find themselves locked in a monolingual society. How strange that, instead of viewing those who speak other languages as welcome assets to our nation, some seem eager to erase linguistic diversity.

Multicultural Education

Students in many urban and suburban schools speak scores of languages. In some urban communities, students of color comprise 70 to more than 90 percent of school enrollment. A successful teacher in these communities will need to bridge possible racial, cultural, and language differences. In fact, even in very stable, overwhelmingly white school districts where all students share apparently similar backgrounds and are native speakers, cross-cultural knowledge is important. Many of these students will graduate, leave these communities, and work and live in more diverse areas. The success of their transition may depend on what they learned—or did not learn—in school. Moreover, communities that appear uniform and static may have differences in religion, social class, gender, and sexuality. The controversial question facing the nation: how best to teach our multicultural students?

Focus Question 5
What are the purposes and approaches of multicultural education?

The Multiculturalism Debate

You enter teaching in a time of harsh and divisive "culture wars," as people argue about how diversity should be recognized in schools.[26] Some worry that overemphasizing diversity may pull us apart, and fear that multiculturalism will lead to a Dis-United States. Adversaries of multiculturalism point to Yugoslavia and Czechoslovakia, nations dissolved by the power of ethnic differences. They argue for a uniform national identity and urge schools to promote one set of common beliefs based on our English and European traditions. In their eyes, time spent teaching about different cultures poses a double threat: pulling apart the national fabric while taking time from important academic subjects like math and reading. They would prefer that students focus on academic achievement and adopt what they see as core values of the United States.

Others claim that multiculturalism is the nation's future. They believe that schools can no longer ignore or devalue cultural and ethnic differences, either in this country or throughout the world. National demographics are changing, and schools must recognize these changes. They argue that current practices are failing in their mission to unite and educate all our students equitably and point to statistics like these to underscore their point:[27]

- Although schools were ordered to desegregate in the 1954 *Brown* decision, since the 1980s, schools have been resegregating.
- Since the 1990s, the segregation of students of every racial group has increased.
- Nationally, Asian Americans are more likely than students of other races to attend multiracial schools.

- White students are the least likely to attend multiracial schools and are the most isolated group.
- More than three-quarters of intensely segregated schools are also high-poverty schools.
- High school graduation rates are around 70 percent, and in many communities only 50 or 60 percent of Hispanic American, African American, and Native American students are graduating from high school.

Is multicultural education part of the answer to these troubling statistics? Perhaps multiculturalism itself, specifically Eastern thought, can offer an answer. A sacred belief of the Hindu religion is "We are one," that all humans are connected. A second Hindu truth is "Honor one another," emphasizing the importance of appreciating our differences. These Hindu beliefs are held simultaneously and are not viewed as mutually exclusive. Perhaps the key to moving ahead and avoiding yet another culture war is for us to learn balance, to honor our national commonalities as we celebrate our group and individual differences.

Approaches to Multicultural Education

When multiculturalism began, the focus was on fighting racism. Over time, these programs expanded to confront not only racism, but also injustices based on gender, social class, disability, and sexual orientation. Today, there are many dimensions to **multicultural education,** including (1) *expanding the curriculum* to reflect America's diversity; (2) *using teaching strategies* that are responsive to different learning styles; (3) *supporting the multicultural competence of teachers* so they are comfortable and knowledgeable working with students and families of different cultures; and (4) *a commitment to social justice,* promoting efforts to work and teach toward local and global equity.

Multiculturalism has come to mean different things to different educators.[28] Some focus on *human relations,* activities that promote cultural and racial understanding among different groups. Others teach *single-group studies,* which you may know as Black Studies, Hispanic Studies, or Women's Studies programs. Some educators believe multicultural education is all about creating close links between home and school so that minority children can succeed academically, an approach termed *teaching the culturally different.* Another tack, called simply *multicultural,* promotes different perspectives based on race, class, and culture; in a sense, developing new eyes through which students learn. And finally, the *multicultural reconstructionist* approach mobilizes students to examine and work to remediate social injustices. As you can see, multicultural education can mean different things to different people.

James Banks focuses specifically on developing a multicultural curriculum.[29] Banks believes that one way to achieve greater understanding and more positive attitudes toward different groups is to integrate and broaden the curriculum to make it more inclusive and action oriented. He defines four approaches to a multicultural curriculum that are related to several proposed by others[30] (Figure 3.4). As you read each description, consider if any of these approaches were used in your own schooling.

1. Multicultural education often begins with the *contributions approach,* in which the study of ethnic heroes (for example, Sacagawea, Rosa Parks, or Booker T. Washington) is included in the curriculum. At this superficial contributions level, one might also find "food and festivals" being featured or holidays such as Cinco de Mayo being described or celebrated.

2. In the *additive approach,* a unit or course is incorporated, often but not always during a "special" week or month. February has become the month to study African Americans, and March has been designated "Women's History Month." Although these dedicated weeks and months offer a respite from the typical curricular material, no substantial change is made to the curriculum as a whole.

3. In the *transformation approach,* the entire Eurocentric nature of the curriculum is changed. Students are taught to view events and issues from diverse ethnic and cultural perspectives. For instance, the westward expansion of Europeans can be seen as manifest destiny through the eyes of European descendants, or as an invasion from the east through the eyes of Native Americans.

4. The fourth level, *social action,* goes beyond the transformation approach. Students not only learn to view issues from multiple perspectives, but also become directly involved in solving related problems. At this level, a school would address social and economic needs here and abroad, advocate human rights and peace, and work to ensure that the school building and activities did not harm the environment. Rather than political passivity, the typical by-product of many curricular programs, this approach promotes decision making and social action to achieve multicultural goals and a more vibrant democracy.

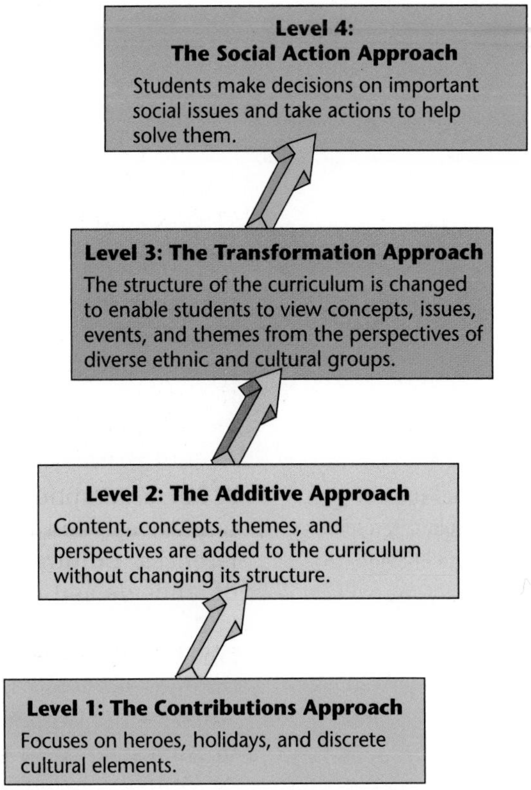

Multicultural education also seeks to help all students develop more positive attitudes toward different racial, ethnic, cultural, and religious groups. According to a 1990s survey of more than 1,000 young people between the ages of 15 and 24 conducted by People for the American Way, most respondents felt their attitudes toward race relations were healthier than those of their parents. Yet about half described the state of race relations in the United States as generally bad. Fifty-five percent of African Americans and whites said they were "uneasy" rather than "comfortable" in dealing with members of the other racial group.[31] If you are thinking that the 1990s were a while ago, and perhaps things have changed since then, they have not. The 2008 presidential elections gave the entire nation a chance to talk about race, and perhaps learn more, but if the media is any indication, that conversation did not happen. Although most Americans took pride in electing a multiracial president, the media gave little in-depth coverage to race. "Black and white people have a different notion of the need to talk about race," notes *Chicago Tribune* reporter Clarence Page. Ninety-two percent of journalists reported

Level 4: The Social Action Approach
Students make decisions on important social issues and take actions to help solve them.

Level 3: The Transformation Approach
The structure of the curriculum is changed to enable students to view concepts, issues, events, and themes from the perspectives of diverse ethnic and cultural groups.

Level 2: The Additive Approach
Content, concepts, themes, and perspectives are added to the curriculum without changing its structure.

Level 1: The Contributions Approach
Focuses on heroes, holidays, and discrete cultural elements.

FIGURE 3.4
Banks's approach to multicultural education.

REFLECTION: Think back to your own schooling. At which of Banks's levels would you place your own multicultural education? Provide supporting evidence. As a teacher, which of these levels do you want to reach and teach? Explain.

that when it came to covering race relations, the media was not doing its job effectively.[32]

Another indication of how slowly we are dealing with the race issue is school desegregation. Students are more segregated today than any time since the Civil Rights movement.[33] Segregated housing patterns and federal courts no longer willing to attend to this problem have left most American schoolchildren segregated by race and class, and ignorant of one another's cultures, languages, and experiences. How to encourage students to become more "comfortable" with one another depends at least in part on the skills and insights the teacher brings to the classroom, what some term *culturally responsive teaching*.

Culturally Responsive Teaching

Focus Question 6
Why is culturally responsive teaching important?

A key assumption of multicultural education is that students learn in different ways and that effective teachers recognize and respond to these differences. **Culturally responsive teaching** focuses on the learning strengths of students and mediates the frequent mismatch between home and school cultures. Gloria Ladson-Billings, a professor at the University of Wisconsin, offers a powerful example of culturally relevant teaching. She wanted to find out what behaviors make some teachers successful with African American children, while others are not. She asked parents and principals in four schools serving primarily African American students to nominate "excellent teachers," teachers they would rate as successful. As you might expect, principals chose teachers who had low numbers of discipline referrals, high attendance rates, and high standardized test scores. Parents, on the other hand, selected teachers who were enthusiastic, respectful, and understood that students need to operate in both the white world and their local community. Nine teachers, white and black, made both lists, and eight of them agreed to participate in her study. After several years of observations and interviews, she was baffled: their personalities, teaching strategies, and styles were entirely different; there seemed to be no common patterns. She was close to throwing in the towel when she finally saw the subtle, but striking, commonalities.

First, all of these eight teachers had chosen to teach in these more challenging schools and felt responsible for the academic success of each student. Second, they were sensitive to race discrimination in society; they actively fought bias and prejudice and wanted their students to do the same. For example, some of these teachers had students rewrite out-of-date textbooks or work on projects to improve their community. And finally, the teachers viewed both the home and school as connected, and seized opportunities to learn from their neighborhoods. They honored the crafts and traditions in the community, inviting parents to share traditional cooking in the school. One teacher allowed students to use "home English" in class but required that students also master Standard English. Students were expected to learn both languages well. Teachers realized that they, too, were learners and needed to be open to new information. Gloria Ladson-Billings developed three promising culturally responsive principles for teaching not only African American children, but also others:[34]

1. **Students must experience academic success, which leads to a stronger self-esteem. Esteem is built on solid academic accomplishment.** We intuitively know that students who do not feel good about themselves have a tough time in (and beyond) school. But this is not enough. For school success, students' self-esteem needs to be built on solid academic accomplishment. Teachers must create lessons that are responsive to student learning styles *and* allow student mastery of the basic knowledge and skills necessary for success in today's society. The bottom line: students feel good about themselves when there is real academic progress.

2. **Students should develop and maintain cultural competence, and the student's home culture is an opportunity for learning.** Too many teachers have been taught only about classroom teaching skills and not about community outreach possibilities. Ladson-Billings's research teaches us that we must expand our concept of the classroom to include the community. When there is friction between school and home, academic progress suffers. Put more positively, when teachers move beyond their classroom and integrate learning with the local community, they can create a more positive, seamless, and mutually supportive academic environment. For example, a local African storyteller can visit the class and relate an African folktale. Students could use the experience as a springboard for their writing or drawing. Or a local politician could be invited to class to share his or her public service work, challenging students to develop their own vision of community service and social activism. Following the presentation, students might do just that: organize a class project to improve the quality of community life. Identifying community resources and connecting classroom activities to those resources are keystones to creating a fruitful academic climate for students.

3. **Students must develop critical consciousness and actively challenge social injustice.** A culturally relevant teacher needs to do more than connect with student needs and the local community; a culturally relevant teacher also works to improve the quality of life in the school and community. Do you remember the disconnect you may have felt between life in school, the world you read about in textbooks, and "the real world" you lived in? Schools too often live in a sanitized bubble, separate from the world's problems. Culturally relevant teachers break that bubble and, along with their students, work to improve the quality of life. For instance, if school textbooks are weak and dated, a teacher might encourage students to rewrite them. The result would be more realistic and current texts, as well as student practice in writing. Or perhaps there are serious health problems in the community. Students might volunteer to attract additional resources to the community health clinic and in the process learn how local government works. Confronting and eliminating real social problems is the third component of a culturally relevant classroom.

As you prepare to teach, it is helpful for you to consider what it means to be a culturally responsive teacher, to broaden your view of what it takes to be successful in the classroom. Let's take a moment to think about what this means for your own teacher preparation. To be competent in each of Ladson-Billings's three points, you will need to acquire certain skills, attitudes, and knowledge. What teaching *skills* will you need to be a culturally responsive teacher for all your students? You will want to diagnose different student needs and plan for different learning styles. You will want to develop critical thinking skills and include all your students in an equitable manner. You will even want to make certain that you can be silent and listen to the answers that are volunteered by all the students (a skill called "wait time"). Studies show that even teachers with the best of intentions too often fail to use these skills. (We describe equitable teaching skills later in this text in Chapter 11, "Becoming an Effective Teacher.")

What *attitudes* will you need to be a culturally responsive teacher? How do you approach teaching students whose background may be quite different from your own? Because most of us have grown up in a segregated community, there is an excellent chance that most of your friends are similar to you in race, class, and ethnicity. You probably share a common set of values and opinions, seeing the world through a lens forged in your own socialization. As you prepare to teach, you may want to make an extra effort to move out of your familiar milieu and seek different views. The more voices you hear, the more likely you will be able to appreciate different life experiences and develop attitudes that are accepting of people who at first glance may seem very different from you.

Finally, as you prepare to teach, you will want to acquire *knowledge* about different group experiences in order to be a culturally responsive teacher. You already bring to the classroom some knowledge of other groups, but this knowledge is limited, and some of it may be inaccurate. You will want to educate yourself about your future students and the educational implications of their cultural backgrounds. This chapter helps you move down that path. For example, many African American communities often emphasize aural and participatory learning over writing. If you ignore this insight and use only writing activities in class, student performance may suffer.[35] As another example, research suggests that many girls and women personalize knowledge and prefer learning through experience and first-hand observation.[36] Creating personal connections and examples may increase the success of your female students. In fact, responding to all types of student diversity is simply good teaching. A Head Start teacher in Michigan, in this case teaching poor, white, rural students, shares her view of culturally responsive teaching:

> I believe that it is my responsibility to learn as much as I can about the child's family and their culture and then implement that into my classroom, so that the child can see his/her culture is a part of our classroom and that I respect them and their family and their culture. It can be hard; I don't want to present any new stereotypes to these kids, so I ask the parents a lot of questions. Sometimes I get the answers and sometimes I don't, but at least they see I am trying.[37]

The challenge for teachers is to acquire useful and accurate cultural insights that help connect classroom and the culture, while avoiding the trap of stereotypic thinking. What's the difference between a useful cultural insight and a damaging stereotype? That critical distinction is explored in the next section.

Stereotypes

The way we use the terms stereotype and generalization can be very confusing, so let's try to be more precise. **Stereotypes** are absolute beliefs that all members of a group have a fixed set of characteristics. The word *stereotype* originated in the print shop. It is literally a type—a one-piece plate that repeats a pattern with no individuality. Today's cultural stereotypes also ignore individuality and are repeatedly applied to all members of a group. People who use stereotypes try to

WHAT YOU CAN DO TO LEARN ABOUT YOUR STUDENTS

1. Walk around the neighborhoods where your students live. If your students are older, they can be your guides. (They love doing this!)

2. Learn how to ask culturally acceptable questions. Your colleagues at school can be a big help here.

3. Before you start teaching, learn about the history and the cultures of the students you will serve.

4. Schedule home visits. Be open, honest, and humble, and tell families that such visits can help you be a more effective teacher.

5. Build community in your class by inviting parents to school to share their cultures.

6. In many cultures, teachers are invited to community and family events. Go! This can be an incredibly fulfilling (and delicious) part of your job!

7. If your students are immigrants, connect with community centers or refugee assistance organizations and ask questions like: "As these children's teacher, what do you think are the most important things for me to know?"

8. Get specific information about each of your students. Mexican American children born in the United States are quite different from Nicaraguan children who just arrived here. Avoid assumptions.

9. Talk to your colleagues and ask them about the mistakes they made in their own teaching—mistakes you can work to avoid.

10. In the beginning of the year, have a potluck and connect with students, families, and the community. Breaking bread together nourishes the body and the soul.

How can that experience help you in your teaching?

Adapted from Elena Aguilar, "Teaching Secrets: When the Kids Don't Share Your Culture," *Teacher Magazine*, July 14, 2010.

REFLECTION: Have you ever visited or lived in another culture? How did you learn about it?

save time by short-circuiting the thinking process, just like the original stereotype saved time in the printing process. A set of characteristics with no qualifiers is attributed to individuals based on their membership in a group. Simplistic sentences are used with words like "all Hispanics are" and are applied to every member of the group without distinction. Actually, stereotypes are examples of sloppy thinking that undermine the critical reflection that we want our students to develop. For example, a stereotype might naively proclaim that Hispanics are poor students, Asians are math geniuses, Jews are wealthy, and African Americans are great athletes. Stereotypes are impervious to contradictory information. Find a poor Jew, a Hispanic with a doctorate, an Asian dropping out of school, or an unathletic African American and each is thought to be an anomaly, the exception to the rule. The rule, the stereotype, endures. Stereotypes not only hurt people, they block learning. Stereotypic thinking obstructs a search for new information—not just "contradictory" information, but any information that might add to the complex, rich understanding of an individual or a group. Stereotypes ignore nuances, qualifiers, and subtleties that might more accurately characterize the group. This willingness to engage in complex thinking is what students need; unfortunately, stereotypes short-circuit thoughtful reflection.

Stereotype Threat Let's look at an example of how damaging stereotypes can be. Opinion polls suggest that about half of white America endorses common stereotypes about blacks and Hispanics, such as the belief that they are not very intelligent. Such stereotypes influence expectations and behaviors not only of whites who hold them, but also of blacks and Hispanics who must live in a society marked by such beliefs. For example, an African American called on in class realizes that an incorrect answer may confirm the stereotype of inferior intelligence. For this student, speaking in class can be risky. As you might imagine, the risk intensifies on high-stakes tests. Consider the following studies: African American and white college students were asked to take a difficult standardized verbal examination. In the control group, the test was presented in a typical way, as a measure of intelligence. In the experimental group, the students were told that ability was not being assessed; rather, the psychology of their verbal problem-solving was being researched. The two groups were matched so that student abilities, time to take the test, and the test itself were similar. In the nonthreatening experimental groups, black test takers solved about twice as many problems as the ones in the control group; the white students solved the same number in both groups. In a similar study, researchers found that simply asking students to record their race before taking a test had a similar devastating impact on black performance.[38]

This dramatic outcome has been termed **stereotype threat,** a measure of how social context, such as self-image, trust in others, and a sense of belonging, can influence academic performance. When an individual is aware of a stereotype, he or she is more likely to behave like the stereotype than if it did not exist. Studies indicate that students who care the most about their academic performance are the most vulnerable to stereotype threat. Stereotype threat may explain in part why African Americans (and others) perform better in college than their SAT scores predict, and why standardized test scores can be so misleading. Nor are blacks alone. Latinos on English tests, females on math tests, and elderly people on short-term memory tests also fall victim to stereotype threat. In fact, even students with strong test scores can fall prey. White male engineering students with very high SAT scores were told that their performance on a test would help researchers understand the math superiority of Asians. Hearing about the comparison to strong Asian students, their scores fell. None of us is immune from stereotype threat.

Stereotypes limit students by teaching them that intellect is a fixed trait, that some groups are naturally brighter than others, and that their future was determined at birth. The belief that group differences are unchangeable is not a helpful construct for teachers. A person's intellect, like a person's brain, grows and changes. Human potential is amazing. If students see their brain and their intellect as muscles that can be taught to grow and become stronger, stereotype threat is diminished, and test scores rise.[39] Imagine the impact of stereotypes not only on intellectual performance, but also on other characteristics. Teaching also deals with ethics, values, and character of students, and damaging stereotypes can inhibit this learning as well. Fortunately, stereotype threat can be overcome with proper instruction.[40]

You can diminish stereotype threat by ensuring that your curriculum represents diversity across race, ethnicity, gender, religion, and socioeconomic class. Or perhaps you prefer to confront the problem directly: explain stereotype threat in class and explore with your students strategies to neutralize it. The one thing you do not want to do is ignore the damage done by stereotype threat.

Generalizations

Generalizations recognize that there are trends over large numbers of people. Members of religious, racial, or ethnic groups share certain experiences and may share certain similarities. Generalizations offer insights, not hard and fast conclusions like stereotypes, and unlike a stereotype, a generalization does not assume that everyone in a group has a fixed set of characteristics. So the generalization that many Japanese value and seek higher education still holds if one encounters a Japanese dropout who dislikes school. The generalization is never intended to be applied to all; it is open to modification as new information is gathered, and there are always exceptions. Note that generalizations use words like "many," "often," or "tend to." Moreover, whereas stereotypes view people in one group or another, generalizations recognize that people belong to many groups simultaneously. Some Jews are Hispanic, some are Asian, and some are Arab, yet they are all Jews.

Generalizations offer us a hunch or clue about a group, and sometimes these clues are useful in planning for teaching. When you begin teaching you may know very little about your students, and a generalization offers a useful starting point. Think of it as an educated guess. As you learn more and more about each student, you will realize which generalizations are appropriate and which are not.

How can we use generalizations to develop culturally responsive teaching? Let's assume that a teacher has many Native American students in class; the teacher does some research and discovers that most Native American students prefer to learn in a cooperative group, valuing community and family over individual competition. Rather than teaching in the familiar teacher-centered manner, she modifies her plan and creates student groups to work on several academic topics. Using open-ended questions, she asks the groups to share their experiences, and patiently waits for each group response, realizing that Native American children may prefer to carefully consider their comments and compose their thoughts. When she can, the teacher uses natural phenomena in her explanations, because Native Americans often value both natural and supernatural forces. She may also integrate Indian words, symbols, or legends as appropriate. By building the learning on sharing rather than competition, and on valuing tribal experiences and beliefs, the teacher is increasing her chance of connecting with most of her students.[41] Since generalizations are flexible, the teacher is free to use a different approach with some or all of her students if she later discovers that they prefer a different learning style.

As you become a more experienced teacher, you will become more skilled at confronting all kinds of limiting stereotypes, developing useful teaching generalizations, and becoming a more culturally responsive teacher. In fact, let's start that process right now.

www.mhhe.com/
sadkerbrief3e
INTERACTIVE ACTIVITY
Multicultural Literacy.
Match multicultural
terms with their
descriptions.

Today's Classroom

Consider yourself a teacher working with the nation's diverse students. If you are teaching in a community that reflects the nation's population, your class of 40 students might include the following:[42]

17 white children

  6 Hispanic American children

    6 children who do not speak English at home

      5 poor children

        5 African American children

          1 Asian American child

Focus Question 7
How can teachers use cul-
turally responsive teaching
strategies?

The class might also include a Jewish, Native American, or Arab heritage child, not to mention multiracial or biracial students. Although we lack firm statistics concerning the number of lesbian, gay, bisexual, or transgendered children, estimates are that perhaps two or three of your students would fall into these categories. Planning for this class is quite a challenge!

The reality is that hyper-segregation of our schools makes it unlikely that you will be teaching students from all of these groups in the same class at the same time. Unlikely, but not impossible. And certainly, over time, you may teach many if not all of them.

Consider these three students. What assumptions do you make about them based on this photo? Are these assumptions based on stereotypes?

Meet Your Seventh-Grade Class

In this section, we profile eight students—students similar to ones you may someday teach. Each student is from a cultural, ethnic, racial, or other group, bringing to your class a rich history and different learning preferences. It is important to keep in mind that each student is an individual, and any generalizations you make initially may change over time. But for now, let's take step one of culturally responsive teaching and learn about our students. For each student, we ask you to identify a generalization that might influence your teaching and enhance learning. As you read each student's description, you will encounter hints about potential generalizations. You may want to draw on your own knowledge as well. When you teach, you will want to learn more about your students through reading and personal interactions. But for now, let's establish your baseline—what you know about groups as you begin your teacher education program—and what you will want to learn in the future.

This exercise is not simple. You may be pushed beyond your comfort zone, and formulating generalizations will be a demanding task. If you are baffled, venture your best guess. At the end of the section we shall provide you with sample generalizations that should help you think in new and constructive ways.

We will start you off by suggesting a few generalizations for the first student, Lindsey Maria Riley, who is Navajo. Then you are on your own. Try to identify at least one generalization for each of the other students. Later in the section you can compare your responses to our suggestions.[43] Now, meet (and begin thinking about) your students.

Lindsey Maria Riley (Navajo)

Lindsey grew up in a small, poor town in the Southwest. Although Lindsey did not live on a reservation, her family adhered to traditional Navajo ways. Lindsey followed tradition when not at school and spent time mostly with girls and women learning to cook, make pottery, and weave at an early age. Navajo boys would hunt, make tools, and live more physical lives, quite separate from the girls. Lindsey's family did not have a lot of money and received assistance for her school supplies from Save the Children, a nonprofit organization. Lindsey enjoyed the school she attended that was run by the Bureau of

Indian Affairs. But this year, her family moved to your community and she is a new student in your class.

Most of the other students in your class have seen Indians only in movies, like *The Last of the Mohicans,* or on television. Some of Lindsey's classmates believe that Indians lived a long time ago on the frontier and are surprised to learn they still exist. Some have heard their parents say that Indians make a fortune running casinos. But neither casinos nor movies explain Lindsey. And Lindsey does not explain herself—she does not talk much. The students in your class like Lindsey, although they haven't really figured her out. To put it politely, Lindsey is a curiosity to them.

You recently asked the class to write a brief report on a president for Presidents' Day. Lindsey never handed in her report. When you asked her about it, she said that all the presidents had done bad things to her people and that she would rather report on a different topic. Today, she told you that the school mascot, an Indian chief, bothers her.

Potentially Useful Generalization:_____

Sample Response [Note: Native Americans are not one group but hundreds of tribal nations with different languages and beliefs. Learning about tribal distinctions is a useful first step for teachers and students.] In this sample response, we will offer you a series of possible and well-accepted generalizations, but there are others as well. If we do not mention your generalization, you may want to research it to see if you are correct.

Potentially Useful Generalization: Many tribes revere modesty. Group, rather than individual, recognition is typically preferred, as is cooperation over competition and patience rather than immediate gratification (qualities too often lost in contemporary classrooms). Additionally, visual and artistic learning and "hands-on learning" are valued by many tribal cultures. Using American Indian cultural beliefs and insights during a lesson can help Native American students feel connected to the academic program. The supernatural, intuition, and spiritual beliefs are valued by many tribes and could also be incorporated in classroom instruction.

[In terms of the casino-to-riches stereotype mentioned in the profile, less than 1 percent of Indians work in casinos, and the casino profits often go to schools and community improvement projects.]

Marcus Griffin (African American)

Marcus is in your class because of your school district's policy to voluntarily bus African American students from across the county line, a rare event these days. He lives with his mother, who works at the post office, about 10 miles from school. His older brother never attended this school; in fact, he never graduated from high school. You hear rumors that he is in and out of trouble. Marcus has only a few friends in class, a situation made worse by the bus schedule. After his last class, he hurries to catch his bus for the long ride home. Because of this schedule, he cannot participate in after-school activities, sports, and clubs. Marcus's neighborhood friends do not really talk much about school. They do not like the fact that Marcus chooses to bus to a white community instead of hanging out with them. Marcus feels that he is growing further and further away from his roots.

Marcus loves reading and writing, but feels like an alien in his new school. Virtually everything he sees or reads in school is about the history, accomplishments, and interests of whites. Only rarely are his people discussed, and then it is not in a very positive light. Marcus finds the teachers in your school pretty serious, and he decides not to rock the boat by suggesting different ideas in class. There is only one African American teacher in your school and only a few black students. Marcus would like to go to college, but his family's finances are limited. Some of the black kids talk about going to college on an athletic scholarship, but Marcus is not very athletic. You wish that you could connect with him, but when you try, he rarely looks at you. Like several other students in your school, he sometimes interrupts in class, a habit you find annoying. You hope for the best for Marcus, but you are not optimistic.

Potentially Useful Generalization:_____

Ana Garcia (Mexican American)

Ana Garcia is one of the warmest and most involved students in your class. She is one of those students who actually hugs people, including you! She loves to ask questions, works closely with her peers, and seems eager to explore new topics. Her favorite topic is history. Ana loves doing class projects, yet she is quite modest about her work.

Although Ana was born in the United States, her parents, who work as laborers, emigrated from Mexico. Ana is the only one in her family who speaks any English, but most of the time she speaks Spanish with friends and family. Unfortunately, despite her motivation, Ana's English language skills lag behind those of her peers, and the gap seems to be widening. Since you do not speak Spanish, you suggest that she participate in some of the after-school activities where she might have more opportunities to work on her English. Ana listens to your advice, but explains that she goes right home after school to care for her younger siblings. Although Ana loves school, you get the sense that she is getting frustrated and is already focusing on her future family responsibilities and becoming a mother.

Potentially Useful Generalization:_____

Kasem Pravat (Asian American from Thailand)

Kasem is a very pleasant student who seems content in your class. He is always respectful and calm. Kasem works very hard. His papers are done with great care, and his test grades are strong. The one skill you would like him to develop is speaking up in class. Sometimes, he seems painfully shy.

You met Kasem's family briefly before school started, and they impressed you as agreeable, patient, and hard-working people. Kasem reflects those values. His family came from Thailand only recently, but because Kasem studied English in Thailand, his language adjustment here was relatively smooth. His favorite subject is math, and he is already talking about majoring in engineering in college. Kasem is one of the few students in your middle school class who is not only talking about college, but has already identified a major.

Kasem is protective and caring of his younger sister, Keyo, who is in the neighboring elementary school.

Potentially Useful Generalization:_____

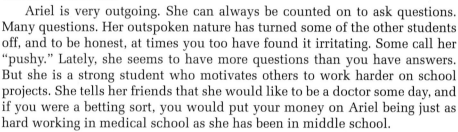

Ariel Klein (Jewish American)

Ariel is an excellent student, in part because she is so hard working. Ariel's family is originally from an Orthodox Jewish neighborhood in New York City. Your community does not have an Orthodox synagogue for observant Jews who want to strictly follow their faith, so the Kleins now practice the more secular Conservative Judaism. Maintaining a kosher home has proven too difficult for the family because the nearest kosher food store is almost two hours away. Ariel and her family still observe Rosh Hashanah and Yom Kippur, which caused a major disruption in September when those holidays kept her from taking your academic skills assessment test. It was very difficult scheduling a retest because the arranged make-up day was the following Saturday, her Sabbath. After several delays, she finally took the exam in the main office over two weekdays, but had to miss two more days of class, which troubled her.

Ariel is very outgoing. She can always be counted on to ask questions. Many questions. Her outspoken nature has turned some of the other students off, and to be honest, at times you too have found it irritating. Some call her "pushy." Lately, she seems to have more questions than you have answers. But she is a strong student who motivates others to work harder on school projects. She tells her friends that she would like to be a doctor some day, and if you were a betting sort, you would put your money on Ariel being just as hard working in medical school as she has been in middle school.

Potentially Useful Generalization:_____

Mary Goode (rural white)

Mary grew up in a small town tucked away in the mountains of West Virginia. She attended a local elementary school with an enrollment of only 120 students in grades 1–8. Mary went through the first six years of elementary school with pretty much the same close group of 13 classmates. Her school had only nine classes and nine teachers. However, only a few teachers stayed during her entire time at the school. Because she helped out in the local food co-op, Mary knew virtually all of the families in town. The few she missed during the weekdays at the co-op she would see at church on Sunday. Her parents talked about her brother doing well in high school and then perhaps opening a business. For Mary, the conversation revolved around potential suitors and someday converting her parents into grandparents.

When Mary moved to your much larger community, she was overwhelmed. She says that she was never with so many students in one school or in one class in her life, and you suspect this might be why she is overwhelmed. You also think she might be reacting to the fact that the children in this town are all so different from those in her old town. Mary is now quite introverted and rarely speaks, in part because some students make fun of her accent. She is self-conscious about her background and all the things she does not seem to know that everyone else knows. Her clothes draw special attention by the other girls who explain how "yesterday" they are. When you finally meet her parents, they are very quiet and also a bit overwhelmed. They were reticent to come to school. Although Mary takes her school work seriously and is doing fine right now, you are concerned that she may get lost in this new crowd, perhaps turn off from school or, worse yet, drop out.

Potentially Useful Generalization:_____

Ibrahim Mouawad (Arab American)

Although Ibrahim has lived in your community his entire life, many see him as a foreigner. His family was one of the few who invited you over for dinner, and you still recall how warm they were toward you. The food was wonderful, although the names of some of those dishes fled your mind quickly.

When students ask Ibrahim where he is from, he says the Middle East, but avoids identifying a particular country. Since the September 11, 2001, attack and the war in Iraq, your community has been wary of the few Arab families living here. You can see that tension in the eyes and behaviors of some of your students. You find yourself paying a little more attention when Ibrahim and Ariel are in the same group or have extended interactions together. You, too, have been influenced by the Arab-Israeli conflict. Perhaps you are overreacting, but you wonder if Ibrahim's unnamed country is Palestine or Iraq.

Ibrahim enjoys school, and although quiet in class, he is extremely polite to you and his classmates. But it is clear that he does not always "fit in." During Ramadan, a Muslim religious time for fasting, for example, he avoided the cafeteria during lunch. No one talked much about it, but you wonder what it must be like to smell food and see everyone else eating while you are fasting. Lunchtime saw him sitting by himself for the whole month of Ramadan. Like Ariel, Ibrahim has real problems with cafeteria foods, which make no allowances for Jewish or Muslim dietary laws.

Potentially Useful Generalization:_____

Carlos Martinez (Gay)

Carlos always felt different from other boys. A year ago he realized that he was gay. His mom and dad had divorced when he was younger, and he is now estranged from his father, who is uncomfortable with Carlos's sexual orientation. His mother continues to accept him for who he is and relies on him to help care for his younger sister. Carlos is now in your class and he is doing well. Schoolwork has always been easy for him, but he and his friends are concerned about hateful comments, like "fag," they sometimes hear in the hallways. They decided to start a Gay-Straight Alliance (GSA) to educate their peers.

After it was approved by the principal, the GSA began planning a fundraiser to buy holiday gifts for underprivileged children in the community. When word reached a conservative community group, however, protests began pouring into the superintendent's office that the middle school has a "gay club that is promoting homosexuality."

The GSA was invited to speak at the school board meeting. Though a small group of parents complained about the GSA, the school board members were impressed with the maturity and compassion displayed by Carlos and the other students. The school board voted to affirm the right of the GSA, and other student clubs, like the Bible Club, to meet in the school. You are excited that next month, Carlos will be speaking at the state capitol to testify before the House Education Committee in support of antibullying legislation. But you worry, and hope that no backlash will follow him here.

Potentially Useful Generalization:_____

So how did you do? Some of these scenarios may have been more challenging than others, and noting all the possible generalizations would be a Herculean task. Before we share our responses, look back at yours. Were some generalizations easier to identify than others? Or were all a challenge? What does that tell you about your own education, about what you have experienced and learned about other groups? Now you have an idea of what you need to learn to become more culturally knowledgeable. If you struggled with creating generalizations, you will want to learn more about different groups so that you can one day become a more effective culturally responsive teacher. Here are some generalizations for each student:

Marcus Griffin (African American)

Potentially Useful Generalizations: Research concerning African Americans indicates that many benefit from kinesthetic and activity-oriented learning; others have a strong oral language tradition—calling out in class may reflect interest and involvement, not rudeness; they tend to value imagination, imagery, and humor in learning; they also may value spirituality rather than a mechanistic approach to life. Also, not looking directly at an adult is often a sign of respect in this community.

Ana Garcia (Mexican American)

Potentially Useful Generalizations: One generalization is that many Mexican American students feel a loyalty and commitment to the family. Another is that many adhere to traditional gender roles in a patriarchal family. Mexican American students often prefer to work in peer groups rather than alone, and prefer structured learning environments. The high school dropout rates of Latinos and Latinas are very high, with estimates ranging from 40 to 50 percent.

Kasem Pravat (Asian American from Thailand)

Potentially Useful Generalizations: [Note: Generalizations about Asian Americans are by nature a "broad brush" because Americans group Japanese, Indians, Chinese, Pakistanis, Indonesians, and Vietnamese—about half the world population—under the term "Asian." Learning about each unique culture and country is critical.] Thais typically honor their national independence, many are fatalistic, and they may be offended by someone touching their head, the most sacred part of their body. Many cast their eyes down as a sign of respect. Thais often value self-discipline and academic success, seek cooperation and reconciliation, can be quite modest, might work hard to avoid confrontation, are often quiet, and typically revere teachers.

Ariel Klein (Jewish American)

Potentially Useful Generalizations: Jewish families in general are strong supporters of education, and children are often academically diligent with high career expectations. Jewish holidays can conflict with school calendars because schools are scheduled to conform to Christian holidays; observant Jews are unable to attend school functions on Friday nights and Saturdays, and may not be able to eat in the cafeteria. Jewish–Gentile conflict has existed for centuries and provides a disturbing undercurrent of anti-Semitism in some communities. Most Jews live in urban communities and on the east and west coasts.

Mary Goode (rural white)

Potentially Useful Generalizations: About one in five students attend rural schools; they are more likely to graduate from high school than urban or suburban students, but are less likely to attend college. Rural white students typically attend smaller schools and may struggle in a larger school community. Appalachian families are often traditional and patriarchal, with boys being favored.

Ibrahim Mouawad (Arab American)

Potentially Useful Generalizations: Arab homelands, rich heritage, and historical contributions are often discounted in the West and in the curriculum. Also, cultural, linguistic, religious, and national distinctions are typically ignored. (The word *Arabs* refers to different nationalities, religions, and ethnic groups connected by a common language and culture.) Close family relationships and respect for elders are common. Arabs are often generous and hospitable to friends and even strangers. Arabs often excel in math.

Carlos Martinez (Gay)

Potentially Useful Generalizations: LGBT students are often "overachievers" and show a high degree of creativity and energy. They are often committed to resolving social injustice. Some LGBT students, however, prefer to remain closeted.

One last reminder: these generalizations offer you a starting point, a place where research suggests you are most likely to reach success. But after you get to know your students, each student becomes an individual and will not always "fit" the generalization. So after working with Ibrahim for several months, if you discover that despite the generalization about Arab proficiency in math, Ibrahim is struggling in that subject, then, of course, you would offer extra instruction in math. Individual needs always trump group tendencies.

Diversity Assets

After you begin to formulate generalizations, you will realize that learning about students and their unique backgrounds can be a growth experience for the entire class, including the teacher. Even casual interactions can enhance learning for all, because each group brings rich and unique insights to school. These insights and experiences, these different ways of knowing and seeing the world, are *diversity assets.*

Let's visit those eight students in your class one more time. In each case, we will suggest a potential asset that the student's background may bring to your class, a way that this student's culture enriches learning:

Lindsey may be able to share her people's reverence for the earth and stewardship of the environment, their spiritual insights, artistic talents, oral traditions, and preference for cooperative learning. Perhaps her tribe's warm interpersonal relationships will help build the class community.

Marcus may offer a "lens" to help others see invisible white privilege. Perhaps Marcus will share a history of oral traditions and be another voice for cooperative learning.

Ana can contribute a second language, helping monolingual students broaden their linguistic horizons. Mexican American warmth and loyalty may also help create a class community.

Kasem can share yet another language and culture, a culture that may also enhance class cohesion. He may also model academic persistence for others.

Ariel may support Kasem in promoting an academic focus and class dialogue. She may also offer insights into one of the world's oldest religions and cultures, and help others see how Christian beliefs and practices shape "secular" practices in the United States.

Mary can offer insights into life in rural America and may be particularly resourceful because growing up in a rural community often fosters independence. Rural life also encourages a closer community, sometimes lost in today's fast-paced lifestyles.

Ibrahim brings another language to class and may provide insights into the rich Arab culture and history, particularly crucial in today's world of ethnic and religious intolerance.

Carlos may be striving toward social justice and equality in the face of adversity. In communities with little racial or ethnic diversity, Carlos may offer a diversity opportunity, a way to learn from the experiences and insights of others.

These students offer what a textbook or a curriculum cannot: a human connection to the world's diversity. Along with honoring their backgrounds and insights, their individual choices must be honored as well. Some teachers fall into the trap of inviting a Navajo, an African American, or a Mexican American student to be the voice of their people. How do black Americans feel about this, or what do Hispanics think about this? Crowning a black or Hispanic student as a spokesperson is unwise; one student cannot and should not speak for an entire group, and such a request can make a student feel uncomfortable. But as students volunteer their stories and opinions, and communicate informally with each other, their diversity assets will enrich learning for all.

Teaching Skills

Recognizing the experiences and histories of all your students is an important first step in creating a climate that honors and celebrates diversity. Your teaching behaviors should also reinforce your commitment to equity. All students benefit when they feel safe, their unique needs and interests are recognized, and they are part of classroom discourse. Teachers need to share their time and talent fairly, offering helpful feedback and encouragement to each student, and ensuring that the curriculum is meaningful. We will describe equitable teaching skills in Chapter 11, but here are some suggestions for effective and equitable teaching strategies. To help you remember them, we created the acronym *DIVERSE.*

D*iverse instructional materials:* Some say that an effective curriculum is both a window and a mirror. Are all your students able to see themselves in your curricular mirror? Are all parts of the world seen through your curricular window? Are diverse thoughts, views, and people woven into the curriculum? Do class and school displays reflect all the world's cultures and peoples?

MYTHS ABOUT CULTURALLY RESPONSIVE TEACHING

MYTH 1—CULTURALLY RESPONSIVE TEACHING IS A NEW APPROACH INTENDED TO MEET THE NEEDS OF POOR, URBAN STUDENTS OF COLOR.

Teaching has always been culturally responsive, but primarily responsive to the values of white, European American, middle-class students. That is why schools historically have emphasized individual success more than group success, strict adherence to time schedules, knowledge valued through analytical reasoning, self-sufficiency, and even dress codes. More inclusive culturally responsive teaching embraces the values and experiences of other cultures as well.

MYTH 2—ONLY TEACHERS OF COLOR CAN ACTUALLY BE CULTURALLY RESPONSIVE TO STUDENTS OF COLOR.

Race is not an obstacle to culturally responsive teaching; ignorance is. Through teacher training, teachers of any cultural background can gain the knowledge, skills, and attitudes needed to teach children from diverse cultures. In turn, because most teachers are white, they can share important lessons about the dominant culture.

MYTH 3—CULTURALLY RESPONSIVE TEACHING IS LITTLE MORE THAN A COLLECTION OF TEACHING IDEAS AND PRACTICES TO MOTIVATE STUDENTS OF COLOR.

Culturally responsive teaching offers a new way of looking at the roles of teachers and students. Culturally relevant teachers are committed to valuing the experiences of their students and working toward a more just society, far more profound goals than simply a collection of teaching ideas.

MYTH 4—CULTURALLY RELEVANT TEACHERS MUST MASTER ALL THE CRITICAL DETAILS OF MANY CULTURES.

It is unrealistic to expect teachers to master the intricacies of many cultures. But over time, thoughtful teachers will abandon simplistic, stereotypic thinking as they gain insights into cultural differences that influence behavior and learning.

MYTH 5—CULTURALLY RELEVANT TEACHING CATEGORIZES CHILDREN, WHICH FEEDS STEREOTYPIC THINKING.

Actually, culturally relevant teaching reduces stereotypic thinking by asking teachers to be reflective. They must consider student experiences and backgrounds, create teaching opportunities that respond to student learning styles, hold high expectations for all students, and help students experience academic success.

SOURCE: Adapted from Jacqueline Jordan and Beverley Jeanne Armento, *Culturally Responsive Teaching: Lesson Planning for Elementary and Middle Grades* (Boston: McGraw-Hill, 2001). Used with permission.

REFLECTION: Why do you think these myths are so prevalent? What additional myths about culturally relevant teaching can you add? How has your understanding of culturally relevant teaching expanded by reading this chapter?

Inclusive: Does your teaching provide opportunities for each student, especially those very quiet students, to participate in class discussions? Sometimes careful planning, thoughtful selection of particular students to respond, and patience can encourage even shy students to participate. Every student deserves a public voice and should be heard.

Variety: Using different teaching strategies—learning styles, sensory channels, and intelligences—can do wonders to involve all. Kinesthetic and artistic activities, cooperative learning, and other approaches honor different ways of learning and allow each student to experience success.

Exploration: Teachers should encourage students to explore new cultures and beliefs, and be open themselves to new ideas. Learning how different peoples view the world can unlock student (and teacher) minds.

Reaction: Often, teacher feedback is given too quickly, with little thought, and is of little help. Each student deserves the teacher's specific, timely, honest, and precise comments. With effective feedback, patience, encouragement, and high expectation, all children can learn, and can learn well.

Safety: Without safety and security, little learning is possible. Offensive comments about religion, race, ethnicity, or sexuality and verbal or physical bullying should be quickly confronted and stopped by the teacher.

Evaluation: Teachers often forget that the achievement tests, aptitude tests, and high-stakes tests are often designed for white, middle-class culture. Teachers should consider a variety of evaluation strategies to assess the unique strengths of each student. Evaluation can assist in student diagnosis and planning effective instruction. It can serve a more constructive purpose than simply ranking and rating students.

These skills should help you to reach out to all your students. While they promote equity, they also promote good teaching. How fortunate we are that equitable teaching skills are also effective teaching skills.

We Are One

In this chapter, we recognize that group differences offer a way of broadening our perspective on what it means to be truly educated. We should treat our wondrous diversity "as one of the most exciting parts of our education—an enormous opportunity to see the world in new ways and understand more about humanity. What is education about if not that?"[44]

As Hindu tradition reminds us, as we honor one another's differences, we need also to honor what we hold in common. So let's close this chapter by recognizing that we are all part of the human family. In his 1963 commencement speech at American University, John F. Kennedy said: "For in the final analysis, our most basic common link is that we all inhabit this small planet, we all breathe the same air, we all cherish our children's futures, and we are all mortal." Those words still ring true today. According to genome research, human beings are 96 percent alike, no matter where we live, no matter what experiences we have, no matter our color, our language, or our God.[45] Yes, we can do both: honor our common humanity and the richness of our differences.

An eighth-grade language arts teacher shared Langston Hughes's poem "I, Too, Sing America" with her students, and asked her students to create a similar poem based on their own experiences.[46] Her students wrote remarkable poems that underscored the continuing racism and sexism in society, as well as profound universal desires to accept and be accepted by others. We use this same activity in our teacher education classes, and each year we learn from our students. Here are two poems written by our teacher education students. You can find more poems on the text website, and we invite you to write and submit your own.

I, too, am an American
I am the trusting farm girl who grew up knowing no strangers
I ventured to the city, where they tell me I am too naïve
But I am not what my white, non-diverse, God-fearing, conservative roots
suggest
I have experiences with the good and the bad this world has to offer
Yet, each day I choose to smile and look for the good
Maybe
I am the beginning of this cycle
One smile, one act of trust, one stranger turned friend at a time

I, too, am an American.

—Lacey Rosenbaum

I, too, am an original American.
But concealed by my blond locks
and ocean deep blue eyes,
Red Man's blood
courses through these veins.
Undetected.
The White Man joke about the gamble
they think they are safe
"I can spot an ingine a mile a way!"
They spout without a single thought.
Then I smile
and take their then trembling hand
"Rainwater, and yes, it's Cherokee"
is all I say
as I walk away.
I am an Original American.

—Mandie Rainwater

SUMMARY

CHAPTER REVIEW

Go to the Online Learning Center to take a chapter self-quiz, practice with key terms, and review concepts from the chapter.

www.mhhe.com/
   sadkerbrief3e

1. In what ways are U.S. schools failing culturally diverse students?

Today, about 1 in 10 Americans is foreign born, and the native language of well over 30 million Americans is a language other than English. By 2030, half of all schoolchildren will be of color. Hispanic American, Native American, and African American students score consistently lower on standardized tests than do their Asian American and white classmates. Yet, almost half of the nation's historically under-resourced populations, Hispanic American, African American, and Native American, are not graduating from high school. Students from low-income families are far more likely to drop out of school than are the children of the wealthy. Part of this diversity now includes sexual orientation. Students need to understand that discrimination against gays is not to be tolerated, and teachers must provide a safe place for all students.

2. How do deficit, expectation, and cultural difference theories explain disparate academic performance among various racial, ethnic, and cultural groups?

Most white Americans believe that schools offer equitable educational opportunities to all children, and do not "see" the invisible privileges that many enjoy. Deficit, expectation, and cultural difference theories offer various explanations for the academic gaps that characterize different group performances in America's schools.

3. How do phrases like "melting pot" and "cultural pluralism" both capture and mask American identity?

Traditionally, Americans viewed their identity as a simplistic *melting pot,* where the historical and cultural differences of immigrants are lost and a new American is forged. The cultural pluralism image views Americans as honoring their past cultures as well as their new nationality. Perhaps both are simplistic perceptions, but they influence people's mindset a great deal.

4. What are the political and instructional issues surrounding bilingual education?

In *Lau v. Nichols* (1974), the Supreme Court ruled that schools were deficient in their treatment of students with limited English proficiency. Many schools subsequently established a variety of bilingual programs. Some programs teach students in their native language until they learn English (the transitional approach), others teach in both languages (the maintenance approach), and some use English as a Second Language (ESL). Studies suggest that many bilingual programs often fall short of their goals, and some critics advocate fast-paced immersion (also termed "submersion"), an effort supported by those who want English to be declared the "official" American language. The future direction of bilingual education may be as much a political determination as an instructional one.

5. **What are the purposes and approaches of multicultural education?**

   Multicultural education has multiple purposes, including *expanding the curriculum* to reflect the national diversity; *expanding teaching strategies* to respond to different learning styles; promoting the *multicultural competence of teachers;* and *a commitment to social justice,* to work and teach toward local and global equity. James Banks identifies four levels of a multicultural curriculum: contributions, additive, transformation, and social action. Those opposed to multicultural education fear it emphasizes differences at the expense of national unity and takes time from critical academic subjects.

6. **Why is culturally responsive teaching important?**

   As the United States' demographics become increasingly diverse, teachers will be expected to understand the needs and cultural learning styles of students with backgrounds very different from their own. Culturally responsive teaching focuses on mediating the frequent mismatch between the home and school cultures. Understanding and rejecting stereotypes and formulating generalizations about groups and their educational assets can offer a practical introduction for planning instruction.

7. **How can teachers use culturally responsive teaching strategies?**

   In addition to recognizing cultural learning styles and bridging school and community cultures, a number of specific teaching strategies are also suggested. These range from an inclusive curriculum reflecting all groups, to inclusive classroom interactions where all students, even quiet ones, contribute to the learning community. Tomorrow's teachers will need to plan for diversity, which means using a variety of classroom strategies and techniques to respond to different learning styles.

KEY TERMS AND PEOPLE

assimilation (enculturation), 70

James Banks, 78

bilingual education, 71

cultural difference theory, 67

cultural pluralism, 70

culturally responsive teaching, 80

culture, 61

deficit theory, 67

dual-language instruction, 73

English as a Second Language (ESL), 73

English language learners (ELL), 72

English-only movement, 74

ethnicity, 61

expectation theory, 67

generalizations, 84

immersion, 73

language submersion, 71

Lau v. Nichols, 72

maintenance (developmental) approach, 73

multicultural education, 78

multiracial, 61

race, 61

stereotypes, 82

stereotype threat, 84

transitional approach, 73

DISCUSSION QUESTIONS AND ACTIVITIES

1. Observe a classroom, noting how many times teachers call on each student. Compare the amount of attention each student receives. Now determine group representation in the classroom. Does one group (boys or whites or native-English speakers) get more than its fair share of teacher attention? The online observation guide can be helpful in this activity.

WEB-*TIVITIES*

Go to the Online Learning Center to do the following activities:
1. Today's Students: Patterns of Diversity
2. Native American Education Today
3. Black Americans and Desegregation
4. Multicultural Education
5. Bilingual Education

2. How do you react to the various issues raised in this chapter? On a separate sheet of paper complete the following sentences as honestly as you can. If you wish, share your responses with your classmates.

- To me, the phrase *invisible race privilege* means . . .
- A great example of expectation theory is . . .

3. Given demographic trends, pick a region of the country and a particular community. Develop a scenario of a classroom in that community in the year 2030. Describe the students' characteristics and the teacher's role. Is that classroom likely to be affected by changing demographics? How are cultural learning styles manifested in the way the teacher organizes and instructs the class?

4. Choose a school curriculum and suggest how it can be changed to reflect one of the four approaches to multicultural education described by Banks. Why did you choose the approach you did?

5. Discuss the two main approaches to bilingual education in the United States: transitional and maintenance. Which do you favor, and why?

YOUR CD-ROM: THE *TEACHERS, SCHOOLS, AND SOCIETY READER* WITH CLASSROOM OBSERVATION VIDEO CLIPS

Articles, Case Studies, and Videos correspond to chapter content and are not always in numeric order. Go to your *Teachers, Schools, and Society Reader* CD-ROM to:

Read Current and Historical Articles

9. "I, Too, Am an American: Preservice Teachers Reflect upon National Identity," Nancy Gallavan, *Multicultural Teaching*, Spring 2002.

10. "The Threat of Stereotype," Joshua Aronson, *Educational Leadership*, November 2004.

11. "How Good Are the Asians: Refuting Four Myths About Asian-American Academic Achievement," Yong Zhao and Wei Qiu, *Phi Delta Kappan*, January 2009.

47. "Autobiography of a Teacher: A Journey Toward Critical Multiculturalism," Sarah J. Ramsey, *Scholar-Practitioner Quarterly* 2, no. 3, 2004.

Analyze Case Studies

5. **Helen Franklin:** A teacher who uses parents as volunteers to help with her unique classroom organization notices that a parent volunteer who has questioned the teacher's methods will work only with white students.

6. **Leigh Scott:** A teacher gives a higher-than-earned grade to a mainstreamed student on the basis of the boy's effort and attitude and is confronted by a black student with identical test scores who received a lower grade and who accuses her of racism.

Observe Teachers, Students, and Classrooms in Action

5. **High School Students Discuss Issues They Face as Immigrants**
See page 68 of this text for a description of this video. You'll find the video on the CD Reader and at the Online Learning Center.

www.mhhe.com/
sadkerbrief3e

STUDENT LIFE IN SCHOOL AND AT HOME

chapter 4

Focus Questions

1. What rituals and routines shape classroom life?
2. How is class time related to student achievement?
3. How does the teacher's gatekeeping function influence classroom roles?
4. What is tracking, and what are its advantages and disadvantages?
5. How do gender and peer groups influence children in elementary and middle school?
6. In what ways does the adolescent culture shape teenage perceptions and behaviors?
7. What impact do changing family patterns and economic issues have on children and schools?
8. How can educators respond to social issues that place children at risk?

WHAT DO YOU THINK? What Was Your School Experience Like? See how it compares to that of your colleagues.

www.mhhe.com/
sadkerbrief3e

Chapter Preview

School is a culture. Like most cultures, it is filled with its own unique rituals, traditions, and its own set of norms and mores. In school even the familiar, like time, is made new. Time is told by subjects ("Let's talk before math") or periods ("I'm going home after seventh period"). Students are pinched into passive roles, following schedules created by others, sitting still rather than being active, and responding to teacher questions, but seldom asking any of their own. Such a system challenges and confines both teachers and students. Peer groups create friendships and popularity, a strong subculture that make winners and losers of us all—at least for a brief time. Adults pick up where children leave off, assigning students to what amounts to an academic caste system through *de facto* tracking or ability grouping. While adults focus on academics, many adolescents and preadolescents are focused on relationships and sexuality.

Economic and social factors are also powerful forces in today's classrooms and have reshaped the family unit. New family patterns abound, challenging the traditional view of the mother, father, and two children (did we forget the dog?) as the "typical" American family. With these changes, economic and social problems threaten our children and challenge teachers. We will describe these challenges—such as poverty, obesity, and bullying—so that educators can work to create schools that are safe havens and institutions of hope.

Rules, Rituals, and Routines

Schools create their own cultures, replete with norms, rituals, and routines. Even simple tasks, like distributing textbooks, are clothed with cultural cues, but they are cues that differ for students and teachers.

Focus Question 1
What rituals and routines shape classroom life?

"Come Right Up and Get Your New Books": A Teacher's Perspective

"Okay, class, quiet down," said Mr. Thompson. "As you can see, the poetry books we've been waiting for have finally arrived. All right, you can cut out the groans. Give the books a fair trial before you sentence them. I'd like the first person in each row to come up, count out enough books for his or her row, and hand them out."

Six students charged to the front and made a mad grab for the books. In the ensuing melee, one stack of books went crashing to the floor.

"Hey, kids, take it easy. When you get your texts, write your name and room number in the stamped box inside the cover." Mr. Thompson turned his attention to the several hands waving in the air.

"Yes, Jessica?"

"I can't fill in my name because my pencil just broke. Can I sharpen it?"

"Go ahead. Jamie?"

"My pencil's broken too. Can I sharpen mine?"

"Yes, but wait until Jessica sits down. Let me remind you that you're supposed to come to class prepared. Now there will be no more at the pencil sharpener today. Scott?"

"Can I use the hall pass?"

"Is this absolutely necessary? All right then [responding to Scott's urgent nod]. After you get your book and fill in the appropriate information, turn to the poem on page 3. It's called 'Stopping by Woods on a Snowy Evening,' and it's by Robert Frost, one of America's most famous poets. Yes, Rosa?"

"I didn't get a book."

"Okay, Rosa. Go down to the office and tell Mrs. Goldberg that we need one more of the new poetry anthologies. Now, as I was about to say, I'd like you to think about the questions that I've written on the board: How does the speaker in this poem feel as he looks at the snow filling up the deserted woods? Why does he wish to stop, and what makes him realize that he must go on? April! Maxine! This is not a time for your private chat room. This is a silent reading activity—and I do mean silent. Okay, class, I think most of you have had enough time to read the poem. Who has an answer for the first question? Jordan?"

"Well, I think the guy in this poem really likes nature. He's all alone, and it's private, with no people around to interrupt him, and he thinks the woods and the snow are really beautiful."

"Jordan, that's an excellent response. You've captured the mood of this poem. Maxine?"

"I think he wants to stop because . . ."

Maxine's answer was cut short by the abrasive ring of the fourth-period bell.

"For homework, I'd like you to answer the remaining questions. Alice?"

"Is this to hand in?"

"Yes. Any other questions? Okay, you'd better get to your next-period class."

As the last student left, Rick Thompson slumped over his desk and wearily ran his fingers through his hair. As he looked down, he spotted the missing poetry anthology under his desk, a victim of the charge of the book brigade. The whole lesson was a victim of the book brigade. He had been so busy getting the books dispensed and fielding all the interruptions that he had forgotten to give his brief explanation on the differences between prose and poetry. He had even forgotten to give his motivating speech on how interesting the new poetry unit was going to be. Well, no time for a postmortem now. Stampede-like noises outside the door meant the fourth-period class was about to burst in.

"Come Right Up and Get Your New Books": A Student's Perspective

From her vantage point in the fourth seat, fifth row, Maxine eyed the stack of new books on the teacher's desk. She knew they were poetry books because she had flipped through one as she meandered into the room. She didn't care that it wasn't "in" to like poetry; she liked it anyway.

Maxine settled into her seat and began the long wait for her book. Her thoughts wandered: "Mr. Thompson seems like he's in some kind of daze, just staring at the new books like he's zoned out. Wonder what's bugging him. Good enough, the first kids in each row are heading up to get the books. Oh, right, they're getting into a brawl over handing out the stupid books. What a bunch of jerks; they must think they're funny or something. Now it'll be one row at a time and will take forever. I suppose I can start my math homework or write some letters."

Maxine got several of her math problems solved by the time her poetry anthology arrived, along with instructions to read the poem on page 3. She skimmed through the poem and decided she liked it. She understood how Robert Frost felt, watching the snowy woods and wanting to get away from all the hassles. It sure would be nice to read this poem quietly somewhere without listening to kids going on about pencil sharpeners and hall passes and seat changes. As she turned around to share her observation about hassles with April Marston, Mr. Thompson's sharp reprimand interrupted her. She fumed to herself, "Private chat room. What's with him? Half the class is talking, and old Eagle Eyes Thompson has to pick on me. And they're all talking about the football game Saturday. At least I was talking about the poem. Oh well, I'd better answer one of those questions on the board and show him that I really am paying attention."

Maxine waved her hand wildly, but Jordan got called for question 1. Maxine shot her hand in the air again for a chance at question 2. When Mr. Thompson called on her, she drew a deep breath and began her response. Once again, she was interrupted in midsentence, this time by the fourth-period bell.

"I really knew the answer to that question," she muttered under her breath. "Now we have to write all the answers out. Boring. Well, next period is science and we're supposed to be giving lab reports. Maybe we'll have a chance to finish the English homework there."

Watching the Clock

You have just read two replays of a seventh-grade English lesson, one from the vantage point of the teacher, the other from the vantage point of a student. Mr. Thompson and Maxine play different roles, which cause them to have very different experiences in this class. Mr. Thompson was continually leap-frogging from one minor crisis to the next; Maxine was sitting and waiting.

In his perceptive book titled *Life in Classrooms*, **Philip W. Jackson** describes how time is spent in school.[1] He suggests that, whereas teachers are typically very busy, students are often caught in patterns of delay that force them to do nothing. Jackson notes that a great deal of teachers' time is spent in noninstructional busywork, such as keeping time and dispensing supplies. In the slice of classroom life you just read, Mr. Thompson spent a substantial part of the class time distributing new texts. Indeed, most teachers spend a good deal of time giving out things: paper, pencils, art materials, science equipment, CDs, exam booklets, erasers, happy faces, special privileges—the list goes on and on. The classroom scene described also shows Mr. Thompson greatly involved in timekeeping activities. Within the limits set by school buzzers and bells, he determines when the texts will be distributed, when and for how long the reading activity will take place, and when the class discussion will begin.

What do students do while teachers are busy organizing, structuring, talking, questioning, handing out, collecting, timekeeping, and crisis hopping? According to Jackson's analysis, they do little more than sit and wait.[2] They wait for the materials to be handed out, for the assignment to be given, for the questions to be asked, for the teacher to call on them, for the teacher to react to their response, and for the slower class members to catch up so that the activity can change. They wait in lines to get drinks of water, to get pencils sharpened, to get their turn at the computer, to go to the playground, to get to the bathroom, and to be dismissed from class. If students are to succeed in school, they must be able to cope with continual delay as a standard operating procedure.

One plea that is rarely granted is that of talking to classmates beyond controlled learning activities. Like the character from Greek mythology, Tantalus, who was continually tempted with food and water but was not allowed to eat or drink, students are surrounded by peers and friends but are restrained from communicating with them. Furthermore, while trying to concentrate on work and to ignore social temptations, students are beset by frequent interruptions—the public address system blaring a message in the middle of an exam, the end-of-class bell interrupting a lively discussion, a teacher's reprimand, or a student's question derailing a train of thought.

What are the pluses and pitfalls of posting a schedule like this? Do you recall your own feelings as a student about the routine and regimentation of school life?

Consider how Maxine in Mr. Thompson's English class had to cope with delay, denial of desire, social distraction, and interruptions. She waited for the delivery of her new text. She waited to be called on by the teacher. Her attempt to concentrate on reading the poem was disturbed by frequent interruptions. Her brief communication with a classmate was interrupted by a reprimand. Her head was filled with ideas and questions. In short, there was a lot she would like to have said, but there was almost no opportunity to say it.

Educators concerned about school improvement have called attention to the inefficient use of time in school, claiming that we lose between one-quarter and one-half of the time available for learning through attendance problems, noninstructional activities (such as class changes and assemblies), administrative and organizational activities, and disruptions caused by student misbehavior.[3]

Focus Question 2

How is class time related to student achievement?

In a classic study of schools, **John Goodlad** found a fair degree of consistency in how time is spent in different activities as children go through the grades. As Figure 4.1 illustrates, about 2 percent of time is spent on social activities, 2 to 5 percent on behavior management, 20 percent on routines, and 74 percent on instruction.

In Goodlad's study, although there was a general consistency in how time was spent at different levels of schooling, one of the most astonishing findings was the enormous variation in the *efficiency* with which different schools used time. When examining the hours per week allocated to subject-matter learning, time ranged from a low of 18.5 hours in one school to a high of 27.5 hours in another. Goodlad was also surprised at the limited amount of time spent on the academic staples, such as reading and writing. He found that only 6 percent of time in elementary school was spent on reading. This dropped to a minuscule 2 percent at the high school level. In contrast, the amount of time students spent listening to teacher lectures and explanations

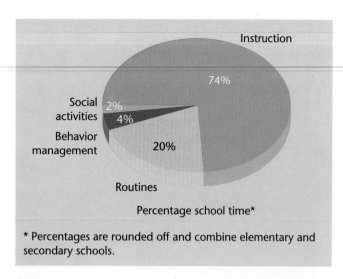

FIGURE 4.1

School time.

SOURCE: From John Goodlad, *A Place Called School* Copyright © 1984 The McGraw-Hill Companies, Inc. Reprinted with permission of The McGraw-Hill Companies, Inc.

REFLECTION: About three-fourths of class time is spent in instruction. Does that seem high, low, or about right? The instruction category is quite broad. How might you break it down into more meaningful subcategories?

Focus Question 3

How does the teacher's gatekeeping function influence classroom roles?

increased from approximately 18 percent in elementary school to more than 25 percent in high school.[4] We would like Goodlad's study to be replicated in today's schools to see if we are more—or less—efficient in the use of instructional time.[5]

While the business world may suggest "time is money," for educators, time is learning. As one teacher points out:

> Time is the currency of teaching. We barter with time. Every day we make small concessions, small trade-offs, but, in the end, we know it's going to defeat us. After all, how many times are we actually able to cover World War I in our history courses before the year is out? We always laugh a little about that, but the truth is the sense of the clock ticking is one of the most oppressive features of teaching.[6]

There is a limited amount of time set aside for the school day. Research shows that when more time is allocated to subject-matter learning, student achievement increases.[7] When this valuable resource is spent handing out supplies or reprimanding misbehavior, it is lost for learning. Looked at from this perspective, Mr. Thompson's class was not only frustrating, but also deprived students of a precious and limited resource—the time to learn.

The Teacher as Gatekeeper

Teachers are typically involved in more than one thousand verbal exchanges with their students every day.[8] Count the number of verbal exchanges Mr. Thompson had with his students during our abbreviated classroom scene and you will get some idea of how much and how often teachers talk. One of the functions that keeps teachers busiest is what Philip Jackson terms **gatekeeping.** As gatekeepers, teachers must determine who will talk, when, and for how long, as well as the basic direction of the communication.

Consider what effect patterns of classroom interaction have on both teachers and students:

- Roughly two-thirds of classroom time is taken up by talk; two-thirds of that talk is by the teacher.[9]
- In the typical "pedagogical cycle," teachers structure (lecture and direct), question, and react to student comments. Teachers initiate about 85 percent of these verbal cycles.[10]
- While questioning signals curiosity, it is the teachers, not the learners, who do the questioning, asking as many as 348 questions a day.[11] The typical student rarely asks a question.[12]
- Most classroom questions require that students use only rote memory.[13]
- Students are not given much time to ask, or even answer, questions. Teachers usually wait less than a second for student comments and answers.[14]
- Teachers interact less and less with students as they go through the grades.[15]

THE PATTERNS OF THE CLASSROOM

After observing in more than 1,000 classrooms, John Goodlad and his team of researchers found that the following patterns characterize most classrooms:

- Much of what happens in class is geared toward maintaining order among 20 to 30 students restrained in a relatively small space.
- Although the classroom is a group setting, each student typically works alone.
- The teacher is the key figure in setting the tone and determining the activities.
- Most of the time, the teacher is in front of the classroom, teaching a whole group of students.
- There is little praise or corrective feedback; classes are emotionally neutral or flat places.
- Students are involved in a limited range of activities—listening to lectures, writing answers to questions, and taking exams.

- A significant number of students are confused by teacher explanations and feel that they do not get enough guidance on how to improve.

Goodlad concluded that "the emotional tone of the classroom is neither harsh and punitive nor warm and joyful; it might be described most accurately as flat."

SOURCE: John Goodlad, *A Place Called School* (New York: McGraw-Hill, 1984/2004).

REFLECTION: Goodlad's classic study is now more than two decades old. How many of these findings continue to characterize classroom life? How will you make learning more joyful and engaging?

Ironically, although a major goal of education is to increase students' curiosity and quest for knowledge, it is the teachers, not the students, who dominate and manage classroom interaction. Most classroom interaction patterns do not train students to be active, inquiring, self-reliant learners. Rather, students are too often expected to be quiet and passive, to think quickly (and perhaps superficially), to rely on memory, and to be dependent on the teacher. Silent, passive students have less positive attitudes and lower achievement. Perhaps the challenge new teachers should keep before them is finding a way to turn their gatekeeping role into a benefit for students, instead of a hindrance.

The Other Side of the Tracks

We have seen that teachers function as gatekeepers, controlling the amount and flow of student talk in the classroom. Let's step back a moment and consider an even more basic question: Which students sit (for sit they mainly do) in which classrooms? That very crucial, political decision falls on teachers, counselors, and administrators. Many believe that it is easier for students with similar skills and intellectual abilities to learn together, in *homogeneous* classes. Educators following this belief screen, sort, and direct students based on their abilities, and as a result, send them down different school paths, profoundly shaping their futures. Students of different abilities (low, middle, and high) are assigned to different "tracks" of courses and programs (vocational, general, college-bound, honors, and AP). **Tracking** is the term given to this process, and while some teachers believe that tracking makes instruction more manageable, others believe that it is a terribly flawed system. Either way, tracking is one of the oldest of school traditions.

Focus Question 4
What is tracking, and what are its advantages and disadvantages?

105

PROFILE IN EDUCATION

Jeannie Oakes

Jeannie Oakes became a teacher for a conventional reason, but as a teacher, became an unconventional advocate for social change and equity. Oakes's first-hand experiences as a teacher and a researcher transformed her into one of the leaders in detracking. Her work focuses on not only doing away with tracking, but also increasing the quality of curriculum and instruction for all students. To read a full profile of Jeannie Oakes, go to the Chapter 4 Profile in Education at www.mhhe.com/sadkerbrief3e.

Sociologist Talcott Parsons analyzed school as a social system and concluded that the college selection process begins in elementary school and is virtually sealed by the time students finish junior high.[16] Parsons's analysis has significant implications, for he is suggesting that future roles in adult life are determined by student achievement in elementary school. The labeling system, beginning at an early age, determines who will wear a stethoscope, who will carry a laptop computer, and who will become a low-wage laborer.

Several researchers consider students' social class a critical factor in this selection system. Back in 1929, Robert and Helen Lynd, in their extensive study of Middletown (a small midwestern city), concluded that schools are essentially middle-class institutions that discriminate against lower-class students.[17] Approximately 15 years later, W. Lloyd Warner and his associates at the University of Chicago conducted a series of studies in New England, the deep South, and the Midwest and came to a similar conclusion:

> One group [the lower class] is almost immediately brushed off into a bin labeled "nonreaders, first-grade repeaters," or "opportunity class," where they stay for eight or ten years and are then released through a chute to the outside world to become hewers of wood and drawers of water.[18]

More recently, **Jeannie Oakes's** *Keeping Track* offered a scathing indictment of racial influence on tracking. She found that race more than ability determined which students are placed in which tracks: Black, Hispanic, and Native American students with similar test scores as their White peers are three times more likely to be enrolled in low-track classes. Oakes also documented how these lower-tracked students have fewer learning opportunities and how teachers expect little from them. Their instruction covers less content, involves more drill and repetition, and places more emphasis on classroom management problems.[19]

Students in low-ability tracks have difficulty moving into higher tracks. Ray Rist observed a kindergarten class in an all-black urban school. By the eighth day of class, the kindergarten teacher, apparently using such criteria as physical appearance, socioeconomic status, and language usage, had separated her students into groups of "fast learners" and "slow learners." She spent more time with the "fast learners" and gave them more instruction and encouragement. The "slow learners" got more than their fair share of control and ridicule. The children soon began to mirror the teacher's behavior. As the "fast learners" belittled the "slow learners," the low-status children began to exhibit attitudes of self-degradation and hostility toward one another. This teacher's expectations, formed during eight days at the beginning of school, shaped the academic and social treatment of children in her classroom for the entire year and perhaps for years to come. Records of the grouping that had taken place during the first week in kindergarten were passed on to teachers in the upper grades, providing the basis for further differential treatment.[20]

Consider some additional disturbing facts on race, socioeconomic status, and tracking:

- Teachers with the least experience and the lowest levels of qualifications are assigned to students in the lowest tracks.

- Schools with predominately poor and minority populations offer fewer advanced and more remedial courses in academic subjects.

- Asian, White, and wealthy students are more likely than Black, Hispanic, and poor students to be recommended for advanced classes and gifted programs, even with equivalent test scores.

- Students are more likely to choose their friends from their tracked classes in elementary through high school. These social networks can further entrench racially segregated academic tracks.

- When parents intervene, counselors place middle- and upper-socioeconomic class students with low grades and test scores into higher tracked groups.[21]

Low teacher expectations and unchallenging courses may encourage student passivity and boredom.

Such findings add momentum to the effort to **detrack,** or eliminate tracking practices from the nation's schools. But the task is not easy.

"True," tracking supporters argue, "it would appear more democratic to put everyone in the same class, but such idealism is destined to fail." They contend that it is unrealistic to think everyone can or should master the same material or learn it at the same pace. Without tracking we have *heterogeneous,* or mixed ability classes. Tracking advocates are quick to point out that mixed ability classes have their own set of problems: In heterogeneous classes, bright students get bored while slower students have trouble keeping up, and we lose our most talented and our most needy students. Teachers find themselves grading the brighter students on the quality of their work and the weaker ones on their "effort," which is a big problem (especially with parents!). Teachers get frustrated trying to meet each student's needs but hardly ever hitting the mark. Putting everyone in the same class simply doesn't work.[22]

Detracting advocates, as you might imagine, offer a different take on the issue. "No sorting system is consistent with equality of opportunity. Worse yet, the tracking system is not based on individual ability. It is badly biased in favor of white middle-class America. We must face the reality that poor children, often children of color, come to school far from being ready to learn. And the school, whose job it is to educate all our children, does little to help. The built-in bias in instruction, counseling, curricular materials, and testing must be overcome. Students get shoveled into second-rate courses that prepare them for fourth-rate jobs. Their track becomes "a great training robbery," and the students who are robbed may be ones with great abilities."

While the social pitfalls of tracking have been well documented, its efficacy has not. Students who are placed in low tracks for all subjects fail to academically improve.[23] With little hard evidence supporting tracking, and a growing concern about its negative fallout, it is little wonder that the *term* "tracking" has fallen out of favor. Most schools today instead prefer the term "ability grouping."

Ability grouping sorts students based on capability, but the groupings may well vary by subject. While tracks suggest permanence, ability grouping is more transitory. One year, a student might find herself in a high-ability math group and a low-ability English group. The following year, that same student might be reassigned to a new set of groups. Today, many schools talk about "ability grouping," but sometimes it is only the label that has been changed. Ability grouping becomes *de facto* tracking. (You may want to think of school tracking as a take-off on the federal "witness protection program": a reality functioning under an assumed identity.)

Many educators believe that detracking can work, if it is implemented correctly. Teachers, parents, and students should realize that although students arrive at school from very different backgrounds, learning from each other and together has great advantages. Instruction is best offered through individualized learning, rather than the traditional approach of trying to teach all students simultaneously. Alternative assessments work far better than testing everyone with the same test (compare this view to the current emphasis on standardized tests). In fact, detracked schools can be authentic places of learning, academically challenging to all while teaching a living lesson in democracy. What is needed is time, careful planning, and adequate training for teachers so that they can succeed and all students can learn.[24]

As these arguments suggest, tracking is likely to remain an area of controversy in the years ahead, especially for educators, who find it "the most professionally divisive issue" in the field.[25] One of the ironies of tracking is that it builds on an already divided school culture. What educators do not do to divide students, students often do to themselves.

The Gendered World of Elementary and Middle School

Focus Question 5
How do gender and peer groups influence children in elementary and middle school?

In the first grade, when so much about school seems gigantic and fearful, children look to adults for safety: What am I supposed to do in the classroom? Where do I get lunch? How do I find the bus to ride home from school? Children go to their first-grade teacher not only for this practical information but also for hugs, praise, and general warmth and affection.[26] But by the second grade, a new world emerges, a world where gender shapes identities and relationships and intensifies during the school years. By the second grade, boys break away from teacher dependence and place more importance on their peer group—other boys. Boys claim their own territory on the athletic field and in the lunchroom, and sometimes even challenge the teacher. Male identity and entitlement are strengthened during elementary school years, but not for all boys, not for the boys considered sissies. Over time, many of these excluded males exhibit an increasing number of social, emotional, and academic problems.

Girls spend the first few elementary school years helping the teacher, behaviors that are rewarded, in part, with good report card grades. Girls also form best-friend relationships in which pairs of girls pledge devotion to one another. By the upper elementary grades, girls begin to fantasize about the "cute" boys in their class and about what being married and having a family would be like. Being a good student and having a pleasing personality are important to girls, but by the upper elementary grades, appearance often becomes the key to social status.

Homework Should Be

A MAJOR PART OF A STUDENT'S LIFE BECAUSE . . .

THERE IS TOO MUCH MATERIAL TO BE MASTERED ONLY DURING SCHOOL TIME

Given demands on students to learn more and to increase their test scores, much study and learning needs to take place at home. After all, students are in school for just 5 hours of a 24-hour day.

IT BRINGS PARENTS INTO THE LEARNING PROCESS

School cannot accomplish its goals alone. Students achieve much more when academics are reinforced at home. By providing guidance and monitoring homework, parents demonstrate their support of learning, becoming true partners with teachers. Closing the school–home gap fosters competent and attentive students.

MANY STUDENTS DO NOT USE THEIR TIME WISELY

The average student comes home from school, talks on the phone with friends, "hangs out" at the mall, watches television for hours, and then plays a computer game or two before going to bed. Homework at least gives students something meaningful to do with their time.

LIMITED AND BRIEF BECAUSE . . .

TOO MUCH STRESS IS PLACED ON STUDENTS AS IT IS

Schools have been taken over by this growing obsession with tests. The last thing we need to do is extend this angst to home life. Besides, homework is mostly busywork, unrelated to real learning.

IT FAVORS SOME STUDENTS AND PENALIZES OTHERS

Some children have highly educated parents, home computers, and the resources needed to produce quality homework. Other students have poor and uneducated parents, who may not even speak English, and who may be working two or more jobs. All too often homework is simply a measure of family resources.

MANY STUDENTS DO NOT HAVE THE LUXURY OF EXTRA TIME

Many students go directly from school to their part-time job. Their families may need the money. Other students must care for younger siblings at home while parents are at work. Increasing homework would place an enormous burden on these families.

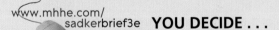

www.mhhe.com/sadkerbrief3e **YOU DECIDE . . .**

Will you be assigning homework? If so, how much do you think is appropriate, and how will homework factor into your assessment of student work? Do you have a plan to handle differences in family resources?

The *gender wall* blocking elementary boys and girls from interacting is stronger than racial barriers. There is more cross-race than cross-sex communication during the elementary school years. As one girl explains:

> If you say you like someone, other kids spread it all over the school and that's embarrassing. . . . If you even sit beside a boy in class, other kids say you like him. And they come to you in the bathroom and tease you about liking the boy. Once some of the girls put J. S. and B. B. on the bathroom walls. That was embarrassing.[27]

Every day, teachers must work to create humane and caring classrooms. When students respond to questions designed to measure their friendship patterns, 10 percent of them emerge as not being anybody's friend (isolates). About half of these are just ignored. The other half become the victims of active peer

YOU BE THE JUDGE

109

FIGURE 4.2

Sociogram: A teacher's tool.

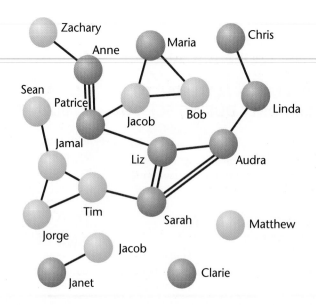

Sociograms provide insights into the social life of a class. In this sociogram, circles represent students, and colors indicate gender. Lines are drawn connecting circles when students interact with one another. Each line reflects a verbal communication: the more lines, the greater number of interactions. In this sociogram, it appears that Anne and Patrice are friends; Liz, Sarah, and Audra may form a clique; while Matthew and Clarie appear to be isolates. Charting several sociograms of these children over time would confirm or refute these initial perceptions.

group rejection and hostility. In fact, elementary school sociometric measures predict social adjustment better than most other personality and educational tests do.[28] These social preferences can be graphically presented in **sociograms** (see Figure 4.2).

Most friendless children are aware of their problem and report feeling lonely and unsuccessful in relating to others. Rejection by the child's peer group is a strong indicator of future problems. Consider the following true story.

Guest Column: Haunted by Racist Attitudes

As graduation time approaches, I am supposed to get nostalgic about my community and my school. I should be thankful for how they have enriched my life, and I should expect to reminisce later on the "great things" about living here. Frankly, in my case, that will not be possible; I'll be trying to forget the bigotry here. Elementary school fostered my negative first impressions. One kid tried to insult me in the halls by calling me "African." My classmates told me to "go back where you came from." (Obviously they had no idea what country this was, but cultural education is another essay.) Often, I was used as an object in a "cooties" game. I was the contaminated one who had to touch all the other pure white-skinned kids. One day after school I was tied to a tree by some boys. The girls just stood around to laugh. They were the friendly ones because at least they did not inflict bodily pain. Wasn't I the naive buffoon to underestimate the burn of psychological humiliation?

Summer meant parks and recreation day camp, and that was hellish. Each day, I was depantsed by some fifth-grade boys in front of the amused campers. I was too embarrassed to tell my parents, and the counselors paid no attention to the foolish games all little boys play. Adult ignorance was by far the most agonizing injustice. In middle school, I sat in front of a boy who constantly whispered, "You f—nigger, black, disgusting" in my ear. Racism was intolerable. The teacher, I guess, disagreed. At least kids are honest. Isn't it amusing how they are little reflections of a community's attitudes? Today, the same people who tormented me as a child walk down the halls faceless. Once a racist reaches a certain age, he realizes that prejudice is not an outright verbal contract. It is subtle and "understood."

Just yesterday my five-year-old sister came home from her preschool and complained, "A girl said she didn't wanna play with me because I'm black." I said, "That's terrible! Did you tell the teacher?" My sister responded, "My teacher said, 'Just ignore her.'"

Yes, I'll have no trouble trying to forget this place.

—Student letter to the school paper[29]

Social exclusion or relational aggression occurs in mixed-sex or same-sex peer groups. In either setting, rejection and isolation can be painful.

An insightful teacher can structure a classroom to minimize negative and hurtful interaction and maximize the positive power of peer group relations. For instance, eliminating social cliques and race- and gender-based segregation is a precursor to successful cooperative groups. An "intentional" teacher often assigns students to seats or to group work to counter pupil favoritism and bias. A teacher's perceptiveness and skill in influencing the social side of school can mean a world of difference in a student's environment. These social needs only grow as students transition into middle school.

Since the 1960s, many policymakers have advocated that middle school—often grades 6, 7, and 8—should be a time when children have a chance to adjust to puberty. Attention to the emotional and physical developmental growth of adolescents is seen as the primary purpose of middle school life. However, some critics see middle schools as having gone "soft," overemphasizing self-esteem building at the expense of academic rigor. Describing the middle school years as the "Bermuda Triangle of American education," such critics call for a return to K–8 schooling and a more discipline-focused curriculum.[30] Because some adolescents struggle with change, they argue that K–8 schools provide stability in neighborhood, building, peers, and staff for parents and students alike. Yet, advocates for middle schools argue that simply changing the grade configuration is no magic bullet. What happens in the classroom is what matters most. Noted one principal, "The challenge for us as middle-school educators in the age of high-stakes testing is to encourage teaching for understanding while addressing the myriad of social and emotional issues."[31] While the future of middle schools is in doubt, one adolescent struggle remains omnipresent: the need to develop an identity, including what it means to be male or female.

"I feel pressure from my parents and teachers to do well in school. But when I do, boys won't ask me to the school dance and even my girlfriends call me a "nerd." So now I talk less in class and don't study as much. The teasing hurts, so it's easier to hide being smart."

"Boys joke around too much so teachers pay more attention by disciplining rather than helping them to learn."

"Boys can't take music class without being called a fag. So I hide my musical talents, like playing Mozart on the keyboard."

"Girls do everything for men in marriage."

Do these words sound like sexist artifacts of the 1950s or 1960s, or perhaps the 1970s? In fact, these are the voices of today's middle-school students. Their words reveal how gender and peer relations play significant roles in their lives, expanding some options, but more often limiting academic and social development. When we asked more than 400 middle schoolers to identify the "best and worst thing about being a boy or girl," their stories lifted the veil on the pervasive sexism in today's schools and society.[32] Students unequivocally had more positive things to say about being a boy than being a girl. Male advantages focused on physical and athletic prowess, underscoring the central role physicality plays for boys. Students also described how boys "naturally" excel at sports: "Boys have more sports available and can play them better. It's fair to say that we are better athletes than girls."

Students also easily described male entitlements: they are listened to more, are naturally smarter, allowed to do more, have the dominant role in marriage, and receive greater respect. More than 1 in 10 students wrote that one of the best things about being a boy was not being a girl, citing the perils of periods, childbirth, pressures to be thin, and limited high-paying career options. Many students identified the worst thing about being a male as "nothing."[33]

Yet middle school boys face challenges, too. When asked to describe the worst thing about being a boy, behavioral aggression and discipline topped the list, followed by poor grades and homophobia. Being a gay boy is now a challenge for middle schools since more gay children are "coming out" at a younger age.[34] A survey of gay, bisexual, and transgender middle-schoolers from across the nation found that 81 percent were regularly harassed, and 39 percent were physically assaulted. Only 29 percent said reporting these activities to authorities resulted in effective intervention.[35]

What are the joys for adolescent girls? In our survey of 400 middle schoolers, appearance was mentioned most often as the best reason for being a girl. Appearance comments included buying clothes, playing with hair styles, and taking beauty treatments, underscoring the need for females to seek approval outside of themselves. One seventh-grade girl vividly captured this salience of appearance: "Clothes make it fun to be a girl. THE perfect outfit can make you feel pretty and worth something." Academic advantage was another "best" reason for being a girl and included two opposing sets of comments, one that spoke to undue favoritism given girls—the "teacher's pet" idea—while the other described the extra effort given by girls and the intellectual satisfaction derived from their higher grades.[36]

Nearly one in five students wrote "nothing" to describe the best thing about being a girl, and students had little difficulty identifying negative aspects of being female. Relational aggression ranked highest with students describing a peer culture of gossip, rumors, and distrust among friends. Girls further expressed frustration at being the "second class gender," describing limited career options, responsibility for domestic chores, and the fear of sexual harassment/rape. At the other end of the spectrum, girls also feel the need to be "supergirls"—everything to everyone all the time. Three-quarters of the girls describe feeling "a lot of pressure" to please everyone. A ninth-grader shared her frustration: "There is way too much pressure to be skinny, popular, athletic, and have a boyfriend. Girls should be respected more as people than so-and-so's girlfriend."[37]

These experiences of middle schoolers are similar for students in urban, suburban, and rural America; in wealthy and poor communities; in schools that are diverse as well as those that are homogeneous. Relational aggression and discipline, appearance, entitlement, and homophobia can create pressures that detract from both the academic emphasis and social well-being of a school community. Schools that do not attend to these issues are placing a number of school goals at risk.

High School: Lessons in Social Change

Nearly 15 million students arrive at 20,000 public high schools every day. These schools run the gamut from decaying buildings plagued by vandalism and drugs to orderly, congenial places with educators who hold positive expectations and high standards for their students. They vary in size from 50 to 5,000 students, who spend days divided into either six or seven 50-minute periods or perhaps fewer, longer blocks of time.[38]

In his book *Is There Life After High School?* Ralph Keyes stirs up the pot of high school memories and draws a very lively picture of what life was like during that time and in that place and state of mind. In researching his book, he asked many people, both the famous and the obscure, about their high school experiences. He was amazed at the vividness and detail with which their memories came pouring out—particularly about the status system, that pattern of social reward and recognition that can be so intensely painful or exhilarating. High school was remembered as a caste system of "innies" and "outies," a minutely detailed social register in which one's popularity or lack of it was continually analyzed and contemplated.

For many high school students, peer relationships, not academics, are central to school life. When asked to identify the one best thing about their high school, "my friends" usually ranks at the top of the list. Sports activities ranked second. "Nothing" ranked higher than "classes I'm taking" and "teachers."[39] When asked to describe her school, one high school junior said,

> The classes are okay, I guess. Most of the time I find them pretty boring, but then I suppose that's the way school classes are supposed to be. What I like most about the place is the chance to be with my friends. It's nice to be a part of a group. I don't mean one of the clubs or groups the school runs . . . But an informal group of your own friends is great.[40]

David Owen is an author who returned to high school undercover to study peer culture. Posing as a student who had just moved into the area, he enrolled in what he calls a typical American high school, approximately two hours out of New York City. He was struck by the power of the peer group and how socially ill at ease most adolescents are. He likened adolescents to

Focus Question 6
In what ways does the adolescent culture shape teenage perceptions and behaviors?

www.mhhe.com/
sadkerbrief3e
INTERACTIVE ACTIVITY
How Cool Are You? Test how much of today's slang you understand.

Peer groups tend to define the quality of students' school life.

adults visiting a foreign country and a different culture. Experimenting with new behavior, they are terrified of being noticed doing something stupid:

> Being an adolescent is a full-time job, an all-out war against the appearance of awkwardness. No one is more attentive to nuance than a seventeen-year-old. . . . When a kid in my class came to school one day in a funny-looking pair of shoes that one of his friends eventually laughed at, I could see by his face that he was thinking, "well, that does it, there goes the rest of my life."[41]

For those who remember jockeying unsuccessfully for a place within the inner circle of the high school social register, it may be comforting to learn that the tables do turn. Few studies show any correlation between high status in high school and later achievement as an adult. Those who are voted king and queen of the prom or most likely to succeed do not appear to do any better or any worse in adult life than those whose yearbook description is less illustrious. What works in that very insular adolescent environment is not necessarily what works in the outside world. One researcher speculates that it is those on the "second tier," those in the group just below the top, who are most likely to succeed after high school. He says, "I think the rest of our lives are spent making up for what we did or did not do in high school."[42]

Being part of a group continues to be a challenge for today's adolescents. While historically entire communities participated in child care and extended families guided and monitored children, today this familial social fabric has disappeared. With increased mobility, the generations have been separated. Two-parent wage earners provide less supervision, adding to the stress of growing up in America.

In *A Tribe Apart: A Journey Into the Heart of American Adolescence*, Patricia Hersch shares the story of three years she spent with seventh through twelfth graders in suburban Reston, Virginia.[43] What Hersch discovered was troubling: the development of a more isolated, intense, and perilous adolescent culture, where drugs, alienation, and violence represent ongoing threats. It is a teenage society unknown to many parents. Contemporary adolescent friendships appear to be more fluid: teenagers may have one group of friends in a drama club, another from math class, and a third set from sports activities. Today cross-gender friendships are also more common as boys and girls do a better job of developing relationships without the need for a romantic attachment.

But even as the number of friendships grows, the quality of adolescent relationships remains a problem. Today's teenagers, both girls and boys, report that although they have many friends, they lack intimate, close friends. Teenagers say that there is no one that they can really confide in, no one with whom to share their deepest thoughts. In the midst of a crowd, they feel alone and stressed. It is a disturbing admission, and some educators believe that schools can and should do something about it.

Classroom Observation

6. Three High School Girls Discuss Adolescent Self-Concept at Age 16

Understanding your students and the issues they face is an important part of being an effective teacher. Adolescents particularly struggle with self-esteem. In this observation you will observe adolescent girls as they discuss how their self-esteem fluctuates and is more influenced by the opinions of friends than family.

Classroom Observation videos are available on the CD Reader and at the Online Learning Center.

www.mhhe.com/
sadkerbrief3e

Social Challenges Come to School

Have you ever felt the cold slap of rejection because of your social class? Have you ever denied a family history that includes divorce, domestic violence, or unplanned pregnancy? Has your life been touched by depression, substance abuse, or bullying? Children across all racial, ethnic, and socioeconomic backgrounds may be plagued by such difficulties, affecting their academic and emotional well-being. Your students will likely carry these struggles and concerns with them as they walk through your classroom door. While schools and teachers cannot completely solve these social issues (as much as we may try), education can bring purpose, hope, and empowerment to our most troubled youth.

Focus Question 7
What impact do changing family patterns and economic issues have on children and schools?

Family Patterns

Not too many years ago, the Andersons of *Father Knows Best* lived through weekly, if minor, crises on television; Dick and Jane lived trouble-free lives with their parents and pets in America's textbooks; and most real families contained a father, mother, and perhaps three children confronting life's trials and tribulations as a family unit. Mothers stayed at home and fathers went to work. Out-of-wedlock children and pregnant, unmarried teenagers were hidden from the public's attention. Divorce was rare.

But today's family bears little resemblance to these images. Only two-thirds of children today live in two-parent families, with children of color far less likely than their white peers to live with both parents (Figure 4.3). Nearly one in four children live only with their mothers, 5 percent live only with their fathers, and 5 percent live with neither parent. Half of those children living with no parent are being raised by a grandparent.[44] Research shows that children from single-parent families are less likely to achieve and more likely to be expelled or suspended.[45]

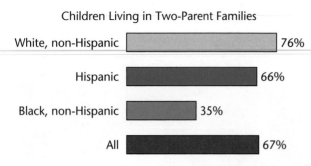

Children Living in Two-Parent Families

White, non-Hispanic   76%

Hispanic   66%

Black, non-Hispanic   35%

All   67%

FIGURE 4.3

The changing American family.

SOURCE: Federal Interagency Forum on Child and Family Statistics, America's Children: Key National Indicators of Well-Being, 2010.

REFLECTION: What factors might account for these family differences across racial groups?

Generally, our families are getting smaller, older, and more diverse. Families most often have two children or fewer, and these children are born to increasingly older and more educated mothers. Today, one in seven children is born to a mother at least 35 years old, and more than 50 percent of new mothers have at least some college education.[46] More than half of American families are remarried or recoupled, including half of our children. Step-families consist of biological and legal relationships with stepparents, stepsiblings, multiple sets of grandparents, and what often becomes a confusing array of relatives from old and new relationships.[47] Other families are created through cross-cultural and racial unions. It was only in 1967 that the Supreme Court overruled antimiscegenation laws, which had banned interracial marriage.

Although Americans still prefer marriage, the past two decades have seen the number of unmarried couples living together more than double, including both opposite- and same-sex partners. In fact, 41 percent of births today are to unmarried mothers, an increase from 28 percent in 1990.[48] **Alternative families** refers to family lifestyles other than a married male and female living with their children. Alternative families can consist of a single parent with children; biological parents who are not married; relatives or friends acting as child guardians; same-sex couples sharing parenting roles; nonmarried couples living as families; or serial relationships with continually changing partners. Yet, children in nontraditional families may feel discomfort as they learn from a curriculum that continues to feature the conventional family structure. Clearly, many schools have a way to go before they successfully integrate all family structures into family life.

Wage Earners and Parenting

For the first time in our nation's history, women comprise half of all U.S. workers. In fact, women with children are the primary breadwinners or co-breadwinners in nearly two-thirds of American families. Back in 1960, a minority of women with children worked outside the home. Today, eighty percent of women with children between the ages of 6 and 17 work outside the home, and more than 60 percent of moms with children 6 or younger work in the salaried workforce. One trend that hasn't changed is paying women less. Although equal pay has been the law since 1963, employers still find ways to pay women less, even when education, skills, and experience are the same.[49]

Although parenting responsibilities still fall more on women (between 16–20 hours a week), today more and more fathers are also assuming parenting responsibilities (about 8 to 10 hours a week). Working fathers and mothers desire more flexible work schedules, equal pay, redesigned family and medical leave, and comprehensive child care policies.[50]

Latchkey Kids

Jennifer unlocked her door quickly, raced inside, and shut it loudly behind her. She fastened the lock, threw the bolt, dropped her books on the floor, and made her way to the kitchen for her usual snack. Within a few minutes, Jennifer was ensconced on the sofa, the television on and her stuffed animals clutched firmly in her hand. She decided to do her homework later. Her parents would be home then, and she tried not to spend too much time thinking about being lonely. She turned her attention to the television, to spend the next few hours watching talk shows.

Jennifer is a latchkey kid, one of the 4 million children left to care for themselves after school. The term **latchkey** was coined to describe children who carry a key on a cord or chain around their necks to unlock their home door. These children are often from single-parent homes or families with two working parents, few extended family members, and no affordable, high-quality child care facilities nearby. Latchkey kids are found in all racial and socioeconomic groups, but the more educated the parents, the more likely they are to have a latchkey child. The average latchkey child is left alone two and a half hours per day, with most of that time devoted to watching television or playing video games. Unsupervised children are more likely to suffer with depression, smoke cigarettes and marijuana, and drink alcohol. They are also more likely to be the victims of crimes.[51]

Divorce

Although today divorce is common (more than half of new marriages end in divorce), it is hardly routine. The underlying stress can increase a child's anguish. Along with the emotional trauma of changing family dynamics, divorce can also create financial worries. The divorced mom often struggles with a severe loss of income. Children living only with their mothers are five times more likely to live in poverty than children living in a married household.[52] Children who have experienced divorce may exhibit a variety of problem behaviors. Symptoms from depression to aggression diminish school performance. Children often go through a classic mourning process similar to that experienced after a death in the family. However, most children are resilient and can rebound from the trauma of divorce, with 80 to 90 percent recovering in about a year. Teachers should give children the chance to express their feelings about divorce and let them know they are not alone in their experience.[53]

Poverty

Today, children are the poorest group in our society, and current programs and policies are woefully inadequate to meet their growing needs. Stanford's Michael Kirst sums it up this way:

> Johnny can't read because he needs glasses and breakfast and encouragement from his absent father. Maria doesn't pay attention in class because she doesn't understand English very well and she's worried about her father's drinking and she's tired from trying to sleep in her car. Dick is flunking because he's frequently absent. His mother doesn't get him to school because she's depressed because she lost her job. She missed too much work because she was sick and could not afford medical care.[54]

The more than one in five American children living in poor families are among the poorest in all developed nations. Poverty touches the lives of children across all diverse racial and ethnic backgrounds, and particularly jeopardizes the well-being of black, Hispanic, and Native American youth. Children in poverty often have to cope with issues that other children (and many adults) seldom, if ever, contemplate. Most parents of poor children work, but they don't earn enough to provide their families with basic necessities—adequate food, shelter, child care, and health care. When children are poor, they are more likely to drop out of school and be involved in violent crime, early sexual activity, and drugs. Children, with little voice and no votes, are among the first to lose services. More than 7.5 million children under age 18 have no medical coverage.[55] In short, poverty puts children at risk.

Poor children enter school with distinct disadvantages. Poor children are more often in single-parent families, typically receive less adult attention, have fewer books to read, and are not read to as often. As a consequence, they are not exposed to complex language or large vocabularies, a deficit when entering school. (See Figure 4.4.) Their neighborhoods have fewer adults with professional careers who can serve as role models. In fact, simply getting out of the neighborhood to visit museums or zoos or cultural activities is difficult. Such isolation deprives these children of experiences beyond the familiar and also chips away at their self-confidence.[56] Their neighborhood reality is often filled with crime and drugs, so safety concerns can dominate daily existence. It is no surprise that research reveals how chronic stress from growing up poor can impair cognitive development.[57] Each of these disadvantages makes only a small contribution to the educational struggles of poor children, but cumulatively they can easily overwhelm.

How can teachers understand the unique needs of children living in poverty? We can start by realizing that poverty itself is a culture. The concept of the *culture of poverty* was coined by anthropologist Oscar Lewis and describes how people in poverty often have their own behavioral norms, communication skills, and even ways of viewing the world.[58] Since schools tend to reflect middle-class values, the culture of poverty can clash with school culture. This culture clash often alienates the poor from school, and school from the poor.

Here is an example of how class differences can hinder poor children even before they enter school. Researcher Shirley Brice Heath found that the number and the nature of verbal interactions in families varies according to

REFLECTION: Do these numbers surprise you? What actions can you as a teacher take to improve access to books for children from poverty?

FIGURE 4.4

Books and socioeconomic class.

SOURCE: Adapted from Royal Van Horn, *Bridging the Chasm between Research and Practice: A Guide to Major Educational Research* (Lanham, MD: Rowman and Littlefield Education, 2008), p. 32.

socioeconomic status. In lower-class families, interactions between adults and children are fewer than in middle-class families, and the purpose is information driven. For example, a parent may ask a child, "Where is your sister?" or "Have you finished your homework?" For middle-class children, family interactions are more numerous and closely resemble school interactions. A parent may ask a child to identify an object or a word, share his or her opinion, or read together. Middle-class students who have had such interactions at home have in a sense been in training for school and arrive there better prepared.[59] It is not that poor children are less capable or intelligent; it is that what they bring to school is different. Students from poverty lack the experiences and the strategies expected for success in school. Think about the struggle an upper- or middle-class child would have in a poor neighborhood.

Teachers need to avoid what has been termed "soft bias," the lowering of academic expectations for poor children. Strategies may differ, but academic goals and expectations should remain high. What kind of strategies might be useful? We discussed that poor children typically have a limited vocabulary, less than half the words of more affluent students, so working with poor children on expanding their vocabulary not only reduces the language deficit but also uses words to take the child beyond the local neighborhood to see a broader world perspective.[60] Another teaching strategy is to involve poor students in after-school programs to expand their cultural, artistic, and athletic opportunities while keeping them in a safe environment for a longer part of the day. Extracurricular activities can also help forge new and constructive peer relationships. In fact, you may want to check the culturally relevant teaching strategies described in Chapter 3, for many of those strategies also work with students living in poverty.

One of the most common misperceptions of the poor is that they do not value education. When poor parents do not attend a back-to-school night or if they miss a parent-teacher meeting, many in the middle class assume that the parents are not committed to education. In reality, these absences may be due to working several jobs, struggling with unreliable transportation, or simply navigating the challenges of middle-class norms.

Karen Arnold and her colleagues studied just how subtle and devastating the clash of norms can be when poor students are admitted to college but many end up never attending.[61] The world of postsecondary education and professional careers is a new one for low-income, first-generation college students, and they often lack the implicit knowledge that middle- and upper-class students take for granted. Counselors report that poor students "are gathering bits and pieces of information from people who don't really know anything." In one case, a student decided over the summer to apply to Northwestern University because he assumed it was the California branch of Northeastern University. Another senior reported: "I found a scholarship on E-bay. Should I buy it?" After all, he said, "it was a $1,000 scholarship offer for only $500. Wasn't that a good deal?" In the absence of nuanced knowledge of colleges common to middle-class students, poor students sometimes make decisions that are based on misinformation.

Financial fears also loom large. As one counselor explained: "For them, $4,000 a year of loans is huge. Some parents and kids can't see debt as an investment. Even if they understand it, they don't believe it." As one student explained: "I don't think I want to go to college and be in debt the rest of my life." Families willing to take out loans may run into another problem: no credit-worthy family member able to cosign a loan document. Even if college were free, it can be costly. Many students contribute a significant portion of their family's income; with a student at college, the family can experience a painful financial setback.

Along with economic anxiety, safety concerns also emerge. As a daughter of a Dominican father explained, "They thought New York was too far, too dangerous, too expensive. [Dad] was really strict. He didn't want me to go." For the poor, first-generation college student, going away to a four-year college may be a frightening prospect, and a local community college can be seen as a safer option. "Transferring is part of their plan," a counselor reported. As one student related the situation, his family suggested, ". . . 'why don't you go to a community college and transfer?' They don't see the importance, I guess, of going to a four-year. Going to a very nice school." Even positive family messages can imply failure far from home, as one student's grandmother advised: "If you don't do anything else, go to college. If you don't make it, at least you can say you went."

This shaky road to college need not be the case. Research suggests that to navigate the road into college, poor students need specific guidance on taking college entrance examinations and completing financial aid applications. It is also important to have counselors available during that critical summer as they transition to that brave new world called college. Counselors can reduce the fears and confusion about college.[62] Clearly, treating poor students as though they were middle-class is a costly injustice.

Hidden America: Homeless Families

Homelessness may conjure up images of cardboard boxes, sleeping bags, and heating grates. The realities are more complex. By federal definition, "homeless child and youth includes minors living in shelters with or without family, doubling up with friends or extended family, settling into motels, campgrounds, trailer parks, or living in vehicles." The strain on families as they face declining fortunes can be soul draining. Survival needs such as food, safety, and shelter become daily struggles.

America's estimated 1.35 million homeless children are urban, suburban, and rural and of every racial and ethnic background. Most experts agree that the true number of homeless children is much greater because official numbers do not count the indefinite number of families living on the edge of foreclosure and eviction.[63] These youth face significant school challenges. Although most attend school, there is constant turmoil and frequent transfers. Many arrive at school hungry, tired, distracted, and lacking even rudimentary study facilities. Add to this equation the drugs, crimes, violence, and prostitution often found in their lives, and it is clear that these children struggle against overwhelming odds. Children whose address has been in flux for more than a year are subject to developmental delays four times greater than their peers, are twice as likely to repeat a grade, and twice as likely to be identified as learning disabled.[64]

In 1987, Congress passed the **McKinney-Vento Homeless Assistance Act,** providing the homeless with emergency food services, adult literacy programs, access to schooling, job training, and other assistance. In the past, school districts had required proof of residency, birth certificates, and proof of

HELPING HOMELESS STUDENTS SUCCEED

The National Center for Homeless Education suggests several strategies to address the unique needs of homeless students. Teachers can

- Assign a "buddy" to introduce new students to the classroom and school
- Create a stable learning environment with structured routine
- Make time to individually welcome and talk with new students
- Assess students' interests to hook them into learning
- Have available different levels of reading materials on the same content

- Keep a supply of healthy snacks and extra school supplies
- Connect students with community support services, such as tutoring programs.

SOURCE: Adapted from Helena Holgersson-Shorter, "Helping the Homeless," *Teaching Tolerance* (Fall 2010), pp. 47–50.

REFLECTION: Have you ever encountered the homeless? What were your reactions? How have those reactions changed or stayed the same? How might they influence your teaching?

immunization—simple tasks for most families, but enough to keep many homeless children out of school. Renewed in 2002, McKinney-Vento eliminated many such barriers, allowing students to enroll immediately without proof of a permanent address. Homeless students also have the right to participate in all extracurricular activities as well as all support programs, including meal services, before- and after-school care, special education, and gifted programs. School districts must provide transportation so that highly mobile students can stay in the same school, a place of familiar faces and stability. McKinney-Vento also mandates that school districts provide a homeless liaison to connect families to appropriate social and educational services.[65] Despite this progress, and the potential of schools to be a stabilizing force, the educational needs of the nation's homeless children often go unmet.

Children: At Promise or At Risk?

It was not too long ago that family life was captured by simplistic TV images, with problems easily solved in fewer than 30, almost commercial-free, minutes. In the mid-1900s, teachers were concerned about students talking out of turn, chewing gum, making noise, running in the halls, cutting in line, and violating dress codes. Half a century later, teachers' top student concerns reflect the devastating changes in the lives of their pupils: drug and alcohol abuse, pregnancy, suicide, bullying, dropping out, and weight issues.

Many teenagers smoke, do drugs (prescription and nonprescription), and engage in unprotected sex. Adolescents view this period between childhood and adulthood as a time for fun, and being adolescents, they feel protected by their own youth, by a sense of invulnerability. A second group of teenagers take similar risks for different reasons: They believe they have little to lose. Native American, Hispanic, black, and low-income teens may more often than whites view the future with a sense of hopelessness, a fatalistic belief that risky behavior is not so risky if life offers few options, if death may come at any time.[66]

Focus Question 8
How can educators respond to social issues that place children at risk?

Dropping Out

Lamar was finishing junior high school with resignation and despair. He had just managed to squeak through Beaton Junior High with poor grades and no understanding of how this frustrating experience would help him. He wasn't good at schoolwork and felt that the classes he had to sit through were a waste of time. He wanted to end these long, boring days, get a job, and get a car. He'd had enough of school.

Lamar is a good candidate to join the nation's dropouts. In fact, students who are poor are six times more likely to drop out than wealthy ones, and students whose parents do not value schooling are also on the "most-likely-to-drop-out" list. Typically, dropping out is a long-term process with academic warning signs. Students who eventually drop out often start struggling academically in the first grade, are likely to repeat a grade at least once, frequently transfer between different elementary and middle schools, and attend poor schools.[67] One teacher described the academic slide of dropouts like this: "Kids who fail math or English in 6th grade go on to start failing *everything* in ninth grade."[68]

Are you surprised to learn that nationwide slightly more than 70 percent of students graduate from high school? Every 11 seconds another student gives up on school, resulting in more than 1 million American high school students who drop out every year. Racial, ethnic, and gender patterns offer an even more disturbing picture of educational attainment (see Figure 4.5).[69] Most students don't drop out because they can't do the work. In fact, nearly 90 percent have passing grades when they leave school. The major reason

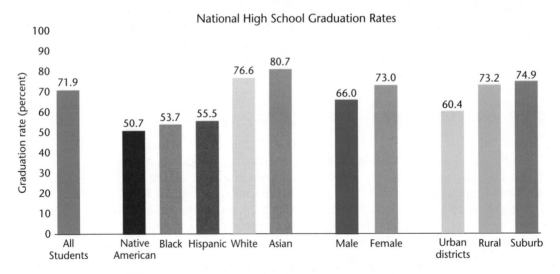

FIGURE 4.5

National graduation rates.

SOURCE: Editorial Projects in Education Research Center, June 2010.

REFLECTION: What strategies would you suggest to improve graduation rates? Do these strategies vary based on the race, gender, and socioeconomic status of students? Why or why not?

for opting out? Classes are too boring, and students feel academically disengaged. Others are more worried about pregnancy, family issues, or financial concerns. Indeed, the immediate monetary rewards of the workplace lure some students. Yet, dropouts earn an average of $10,000 less a year than high school graduates and are far more likely to need government assistance or end up in jail. Many educators believe that the dropout rate can be reduced through early intervention, early literacy programs, one-on-one instruction, mentoring and tutoring, more relevant curricular materials, service learning, and family involvement.[70]

Sexuality and Teenage Pregnancy

Who can blame today's adolescents for being confused about sexuality? On the one hand, they see a "green light," as they are bombarded with suggestive advertising, graphic movies, bawdy television shows, and sexualized cable channels. Contraceptives, including the morning-after pill, offer pregnancy safeguards that did not exist just a few years ago. Then students see a bright "red light" of morality standards preaching abstinence and the looming threat of sexually transmitted diseases (STDs). So how do schools respond to this conflict?

What students learn (or do not learn) in school about sex depends on the school they attend. More than a third of schools follow an "abstinence only" sex education curriculum, emphasizing no sex before marriage. Contraception in these programs is a nontopic, and these programs are not particularly effective. A study of nine abstinence-focused programs found that the information being taught was inaccurate, outdated, and biased against reproductive choice options. Teens' sexual behavior, pregnancy rates, and frequency of contracting STDs usually remained steady or increased following completion of abstinence-only courses[71] Other school districts embrace a more comprehensive approach, stressing abstinence but also teaching about contraception. A national survey found that 90 percent of middle and high school students and their parents support such a comprehensive approach.[72] In 2010, the federal government reversed its decade long policy of limiting funds to abstinence-only sex education programs and began funding more comprehensive sex education in schools, ranging from abstinence to the use of contraception. Hopefully this change will help ease staggering teen sexuality statistics: Rates of pregnancy and STDs in this nation are the highest in the industrialized world, and nearly half of high school students are sexually active.[73]

Substance Abuse: Drinking, Drugs, and Smoking

"You won't see the drug culture here unless you know what to look for. You'll get a lot of parent and school denial, but the reputation of this school is 'cocaine heaven.'"

"On an average week, I gross over $2,000 dealing drugs at this school."

These statements from high school students add a personal dimension to official reports indicating that the United States has the highest rate of teenage drug use of any industrialized nation in the world. Substance abuse ranges from alcohol and chewing tobacco to inhalants, cocaine, and LSD, to food abuse, from dieting to obesity. Almost two-thirds of high school students and one in three middle schoolers say drugs are used, kept, and sold in their schools and are easily available. Only 43 percent of students believe that their school is drug-free.[74]

Although alcohol, cigarette smoking, and marijuana use among teenagers are at historic lows, they remain serious problems for our youth. Alcohol represents by far the most widespread form of substance abuse. More than two-thirds of high school seniors admit to drinking. The pattern of abuse starts early: more than one-third of eighth-graders report drinking within the last year, and nearly one-quarter of high school seniors admits to repeated binge drinking. Cigarette smoking is down for the population as a whole, yet more than a million young people start smoking each year. Teens, though, understand that smoking is bad for their health, and very few believe the harmful effects of smoking have been exaggerated. Teens believe just the opposite about marijuana. The majority of students believe that marijuana is safe to regularly smoke, and use of the drug is growing. More than one in four teens used the drug at least once in the past year. Asked whether they had used other illicit drugs such as Ecstasy, cocaine, and heroin, 25 percent of seniors and nearly 1 in 10 eighth-graders said yes. More than half of all students will try an illicit drug by the time they finish high school.[75]

Researchers are discovering a cultural shift in drug abuse among teens with the increased use of inhalants, diet pills, sedatives, and prescription drugs. Although marijuana is the most popular choice for teens trying drugs for the first time, prescription drugs and inhalants are a close second and third.[76] Today's youth grow up in a world where it is routine to reach for a prescription bottle to enhance performance, to focus better in school, and to stay awake or calm down. Not surprisingly, prescription painkillers such as Vicodin and Oxycontin are abused by 1 in 10 high schoolers. One million teens ages 12 to 17 years have tried an inhalant—such as glue, paint, felt-tip markers, and air fresheners—to get high.[77]

What leads youth to substance abuse? Some blame the mixed messages children receive. Although parents and teachers may talk about the physical, emotional, and academic dangers, the media and pop culture often glorify alcohol and other drugs as methods for coping with stress and loneliness or to improve performance. Other contributing factors include family instability and the materialistic, success-driven nature of our culture that creates tremendous pressure on youth (and adults). Interestingly, students who consider themselves popular are more likely to use drugs, drink, and smoke than their unpopular peers. Yet, the problems of substance abuse are all too real for many students. When asked to describe their greatest concern, teens frequently cite the pressure to use drugs ahead of social and academic pressures.[78] We know all too well that substance abuse paves a risky, downward path:

- Grades go down as alcohol consumption and drug use go up.
- The more teenagers drink and use drugs, the more likely they are to be involved in violent crime, such as murder, rape, or robbery, either as victim or perpetrator.
- Alcohol and drug abuse is associated with more unplanned pregnancies, more sexually transmitted diseases, and more HIV infections than any other single factor.
- Approximately 50 percent of all youth deaths from drowning, fires, suicide, and homicide are alcohol related.[79]

7. Three High Schools Talk about Drugs at Age 15

Understanding your students and the issues they face is an important part of being an effective teacher. Too many of today's adolescents will have some contact, direct or indirect, with illegal substances before they graduate from high school. In this observation you will observe three teenage girls discussing drug use at their school and that fact that they believe that most of the kids in their school have at least experimented with marijuana.

Classroom Observation videos are available on the CD Reader and at the Online Learning Center.

www.mhhe.com/
sadkerbrief3e

Schools often adopt programs such as Drug Abuse Resistance Education (D.A.R.E.) to help youth understand the facts about drugs and cope with peer pressures. Funded and run by local police departments, D.A.R.E. costs school districts very little and is popular in schools nationwide. Yet research reveals that D.A.R.E. and its "Just Say No" message are largely ineffective in curtailing drug use. Similar criticism has been leveled on the U.S. Department of Education's Safe and Drug-Free Schools program.[80] Given the poor track record of these national programs, many local schools choose to develop their own substance abuse curricula and policies.

Obesity and Eating Disorders

What does more than 50 hours a week watching television, playing video and computer games, and eating junk food get you? Pounds, lots of extra pounds. Nine million American children ages 6 to 19—one in three—are overweight or obese. (See Figure 4.6). The trends start early: Nearly one in five 4-year-olds is obese. At special risk are children from low socioeconomic backgrounds, as well as Hispanic, black, and Native American youth whose obesity rates are often 50 percent greater than those of their peers. The consequences of obesity are staggering. Besides potential health problems such as diabetes, arthritis, and heart disease, overweight children are more likely to have low self-esteem and be absent from school. Overweight students, particularly girls, are more likely to engage in sexual activity earlier and without protection and are less likely to attend college.[81]

Schools often make the problem worse. Faced with pressures to improve test scores, school leaders often try to increase academic classroom time by eliminating recess or physical education (despite evidence showing that exercise improves academic performance). Only 4 percent of elementary schools, 8 percent of middle schools, and 2 percent of high schools provide daily physical education.[82] School meals fail, too. The National School Lunch Program, signed into law by President Truman in 1946, was designed to feed hungry

FIGURE 4.6

Overweight and obese children.

SOURCE: U.S. Department of Health and Human Services (2010).

REFLECTION: Why do you think Minnesota, Utah, and Oregon have the lowest rates of overweight and obese children? Why do states in the Southeast face the greatest challenge?

In an effort to promote healthy eating, First Lady Michelle Obama invites students to create a vegetable garden on the White House Lawn. What role, if any, should schools have in promoting a healthy life style?

children who needed extra calories. Today it serves 31 million kids, most of whom don't. Although school meals are subsidized by the government and should follow nutritional standards, that doesn't always translate into apples and cucumbers. More than 40 percent of schools do not offer any fresh fruits or raw vegetables on a daily basis. What's more, vending machines, some stocked with cookies and soda, can be found in nearly all middle and high schools.[83] But these nutritional failings may change. The Healthy, Hunger-free Kids Act of 2010 gives the federal government power to set new nutrition standards for all food served in schools, from lunchrooms to vending machines. (See Table 4.1) We encourage you to see if your school follows these recommendations.

The good news? Some schools are stepping up to this challenge by planting organic gardens and harvesting the food that they use for school lunches and selling it at their own farmers' markets. Some ban vending machines completely, while others are filling them with low sugar and salt snacks, juices, and water. Several major school food suppliers are doubling the amount of fresh produce they provide. First Lady Michelle Obama initiated the Let's Move campaign to encourage parents, school leaders, PTAs, food manufacturers, and elected officials to make physical activity and healthy foods an integral part of school life.

But obesity is not our only weight issue. Some children are taught by our culture that you cannot be too thin, and they take drastic measures to diminish their bodies. Eating disorders among youth are on the rise, and an estimated 11 million Americans struggle with anorexia and bulimia, 90 percent of whom are females and 10 percent are males between the ages of 12 and 20. Anorexia is the third most common chronic illness among adolescents.[84] For

A Typical School Lunch Before and After the Passage of Healthy, Hunger-Free Kids Act of 2010.	
Old Menu	Proposed New Menu
Bean and cheese burrito (5.3oz)	Sub sandwich (1 oz turkey, ½ oz low-fat
with mozzarella cheese (1 oz)	cheese on whole wheat roll)
Applesauce (1/4 cup)	Refried beans (1/2 cup)
Orange juice (4 oz)	Jicama (1/4 cup)
Low-fat (1%) chocolate milk (8 oz)	Green pepper strips (1/4 cup)
	Cantaloupe wedges (1/2 cup)
	Low-fat ranch dip (1 oz)
	Reduced mayonnaise (1oz)
	Low-fat (1%) milk (8 oz)
Old Menu	Proposed New Menu
Cheese pizza (1 slice)	Whole-wheat cheese pizza (1 slice)
Tater tots (1/2 cup)	Baked sweet-potato fries (1/2 cup)
Ketchup (2 tablespoons)	Grape tomatoes, raw (1/4 cup)
Canned pineapple (1/2 cup)	Applesauce (1/2 cup)
Low-fat (1%) chocolate milk (8 oz)	Low-fat (1%) milk (8 oz)
	Low-fat ranch dip (1 oz)

TABLE 4.1 What's in a meal?

SOURCE: United States Department of Agriculture, Healthy, Hunger-free Kids Act (2010), available at www .usda.gov.

REFLECTION: What are your impressions about the new school nutrition guidelines? Who might oppose these changes?

most kids, eating disorders typically start when they are 11 to 13 years old, but can begin much earlier. Almost half (42 percent) of first- to third-grade girls want to be thinner, and 81 percent of 10-year-olds are afraid of being fat. The number-one wish of girls 11–17 years old is to lose weight.[85] Persistent, chronic dieting puts an enormous stress on teenagers, one that takes a toll on physical well-being and the energy needed to learn in school.

While movies, magazines, and television tell females that being thin is the ticket to success, males often receive a different message: bulk up those muscles and flatten those abs! Boys say, "I'm getting into shape," not, "I'm fat and need to go on a diet." Yet the fitness quest can quickly turn life-threatening. Males are about 10 percent of those struggling with anorexia, bulimia, or binge eating. The number may be much higher because males believe that food issues are "female issues" and are likely to deny or fail to recognize their own struggles with eating.

More than ever, U.S. boys are trying to find designer bodies not just by dieting or going to the gym, but also from steroids. Nearly half a million boys are taking steroids, and boys as young as 10 are bulking up simply because they want to look good. While steroids can guarantee a rack of rippling muscles, many of these substances can stifle bone growth and lead to cancer, hair loss, acne, and testosterone-driven rage.[86]

Americans of all ages have a long way to go in freeing themselves from media images of one ideal body type. Healthy bodies come in many shapes, and it is not necessary for all females to be incredibly thin or all males to look like professional athletes.

Youth Suicide

A closely knit New Jersey community across the Hudson River from Manhattan was viewed as a model town. The high school frequently won the state football championship, the police department won awards for its youth-assistance programs, and the town was known for the beauty of its parks and safety of its streets. On an early Wednesday morning in March, the citizens of Bergenfield woke up to discover that four of their teenagers had locked themselves in a garage, turned on a car engine, and left a note requesting that they be buried together. The group suicide brought the total of teen suicides in Bergenfield to eight that year.

In the past three decades, while the general incidence of suicide has decreased, the rate for those between the ages of 15 and 24 has tripled. Suicide is the third most common cause of death among adolescents, and many health specialists suspect it is seriously underreported. Every day, 11 adolescents will take their own lives. Differences in suicidal behavior can vary across gender and ethnic groups. Native Americans have the highest suicide rate of all racial and ethnic groups. While females are three times more likely to attempt suicide, males are four times more likely to die from an attempt. Particularly at risk are substance abusers, teens questioning their sexuality, victims of bullying, academic achievers, and girls who have been physically or sexually abused.[87]

What should teachers look for? Depression often precedes suicide attempts. Manifestations include persistent sadness, boredom or low energy, loss of interests in favorite pastimes, irritability, physical complaints and illness, serious changes in sleeping and eating, and school avoidance or poor performance.[88] To date, teachers and parents have not done well in preventing youth depression and suicide.

Bullying

Loser and *Fag* are scribbled on binders littering a classroom. A huddle of popular girls glare at the classmate they've chosen as outsider of the week. A broad-shouldered ninth-grade boy shoves his scrawny, bespectacled friend of yesterday into the stretch of lockers.[89]

Bullying. Though we bemoan such behavior, it's almost as if we expect it from adolescents, even young children. Although metal detectors and extra security measures have sharply reduced school violence, bullies still stalk. Cell phones, social networks, and online game rooms have joined playgrounds, hallways, cafeterias, and school buses as places where students interact informally with little adult supervision—prime areas for bullying. One-third to one-half of America's children report being bullied at school. In a typical classroom of 20 students, 2 or 3 come to school every day fearing being bullied, harassed, or worse. The most likely targets are gay students, or students perceived as gay. While most youth describe bullying as harmful, a gap exists between this belief and students' behaviors. More than 40 percent of students admit to bullying a classmate at least once; more than half have witnessed bullying and not stopped or reported it.[90]

Bullies seek control over others by taking advantage of imbalances in perceived power, such as social status, greater size, and physical strength. Bullies can use physical force or threats, but sticks and stones aren't the only tools. Social weapons, such as public humiliation, intimidation, taunts and teases, name-calling, gossip-mongering, and exclusion, can cut children much deeper. The ways students are tormented and ostracized by one another, often in the guise of being cool or hip, are the stuff of teenage nightmares: being made the butt of a clique's disdain, not being invited to the party everyone is talking about, and increasingly, being eviscerated in nasty instant messages over the Internet.

Cyberbullying is a relatively new phenomenon. The word didn't even exist a decade ago, but the problem is pervasive in children's lives today, with increasingly deadly consequences. Half of all students report being bullied online.[91] Noted one teacher:

> You can pass around a note to classmates making fun of a peer, and it stays in the room. But when you post that same note online, thousands can see it. The whole world becomes witness and is invited to participate. Wherever kids go with their computers or phones, which is nearly everywhere, the bullies come with them.[92]

Through e-mail, texting, blogs, Facebook, Twitter, and electronic gadgets like camera cell phones, cyberbullies forward and spread hurtful images and/or messages to harass, humiliate, or threaten. Bullies use this technology to harass victims at all hours, in wide circles, and at warp speed. At least half of adolescents report being targeted by a cyberbully. Those experiences yield damaging consequences, from a decline in academic performance to poor self-esteem to thoughts of suicide. Studies find that cyberbullying victims are twice as likely to attempt suicide compared to students not targeted online.[93] (For more about cyberbullying, see Contemporary Issues: A View from the Field.)

Bullying has been an accepted school tradition for decades, if not centuries, often because so many educators accepted the myths surrounding bullying: only a small number of children are affected, students are just "tattling, it's a natural behavior," and "boys will be boys." But these myths are dangerous. Boys *and* girls engage in bullying, though often with different behaviors. Boys are more likely to engage in physical bullying, while girls often revert to relational bullying, such as gossip and exclusion. Both are likely to cyberbully. Bullying is linked to academic difficulties, withdrawal from activities, depression, and eating disorders. Too many students are bullied into suicide. And children who bully are more likely to get into fights, vandalize property, and drop out of school. The cost of bullying is high, and schools are finally "getting it." Half of public school principals say bullying is a serious problem in their schools, ranking it above such other issues as peer pressure to use drugs and alcohol and ethnic and racial differences among students.[94]

Courts are sending the message that bullying is not protected by freedom of expression, and more than 40 states have laws against bullying in school.[95] Massachusetts, for example, defines bullying as both cyberbullying and any act that creates a "hostile learning environment." In that state, even bullying done away

A VIEW FROM THE FIELD: CYBERBULLYING

Nadia*, 24, teaches seventh-grade reading, writing, and history in a suburb outside Chicago. Though she's been teaching for only two years, she's already witnessed several incidents of cyberbullying at her school. "It was recently brought to the attention of the teachers and staff that one student used his cell phone to record girls at our school and then placed these videos on YouTube," Sheila explains.

> I believe the title said something to the effect of "Fat Girls at our School Just Being Fat." Just two weeks ago, three boys ganged up on another male student. Two of the boys participated in the actual assault while the third student took a video of it on his cell phone. Another student [pretended to be a teacher] and created a MySpace page for "the teacher" which painted her in an extremely unfavorable light. Another girl via Instant Messenger has repeatedly bullied one girl in my class. It seems as though these kids grow very courageous when they do not have to say things face-to-face.

Nadia's school has gone beyond simple reprimands to deal with cyberbullying.

> I definitely address all types of bullying in my class and will not stand for it. My school administrators deal with specific incidents: parents are called in, the student is required to shut down the website or at least get rid of all objectionable material, and a suspension is given. We have a police liaison who deals with a variety of issues at our school. Her job description now includes surfing student MySpace pages and checking for signs of bullying and harassment. Next year we will be introducing the Positive Behavioral and Intervention Supports system. I think my school will benefit from this as I see a definite need for it right now. Although I am very near in age to my students, with a difference of 10 to 11 years, I am shocked to see all that is out there! I consider myself to be pretty technologically savvy, but never would have thought to use this tool as a form of humiliation or aggression against others. I would love to learn more about what the classroom teacher can do to address and prevent these issues.

Nadia earned a B.S. in elementary education from Illinois State University. To learn more about the Positive Behavioral and Intervention Supports system, please visit www.pbis.org.

* Name has been changed.

from the school can be punishable if the learning environment is affected. Teachers are required to report any instance of bullying to the school principal, who must take action. Furthermore, every school in the state is required to provide age-appropriate antibullying instruction.

School leaders are also stepping up, sending the message that bullying will not be tolerated and creating a climate where students know there are adults they can trust and to whom they can safely report information. Effective antibullying practices ask teachers to be involved and interested in students; set firm limits on unacceptable behavior; apply consistent nonpunitive, nonphysical sanctions; and act as authorities and positive role models. At one Illinois school district students can call an anonymous tip line to report instances of bullying. The school system's policy handbook makes clear that staff members must report acts of bullying and protect students who report bullying from retaliation.[96]

Creating a safe school climate is the first step in effective teaching. Another is teaching empathy and community building throughout the curriculum. Schools have devised some interesting ways of doing this. In one New York school, English classes discuss whether Friar Laurence was empathetic to Romeo and Juliet. In other schools, students share snacks and board games with four autistic classmates, or receive recognition for sitting with a new student at lunch or helping a panicked classmate on the rock-climbing wall. To help students better relate to life with a disability, a common assignment asks students to spend a day in a wheelchair and then write a short story or poem about the experience. Meditation and yoga are increasingly offered to promote compassion and kindness. Schools are also implementing peer

8. Characteristics of Children Who Bully

Being aware of the characteristics of bullying is an important first step in creating a safe classroom. In this observation you will observe an interview with Dr. Espelage, an educational psychologist, in which bullying behavior and its characteristics are defined and the sex differences in bullying behavior described.

Classroom Observation Videos are available on the CD Reader and at the Online Learning Center.

www.mhhe.com/
sadkerbrief3e

mediation programs to help reduce bullying and school violence. Students are trained to help classmates peacefully solve problems, becoming empowered advocates against bullying.[97]

As our awareness of bullying increases, some educators are offering new ways to address the issues. For example, Colby College Professor Lyn Mikel Brown recommends a deeper look at the factors underlying bullying. Accordingly to Brown, educators need to:

- *Talk accurately about behavior.* Bullying is a broad term. If it's sexual harassment, call it sexual harassment; if it's homophobia, call it homophobia. Calling behaviors what they are encourages more complex and meaningful solutions.

- *Move beyond the individual.* To understand why a child uses aggression toward others, it's important to understand what impact race, ethnicity, social class, gender, religion, and ability has on his or her daily experiences in school. How do these realities affect the kinds of attention and resources a child receives, where he fits in, or whether she feels marginal or privileged in school?

- *Stop labeling students.* Bully prevention programs typically put kids into three categories: bullies, victims, and bystanders. Labeling focuses on the child as the problem, downplaying the roles of parents, teachers, the school system, a powerful media culture, and societal injustices children experience every day. Labels also simplify the issue: We are all complex individuals with the capacity to do harm and to do good.

- *Accentuate the positive.* Instead of labeling kids, affirm their strengths and believe that they can do good, brave, remarkable things. The path to safer, less violent schools lies less in adults' control over children than in appreciating their need to have more control in their lives, to feel important, to be visible, to have an effect on people and situations.[98]

We don't have to accept bullying as a part of growing up. Teaching acceptance and kindness toward others can be as much a part of schools as algebra or social studies.

CHAPTER REVIEW

Go to the Online Learning Center to take a chapter self-quiz practice with key terms, and review concepts from the chapter.

www.mhhe.com/
sadkerbrief3e

1. **What rituals and routines shape classroom life?**

   Students spend much of their time sitting still and waiting, denying their needs, and becoming distracted.

2. **How is class time related to student achievement?**

   John Goodlad and others have documented that while some teachers use instructional time efficiently, others are sidetracked by behavioral problems and administrative routine.

3. **How does the teacher's gatekeeping function influence classroom roles?**

   Phil Jackson and others have shown that while a major goal of education is to increase students' curiosity, teachers are the gatekeepers who determine what will be learned and who will be actively involved.

4. **What is tracking, and what are its advantages and disadvantages?**

   The practice of placing students into a specific class based on ability is called tracking, but Jeannie Oakes and other scholars have found that a disproportionate number of poor children and students of color are tracked as slow learners and receive weaker teachers and fewer opportunities. Supporters of detracking call for more individualization of instruction, more authentic learning, and less reliance on a "one size fits all" view of teaching.

5. **How do gender and peer groups influence children in elementary and middle school?**

   Peer pressure wields great power in and out of school, and a gender wall rigidly segregates children in the elementary and middle school years.

6. **In what ways does the adolescent culture shape teenage perceptions and behaviors?**

   Sociologist James Coleman described high school as an intense, almost "closed" social system, where peer status dominates, while author Patricia Hersch is troubled by the lack of community or parental values on the young.

7. **What impact do changing family patterns and economic issues have on children and schools?**

   More than one in five U.S. children lives in poverty, a condition that frequently short circuits educational promise. Divorce, remarriage, and nontraditional family patterns have restructured the family and the home–school connection.

8. **How can educators respond to social issues that place children at risk?**

   Sexuality, substance abuse, disordered eating, and bullying are just a few of the social and health issues faced by today's youth. Teachers are challenged to create classrooms where bias, hatred, and misinformation are replaced by a sense of security, trust, and truthful information concerning health, relationships, and sex education.

KEY TERMS AND PEOPLE

1. Observe in a local elementary school. What are the rules and regulations that students must follow? Do they seem reasonable or arbitrary? Do students seem to spend a large amount of time waiting? Observe one student over a 40-minute period and determine what portion of those 40 minutes she or he spends just waiting.

2. Do you think that tracking is a valid method for enhancing student performance? Or do you think it is a mechanism for perpetuating inequality of opportunity based on social class, race, or sex? Debate someone in your class who holds an opposing point of view.

3. We have noted the vividness and detail with which many people recall their high school years. Try to answer the following:

   • Who was voted most likely to succeed in your high school class? (Do you know what he or she is doing today?)

   • What was your happiest moment in high school? Your worst?

   • Name five people who were part of the "in crowd" in your class. What were the "innies" in your high school like?

   • Is there any academic experience in high school that you remember vividly? If so, what was it?

4. Research the issue of adolescent alienation. Make some recommendations on how schools could get students to become more involved in academic and extracurricular activities.

5. What can schools do to address each of the following issues?

   • Poverty

   • Single-parent families

   • Alternative families

   • Substance abuse

   • Dropping out

   • Obesity and eating disorders

   • Bullying

WEB-*TIVITIES*

Go to the Online Learning Center to do the following activities:
1. Gender Equity: The Work of Myra Sadker
2. Hidden America: Homeless Families
3. Children: At Promise or at Risk?

YOUR CD-ROM: THE *TEACHERS, SCHOOLS, AND SOCIETY READER* WITH CLASSROOM OBSERVATION VIDEO CLIPS

Articles, Case Studies, and Videos correspond to chapter content and are not always in numeric order. Go to your *Teachers, Schools, and Society Reader* CD-ROM to:

Read Current and Historical Articles

12. "Teaching Themes of Care, Nel Noddings," *Phi Delta Kappan,* May 1995.

13. "The Engaged Classroom," Sam M. Intrator, *Educational Leadership,* September 2004.

14. "Dealing with Rumors, Secrets, and Lies: Tools of Aggression for Middle School," Betsy Lane, *Middle School Journal,* January 2005.

15. "The Myth of the Culture of Poverty," Paul Gorski, *Educational Leadership*, April 2008.

16. "Everyday Pedagogy: Lessons from Basketball, Track, and Dominoes," Na'ilah Suad Nasir, *Phi Delta Kappan*, March 2008.

Analyze Case Studies

7. **Marsha Warren:** A teacher is overwhelmed by the problems created by her students, including eight children who have unique home problems and personal situations that are affecting their schooling.

8. **Anne Holt:** This case follows an experienced teacher through her morning routine with a diverse group of first-grade children. The case presents a detailed look at her organization and the climate she creates in the classroom.

Observe Teachers, Students, and Classrooms in Action

6. Three High School Girls Discuss Adolescent Self-Concept at Age 16

7. Three High Schools Talk about Drugs at Age 15

8. Characteristics of Children Who Bully

See pages 115, 125, and 131 of this text for descriptions of these videos. You'll find the videos on the CD Reader and at the Online Learning Center.

www.mhhe.com/
sadkerbrief3e

THE MULTICULTURAL HISTORY OF AMERICAN EDUCATION

chapter 5

Focus Questions

1. What was the nature and purpose of colonial education?

2. How did the Common School Movement influence the idea of universal education?

3. What developments mark the educational history of Native Americans?

4. How did teaching become a "gendered" career?

5. How did secondary schools evolve?

6. What were the main tenets of the Progressive Education movement?

7. What role has the federal government played in American education?

8. How did history shape the educational experiences of African Americans, Hispanics, Asian Americans/Pacific Islanders, and Arab Americans?

9. What educational barriers and breakthroughs have girls and women experienced?

10. Who are some of the influential educators who have helped fashion today's schools?

WHAT DO YOU THINK? How much do you already know about the history of education? Before reading the chapter, take a quiz that includes some "basics" and fun facts.

www.mhhe.com/
sadkerbrief3e

Chapter Preview

Understanding the history of America's schools offers you perspective—a sense of your place in your new profession. Your classroom is a living tribute to past achievements and sacrifices.

In this chapter, you will discover how social class, race, ethnicity, gender, and religion influenced American education throughout history. Education during the colonial period was intended to further religious goals and was offered primarily to white males—typically, wealthy white males. Over time, educational exclusivity diminished, but, even today, wealth, race, and gender continue to impact educational quality. To a great extent, the story of American education is a battle to open the schoolhouse door to more and more of our citizens. In this chapter, we share the story of the struggle to have America honor its commitment to equality.

The complex network of expectations surrounding today's schools is the product of a society that has been evolving for over three centuries. Individuals, groups, and the government all have contributed to making public schools more accessible. Benjamin Franklin, Horace Mann, Emma Hart Willard, and Mary McLeod Bethune, for example, fought to free America from historical biases. Federal laws were designed to create more equitable and effective educational opportunities. Today, the federal focus is to increase school competition, identify failing schools, and either "fix" them or replace them. But the notion of competition and standards is only the most recent chapter in the story of our nation's schools. In the colonial era, the goals were simpler: to teach the Scriptures and to develop a religious community. We will begin by looking into the classroom of Christopher Lamb, a New England teacher in one of the earliest American schools, more than three centuries ago.

Christopher Lamb's Colonial Classroom

The frigid wintry wind knifed through Christopher Lamb's coat, chilling him to the bone as he walked in the predawn darkness. The single bucket of firewood that he lugged, intended to keep his seventeenth-century New England schoolroom warm all day, would clearly not do the job. After the fire was started, Christopher focused on his other teaching tasks: carrying in a bucket of water for the class, sweeping the floor, and mending the ever so fragile pen points for the students. Margaret, who loved school, was the first student to arrive. Margaret, like most girls, would stay in school for only a year or two to learn to read the Bible so that she could be a better wife and mother. She might even learn to write her name before she left school. But that was really not important for girls. The other students found their way to either the boys' bench or the girls' bench, where, in turn, they read their Testament aloud.

Christopher was amazed at how poorly some students read, tripping over every other word. The last student to finish, Benjamin, slowly rose from the bench, cringing. Christopher called out, "Lazy pupil," and a chorus of children's voices chimed in: "Lazy pupil. Lazy pupil. Lazy pupil." Benjamin, if not totally accustomed to the taunts, was no longer crushed by them, either. After the recitation and writing lessons, all the children were lined up and examined, to make certain they had washed and combed. For 10 minutes, the class and teacher knelt in prayer. Each student then recited the day's biblical lesson.

Christopher Lamb had been an apprentice teacher for five years before accepting this position. He rejected the rod approach used so frequently by

his master teacher. Using the children to provide rewards and punishments was far more effective than welts and bruises, marks left by a teacher's rod. Yes, Christopher was somewhat unorthodox, perhaps even a bit revolutionary, but the challenges of contemporary seventeenth-century society demanded forward-thinking educators, such as Christopher Lamb.

Focus Question 1
What was the nature and purpose of colonial education?

Colonial New England Education: God's Classrooms

One of the striking differences between Christopher Lamb's room and today's typical public school is the role of religio The religious fervor that drove the Puritans to America also provide religious education for their young, making New Eng of American education. In Christopher Lamb's time, school wa souls. Education provided a path to heaven, and reading, wr development all revolved around the Bible.

Early colonial education, both in New England and in often began in the home. (Today's home schooling moveme approach.) The family was the major educational resource for the first lessons typically focused on reading. Values, manner and even vocational skills were taught by parents and gran instruction eventually became more specialized, and some to devote their time to teaching, converting their homes into "dames" taught reading, writing, and computation, and their known as **dame schools.** A "dame," or well-respected woman in education, became (for a fee) the community's teacher.

An apprenticeship program rounded out a child's colonial education. While boys, sometimes as young as 7 years of age, were sent to live with masters who taught them a trade, girls typically learned homemaking skills from their mothers. Apprenticeship programs for boys involved not only learning skilled crafts but also managing farms and shops. Many colonies required that masters teach reading and writing as well as vocational skills. The masters served *in loco parentis*—that is, in place of the child's parent. The competencies of the masters guiding apprentices varied greatly, as did the talents of family members, dames, ministers, and others fulfilling the teaching role. Not surprisingly, this educational hodgepodge did not always lead to a well-educated citizenry; a more formal structure was needed.

Twenty-two years after arriving in the New World, the Puritans living in the Commonwealth of Massachusetts passed a law requiring that parents and masters of apprentices be checked periodically to ensure that children were being taught properly. Five years later, in 1647, Massachusetts took even more rigorous measures to ensure the education of its children. The Massachusetts Law of 1647, more

[handwritten notes:] Christopher Lamb preferred to not beat his students. Believed rewards & punishment was more effective.

Dame Schools: Women, or "Dames" who loved teaching turned their home into a DS. often became community teacher. Children as young as 7 did apprenticeships, the apprents became the "in loco parentis" meaning in place of parent

this colonial recitation lesson includes a boy sitting in the corner with a dunce cap. By today's standards, "time out" back then was quite humiliating.

commonly known as the **Old Deluder Satan Law**—the Puritans' attempt to thwart Satan's trickery with Scripture-reading citizens—required that

- Every town of 50 households must appoint and pay a teacher of reading and writing.
- Every town of 100 households must provide a (Latin) grammar school to prepare youths for the university, under a penalty of £5 for failure to do so.[1]

By 1680, such laws had spread throughout most of New England. The settlement patterns of the Puritans, who lived in towns and communities rather than scattered throughout the countryside, made establishing schools relatively uncomplicated. After learning to read and write, most girls returned home to practice the art of housekeeping. Boys who could afford to pay for their education went on to a **Latin grammar school.** In 1635, only 15 years after arriving in America's wilderness, the Puritans established their first Latin grammar school in Boston. The Boston Latin Grammar School was not unlike a "prep" school for boys and was similar to the classical schools of Europe. The Boston Latin Grammar School was a rather exclusive school for boys of wealth, charging tuition to teach boys between the ages of 7 and 14.

Many consider the Boston Latin Grammar School to be the first step on the road to creating the American high school, although the school's curriculum reflected European roots. Students were expected to read and recite (in Latin, of course) the works of Cicero, Ovid, and Erasmus. In Greek, they read the works of Socrates and Homer. (Back to basics in colonial times meant back to the glory of Rome and Greece.) By the eighteenth century, the grammar school had incorporated mathematics, science, and modern languages. Classes started at 7 A.M., recessed at 11 A.M., and picked up from 1 P.M. until 5 P.M. Graduates were expected to go on to college and become colonial leaders, especially ministers.

Within a year of the founding of the Boston Latin Grammar School, Harvard College was established specifically to prepare ministers. Founded in 1636, Harvard was the first college in America, the jewel in the Puritans' religious and educational crown.[2]

For attendance at exclusive schools, such as Boston Latin Grammar, or at college, wealth was critical. The least desirable educational and apprenticeship opportunities were left to the poor. Some civic-minded communities made basic education in reading and writing more available to the poor, but only to families who would publicly admit their poverty by signing a "Pauper's Oath." Broadcasting one's poverty was no less offensive in colonial times than today, and many chose to have their children remain illiterate rather than sign such a public admission. The result was that most poor children remained outside the educational system.

Blacks, in America since 1619, and Native Americans were typically denied educational opportunities. In rare cases, religious groups, such as the Quakers, created special schools for children of color.[3] But these were the exceptions. Girls did not fare much better. After they had learned the rudiments of reading and writing, girls were taught the tasks related to their future roles as mother and wife. They were taught various handicrafts. Girls memorized the alphabet and then learned to stitch and display their accomplishments. They also learned to reproduce and attractively display religious

his master teacher. Using the children to provide rewards and punishments was far more effective than welts and bruises, marks left by a teacher's rod. Yes, Christopher was somewhat unorthodox, perhaps even a bit revolutionary, but the challenges of contemporary seventeenth-century society demanded forward-thinking educators, such as Christopher Lamb.

Focus Question 1
What was the nature and purpose of colonial education?

Colonial New England Education: God's Classrooms

One of the striking differences between Christopher Lamb's colonial classroom and today's typical public school is the role of religion in education. The religious fervor that drove the Puritans to America also drove them to provide religious education for their young, making New England the cradle of American education. In Christopher Lamb's time, school was meant to save souls. Education provided a path to heaven, and reading, writing, and moral development all revolved around the Bible.

Early colonial education, both in New England and in other colonies, often began in the home. (Today's home schooling movement is not a new approach.) The family was the major educational resource for youngsters, and the first lessons typically focused on reading. Values, manners, social graces, and even vocational skills were taught by parents and grandparents. Home instruction eventually became more specialized, and some women began to devote their time to teaching, converting their homes into schools. These "dames" taught reading, writing, and computation, and their homes became known as **dame schools**. A "dame," or well-respected woman with an interest in education, became (for a fee) the community's teacher.

An apprenticeship program rounded out a child's colonial education. While boys, sometimes as young as 7 years of age, were sent to live with masters who taught them a trade, girls typically learned homemaking skills from their mothers. Apprenticeship programs for boys involved not only learning skilled crafts but also managing farms and shops. Many colonies

This colonial recitation lesson includes a boy sitting in the corner with a dunce cap. By today's standards, "time out" back then was quite humiliating.

required that masters teach reading and writing as well as vocational skills. The masters served *in loco parentis*—that is, in place of the child's parent. The competencies of the masters guiding apprentices varied greatly, as did the talents of family members, dames, ministers, and others fulfilling the teaching role. Not surprisingly, this educational hodgepodge did not always lead to a well-educated citizenry; a more formal structure was needed.

Twenty-two years after arriving in the New World, the Puritans living in the Commonwealth of Massachusetts passed a law requiring that parents and masters of apprentices be checked periodically to ensure that children were being taught properly. Five years later, in 1647, Massachusetts took even more rigorous measures to ensure the education of its children. The Massachusetts Law of 1647, more

commonly known as the **Old Deluder Satan Law**—the Puritans' attempt to thwart Satan's trickery with Scripture-reading citizens—required that

- Every town of 50 households must appoint and pay a teacher of reading and writing.
- Every town of 100 households must provide a (Latin) grammar school to prepare youths for the university, under a penalty of £5 for failure to do so.[1]

By 1680, such laws had spread throughout most of New England. The settlement patterns of the Puritans, who lived in towns and communities rather than scattered throughout the countryside, made establishing schools relatively uncomplicated. After learning to read and write, most girls returned home to practice the art of housekeeping. Boys who could afford to pay for their education went on to a **Latin grammar school.** In 1635, only 15 years after arriving in America's wilderness, the Puritans established their first Latin grammar school in Boston. The Boston Latin Grammar School was not unlike a "prep" school for boys and was similar to the classical schools of Europe. The Boston Latin Grammar School was a rather exclusive school for boys of wealth, charging tuition to teach boys between the ages of 7 and 14.

Many consider the Boston Latin Grammar School to be the first step on the road to creating the American high school, although the school's curriculum reflected European roots. Students were expected to read and recite (in Latin, of course) the works of Cicero, Ovid, and Erasmus. In Greek, they read the works of Socrates and Homer. (Back to basics in colonial times meant back to the glory of Rome and Greece.) By the eighteenth century, the grammar school had incorporated mathematics, science, and modern languages. Classes started at 7 A.M., recessed at 11 A.M., and picked up from 1 P.M. until 5 P.M. Graduates were expected to go on to college and become colonial leaders, especially ministers.

Within a year of the founding of the Boston Latin Grammar School, Harvard College was established specifically to prepare ministers. Founded in 1636, Harvard was the first college in America, the jewel in the Puritans' religious and educational crown.[2]

For attendance at exclusive schools, such as Boston Latin Grammar, or at college, wealth was critical. The least desirable educational and apprenticeship opportunities were left to the poor. Some civic-minded communities made basic education in reading and writing more available to the poor, but only to families who would publicly admit their poverty by signing a "Pauper's Oath." Broadcasting one's poverty was no less offensive in colonial times than today, and many chose to have their children remain illiterate rather than sign such a public admission. The result was that most poor children remained outside the educational system.

Blacks, in America since 1619, and Native Americans were typically denied educational opportunities. In rare cases, religious groups, such as the Quakers, created special schools for children of color.[3] But these were the exceptions. Girls did not fare much better. After they had learned the rudiments of reading and writing, girls were taught the tasks related to their future roles as mother and wife. They were taught various handicrafts. Girls memorized the alphabet and then learned to stitch and display their accomplishments. They also learned to reproduce and attractively display religious

his master teacher. Using the children to provide rewards and punishments was far more effective than welts and bruises, marks left by a teacher's rod. Yes, Christopher was somewhat unorthodox, perhaps even a bit revolutionary, but the challenges of contemporary seventeenth-century society demanded forward-thinking educators, such as Christopher Lamb.

Focus Question 1
What was the nature and purpose of colonial education?

Colonial New England Education: God's Classrooms

One of the striking differences between Christopher Lamb's colonial classroom and today's typical public school is the role of religion in education. The religious fervor that drove the Puritans to America also drove them to provide religious education for their young, making New England the cradle of American education. In Christopher Lamb's time, school was meant to save souls. Education provided a path to heaven, and reading, writing, and moral development all revolved around the Bible.

Early colonial education, both in New England and in other colonies, often began in the home. (Today's home schooling movement is not a new approach.) The family was the major educational resource for youngsters, and the first lessons typically focused on reading. Values, manners, social graces, and even vocational skills were taught by parents and grandparents. Home instruction eventually became more specialized, and some women began to devote their time to teaching, converting their homes into schools. These "dames" taught reading, writing, and computation, and their homes became known as **dame schools**. A "dame," or well-respected woman with an interest in education, became (for a fee) the community's teacher.

An apprenticeship program rounded out a child's colonial education. While boys, sometimes as young as 7 years of age, were sent to live with masters who taught them a trade, girls typically learned homemaking skills from their mothers. Apprenticeship programs for boys involved not only learning skilled crafts but also managing farms and shops. Many colonies required that masters teach reading and writing as well as vocational skills. The masters served *in loco parentis*—that is, in place of the child's parent. The competencies of the masters guiding apprentices varied greatly, as did the talents of family members, dames, ministers, and others fulfilling the teaching role. Not surprisingly, this educational hodgepodge did not always lead to a well-educated citizenry; a more formal structure was needed.

Twenty-two years after arriving in the New World, the Puritans living in the Commonwealth of Massachusetts passed a law requiring that parents and masters of apprentices be checked periodically to ensure that children were being taught properly. Five years later, in 1647, Massachusetts took even more rigorous measures to ensure the education of its children. The Massachusetts Law of 1647, more

This colonial recitation lesson includes a boy sitting in the corner with a dunce cap. By today's standards, "time out" back then was quite humiliating.

commonly known as the **Old Deluder Satan Law**—the Puritans' attempt to thwart Satan's trickery with Scripture-reading citizens—required that

- Every town of 50 households must appoint and pay a teacher of reading and writing.
- Every town of 100 households must provide a (Latin) grammar school to prepare youths for the university, under a penalty of £5 for failure to do so.[1]

By 1680, such laws had spread throughout most of New England. The settlement patterns of the Puritans, who lived in towns and communities rather than scattered throughout the countryside, made establishing schools relatively uncomplicated. After learning to read and write, most girls returned home to practice the art of housekeeping. Boys who could afford to pay for their education went on to a **Latin grammar school.** In 1635, only 15 years after arriving in America's wilderness, the Puritans established their first Latin grammar school in Boston. The Boston Latin Grammar School was not unlike a "prep" school for boys and was similar to the classical schools of Europe. The Boston Latin Grammar School was a rather exclusive school for boys of wealth, charging tuition to teach boys between the ages of 7 and 14.

Many consider the Boston Latin Grammar School to be the first step on the road to creating the American high school, although the school's curriculum reflected European roots. Students were expected to read and recite (in Latin, of course) the works of Cicero, Ovid, and Erasmus. In Greek, they read the works of Socrates and Homer. (Back to basics in colonial times meant back to the glory of Rome and Greece.) By the eighteenth century, the grammar school had incorporated mathematics, science, and modern languages. Classes started at 7 A.M., recessed at 11 A.M., and picked up from 1 P.M. until 5 P.M. Graduates were expected to go on to college and become colonial leaders, especially ministers.

Within a year of the founding of the Boston Latin Grammar School, Harvard College was established specifically to prepare ministers. Founded in 1636, Harvard was the first college in America, the jewel in the Puritans' religious and educational crown.[2]

For attendance at exclusive schools, such as Boston Latin Grammar, or at college, wealth was critical. The least desirable educational and apprenticeship opportunities were left to the poor. Some civic-minded communities made basic education in reading and writing more available to the poor, but only to families who would publicly admit their poverty by signing a "Pauper's Oath." Broadcasting one's poverty was no less offensive in colonial times than today, and many chose to have their children remain illiterate rather than sign such a public admission. The result was that most poor children remained outside the educational system.

Blacks, in America since 1619, and Native Americans were typically denied educational opportunities. In rare cases, religious groups, such as the Quakers, created special schools for children of color.[3] But these were the exceptions. Girls did not fare much better. After they had learned the rudiments of reading and writing, girls were taught the tasks related to their future roles as mother and wife. They were taught various handicrafts. Girls memorized the alphabet and then learned to stitch and display their accomplishments. They also learned to reproduce and attractively display religious

sayings, on the road to becoming good Christian wives and mothers. As much as we value these beautiful samplers today, they are a sad reminder of a time when they marked the academic finish line for girls, the diploma of a second-rate education, a depressing denial of equal educational rights. Later in this chapter, we will describe in detail the barriers separating many Americans from quality education.

Location greatly influenced educational opportunities. The northern colonies were settled by Puritans who lived in towns and communities relatively close to one another. Their religious fervor and proximity made the creation of community schools dedicated to teaching the Bible a predictable development.

In the middle colonies, the range of European religious and ethnic groups created, if not a melting pot, a limited tolerance for diversity.[4] Various religious groups established schools, and apprenticeships groomed youngsters for a variety of careers, including teaching. In the middle colonies, the development of commerce and mercantile demands promoted the formation of private schools devoted to job training. By the 1700s, private teachers and night schools were functioning in Philadelphia and New York, teaching accounting, navigation, French, and Spanish.

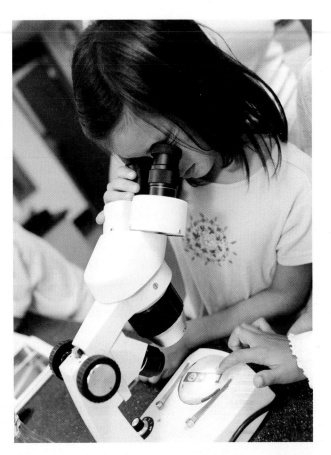

Identify some of the educational opportunities available to girls and minorities since colonial times, as well as some continuing limitations.

The first city in North America was St. Augustine, Florida, where there is evidence that the Spanish settlers established schools. In terms of education, the southern English colonies trailed behind. The rural, sparsely populated southern colonies developed an educational system that was responsive to plantation society. Wealthy plantation owners took tutors into their homes to teach their children not only basic academic skills but also the social graces appropriate to their station in life. Plantation owners' children learned the proper way to entertain guests and "manage" slaves, using such texts as *The Complete Gentleman*. Wealthy young men seeking higher education were sent to Europe. Girls made do with just an introduction to academics and a greater focus on their social responsibilities. Poor white children might have had rudimentary home instruction in reading, writing, and computation. Black children made do with little if any instruction and, as time went by, encountered laws that actually prohibited their education entirely.[5]

Education has come a long way from colonial days and from Christopher Lamb's class—or has it? Consider the following:

1. The colonial experience established many of today's educational norms:
   - Local control of schools
   - Compulsory education
   - Tax-supported schools
   - State standards for teaching and schools

2. The colonial experience highlighted many of the persistent tension points challenging schools today:
   - What is the role of religion in the classroom?
   - How can we equalize the quality of education in various communities?
   - How can the barriers of racism, sexism, religious intolerance, and classism be eliminated, so that all children receive equal educational opportunity?
   - How can we prepare the most competent teachers?

A New Nation Shapes Education

The ideas that led to the American Revolution revolutionized our schools. European beliefs and practices, which had pervaded America's schools, were gradually abandoned as the new national character was formed. None of these beliefs had been more firmly adhered to than the integration of the state and religion.

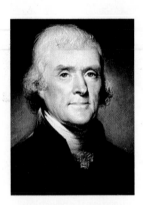

In addition to serving two terms as President of the United States, Thomas Jefferson was the colonial era's most eloquent spokesperson for education and was the founder of the University of Virginia.

In sixteenth- and seventeenth-century England, the Puritans' desire to reform the Church of England was viewed as treason. The Puritans encountered both religious and political opposition, and they looked to the New World as an escape from persecution. However, they came to America not to establish religious freedom, as our history books sometimes suggest, but to establish their own church as supreme, both religiously and politically. The Puritans were neither tolerant of other religions nor interested in separating religion and politics. Nonconformers, such as the Quakers, were vigorously persecuted. The purpose of the Massachusetts colony was to establish the "true" religion of the Puritans, to create a "new Israel" in America. Schools were simply an extension of the religious state, designed to teach the young to read and understand the Bible and to do honorable battle with Satan.

During the 1700s, American education was reconstructed to meet broader, nonsectarian goals. Such leaders as **Thomas Jefferson** wanted to go beyond educating a small elite class or providing only religious instruction. Jefferson maintained that education should be more widely available to white children from all economic and social classes. Public citizens began to question the usefulness of rudimentary skills taught in a school year of just three or four months. They questioned the value of mastering Greek and Latin classics in the Latin grammar schools, when practical skills were in short supply in the New World.

In 1749, **Benjamin Franklin** penned *Proposals Relating to the Youth of Pennsylvania,* suggesting a new kind of secondary school to replace the Latin grammar school—the **academy.** Two years later, the Franklin Academy was established, free of religious influence and offering a variety of practical subjects, including mathematics, astronomy, athletics, navigation, dramatics, and bookkeeping. Students were able to choose some of their courses, thus setting the precedent for elective courses and programs at the secondary level. In the late 1700s, it was the Franklin Academy and not the Boston Latin Grammar School that was considered the most important secondary school in America.[6]

The Franklin Academy accepted both girls and boys who could afford the tuition, and the practical curriculum became an attractive innovation. Franklin's Academy sparked the establishment of 6,000 academies in the century that followed, including Phillips Academy at Andover, Massachusetts (1778), and Phillips Exeter Academy in Exeter, New Hampshire (1783). The original Franklin Academy eventually became the University of Pennsylvania.

Jefferson's commitment to educating all white Americans, rich and poor, at government expense, and Franklin's commitment to a practical program of nonsectarian study offering elective courses severed American educational thought from its European roots. Many years passed before these ideas became widely established practices, but the pattern for innovation and a truly American approach to education was taking shape.

The Common School Movement

During the early decades of the nineteenth century, the democratic ideal became popular as many "common people"—immigrants, small farmers, and urban laborers—demanded greater participation in the democracy. With the election of Andrew Jackson in 1828, the voices of many poor white people were heard, particularly their demands for educational access. Many more decades would pass before additional voices—particularly those of people of color—would also be heard.

Horace Mann became the nation's leading advocate for the establishment of a **common school** open to all. Today we know this common school as the public **elementary school.** Historians consider Horace Mann to be the outstanding proponent of education for the common person (the common school movement), and he is often referred to as "the father of the public school." Mann helped create the Massachusetts State Board of Education and in 1837 became its secretary, a position similar to today's state superintendent of schools. In this role, Mann began an effort to reform education, believing that public education should serve both practical and idealistic goals. In practical terms, both business and industry would benefit from educated workers, resulting in a more productive economy. In idealistic terms, public schools should help us identify and nurture the talents in poor as well as wealthy children, and schools should ameliorate social disharmony.[7] Mann decried the rifts between rich and poor, Calvinists and religious reformers, new Irish immigrants and native workers. A common school instilling common and humane moral values could reduce such social disharmony (a popular belief today as well). Mann attempted to promote such values, but he encountered strong opposition when the values he selected revealed a distinct religious bias, one that offended Calvinists, atheists, Jews, Catholics, and others. His moral program to create a common set of beliefs had the opposite impact, igniting a dispute over the role of religion in school.

The idea of public education is so commonplace today that it seems difficult to imagine another system. But Horace Mann, along with such allies as Henry Barnard of Connecticut, fought a long and difficult battle to win the acceptance of public elementary schools. The opposition was powerful. Business interests predicted disaster if their labor pool of children were taken away. Concerned taxpayers protested the additional tax monies needed to support public education. There was also the competition. Private schools and religious groups sponsoring their own schools protested the establishment of free schools. Americans wondered what would become of a nation in

Focus Question 2
How did the Common School Movement influence the idea of universal education?

which everyone received an elementary education. Would this not produce overeducated citizens, questioning authority and promoting self-interest? The opposition to public elementary schools was often fierce, but Horace Mann and his allies prevailed.

As he fought for public schools for all, Mann also waged a battle for high-quality schools. He continually attempted to build new and better schools, which was a problem because so many Massachusetts schools were in deplorable condition. By publicly disseminating information about which communities had well-built or poorly built schools, he applied public pressure on districts to improve their school buildings. He worked for effective teacher training programs as well and promoted more stringent teacher licensing procedures. As a result of his efforts, several **normal schools** were founded in Massachusetts, schools devoted to preparing teachers in pedagogy—the best ways to teach children. He also championed newer teaching methods designed to improve and modernize classroom instruction. He opposed the routine practice of corporal punishment and sought ways to positively motivate students to learn. Mann emphasized practical subjects useful to children and to adult society, rather than the mastery of Greek and Latin. Mann saw education as a great investment, for individuals and for the country, and he worked for many years to make free public education a reality. He worked for the abolition of slavery, promoted women's educational and economic rights, and even fought alongside the temperance movement to limit the negative impact of alcohol. He was not only a committed educator but a committed reformer as well.

By the time of the Civil War, this radical notion of the public elementary school had become widespread and widely accepted. Educational historian Lawrence Cremin summarized the advance of the common school movement in his book *The Transformation of the School:*

> A majority of the states had established public school systems, and a good half of the nation's children were already getting some formal education. Elementary schools were becoming widely available; in some states, like Massachusetts, New York, and Pennsylvania, the notion of free public education was slowly expanding to include secondary schools; and in a few, like Michigan and Wisconsin, the public school system was already capped by a state university. There were, of course, significant variations from state to state and from region to region. New England, long a pioneer in public education, also had an established tradition of private education, and private schools continued to flourish there. The Midwest, on the other hand, sent a far greater proportion of its school children to public institutions. The southern states, with the exception of North Carolina, tended to lag behind, and did not generally establish popular schooling until after the Civil War.[8]

Native American Tribes: The History of Miseducation

Focus Question 3
What developments mark the educational history of Native Americans?

While the notion of universal education, especially at the elementary level, spread slowly among Americans of European ancestry, many who lived here were not European. In fact, Europeans were the late arrivals. It has been estimated that 50 to 100 million Native Americans occupied both North and South America before Columbus arrived.[9] Within a relatively brief time,

EARLY TEXTBOOKS

A rich variety of textbooks, media, library books, and computer software provide today's teachers with curricular resources unimaginable just a few years ago. As a teacher, you will come across references to some of the limited but influential curriculum materials of the past. Here is a brief profile of the best-known instructional materials from yesterday's schools.

HORNBOOK

The most common teaching device in colonial schools, the **hornbook** consisted of an alphabet sheet covered by a thin, transparent sheet made from a cow's horn. The alphabet and the horn covering were tacked to a paddle-shaped piece of wood and often hung by a leather strap around the student's neck. Originating in medieval Europe, the hornbook provided colonial children with their introduction to the alphabet and reading.

NEW ENGLAND PRIMER

The first real textbook, the **New England Primer** was a tiny 2½- by 4½-inch book containing 50 to 100 pages of alphabet, words, and small verses accompanied by woodcut illustrations. First published in 1690, it was virtually the only reading text used in colonial schools until about 1800. The Primer reflected the religious orientation of colonial schools. A typical verse was

In Adam's Fall
We sinned all.
Thy Life to mend,
This Book attend
The idle fool
Is whipt at School.

AMERICAN SPELLING BOOK

The task undertaken by Noah Webster was to define and nourish the new American culture. His **American Spelling Book** replaced the *New England Primer* as the most common elementary textbook. The book contained the alphabet, syllables, consonants, rules for speaking, readings, short stories, and moral advice. The bulk of the book was taken up by lists of words. Royalty income from the sale of millions of copies of this book supported Webster in his other efforts to standardize the American language, including his best-known work, which is still used today, the *American Dictionary*.

MCGUFFEY READERS

William Holmes McGuffey was a minister, professor, and college president who believed that clean living, hard work, and literacy were the virtues to instill in children. He wrote a series of readers that emphasized the work ethic, patriotism, heroism, and morality. It is estimated that more than 100 million copies of *McGuffey Readers* educated several generations of Americans between 1836 and 1920. **McGuffey Readers** are noteworthy because they were geared for different grade levels and paved the way for graded elementary schools.

REFLECTION: Can you detect the morals and traditional values being promoted in today's texts? Can you cite any examples?

---

more than 90 percent of them would be dead from disease, starvation, and conquest. The survivors in the United States would soon experience what many describe as an attempt to kill their culture through education.[10] Church missionaries educated native peoples to abandon their history and language in order to become "civilized Christians." Native beliefs, customs, and languages were systematically ridiculed and repressed.[11]

Despite adverse conditions, Native Americans achieved some extraordinary educational accomplishments. For example, when their oral traditions and beliefs were discredited, Sequoyah revealed a hidden Cherokee syllabary that was developed by ancient tribal elders years earlier. This syllabary permitted the Cherokee language to be written. Books were published

School Mascots

SHOULD CHANGE WITH THE TIMES BECAUSE . . .

MASCOT NAMES CAN BE HURTFUL

A pep rally featuring chanting "Indians" shaking rubber tomahawks trivializes meaningful rituals and cultural differences. Names such as the "Lady Bucks" or "Tiger-ettes" perpetuate an image of female inferiority and the second-class status of their sports.

MASCOT NAMES PROMOTE VIOLENCE

Stands filled with "Pirates" wielding sabers and chanting insults bring us all closer to potential violence and injury. Mascots should build a positive climate, not a destructive one.

WE SHOULD SET AN EXAMPLE FOR STUDENTS

We must teach by example, and changing offensive mascot names gives us that opportunity. By adopting names like "Freedom" or "Liberty," we teach our children how names can model our historical best, not our historical bigotries, and how adults can learn from past mistakes.

SHOULD NOT CHANGE OVER TIME BECAUSE . . .

IT'S JUST A NAME

There are more important issues to address than changing names of athletic teams. Exaggerated complaints about mascot names consume hours of school board meetings and only show how political correctness is driving the times.

MASCOT NAMES BUILD SCHOOL SPIRIT

Proud mascot names like the "Patriots" highlight courage and bravery. Mascot names instill school spirit, a trait sorely needed by today's young people.

TRADITION MATTERS

Some things really do need to stay the same. Building a positive and stable school community is hard enough with people constantly moving and families splitting. School mascot names provide stability, and do not mindlessly mirror every passing fad.

www.mhhe.com/sadkerbrief3e **YOU DECIDE . . .**

You and your classmates may want to share your own experiences on this hot-button issue. Should any mascot names be changed? Which names and why (or why not)? Brainstorm positive team names and mascots.

This may be more challenging than you think. To understand more about mascots and American Indians, visit www.racismagainstindians.org.

in Cherokee; Cherokee schools became bilingual; and the Cherokee nation wrote, edited, and published the *Cherokee Phoenix,* a bilingual weekly newspaper. However, as federal interventions became more systematic, the tribes' control over their own education diminished.

After the Civil War, the federal government, through the Bureau of Indian Affairs (BIA), continued to use education as a tool of cultural conquest. Indian reservations saw more white superintendents, farm agents, teachers, inspectors, and missionaries. The largest of the tribes, the Navajos, despite their years of resistance, were assigned to a reservation. The treaty with the Navajos promised that schools would be built to educate their children. In 1892, almost 20 years after the treaty was signed, Indian boarding schools were established to assimilate young Native Americans into the dominant European American values: veneration of property, individual competition, European-style domesticity, toil, and European standards of dress.

Many Native Americans refused to send their children to reservation schools. Arrest and kidnapping were common practices in forcing Native

American children to attend. Rations were often withheld from parents as a means of compelling them to send their children to school.

After 1920, there was an increase in political and legal activity as Native Americans fought for tribal and educational rights. Native Americans challenged the federal government for violating treaties, including failure to provide adequate education. The federal courts were not responsive. Greater gains at the state level were made, and in several court cases Native Americans won the right to attend public schools.[12]

Today, more than half of the Native Americans in this country do not live on reservations, and their youngsters have become invisible children of color in urban centers. As the students have been desegregated across neighborhoods, they have lost their "critical mass," which is often associated with higher achievement.[13]

The recent decades have witnessed continued activity by Native Americans to win control of the reservations, including the schools. The tribes feel strongly that such control will maintain cultural identity, as well as increase the academic achievement of their children. The vast majority of Indian children are educated in public schools. Most other Native youth are clustered in programs under the advisory of the BIA or private schools.

The following Ancient Digger Indian proverb captures the last two centuries of Indian tribal education:

> In the beginning, God gave to every people a cup of clay, and from this cup they drank their life. They all dipped in the water, but their cups were different. Our cup is broken now. It has passed away.

Spinsters, Bachelors, and Gender Barriers in Teaching

Although today's popular perception is that teaching is predominantly a female career, in fact, men dominated teaching well into the mid-nineteenth century. Teaching was a **gendered career,** and it was gendered "male." Although a few women taught at home in dame schools, the first women to become teachers in regular school settings, earning a public salary, were viewed as gender trespassers, "unsexed" by their ambition, and considered masculine. Concerned by this negative characterization, early feminists such as Catherine Beecher implored female teachers to accentuate their feminine traits, highlight their domestic skills, and continue their preparation for marriage.[14] Despite the national reluctance to allow women into the workforce, and despite the perception that teachers should be male, the demand for more and inexpensive teachers created by common schools made the hiring of women teachers inevitable.

By the early part of the twentieth century, women constituted upwards of 90 percent of teachers. But not all women were equally welcome. School districts preferred "spinsters," women unmarried and unlikely to marry. Such women would not suffer the dual loyalties inherent in "serving" both husband and employer. Unmarried women were hired so frequently in the late nineteenth and early twentieth centuries that teaching and spinsterhood became synonymous. Cartoonists, authors, and reporters made the spinster schoolteacher a cultural icon. Boarding and rooming houses, and eventually small

Focus Question 4

How did teaching become a "gendered" career?

apartments, sometimes called *teacherages,* were built to provide accommodations for this new class of workers. Teaching was gendered again, but now it was gendered "female."

As women came to dominate teaching, the gender tables were turned, and a new concern arose: the fear that female teachers were "feminizing" boys. There were demands to bring men back to teaching and to halt the "feminization" of young schoolboys. President Theodore Roosevelt added a touch of racism to the debate, arguing that since so many white women were choosing teaching over motherhood, they were committing "race suicide," and the continuance of the white race was in jeopardy.[15] School districts responded by actively recruiting male teachers, and male educators carved out their own niches in school systems. Administration, coaching, vocational education, and certain high school departments, specifically science and math, became male bastions.

For women, teaching meant economic and financial liberation. But not without cost. The dedicated teaching spinsters of the nineteenth century became the object of ridicule in the twentieth century. Women choosing teaching over motherhood were considered unnatural by a mostly male cadre of psychologists, physicians, and authors. Articles and books began to appear early in the twentieth century arguing that being unmarried caused women to be spiteful, hateful, and disgusting. The eminent psychologist G. Stanley Hall wrote an article titled "Certain Degenerative Tendencies among Teachers," explaining why unmarried women were frustrated, bitter, and otherwise unpleasant. Political opinions parading as research soon appeared, claiming that as many as half of all single teachers were lesbians. Stage shows and movies picked up the theme, portraying lesbian relationships in and beyond school settings. The National Education Association reacted by campaigning for school districts to drop their ban against hiring married women. But when the Depression hit in the 1930s, the idea of hiring wives and creating two-income families was anathema: the scarce jobs were to be funneled to women living alone or to men, the family "breadwinners." It was not until the end of World War II that most school districts even employed married women.

Men who remained in teaching also paid a price. Conventional wisdom early in the twentieth century held that effeminate men were gay men, and that gay men were naturally drawn to teaching. Worse yet, gay men were considered to be a teaching time bomb, because they would be poor role models for children. All male teachers became suspect, and few were drawn to teaching. School districts avoided hiring men who did not possess a clearly masculine demeanor. (Married men with children were preferred.) The Cold War and the accompanying McCarthy anti-Communist scare of the 1950s declared war on liberal ideas and unconventional choices: Homosexuality was seen as a threat to America. "There was a list of about twenty-one things that you could be fired for. The first was to be a card-carrying Communist, and the second was to be a homosexual."[16] Single teachers declared their "healthy" heterosexuality, and gay teachers stayed hidden. During this time, the number of married teachers doubled.

Although gender straightjackets have recently loosened, sex stereotypes, myths, and bigotry against gays continue to restrict and confine both women and men. Men drawn to teaching young children and women seeking leadership roles confront both barriers and social sanctions. Gay and lesbian

A VIEW FROM THE FIELD: MALE TEACHERS

As an elementary school teacher, Kyle Birstler, 25, is unusual: he is one of only five male teachers at Jackson Road Elementary School in Silver Spring, Maryland. But Kyle feels that the fact that he is a male elementary teacher makes a difference to his students.

> In my first year of teaching I was given a class that I've now become quite accustomed to: a class of all or almost all boys, most of them from broken homes with absent father figures. These students can be tough, but sometimes it takes a man's approach, or just the presence, to win them over. Every year, I have had students lose their tough guy images and come talk to me about what is going on in their lives. I chose to teach in this school because it is a Title I school; I knew there were needs that I hoped to be able to meet.

Kyle was drawn to teaching at an early age by the compassion of a concerned teacher.

> I had wanted to be a paleontologist when I was growing up. I wanted to discover dinosaurs and name them after myself. On a first-grade field trip I met a real paleontologist and I told him my dream. He told me my dream was next to impossible. I cried and my first-grade teacher comforted me. Next thing you know, I wanted to teach. I have always wanted to teach younger students but during my student teaching I worked in a phenomenal fifth-grade classroom; I was hooked. I couldn't believe how independent the students could be. It was very fun and I've been teaching fifth grade since.

Though Kyle feels that the challenges he faced as a new teacher had more to do with his inexperience than his gender, he does advise new male teachers to find confidants.

> I'd advise male teachers to find mentors of their own, a professor or a male teacher in their building. They'll want a buddy to talk to and bounce ideas off of, and sometimes it's nice to get away. I know the things I learned in my first week of being in the classroom far outweighed anything I learned in the university setting. I was one of three men in my program and it (the issue of men as early childhood educators) simply didn't come up. In general, I think you cannot learn enough about classroom management and the social and emotional issues that impact your students. It's the hardest, most exciting job I can think of.

Kyle Birstler graduated from American University in Washington, D.C.

---

teachers (and students) frequently endure hurtful comments and discriminatory treatment. As long as these gender and sexual barriers persist, we are all the poorer. (See Contemporary Issues: A View from the Field.)

The Secondary School Movement

With Mann's success in promoting public elementary schools, more and more citizens were given a basic education. In 1880, almost 10 million Americans were enrolled in elementary schools, and, at the upper levels of schooling, both private and public universities were established. But the gap between the elementary schools and the universities remained wide.

Massachusetts, the site of the first tax-supported elementary schools and the first college in America, was the site of the first free secondary school. Established in Boston in 1821, the **English Classical School** enrolled 176 students (all boys); shortly thereafter, 76 students dropped out. The notion of a public high school was slow to take root. It was not until 1852 that Boston was able to maintain a similar school for girls. The name of the boys' school was changed to The English High School and, even more simply, Boys' High School, to emphasize the more practical nature of the curriculum.

As secondary schools spread, they generally took the form of private, tuition-charging academies. Citizens did not view the secondary schools as

Focus Question 5
How did secondary schools evolve?

we do today, as a free and natural extension of elementary education.[17] On the eve of the Civil War, more than a quarter of a million secondary students were enrolled in six thousand tuition-charging private academies. The curricula of these academies varied widely, some focusing on college preparation and others providing a general curriculum for students who would not continue their studies. For those wanting to attend college, these academies were a critical link. In academies founded for females or in coeducational academies, "normal" courses were often popular. The normal course prepared academy graduates for teaching careers in the common schools. A few academies provided military programs of study.

A major stumbling block to the creation of free high schools was public resistance to paying additional school taxes (sound familiar?). But, in a series of court cases, especially the **Kalamazoo Michigan case** in 1874, the courts ruled that taxes could be used to support secondary schools. In Michigan, citizens already had access to free elementary schools and a state-supported university. The courts saw a lack of rationality in not providing a bridge between the two. The idea of public high school slowly took hold.

During the last half of the nineteenth century, the nation moved from agrarian to industrial, from mostly rural to urban, and people viewed the elementary school as inadequate to meet the needs of a more sophisticated and industrialized society. More parents viewed the high school as an important stepping-stone to better jobs. With the gradual decrease in demand for teenage workers, high school attendance grew. Half a century earlier, the public elementary school had reflected the growing dreams and aspirations of Americans and their changing economy. Now the public high school was the benchmark of these changes.

Although the high school grew in popularity, it did not meet the needs of all its students, especially the younger ones. The junior high school, first established in 1909 in Columbus, Ohio, included grades 7, 8, and 9 and was designed to meet the unique needs of preadolescents. More individualized instruction, a strong emphasis on guidance and counseling, and a core curriculum were designed to respond to the academic, physiological, social, and psychological characteristics of preadolescents. The junior high school concept was further refined in the middle school, which included grades 5–8. Created in 1950, the middle school was built on the experiences of the junior high school, while stressing team teaching and interdisciplinary learning, de-emphasizing the senior high school's heavy emphasis on both subject matter mastery and competitive sports. Middle schools continue to replace junior high schools, but the academic effectiveness of both types of schools is often questioned.[18] (See Chapter 4 for an in-depth discussion of middle schools)

John Dewey and Progressive Education

Focus Question 6
What were the main tenets of the Progressive Education movement?

John Dewey was possibly the most influential educator of the twentieth century—and one of the most controversial. Some saw him as a savior of U.S. schools; others accused him of nearly destroying them. Rather than become engrossed in the heated controversy surrounding Dewey, however, let us look at progressivism, the movement with which he is closely associated, and later in this text, explore the philosophy behind progressivism.

THE DEVELOPMENT OF AMERICAN SCHOOLS

ELEMENTARY SCHOOLS

Dame schools (1600s) These private schools taught by women in their homes offered child care for working parents willing to pay a fee. The dames who taught here received meager wages, and the quality of instruction varied greatly.

Local schools (1600s–1800s) First started in towns and later expanded to include larger districts, these schools were open to those who could afford to pay. Found generally in New England, these schools taught basic skills and religion.

Itinerant schools (1700s) and tutors (1600s–1900s) Rural America could not support schools and full-time teachers. As a result, in sparsely populated New England, itinerant teachers carried schooling from village to village; they lived in people's homes and provided instruction. In the South, private tutors taught the rich. Traveling teachers and tutors, usually working for a fee and room and board, took varying levels of education to small towns and wealthy populations.

Private schools (1700s–1800s) Private schools, often located in the middle colonies, offered a variety of special studies. These schools constituted a true free market, as parents paid for the kind of private school they desired. As you might imagine, both the curricula and the quality of these schools varied greatly.

Common schools (1830–present) The common school was a radical departure from earlier ones in several ways. First, it was free. Parents did not have to pay tuition or fees. Second, it was open to all social classes. Previously, schools usually taught either middle-class or upper-class children. Horace Mann's common school was intended to bring democracy to the classroom. By the mid-nineteenth century, kindergarten was added. In the past few decades, many common schools, now called elementary schools, have added Head Start and other prekindergarten programs.

SECONDARY SCHOOLS

Latin grammar schools (1600s–1700s) These schools prepared wealthy men for college and emphasized a classical curriculum, including Latin and some Greek. From European roots, the curriculum in these schools reflected the belief that the pinnacle of civilization was reached in the Roman Empire.

English grammar schools (1700s) These private schools moved away from the classical Latin tradition to more practical studies. These schools were viewed not as preparation for college but as preparation for business careers and as a means of instilling social graces. Some of these schools set a precedent by admitting white girls, thus paving the way for the widespread acceptance of females in other schools.

Academies (1700s–1800s) The academies were a combination of the Latin and English grammar schools. These schools taught English, not Latin. Practical courses were taught, but history and the classics were also included. Some academies emphasized college preparation, while others prepared students to enter business and vocations.

High schools (1800s–present) These secondary schools differed from their predecessors in that they were free; they were governed not by private boards but by the public. The high school can be viewed as an extension of the common school movement to the secondary level. High schools were open to all social classes and provided both precollege and career education.

Junior high schools (1909–present) and middle schools (1950s–present) Junior high schools (grades 7–9) and middle schools (grades 5–8) were designed to meet the unique needs of preadolescents and to prepare them for the high school experience.

REFLECTION: If you were responsible for creating a new school based on contemporary needs, what kind of school would you create?

As early as 1875, Francis Parker, superintendent of schools in Quincy, Massachusetts, introduced the concepts of progressivism in his schools, and by 1896, John Dewey had established his famous laboratory school at the University of Chicago. But it was not until the 1920s and 1930s that the progressive education movement became more widely known. During the 1920s and 1930s, the Dalton and Walden schools in New York, the Beaver Country Day School in Massachusetts, the Oak Lane Country Day School in Pennsylvania, and laboratory schools at Columbia and Ohio State universities began to challenge

Classroom Observation

John Dewey believed in learning by doing, one of the key-stones of progressive education. In this observation you will observe students in an American civics class learning about the law by role-playing different legal cases. In this instance, the students are arguing the pledge of allegiance case.

Classroom Observation videos are available on the CD Reader and at Online Learning Center.

www.mhhe.com/
        sadkerbrief3e

traditional practices. The progressive education approach soon spread to suburban and city public school systems across the country. Various school systems adapted or modified progressive education, but certain basic features remained constant, and elements of progressive education can still be found in many schools.

Progressive education included several components. First, it broadened the school program to include health concerns, family and community life issues, and a concern for vocational education. Second, progressivism applied new research in psychology and the social sciences to classroom practices. Third, progressivism emphasized a more democratic educational approach, accepting the interests and needs of an increasingly diverse student body.

This model of education assumed that students learn best when their learning follows their interests. Progressivists believe that knowledge is not an inert body of facts to be committed to memory; rather, it consists of experiences that should be used to help solve present problems. Passively listening to the teacher, according to the progressive movement, is not the most effective learning strategy. Students' interests should serve as a springboard to understanding and mastering contemporary issues. The role of the teacher is to identify student needs and interests and provide an educational environment that builds on them. In fact, progressive education shares some characteristics with problem-based and authentic learning, popular innovations in some of today's schools.

Although not involved in all the progressive education programs, John Dewey, in many minds, is the personification of progressive education, as well as its most notable advocate. In no small part, this is due to the tens of thousands of pages that Dewey wrote during his long life. (Dewey was born on the eve of the Civil War in 1859 and died during the Korean War in the early 1950s.) Toward the end of Dewey's life, both he and progressive education came under strong attack.

The criticism of Dewey and progressive education originated with far-right political groups, for it was the era of Senator Joseph McCarthy and his extremist campaign against communism. Although McCarthy's hunt for communists was primarily directed at the government and the military, educators were not immune. Some viewed progressive education as an atheistic, un-American force that had all but destroyed the nation's schools. Because students were allowed to explore and question, many critics were able to cite examples of how traditional values were not being taught. Although these critics were generally ignorant of Dewey's ideas and progressive practices, a second group was more responsible in its critique.

This second wave of criticism came not from the radical right but from individuals who felt that the school curriculum was not academically sound. Hyman Rickover, a famous admiral and developer of the nuclear submarine, and Arthur Bestor, a liberal arts professor, were among the foremost critics decrying the ills of progressive education. They called for an end to "student-centered" and "life-adjustment" subjects and a return to a more rigorous study of traditional courses. While the arguments raged, the launching of *Sputnik* by the Soviet Union in 1957 put at least a temporary closure on the debate. The United States was involved in a space race with the Soviets, a race to educate scientists and engineers, a race toward the first moon landing. Those arguing for a more rigorous, science- and math-focused curriculum won the day. Although many still argued vociferously over the benefits and shortcomings of progressive education, traditionalists were setting the direction for the nation's curriculum.

Before leaving progressive education, however, it will be beneficial to examine one of the most famous studies of the progressive movement. The Progressive Education Association, formed in 1919, initiated a study during the 1930s that compared almost 3,000 graduates of progressive and of traditional schools as they made their way through college. The study, called the Eight-Year Study, was intended to determine which educational approach was more effective. The results indicated that graduates of progressive schools:

1. Earned a slightly higher grade point average
2. Earned higher grades in all fields except foreign languages
3. Tended to specialize in the same fields as more traditional students
4. Received slightly more academic honors
5. Were judged to be more objective and more precise thinkers
6. Were judged to possess higher intellectual curiosity and greater drive

The Federal Government

As World War II drew to a close, the United States found itself the most powerful nation on earth. For the remainder of the twentieth century, the United States reconstructed a war-ravaged global economy while confronting world communism. In fact, the United States viewed education as an important tool in accomplishing these strategic goals. When the Soviets launched *Sputnik,* for example, the government enlisted the nation's schools in meeting this new challenge. Consequently, Congress passed the **National Defense Education Act (NDEA)** in 1958 to enhance "the security of the nation" and to develop "the mental resources and technical skills of its young men and

Focus Question 7

What role has the federal government played in American education?

women." The NDEA supported the improvement of instruction and curriculum development, funded teacher training programs, and provided loans and scholarships for college students that allowed them to major in subjects deemed important to the national defense (such as teaching). However, looking back in history, it is not at all clear how the federal government was legally able to do this. After all, the framers of the Constitution made their intentions clear: Education was to be a state responsibility, and the federal government was not to be involved. How did the NDEA and other federal acts come to pass?

Many people are unaware that the responsibility for educating Americans is not even mentioned in the Constitution. Under the **Tenth Amendment,** any area not specifically stated in the Constitution as a federal responsibility is automatically assigned to the states. Why was education a nontopic? Some historians believe that, because the individual colonies had already established disparate educational systems, the framers of the Constitution did not want to create dissension by forcing the states to accept a single educational system. Other analysts believe that education was deliberately omitted from the Constitution because Americans feared control of the schools by a central government, any central government, as had been the case in Europe. They saw central control as a possible threat to their freedom. Still others suggest that the framers of the Constitution, in their haste, bartering, and bickering, simply forgot about education (what a depressing thought!). Whatever the reason, distinct colonial practices continued, as each state created its own educational structure—its own approach for preparing teachers and funding schools.

Over time, however, the federal government discovered ways to influence education. As early as the revolutionary period, the new nation passed the **Land Ordinance Act** of 1785 and the **Northwest Ordinance** of 1787. These acts required townships in the newly settled territories bounded by the Ohio and Mississippi Rivers and the Great Lakes to reserve a section of land for educational purposes. The ordinances contained a much-quoted sentence underscoring the new nation's faith in education: "Religion, morality, and knowledge being necessary to good government and the happiness of mankind, schools and the means of education shall forever be encouraged."

The federal government also exerted its influence through targeted funding, or categorical grants. By using federal dollars for specific programs, the government was able to create new colleges and universities, to promote agricultural and industrial research efforts, and to provide schools for Native Americans and other groups. During the Great Depression of the 1930s, the federal government became even more directly involved with education, constructing schools, providing free lunches for poor children, instituting part-time work programs for high school and college students, and offering educational programs to older Americans. With unemployment, hunger, and desperation rampant in the 1930s, states welcomed these federal efforts. More and more Americans were coming to realize that some educational challenges were beyond the resources of the states. But federal involvement in education was sometimes resisted by states and local communities. In the case of African American education, it took nearly a century for the federal government to move forcefully to end racial segregation. And then, a few decades later, most students found themselves once again racially segregated.

Black Americans: The Struggle for a Chance to Learn

Much of the history of African American education in the United States has been one of denial. The first law prohibiting education of slaves was passed in South Carolina in 1740. During the next hundred years, many states passed similar and even stronger compulsory-ignorance laws. For example, an 1823 Mississippi law prohibited six or more Negroes from gathering for educational purposes. In Louisiana, an 1830 law imposed a prison sentence on anyone caught teaching a slave to read or write. However, because education has always been integral to African Americans' struggle for equal opportunity, they risked the penalties of these laws and even the dangers of violence for a chance to learn. They formed clandestine schools throughout most large cities and towns of the South. Suzie King Taylor described what it was like to attend one of those secret schools in Savannah, Georgia:

> We went every day about nine o'clock with our books wrapped in paper to prevent the police or white persons from seeing them. We went in, one at a time, through the gate, into the yard to the L Kitchen which was the schoolroom.[19]

The Civil War brought an end to policies of compulsory ignorance and an affirmation of black people's belief in the power of education. Most of the schooling of African Americans immediately following the Civil War was carried out by philanthropic societies. These associations worked with the Freedmen's Bureau, a federal agency established to provide various services, including the establishment of schools. School staffs were usually a mixture of instructors from the North, blacks of Caribbean island heritage, and formerly enslaved literate blacks.

Many white Southerners responded to the education of blacks with fear and anger. Sometimes there was terrorism against black schools. State after state passed laws that explicitly provided for segregated schools. With the 1896 **Plessy v. Ferguson** Supreme Court decision, segregation became a legally sanctioned part of the American way of life. In this landmark case, the Court developed the doctrine of **separate but equal.** Separate but equal initially legalized separate railway passenger cars for black and white Americans, and was also used to justify a legally segregated school system, which in many states lasted for more than half a century.

"Separate but equal" was not equal. In 1907, Mississippi spent $5.02 for the education of each white child but only $1.10 for each black child. In 1924, the state paid more than $1 million to transport whites long distances to schools. No money was spent for blacks, and for them a daily walk of more than 12 miles was not out of the question. Attending schools without enough books, seats, space, equipment, or facilities taught African American children the harsh reality of "separate but unequal." In the South, a dual school system based on race was in existence. This was **de jure segregation**—that is, segregation by law or by official action.

In the North, school assignments were based on both race and residence. **De facto (unofficial) segregation** occurred as the result of segregated residential patterns, patterns that were often prompted by discriminatory real estate practices. As housing patterns changed, attendance zones were often redrawn to ensure the separation of white and black children in schools. Even in schools that were not entirely segregated, black children were routinely placed in

Focus Question 8
How did history shape the educational experiences of African Americans, Hispanics, Asian Americans/Pacific Islanders, and Arab Americans?

Scenes like this one became commonplace all across America in the years following the landmark *Brown v. Board of Education of Topeka* decision in 1954 and the passage of the Civil Rights Act in 1964.

special classes or separate academic tracks, counseled into low-status careers, and barred from extracurricular activities. Whatever the obstacle, however, African Americans continued their struggle for access to quality education. As W. E. B. DuBois noted: "Probably never in the world have so many oppressed people tried in every possible way to educate themselves."[20]

Political momentum for civil rights reform grew with the participation of African Americans in World War II and the 1954 Supreme Court decision that schools must desegregate "with all deliberate speed." In **Brown v. Board of Education of Topeka** (Kansas), the court ruled unanimously that "in the field of public education the doctrine of 'separate but equal' has no place. Separate educational facilities are inherently unequal." Yet a decade after Brown, almost 91 percent of all African American children in the South still attended all-black schools.

In 1964, President Johnson and Congress moved boldly to eradicate racial segregation. The Civil Rights Act gave the federal government power to help local school districts desegregate (Title IV), and when necessary, to initiate lawsuits or withhold federal school funds to force desegregation (Title VI). The Civil Rights Act produced more desegregation in the next four years than the Supreme Court's Brown decision had in the preceding decade. All branches of the federal government now moved in concert to desegregate the nation's schools.

During the late 1960s and early 1970s, the Supreme Court also attacked de facto segregation stemming from racially imbalanced neighborhoods. Courts supported busing, racial quotas, and school pairing to eradicate school segregation in both the North and the South. But opposition to these measures grew, and school districts began to experiment with magnet schools, choice plans, and voluntary metropolitan desegregation, remedies more acceptable to many school families.

Even as some schools became more racially balanced, a new barrier to equality appeared. In the same school building, black students and white students found themselves separated by tracking, treated differently by teachers and administrators, and even gravitating to different areas of the school.[21] This within-school segregation was termed **second-generation segregation.** In the 1960s, the Kerner Commission warned: "Our nation is moving toward two societies, one black, and one white—separate and unequal." The commission charged that white society must assume responsibility for the black ghetto. "White institutions created it, white institutions maintain it, and white society condones it."[22]

But the Kerner Commission's warning was not heeded. As the century drew to a close, affirmative efforts such as busing were abandoned, and in the Hopwood (1996) and the University of Michigan decisions (2003), firm racial set-asides for college and law school admissions were eliminated. Although the courts said that race could be a factor in promoting student diversity, it could not be a major factor. In a 2007 ruling, the Supreme Court further backed away from desegregation efforts by striking down plans in Seattle and Louisville that used race to assign K-12 students to public schools.[23]

The consequences of these actions are now evident in the nation's schools, as residential patterns and the diminished legal pressures have resegregated the nation's schools. Today's students are more segregated than they were four decades ago, with white students experiencing the most segregated educational environment.[24] Should desegregation still be a goal? Has its time passed? Some believe that even the idea that African American or Latino children can learn effectively only when they sit next to a white student is demeaning. Others see segregation as a way to protect African American and Latino cultures.

Researcher Gary Orfield of the UCLA Civil Rights Project does not agree. His research suggests that students who attend integrated schools are more comfortable with peers from diverse racial, cultural, and socioeconomic backgrounds and more understanding of different points of view. As schools resegregate, these benefits are lost. Others argue that racial isolation puts minority children in poorer schools with less experienced teachers, weaker precollegiate courses, and lower achievement and graduation rates.[25] As one advocate for desegregation decried, "[African Americans] who favor resegregation are doing whites the great favor of relieving both their guilty conscience and their pocketbooks."[26]

Hispanics: Growing School Impact

More than 45 million Hispanics live in the United States, including Puerto Rico, up more than 75 percent since 1980. Most Hispanics living in the United States are U.S. citizens and constitute 16 percent of the nation's population, the largest minority group in the nation.[27] Because many Latinos immigrate to the United States to escape economic and political repression, they do not all enter the country legally. Consequently, their numbers may be underestimated. Ongoing legal and illegal immigration, together with high birth rates for young families in their childbearing years, have made Hispanics the youngest and fastest-growing school-age population in the United States. By 2050, Hispanic children will represent more than half of all students.[28] Latino children confront numerous educational barriers. As early as kindergarten, Hispanic students are less able than their white peers to identify colors, recognize letters, count to 50, or write their first name. Approximately half of Hispanics drop out of school.[29]

Hispanics consist of several subgroups, which share some characteristics, such as language, but differ in others, such as race, location, age, income, and educational attainment. The three largest Hispanic subgroups are Mexican Americans, Puerto Ricans, and Cuban Americans. There is also significant representation from other Latin American and Caribbean countries, such as the Dominican Republic, El Salvador, Nicaragua, and Honduras, (see Figure 5.1). In contrast to these new immigrants, many from war-torn or poverty-stricken countries, there is also an "old" population of Mexican and Spanish descent living in the Southwest with a longer history on this continent than those who trace their ancestors to the New England colonies. Let's briefly look at some of the groups that compose the Hispanic community.

PROFILE IN EDUCATION:

Marian Wright Edelman

Marian Wright Edelman is a voice for children. With views shaped by parents devoted to service and an upbringing in the segregated South, Edelman founded the Children's Defense Fund (CDF) in 1973 to ensure that every child has a Healthy Start, a Head Start, a Fair Start, a Safe Start, and a Moral Start in life. To read a full profile of Marian Wright Edelman, go to the Chapter 5 Profile in Education at www.mhhe.com/sadkerbrief3e.

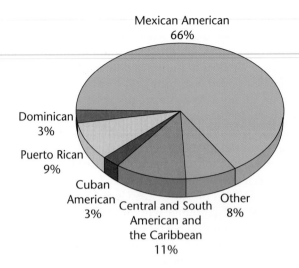

Mexican American 66%
Dominican 3%
Puerto Rican 9%
Cuban American 3%
Central and South American and the Caribbean 11%
Other 8%

U.S. HISPANIC SUBGROUPS

Mexican Americans

At the end of the United States' war with Mexico (1846–1848), the Mexicans who decided to stay in the new U.S. territories were guaranteed full citizenship. By 1900, approximately 200,000 Mexican Americans were living in the Southwest, having built the cities of Los Angeles, San Diego, Tucson, Albuquerque, Dallas, and San Antonio. The devices that were used to deny educational opportunity to Mexican Americans were similar to those imposed on African Americans. By 1920, a pattern of separate and unequal Mexican American schools had emerged throughout the Southwest.

Then, as now, significant numbers of Mexican American families migrated once or twice a year, exploited as a source of cheap labor in rural, agricultural communities. With constant transitions, children's learning suffered. One superintendent in Texas, reflecting deeply engrained prejudice, argued that education was actually dangerous for Mexican Americans:

Most of our Mexicans are of the lower class. They transplant onions, harvest them, etc. The less they know about everything else, the better contented they are . . . so you see it is up to the white population to keep the Mexican on his knees in an onion patch. . . . This does not mix well with education.[30]

In the late 1960s, Cesar Chavez led the fight of migrant Mexican American laborers to organize themselves into a union and to demand a more responsive education that included culture-free IQ tests, instruction in Spanish, smaller classes, and greater cultural representation in the curriculum.

Today, more than one in four public schools enroll migrant students, mostly Mexican Americans. The greatest numbers are in California, Illinois, Texas, and Arizona.[31]

Puerto Ricans

During the nineteenth century, many of the Puerto Ricans in the United States were highly respected political exiles striving for the independence of their homeland. But all that changed in 1898, when Puerto Rico was acquired from Spain and became a territory of the United States. Citizenship, through the Jones Act in 1917, provided free movement between the continent and the island. Migration to the mainland peaked during the 1950s, with the majority of Puerto Ricans settling in New York City. Currently, about half the Puerto Rican population lives within the 50 states, and the other half lives in Puerto Rico.[32] The frequent passage between the island and the United States, as families search for a better economic life, makes schooling all the more difficult for Puerto Rican children.

Cuban Americans

Following the Castro-led revolution in the 1950s, Cuban immigration to the United States increased significantly. During the 1960s, Cubans who settled in the United States were primarily well-educated, professional, and middle- and upper-class. By 1980, 800,000 Cubans—10 percent of the population of Cuba—were living in the United States. For the most part, Cubans settled in Miami and other locations in southern Florida, but there are also sizable populations in New York, Philadelphia, Chicago, Milwaukee, and Indianapolis. Cubans, considered one of the most highly educated people in American immigration history, tend to be more prosperous and more conservative than most of the other Latino groups.[33] In the second immigration wave, during the 1980s, there were many more black and poor Cubans, who have not been accepted as readily into communities in the United States.

Asian Americans and Pacific Islanders: The Magnitude of Diversity

The term "Asian Americans and Pacific Islanders" embraces peoples from nations as diverse as India, Vietnam, China, Pakistan, Korea, Samoa, and Japan, and Native Hawaiians, about half the world's population. More than 15 million Americans have roots in Asia, although demographers predict that this figure will increase severalfold by the year 2050.[34] As a group these Americans have attained a high degree of educational and economic success. This section describes the differing experiences of four of the largest Asian immigrant groups—Chinese, Filipinos, Asian Indians, and Japanese—as well as problems faced by refugees from Southeast Asia.[35]

Many of these cultures hold education in high esteem, and well-mannered, respectful, and studious Asian American students have earned themselves the moniker of *model minority*. In kindergarten, Asian American children consistently outscore their peers in both reading and math.[36] More than 50 percent of Asian American/Pacific Islanders graduate from college. One year after graduation, they have a higher starting salary than any racial or ethnic group.[37] However, diversity within the Asian community is often overlooked, and as with many stereotypes, misconceptions abound. Fewer than half of Vietnamese and Samoan Americans graduate from high school, and Asian New Wavers reflect the current countercultural pattern, with baggy pants, combat boots, and dyed hair, challenging the model minority stereotype.[38]

Chinese Americans

When the Chinese first began immigrating to the West Coast in the 1850s, they were mostly young, unmarried men who left China, a country ravaged by famine and political turmoil, to seek their fortune in the "Golden Mountains" across the Pacific and then take their wealth back to their homeland. The California gold mines were largely depleted by the time they arrived, and after the completion of the transcontinental railroad signaled a loss of jobs for Chinese laborers, many found that the hope of taking fortunes home to their families in China was an impossible dream.

By 1880, approximately 106,000 Chinese had immigrated to the United States, fueling a vicious reaction: "The Chinese must go." With the passage of the Immigration Act of 1882, along with a series of similar bills, further Chinese immigration was blocked. The Chinese already in this country responded to increasing physical violence by moving eastward and consolidating into ghettos called Chinatowns. Inhabited largely by male immigrants, these ghettos offered a grim and sometimes violent lifestyle, one with widespread prostitution and gambling. Chinatowns, vestiges of century-old ghettos, can still be found in many of America's cities.

In 1949, the institution of a Communist government in mainland China caused Congress to reverse more than a century of immigration quotas, naturalization, and antimiscegenation laws and grant refugee status to 5,000 highly educated Chinese in the United States. Despite facing active prejudice and discrimination, Chinese Americans today have achieved a higher median income and educational level than that of white Americans.

Filipino Americans

After the 1898 Spanish-American War, the United States acquired the Philippines. Filipinos, viewed as low-cost labor, were recruited to work in the fields of Hawaii and the U.S. mainland. Thousands left the poverty of their islands to seek economic security.

With a scarcity of women (in 1930, the male–female ratio was 143 to 1) and the mobility of their work on farms and as fieldhands, the Filipinos had difficulty establishing cohesive communities. Like other Asian immigrants, they came with the goal of taking their earnings back to their homeland; like other Asian immigrants, most found this an impossible dream.

Because of their unique legal status (the United States had annexed the Philippines in 1898), Filipinos were not excluded as aliens under the Immigration Act of 1924. However, the Tydings-McDuffie Act of 1934 was a victory for those who wanted the Filipinos excluded from the United States. Promising independence to the Philippines, this act limited immigration to the United States to 50 Filipinos per year.

All that changed in 1965, when a new immigration act allowed a significant increase in Filipino immigration. Between 1970 and 1980, the Filipino population in the United States more than doubled. The earlier presence of the U.S. military in Manila generated an educated elite who spoke English, studied the American school curriculum, and moved to the United States with professional skills, seeking jobs commensurate with their training. Concentrated in urban areas of the West Coast, Filipinos are the second-largest Asian American ethnic group in the United States.

Although often grouped together, Asian Americans and Pacific Islanders reflect great ethnic and cultural diversity.

Asian Indian Americans

Traders from India arrived in New England in the 1880s, bartering silks and spices. Intellectuals Henry David Thoreau, Ralph Waldo Emerson, and E. M. Forester (*Passage to India*) gravitated to the culture, religion, and philosophy of the Eastern purveyors. On the West Coast, Indians from Punjab migrated to escape British exploitation, which had forced farmers to raise commercial rather than food crops. With farming conditions in California similar to those in India, Punjabees became successful growers and landowners. They were destined to lose their lands, however, and even their leasing rights, under the California Alien Land Law, which recalled the ownership of land held by Indians and Japanese.

In addition to legal restrictions, Indian laborers were attacked by racist mobs in Bellingham, Washington, in 1907, triggering other riots and expulsions throughout the Pacific region. U.S. government support for British colonial rule in India became the rationale to further restrict Indian immigration. It was not until 1946 that a law allowing Indian naturalization and immigration was passed. During the past three decades, tens of thousands of Indians have arrived in America. Most Indians are extremely well educated, and many are professionals. Their educational and income levels are the highest of any group in the United States, including other Asians.[39]

Japanese Americans

Only when the Japanese government legalized emigration in 1886 did the Japanese come to the United States in significant numbers. For example, in 1870, records show only 50 Japanese in the United States, but by 1920, the number had increased to more than 110,000.

With the immigration of the Chinese halted by various exclusion acts, Japanese immigrants filled the need for cheap labor. Like the Chinese, the early Japanese immigrants were males who hoped to return to their homeland with fortunes they earned in the United States. For most, this remained an unfulfilled dream. Praised for their willingness to work when they first arrived in California, the Japanese began to make other farmers nervous with their great success in agriculture and truck farming. Anti-Japanese feelings became prevalent along the West Coast. Such slogans as "Japs must go" and warnings of a new "yellow peril" were frequent. In 1924, Congress passed an immigration bill that halted Japanese immigration to the United States.

After Japan's attack on Pearl Harbor on December 7, 1941, fear and prejudice about the "threat" from Japanese Americans were rampant. On February 19, 1942, President Franklin Roosevelt issued Executive Order No. 9006, which declared the West Coast a "military area" and established federal "relocation" camps. Approximately 110,000 Japanese, more than two-thirds of whom were U.S. citizens, were removed from their homes in the "military area" and were forced into 10 internment camps in California, Idaho, Utah, Arizona, Wyoming, Colorado, and Arkansas. Located in geographically barren areas, guarded by soldiers and barbed wire, these internment camps made it very difficult for the Japanese people to keep their traditions and cultural heritage alive. Almost half a century later, the U.S. government officially acknowledged this wrong and offered a symbolic payment ($20,000 in reparations) to each victim.

Despite severe discrimination in the past, today's Japanese Americans enjoy both a high median family income and educational attainment. Their success is at least partially due to traditional values, a heritage some fear may be weakened by increasing assimilation.

Southeast Asian Americans

Before 1975, the United States saw only small numbers of immigrants from Southeast Asia, including Vietnam, Laos, and Kampuchea/Cambodia. Their arrival in greater numbers was related directly to the end of the Vietnam War and resulting Communist rule.

The refugees came from all strata of society. Some were wealthy; others were poverty stricken. Some were widely traveled and sophisticated; others were farmers and fishing people who had never before left their small villages. Most came as part of a family, and almost half were under age 18 at the time of their arrival. Refugee camps were established to dispense food, clothing, medical assistance, and temporary housing, as well as to provide an introduction to U.S. culture and to the English language.

By December 1975, the last refugee camp had closed and the U.S. government had resettled large numbers of Southeast Asians across the nation without too high a concentration in any one location. This dispersal was well intentioned but often left the refugees feeling lonely and isolated. In fact, many moved from original areas of settlement to cities where large numbers of Asian Americans were already located.

A second wave of Southeast Asian refugees followed in the years after 1975. Cambodians and Laotians migrated to escape poverty, starvation, and political repression in their homelands. Many tried to escape in small fishing boats not meant for travel across rough ocean seas. Called *boat people* by the press, almost half of them, according to the estimates, died before they reached the shores of the United States.

Similar to war refugees from Latin America, these children brought memories of terrible tragedy to school. For example, a teacher in San Francisco was playing hangman during a language arts lesson. As the class was laughing and shouting out letters, she was shocked to see one child, a newcomer, in tears. The girl spoke so little English she could not explain the problem. Finally, another child translated. The game had triggered a traumatic memory. In Cambodia, the girl had watched the hanging of her father.[40] Since the fall of Saigon in 1975, more than 1.4 million Southeast Asians have resettled in the United States. Their struggle to find a place in this society remains conflicted as most Americans associate Vietnam with war.

www.mhhe.com/
sadkerbrief3e
INTERACTIVE ACTIVITY
Multicultural Literacy.
Match multicultural terms
with their descriptions.

Arab Americans: Moving Beyond the Stereotype

Misunderstanding and intolerance have been all-too-common facts of life for the more than 3 million Americans of Arab descent. Arab Americans' quality of life is often influenced by events taking place in other parts of the world. The Iraq Wars, assaults on the terrorist camps in Taliban-ruled Afghanistan, the September 11, 2001, attacks on the World Trade Center and the Pentagon, and the continuing conflict between Israelis and Palestinians create tension and anxiety for Americans of Arab descent. While these news events are troubling enough, media portrayals can exacerbate the problem. Books and movies depict a strange melange of offensive Arab caricatures: greedy billionaires, corrupt sheiks, immoral terrorists, suave oil cartel magnates, and even romantic, if ignorant, camel-riding Bedouins. Nor are children's books immune from such characterizations. Caroline Cooney's *The Terrorist,* a popular book for children in grades 5 through 10, is the fictional tale of an American teenager who tries to find the Arab terrorist responsible for her younger brother's death. It is not surprising that polls taken as far back as the 1980s reveal that most Americans perceive Arabs as anti-American, warlike, anti-Christian, and cunning. Such beliefs seem entrenched: In 2010, less than half of all Americans expressed a favorable view of Arabs.[41] The challenge to educators could not be clearer. Students and teachers need to learn about Arab Americans, as well as the Arab world.

The first wave of Arab immigrants, mostly from Syria and Lebanon, came to America at the end of the nineteenth century for the same reasons that have driven so many immigrants: political freedom and economic opportunity. Toledo, Ohio, Detroit, Michigan, and New York became important centers of Arab immigration, and business became the economic mainstay of this first wave. Other waves of immigration followed, one just after World War II, and the third as a result of the Palestinian–Israeli conflict. Arabs continue to arrive from over a score of countries in northern Africa and southwestern Asian. Although Arab Americans live in all 50 states, they typically settle in major U.S. urban centers such as New York, Los Angeles, Chicago, Detroit, and Washington, DC (see Figure 5.2).

Many Americans confuse Arabs and Muslims, mistaking Islam, a religion, with Arabs, a cultural group. While Islam is the predominant religion of the Middle East, and most Arabs living there are Muslims, there are also millions of Christian Arabs (as well as those who are Jewish or Druze). In the

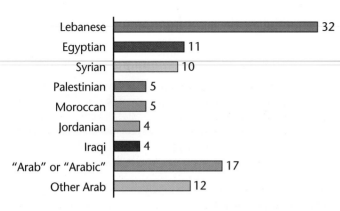

FIGURE 5.2
Arab Americans by ancestry.

Note: "Other Arab" includes Yemeni, Kurdish, Algerian, Saudi, Tunisian, Kuwaiti, Libyan, Berber, Emirati (United Arab Emirates), Omani, Bahraini, Alhuceman, Bedouin, Rio de Oro, and the general terms Middle Eastern and North African.

SOURCE: Arab American Institute, Demographics 2010, available at www.aaiusa.org.

REFLECTION: As a teacher, what steps can you take to help your students appreciate the diversity obscured by broad labels such as "Arab American"?

United States, the vast majority of the 3 million Arab Americans are Christian. And, in contrast, the majority of America's 8 million Muslims are not Arab. While Arabs practice different religions, they do share the same language and culture, a culture that is at times in conflict with Western values.[42]

Such differences can create friction in and beyond school. For example, Arabs enjoy close social proximity, and members of the same sex often walk arm-in-arm or hold hands, behaviors at odds with American practice. Features of the Arabic language, including loudness and intonation, may be perceived in America as too loud, and even rude. Although punctuality is considered a courtesy in the United States, being late is not considered a sign of disrespect in Arab culture. In addition to these cultural disconnects, more profound differences emerge, such as the disparity between the role of women in Arab society and the role of women in Western society. Many Arab nations cast women in an inferior position, denying them education, inheritance, and power. Saudi Arabia, for example, still forbids women to drive, prohibits co-education, and requires that women wear veils in public. Arranged marriages and polygamy are practiced in several Arab nations. While the birth of a son is celebrated in conventional Arab families, the birth of a daughter may be met with silence.[43] Yet, change is also sweeping part of the Arab world. Several Arab states have opened schools and the workplace to women, with dramatic results.

Today, students of Arab heritage can be found in all 50 states, and as a group, do well in American schools. The proportion of Arab Americans who graduate from high school and who attend college is higher than the national average, and Arab Americans earn postgraduate degrees at a rate nearly double the national average.[44] Yet they still face challenges. They learn from textbooks that have little if anything to say about their history or experiences. American teachers lack basic information about Arab culture, which may present problems. For example, a traditional Arab student may be troubled or confused in an American school where women can be both teachers and principals. In a similar way, an American teacher who criticizes an Arab student in public may have unintentionally erected a wall of hard feelings. Arabs put a lot of emphasis on personal and family honor, and public ridicule is a serious matter.

If the Arab student happens to be of the Muslim faith, additional issues emerge. Muslims discover that while schools typically celebrate Christmas, they ignore Muslim holidays. For instance, during Ramadan, Muslims fast for a month during daylight hours, yet few schools recognize this observance, much less make provision for it. In terms of dietary restrictions, school cafeterias serve, but do not always label, pork products, a food Muslims are prohibited from eating. Clearly, Arab and Muslim American students are all but invisible in the official and hidden curriculum of most American schools. Teacher training, curricular revision, and a greater understanding of these cultural and religious issues are needed if equal educational opportunities are to become a reality for these Americans.

ELUSIVE HISTORY

Napoleon said that history is a myth that we agree to believe; Henry Ford thought history was "bunk"; Mark Twain was even more cynical, characterizing the very ink used to write history as "fluid prejudice." History always has a bias because only one side writes it, and more often than not, it is the side of power. Let's take the Civil War as an example. Most of us were taught that the Civil War was fought over states' rights, or slavery, or two colliding economic systems. (Which one were you taught?) But in *A People's History of the Civil War* (2005) by David Williams, we learn a very different story, a story of greed and class warfare. Poor southern farmers and northern factory workers were exploited and drafted to fight and often died in a war many opposed. Wealthy southerners and northerners were protected from the bloodshed by law, but used the war as an opportunity to grow their fortunes. Northern factory owners gladly bought southern cotton to make uniforms, because trading with the enemy to make a profit was fine for both sides. But profits did not mean quality products. In fact, the word "shoddy" comes from the Civil War. Back then, shoddy was a grade of cotton, the lowest quality cotton. When used to make uniforms, the uniforms would quickly disintegrate. It wasn't long before "shoddy" was applied to the poor quality of most things sold to the governments, north and south.

This may not be the Civil War history many of us learned, but Williams provides an abundance of primary source documents to support his findings. When you teach history, as well as some other subjects, you may want to leave your prelearned ideas outside the classroom and start fresh along with your students. Primary sources like original letters, correspondence, eyewitness reports, and print and media accounts will likely offer a more complete and accurate perspective than a single textbook version. (Even this one!)

REFLECTION: What are the advantages of working with primary sources to help students reach their own insights? What are the downsides of this kind of learning?

Women and Education: A History of Sexism

Focus Question 9
What educational barriers and breakthroughs have girls and women experienced?

The peopling of America is a story of voluntary immigration and forced migration. The story of women's struggle for educational opportunity may be just as hard to uncover but equally important to reclaim.

For almost two centuries, girls were barred from America's schools.[45] Although a woman gave the first plot of ground for a free school in New England, female children were not allowed to attend the school. In 1687, the town council of Farmington, Connecticut, voted money for a school "where all children shall learn to read and write English." However, the council quickly qualified this statement by explaining that "all children" meant "all males." In fact, the education of America's girls was so limited that fewer than a third of the women in colonial America could even sign their names. For centuries, women fought to open the schoolhouse door.

In colonial America, secondary schools, called female seminaries, appealed to families financially able to educate their daughters beyond elementary school. **Emma Hart Willard** wrote and disseminated her views on opening higher education to women and won favorable responses from Thomas Jefferson, John Adams, and James Monroe. Eventually, with local support, she opened the Troy Female Seminary, devoted to preparing professional teachers, thus providing a teacher education program years before the first normal (teacher training) school was founded. In Massachusetts, Mary Lyon created Mount Holyoke, a seminary that eventually became a noted women's college. Religious observance was an important part of seminary life in institutions such as Mount Holyoke. Self-denial and strict discipline were

Historically, low teacher salaries can be traced back to the late nineteenth century, when communities found that they could hire capable women teachers for far less than what men teachers were paid.

considered important elements of molding devout wives and Christian mothers. By the 1850s, with help from Quakers such as Harriet Beecher Stowe, Myrtilla Miner established the Miner Normal School for Colored Girls in the nation's capital, providing new educational opportunities for African American women. While these seminaries sometimes offered superior educations, they were also trapped in a paradox they could never fully resolve: They were educating girls for a world not ready to accept educated women. Seminaries sometimes went to extraordinary lengths to reconcile this conflict. Emma Willard's Troy Female Seminary was devoted to "professionalizing motherhood" (and who could not support motherhood?). But, en route to reshaping motherhood, seminaries reshaped teaching.

For the teaching profession, seminaries became the source of new ideas and new recruits. Seminary leaders, such as Emma Hart Willard and Catherine Beecher, wrote textbooks on how to teach and on how to teach more humanely than was the practice at the time. They denounced corporal punishment and promoted more cooperative educational practices. Because school was seen as an extension of the home and another arena for raising children, seminary graduates were allowed to become teachers—at least until they decided to marry. More than 80 percent of the graduates of Troy Female Seminary and Mount Holyoke became teachers. Female teachers were particularly attractive to school districts—not just because of their teaching effectiveness but also because they were typically paid one-third to one-half of the salary paid to male teachers.

By the end of the Civil War, a number of colleges and universities, especially tax-supported ones, were desperate for dollars. Institutions of higher learning experienced a serious student shortage due to Civil War casualties, and women became the source of much-needed tuition dollars.

Female funding did not buy on-campus equality. Women often faced separate courses and hostility from male students and professors. At state universities, male students would stamp their feet in protest when a woman entered a classroom.

In *Sex in Education* (1873), Dr. Edward Clarke, a member of Harvard's medical faculty, argued that women attending high school and college were at risk because the blood destined for the development and health of their ovaries would be redirected to their brains. The stress of study was no laughing matter. Too much education would leave women with "monstrous brains and puny bodies . . . flowing thought and constipated bowels." Clarke recommended that females be provided with a less-demanding education, easier courses, no competition, and "rest" periods, so that their reproductive organs could develop. He maintained that allowing girls to attend such places as Harvard would pose a serious health threat to the women themselves, with sterility and hysteria potential outcomes.

Classroom Observation

4. Author David Sadker Identifies Classroom Bias Through Role Play

David Sadker (coauthor of *Teachers, Schools, and Society*) often works with school administrators and teachers to demonstrate, through a role-play, several issues of bias that can overwhelm a classroom. In this observation, you will see David Sadker give one of these classroom bias workshops.

Classroom Observation Videos are available on the CD Reader and at the Online Learning Center.

www.mhhe.com/
sadkerbrief3e

M. Carey Thomas, future president of Bryn Mawr and one of the first women to earn a Ph.D. in the United States, wrote in her diary about the profound fears she experienced as she was studying: "I remember often praying about it, and begging God that if it were true that because I was a girl, I could not successfully master Greek and go to college, and understand things, to kill me for it."[46] In 1895, the faculty of the University of Virginia concluded that "women were often physically unsexed by the strains of study." Parents, fearing for the health of their daughters, often placed them in less demanding programs reserved for females, or kept them out of advanced education entirely. Even today, the echoes of Clarke's warning resonate, as some people still see well-educated women as less attractive, view advanced education as "too stressful" for females, or believe that education is more important for males than for females.

In the twentieth century, women won greater access to educational programs at all levels, although well into the 1970s gender-segregated programs were the rule. Even when females attended the same schools as males, they often received a less valuable education. Commercial courses prepared girls to become secretaries, and vocational programs channeled them into cosmetology and other low-paying occupations. After World War II, it was not unusual for a university to require a married woman to submit a letter from her husband, granting her permission to enroll in courses, before she would be admitted. By the 1970s, with the passage of Title IX of the Education Amendments of 1972, females saw significant progress toward gaining access to educational programs, but not equality. The opening of Title IX states:

> No person in the United States shall, on the basis of sex, be excluded from participation in, be denied the benefits of, or be subjected to discrimination under any education program or activity receiving federal financial assistance.

Classroom Observation

4. Author David Sadker Identifies Classroom Bias Through Role Play, Continued.

In this observation you will see a discussion that follows David Sadker's role-play. The discussion analyzes both the subtle and not-so-subtle forms of bias that emerged from the role-play in the previous segment.

Classroom Observation Videos are available on the CD Reader and at the Online Learning Center.

www.mhhe.com/
sadkerbrief3e

The law is straightforward, but misperceptions are common. For example, many equate Title IX only with athletics, yet the law prohibits gender discrimination in admissions, treatment of students, counseling, financial aid, employment, and health benefits, to name but a few. Nor is Title IX only about females; males are protected from gender discrimination as well. Ignorance of the law is widespread, one reason why it is so rarely enforced. In fact, in over three decades since Title IX became law, no school has ever been financially penalized by the federal government for violating Title IX.

Unfortunately, sexism still thrives in today's classrooms, affecting attitudes and careers.[47] Nursing, teaching, library science, and social work continue to be predominantly female while engineering, physics, and computer science are male domains. Even in medicine and law, where women have made progress, they find themselves channeled into the least prestigious, least profitable specialties. A "glass wall" still divides the sexes, and some call for the glass wall to become permanent, believing that males and females are so different that the nation should return to single-sex schools, an idea that was popular in colonial America, bringing us full circle in this chapter.

At the beginning of the chapter, we peeked into Christopher Lamb's colonial classroom to watch our school traditions take root. Unfortunately, one such tradition was that education was reserved for some and denied to others. We still struggle to create fair schools. In a sense, today's teachers stand on the shoulders of Christopher Lamb and other educators as each generation makes its own contribution to creating fairer, more effective schools. We have chosen to conclude this chapter with a Hall of Fame, a small tribute to those whose shoulders we stand on.

EDUCATION MILESTONES

SEVENTEENTH CENTURY

Informal family education, apprenticeships, dame schools, tutors

1635	Boston Latin Grammar School
1636	Harvard College
1647	Old Deluder Satan Law
1687–1890	*New England Primer* published

EIGHTEENTH CENTURY

Development of a national interest in education, state responsibility for education, growth in secondary education

1740	South Carolina denies education to blacks.
1751	Franklin Academy in Philadelphia opens.
1783	Noah Webster's *American Spelling Book*
1785, 1787	Land Ordinance Act, Northwest Ordinance

NINETEENTH CENTURY

Increasing role of public secondary schools, increased but segregated education for women and minorities, attention to teacher preparation

1821	Emma Willard's Troy Female Seminary opens.
1821	First public high school opens in Boston.
1823	First (private) normal school opens in Vermont.
1827	Massachusetts requires public high schools.
1837	Horace Mann becomes secretary of board of education in Massachusetts.
1839	First public normal school in Lexington, Massachusetts
1855	First kindergarten (German language) in United States
1862	Morrill Land Grant College Act
1874	Kalamazoo case (legalizes taxes for high schools)
1896	*Plessy v. Ferguson* Supreme Court decision supports racially separate but equal schools.

TWENTIETH CENTURY

Increasing federal support for educational rights of under-achieving students; increased federal funding of categorical education programs

1909	First junior high school in Columbus, Ohio
1919	Progressive education programs
1932	New Deal education programs
1944	G.I. Bill of Rights
1950	First middle school in Bay City, Michigan
1954	*Brown v. Board of Education of Topeka* Supreme Court decision outlaws racial segregation in schools.
1957	*Sputnik* leads to increased federal education funds.
1958	National Defense Education Act funds science, math, and foreign language programs.
1964–1965	Job Corps and Head Start are funded.
1972	Title IX prohibits sex discrimination in schools.
1975	Public Law 94-142, Education for All Handicapped Children Act (renamed Individuals with Disabilities Education Act, 1991).
1979	Cabinet-level Department of Education is established.
1990–present	Increased public school diversity and competition through charter schools, for-profit companies, open enrollment, and online options. Educational goals, standards, and testing are promoted.

TWENTY-FIRST CENTURY

2001	Passage of No Child Left Behind Act

SOURCE: Joel Spring, *American Education,* 14th edition (New York: McGraw-Hill, 2009).

REFLECTION: What milestones do you believe will occur in the years ahead?

Hall of Fame: Profiles in Education

Focus Question 10

Who are some of the influential educators who have helped fashion today's schools?

A "hall of fame" recognizes individuals for significant contributions to a field. Football, baseball, rock and roll, and country music all have halls of fame to recognize outstanding individuals. We think education is no less important and merits its own forum for recognition. In fact, Emporia State University in Kansas houses a Teachers' Hall of Fame. Following are the nominations we would offer to honor educators who we believe should be in a hall of fame.

Obviously, not all influential educators have been included in these brief profiles, but it is important to begin recognizing significant educational contributions. Indirectly or directly, these individuals have influenced your life as a student and will influence your career as a teacher.

For establishing the kindergarten as an integral part of a child's education—

Friedrich Froebel (1782–1852). Froebel frequently reflected on his own childhood. Froebel's mother died when he was only nine months old. In his recollections, he developed a deep sense of the importance of early childhood and of the critical role played by teachers of the young. Although he worked as a forester, chemist's assistant, and museum curator, he eventually found his true vocation as an educator. He attended Pestalozzi's institute and extended Pestalozzi's ideas. He saw nature as a prime source of learning and believed that schools should provide a warm and supportive environment for children.

In 1837 Froebel founded the first **kindergarten** ("child's garden") to "cultivate" the child's development and socialization. Games provided cooperative activities for socialization and physical development, and such materials as sand and clay were used to stimulate the child's imagination. Like Pestalozzi, Froebel believed in the importance of establishing an emotionally secure environment for children. Going beyond Pestalozzi, Froebel saw the teacher as a moral and cultural model for children, a model worthy of emulation (how different from the earlier view of the teacher as disciplinarian).

In the nineteenth century, as German immigrants came to the United States, they brought with them the idea of kindergarten education. Margarethe Schurz established a German-language kindergarten in Wisconsin in 1855. Elizabeth Peabody started the first English-language kindergarten and training school for kindergarten teachers in Boston in 1860.

For her integrity and bravery in bringing education to African American girls—

Prudence Crandall (1803–1889). Born of Quaker parents, Prudence Crandall received her education at a school in Providence, Rhode Island, founded by an active abolitionist, Moses Brown. Her upbringing within Quaker circles, in which discussions of abolition were common, may have inspired her interest in racial equality, an interest that led her to acts of personal courage as she strove to promote education among people of all colors.

After graduating from the Brown Seminary around 1830, Crandall taught briefly in Plainfield, Connecticut, before founding her own school for girls in the neighboring town of Canterbury. However, her decision to admit a black girl, Sarah Harris, daughter of a neighboring farmer, caused outrage. Although

African Americans in Connecticut were free, a large segment of the white population within Canterbury supported the efforts of the American Colonization Society to deport all freed blacks to Africa, believing them to be inherently inferior. Many were adamant that anything but the most basic education for African Americans would lead to discontent and might encourage interracial marriage. The townspeople voiced fears that Crandall's school would lead to the devaluation of local property by attracting a large number of blacks to the area. Prudence Crandall was pressured by the local population to expel Sarah Harris. However, she was determined to defy their wishes. When the wife of a prominent local clergyman suggested that if Harris remained, the school "could not be sustained," Crandall replied, "Then it might sink then, for I should not turn her out."

When other parents withdrew their children, Crandall advertised for pupils in *The Liberator,* the newspaper of abolitionist William Lloyd Garrison. A month later, the school reopened with a student body composed of 15 black girls. However, the townspeople made life difficult for Crandall and her students. Supplies were hard to obtain, and Crandall and her pupils faced verbal harassment, as well as being pelted with chicken heads, manure, and other objects. Nonetheless, they persisted.

In 1833, only one month after Crandall had opened her doors to African American girls, the Connecticut legislature passed the notorious "Black Law." This law forbade the founding of schools for the education of African Americans from other states without the permission of local authorities. Crandall was arrested and tried. At her trial, her counsel advised the jury, "You may find that she has violated an act of the State Legislature, but if you also find her protected by higher power, it will be your duty to acquit." Her conviction was later overturned on appeal, but vandalism and arson continued. When a gang stormed the school building with clubs and iron bars, smashing windows and rendering the downstairs area uninhabitable, the school finally was forced to close.

Prudence Crandall's interest in education, racial equality, and women's rights continued throughout her life. Several of her students continued her work, including her first African American student, Sarah Harris, who taught black pupils in Louisiana for many years.[48]

For her work in identifying the educational potential of young children and crafting an environment in which the young could learn—

Maria Montessori (1870–1952). Montessori was no follower of tradition, in her private life or in her professional activities. Shattering sex-role stereotypes, she attended a technical school and then a medical school, becoming the first female physician in Italy. Her work brought her in contact with children regarded as mentally handicapped and brain damaged, but her educational activities with these children indicated that they were far more capable than many believed. By 1908, Montessori had established a children's school called the Casa dei Bambini, designed to provide an education for disadvantaged children from the slums of Rome.

Montessori's view of children differed from the views held by her contemporaries. Her observations led her to conclude that children have an inner need to work at tasks that interest them. Given the right materials and tasks, children need not be rewarded and punished by the teacher. In fact, she believed that children prefer work to play and are capable of sustained periods of concentration. Young children need a carefully prepared environment in order to learn.

Montessori's curriculum reflected this specially prepared environment. Children learned practical skills, including setting a table, washing dishes, buttoning clothing, and displaying basic manners. They learned formal skills, such as reading, writing, and arithmetic. Special materials included movable sandpaper letters to teach the alphabet and colored rods to teach counting. The children developed motor skills as well as intellectual skills in a carefully developed sequence. Montessori worked with each student individually, rather than with the class as a whole, to accomplish these goals.

The impact of Montessori's methods continues to this day. Throughout the United States, early childhood education programs use Montessori-like materials. A number of early childhood institutions are called Montessori schools and adhere to the approach she developed almost a century ago. Although originally intended for disadvantaged students, Montessori's concept of carefully preparing an environment and program to teach the very young is used today with children from all social classes.

For her contributions in moving a people from intellectual slavery to education—

Mary McLeod Bethune (1875–1955). The first child of her family not born in slavery, Bethune rose from a field hand, picking cotton, to an unofficial presidential adviser. The last of 17 children born to South Carolina sharecroppers, she filled the breaks in her fieldwork with reading and studying. She was committed to meeting the critical need of providing education to the newly freed African Americans, and when a Colorado seamstress offered to pay the cost of educating one black girl at Scotia Seminary in Concord, New Hampshire, she was selected. Bethune's plans to become an African missionary changed as she became more deeply involved in the need to educate newly liberated American blacks.

With $1.50, five students, and a rented cottage near the Daytona Beach city dump in Florida, Bethune founded a school that eventually became Bethune-Cookman College. As a national leader, she created a number of black civic and welfare organizations, serving as a member of the Hoover Commission on Child Welfare, and acting as an adviser to President Franklin D. Roosevelt.

Mary McLeod Bethune demonstrated commitment and effort in establishing a black college against overwhelming odds and by rising from poverty to become a national voice for African Americans.

For her creative approaches placing children at the center of the curriculum—

Sylvia Ashton-Warner (1908–1984). Sylvia Ashton-Warner began her school career in her mother's New Zealand classroom, where rote memorization constituted the main avenue for learning. The teaching strategies that Ashton-Warner later devised, with their emphasis on child-centered learning and creativity in the classroom, stand in opposition to this early experience.

Ashton-Warner was a flamboyant and eccentric personality; throughout her life, she considered herself to be an artist rather than a teacher. She focused on painting, music, and writing. Her fascination with creativity was apparent in the remote New Zealand classrooms, where she encouraged self-expression among the native Maori children. As a teacher, she infuriated authorities with her absenteeism and unpredictability, and in official ratings she was never estimated as above average in her abilities. However, during the peak years of her teaching career, between 1950 and 1952, she developed innovative teaching techniques that influenced teachers around the world and especially in the United States.

Realizing that certain words were especially significant to individual pupils because of their life experiences, Ashton-Warner developed her "key vocabulary" system for teaching reading to young children. Words drawn from children's conversations were written on cards. Using these words, children learned to read. Ashton-Warner asserted that the key to making this approach effective lay in choosing words that had personal meaning to the individual child: "Pleasant words won't do. Respectable words won't do. They must be words organically tied up, organically born from the dynamic life itself. They must be words that are already part of the child's being."

Bringing meaning to children was at the center of Ashton-Warner's philosophy. This belief provided the foundation of several reading approaches and teaching strategies used throughout the United States. Her work brought meaning to reading for millions of children. In her best-selling book, *Teacher,* she provided many future teachers with important and useful insights. Her emphasis on key vocabulary, individualized reading, and meaningful learning is evident in classrooms today in America and abroad.

For his work in identifying the crippling effects of racism on all American children and in formulating community action to overcome the educational, psychological, and economic impacts of racism—

Kenneth Clark (1914–2005). Kenneth Clark attended schools in Harlem, where he witnessed an integrated community become all black and felt the growing impact of racism. He attended Howard University, was the first African American to receive a doctorate in psychology from Columbia University, and in 1960 became the first black to be tenured at City College of New York. His concern with the educational plight of African Americans generally, and the Harlem community in particular, was always central in his professional efforts.

Beginning in the 1930s, Clark and his wife, Mamie Phipps Clark, assessed black children's self-perceptions. They bought black dolls for 50 cents each at a store in Harlem, one of the few places where black dolls could be purchased. They showed black and white children two white dolls and two black dolls, and asked the children to pick out the "nice" doll, the "pretty" doll, and the "bad" doll. Both groups tended to pick the white dolls as nice and pretty, and the black doll as bad. He repeated the study in the 1950s in South Carolina, where white students received far more funds for education than black children. The results were similar. He concluded that the lesson of black inferiority was so deep in society that even young black children understood it and believed it. As Clark noted, "A racist system inevitably destroys and damages human beings; it brutalizes and dehumanizes blacks and whites alike." In Brown v. the Topeka Board of Education (1954), the Supreme Court cited Clark's "doll" study in deciding that "separate was inherently unequal."

For his global effort to mobilize education in the cause of social justice—

Paulo Reglus Neves Freire (1921–1997). Abandoning a career in the law, Brazilian-born Freire committed himself to the education of the poor and politically oppressed. His efforts moved literacy from an educational tool to a political instrument.

Freire denounced teacher-centered classrooms. He believed that instructor domination denied the legitimacy of student experiences and treated students as secondary objects in the learning process. He termed such instruction "banking" education, because the students become little more than passive targets of the teacher's comments. Freire championed a critical pedagogy, one that places the student at the center of the learning process. In Freire's pedagogy, student dialogues, knowledge, and skills are shared cooperatively, legitimizing the experiences of the poor. Students are taught how to generate their own questions, focus on their own social problems, and develop strategies to live more fruitful and satisfying lives. Teachers are not passive bystanders or the only source of classroom wisdom. Freire believed that teachers should facilitate and inspire, that teachers should "live part of their dreams within their educational space." Rather than unhappy witnesses to social injustice, teachers should be advocates for the poor and agents for social change. Freire's best known work, ***Pedagogy of the Oppressed,*** illustrated how education could transform society.

Freire's approach obviously threatened the social order of many repressive governments, and he faced constant intimidation and threats. Following the military overthrow of the Brazilian government in 1964, Freire was jailed for "subversive" activities and later exiled. In the late 1960s, while studying in America, Freire witnessed racial unrest and the antiwar protests. These events convinced Freire that political oppression is present in "developed nations" as well as third-world countries, that economic privilege does not guarantee political advantage, and that the pedagogy of the oppressed has worldwide significance.

www.mhhe.com/
sadkerbrief3e

INTERACTIVE ACTIVITY
Who Am I?
Using hints, determine the identity of famous educational figures.

Now that you have learned about these important figures in education, we invite you to read about some additional Hall of Famers in the Profiles in Education section in Chapter 5 on the Online Learning Center.

 Comenius (1592–1670), profiled for his pioneering work in identifying developmental stages of learning and his support of universal education.

 Jean-Jacques Rousseau (1712–1778), profiled for his work in distinguishing schooling from education and for his concern with the stages of development.

 Johann Heinrich Pestalozzi (1746–1827), profiled for his recognition of the special needs of the disadvantaged and his work in curricular development.

 Johann Herbart (1776–1841), profiled for his contributions to moral development in education and for his creation of a structured methodology of instruction.

 Emma Hart Willard ((1787–1870), profiled for opening the door of higher education to women and for promoting professional teacher preparation.

 Horace Mann (1796–1859), profiled for establishing free public schools and expanding the opportunities of poor as well as wealthy Americans, and for his vision of the central role of education in improving the quality of American life.

 John Dewey (1859–1952), profiled for his work in developing progressive education, for incorporating democratic practices in the educational process.

 Jean Piaget (1896–1980), profiled for his creation of a theory of cognitive development.

 Burrhus Frederick (B. F.) Skinner (1904–1990), profiled for his contributions in altering environments to promote learning.

SUMMARY

CHAPTER REVIEW

Go to the Online Learning Center to take a chapter self-quiz, practice with key terms, and review concepts from the chapter.

www.mhhe.com/
sadkerbrief3e

1. **What was the nature and purpose of colonial education?**

   Colonial education took place in homes, including the dame schools; in churches; and through apprentice programs. Thomas Jefferson and Benjamin Franklin viewed the new nation's schools as a continuation of democratic principles and as a break from classist European traditions, although instruction was typically dominated by religious teachings. From colonial times to the present, continuing educational disputes include the role of religion in schools; local control and state standards; and inequities in educational opportunities for women, people of color, and the poor.

2. **How did the Common School Movement influence the idea of universal education?**

   Nineteenth-century leader Horace Mann fought for the establishment of the common school for all children, and for quality teacher education. He believed that education should develop the talents of the poor as well as the wealthy.

3. **What developments mark the educational history of Native Americans?**

   In the early years, Native Americans (or Indians) were attacked by disease and warfare, and almost annihilated. During the nineteenth century, schools were used to "civilize" them into Western ways, degrading their culture, beliefs, and languages. Although most Native Americans are currently in public schools, some are educated in private schools or through schools run by the Bureau of Indian Affairs (BIA).

4. **How did teaching become a "gendered" career?**

   Although teaching was initially "gendered" male, the advent of the common school created a demand for a large number of inexpensive teachers, and women were recruited and soon dominated teaching. Today's teachers continue to encounter sexism.

5. **How did secondary schools evolve?**

   The first publicly supported secondary school was the English Classical School in Boston. Not until 1874 in the Kalamazoo case was the legal basis for high school funding established. By the twentieth century, junior high and middle schools were created.

6. **What were the main tenets of the Progressive Education movement?**

   Progressivism, led by John Dewey, emphasized learning by doing and shaping curricula around children's interests.

7. **What role has the federal government played in American education?**

   While the Constitution leaves the responsibility for schooling to the states, the federal government has played an increasing role in education over the past century, promoting teacher training, science and math instruction, and desegregation. More recently, the emphasis has been on school standards and testing.

8. **How did history shape the educational experiences of African Americans, Hispanics, Asian Americans/Pacific Islanders, and Arab Americans?**

   Despite a national commitment to educate all citizens, bias and discrimination characterize the histories of many ethnic and racial groups. The doctrine of "separate but equal" (Plessey v. Ferguson) was the law of the land until the 1954 Brown decision. Today, more than half a century after Brown, de facto resegregation has again separated black and white. Hispanics (or Latinos) are now the largest minority group in the United States and face challenges in a culture that often fears people who speak another language. Asian is a broad label assigned to several billion people from a score of nations, and Asian Americans and Pacific Islanders are a rapidly growing population. Students from China, Japan, and India are stereotyped as model minorities, a label that often masks the impact of prejudice on these children. Many Americans confuse Arabs and Muslims, mistaking Islam, a religion, with Arabs, a cultural group.

9. **What educational barriers and breakthroughs have girls and women experienced?**

   For much of this nation's history, females were denied access to or segregated within schools. Although options have improved dramatically for girls and women, much of that progress due to Title IX, subtle bias continues to send boys and girls down different career paths.

10. **Who are some of the influential educators who have helped fashion today's schools?**

    In this chapter and online, noted educators from eighteenth-century Rousseau to twentieth-century Freire are profiled.

KEY TERMS AND PEOPLE

KEY TERMS

academy, 140

American Spelling Book, 143

Brown v. Board of Education of Topeka, 154

common school, 141

dame schools, 137

de facto segregation, 153

de jure segregation, 153

elementary school, 141

English Classical School, 147

gendered career, 145

hornbook, 143

in loco parentis, 137

Kalamazoo, Michigan, case, 148

kindergarten, 168

Land Ordinance Act, 152

Latin grammar school, 138

McGuffey Readers, 143

National Defense Education Act (NDEA), 151

New England Primer, 143

normal schools, 142

Northwest Ordinance, 152

Old Deluder Satan Law, 138

Pedagogy of the Oppressed, 172

Plessy v. Ferguson , 153

progressive education, 150

second-generation segregation, 154

separate but equal, 153

Tenth Amendment, 152

KEY PEOPLE

You'll find the stories of key people listed below both in the text and at the Online Learning Center.

www.mhhe.com/
sadkerbrief3e

Sylvia Ashton-Warner, 170

Mary McLeod Bethune, 170

Kenneth Clark, 171

Comenius, online, 173

Prudence Crandall, 168

John Dewey, online, 148, 173

Benjamin Franklin, 140

Paulo Reglus Neves Freire, 172

Friedrich Froebel, 168

Johann Herbart, online, 173

Thomas Jefferson, 140

Horace Mann, online, 173

Maria Montessori, 169

Johann Heinrich Pestalozzi, online, 173

Jean Piaget, online, 173

Jean-Jacques Rousseau, online, 173

Burrhus Frederick (B. F.) Skinner, online, 173

Emma Hart Willard, online, 163, 173

1. In the colonial period, a number of factors influenced the kind of education you might receive. Describe how the following factors influenced educational opportunities:

   - Geography
   - Wealth
   - Race/ethnicity
   - Gender

2. Progressive education has sparked adamant critics and fervent supporters. Offer several arguments supporting the tenets of progressivism, as well as arguments against this movement.

3. In what ways are terms like Native Americans, African Americans, Asian Americans, Hispanic Americans, or Arab Americans helpful? In what ways are these labels misleading?

4. Identify the contributions made by the following educators, whom some might consider candidates for the Hall of Fame: Septima Poinsette Clark, Madeline C. Hunter, Charlotte Hawkins Brown, Johnetta Cole, Joyce Ladner, Henri Mann.

5. Some teacher preparation programs do not consider or discuss the history of education, while other programs devote courses to reviewing and analyzing educational history. Set up a debate (or use another academic controversy strategy) arguing the pros and cons of the following proposition. Resolved: Teacher preparation programs should focus on current issues and not consider the history of education.

YOUR CD-ROM: *THE TEACHERS, SCHOOLS, AND SOCIETY READER* WITH CLASSROOM OBSERVATION VIDEO CLIPS

Articles, Case Studies, and Videos correspond to chapter content and are not always in numeric order. Go to your *Teachers, Schools, and Society Reader* CD-ROM to:

Read Current and Historical Articles

25. Text excerpts from *Narrative of the Life of Frederick Douglass: An American Slave.*

26. Text excerpts from *The Education of Free Men*, Horace Mann.

27. *What We Don't Know Can Hurt Them: White Teachers, Indian Children*, Bobby Ann Starnes, *Phi Delta Kappan*, January 2006.

28. "Reviving the Goal of An Integrated Society: A 21st Century Challenge," by Gary Orfield, *The Civil Rights Project*, January 14, 2009.

Analyze Case Studies

13. Hamilton High: From the 1950s through the 1980s, this case presents how a school has changed in reaction to societal and educational changes.

Observe Teachers, Students, and Classrooms in Action

12. **Classroom Observation: Progressivism in Action: A Classroom Lesson**

 4. **Classroom Observation: Author David Sadker Identifies Classroom Bias Through Role Play**

See pages 150, 165, and 166 of this text for descriptions of these videos. You'll find the videos on the CD Reader and at the Online Learning Center.

www.mhhe.com/
sadkerbrief3e

WEB-*TIVITIES*

Go to the Online Learning Center to do the following activities:

1. Historical Events and Trends: Shaping American Education
2. American Schools of the Past: A Day in the Life
3. Early Textbooks
4. The Education Hall of Fame

chapter 6

PHILOSOPHY OF EDUCATION

Focus Questions

1. What is a philosophy of education, and why should it be important to you?

2. How do teacher-centered philosophies of education differ from student-centered philosophies of education?

3. What are some major philosophies of education in the United States today?

4. How are these philosophies reflected in school practices?

5. What are some of the psychological and cultural factors influencing education?

6. What were the contributions of Socrates, Plato, and Aristotle to Western philosophy, and how are their legacies reflected in education today?

7. How do metaphysics, epistemology, ethics, political philosophy, aesthetics, and logic factor into a philosophy of education?

www.mhhe.com/
sadkerbrief3e

WHAT DO YOU THINK? What Is Your Philosophy of Education? Take an electronic version of the quiz on pages 181-182. Then, submit your responses to see how they compare to those of your colleagues.

Chapter Preview

The root for the word **philosophy** is made up of two Greek words: *philo,* meaning "love," and *sophos,* meaning "wisdom." For thousands of years, philosophers have been wrestling with fundamental questions: What is most real—the physical world or the realm of mind and spirit? What is the basis of human knowledge? What is the nature of the just society? Educators must take stances on such questions before they can determine what and how students should be taught.

Because educators do not always agree on the answers to these questions, different philosophies of education have emerged. Although there are some similarities, profound differences exist in the way leading educators define the purpose of education, the role of the teacher, the nature of the curriculum and assessment, and the method of instruction.

This chapter is intended to start you on a path of thoughtfully considering your values and beliefs. Five influential philosophies will be described, and you will see how each can shape classroom life. We invite you to consider how psychological and cultural beliefs can also affect schools. We then revisit the roots of Western philosophy with three ancient Greeks as our guides: Socrates, Plato, and Aristotle. Finally, we briefly examine the building blocks of philosophy, the divisions within philosophy that focus on questions pertinent to educators (What is of worth? How do we know what we know?). The ideas in this chapter will spark some very basic questions about your role in the classroom and the school's role in society. Your answers to these questions will help you frame your philosophy of education.

Finding Your Philosophy of Education

What is a philosophy of education? Do you have one? Do you think it matters? If you are like most people, you probably have not given much thought to philosophy, in education or elsewhere. Being a practical person, you may be more concerned with other questions: Will I enjoy teaching? Will I be good at it? How will I handle discipline problems? Believe it or not, underlying the answers to these practical questions *is* your philosophy of education.

At this point, your philosophy may still be taking shape (not a bad thing). Your beliefs may reflect an amalgam of different philosophies. Unfortunately, they may also be filled with inconsistencies. To help you shape a coherent and useful educational philosophy, you must consider some basic—and very important—questions, such as:

What is the purpose of education?

What content and skills should schools teach?

How should schools teach this content?

What are the proper roles for teachers and students?

How should learning be measured?

Still not sure what a philosophy of education is all about, or how it shapes classroom and school life? Let's listen to some teachers discussing the direction a new charter school should take. You'll see that each teacher has very clear ideas about what schools are for, what students should learn, and how teachers should teach.

Hear that noise coming from the faculty room down the hall? Your potential colleagues sometimes get a bit loud as they debate the possible directions

Focus Question 1
What is a philosophy of education, and why should it be important to you?

for the new charter school. As you listen in, try to sort out which of these educational directions appeals to you.

JACK POLLACK: I am so excited! This new charter school can be just what we need, a chance to raise our test scores and reestablish a positive reputation for the quality of public education! It's all about tough standards and high test scores. Let's face it, we are competing in a global economy, against nations whose students outscore ours on the standardized tests that matter. It's embarrassing. I'd love to see a strict code of conduct, demanding math, science, and humanities courses, and no silly electives. It's all about rigorous standards!

MYRA MILLER: Jack, you and I both would like to teach in a more rigorous schools, but the truth is I am fed up with testing. I'll tell you a secret: I don't much care whether South Korean kids or those at the Country Day School score better than us on those silly multiple-choice tests. Kids thirst for meaningful ideas. The school I envision would focus on classic works of literature and art. How about a school where we discuss great books like *Moby Dick, The Old Man and the Sea,* Plato's *Republic,* and Homer's *Iliad?* I want to create students who know not only *how* to read, but who *want* to read, and best of all, know how to *think.*

MARK WASHINGTON: I agree with Myra that we need to move beyond today's tyranny of testing, but Hemingway and Homer are not the answers. Our job as teachers is to make certain that our students can do well in the real world. When I was in eighth grade, my class took a three-week train trip throughout the Midwest. We researched and planned where to go; figured out how to read train schedules; used maps; and ended up learning math, history, geography, and writing. Talk about an integrated curriculum! I want students to learn how to solve real-world problems, not just answer test questions or discuss books.

TED GOODHEART: At last, reality! But there are more pressing social needs than a train trip. I want students to do more than simply fit into society; I want them to leave the world a better place than they found it. One out of five U.S. children is born into poverty. I want to teach kids to make a difference. Rather than insulate them from real-world problems, we should help our kids develop a social conscience and the political skills needed to improve our society. Teaching in a socially responsible charter school would be my dream.

CARA CAMUS: Everyone in this room has been trying to design a charter school backward. Let's set aside what we as teachers want and consider a revolutionary idea: building a school based on what students want. I would like our charter schools staffed by teachers who are skilled in facilitating and counseling children to reach their personal goals. Believe it or not, I trust students, and I would give every child (even the youngest or least able) an equal voice in decision making. We have forgotten the purpose of schools: to help students find their way.

As you might have suspected, these teachers are not only discussing different approaches to a proposed charter school, they are also shedding light on five major educational philosophies. Do any of these diverse views sound attractive to you? Do any sound particularly unappealing? If so, note which of these teachers you thought reflected your own beliefs, and which were really off the mark. If you found that you had strong opinions—pro or con—about one or more of these teachers' positions, then you are beginning to get in touch with your educational philosophy. Let's leave the faculty room conversation and take a closer, more orderly look at your own philosophical leanings. The following inventory can help you sort out tenets of your educational philosophy.

Inventory of Philosophies of Education

As you read through each of the following statements about schools and teaching, decide how strongly you agree or disagree. In a bit, we will help you interpret your results. Write your response to the left of each statement, using the following scale:

5 Agree strongly

4 Agree

3 Neither agree nor disagree

2 Disagree

1 Disagree strongly

_____ 1. A school curriculum should include a common body of information that all students should know.

_____ 2. The school curriculum should focus on the great ideas that have survived through time.

_____ 3. The gap between the real world and schools should be bridged through field trips, internships, and adult mentors.

_____ 4. Schools should prepare students for analyzing and solving the social problems they will face beyond the classroom.

_____ 5. Each student should determine his or her individual curriculum, and teachers should guide and help them.

_____ 6. Students should not be promoted from one grade to the next until they have read and mastered certain key material.

_____ 7. Schools, above all, should develop students' abilities to think deeply, analytically, and creatively, rather than focus on transient concerns like social skills and current trends.

_____ 8. Whether inside or outside the classroom, teachers must stress the relevance of what students are learning to real and current events.

_____ 9. Education should enable students to recognize injustices in society, and schools should promote projects to redress social inequities.

_____ 10. Students who do not want to study much should not be required to do so.

_____ 11. Teachers and schools should emphasize academic rigor, discipline, hard work, and respect for authority.

_____ 12. Education is not primarily about workers and the world economic competition; learning should be appreciated for its own sake, and students should enjoy reading, learning, and discussing intriguing ideas.

_____ 13. The school curriculum should be designed by teachers to respond to the experiences and needs of the students.

_____ 14. Schools should promote positive group relationships by teaching about different ethnic and racial groups.

_____ 15. The purpose of school is to help students understand themselves, appreciate their distinctive talents and insights, and find their own unique place in the world.

_____ 16. For the United States to be competitive economically in the world marketplace, schools must bolster their academic requirements to train more competent workers.

_____ 17. Teachers ought to teach from the classics, because important insights related to many of today's challenges and concerns are found in these Great Books.

_____ 18. Because students learn effectively through social interaction, schools should plan for substantial social interaction in their curricula.

_____ 19. Students should be taught how to be politically literate, and learn how to improve the quality of life for all people.

_____ 20. The central role of the school is to provide students with options and choices. The student must decide what and how to learn.

_____ 21. Schools must provide students with a firm grasp of basic facts regarding the books, people, and events that have shaped the nation's heritage.

_____ 22. The teacher's main goal is to help students unlock the insights learned over time, so they can gain wisdom from the great thinkers of the past.

_____ 23. Students should be active participants in the learning process, involved in democratic class decision making and reflective thinking.

_____ 24. Teaching should mean more than simply transmitting the Great Books, which are replete with biases and prejudices. Rather, schools need to identify a new list of Great Books more appropriate for today's world and prepare students to create a better society than their ancestors did.

_____ 25. Effective teachers help students to discover and develop their personal values, even when those values conflict with traditional ones.

_____ 26. Teachers should help students constantly reexamine their beliefs. In history, for example, students should learn about those who have been historically omitted: the poor, the non-European, women, and people of color.

_____ 27. Frequent objective testing is the best way to determine what students know. Rewarding students when they learn, even when they learn small things, is the key to successful teaching.

_____ 28. Education should be a responsibility of the family and community, rather than delegated to formal and impersonal institutions, such as schools.

A	B	C	D	E
Essentialism (Jack)	Perennialism (Myra)	Progressivism (Mark)	Social Reconstructionism (Ted)	Existentialism (Cara)
1. _____	2. _____	3. _____	4. _____	5. _____
6. _____	7. _____	8. _____	9. _____	10. _____
11. _____	12. _____	13. _____	14. _____	15. _____
16. _____	17. _____	18. _____	19. _____	20. _____
21. _____	22. _____	23. _____	24. _____	25. _____
Scores _____	_____	_____	_____	_____

Interpreting Your Responses

Write your responses to statements 1 through 25 in the following columns, and tally up your score in each column. (We will return to items 26 to 28 in a bit.) Each column is labeled with a philosophy and the name of the teacher who represented that view in this chapter's opening scenario (the charter school discussion). The highest possible score in any one column is 25, and the lowest possible score is 5. Scores in the 20s indicate strong agreement, and scores below 10 indicate disagreement with the tenets of a particular philosophy.

Your scores in columns A through E, respectively, represent how much you agree or disagree with the beliefs of five major educational philosophies: essentialism, perennialism, progressivism, social reconstructionism, and existentialism. Check back to see if your scores reflect your initial reactions to these teachers' points of view. For example, if you agreed with Jack's proposal to create an "Academy," then you probably agreed with a number of the statements associated with essentialist education, and your score in this column may be fairly high.

Compare your five scores. What is your highest? What is your lowest? Which three statements best reflect your views on education? Are they congruent and mutually supporting? Looking at the statements that you least support, what do these statements tell you about your values? You may notice that your philosophical leanings, as identified by your responses to statements in the inventory, reflect your general outlook on life. For example, your responses may indicate whether you generally trust people to do the right thing, or if you believe that individuals need supervision. How have your culture, religion, upbringing, and political beliefs shaped your responses to the items in this inventory? How have your own education and life experiences influenced your philosophical beliefs?

Now that you have begun to examine varying beliefs about education, you may even want to lay claim to a philosophical label. But what do these philosophical labels mean? In the following pages we will introduce you to all five of these educational philosophies and look at their impact in the classroom.

www.mhhe.com/
sadkerbrief3e

INTERACTIVE ACTIVITY
Where Do You Stand on the Philosophy Spectrum?
Note where you think your philosophy of education falls, and compare where you stand to where your colleagues do.

Five Philosophies of Education

Focus Questions 2–4

How do teacher-centered philosophies of education differ from student-centered philosophies of education? What are some major philosophies of education in the United States today? How are these philosophies reflected in school practices?

Essentialism, perennialism, progressivism, social reconstructionism, and existentialism. Taken together, these five schools of thought do not exhaust the list of possible educational philosophies you may consider, but they present strong frameworks for you to refine your own educational philosophy. We can place these five philosophies on a continuum, from teacher-centered (some would say "authoritarian") to student-centered (some would characterize as "permissive").

Let's begin our discussion with the teacher-centered philosophies, for they have exerted significant influence on American education during the past two decades.

Teacher-Centered Philosophies

Traditionally, *teacher-centered philosophies* emphasize the importance of transferring knowledge, information, and skills from the older (presumably wiser) generation to the younger one. The teacher's role is to instill respect for authority, perseverance, duty, consideration, and practicality. When students demonstrate through tests and writings that they are competent in academic subjects and traditional skills, and through their actions that they have disciplined minds and adhere to traditional morals and behavior, then both the school and the teacher have been successful. (As discussed in Chapter 9, these philosophies view the primary purpose of education as "passing the cultural baton.") The major teacher-centered philosophies of education are essentialism and perennialism.

Essentialism

Essentialism strives to teach students the accumulated knowledge of our civilization through core courses in the traditional academic disciplines. Essentialists aim to instill students with the "essentials" of academic knowledge, patriotism, and character development. This traditional or **back-to-basics** approach is meant to train the mind, promote reasoning, and ensure a common culture among all Americans.

American educator **William Bagley** popularized the term *essentialism* in the 1930s,[1] and essentialism has been a dominant influence in American education since World War II. Factors such as the launching of *Sputnik* in 1957, the 1983 report *A Nation at Risk,* the rise of standardized testing, intense global economic competition, and increased immigration into the United States have all kept essentialism at center stage. Some educators refer to the present period as neoessentialism because of the increased core graduation requirements, stronger standards, and more testing of both students and teachers.

Not all essentialists are the same. Allan Bloom, the author of *The Closing of the American Mind,* contends that immigration and multiculturalism threaten the traditional "American" identity. He advocates for a time-honored, Anglo-Saxon curriculum reflecting European traditions. On the other hand, noted essentialist **E. D. Hirsch, Jr.** advocates for a more inclusive curriculum that offers all students a shared knowledge, a common curriculum (not unlike

Horace Mann's idea of a common school). Hirsch authored *Cultural Literacy: What Every American Needs to Know* and *The Knowledge Deficit,* and he suggests facts and ideas that might be included in his curriculum. Although people refer to his work by the popular title of his book, cultural literacy, he prefers to call it core knowledge, a knowledge that would be shared by all Americans.[2] (See Chapter 10 for an in-depth discussion on the works of Bloom and Hirsch.)

The current emphasis on pen-and-paper testing is an example of essentialism in action.

Most of you reading this chapter have been educated in essentialist schools. You were probably required to take many courses in English, history, math, and science, but were able to enroll in only a few electives. Such a program would be typical in an essentialist school.

The Essentialist Classroom Essentialists urge that traditional disciplines such as math, science, history, foreign language, and literature form the foundation of the curriculum, which is referred to as the **core curriculum.** Essentialists frown upon electives that "water down" academic content. Elementary students receive instruction in skills such as writing, reading, measuring, and computing. Even when studying art and music, subjects most often associated with the development of creativity, students master a body of information and basic techniques, gradually moving to more complex skills and detailed knowledge. Only by mastering the required material are students promoted to the next higher level.

Essentialists maintain that classrooms should be oriented around the teacher, who should serve as an intellectual and moral role model for the students. The teachers or administrators decide what is most important for the students to learn and place little emphasis on student interests, particularly when such interests divert time and attention from the academic curriculum. Essentialist teachers rely on test scores to evaluate progress. Essentialists expect that students will leave school possessing not only basic skills and an extensive body of knowledge, but also disciplined, practical minds, capable of applying schoolhouse lessons in the real world.

Essentialism in Action: Rancho Elementary School Rancho Elementary School in Marin County, California, proudly promotes its essentialist philosophy, and announces on its web page that "students will participate in a highly enriched environment exposing them to rigorous academics, foreign language, citizenship/leadership opportunities, and grade appropriate technology." Its mission is the acquisition of basic skills through direct instruction in the core academic areas, including reading through phonics. As a testament to its success, the school boasts high test scores. Beyond academics, the school also emphasizes "firm, consistent discipline" and close parent–teacher relationships.

If you do not live in Marin County, you may not have heard of Rancho, but you may have heard of a school belonging to the Coalition of Essential Schools; 150 schools nationwide are members. But don't be misled by the

13. Essentialism in Action: A Classroom Lesson

It is hard to visualize how different philosophies might manifest themselves in the classroom. In this observation you will see essentialism in action as an elementary teacher organizes an exciting class competition based on a television game. The involvement and excitement of the students is apparent.

Classroom Observation Videos are available on the CD Reader and at the Online Learning Center.

www.mhhe.com/
sadkerbrief3e

name. Although these schools promote intellectual rigor, test students for mastery of information, and emphasize strong thinking skills across subjects, they are not pure examples of essentialism. The schools do not share a fixed core curriculum, they emphasize the study of single topics or issues in depth, and incorporate components of perennialism, which brings us to the other teacher-centered philosophy.

Perennialism

Perennialism is a cousin to essentialism. Both advocate teacher-centered classrooms. Both tolerate little flexibility in the curriculum. Both implement rigorous standards. Both aim to sharpen students' intellectual powers and enhance their moral qualities. So what are the differences?

Perennialists organize their schools around books, ideas, and concepts, and criticize essentialists for the vast amount of factual information they require students to absorb in their push for "cultural literacy." Perennial means "everlasting"—a perennialist education focuses on enduring themes and questions that span the ages. Perennialists recommend that students learn directly from the **Great Books**—works by history's finest thinkers and writers, books as meaningful today as when they were first written.

Perennialists believe that the goal of education should be to develop rational thought and to discipline minds to think rigorously. Perennialists see education as a sorting mechanism, a way to identify and prepare the intellectually gifted for leadership, while providing vocational training for the rest of society. They lament the change in universities over the centuries, from institutions where a few gifted students (and teachers) rigorously pursued truth for its own sake, to a glorified training ground for future careers.

Those of you who received a religious education might recognize the perennialist philosophy. Many parochial schools reflect the perennialist tradition with a curriculum that focuses on analyzing great religious books (such as the *Bible, Talmud,* or *Koran),* discerning moral truths, and honoring these moral values. In the classroom description that follows, we will concentrate on secular perennialism as formulated in the twentieth-century United States by such individuals as Robert Hutchins and Mortimer Adler.

In a perennialist classroom, primary sources rather than textbooks are the center of learning

The Perennialist Classroom As in an essentialist classroom, students in a perennialist classroom spend considerable time and energy mastering the three "Rs," reading, 'riting, and 'rithmetic. Greatest importance is placed on reading, the key to unlocking the enduring ideas found in the Great Books. Special attention is given to teaching values and character training, often through discussion about the underlying values and moral principles in a story. (Former Secretary of Education Bill Bennett wrote a collection of such stories titled *Book of Virtues.*) High school marks an increase in academic rigor as more challenging books are explored, including works of Darwin, Homer, and Shakespeare. Few elective choices are allowed. In an extreme example, in his *Paideia Proposal,* published in 1982, **Mortimer Adler** proposed a single elementary and secondary curriculum for all students, with no curricular electives except in the choice of a second language.

Electives are not the only things perennialists go without. You find few if any textbooks in a perennialist class. **Robert Hutchins,** who as president of the University of Chicago introduced the Great Books program, once opined that textbooks "have probably done as much to degrade the American intelligence as any single force."[3] Because perennialist teachers see themselves as discussion seminar leaders and facilitators, lectures are rare. Instead, students are guided through intense questioning to reveal new insights. Current concerns like multiculturalism, gender stereotypes, or computer technology would find no place in a perennialist curriculum.

While critics chastise perennialists for the lack of women, people of color, and non-Western ideas in the Great Books they teach, perennialists are unmoved by such criticism. To them, "training the mind" is ageless, beyond demographic concerns and transient trends. As Mortimer Adler wrote:

> The Great Books of ancient and medieval as well as modern times are a repository of knowledge and wisdom, a tradition of culture which must initiate each generation.[4]

Perennialism in Action: St. John's College The best-known example of perennialist education today takes place at a private institution unaffiliated with any religion: St. John's College, founded in 1784 in Annapolis, Maryland (www.sjcsf.edu). St. John's College adopted the Great Books as a core curriculum in 1937 and assigns readings in the fields of literature, philosophy and theology, history and the social sciences, mathematics and natural science, and music. Students write extensively and attend seminars twice weekly to discuss assigned readings. They also complete a number of laboratory

ESSENTIALISTS AND PERENNIALISTS: DIFFERENT CORE CURRICULA

Although both essentialism and perennialism promote a traditional approach to education, these teacher-centered philosophies draw their curricula from different sources. The first column includes excerpts from a typical essentialist list (we included a few words and phrases under the letter "c"); the second column samples the perennialists' Great Books curriculum. Remember, these are only a few items from very long lists!

THE LIST (ESSENTIALISM)

centigrade
cerebellum
carry coals to Newcastle
capital expenditure
Cèzanne
Canberra
Caesar Augustus
Candide
cast pearls before swine
cadre
catharsis
carbon dioxide
carte blanche
Caruso, Enrico
cathode ray tube

GREAT BOOKS (PERENNIALSIM)

The Bible
Geoffry Chaucer, *Canterbury Tales*
Charles Dickens, *Oliver Twist*
F. Scott Fitzgerald, *The Great Gatsby*
Homer, *The Iliad*
Henry James, *In the Cage*
James Joyce, *Ulysses*
The Koran
Karl Marx, *Das Kapital*
Herman Melville, *Moby Dick*
Thomas Paine, *Common Sense*
Plato, *Charmides*
Jonathan Swift, *Gulliver's Travels*
Virginia Woolf, *Night and Day*
Leo Tolstoy, *War and Peace*

REFLECTION: Does this list make you feel culturally literate—or illiterate? Do you believe that lists like this one should be important? Why or why not?

---

experiences and tutorials in language, mathematics, and music, guided by the faculty, who are called *tutors.* Seniors take oral examinations at the beginning and end of their senior year and write a final essay that must be approved before they are allowed to graduate.

Although grades are given in order to facilitate admission to graduate programs, students receive their grades only upon request and are expected to learn only for learning's sake. Since the St. John's experience thrives best in a small-group atmosphere, the college established a second campus in 1964 in Santa Fe, New Mexico, to handle additional enrollment.

Student-Centered Philosophies

Student-centered philosophies are less authoritarian, less concerned with the past and "training the mind," and more focused on individual needs, contemporary relevance, and preparing students for a changing future. Progressivism, social reconstructionism, and existentialism place the learner at the

Teacher- versus Student-Centered Approaches to Education

TEACHER-CENTERED APPROACHES ARE BEST BECAUSE . . .

AFTER CENTURIES OF EXPERIENCE, WE KNOW WHAT TO TEACH

From Plato to Orwell, great writers and thinkers of the past light our way into the future. We must pass our cherished cultural legacy on to the next generation.

TEACHERS MUST SELECT WHAT IS WORTH KNOWING

The knowledge explosion showers us with mountains of new, complex information on a daily basis. Selecting what students should learn is a daunting challenge. Teachers, not students, are trained and best equipped to determine what is of value. To ask students to choose what they should learn would be the height of irresponsibility.

SCHOOLS MUST BE INSULATED FROM EXTERNAL DISTRACTIONS

Students can be easily distracted by the "excitement" of contemporary events. While academic and rigorous school-based learning may be less flashy and less appealing, in the long run, it is far more valuable. After schoolwork has been mastered, students will be well prepared to leave the sanctuary of learning and confront the outside world.

WE ARE FALLING BEHIND OTHER NATIONS

U.S. student performance on international tests lags behind that of students from other nations. We have grown "educationally soft," lacking the challenging teacher-centered curriculums that other nations use. Only by creating a tough and demanding curriculum can we hope to compete with other nations.

COMPETITION AND REWARDS ARE IMPORTANT FOR MOTIVATING LEARNERS

Most people want and need to be recognized for their effort. Students are motivated to earn good report card grades and academic honors, to "ace" the SATs and be admitted to a prestigious college. Competition to earn high grades is the

STUDENT-CENTERED APPROACHES ARE BEST BECAUSE . . .

GENUINE LEARNING ORIGINATES WITH THE LEARNER

People learn best what they want to learn, what they feel they should or need to learn. Students find lessons imposed "from above" to be mostly irrelevant, and the lessons are quickly forgotten.

THEY BEST PREPARE STUDENTS FOR THE INFORMATION AGE

The knowledge explosion is actually a powerful argument for student-directed learning. Teachers can't possibly teach everything. We must equip students with research skills, then fan the flames of curiosity so they will want to learn for themselves. Then students can navigate the Information Age, finding and evaluating new information.

EDUCATION IS A VITAL AND ORGANIC PART OF SOCIETY

The most important lessons of life are found not on the pages of books or behind the walls of a school, but in the real world. Students need to work and learn directly in the community, from cleaning up the environment to reducing violence. Social action projects and service learning can offer a beacon of hope for the community while building compassionate values within our students.

MULTIPLE CHOICE TESTS ARE NOT AN OLYMPIC EVENT

Education is not a competition, and academic tests are not a new Olympic event where youngsters have to get the highest score to please the cheering crowd. National success will come from living up to our beliefs, not "beating" the children of some other nation on a multiple choice test.

MEANINGFUL REWARDS DO NOT COME FROM ACADEMIC COMPETITIONS

Grades, funny stickers, and social approval are poor sources of motivation. Authentic learning rests on a more solid foundation: intrinsic motivation. Real success comes from an inner drive, not from artificial rewards. Schools

continued

TEACHER-CENTERED APPROACHES ARE BEST BECAUSE . . .	STUDENT-CENTERED APPROACHES ARE BEST BECAUSE . . .

engine that drives successful school performance. Competition and rewards also drive the nation's productive workforce.

DISCIPLINED MINDS, RESPECTFUL CITIZENS

Students who listen thoughtfully and participate respectfully in classroom discussions learn several important lessons. For one, they learn the worth and wisdom of Western culture. They also learn to appreciate and to honor those who brought them this heritage, the guardians of their freedom and culture: their teachers.

need to develop students' inner motivation and stress student cooperation, not competition.

HUMAN DIGNITY IS LEARNED IN DEMOCRATIC CLASSROOMS

Democracy is learned through experience, not books. Students flourish when they are respected; they are stifled when they are told what and how to think. As students manage their own learning, they master the most important lesson any school can teach: the importance of the individual's ideas.

www.mhhe.com/
sadkerbrief3e **YOU DECIDE . . .**

Do you find yourself influenced more by the arguments supporting teacher-centered approaches, or those advocating student-centered approaches? Are there elements of each that you find appealing? How will your classroom practices reflect your philosophy?

center of the educational process: Students and teachers work together on determining what should be learned and how best to learn it. School is not seen as an institution that controls and directs youth, or works to preserve and transmit the core culture, but as an institution that works with youth to improve society or help students realize their individuality.

Progressivism

Progressivism organizes schools around the concerns, curiosity, and real-world experiences of students. The progressive teacher facilitates learning by helping students formulate meaningful questions and devise strategies to answer those questions. Answers are not drawn from lists or even Great Books; they are discovered through real-world experience. Progressivism is the educational application of a philosophy called pragmatism. According to **pragmatism,** the way to determine if an idea has merit is simple: test it. If the idea works in the real world, then it has merit. Both pragmatism and progressivism originated in America, the home of a very practical and pragmatic people. John Dewey refined and applied pragmatism to education, establishing what became known as progressivism.

John Dewey was a reformer with a background in philosophy and psychology who taught that people learn best through social interaction in the real world. Dewey believed that because social learning had meaning, it endured. Book learning, on the other hand, was no substitute for actually doing things. Progressivists do not believe that the mind can be disciplined through reading Great Books, rather that the mind should be trained to analyze experience thoughtfully and draw conclusions objectively.

Dewey saw education as an opportunity to learn how to apply previous experiences in new ways. Dewey believed that students, facing an ever-changing world, should master the scientific method: (1) Become aware of a problem; (2) define it; (3) propose various hypotheses to solve it; (4) examine the consequences of each hypothesis in the light of previous experience; and (5) test the most likely solution. (John Dewey is also discussed in Chapter 5.)

Dewey regarded democracy and freedom as far superior to the political ideas of earlier times. Dewey saw traditional, autocratic, teacher-centered schools as the antithesis of democratic ideals. He viewed progressive schools as a working model of democracy. Dewey wrote:

> To imposition from above is opposed expression and cultivation of individuality; to external discipline is opposed free activity; to learning from texts and teachers, learning through experience; to acquisition of isolated skills and techniques by drill is opposed acquisition of them as means of attaining ends which make direct vital appeal; to preparation for a more or less remote future is opposed making the most of the opportunities of present life; to statistics and materials is opposed acquaintance with a changing world.[5]

The Progressive Classroom Walk into a progressivist classroom, and you will not find a teacher standing at the front of the room talking to rows of seated students. Rather, you will likely see children working in small groups, moving about and talking freely. Some children might be discussing a science experiment, while another group works on a model volcano, and a third prepares for a presentation. Interest centers would be located throughout the room, filled with books, materials, software, and projects designed to attract student interest on a wide array of topics. Finally you notice the teacher, walking around the room, bending over to talk with individual students and small groups, asking questions and making suggestions. You sense that the last thing on her mind is the standardized state test scheduled for next week.[6]

Progressivists build the curriculum around the experiences, interests, and abilities of students, and encourage students to work together cooperatively. Teachers feel no compulsion to focus their students' attention on one discrete discipline at a time, and students integrate several subjects in their studies. Thought-provoking activities augment reading, and a game like Monopoly might be used to illustrate the principles of capitalism versus socialism. Computer simulations, field trips, and arts-based learning offer realistic learning challenges for students and build on students' multiple intelligences.

Learning by doing is a touchstone of progressivism

Progressivism in Action: The Laboratory School In 1896, while a professor at the University of Chicago, Dewey founded the **Laboratory School** as a testing ground for his educational ideas. Dewey's writings and his work with the Laboratory School set the stage for the progressive education movement. Based on the view that educators, like scientists, need a place to test their ideas, Dewey's Laboratory School eventually became the most famous experimental school in the history of U.S. education, a place where thousands observed Dewey's innovations in school design, methods, and curriculum. Although the school remained under Dewey's control for only eight years and never enrolled more than 140 students (ages 3 to 13) in a single year, its influence was enormous.

Dewey designed the Lab School with only one classroom but with several facilities for experiential learning: a science laboratory, an art room, a woodworking shop, and a kitchen. Children were likely to make their own weights and measures in the laboratory, illustrate their own stories in the art room, build a boat in the shop, and learn chemistry in the kitchen. They were unlikely to learn through isolated exercises or drills, which, according to Dewey, students consider irrelevant. Because Dewey believed that students learn from social interaction, the school used many group methods, such as cooperative model-making, field trips, role-playing, and dramatizations. Dewey maintained that group techniques make the students better citizens, developing, for example, their willingness to share responsibilities.

Children in the Laboratory School were not promoted from one grade to another after mastering certain material. Rather, they were grouped according to their individual interests and abilities. For all its child-centered orientation, however, the Laboratory School remained hierarchical in the sense that the students were never given a role comparable to that of the staff in determining the school's educational practices.

Social Reconstructionism

Social reconstructionism encourages schools, teachers, and students to focus their studies and energies on alleviating pervasive social inequities and, as the name implies, reconstruct society into a new and more just social order. Although social reconstructionists agree with progressivists that schools should concentrate on the needs of students, they split from progressivism in the 1920s after growing impatient with the slow pace of change in schools and in society. **George Counts,** a student of Dewey, published his classic book, *Dare the Schools Build a New Social Order?,* in which he outlined a more ambitious, and clearly more radical, approach to education. Counts's book, written in 1932, was no doubt influenced by the human cost of the Great Depression. He proposed that schools focus on reforming society, an idea that caught the imagination and sparked the ideals of educators both in this country and abroad.

Social challenges and problems provide a natural (and moral) direction for curricular and instructional activities. Racism, sexism, environmental pollution, homelessness, poverty, substance abuse, homophobia, AIDS, and violence are rooted in misinformation and thrive in ignorance. Therefore, social reconstructionists believe that school is the ideal place to begin ameliorating social problems. The teacher's role is to explore social problems, suggest alternate

In social reconstructionism, students not only learn by doing, they learn to make the world a better, more just place to live.

perspectives, and facilitate student analysis of these problems. Although convincing, cajoling, or moralizing about the importance of addressing human tragedy would be a natural teacher response, such adult-led decision making flies in the face of reconstructionist philosophy. A social reconstructionist teacher must model democratic principles. Students and teachers are expected to live and learn in a democratic culture; the students themselves must select educational objectives and social priorities.

The Social Reconstructionist Classroom A social reconstructionist teacher creates lessons that both intellectually inform and emotionally stir students about the inequities that surround them. A class might read a book and visit a photojournalist's exhibit portraying violent acts of racism. If the book, exhibit, and the class discussion that follows move the students, the class might choose to pursue a long-term project to investigate the problem. One group of students might analyze news coverage of racial and ethnic groups in the community. Another student group might conduct a survey analyzing community perceptions of racial groups and race relations. Students might visit city hall and examine arrest and trial records to determine the role race plays in differential application of the law. Students might examine government records for information about housing patterns, income levels, graduation rates, and other relevant statistics. The teacher's role would be as facilitator: assisting students in focusing their questions, developing a strategy, helping to organize visits, and ensuring that the data collected and analyzed meet standards of objectivity. Throughout, the teacher would be instructing students on research techniques, statistical evaluation, writing skills, and public communications.

In a social reconstructionist class, a research project is more than an academic exercise; the class is engaged in a genuine effort to improve society. In this case, the class might arrange to meet with political leaders, encouraging them to create programs or legislation to respond to issues the students uncovered. The students might seek a *pro bono* attorney to initiate legal action to remedy a social injustice they unmasked. Or perhaps the students might take their findings directly to the media by holding a press conference. They might also create a web page to share their findings and research methods with students in other parts of the country or other parts of the world. How would the teacher decide if the students have met the educational goals? In this example, an objective, well-prepared report would be one criterion, and reducing or eliminating a racist community practice would be a second measure of success. (See Contemporary Issues: A View from the Field to learn how an entire school and an individual teacher follow the social reconstructionist philosophy to improve the environment.)

Social Reconstructionism in Action: Paulo Freire **Paulo Freire** believed that schools were just another institution perpetuating social inequities while serving the interests of the dominant group. Like social reconstructionism itself, Freire's beliefs grew during the Great Depression of the 1930s, when he experienced hunger and poverty firsthand. Influenced by Marxist and neo-Marxist ideas, Freire accused schools of perpetuating the status quo views of the rich and powerful "for the purpose of keeping the masses submerged and content in a culture of silence."[7] Schools were endorsing **social Darwinism,**

PROFILE IN EDUCATION

Jane Roland Martin

Jane Roland Martin advocates the development of "schoolhomes" that support what she calls the 3 Cs—caring, concern, and connection. Her social reconstructionist vision focuses on fostering students' individual emotional and cognitive needs. To read a full profile of Jane Roland Martin, go to the Chapter 6 Profile in Education at www.mhhe.com/sadkerbrief3e.

A VIEW FROM THE FIELD: GREENING SCHOOLS

Sidwell Friends Middle School in Washington, D.C., is one of a few, but growing number of green schools. Guided by its Quaker values, Sidwell Friends is committed to practicing responsible environmental stewardship. The building itself has achieved a LEED Platinum green certification, the highest level awarded.

Every aspect of the building has been constructed or remodeled with an eye toward conservation and sustainability. Photovoltaic panels on the roof provide 5 percent of the school's energy, which helps power the computer lab. On the rooftop garden, students grow herbs and vegetables for their school lunches. A constructed wetland in front of the school looks like an attractive, sloping landscape with a variety of plants, but it is much more. The school's wastewater flows below, filtered and cleaned by the plants and microorganisms, and then is recycled and used in the school's toilets. Skylights and reflective panels maximize the natural light in classrooms, a renovation that has been shown to improve academic performance. The windows, with their light-filtering shades, are the single most energy-efficient step employed in the building: Sidwell uses 10 to 15 percent of the energy of a comparable building to light the school. Even the siding on the building is green; the wood cladding is made from reclaimed cedar wine casks. Sidwell Friends represents an amazing institutional commitment to environmental sustainability. Educators use these building innovations as teaching tools, to help students understand the importance of protecting our planet. More and more, teachers across the nation are also promoting green living. Take, for example, Andy Stephens.

Andy Stephens, 26, is a science teacher at CALS Early College High School in Los Angeles. Andy's school is not a certified green school but he incorporates environmental education into his curriculum.

> We focus on the impacts we have at our school in terms of energy usage, transportation, waste, recycling, and indoor air quality. In a culminating project, I work with a team of teachers to create an interdisciplinary (math, science, history, English) action project that includes a research paper, civic action, presentation, and reflection. Students look at the science behind an issue, mathematically analyze data, write about the history of the issue, and take action.

Andy also leads the school's environmental club, the Mean Green Team. The club's many activities include beach cleanups and peer education.

Andy was actively interested in the environment before becoming a teacher. He was an avid hiker, hunter, and fisherman growing up in Washington. "I was galvanized towards action at a young age thanks to many outdoor experiences and my connection to the land."

More information about Sidwell Friends School and its green building can be found at www.sidwell.edu.

Andy Stephens has a BA in economics from Occidental College and completed his master's in science education at California State University Northridge in 2008.

the idea that society is an ingenious "sorting" system, one in which the more talented rise to the top, while those less deserving find themselves at the bottom of the social and economic pecking order. The conclusion: Those with money deserve it, those without money deserve their lot in life, and poverty is a normal, preordained part of reality.

Freire rejected this conclusion. He did not believe that schools should be viewed as "banks," where the privileged deposit ideas like social Darwinism to be spoon-fed into the limited minds of the dispossessed. He envisioned schools as a place where the poor can acquire the skills to regain control of their lives and influence the social and economic forces that locked them in poverty in the first place. Freire engaged the poor as equal partners in dialogues that explored their economic and social problems and possible solutions. Freire believed in **praxis,** the doctrine that when actions are based on sound theory and values, they can make a real difference in the world. (It is no accident that the term praxis is also the name given to the teacher competency tests required by many states.) Freire's ideas took hold not only in his native Brazil, but in poor areas around the globe. As poor farm workers became literate and aware, they organized for their self-improvement, and began to work for change. It is not surprising that the autocratic leaders of his country eventually forced him into exile, for he had turned schooling into a liberating force. (For a biography of Paulo Freire, see the Hall of Fame: Profiles in Education in Chapter 5.)

Existentialism

Existentialism, the final student-centered philosophy we shall discuss, places the highest priority on students directing their own learning. **Existentialism** asserts that the purpose of education is to help children find meaning and direction in their lives, and it rejects the notion that adults should or could direct meaningful learning for children. Existentialists do not believe that "truth" is objective and applicable to all. Instead, each of us must look within ourselves to discover our own truth, our own purpose in life. Teaching students what adults believe they should learn is neither efficient nor effective; in fact, most of this "learning" will be forgotten. Instead, each student should decide what he or she needs to learn, and when to learn it. As the Buddhist proverb reminds us: When the student is ready, the teacher will appear.

There is little doubt that for many readers this is the most challenging of all the philosophies, and schools built on this premise will seem the most alien. We are a culture very connected to the outside world, and far less connected to our inner voice, or as an existentialist might say, our essence. We compete with each other for material goods, and we are distracted by hundreds of cable channels, iPods, and a constant array of external stimuli. Thinking about why we are here and finding our purpose in life is not what schools typically do, but existentialists believe it is precisely what they should do. Schools should help each of us answer the fundamental questions: Why am I here? What is my purpose?

The Existentialist Classroom Existentialism in the classroom is a powerful rejection of traditional, and particularly essentialist thinking. In the existentialist classroom, subject matter takes second place to helping the students understand and appreciate themselves as unique individuals. The teacher's role is to help students define their own essence by exposing them to various paths they may take in life and by creating an environment in which they can freely choose their way. Existentialism, more than other educational philosophies, affords students great latitude in their choice of subject matter and activity.

The existentialist curriculum often emphasizes the humanities as a means of providing students with vicarious experiences that will help unleash their creativity and self-expression. For example, existentialists focus on the actions of historical individuals, each of whom provides a model for the students to explore. Math and the natural sciences may be deemphasized because their subject matter is less fruitful for promoting self-awareness. Career education is regarded more as a means of teaching students about their potential than of teaching a livelihood. In art, existentialism encourages individual creativity and imagination more than it does the imitation of established models.

Existentialist learning is self-paced, self-directed, and includes a great deal of individual contact with the teacher. Honest interpersonal relationships are emphasized; roles and "official" status are deemphasized. According to philosopher Maxine Greene, teachers themselves must be deeply involved in their own learning and questioning: "Only a teacher in search of his freedom can inspire a

	Focus of Curriculum	Sample Classroom Activity	Role of Teacher	Goals for Students	Educational Leaders
Student-Centered Philosophies					
Progressivism	Flexible; integrated study of academic subjects around the needs and experiences of students	Learning by doing—for example, students plan a field trip to learn about history, geography, and natural science	Guide and integrate learning activities so that students can find meaning	To become intelligent problem solvers, socially aware citizens who are prepared to live comfortably in the world	John Dewey, Nel Noddings
Social Reconstructionism	Focus on social, political, and economic needs; integrated study of academic subjects around socially meaningful actions	Learning by reconstructing society—for example, students work to remove health hazards in a building housing the poor	Provide authentic learning activities that both instruct students and improve society	To become intelligent problem solvers, to enjoy learning, to live comfortably in the world while also helping reshape it	George S. Counts, John Brameld, Jane Roland Martin
Existentialism	Each student determines the pace and direction of his or her own learning	Students choose their preferred medium—such as poetry, prose, or painting—and evaluate their own performance	One who seeks to relate to each student honestly; skilled at creating a free, open, and stimuating environment	To accept personal responsibility; to understand deeply and be at peace with one's own unique individuality	A. S. Neill, Maxine Greene
Teacher-Centered Philosophies					
Essentialism	Core curriculum of traditional academic topics and traditional American virtues	Teacher focuses on "essential" information or the development of particular skills	Model of academic and moral virtue; center of classroom	To become culturally literate individuals, model citizens educated to compete in the world	William Bagley, E. D. Hirsch, Jr., William Bennett
Perennialism	Core curriculum analyzing enduring ideas found in Great Books	Socratic dialogue analyzing a philosophical issue or the meaning of a great work of literature	Scholarly role model; philosophically oriented, helps students seek the truth for themselves	To increase their intellectual powers and to appreciate learning for its own sake	Robert Hutchins, Mortimer Adler

TABLE 6.1 Five philosophies of education.

REFLECTION: How many of these philosophies have you experienced in your own education? Describe the circumstances. Would you like to encounter others as a student? a teacher? Explain.

student to search for his own." Greene asserts that education should move teachers and students to "wide awakeness," the ability to discover their own truths.[8]

Although elements of existentialism occasionally appear in public schools, this philosophy has not been widely disseminated. In an age of high-stakes tests and standards, only a few schools, mostly private, implement existentialist ideas. Even Summerhill, the well-known existentialist school founded in England by A. S. Neill in 1921, struggles to persevere with its unusual educational approach.

Existentialism in Action: The Sudbury Valley School Visit Sudbury Valley School just outside of Boston, Massachusetts; look around, look closely, and you still may not see the school. The large building nestled next to a fishing pond on a 10-acre campus looks more like a mansion than a school. Walk inside, and you will find students and adults doing pretty much as they please. Not a "class" in sight. Some people are talking, some playing, some reading. A group is building a bookcase over there, a student is working on the computer in the corner, another is taking a nap on a chair. All ages mix freely, with no discernable grade level for any activity. In fact, it is even difficult to locate the teachers. If there is a curriculum, it is difficult to detect. Instead, the school offers a wide variety of educational options, including field trips to Boston, New York, and the nearby mountains and seacoast, and the use of facilities that include a laboratory, a woodworking shop, a computer room, a kitchen, a darkroom, an art room, and several music rooms.

Sudbury Valley provides a setting, an opportunity, but each student must decide what to do with that opportunity. Students are trusted to make their own decisions about learning. The school's purpose is to build on the students' natural curiosity, based on the belief that authentic learning takes place only when students initiate it. The school operates on the premise that all its students are creative, and each should be helped to discover and nurture his or her individual talents.

Sudbury Valley is fully accredited, and the majority of Sudbury Valley's graduates have continued on to college. The school accepts anyone from 4-year-olds to adults and charges low tuition, so as not to exclude anyone. Evaluations or grades are given only on request. A high school diploma is awarded to those who complete relevant requirements, which mainly focus on the ability to be a responsible member of the community at large. More than 30 schools follow the Sudbury model, including schools in Canada, Europe, Israel, and Japan.[9]

Can Teachers Blend These Five Philosophies?

Some of you might be drawn to (and let's face it, sometimes repelled by) one or more of these philosophies. A social reconstructionist idea like students learning as they work to improve the world sounds perfect to some of us, while a more traditional approach focused on reading and discussing Great Books is a dream come true to others. But for many, elements from both of these approaches are appealing. So you might be wondering if this is an either/or proposition; must we be purists and choose one philosophy, or can we mix and match, blending two or more philosophies?

VOICES OF THE FIVE PHILOSOPHIES

YESTERDAY'S VOICES

William Bagley (1874–1946) *Essentialism* Bagley believed that the major role of the school is to produce a literate, intelligent electorate; he argued against electives while stressing thinking skills to help students apply their academic knowledge.

Robert M. Hutchins (1899–1979) *Perennialism* During the 16 years he served as president of the University of Chicago, Hutchins abolished fraternities, football, and compulsory attendance, and introduced the Great Books program.

John Dewey (1859–1952) *Progressivism* A founder of progressivism, Dewey not only worked to democratize schools, he also fought for women's suffrage and the right of teachers to form unions.

George S. Counts (1907–1974) *Social Reconstructionism* Counts viewed education as an important tool to counter social injustices, and, if educators questioned their own power to make critical decisions, Counts's plea was to "Just do it!"

A. S. Neill (1883–1973) *Existentialism* Neill's attitude toward education stemmed from his own problems as a student, problems which fueled his creation of Summerhill, a school that encouraged youngsters to make their own decisions about what and when to learn.

TODAY'S VOICES

E. D. Hirsch, Jr. (1928–) *Essentialism* He established the Core Knowledge Foundation to develop a prescribed curriculum in subject areas, including technology. Visit your local bookstore and browse through his books delineating what educated people should know.

Mortimer Adler (1902–2001) *Perennialism* He renewed interest in perennialism with the publication of *The Paideia Proposal* (1982). Adler advocated that all students be educated in the classics and that education be a lifelong venture.

Nel Noddings (1929–) *Progressivism* She believes that an ethic of care can best be cultivated when the curriculum is centered around the interests of students. Schools are challenged to nourish the physical, spiritual, occupational, and intellectual development of each child.

bell hooks (1952–) *Social Reconstructionism* Her theory of education, *engaged pedagogy,* helps students and teachers develop a critical consciousness of race, gender, and class biases. A prolific writer, her books include *Ain't I a Woman: Black Women and Feminism* (1981) and *Teaching to Transgress: Education as the Practice of Freedom* (1994).

Maxine Greene (1917–) *Existentialism* She believes that it is crucial for students and teachers to create meaning in their lives. Greene sees the humanities and the arts as catalysts for moving people to critical awareness and conscious engagement with the world.

REFLECTION: How do historical and political events influence which of these voices are heard? Which voices are being heard in public policy circles today, and which are not?

As you probably have guessed, people differ on the answer, which means you get to think it through and come to your own conclusion. Some schools blend several philosophies. For example, the YES College Preparatory School in Houston and Wakefield High School in Maryland mix several philosophies in their programs. There is both traditional academic emphasis on content mastery, with many AP tests being offered, as well as a more progressive approach as students create independent senior projects. Faculty and students seem to appreciate the blending. But others are not so sure this is a good idea.

Advocates of a purist model argue that although blending sounds like a comfortable and reasonable compromise, much is lost. For example, if we want children to be independent problem solvers, then we must promote that approach. Blending independent problem solving with a traditional philosophy of teachers telling students what they are to learn does not work. Either students are taught how to think for themselves, or they are told what to think, and compromise is not an option. More traditional teachers have their reservations as well. They fear that much of progressive education, although replete with lofty goals, actually leads to little real learning. They claim that blending student-centered philosophies with a demanding traditional curriculum actually dilutes learning.[10] As you consider where you want to teach geographically, you might also want to consider where you want to teach philosophically. Are you comfortable with the school's educational philosophy? If you have some freedom in structuring your classroom, which philosophy or philosophies will you follow? Are you a purist, or will you be blending several philosophies?

Psychological Influences on Education

While essentialism, perennialism, progressivism, social reconstructionism, and existentialism are influential philosophies of education, they are far from the only forces shaping today's schools. The following descriptions offer a glimpse into some other ideas guiding current school practices.

Focus Question 5
What are some of the psychological and -cultural factors influencing education?

Constructivism

Constructivism, like existentialism, puts the learner at the center of the educational stage. **Constructivism** asserts that knowledge cannot be handed from one person to another (from a teacher to a learner), but must be *constructed* by each learner through interpreting and reinterpreting a constant flow of information. Constructivists believe that people continually try to make sense and bring order to the world.

Built on the work of Swiss and Russian psychologists, Jean Piaget and Lev Vygotsky, constructivism reflects the cognitive psychologists' view that the essence of learning is the constant effort to assimilate new information. In a constructivist classroom, the teacher builds knowledge in much the same way, gauging a student's prior knowledge and understanding, then carefully orchestrating cues, penetrating questions, and instructional activities that challenge and extend a student's insight. Teachers can use **scaffolding,** that is, questions, clues, or suggestions that help a student link prior knowledge to the new information. The educational challenges facing students in a constructivist classroom could be creating a new way to handle a math problem, letting go of an unfounded bias about an ethnic group, or discovering why women's contributions seem all but absent in a history textbook. In a constructivist classroom, students and teachers constantly challenge their own assumptions. (If you check back to the philosophy inventory, see how you responded to item 26, which captured this aspect of constructivism.)

Although constructivism runs counter to the current emphasis on uniform standards and testing, it is enjoying popularity, especially among school reformers. Perhaps part of the reason for its growing acceptance is that constructivism dovetails with authentic learning, critical thinking, individualized instruction, and project-based learning.

Behaviorism

In stark contrast to both existentialism and constructivism, **behaviorism** is derived from the belief that free will is an illusion, and that human beings are shaped entirely by their environment. Alter a person's environment, and you will alter his or her thoughts, feelings, and behavior. People act in response to physical stimuli. We learn, for instance, to avoid overexposure to heat through the impulses of pain our nerves send to our brain. More complex learning, such as understanding the material in this chapter, is also determined by stimuli, such as the educational support you have received from your professor or parents and the comfort of the chair in which you sit when reading this chapter.

Harvard professor **B. F. Skinner** became the leading advocate of behaviorism, and he did much to popularize the use of positive reinforcement to promote desired learning. Behaviorists urge teachers to use a system of reinforcement to encourage desired behaviors, to connect learning with pleasure and reward (a smile, special privilege, or good grades). In a program termed **behavior modification,** extrinsic rewards are gradually lessened as the student acquires and masters the targeted behavior. By association, the desired behavior now produces its own reward (self-satisfaction). This process may take minutes, weeks, or years, depending on the complexity of the learning desired and on the past environment of the learner. The teacher's goal is to move the learner from extrinsic to intrinsic rewards. (If you check the inventory at the chapter's opening, behaviorism was represented by statement 27. How did you respond?)

Critics of behaviorism decry behaviorists' disbelief in the autonomy of the individual. They ask, Are people little more than selfish "reward machines"? Can clever forces manipulate populations through clever social engineering? Are educators qualified to exert such total control of students? Those who defend behaviorism point to its striking successes. Behaviorism's influence is apparent in the joy on students' faces as they receive visual and auditory rewards via their computer monitor, or in the classroom down the hall where special needs learners make significant progress in a behaviorist-designed curriculum.

www.mhhe.com/
sadkerbrief3e

INTERACTIVE ACTIVITY
What Philosophy or Approach Is This? Read scenarios and match the philosophy or approach being exhibited.

Cultural Influences on Education

Most of the ideas and philosophies discussed in this chapter are drawn from Western culture. As a nation, we rarely identify or reflect on the ideas that derive from many parts of Asia, Africa, and Latin America. We are guilty of **ethnocentrism,** the tendency to view one's own culture as superior to others, and (perhaps worse) a failure to consider other cultures at all. Let's broaden our view and examine education as practiced in other cultures.

In much of the West, society's needs dictate educational practices, such as statewide standards, national goals, and high-stakes testing. In the rest of the world, that is to say, in most of the world, the child's education is primarily a concern of the family, not the society. A child's vocational interests, for example, might mirror the occupation of a parent or be built around the unique interest or talent of the child, rather than respond to the broader employment market or societal priorities. Family and community are foremost; the nation is a weaker influence.

In Western society, formal schools, formal certification, and degrees are valued; in other societies, more credence is placed on actual knowledge and mastery rather than educational documentation. The notion of *teachers* and *nonteachers* is foreign in many cultures because all adults and even older children participate in educating the young. Children learn adult roles through observation, conversation, assisting, and imitating, all the while absorbing moral, intellectual, and vocational lessons. This shared educational responsibility is called **informal education.**[11] (What does calling this practice "informal education" reveal about Western values and assumptions? Would someone in a culture practicing this integrated education call it "informal education"?) In the process, adults also learn a great deal about the children in the community. Strong bonds are forged between the generations. (As you probably already concluded, item 28 on our opening inventory describes informal education. You might want to check your answer to that statement.)

Oral traditions enjoy particular prominence in many parts of the world, even in literate societies where reading and writing are commonplace and valued. In the **oral tradition,** spoken language becomes a primary method for instruction: Word problems teach reasoning skills; proverbs instill wisdom; and stories, anecdotes, and rhymes teach lessons about nature, history, religion, and social customs. The oral tradition refines communication and analytical skills, and reinforces human connections and moral values. Not infrequently, religious and moral lessons were passed on initially through oral communication, only later to be written. In fact, the word Qur'an (Koran) is often translated as "the Recitation."

The practices and beliefs of peoples in other parts of the world offer useful insights for enhancing—or questioning—our own educational practices, but they are insights too rarely considered, much less implemented. Perhaps this will change in the years ahead as immigration continues to bring these ideas to our communities, and technological advances bring all world cultures closer together. For now, however, our education philosophies are rooted in the ideas and thoughts of Western thinkers. Let's visit some of these powerful, legendary thinkers and their enduring contributions.

The Three Legendary Figures of Classical Western Philosophy

Focus Question 6

What were the contributions of Socrates, Plato, and Aristotle to Western philosophy, and how are their legacies reflected in education today?

To understand Western philosophy, we must look back to the birthplace of Western philosophy—ancient Greece. Specifically, we must begin with a trio of philosopher-teachers: Socrates, Plato, and Aristotle. Together they laid the foundation for most of Western philosophy. It is likely that you are familiar with at least their names. Let's review their lasting contributions to the world of philosophy.

The name of **Socrates** is practically synonymous with wisdom and the philosophical life. Socrates (469–399 B.C.E.) was a teacher without a school. He walked about Athens, engaging people in provocative dialogues about questions of ultimate significance. Socrates is hailed as an exemplar of human virtue whose goal was to help others find the truths that lie within their own minds. In that regard, he described himself as a "midwife"; today we call his approach the **Socratic method.** By repeatedly questioning, disproving, and testing the thoughts of his pupils on such questions as the nature of "love" or "the good," he helped his students reach deeper, clearer ideas.

Socrates' method did not just promote intellectual insights in his students; it also challenged the conventional ideas and traditions of his time. Socrates offended many powerful people and was eventually charged with corrupting the youth of Athens. Even in this, Socrates provides a lesson for today's teachers: challenges to popular convention may lead to community opposition and sanctions. (Luckily, sanctions today are less severe than those meted out to Socrates, who was condemned to death for his "impiety.")

We know about Socrates and his teachings through the writings of his disciples, one of whom was **Plato** (427–347 B.C.E.). Plato's writing is renowned for its depth, beauty, and clarity. His most famous works were dialogues, conversations between two or more people, that present and critique various philosophical viewpoints. Plato's dialogues feature Socrates questioning and challenging others and presenting his own philosophy. After Socrates was put to death, Plato became disillusioned with Athenian democracy and left the city for many years. Later, he returned to Athens and founded the **Academy,** considered by some to be the world's first university.

Plato held that a realm of eternally existing "ideas" or "forms" underlies the physical world. In Plato's philosophy, the human soul has three parts: intellect, spirit, and appetite (basic animal desires). Plato believed that these faculties interact to determine human behavior. Plato urged that the intellect, the highest faculty, be trained to control the other two. For a look at Plato's famous "Allegory of the Cave," from *The Republic,* setting out his political philosophy (he envisioned a class of philosopher-kings that would rule over the warriors and the common people), visit the Online Learning Center.

Just as Plato studied under Socrates, **Aristotle** (384–322 B.C.E.) studied under Plato. Aristotle entered Plato's Academy at age 18 and stayed for 20 years. In 342 B.C.E., Aristotle went to northern Greece and, for several years, tutored a young boy named Alexander, later known as Alexander the Great. After educating Alexander, Aristotle returned to Athens to set up his own school, the *Lyceum,* adjacent to Plato's Academy.

The depth and breadth of Aristotle's ideas were unsurpassed in ancient Western civilization. In addition to tackling philosophical questions, Aristotle wrote influential works on biology, physics, astronomy, mathematics,

WHY WE REMEMBER SOCRATES, PLATO, AND ARISTOTLE

- **Socrates.** His philosophical lifestyle; the Socratic method, in which students are provocatively questioned so that they can rethink what they believe; his noble death
- **Plato.** Discussions of philosophy through eloquent dialogues; the theory of "forms," or "ideas," that exist in an eternal, transcendent realm; a vision of utopia, where an elite group of philosopher-kings rules over other members of society

- **Aristotle.** The breadth of his knowledge; the synthesis of Plato's belief in the eternal "forms" and a scientist's belief in the "real" world that we can see, touch, or smell; the theory of the Golden Mean (everything in moderation)

REFLECTION: How might your current classroom instruction change if your education professor was Dr. Socrates, Plato, or Aristotle?

psychology, and literary criticism. Aristotle placed more importance on the physical world than did Plato. Aristotle's teachings can, in fact, be regarded as a synthesis of Plato's belief in the universal, spiritual forms, and a scientist's belief that each animal, vegetable, and mineral we observe is undeniably real.

Aristotle also won renown for his ethical and political theories. He wrote that the highest good for people is a virtuous life, fully governed by the faculty of reason, with which all other faculties are in harmony. Aristotle promoted the doctrine of the *Golden Mean,* or the notion that virtue lies in a middle ground between two extremes. Courage, for example, is bordered on the one side by cowardice and on the other side by foolhardiness.

Many of the ideas first formulated by Socrates, Plato, and Aristotle have long been integrated into Western culture and education.

Basic Philosophical Issues and Concepts

Philosophy has many subdivisions that are of particular significance to educators: metaphysics, epistemology, ethics, political philosophy, aesthetics, and logic (see Figure 6.1). These fields are where key educational questions are

Focus Question 7
How do metaphysics, epistemology, ethics, political philosophy, aesthetics, and logic factor into a philosophy of education?

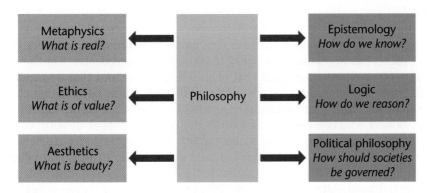

FIGURE 6.1
Branches of philosophy.

REFLECTION: This view of philosophy is like a tree, with rich branches for further study.

raised, including: How do we know what we know? What is of value? What is education's role in society? As you ponder these questions, you should find elements of your philosophy of education coming into sharper focus.

Metaphysics and Epistemology

Metaphysics deals with the origin and structure of reality. Metaphysicians ask: What really is the nature of the world in which we live? **Epistemology** examines the nature and origin of human knowledge. Epistemologists are interested in how we use our minds to distinguish valid from illusory paths to true knowledge. It may be easiest to remember the scope of these closely related disciplines by considering that epistemology and metaphysics address, respectively, *how* we know (epistemology) *what* we know (metaphysics) about reality.

Is Reality Composed Solely of Matter? One of the most basic metaphysical issues is whether anything exists other than the material realm that we experience with our senses. Many philosophers assert the existence only of the physical, affirming fundamentally the existence of matter, a philosophy called **materialism.** By emphasizing in their curriculum the study of nature through scientific observation, modern public schools clearly deem that the material world is real and important. Other philosophers contend that the physical realm is but an illusion. They point out that matter is known only through the mind. This philosophy is called spiritualism or **idealism.** Educators responding to ideals believe that the physical world exists to teach us higher principles and meaningful lessons, but life is far more than a drive to acquire physical things. Spiritual leaders like Jesus and Gandhi have taught these lessons. Educators focused on idealism might teach students the importance of finding their place and purpose in the world, the importance of helping one another, and the need to protect the environment rather than abuse it. A third group of philosophers asserts that reality is composed of both materialism and idealism, body and mind, a belief associated with French philosopher René Descartes and called **Cartesian dualism.**

Is Reality Characterized by Change and Progress? Metaphysicians question whether nature is constantly improving through time. The belief that progress is inevitable is widely held in the United States. On the other hand, some philosophers hold that change is illusory and that a foundation of timeless, static content underlies all reality. Still others believe that change is cyclical, swinging widely from one side of center to the opposing side.

Teachers who believe in the inevitability of progress seek new approaches to teaching and new subjects to be taught, thereby "keeping up with the times." Other teachers, less enamored with change, pay little heed to current trends and technologies. They may prefer to teach everlasting, timeless truths discovered by great thinkers, such as Plato and Aristotle. Finally, some teachers suggest that, with change such a constant, it is pointless to try to keep pace. They choose to ignore these cycles and to select the teaching methods they find most comfortable.

What Is the Basis of Our Knowledge? Empiricism holds that sensory experience (seeing, hearing, touching, and so on) is the source of knowledge. Empiricists assert that we experience the external world by sensory perception; then, through reflection, we conceptualize ideas that help us interpret that world. For example, because we have seen the sun rise every day, we can formulate the belief that it will rise again tomorrow. The empiricist doctrine that knowledge is gained most reliably through scientific experimentation may be the most widely held belief in Western culture. People want to hear the latest research or be shown documentation that something is true. Teachers expect students to present evidence before drawing conclusions. Even children demand of one another: "Prove it."

Rationalism emphasizes the power of reason—in particular, logic—to derive true statements about the world, even when such realities are not detected by the senses. Rationalists point out that the field of mathematics has generated considerable knowledge that is not based on our senses. For example, we can reason that 7 cubed equals 343 without having to count 7 times 7 times 7 objects to verify our conclusion experientially. Whereas educational empiricists would support hands-on learning activities as the primary source for discovery and validation of information, rationalists would encourage schools to place a greater emphasis on teaching mathematics, as well as such nonempirical disciplines as philosophy and logic.

Ethics, Political Philosophy, and Aesthetics

Whereas metaphysics focuses on what "is," ethics, political philosophy, and aesthetics are concerned with what "ought to be." In these disciplines, philosophers grapple with the issue of what we should value. As you read on, consider the place of ethics, political philosophy, and aesthetics in the classroom.

Ethics is the study of what is "good" or "bad" in human behavior, thoughts, and feelings. It asks: What is the good life? How should we treat each other? (What should schools teach children about what is "good" and what is "bad"?)

Political philosophy analyzes how past and present societies are arranged and governed and proposes ways to create better societies in the future. (How might schools engage in an objective evaluation of current governments, including our own?)

Aesthetics probes the nature of beauty. It asks: What is beauty? Is beauty solely in the eyes of the beholder? Or are some objects, people, and works (music, art, literature) objectively more beautiful than others? (How can teachers help students understand how their personal experiences, peer group values, and cultural and ethnic history shape their standards of what is beautiful?)

Logic

Logic is the branch of philosophy that deals with reasoning. Logic focuses on how to move from a set of assumptions to valid conclusions and examines

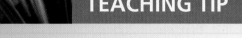

WRITING YOUR PHILOSOPHY STATEMENT

Writing your philosophy of teaching statement can feel like a daunting experience, but it's a lot more manageable when you do it one step at a time. Here a few ideas to help you get started.

1. Review the philosophies described in this chapter. Which one(s) most closely aligns with your beliefs about education? Why?
2. Now, ask yourself some specific questions about learning, teaching, and schools:

   • What qualities do good teachers have?
   • What is the role of a teacher?
   • The role of a student?
   • What adjectives describe your teaching style?
   • What is the most effective way to motivate students?
   • What should students learn in school?

   • What is the most effective way to assess student learning?
   • What is the purpose of school?

   Your answers to these questions are the beginning of your philosophy statement! A philosophy of teaching statement might be just one or two typed pages, but collecting your thoughts into a single document helps you reflect on how you will apply your knowledge and insights to your actual teaching practice. Your philosophy is a work in progress. As your teaching experience grows and reflections deepen, see how much your ideas change, or stay the same.

   REFLECTION: What new insights did you learn about yourself, teaching, or learning from drafting your philosophy statement?

the rules of inference that enable us to frame our propositions and arguments. While epistemology defines reasoning as one way to gain knowledge, logic defines the rules of reasoning.

Schools teach children to reason both deductively and inductively. When teaching **deductive reasoning,** teachers present their students with a general rule and then help them identify particular examples and applications of the rule. Inductive reasoning works in the opposite manner. When teaching **inductive reasoning,** teachers help their students draw tentative generalizations after having observed specific instances of a phenomenon.

A teacher who explains the commutative property of addition $(a + b = b + a)$ and then has the student work out specific examples of this rule (such as $3 + 2 = 2 + 3$) is teaching deductive reasoning. Contrast this with a teacher who begins a lesson by stating a series of addition problems of the form $3 + 2 = 5$ and $2 + 3 = 5$, then asks, "What do you notice about these examples?" If students can draw a generalization about the commutative property of addition, they are reasoning inductively. While math is a natural field to isolate examples of deductive and inductive reasoning, logic equips students to think more precisely in virtually any field.

Your Turn

[I]n modern times there are opposing views about the practice of education. There is no general agreement about what the young should learn either in relation to virtue or in relation to the best life; nor is it clear whether their education ought to be directed more towards the intellect than towards the character of the soul. . . . [A]nd it is not certain whether training should be directed at things useful in life, or at those conducive to virtue, or at nonessentials. . . . And there is no agreement as to what in fact does tend towards virtue. Men [sic] do not all prize most highly the same virtue, so naturally they differ also about the proper training for it.[12]

—**Aristotle**

More than 2,300 years later, we still find that reasonable people can come to entirely different points of view on all kinds of issues in education. (Remember the faculty charter school discussion at the beginning of the chapter?) If everyone agreed on what should be taught, and how to teach it, there might be just one philosophy of education. But it is not so simple.

Rereading the inventory statements at the beginning of this chapter can help you determine if one of the five major philosophies speaks for you. You may be more eclectic in your outlook, picking and choosing elements from different philosophies. Your responsibility as an educator is to wrestle with tough questions, to bring your values to the surface, and to forge a coherent philosophy of education.

You might say that a clear philosophy of education is to a teacher what a blueprint is to a builder—a plan of action; reassurance that the parts will fit together in a constructive way. With a clear philosophy of education, you will not ricochet from one teaching method to another, and will not confuse students, parents, and administrators with conflicting messages about the role of students and teacher in the classroom. If you have a well-honed philosophy of education, you will be better able to assess whether you will find a comfortable fit in a school and a community. Simply put, a philosophy brings purpose and coherence to your work in the classroom.

SUMMARY

1. **What is a philosophy of education, and why should it be important to you?**

   Behind every school and every teacher is a philosophy of education that reflects the purpose of schooling and the role of the teacher.

2. **How do teacher-centered philosophies of education differ from student-centered philosophies of education?**

   Teacher-centered philosophies, like essentialism and perennialism, are traditional and emphasize the values and knowledge that have survived through time. Student-centered philosophies focus on individual needs, contemporary relevance, and a future orientation.

3. **What are some major philosophies of education in the United States today?**

   Essentialists emphasize a strong core curriculum, and perennialists value Great Books and stress eternal truths. Progressivists focus on the needs of the students, and social reconstructionists directly confront societal ills. Existentialism focuses on the need for students to shape their own futures.

4. **How are these philosophies reflected in school practices?**

   Essentialism and perennialism give teachers the power to choose the curriculum and construct classroom activities. Progressivism, social reconstructionism, and existentialism focus on student interests and view the teacher as a guide.

CHAPTER REVIEW

Go to the Online Learning Center to take a chapter self-quiz, practice with key terms, and review concepts from the chapter.

www.mhhe.com/
sadkerbrief3e

5. What are some of the psychological and cultural factors influencing education?

Constructivist teachers carefully orchestrate cues, classroom activities, and penetrating questions to push students to higher levels of understanding. Skinner "teaches" behavior through an extrinsic reward system. Informal and oral education offer useful insights from non-Western cultures.

6. What were the contributions of Socrates, Plato, and Aristotle to Western philosophy, and how are their legacies reflected in education today?

Socrates used persistent questions to help students clarify their thoughts (Socratic method). Plato crafted eloquent dialogues that present different philosophical positions. Aristotle provided a synthesis of Plato's belief in the universal, spiritual forms, and a scientist's belief in the physical world.

7. How do metaphysics, epistemology, ethics, political philosophy, aesthetics, and logic factor into a philosophy of education?

Metaphysics poses curricular choices: Should we study the natural world, or focus on spiritual or ideal forms? Epistemology influences teaching methods and asks how we know. Ethics is the study of what is "good" or "bad" in human behavior. Political philosophy asks: How will a classroom be organized, and what will that say about who wields power? Aesthetics raises the issue: What works are valuable?

KEY TERMS AND PEOPLE

KEY TERMS

Academy, 202

aesthetics, 205

back-to-basics, 184

behavior modification, 200

behaviorism, 200

Cartesian dualism, 204

constructivism, 199

core curriculum, 185

deductive reasoning, 206

empiricism, 205

epistemology, 204

essentialism, 184

ethics, 205

ethnocentrism, 201

existentialism, 195

Great Books, 186

idealism, 204

inductive reasoning, 206

informal education, 201

Laboratory School, 191

logic, 205

materialism, 204

metaphysics, 204

oral tradition, 201

perennialism, 186

philosophy, 179

political philosophy, 205

pragmatism, 190

praxis, 194

progressivism, 190

rationalism, 205

scaffolding, 199

social Darwinism, 193

social reconstructionism, 192

Socratic method, 202

KEY PEOPLE

Mortimer Adler, 187, 198

Aristotle, 202

William Bagley, 184, 198

George Counts, 192, 198

John Dewey, 190, 198

Paulo Freire, 193

Maxine Greene, 198

E. D. Hirsch, Jr., 184, 198

bell hooks, 198

Robert Hutchins, 187, 198

A. S. Neill, 198

Nel Noddings, 198

Plato, 202

B. F. Skinner, 200

Socrates, 202

DISCUSSION QUESTIONS AND ACTIVITIES

1. Suppose that you are a student who must choose one of five schools to attend. Each reflects one of the five major philosophies. Which would you choose and why? Which school would you choose to work in as a teacher? Why?

2. Interview a teacher who has been teaching for several years. Find out what that teacher's philosophy was when he or she started teaching and what it is today. Is there a difference? If so, try to find out why.

3. Reread the five statements by the teachers in the faculty room at the beginning of the chapter. In what areas do you think these teachers could agree? In what areas are their philosophies distinct and different? What do you predict will be the result of their meeting? Which of the statements by the five teachers do you agree with most?

4. How would you describe your own philosophy of education? Imagine you are a teacher. Create a 3-minute speech that you would give to parents on back-to-school night that outlines your philosophy of education and identifies how it would be evident in the classroom.

5. The ideas in this chapter could be dramatically expanded by including Far Eastern and Middle Eastern philosophy. Consider the following additions: Buddhism, Confucianism, Hinduism, Islam, Jainism, Judaism, Mohammedanism, Shintoism, Taoism, and Zen Buddhism. Research and briefly describe each of these. What has been (or might be) the impact of these ideas on our present educational philosophies?

WEB-*TIVITIES*

Go to the Online Learning Center to do the following activities:

1. What Is Your Philosophy of Education?
2. Philosophies of Education
3. Progressivism and Dewey's Laboratory School
4. Existentialism
5. Behaviorism

YOUR CD-ROM: THE *TEACHERS, SCHOOLS, AND SOCIETY READER* WITH CLASSROOM OBSERVATION VIDEO CLIPS

Articles, Case Studies, and Videos correspond to chapter content and are not always in numeric order. Go to your *Teachers, Schools, and Society Reader* CD-ROM to:

Read Current and Historical Articles

29. Text excerpts from *Experience and Education,* John Dewey.

30. "Pathways to Reform: Start with Values," David Ferrero, Jr., *Educational Leadership,* February 2005.

31. Text excerpts from *Escape from Childhood,* John Holt, E. P. Dutton, 1974. The excerpt is taken from *Taking Sides,* 2009.

32. "Dewey, Freire, and Pedagogy for the Oppressor," Rick A. Breault, *Multicultural Education,* Spring 2003.

Analyze Case Studies

14. **Brenda Forester:** A preservice education student is concerned that one of her methods classes will not prepare her for teaching. Her philosophy of education is challenged when she observes a writing process classroom.

15. **Michael Watson:** A teacher finds that the assistant principal's evaluation of his class calls into question his teaching style as well as his philosophy of

education. The evaluation suggests that his style and rapport with the students are getting in the way of his being more demanding.

Observe Teachers, Students, and Classrooms in Action

Classroom Observation

13. Essentialism in Action: A Classroom Lesson
See page 186 of this text for a description of this video. You'll find the video on the CD Reader and at the Online Learning Center.

www.mhhe.com/
sadkerbrief3e

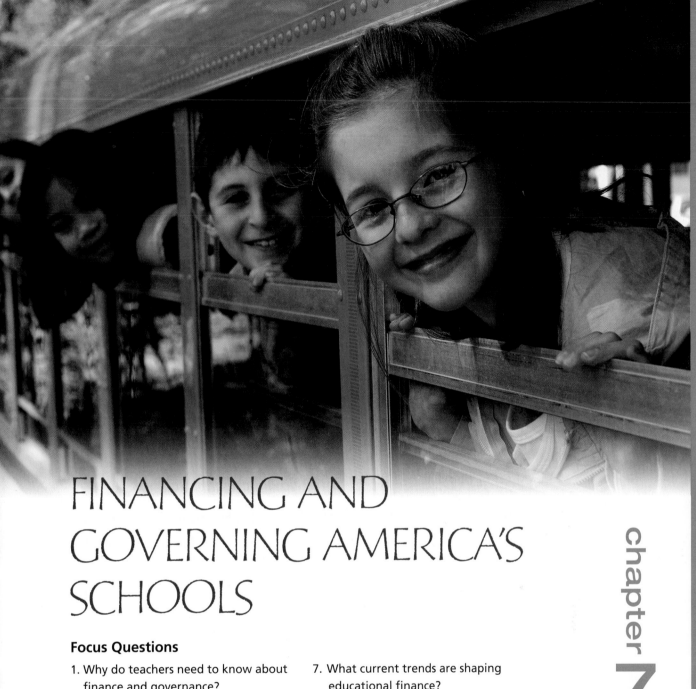

FINANCING AND GOVERNING AMERICA'S SCHOOLS

chapter 7

Focus Questions

1. Why do teachers need to know about finance and governance?
2. How is the property tax connected to unequal educational funding?
3. What is the distinction between educational equity and educational adequacy?
4. What are the sources of state revenues?
5. How does the federal government influence education?
6. How does commercialization at home and in school affect children?
7. What current trends are shaping educational finance?
8. How do school boards and superintendents manage schools?
9. What is the "hidden" government of schools?
10. How does the business community influence school culture?
11. How are schools being made more responsive to teachers and the community?

WHAT DO YOU THINK? What Costs More? Try your hand at ranking the cost of several items on a state education budget.

www.mhhe.com/
sadkerbrief3e

Chapter Preview

Do you know who pays for U.S. schools, and how? You might be surprised. In this chapter we introduce you to the decentralized, politically charged systems of school funding and school governance in the United States. You will become familiar with the sources of financial inequity in schooling and, more important, learn how reformers are pursuing strategies to keep effective education within the reach of all, not just the very wealthy. Both the formal structure of power in school governance (school boards, school superintendents, and the like) and the informal, hidden government will impact your life in the classroom. By understanding the mechanics behind school finance and governance, you will be more empowered as a classroom teacher and better able to influence decisions that shape the education of our nation's children.

Local and state governments have long grappled with the difficult proposition of raising enough public funds to adequately support education while dodging taxpayer ire over high taxes. Students in wealthy neighborhoods attend modern, well-equipped schools; poorer children make their way to decaying, ill-equipped school buildings in impoverished communities. Courts have forged solutions aimed at reducing these glaring disparities and bringing a measure of fairness to education. Many states are now focusing on guaranteeing that every student receives an adequate and appropriate education.

Day-to-day classroom life is influenced not only by economic issues but also by the ways in which schools are governed. In this chapter, you will learn how schools are managed, officially and unofficially. Your knowledge of educational decision making can be a powerful ally in shaping a successful teaching career.

Follow the Money: Financing America's Schools

Why Should Teachers Care Where the Money Comes From?

Focus Question 1
Why do teachers need to know about finance and governance?

Why should a teacher be concerned much about school finance? (Put another way, why should I want to read this chapter?) Doesn't a teacher's responsibility pretty much start and end at the classroom door?

Sounds reasonable, but here is where the authors jump in. We believe that it is unwise, and even dangerous, for teachers to invest their time and talent in a career where the key decisions are considered beyond their knowledge or influence. Educational finance may well determine not just the quality of life you experience as a teacher, but the very futures of the students you teach. Common sense tells us that the amount of money spent in a school is directly related to how well students learn, but not everyone agrees. What is the wisest way to invest educational dollars—and who should decide?

We believe that teachers should be major participants in financial and governance policy decisions. The current trend toward testing teachers and developing school standards is an example of what happens when teachers are left out of policy circles. The emphasis on standards and testing too often casts the teacher in the role of a technician, implementing other people's goals with the resources other people decide they should have. And in the end, other people evaluate how well teachers (and students) perform. We believe that this system serves neither teachers nor students well. We see teachers as advocates for children, children who themselves are excluded from policy decisions. Teachers and students find themselves the victims of rising educational expectations but limited educational resources. And too many teachers are forced to dig into their own pockets, spending an average of $475 a year on teaching materials.[1] (See Contemporary Issues: A View from the Field.)

Teachers should have a voice, and be a voice for children as well. Consider this chapter a step in that direction and a primer on both the economics and governance of schools.

The Property Tax: The Road to Unequal Schools

> The method of financing public schools . . . can be fairly described as chaotic and unjust.
>
> **—Supreme Court Justice Potter Stewart**

To someone from another country, the way the United States funds its schools must seem bizarre, and certainly unfair. Unlike many other nations, which use a centralized funding system, we have a decentralized system. In fact, we have three levels of government—local, state, and federal—all raising and distributing funds. Currently, the local and state governments share the biggest burden of funding schools, with the federal government responsible for just 6 to 8 percent of the total. What a tangled web we weave when 50 states, 14,000 local governments, and one enormous federal government become involved in funding and managing 90,000 schools.

How did this financial hodgepodge begin? In colonial America, schools were the concern of local communities. Then, at the birth of our nation, the Constitution did not designate a federal role in education, effectively leaving it the responsibility of the states. "Local control" of schools became a well-established tradition, one that still holds sway today.

In the agrarian society of colonial times, wealth was measured by the size of people's farms. So to raise money for schools, colonial towns and districts assessed a **property tax.** Although today only 2 percent of Americans still work the land, the property tax continues to be the major source of school revenue. Today's property taxes are levied on real estate (homes and businesses) and sometimes personal property (cars and boats). Whether a school district will find itself rich in resources or scrambling to make ends meet depends largely on the wealth of the community being taxed. Not surprisingly, a tax on a Beverly Hills mansion raises many more thousands of dollars than a tax on a house in South Central Los Angeles. Communities blessed with valuable real estate can more easily raise funds for their schools. Impoverished communities are not so fortunate. Urban areas struggle the most, suffering not only from lower property values, but also from the need to use those limited resources to fund more social workers, hospitals, mass transit, and other services than their suburban or rural counterparts, a phenomenon known as *municipal overburden.*[2]

Reforming Education Finance

Unequal school funding results in stark differences. In 1968, 48-year-old sheet-metal

Focus Question 2
How is the property tax connected to unequal educational funding?

Steadily increasing property taxes have led to taxpayer protests.

A VIEW FROM THE FIELD: SCHOOLS IN NEED

James Rosenberg, a mergers and acquisitions attorney, founded Adopt-A-Classroom after mentoring a student at a school for physically and mentally delayed children. He couldn't believe the lack of resources available to the school and how much money teachers across the country spend each year on classroom supplies. James wanted to lend a hand. With a law school friend he started Adopt-A-Classroom, partnering underresourced classrooms with caring individuals. An interested donor can visit the website and find a specific classroom to assist or let the organization choose a needy classroom in the donor's community. The teacher receiving the donation can use the funds to shop online with retailers participating in the Adopt-A-Classroom program. If the teacher is unable to locate the needed resources, Adopt-A-Classroom will work with that teacher to fill the request.

Leana Borges, a teacher at P.S. 175 in New York City, has been a recipient of a classroom donation from the organization. "My class has benefited so much from the Adopt-A-Classroom program," Leana writes on the Adopt-A-Classroom website. "We have received plenty of products that we use on a daily basis to help in science class, such as measuring tools, safety tools (goggles), and various math manipulatives. These products have enabled my students to get a clearer understanding of the concepts I have taught." Another teacher, Kristina Kim of Sutro Elementary in San Francisco, found much more than an anonymous donor when she asked for help.

> Little did I know just how big an impact Adopt-A-Classroom would make. When Constance adopted us, she did so for the long haul. For the last two years, she has supported us with her never-ending generosity, impenetrable spirit and enormous heart. Without her, we would not have our new center table, paper cutter, crayons and markers, not to mention all of the little things that we teachers must often purchase with our own money . . . glue, construction paper, scissors. . . . Those "little things" add up. . . . Our kids benefit from her priceless friendship every year, and every year I have the joy and honor of introducing this incredible woman to a whole new class of kids.

VISIT Adopt-A-Classroom at www.adoptaclassroom.org. For a list of other organizations that help classrooms in need, please visit http:// www.donorschoose.org/.

worker Demetrio Rodriguez looked with despair at his children's school in a poor Latino section of San Antonio, Texas. Not only did Edgewood Elementary School lack adequate books and air conditioning, the top two floors were condemned, and barely half the teachers were certified.[3] Ten minutes away, in affluent Alamo Heights, children were taught by certified teachers, in comfortable surroundings with ample materials. The educational cards were stacked against Rodriguez and his neighbors: even though Edgewood residents paid one of the highest tax rates on their property of any Texas community, their property was not worth much. Edgewood raised only $37 per student; Alamo Heights raised $412 per student. Rodriguez went to court, claiming that the system violated the U.S. Constitution's guarantee for equal protection under the law.

In a landmark decision, ***San Antonio v. Rodriguez*** (1973), the Supreme Court ruled against Rodriguez (by one vote, 5-4!), deferring to the long history of local communities funding neighborhood schools. The Court declared that education was not a "fundamental right" under the U.S. Constitution, and that preserving local control was a legitimate reason to use the property tax system. While the Court recognized that educational funding through the property tax was a seriously flawed system, it was left up to the states to change it. It took 16 more years before the Texas Supreme Court would act on the Rodriguez case. By the mid-1980s, Edgewood had neither typewriters nor a playground, but affluent Alamo Heights had computers and a swimming pool. Throughout Texas, per-pupil expenditures ranged from $2,112 in the poorest community to $19,333 in the wealthiest. In *Edgewood v. Kirby* (1989) the Texas Supreme Court issued a unanimous decision that such differences violated the Texas constitution, and ordered Texas to devise a fairer plan.

Reformers had more courtroom success under state constitutions' equal protection clauses. The California Supreme Court, in ***Serrano v. Priest*** (1971), struck down the state's financing system as unconstitutional. The court, faced with the glaring differences between Beverly Hills, spending $1,232 per student, and nearby Baldwin Park, spending only $577 a student, declared that education was a fundamental right under the California constitution and that the property tax system violated equal protection of that right. The court found that heavy reliance on the local property tax "makes the quality of a child's education a function of the wealth of his parents and neighbors. . . . Districts with small tax bases simply cannot levy taxes at a rate sufficient to produce the revenue that more affluent districts produce with a minimum effort." *The Serrano v. Priest* decision ushered in both a wave of litigation in other states and an increase in the state share of school funding[4] (see Figures 7.1 and 7.2). **Robin Hood reformers,** as they were called, won a victory as they took funds from wealthy districts and redistributed the monies to the poorer districts, much like the Robin Hood hero of Sherwood Forest fame. States have used different programs to try to equalize funding. In the foundation program, the state provides funds to ensure that each student receives a minimal or "foundation" level of educational services. Unfortunately, the established minimum is frequently far below actual expenditures. Another approach is the guaranteed tax base program, which adds state funds to poorer districts, helping to reduce economic inequities.

The *Serrano* victory in California was short-lived. Many voters feared tax increases, and wealthy voters revolted as their tax dollars were transported from their own children's schools to faraway poor schools. Proposition 13 was passed to limit the property tax. With decreased tax revenue, California saw its schools go into a rapid decline. California schools were finally becoming equal, but equally bad.

PROFILE IN EDUCATION

Jaime Escalante

Jaime Escalante did not let obstacles constructed by a school district in a low socioeconomic area prevent his students from learning calculus. He launched a calculus AP program in a troubled East Los Angeles school, which resulted in his students passing the AP exam and the launching of a series of other AP classes in the school. While providing inspiration in the 1980s, Escalante's teaching still illustrates what can be achieved by a single teacher. To read a full profile of Jaime Escalante, go to the Chapter 7 Profile in Education at www. mhhe.com/sadkerbrief3e.

FIGURE 7.1

The public education dollar: Where the money comes from.

SOURCE: Public Education Finances, 2008. U.S. Census Bureau, issued June 2010.

REFLECTION: Is the proportion of revenue spent by local, state, and federal governments on education different from your initial perceptions? If you were able to suggest changes in this pie graph, what would they be? Why?

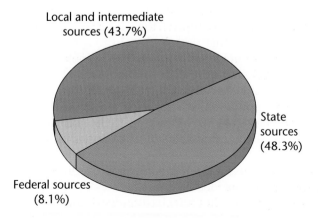

Local and intermediate sources (43.7%)

State sources (48.3%)

Federal sources (8.1%)

FIGURE 7.2

The public education dollar: Where the money goes.

SOURCE: Public Education Finances, 2008. U.S. Census Bureau, issued June 2010.

REFLECTION: Does the distribution of educational funds surprise you? Are there changes that you would suggest?

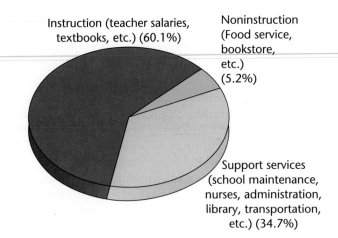

Instruction (teacher salaries, textbooks, etc.) (60.1%)

Noninstruction (Food service, bookstore, etc.) (5.2%)

Support services (school maintenance, nurses, administration, library, transportation, etc.) (34.7%)

From Robin Hood to Adequacy

Focus Question 3
What is the distinction between educational equity and educational adequacy?

As the effort to equalize funding disparities grew, so did the opposition. In New Jersey, for example, the legislature was dominated by wealthy interests and middle-class communities who fought the Robin Hood idea. The state court shut down the schools to force the legislature to distribute more funds to poorer districts. In *Abbott* v. *Burke* (1990, 1998), the state court identified twenty-eight failing districts (known as "Abbott districts") where the rights of poor students were being denied. The court mandated that significantly greater funds be spent to transform their students into "productive members of society."[5]

The *Abbott* cases in New Jersey contributed to a new line of litigation focusing on *educational outcome* (student achievement) rather than *financial input* (per-pupil expenditures). State constitutions do not guarantee that every student is entitled to either an equal education or equal funding, but they do guarantee a basic education to all. States use different words to express this right. Some states require that every student receives an "efficient" education, others a "sound basic" education or a "thorough" education, or that all schools need to be "free and uniform."[6] Together, these constitutional clauses are referred to as **adequate education** guarantees, intended to ensure that all students have the basic skills they need to be effective citizens and compete in the labor market.[7]

States differ dramatically in how they interpret adequate education. In Kentucky, the court ruled that the state's "entire system of common schools was infirm."[8] The Kentucky state legislature launched a new curriculum, statewide performance tests, preschool programs for at-risk students, multiple grades in the same class, and economic incentives for educational progress. New York took a minimalist approach, requiring all schools to provide students with desks and pencils, but not up-to-date science textbooks.[9] States from Wyoming to Ohio endured years of litigation as they struggled to define adequate education.

Perhaps the purest example of the adequacy approach is found in Maryland. Historically, states decided how much money they could afford to spend on education, and then decided how best to distribute those funds. Maryland

"Equity" or "Adequacy"

WE SHOULD SEEK EDUCATIONAL "EQUITY" BECAUSE . . .

MONEY TALKS

The gap between wealthy and poor communities makes a mockery of democracy and fairness. Poor students attend schools with leaking roofs and uncertified teachers; wealthy students learn in schools with computers, swimming pools, and well-paid and qualified teachers. No real democracy can ignore such glaring inequities.

EQUALIZING INPUT IS CRUCIAL

Isn't it strange that those who advocate business values like choice and competition ignore the most fundamental business value of all: money. Wealth creates good schools; poverty creates weak ones. Invest money wisely over a period of time, and watch those once poor schools thrive.

EQUITY IS POWERFUL

Democracy and equity are powerful words representing powerful ideals. Adequacy is a feeble word subject to interpretation and compromise. What's adequate? Is it the ability to read at a high school level, or at an eighth grade level? Does an adequate education lead to a minimum wage job? Only "Equity" can serve as a rallying cry.

WE SHOULD SEEK EDUCATIONAL "ADEQUACY" BECAUSE . . .

MONEY DIVIDES

Robin Hood is dead. Wealthy communities are not going to fund poor ones, happily sending their hard-earned dollars to fund someone else's school. The cornerstone of democracy is local control, and trying to redistribute wealth is fundamentally unfair, and smacks of the approach used by Communists (another failed system).

EQUALIZING INPUT IS INEFFECTIVE

We will never make schools more effective by throwing dollars at them. When California moved toward equitable input, the quality of its public schools deteriorated. Our goal is not to increase school budgets and per-pupil expenditures, but to increase student achievement.

ADEQUACY IS ATTAINABLE

Equity is a powerful dream, but adequacy is an attainable one. We are unlikely to achieve a completely equitable school system, but we can demand reasonable and reachable educational standards. Moreover, we are on firmer legal footing, because state constitutions guarantee not identical expenditures, but an adequate education for all.

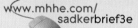

www.mhhe.com/
sadkerbrief3e **YOU DECIDE . . .**

Do you believe that adequacy or equity provides the best foundation for reforming schools? Explain.

Can these approaches be blended, or are they mutually exclusive?

turned that approach upside down. The state appointed a commission that defined adequate education, then computed how much money was needed to achieve it. Adequate education was defined as a school with at least 94 percent student attendance, less than a 4 percent dropout rate, and 70 percent or more of the students passing state achievement tests. Then the state commission studied successful schools that were meeting those goals and found that they were spending about $6,000 per pupil. At the other end of the spectrum, low-performing schools had high numbers of poor children, non-English speakers, and children with special needs. Maryland determined that those schools would require an additional $4,500 per pupil to reach the goals of an adequate education: Maryland would need to add more than a billion education dollars. The state tackled the problem voluntarily, and without litigation.[10]

Maryland calls its program "The Bridge to Excellence" and invested about 80 percent of the additional funds for teacher salaries and hirings, particularly teachers working with poor and special education students, as well as English Language Learners. By 2009, its investment in education seemed to be working. *Education Week* ranked the state's schools first in the nation.[11]

But not every state enjoyed Maryland's success. In many parts of the country, the academic gains were small or nonexistent. In Camden, New Jersey, for example, tens of millions of additional dollars did not improve academic performance, and some argued that the additional funds were not used wisely. Camden was not alone. Court-ordered increases in school funding have not always improved academic performance.[12] Some believe that the slow pace of academic improvement may force the courts to rethink the entire notion of adequate education, asking the question, Does money matter?[13]

Does Money Matter?

> To my knowledge, the U.S. is the only nation to fund elementary and secondary education based on local wealth. Other developed countries either equalize funding or provide extra funding for individuals or groups felt to need it.[14]

Why do Americans tolerate such dramatic inequities in school funding? Here are a few explanations[15]

1. *Local control.* In colonial times, it was left to individual communities in rural America to support their local schools. The Constitution codified this practice, and even after urbanization and suburbanization, Americans continue to believe that local taxes should be used to educate neighborhood children.

2. *Horatio Alger.* The rags-to-riches story of fictional Horatio Alger symbolizes the strongly held American belief that wealth and success are the fruits of individual effort, and that an individual's circumstances are merely obstacles to be overcome. It stands to reason, therefore, that if hard work and motivation alone are responsible for success, poverty comes from a lack of effort and a lack of talent. Individualism absolves communities from any collective responsibility for the poverty of others.

3. *Genetics.* For centuries, genetic differences have been used to explain why some succeed and others fail. The notion that certain groups are genetically deficient is a recurring theme and often promoted in books such as Richard Hernstein and Charles Murray's *The Bell Curve.*

4. *Culture of poverty.* Some believe that poor people live in and are shaped by the problems inherent in impoverished communities, problems that cannot be remedied through additional school funding.

5. *Flawed studies.* Back in the 1960s, the classic Coleman study reported that school quality and funding had less of an effect on student achievement than family background or peer groups, that schools mattered very little. (Note: Such studies have been cited for major methodological flaws.)

6. *Previous funding increases have not resulted in achievement gains.* Critics point out that although education spending has increased, test scores have not. However, most new funds were not for increasing scores, but for specific educational needs, like special education, dropout prevention, expanded school lunch programs, and higher teacher salaries.

Does money matter? Trick question: It depends on how it is spent. Wealthier schools can attract better prepared teachers and create smaller classes, factors that make a difference.[16] Poorer schools cannot afford this.[17] In Illinois, for example, one wealthy district spends about $20,000 more per student (not $20,000 per student, which is amazing, but $20,000 *more* per student) than a poor district in that state.[18] All across America, schools with educational everything continue to exist alongside schools struggling to keep the heat in and the rats out. Research suggests that well-spent funds can reduce the achievement gap, but adequate education does not even attempt to equalize spending; it simply tries to ensure a fundamental level of learning for all students.[19] Despite the Horatio Alger "rags-to-riches" myth, studies show that children born into poor families in the United States are less likely to rise out of poverty than those in other industrialized nations.[20] Schools disappoint the poor, and states need the money to reform them.

States Finding the Money

Let's assume that you have been asked by your (choose one or more of the following): (a) education professor, (b) teacher association, (c) favorite political candidate, or (d) spouse, to find out where states find the money for our schools. Here are some common sources:

Focus Question 4
What are the sources of state revenues?

1. *Sales tax* (a charge added to all sales). Consumers pay a few extra pennies for small purchases or a few extra dollars for large purchases. The sales tax accounts for 30 percent of the typical state's income.[21] More than 40 states use a 2 percent to 8 percent sales tax. Sounds easy, but there are problems: some people avoid the tax by taking their business to a neighboring state. The tax is regressive; that is, it hurts poor families more than rich ones because the poor spend most of their income buying necessities, so most of their money is being taxed.

2. *Personal income tax* (used in more than 40 states). The personal income tax brings in more than 25 percent of state revenues[22] The personal income tax is collected through payroll deductions, money deducted even before you receive your paycheck. The tax is a percentage of income, and each state determines how equally, or unequally, the tax burden falls on the poor, the middle class, and the rich.

3. *Other revenue sources.* Other common state sources of funding include excise taxes (on tobacco, gasoline, and liquor, sometimes known as a *sin tax*), severance tax (based on the state's mineral wealth), motor vehicle license fees, estate or gift taxes, and state lotteries. Although state lotteries offer holders of winning tickets the chance to collect millions in prize money, a disproportionate higher percentage of the poor purchase these long-shot lottery tickets. Most states use lottery revenues to supplement, not fund, parts of an established education budget[23]

Your brief course in "State Finance 101" is over. You can see some of the limits of state revenue sources. For extra credit, can you devise an entirely new scheme to raise state funds? As you can tell from Figure 7.3, states vary widely in how much money is invested in education.

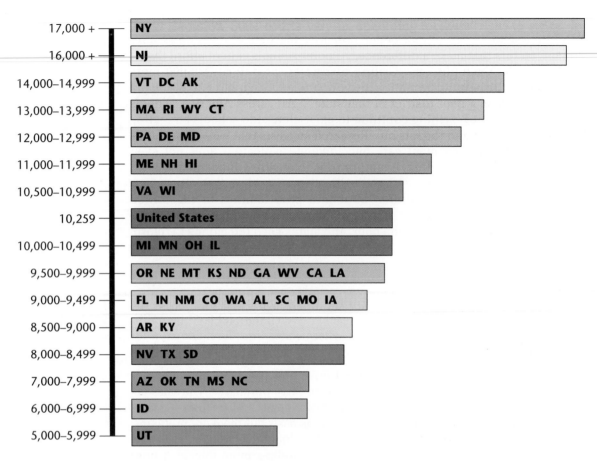

FIGURE 7.3

Per-pupil expenditures for elementary and secondary schools: School year 2007–2008.

SOURCE: 2008 Annual Survey of Local Government Finances—School System, U.S. Census Bureau, April 2007, Updated June 2010.

NOTE: Current expenditures include salaries, employee benefits, purchased services, and supplies, but exclude capital outlay, debt service, facilities acquisition and construction, and equipment.

REFLECTION: Do your teaching plans include any of the states on the top or bottom of this list? Will this spending information influence your decision on where to teach? *For more information on how different states respond to the needs of children, visit www.childrendefense.org.*

The Federal Government's Role in Financing Education

Focus Question 5
How does the federal government influence education?

At this point, some of you might be thinking: Even if every state provided every school district with adequate funding and a great education plan, the economic gaps among the states would still be enormous. If you thought about that, congratulations; you have put your finger on a systemic problem. For instance, students in New York or Connecticut typically receive far more education dollars than students in Mississippi or Arizona, regardless of the state's revenue plan. Because of the Constitution, this is a problem the United States seems unable to correct.

If the Constitution had assigned education as a federal responsibility, we might expect to see the federal government close the economic gap between states. U.S. schools might be centrally financed and governed; or at the very least, the Supreme Court might rule funding inequities among states unconstitutional. But this is not the case. The Supreme Court has ruled that education is not a "fundamental right" under the U.S. Constitution and has left education to the states. Accordingly, the federal government's role in the financing of education is relatively small. In fact, the federal government typically pays only 6 to 9 percent of the nation's educational costs.[24]

However, the federal government still manages to influence schools. How does it do this? One way has been through **categorical grants**—funds directed at specific categories and targeted educational needs. Categorical grants have provided funding for preschool programs for poor children, library construction, acquisition of new technology, education opportunities for veterans, the training of teachers and administrators, educational reform, lunches for low-income youth, and loans to college students. By targeting funds, federal aid, although limited, has had a significant impact on schools.

The federal government also funds schools through **block grants,** large sums of money given directly to the states with few strings attached. Block grants reduce the obligations, rules, and even competition associated with seeking federal dollars. You can see that each type of grant has strengths and weaknesses. Categorical grants give the federal government influence by identifying how federal money should be used. Block grants give the states the power to make those spending decisions.

The federal government also influences education through the courts. For example, the 1954 Supreme Court's *Brown* decision desegregated the nation's schools, a monumental change that affected every state in the union. The civil rights laws that followed increased educational opportunities for students of color, limited speakers of English, students with disabilities, and females. Federal courts matter, and so do targeted federal laws such as *No Child Left Behind* (2001), which ushered in an era of high-stakes testing. (You will read about these laws, court cases, and more in Chapter 8, "School Law and Ethics.") The federal government gets a pretty big bang for its buck, but in 2009, the federal role got even bigger, if only for a limited time.

President Obama took office in January 2009, in the midst of the most profound economic crisis since the Great Depression. To spur the failing economy, he initiated the *American Recovery and Revitalization Act* (*ARRA*), and part of *ARRA* doubled federal aid to schools and prevented the firing of hundreds of thousands of teachers and professors. Education Secretary Arne Duncan set aside billions of dollars for a "Race to the Top" competition to spur school reform.[25] But by 2011, this extra funding ended, and the federal government again became a very minor partner in financing public schools.

Schools, Children, and Commercialism

This section is about the impact of businesses on children and schools, and we want to tell you up front that we are not neutral on this topic. Business dollars are shaping our children, and not in good ways. Along with other writers and educators, the authors of this text have deep reservations about what happens to children when they are targeted by commercial interests and when schools are used for marketing products. We believe that the goal of public education should be to open minds, not turn a profit, and children should be off limits for advertisers and business interests. So as you read this section, you should be aware of our values. But as always, we do present the arguments of those on the other side of this issue in a You Be the Judge feature in Chapter 9, where we explore for-profit schools. We invite you to read both sides of the argument and form your own opinion.

Focus Question 6
How does commercialism at home and in school affect children?

Commercializing Childhood

We have become a nation that places a lower priority on teaching its children how to thrive socially, intellectually, even spiritually, than it does on training them to consume. The long-term consequences of this development are ominous.[26]

Just a few decades ago, the children's advertising industry spent $100 million selling products to kids, mainly through television ads. By 2006, food companies alone spent $1.6 billion marketing carbonated beverages, fast-food restaurants, and breakfast cereals to children.[27] Today, marketing is not just television ads. Computer games, cell phones, MP3 players, DVDs, and even school itself have become advertising hubs. Children are the target for 20 billion advertising dollars annually.

Why the surge in commercializing childhood? Politics, changing lifestyles, and electronic innovation all contribute to this problem. In the 1970s, corporate pressure moved Congress to prohibit the Federal Trade Commission (FTC) from banning television marketing to children under 8 years old. In the 1980s, children's television was deregulated even further, and television programs focused on selling products directly to children. As single-parent and two-working-parent families increased, so did the number of children watching television. Today, almost half of 3-month-old babies regularly watch television, and 10 percent of babies under 1 year of age have a television in their bedroom. The recent surge in personal electronic gadgets means that companies now target ads directly to children on iPods and other devices.[28] Advertisers influence children through product placement (in movies and computer games), brand licensing (a company's brand name placed on other products), viral marketing (advertising done on preexisting social networks), and guerrilla marketing (selling things in unconventional and unexpected places).

Today's children spend a trillion consumer dollars annually. Their allowances, their paychecks, and the influence they exert on parents' spending make them prime targets for advertisers. Marketing experts film children at play, study their behaviors, and analyze their tastes. Based on that research, sophisticated and effective sales pitches are created, and children are persuaded to buy products from fast food to cosmetics.

Are children a legitimate target for advertisers?

Here is one example of how this research shapes the buying habits of children: Advertisers have learned that younger children want to be like older children, so *aspirational marketing* was born. Advertisers intentionally market older products to younger children. Young girls are targeted for sexy adolescent clothes, although they lack the maturity to understand the strong social messages wearing such clothes sends. Abercrombie and Fitch sells thong underpants to 8-year-olds with slogans such as "wink wink" and "eye candy," and girls under 5 go to "spas" such as Sak's Fifth Avenue's Club Libby Lu to get "makeovers."[29] Rather than developing their creativity and self-expression, young girls emulate the older girls they see in *High School Musical* and *Hannah Montana.* The result is that young girls become consumers of weight-reduction products, makeup, clothes, and dating.

For young boys, it is about emulating the physical strength and toughness of older boys, so rough competitions are valued. Young boys watch wrestling matches on television, play violent video games, and sometimes experiment with steroids. The Federal Trade Commission has criticized the entertainment industry for continuing to market R-rated movies, M-rated video games, and explicit-content recordings on television shows and websites with substantial teen audiences.[30] For both genders, sex-role stereotyping is emphasized at the expense of authentic relationships. Creative play, innocence, and connecting with nature, all healthy childhood activities, are lost to commercialism.

Other industrialized nations do not let this happen. Television marketing to children is banned in Norway and Sweden, junk-food ads for the young are banned in Britain, and Greece never allows war toys to be advertised. America's children are virtually defenseless in the face of sophisticated marketing, and they pay a price. Allen Kanner, a clinical child psychologist, finds that children now talk about making money and their friends' clothes and designer labels, but "not the person's human qualities."[31]

Commercialism promotes self-gratification: "It's about me, and I want it now." Happiness is achieved by acquiring things, and one can never have enough things. Such values have led to assaults, as students attacking each other to steal designer jackets or Nike shoes. Marketing to the young teaches all kinds of lessons, few if any of them good. When the marketing occurs at school, the costs are even greater.

Brand Name Education: Should Schools Be Open for Business?

To increase attendance, some schools are offering prizes, paid for by local businesses, just for showing up. For example, in Hartford, Connecticut, a 9-year-old won a raffle for students with perfect attendance and was given the choice of a new Saturn Ion or $10,000. (His parents chose the money.) At Oldham County High School in Kentucky, a high school senior was awarded a canary yellow Ford Mustang. Krispy Kreme doughnuts awards students in Palm Beach County, Florida, a free doughnut for every report card A. Describing his quest for additional school funds, one high school principal noted, "My approach is Leave No Dollar Behind."[32]

Schools also promote specific products by entering "exclusive agreements" so that no competitive products are sold on school grounds. About 75 percent of high schools have signed exclusive soft drink contracts. Coca-Cola

What lesson is being taught in this school environment?

promised Oakland, California, half a million dollars to support a community youth program in return for a 10-year agreement banning the sale of competing soft drinks on city property. Such exclusive contracts may turn out to be a very bad business deal if schools are sued for contributing to America's obesity epidemic,[33] while keeping vendors of healthy snacks and drinks from selling on school grounds.[34]

Branding schools does not stop with products; school districts now sell the naming rights of athletic facilities, school buildings, and offer companies the opportunity to put their corporate logos on textbooks. Sometimes the corporation pays the school for getting students and parents to buy their products. General Mills donates funds to schools according to the number of boxtops turned in or other coupons showing proof of purchase. Channel One broadcasts commercials in school and on school time. Students admit they are more likely to remember the ads than the educational programs. If children grow up with Nike and McDonald's in school, they are likely to stay with those companies as adult consumers. As one critic noted, if you teach business values early enough, children accept it as truth.[35]

Schools and teachers can be persuaded to echo the tactics of advertisers. Tom Farber, an advanced-calculus teacher in San Diego, decided that a good way to pay the cost of photocopying tests was to sell advertising space to local businesses and parents. He charges $10 for an ad on a quiz, $20 for an ad on a test, and $30 for an ad on the final exam. He raised $625 and explained, "When money is tight, you really have to be creative."[36]

These are overt examples of commercialism, but it is wise to remember that the influence of business can be far more subtle. Everyday school practices that seem so familiar also teach students corporate values such as neatness, conformity, and punctuality. As educator Linda Darling-Hammond has noted:

> The short segmented tasks stressing speed and neatness that predominate in most schools, the emphasis on rules from the important to the trivial, and the obsession with bells, schedules, and time clocks are all dug deep into the ethos of late nineteenth-century America, when students were being prepared to work in factories on predetermined tasks that would not require them to figure out what to do.[37]

Commercial interests can overwhelm schools, but we are not helpless. When the Seminole County, Florida, school district was paid by McDonald's to put student report cards in envelopes covered by McDonald's advertising and offering free Happy Meals, almost 2,000 parents protested. The county was forced to stop the practice. Scholastic magazine promoted Bratz items at their book clubs and book fairs. (Bratz is the brand for provocative and sexualized dolls made under suspect labor conditions in China.) More than 5,000 e-mails persuaded Scholastic to stop the practice. Massachusetts and Vermont have introduced legislation to prohibit marketing in school, and citizens and organizations continue to lobby the federal government to regulate childhood commercialization in and beyond school.

Teachers can make an enormous difference as well. Teaching media literacy empowers children to understand and confront the market messages that manipulate them. Classrooms can be places where children discuss the underlying values implicit in consumerism and its impact on the planet and themselves. Rather than sitting by as young lives become focused on consuming, educators can help children connect with healthy alternatives, such as exploring nature, developing creative talents, discovering the joys of community service, and forming authentic relationships. For those who want to learn more about confronting childhood commercialism, we recommend the Campaign for a Commercial Free Childhood as a helpful resource.

What the Future May Hold for School Finance

Today, we are in a period of shifting governmental responsibility for the financing of schools. Reformers are focusing less on financial inequity and more on educational inadequacy. What are some other trends in educational finance, issues that are likely to surface in the years ahead?

Accountability

The public wants to see academic progress for their tax dollars—in short, **accountability.** Schools are often ranked by their students' standardized test scores, as the testing culture persists. Teachers may find their pay determined by student test scores, and tenure more difficult to obtain, or retain.

Choice Programs and the Neighborhood School

The neighborhood school, long a mainstay of public education, is being challenged by school competition and the growth of charter schools. Many neighborhood schools may disappear. (See Chapter 9, "Reforming America's Schools.")

Longer School Day and School Year

A number of charter schools have extended their school day and their school year as one tangible way to improve student performance. Some public schools are now following this trend, but it is difficult to determine what will happen when longer school days and years collide with shrinking educational budgets.[38]

Focus Question 7
What current trends are shaping educational finance?

The Economy's Impact on School Budgets

When the economy takes a downturn, state and local budgets are cut, and education suffers. This means fewer teachers, larger class sizes, and the elimination of sports, extracurricular activities, art, and music. Few state and local governments maintain the financial reserves necessary to avoid such cutbacks.[39]

The Future of Federal Assistance to Education

When the economy went into a serious recession in 2009, the federal government helped the states fund education. But the level of federal financial help was temporary, and the amount of federal help in the future is unclear.

The Rich-Poor School Divide Is Likely to Grow

www.mhhe.com/
sadkerbrief3e

INTERACTIVE ACTIVITY
**Know Your School
Finance Lingo!** Match
economic terms with
educational definitions.

While poor schools struggle, wealthier school districts are developing creative strategies to ensure that their schools are not endangered by funding redistribution plans. Through Parent-Teacher Association donations, online fund-raisers, cooperative agreements with local business endowments, and tax-sheltered private educational foundations, additional educational dollars are provided. Wealthy communities defend such practices as a way to prevent parents from fleeing "to private school if they don't perceive the public education to be excellent."[40]

Decaying Infrastructure

Here we are in the twenty-first century, using schools that were built in the nineteenth. When local governments need to replace these aging buildings, they usually resort to issuing bonds. A **bond** is a certificate of debt issued by a government guaranteeing payment of the original investment plus interest by a specified future date. Bonds give the local communities the money they need to build the schools and 15 to 20 years to pay off the debt.

But for most schools, repair, not replacement, is the remedy for antiquated buildings. Although rewiring for computer and Internet installation is needed, teachers and principals give higher priority to "adequate" heating, lighting, acoustics, ventilation, and air conditioning. The Department of Education estimates that 25,000 schools need major repairs, at an estimated cost of more than $112 billion.[41] In a nationwide survey of elementary and secondary public school principals, more than 40 percent reported that poor building conditions were impairing teacher instruction and student learning.[42] One piece of good news: Polls indicate that the public recognizes the financial need of our schools, suggesting that local bonds will be approved.[43]

Century-old inner-city schools are sad examples of the decaying infrastructure.

FINANCE LESSONS

Learning about school finance is important for educators, but learning about personal finance is useful for everyone, students and teachers alike. Remember your first paycheck? You knew how much you were earning, but when the check appeared, it was way less than you expected. Your $500 a week job was netting you just over $300 a week. Now how did that happen? Things you never heard of, like FICA, seemed to be getting some of your money. (By the way, FICA is how your social security deductions are reported.) Most students leave school woefully unprepared for the everyday world of finance.

This need not be the case. When financial literacy programs are taught, students learn the importance of savings, how compound interest works, when and how to buy items, and what tricks advertisers use to lure customers into an unwise purchase. Students understand the importance of credit scores and how to protect their credit ratings. When financial literacy is acquired, young (and older) adults can navigate the world of finance.

Although financial literacy is increasingly taught in schools, many schools are still without such a program in their curriculum. If your school is one of these, you can make an important difference by accessing relevant financial literacy lesson plans online. (But a word to the wise: Avoid websites that promote a particular bank or financial institution.) One program not aligned with a particular institution is FoolProof. Educators who want to teach financial literacy in their classrooms can sign up for lesson plans at www.fool-proofteacher.com. (And for teachers who need to update their own financial literacy skills, there's Pollinate, at www. pollinateproject.org/.)

REFLECTION: With capitalism so highly valued in U.S. society, how do you explain why the practical world of finance is often missing from the school curriculum?

Commercializing Children and Schools

Many educators and psychologists believe that marketing to the nation's children, especially in school, has an adverse affect on their health and the quality of their lives. Sophisticated marketing techniques create a thirst for consumption and selfishness that replaces healthy, caring, and creative childhood activities. Although other nations protect their young from marketers, the United States has not.

Governing America's Schools

School Governance Quiz

The following quiz should help you focus on how schools are governed. If you are stumped by some of these questions, fear not; the remainder of the chapter is organized around a discussion of these questions and their answers.

1. Most school board members are (choose only one)
   a. White, male, and middle or upper class.
   b. Middle-class women, about half of whom have been or are teachers.
   c. Middle of the road politically, about evenly divided between men and women, and representing all socioeconomic classes.
   d. So diverse politically, economically, and socially that it is impossible to make generalizations.

2. State school boards and chief state school officers are
   a. Elected by the people.
   b. Elected by the people's representatives.
   c. Appointed by the governor.
   d. Appointed by officials other than the governor.

e. All of the above.

f. None of the above.

3. During the past two decades, the influence of local school boards has

a. Increased.

b. Decreased.

c. Remained unchanged.

4. Local school district superintendents are (You may choose more than one.)

a. Often mediating conflicts.

b. Civil service–type administrators.

c. Elected officials.

d. Sometimes powerless figureheads.

5. Who might be considered part of the "hidden school government"? (You may choose more than one.)

a. The school principal.

b. The state school superintendent.

c. The U.S. secretary of education.

d. The school secretary.

e. Parents.

f. The Teacher Arbitration and Labor Relations Board.

6. The influence of the business community in U.S. schools can best be characterized as

a. Virtually nonexistent.

b. Felt only in vocational and commercial programs.

c. Extensive and growing.

d. Usually illegal.

7. In most schools, teachers are expected to

a. Design the policies guiding their schools.

b. Collaborate with principals and district officials to create policies to suit their schools.

c. Comply with policies made by principals and by district and state officials.

d. Comply with policies that seem appropriate and change those that do not.

School Governance Answer Key

1. a   2. e   3. b   4. a, b, d   5. d, e   6. c   7. c

0 to 1 wrong: You receive the Horace Mann Award.

2 wrong: You may want to run for school board.

3 wrong: Read the rest of the chapter carefully.

4 or more wrong: Take detailed notes on this part of the chapter; become a frequent visitor to the text web page; find a friend to quiz you; and whatever you do, stay away from TV quiz shows.

The Legal Control of Schools

Focus Question 8

How do school boards and superintendents manage schools?

The following sections review and discuss the quiz you have just taken, beginning with the first two questions:

1. Most school board members are . . . *white, male, and middle or upper class.*

2. School boards and chief state school officers are . . . *elected by the people, elected by the people's representatives, appointed by the governor, or appointed by officials other than the governor.*

School boards, whether at the state or local level, determine educational policy and their members tend to be male (over 60 percent), white (over 85 percent), and not young (most are 50 years of age or older). In short, school board members look like the leaders we find in corporate America or government.[44] As for the second question, in some states, school boards and chief state school officials are elected; in others, they are appointed. Even the name for the chief state school officer differs from place to place: superintendent, commissioner, or even secretary of education. Why the differences? The **Tenth Amendment** reminds us: "The powers not delegated to the United States by the Constitution, nor prohibited by it to the States, are reserved to the states, respectively, or to the people." More than 200 years ago, the authors of the Constitution did not discuss education, so each state was free to create its own school system. While most nations have a national ministry of education to determine what and how all students will be taught, in our country, each of the 50 states, the District of Columbia, and several U.S. territories make those decisions.

The governor, legislature, state superintendent, or the state school board consider different ideas for improving education. One state might require that all schools have a certain number of computers, and another state might decide that all high school students must pass four years of science. Suppose you apply for a position in a state that passed a new requirement: all new teachers must pass a course in "Instructional Strategies for Improving Student Test Performance." The state superintendent and the state department of education would inform all teacher candidates (including you) of the new course requirement. If you applied to teach in the state, someone in the state department of education would review your transcript to make certain that you had successfully completed the new course on improving test scores before issuing you a teacher's license. If you took that course and completed all the state's requirements, voilá, you will be issued your teacher's license. But (nothing personal) don't expect the state to hire you.

Although states issue teacher licenses, hiring and firing of teachers is done by the local school district, about 14,000 of them across the country. So you don't apply to the state for a teaching position, but to the local district. The district will check to make certain that you have your teacher's license, and then consider you for a position. Figure 7.4 describes these levels of school governance.

State Board of Education The **state board of education** is responsible for formulating educational policy. The members are usually appointed by the governor, but sometimes they are chosen in a statewide election.

Chief State School Officer Called *superintendent, commissioner, secretary of education, or director of instruction,* the **chief state school officer** is responsible for overseeing, regulating, and planning school activities, as well as implementing the policies of the board of education. Like the state school board, the state superintendent is often selected by the board of education but sometimes campaigns for the position in an election.

State Department of Education The **state department of education** performs the administrative tasks needed to implement state policy. This includes licensing teachers, testing student progress, distributing state and federal funds, and seeing that local school systems comply with state laws. The state superintendent manages state department of education activities.

FIGURE 7.4
Structure of a typical
state school system.

REFLECTION: What are
some of the difficulties
in these many levels of
governance? Do you favor
elected or appointed
school boards? Why?

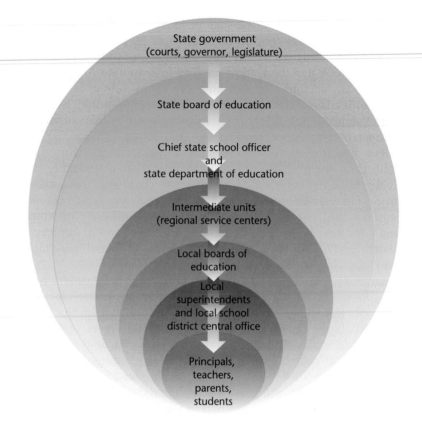

School Districts—Local School Boards and Superintendents All states
except Hawaii have delegated much of the responsibility for local school
operations to local school districts. (Hawaii treats the entire state as a single
school district.) School districts vary in size from those serving only a few students to those with more than a million. Sometimes, local school districts are
grouped into intermediate units as a way to simplify management. Most local
school districts mirror the state organization, with a local school board, superintendent, and office of education. Local school districts may be responsible
for school construction, taxing, budgeting, hiring of school personnel, curriculum decisions, local school policy, and the students' progress. Although
school districts operate at the local level, their authority derives from the
state, and they must operate within the rules and regulations specified by the
state. (A Closer Look: Who Controls What? Levels of Educational Power sum-
marizes the relationships between state and local control of schools.)

State Influence Grows as School Boards Come under Fire

3. During the past two decades, the influence of local school boards has . . .
   decreased.

   Forged in the hamlets of colonial New England, school boards have sym-
bolized small-town democracy. School board meetings evoke the essence of
Americana—the kind painted by Norman Rockwell and made into a Frank
Capra movie titled *Mr. Deeds Elected to the School Board* (starring Jimmy

WHO CONTROLS WHAT? LEVELS OF EDUCATIONAL POWER

STATE GOVERNMENTS

- Levy taxes
- License teachers and other educators
- Set standards for school attendance, safety, and so on
- Outline minimum curricular and graduation standards (sometimes including specific textbooks to be used and competency tests for student graduation and teacher certification)
- Regulate the nature and size of local school districts

LOCAL SCHOOL DISTRICTS

- Implement state regulations and policies
- Create and implement local policies and practices for effective school administration

- Hire school personnel
- Provide needed funds and build appropriate facilities
- Fix salaries and working conditions
- Translate community needs into educational practice
- Initiate additional curriculum, licensing, or other requirements beyond state requirements
- Create current and long-range plans for the school district

REFLECTION: As a classroom teacher, offer some examples of the issues that would lead you to deal with state government. Which issues would send you down a path to the local government?

Stewart as the beleaguered school board president). But Americana aside, many criticize school boards as unresponsive and entrenched bureaucracies.

Part of the problem is that there is little consensus on how school boards should operate.[45] Most school board members view themselves as *trustee representatives,* selected to serve because of their educational expertise and good judgment. But others, including many voters, see school board members as *delegate representatives,* responsible for implementing the will of the public (or being voted out of office if they do not). The type of elections used to select school board members can shape the kind of school board that will emerge. When school boards are selected through "at-large" elections, in which the entire school district votes for all the members of the school board, the school board is expected to represent the interests of the entire community (trustee representatives). But some school districts choose board members to represent the interests of specific neighborhoods (delegate representation).

Districtwide, at-large elections typically result in more elite, politically conservative, and upper-class individuals being elected to school boards. After all, it is the well-established individual who is likely to have the financial resources and educational and business background needed to win a big, districtwide election. Poorer citizens, people of color, and women are less likely to find themselves on at-large school boards. Unfortunately, many citizens feel disenfranchised when it comes to school board elections.

Other criticisms include the following:

- School boards have become *immersed in administrative details,* at the expense of more important and appropriate policy issues. One study of West Virginia school boards showed that only 3 percent of all decisions made concerned policy.
- School boards are *not representing local communities,* but only special interest groups. Elections to the school board receive little public support.

231

Classroom Observation

14. School Board Meeting to Discuss the Application of the Jaime Escalante Charter School

As a teacher, you will be affected by decisions made by your local school board. In this scene you will observe an actual Montgomery County (MD) School Board meeting during which officials struggle with a proposal for the district's first charter school.

Classroom Observation videos are available on the CD Reader and the Online Learning Center.

www.mhhe.com/
    sadkerbrief3e

www.mhhe.com/
sadkerbrief3e

INTERACTIVE ACTIVITY
Who Is in Control? Test your knowledge of who controls different aspects of the school.

In a New York City school board election, for instance, only 7 percent of the voters participated.

- The *politics of local school board elections* have a negative impact on attracting and retaining superintendents and lead to conflict with state education agencies.

- The composition of the boards is *not representative,* with individuals of color, women, the poor, and the young unrepresented or underrepresented.

- School boards have been in the *backseat when it comes to educational change and reform.* As a matter of fact, many school boards do not support current educational reform proposals, and members have lagged behind public opinion on such issues as school choice and charter schools.

- The education of children goes beyond school issues to include health, social, and nutritional concerns. School boards are *too limited in scope* to respond to all the contemporary concerns of children.

- If schools continue to be *financed less from local funds and more from state funds,* local boards could become less influential.

- Many of the new reforms call for *new governance organizations,* site-based management, or choice programs that relegate the school board to a less important, perhaps even unnecessary, role.[46]

Although these criticisms suggest a dismal future for school boards, preparing their obituary may be premature. School boards have endured a long time and may be around long after many of the reform recommendations are forgotten.

The School Superintendent and Principal

4. Local school district superintendents are . . . *often mediating conflicts, civil service–type administrators, sometimes elected and sometimes powerless figureheads.*

The first superintendents were hired to relieve school boards of their growing administrative obligations. The year was 1837, and these new superintendents worked in Buffalo and Louisville. As the nineteenth century progressed, more communities followed this example. Superintendents were expected to supervise and hire teachers, examine students, and buy supplies, which had become too burdensome for the school boards themselves. Superintendents also kept school records, developed examinations, chose textbooks, and trained teachers.

By the twentieth century, the superintendent's role had changed from the board's administrative employee to its most knowledgeable educational expert—from helper to chief executive officer. Today, the superintendent is the most powerful education officer in the school district, responsible for budgets, buildings, new programs, daily operations, long-term goals, short-term results, and recruiting, hiring, demoting, and firing personnel. When things are going well, the superintendent enjoys great popularity. But when things are going poorly, or school board members are not pleased, or local community groups are angry, or teacher organizations turn militant, or . . . you get the picture. When there is a problem, it is usually the head of the system, the superintendent, who gets fired. The superintendent lives and works in a fishbowl, trying to please various groups while managing the school district. It is a very insecure existence of sidestepping controversies, pleasing school board members, responding to critics, juggling many different roles and goals, and living with conflict. In many urban school districts, superintendents serve only a few years before they are fired, resign, or retire.[47] Many believe that this high-visibility, high-stress position is also subject to subtle forms of racism and sexism. About 80 percent of superintendents are male, and more than 90 percent are white.

One need not look hard for the reasons for this turnover. Successful superintendents must win and maintain public support and financing for their schools. This involves forming political coalitions to back their programs and to ward off attacks from those more concerned with rising taxes than with the school budget. In an era in which most citizens in many communities do not have children in schools, this becomes a real test of political acumen. Superintendents find themselves serving on a number of civic committees, speaking to community groups, and being the public relations spokesperson for the school district. Yet, despite feeling high levels of stress, 9 out of 10 superintendents find their work rewarding and believe they made the right career choice.[48]

School superintendents who survive and thrive are the politically savvy administrators who can "read" their school board. In *The School Managers: Power and Conflict in American Public Education*, Donald McCarty and Charles Ramsey provide a useful classification system that matches school board types with different superintendent styles.[49] (See the chart on page 234.)

An effective superintendent must be an effective manager, and a number of new superintendents of large school districts have been selected for their management skills rather than their educational expertise. New York City, San Diego, Seattle, and Los Angeles have chosen generals, lawyers, and a former governor to lead their schools.[50] Although well-known figures may bring visibility and hope, there is no superman to "fix" the problem. An effective superintendent is a good manager who builds solid relationships and persists at the job for more than a few years.[51] And good management is essential. Superintendents have been terminated when textbooks or school buses arrive late. In fact, some school districts have adopted performance-based contracts

School boards in communities that are . . .	Prefer superintendent style that is . . .
Dominated: School boards run by a few local elite who dominate community and school policies	*Functionary:* Follows wishes of the board
Factional: Divided community, competing factions	*Political:* Balances often opposing concerns, avoids appearance of favoritism
Pluralistic: Competition among interest groups	*Advisor:* Moves cautiously as advisor among shifting community coalitions
Inert: No visible power structure, little interest in schools	*Decision maker:* Board relies on superintendent for leadership and decision making

that link superintendent compensation directly to student performance.[52] (Figure 7.5 shows the average salaries of superintendents across the country.)

While the superintendent is the focal point of district pressures, the principal bears the brunt of school pressure. "Stress, testing, and social problems are all in the schools now: AIDS education, security, parenting classes, language programs. There are so many things that they are responsible for that they might not have control over, and it's led to concern about principal burnout."[53] Even at the elementary level, where many consider the stress most tolerable, a typical elementary principal supervises 30 teachers, 14 other staff members, 425 students, and works an average of 9 or 10 hours a day, 54 hours or more a week.[54] Amazingly, 20 percent of principals report spending 5 to 10 hours a week in efforts aimed at a single purpose: avoiding lawsuits.[55] Principal recruiters struggle to overcome persistent racial and ethnic imbalances as well.[56] (Figure 7.6 provides insight into principal demographics.)

These statistics underscore the tough challenges that superintendents and principals face, and you may be wondering, "Why would anyone want these jobs?" Here's one reason: Talented educational leaders take satisfaction from making a real difference in the lives of thousands of students. If you are considering teaching, then making a positive difference in the lives of the

FIGURE 7.5

Average annual salaries of teachers and administrators.

SOURCE: *Salaries & Wages for Professional and support Personnel in Public Schools, 2008-2009*, ERS, www.naesp.org/resources/2/Principal/2009/M-J_p27.pdf

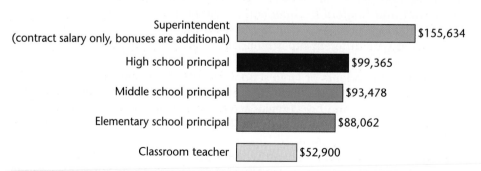

Superintendent (contract salary only, bonuses are additional)	$155,634
High school principal	$99,365
Middle school principal	$93,478
Elementary school principal	$88,062
Classroom teacher	$52,900

REFLECTION: What is the trade off between higher salaries as administrators and their job requirements? Do you think some teachers should be paid more than administrators?

students in your class is a motivator for you. Magnify that and you can see why some are drawn to administration. School districts committed to serious reform know that principals and superintendents can make a difference, and New York City is a case in point. The city established its own Leadership Academy to prepare a new generation of administrators. Once they graduate, these new principals manage schools that have been made smaller to increase their effectiveness. The new principals exert greater authority, control their own budget, and hire their faculty. They also shoulder a greater responsibility for the academic performance of their students and take home a larger paycheck than past administrators. Many of these new principals are only in their 30s. In fact, more than half of New York City's principals are now under 50. Why does the city seek younger (and less experienced) leaders? "I wanted to change the old system," former Schools Chancellor Joel Klein said. "New leadership is a powerful way to do that."[57]

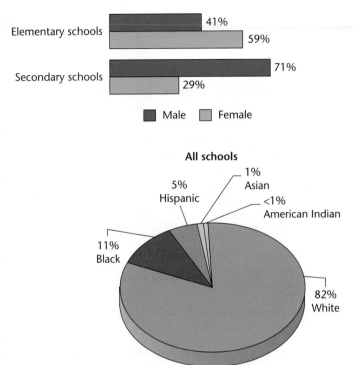

FIGURE 7.6

Public elementary and secondary principals.

SOURCE: National Center for Educational Statistics, "Public and Private School Principals by Selected Characteristics," *Condition of Education, 2010,* Figure 29-1.

Covert Power in Schools

5. Who might be considered part of the "hidden school government" . . . *the school secretary and parents.*

So you think that the school principal is the only one responsible for school personnel decisions, including hiring and firing? Think again. Parents, vocal individuals, the school secretary, and community groups have **covert power** and can bring significant pressure to bear on which teachers stay in a school, and which leave. These unofficial but highly involved people and groups constitute the **hidden government** of schools.[58]

The concept of hidden government is not unique to schools. In fact, most of our institutions, including the White House, have developed their own unique forms of hidden government. There, decision making is often influenced more by old colleagues back home (the "kitchen cabinet") than by the president's official advisers and cabinet members.

How does hidden government operate in schools? Following are some examples.

Example 1 A first-year teacher in a New England junior high school spent long hours after school preparing lessons and working with his students. Admirable as all this appeared, the school secretary, Ms. Hand, advised the teacher not to work with female students after school hours, because "You may get your fingers burned." The teacher smiled, ignored the secretary's advice, and continued providing students with after-school help.

Within a week, the principal called the teacher in for a conference and suggested that the teacher provide extra help to students only if both male and female students were present. The teacher objected to the advice and to the secretary's

REFLECTION: Why are more women principals at the elementary rather than secondary level? What are the challenges faced by schools with white principals and a majority of students of color?

Focus Question 9

What is the "hidden" government of schools?

The school secretary holds a position that can exert significant covert power in his or her pivotal role as the principal's "eyes and ears."

complaining to the principal. The principal responded, "You're new here, and I can understand your concern. But what you have to learn is that Ms. Hand is more than a secretary. She knows this school better than I do. Follow her advice and you'll do just fine."

Lesson: You can't always tell which people hold the real power by their official position.

Lesson: The school secretary is often the eyes and ears of the principal. In some cases, the secretary manages the day-to-day operations of the school.

Example 2 A young teacher in an elementary school in the Midwest was called into the principal's office for a conference. The principal evaluated her teaching as above average but suggested that she maintain greater discipline. Her classroom was simply too noisy, and the students' chairs were too often left in disarray. The conference was over in 10 minutes.

The teacher was offended. She did not feel her classroom was too noisy, and the chairs were always arranged in a neat circle. Moreover, the principal had visited her class for only five minutes, and during that time the students had said hardly a word.

The next day, in the teacher's lounge, all became clear when she discussed the conference with another teacher. The teacher nodded, smiled, and explained:

"Mr. Richards."

"The custodian?"

"Yup. He slowly sweeps the halls and listens for noisy classrooms. Then he tells the principal. He also hates it when the chairs are in a circle, since it makes sweeping harder. Nice straight rows are much easier. Just make sure your classroom is quiet when he's in the halls and have your students put the chairs in neat, straight rows at the end of the day. That's the ticket for getting a good evaluation!"

Lesson: School custodians are often a source of information for principals and of supplies for teachers. They make very helpful allies and powerful adversaries.

Example 3 An elementary school teacher in a rural southern community was put in charge of the class play. Rehearsals were under way when the teacher received a note to stop by the principal's office at 3:00 P.M.

The principal had received a call from a parent who was quite disappointed at the small part her daughter had received in the play. The principal wanted the teacher to consider giving the child a larger part. "After all," he explained, "her mother is influential in the PTA, and her father is one of the town's most successful businessmen. It's silly for you to alienate them. Give her a bigger part. Life will be easier for both of us."

Lesson: Parents can also be influential in school decisions by applying pressure on principals, school boards, and community groups. When you decide to make a stand in the face of parental pressure, choose a significant issue and be able to substantiate your facts.

Focus Question 10
How does the business community influence school culture?

Business and Schools

6. The influence of the business community in U.S. schools can best be characterized as . . . *extensive and growing.*

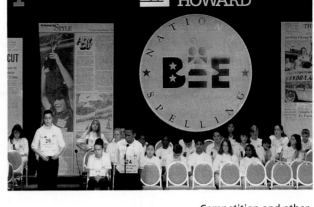

   Business values have long influenced school practices, and decades ago educators adopted a business vocabulary. *Superintendent,* the title originally given to a factory supervisor, was assigned to the school district leader. Both a factory and a school have been called a *plant. Quality control, accountability, management design,* and *efficiency* were also expropriated. Little surprise that a growing number of superintendents come from the business sector. School values often mirror those of business: hard work, competition, dependability, punctuality, neatness, conformity, and loyalty.[59] Companies that formalize a relationship with a school, by dedicating personnel or products or signing exclusive rights contracts, are said to have formed an **educational partnership.** A number of educators express concerns about these developments, an issue we explored earlier in this chapter. But whether we are comfortable or uncomfortable with this trend, "the most far-reaching initiative in education to emerge in recent years is the growing corporate interest in public schools."[60]

Competition and other business-oriented values have become so familiar and pervasive in our schools that we have become inured to them.

Focus Question 11
How are schools being made more responsive to teachers and the community?

Teachers, who know more than most people in the educational chain about the needs and interests of individual students, have often been excluded from school management and policy making.

Making Schools More Responsive

7. In most schools, teachers are expected to . . . *comply with policies made by principals and by district and state officials.*

   While parents, community groups, and the business sector carve out their roles in schools, teachers traditionally have been omitted from meaningful involvement in school governance.

   Teachers, as a rule, do not participate in hiring new teachers, in developing criteria by which their teaching will be evaluated, in setting graduation requirements, or in scheduling classes. One reason is sheer size: Over the past centuries, schools and school districts have continued to grow. Larger districts are considered more cost-effective because they lower the per-pupil expenses, from preparing food to building maintenance, and bigger school districts are able to offer more courses, extracurricular activities, and sports programs.[61] Merging smaller schools and districts into larger ones is called **consolidation.** In 1940, more than 117,000 school districts existed in the United States. Today these are about 14,000.[62] Larger schools and school districts also mean more red tape, greater student alienation, and reduced parent-teacher involvement; in other words, less responsive schools.[63] Many districts are now reversing the trend, creating smaller schools and smaller districts, a process called **decentralization,** or creating charter schools operating without central office involvement.[64]

Classroom Observation

17. Respect and Salary for Teachers

The public views teachers as important but seems unwilling to pay them accordingly. The segment explores some reasons for this by noting a connection between the feminization of teaching and persistent negative stereotypes. In addition, the segment recognizes the "psychic" salary for teachers who love what they do.

www.mhhe.com/
sadkerbrief3e

Beverly High School Teachers
Beverly, MA

In addition to size, top-down decision making by principals and superintendents also contributes to a sense of teacher powerlessness.[65] Efforts to empower teachers include site-based or school-based management and collaborative decision making. **Site-based** or **school-based management** shifts decision making from the central district office to individual schools, and **collaborative decision making** creates teacher committees to share power between the principal and the faculty. If you find yourself teaching in a school using one or both of these approaches, keep in mind that the results have been mixed. Some teachers enjoy making curricular and budgetary decisions, but others feel such participation simply becomes "just another meeting you've got to go to." To complicate these efforts even further, federally mandated tests have preempted many local decisions.[66] One of the challenges facing you as a teacher or an administrator will be to create more responsive and humane school climates, both for yourself and your students.

SUMMARY

CHAPTER REVIEW

Go to the online learning center to take a quiz, practice with key terms, and review concepts from the chapters.

www.mhhe.com/
sadkerbrief3e

1. Why do teachers need to know about finance and governance?

For teachers to influence the direction and policy of schools, they need to become more involved in finance and governance issues.

2. How is the property tax connected to unequal educational funding?

Since neighborhood wealth varies, property taxes have led to unequal educational resources. Robin Hood laws, built on the California *Serrano* decision, attempted to equalize educational funding between wealthy and poor communities, but with only limited success. State courts continue to address these financial inequities.

3. What is the distinction between educational equity and educational adequacy?

Educational *equity*, or Robin Hood laws, moved funds from wealthy districts to poorer ones, creating quite a bit of political opposition in the process. Educational *adequacy* focused less on funding than on educational outcome, like test scores. In the adequacy approach, courts looked at test scores and other performance measures created by the state to ensure that all students were receiving an adequate education.

4. **What are the sources of state revenues?**

   The most common state sources of school funding are property tax, sales tax, personal income tax, and state lotteries.

5. **How does the federal government influence education?**

   The federal government influences schools through court actions, some funding, and specific programs such as No Child Left Behind.

6. **How does commercialization at home and school affect children?**

   Our children are subjected to a constant barrage of advertisements that too often negatively influence their health, diet, and well-being. While other nations protect their young from unrestrained consumerism, we do not, and child obesity is just one price. Schools themselves have been pulled into commercialism, being paid to promote certain companies to children.

7. **What current trends are shaping educational finance?**

   School financing in the future will be influenced by accountability, choice programs, pay for performance, longer school days and school year, the health of the economy, deteriorating school buildings, and the continuing battle over inequitable funding. Whether commercialism targeting children will continue remains to be seen.

8. **How do school boards and superintendents manage schools?**

   The state legislature, state board of education, state superintendent, and state department of education administer schools, but delegate power to local school boards and superintendents. Boards of education formulate education policy, and the superintendent is responsible for implementing those policies.

9. **What is the "hidden" government of schools?**

   Parents, school secretaries, and custodians influence school life and are part of the hidden government of schools.

10. **How does the business community influence school culture?**

    The business community promotes school competitiveness, conformity, and punctuality. Many question the motivation, tactics, and commercialism involved in those efforts.

11. **How are schools being made more responsive to teachers and the community?**

    Some recent trends with school-based management (site-based management), and collaborative decision making, provide teachers with a stronger role in school governance. Consolidation has decreased the number of school districts while increasing the average size of schools, a change that has both supporters and critics.

KEY TERMS AND PEOPLE

DISCUSSION QUESTIONS AND ACTIVITIES

WEB-*TIVITIES*

Go to the Online Learning
Center to do the following
activities:
1. States to the Rescue
2. The Federal Government's
   Role in Financing Education
3. The Legal Control of Schools
4. Superintendents
5. School Boards Under Fire
6. The Business of America
   Is Business
7. Trends in School Governance:
   Educational Partnerships

1. Create a plan for (a) raising funds for education and (b) distributing funds equitably to all school districts within a state.

2. What is your opinion of the "adequacy" argument? Do you have any reservations about this approach? Do you believe that educational expenditures and educational quality are directly related? Support your position.

3. Research the average costs of educating a student in a local district. Discuss with classmates as you compare district programs, tax base, facilities, and student achievement.

4. Which of the four types of school boards would you prefer to serve on, or work for? Why? Which of the four types of school superintendents would you prefer to be, or to work for? Why?

5. Have you had any personal experience in an organization that had both a formal and a "hidden" government? Explain how these governments operated.

YOUR CD-ROM: THE *TEACHERS, SCHOOLS, AND SOCIETY READER* WITH CLASSROOM OBSERVATION VIDEO CLIPS

Articles, Case Studies, and Videos correspond to chapter content and are not always in numeric order. Go to your *Teachers, Schools, and Society Reader* CD-ROM to:

Read Current and Historical Articles

33. "Where Have All the Strong Poets Gone?" Alan C. Jones, *Phi Delta Kappan,* April 2007.

34. "Why Teacher Networks (Can) Work," Tricia Niesz, *Phi Delta Kappan,* April 2007.

35. "Equal Opportunity and the Courts," Michael A. Rebell, *Phi Delta Kappan,* February 2008.

36. "School Funding's Tragic Flaw," Kevin Carey and Marguerite Roza, *Education Sector Reports,* May 15, 2008.

Analyze Case Studies

16. **Kate Sullivan:** A principal faces the problems endemic to the students served by her school, which is located in a very low socioeconomic area. Issues of drugs, poverty, neglect, hunger, and homelessness are compounded by the underfunding for the school.

17. **Jane Vincent:** A teacher is asked by her principal to reconsider her grading of a student whose numerical average for the marking period is just below the department's cutoff score for that grade.

Observe Teachers, Students, and Classrooms in Action

14. **Classroom Observation: School Board Meeting to Discuss and Analyze Application for Jaime Escalante Charter School.**

17. **Classroom Observation: Respect and Salary for Teachers**

See pages 232 and 238 for descriptions of these videos. You'll find the videos on the CD Reader and at the Online Learning Center

www.mhhe.com/
sadkerbrief3e

SCHOOL LAW
AND ETHICS

Focus Questions

1. What are your legal rights and responsibilities as a teacher?

2. What legal rights do students enjoy (and do they have legal responsibilities)?

3. What are the ethical responsibilities of teachers and students?

www.mhhe.com/
sadkerbrief3e

WHAT DO YOU THINK? What Is Your Rights Quotient? Take an electronic version of the quiz starting on page 243.

Chapter Preview

- An honors student sues the school district after being randomly strip searched.
- A teacher is reprimanded for allowing a first grader to read a Bible story to the class.
- A teacher is fired for texting a student.
- A student complains that peer grading of assignments is a violation of privacy.
- A homosexual student sues a school district for discrimination.

Today, lawyers and judges are increasingly a part of school life. In this chapter, you will have the opportunity to respond to actual legal situations that have confronted teachers and students. (Get ready to determine your RQ—Rights Quotient.) Also included are some pragmatic steps for your legal self-defense, steps that you can take to avoid potential problems. But, beyond the nitty-gritty of these legal case studies, we will ask more penetrating questions about right and wrong, questions that go beyond the law, such as: How should teachers deal with ethical issues that emerge in school? Should teachers take positions on moral issues? To handle these important but difficult ethical dilemmas, we will offer some suggestions for ways teachers can organize their classrooms, and themselves.

Classroom Law

You have probably heard it before: The United States is a litigious society. "Take them to court," "I'll sue," and "Have your lawyer call my lawyer" are phrases common in the American lexicon. And actions match words. People sue companies. Companies sue people. Governments sue companies. Companies and people sue governments. We tend to seek redress in the courts for all kinds of problems, from divorce to physical injury, from protecting our beliefs to complying (or not complying) with laws.

Today, parents sue teachers. Students sue teachers. Teachers sue schools. Such a litigious world impacts instruction. Four out of five teachers and nearly that many principals in urban, suburban and rural areas describe *defensive teaching*—meaning that their educational decisions are motivated by a desire to avoid legal challenges. Educators believe that fewer laws would reduce their legal concerns and improve the quality of education.[1]

Despite the growing concern over legal issues, many educators are still unaware of their basic legal rights and responsibilities.[2] This can be a costly professional blind spot.

What rights do you have in the classroom? Consider this exchange between a college professor and a former associate superintendent of public instruction for California:

> SUPERINTENDENT: "Teaching is a privilege, not a right. If one wants this privilege, he or she has to give up some rights."
>
> PROFESSOR: "Just what constitutional rights do people have to give up in order to enter teaching?"
>
> SUPERINTENDENT: "Any right their community wants them to give up."[3]

Although such simplistic attitudes still exist, recent years have seen extraordinary changes in the legal rights of both teachers and students. Once the victims of arbitrary school rules and regulations, today's teachers and students can institute legal action if they believe that their constitutional rights are being threatened. In an increasing number of cases, the courts are finding school administrators guilty of violating the rights of both teachers and students.

As a classroom teacher, what can you legally say and do? Can you freely send text messages to students? What disciplinary methods are acceptable? How does your role as teacher limit your personal life? Knowing the answers to these questions *before* you step into a classroom can help you avoid costly mistakes.

While teachers would like to know definitively what is legal and what is not, courts often set forth standards with such terms as "reasonable care" or "appropriately under the circumstances." Courts try to balance legitimate concerns that can be raised on both sides of an issue. Staying legally up-to-date is an ongoing professional task.

What Is Your Rights Quotient?

The following case studies focus on court cases or federal law.[4] The vignettes are divided into two parts: teachers' rights and students' rights. In each case, an issue is identified, a situation is described, and you are asked to select an appropriate (legal) response. After your selection, the correct response and relevant court decisions or laws are described. Keep track of your rights and wrongs; a scoring system at the conclusion will help you determine your RQ (Rights Quotient). Good luck!

I. Teachers' Rights and Responsibilities

Issue	*Situation 1*
Applying for a position	You did it! You finished student teaching (you were great!) and the school district you most want to teach in has called you for an interview. Mr. Thomas, from the personnel office, seems impressed with your credentials and the interview is going well. He explains that the school district is very committed to its teachers and invests a great deal of resources in training. He wants to make certain that this investment makes sense, so he asks you for your long-range plans with such questions as: "Do you see yourself teaching in this system for a long time?" and "Are you planning to get married or have children in the near future?"

Focus Question 1
What are your legal rights and responsibilities as a teacher?

_____ You answer the questions realizing that the district is entitled to know about your long-range plans.

_____ You avoid answering the questions. You think it's none of his business, but you are worried that you won't get the position.

Legal Decision Not too long ago, school districts regularly considered marital and parenthood status in employment decisions. For women these were critical factors in being offered a job, and the "right" answer was: "No, I am not going to get married or have children." For male candidates, the question was less important and rarely asked. (In fact, married men with families are often highly sought. Brainstorm reasons why.) Now a variety of federal and state laws and court decisions make such inquiries illegal. Interview questions must be related to the job requirements. Questions about race, creed, marital status, sex, religion, age, national origin, physical or other disabilities, and even a request for photographs along with an application are generally illegal. **Title IX of the Education Amendments (1972)** and **Title VII of the Civil Rights Act (1964)** are two federal laws that prohibit many of these practices. In situation 1, the questions are inappropriate and illegal, and you need not answer them. The challenge, of course, is how you could answer such questions without ruining your chances for being offered a position—that is, if you still want the job.[5]

Issue	*Situation 2*
Sexual harassment	After surviving the gender discriminatory interview, you are offered a teaching position and decide to take it. After all, you like the community and the children. You are very excited as you prepare for your first day. You are up an hour early, rehearsing your opening remarks. You enter the school, feeling hopeful and optimistic. You enjoy and respect your new colleagues, but you feel strange around Mr. Gray, the custodian. You share your concerns with the other teachers, but you are alone in your experience. Finally you approach the school principal who assures you that Mr. Gray means no harm, but promises to have a chat with the custodian. You feel good about giving voice to the problem, but soon realize the only thing that has changed is that Mr. Gray no longer empties your classroom trash can. The harassment continues. At the end of the year, you find yourself in counseling and contemplating a leave of absence. You decide that

_____ Your emotional well-being is at risk. You will resign before things get worse.

_____ Enough is enough. You sue the district for damages.

Legal Decision Anita Hill's charges against Supreme Court nominee Clarence Thomas, as well as similar charges against former President Clinton, a stream of senators, and other officials, have awakened millions of Americans to the issue of sexual harassment. The custodian's behavior, both verbal and physical, is clearly an example of this problem. The Supreme Court ruled that under Title IX, victims of sexual harassment are also victims of sex discrimination and can recover monetary damages. Keeping a record of the custodian's behavior and having witnesses will strengthen your case. You certainly can sue, and, if you are successful, you may be awarded significant monetary damages. You can also file a grievance with the Office for Civil Rights, without even having a lawyer. This grievance will launch an investigation of the school's practices.[6]

Along with protecting teachers from sexual harassment and sex discrimination in employment, Title IX prohibits sex discrimination in many areas of education for employees and students, males and females. The law covers federally funded institutions—schools, colleges, vocational training centers, public libraries, and museums—and ensures fairness in athletics, employment, counseling, financial aid, admissions, and treatment in classrooms.

Issue	*Situation 3*
Personal lifestyle	After your first few months, your reputation is established: You are known as a creative and effective teacher and are well liked by students and colleagues (isn't that wonderful!). But your life outside the classroom is not appreciated by school officials. You are single and living with your "significant other." Several school officials have strong feelings about this and believe that you are a poor role model for the students. The school system publicly announces that your cohabitation is having a negative influence on your elementary-age students and suspends you.

_____ You are the victim of an illegal action and should sue to be reinstated.

_____ The school board is within its rights in dismissing you and removing a bad role model from the classroom.

Do you believe that a teacher's sexuality is a legitimate consideration for employment?

Legal Decision This case hinges on how much personal freedom an individual abandons as a teacher and role model for students. Although court decisions have varied, the following general standard should be kept in mind: Does your behavior significantly disrupt the educational process or erode your credibility with students, colleagues, or the community? If the school district can demonstrate that you have disrupted education or have lost credibility, then you may be fired.

In the case outlined here, the teacher sued the school district (*Thompson v. Southwest School District*). The court indicated that until the school district took action to suspend the teacher on grounds of immorality, the public was generally unaware of the teacher's cohabitation with her boyfriend. The court decided that it was unfair of the board of education to make the issue public to gain community support for its position. Furthermore, the court ruled that the teacher's behavior had not interfered with her effectiveness in the classroom. With neither a loss of credibility nor a significant disruption of the educational process, the board lost its case and the teacher kept her job.

HOW PRIVATE IS YOUR PERSONAL LIFE?

Courts are constantly asked to draw the line between a teacher's personal freedom and the community's right to establish teacher behavior standards. Although each case must be judged on its own merits, some trends do emerge. Courts have ruled that the community has the right to fire a teacher for

- Making public homosexual advances to nonstudents
- Incorporating sexual issues into lessons and ignoring the approved syllabus
- Inciting violent protest among students
- Engaging in sex with students
- Encouraging students to attend certain religious meetings
- Allowing students to drink alcohol
- Drinking excessively
- Using profanity and abusive language toward students
- Stealing school property (even if it is returned later)
- Not living within his or her district if that is listed as a condition of employment

On the other hand, courts have ruled that teachers should not be fired for

- Unwed cohabitation
- Private homosexual behavior

- Obesity (unless it inhibits teaching performance)
- Adultery
- Use of vulgar language outside of school
- AIDS or disability

Why are teachers dismissed in some cases and not in others? Often, the standard the courts use is whether the behavior under question reduces teacher effectiveness. Public behavior, or behavior that becomes public, may compromise a teacher's effectiveness. In such cases, the courts find it reasonable and legal to terminate the teacher. If the behavior remains private, if the teacher shows discretion, the teacher's "right to privacy" often prevails.

SOURCE: These examples have been adapted from Louis Fischer, David Schimmel, and Leslie Stallman, *Teachers and the Law,* 8th edition (Prentice Hall, 2010).

REFLECTION: Courts have disagreed on whether the following three situations constitute grounds for dismissal of a teacher. If you were the judge, how would you rule on the following issues?

- Sex-change operation
- Unwed parenthood
- Conviction for shoplifting

What if the teacher's "significant other" was of the same sex? Whether gay and lesbian teachers need legal protection from dismissal based on sexual orientation is a divisive and unsettled debate. Although there is no federal law outlawing sexual orientation discrimination, a growing number of states and nearly 200 cities and counties prohibit such discrimination in employment. Even in places without specific laws protecting gay and lesbian teachers, it is unlikely that they can be dismissed without direct evidence showing that a homosexual lifestyle negatively impacts their teaching.

Court decisions regarding the personal lifestyles of teachers have differed from state to state. Driving while intoxicated or smoking marijuana was found to be grounds for dismissal in one state but not in another, depending on whether the behavior resulted in "substantial disruption" of the educational process. On the other hand, an attempt to dismiss a teacher because she did not attend church was not upheld by the court. In fact, the teacher in this case actually won financial damages against the school district.

What about your personal appearance? What can a school district legally require in terms of personal grooming and dress codes for teachers? Courts have not been consistent in their decisions, although the courts may uphold the legality of dress codes for teachers if the dress requirements are reasonable and related to legitimate educational concerns.[7]

Issue

Teachers'
academic
freedom

Situation 4

As a social studies teacher, you are committed to teaching about the futility of hate and discrimination. You assign your middle-school students the mystery novel *The Terrorist,* a book that evokes strong feelings on ethnic and religious issues. Class discussions and activities focus on challenging stereotypes and creating peaceful responses to violence. Your students find the novel engaging, and class discussions are lively and respectful. But in the post-9/11 climate, some parents are upset, and the school board asks you not to teach such a controversial lesson. Committed to your beliefs, you persist. At the end of the school year, you find that your teaching contract is not renewed.

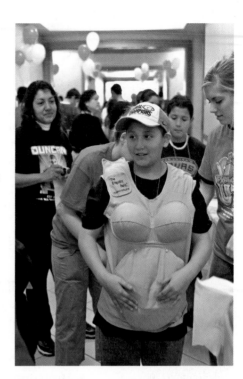

_____ Because you think your academic freedom has been violated, you decide to sue to get your job back.

_____ You realize that the school board is well within its rights to determine curriculum, that you were warned, and that now you must pay the price for your indiscretion.

Academic freedom protects a teacher's right to teach about sensitive issues, such as pregnancy or other sex education topics, as long as the topic is relevant to the course, is not treated in an obscene manner, and is not disruptive of school discipline.

Legal Decision The right to **academic freedom** (that is, to teach without coercion, censorship, or other restrictive interference) is not absolute. The courts will balance your right to academic freedom with the school system's interests in its students learning appropriate subject matter in an environment conducive to learning. Courts look at such factors as whether your learning activities and materials are inappropriate, irrelevant to the subjects to be covered under the syllabus, obscene, or substantially disruptive of school discipline. In this case, the lesson related to ethnic and religious differences appears to be appropriate, relevant, and neither obscene nor disruptive. If you were to sue on the grounds of academic freedom, you would probably get your job back.[8]

Issue

Legal liability
(negligence)

Situation 5

You are assigned to cafeteria duty. Things are pretty quiet, and you take the opportunity to call a guest speaker and confirm a visit to your class. While you are gone from the cafeteria, a student slips on some spilled milk and breaks his arm. His parents hold you liable for their son's injury and sue you for damages.

www.mhhe.com/
sadkerbrief3e

INTERACTIVE ACTIVITY
What Can a Teacher
Be Fired For? Test your
knowledge of teachers'
rights.

_____ You will probably win, since you did not cause the fall and were on educational business when the accident occurred.

_____ The student's parents will win, since you left your assigned post.

_____ The student who spilled the milk is solely responsible for the accident.

_____ No one will win, because the courts long ago ruled that there is no use crying over spilled milk. (You knew that was coming, right?)

Legal Decision In recent years, litigation against teachers has increased dramatically. The public concern over the quality of education, the bureaucratic and impersonal nature of many school systems, and the generally litigious nature of our society have all contributed to this rising tide of lawsuits. Negligence suits against teachers are common. In the cafeteria example, you would be in considerable jeopardy in a legal action. A teacher who is not present at his or her assigned duty might be charged with negligence, unless the absence is "reasonable." The courts are very strict about what is "reasonable" (leaving your post to put out a fire is reasonable, but going to the telephone to make a call is unlikely to be viewed as reasonable). It is a good practice to stay in your classroom or assigned area of responsibility unless there is an emergency.

Teacher liability is an area of considerable concern to many teachers. Courts generally use two standards in determining negligence: (1) whether a reasonable person with similar training would act in the same way and (2) whether or not the teacher could have foreseen the possibility of an injury. Following are some common terms and typical situations related to teacher liability:

- *Misfeasance.* Failure to conduct in an appropriate manner an act that might otherwise have been lawfully performed; for example, unintentionally using too much force in breaking up a fight is **misfeasance.**
- *Nonfeasance.* Failure to perform an act that one has a duty to perform; for example, the cafeteria situation is **nonfeasance,** because the teacher did not supervise an assigned area of responsibility.
- *Malfeasance.* An act that cannot be done lawfully regardless of how it is performed; for example, starting a fistfight or bringing marijuana to school is **malfeasance.**

So what is your "take-away" from this case? Here are some reasonable precautions you can take to avoid liability:

- Establish safety rules for students
- Try to anticipate and avoid dangerous situations
- Warn students of any potential dangers
- Provide proper supervision
- If an accident does occur, document the specifics and how you helped the victim

What is not on this list is liability coverage, but this is a good time to remind you that it is wise to check with your district's personnel office to determine the limits of professional liability protection. Teacher associations and organizations usually offer additional and voluntary liability policies for you. One common risk that teachers unwittingly take is to offer rides to their students for school events. You might want to check your district's liability policy about autos before doing this. Remember, your personal insurance policy may not cover student injuries.[9]

Although liability litigation usually involves physical injury to students because of what a teacher did or failed to do, a new line of litigation, called **educational malpractice,** is concerned with "academic damage." Some students and parents have sued school districts for failing to provide an adequate education. Many courts have rejected these cases, pointing out that many factors affect learning and that failure to learn cannot be blamed solely on the school system.

Issue	*Situation 6*
Teachers' freedom of speech	As a teacher in a small school district, you are quite upset with the way the school board and the superintendent are spending school funds. You are particularly troubled with all the money being spent on high school athletics, since these expenditures have cut into your proposed salary raise. To protest the expenditures, you write a lengthy letter to the local newspaper, criticizing the superintendent and the school board. After the letter is published, you find that the figures you cited in the letter were inaccurate.

The following week, you are called into the superintendent's office and fired for breaking several school rules. You have failed to communicate your complaints to your superiors, and you have caused harm to the school system by spreading false and malicious statements. In addition, the superintendent points out that your acceptance of a teaching position obligated you to refrain from publicizing critical statements about the school. The superintendent says although no one can stop you from making public statements, the school system certainly does not "have to pay you for the privilege." You decide to

_____ Go to court to win back your position.

_____ Chalk it up to experience, look for a new position, and make certain that you do not publish false statements and break school rules in the future.

Legal Decision This situation is based on a suit instigated by a teacher named Marvin Pickering. After balancing the teacher's interests, as a citizen, in commenting on issues of public concern against the school's interests in efficiently providing public services, the Supreme Court ruled in favor of the teacher. It found that the disciplined operation of the school system was not seriously damaged by Pickering's letter and that the misstatements in the letter were not made knowingly or recklessly. Moreover, there was no special need for confidentiality on the issue of school budgets. Hence, concluded the Court, prohibiting Pickering from making his statements was an infringement of his **First Amendment** right to freedom of speech. You, too, would probably win in court if you were to issue public statements on matters of public concern, unless your statements were intentionally or recklessly inaccurate, disclosed confidential material, or hampered either school discipline or your performance of duties.[10]

A teacher's freedom of speech often involves gray areas and may not always come out in the teacher's favor. Consider these two cases. A federal judge ruled that a Southern California public high school history teacher violated the First Amendment when he made disparaging statements during a classroom lecture about Christians and their beliefs and called creationism "religious, superstitious nonsense." The First Amendment prohibits teachers from displaying religious hostility.[11] Can a teacher wear a political button in the classroom? During a recent presidential campaign, many New York City public school teachers wore buttons to school in support of their candidate. Critics argued that the buttons created an environment of intimidation and hostility toward students who did not share their teacher's opinion. The teachers insisted that the students were able to distinguish between personal and institutional views. A federal judge ruled against the teachers.[12]

Issue	*Situation 7*
Copying published material	You read a fascinating two-page article in the *New York Times,* and, since the article concerns an issue your class is discussing, you duplicate the article and distribute it to your students. This is the only article you have distributed in class, and you do not bother to ask either the author or the newspaper for permission to reprint it. You have

_____ Violated the copyright law, and you are liable to legal action.

_____ Not violated any copyright law.

Federal Law   A teacher's ability to freely reproduce and distribute published works is greatly limited by the **Copyright Act.** Under this law, in order to use a published work in class, teachers must write to the publisher or author of the work and obtain written permission. This sometimes requires a permission fee, something that teachers on a limited budget are usually unable to afford. Under certain circumstances, however, teachers may still reproduce published material without written permission or payment. This is called **fair use,** a legal principle that allows the limited use of copyrighted materials. Teachers must observe three criteria in selecting the material: brevity, spontaneity, and cumulative effect.

1. *Brevity.* A work can be reproduced if it is not overly long. It is always wise to contact publishers directly, but typical limits might include the following criteria. Poems or excerpts from poems must be no longer than 250 words. Articles, stories, and essays of less than 2,500 words may be reproduced in complete form. Excerpts of any prose work (such as a book) may be reproduced only up to 1,000 words or 10 percent of the work, whichever is less. Only one illustration (photo, drawing, diagram) may be reproduced from the same book or journal. The brevity criterion limits the length of the material that a teacher can reproduce and distribute from a single work. If you were the teacher in this example and you reproduced only a two-page article, you probably would not have violated the criterion of brevity.

2. *Spontaneity.* If a teacher has an inspiration to use a published work and there is simply not enough time to write for and receive written permission,

the teacher may reproduce and distribute the work. The teacher in our vignette has met this criterion so is acting within the law. If the teacher wishes to distribute the same article during the next semester or the next year, written permission would be required because ample time exists to request such permission.

3. *Cumulative effect.* The total number of works reproduced without permission for class distribution must not exceed nine instances per class per semester. Within this limit, only one complete piece or two excerpts from the same author may be reproduced, and only three pieces from the same book or magazine. Cumulative effect limits the number of articles, poems, excerpts, and so on that can be reproduced, even if the criteria of spontaneity and brevity are met. The teacher in our vignette has not reproduced other works and therefore has met this criterion also.

Under the fair use principle, single copies of printed material may be copied for your personal use. Thus, if you want a single copy for planning a lesson, that is not a problem. Whenever multiple copies are made for classroom use, each copy must include a notice of copyright.

What about DVDs, computer software, and mixed media? These resources, like printed materials, are considered *intellectual property* and are covered by U.S. copyright laws. The growing use of computers prompted the amendment of the Copyright Act in 1990 to prohibit the copying of software for commercial gain. In 1998, Congress further amended the Copyright Act and passed the Digital Millennium Copyright Act to protect the vast amount of material published on the Internet. Text, graphics, web page code, multimedia materials, and even e-mail are copyright protected. Therefore, teachers must follow fair use guidelines when using information obtained from the Internet and gleaned from e-mail attachments. With so much information at our fingertips, both teachers and students need to be aware that all work posted on the Internet is copyright protected, whether or not a specific notice is included. It is always advisable to check with your local school district officials to determine school policy and procedures.[13]

What are the three criteria for fair use of copyrighted materials in your classroom—and can you answer this without peeking at the text?

Issue	Situation 8
Labor rights	Salary negotiations have been going badly in your school district, and at a mass meeting teachers finally vote to strike. You honor the strike and stay home, refusing to teach until an adequate salary increase is provided. During the first week of the strike, you receive a letter from the school board stating that you will be suspended for 15 days without pay at the end of the school year, owing to your participation in the strike. You decide

_____ To fight this illegal, unjust, and costly suspension.

_____ To accept the suspension as a legal action of the school board.

Legal Decision State courts vary in upholding teachers' right to strike. In some states, courts have determined that teachers provide a vital public service and cannot strike. Although more than 30 states have laws that prohibit strikes, many communities choose not to prosecute striking teachers.[14] You need to understand your state laws and community norms to know if you are breaking the law by honoring the strike. The decision to strike is a difficult one. Under what circumstances, if any, you would choose to strike?

In a number of cases, courts have recognized the right of teachers to organize, to join professional organizations, such as the NEA (National Education Association) and the AFT (American Federation of Teachers), and to bargain collectively for improved working conditions. You cannot legally be penalized for these activities. Yet, even though membership in teacher organizations and the right to collective bargaining have been upheld by the courts, some states and communities are adamantly opposed to such organizations and refuse to hire or to renew contracts of teachers who are active in them. Such bias is clearly illegal; nevertheless, it is very difficult to prove in court and, consequently, it is very difficult to stop.[15]

In summary, law and reality do not always coincide. Legally speaking, teachers may be prohibited from striking by state law but are rarely prosecuted or penalized. In some places, active involvement in teacher organizations (albeit legal) may result in discriminatory school board actions. If you choose to strike, join a union, or participate in collective bargaining, do so with the realization that such activity may make you liable to legal sanctions or, at the very least, community hostility.[16]

II. Students' Rights and Responsibilities

Focus Question 2

What legal rights do students enjoy (and do they have legal responsibilities)?

Issue	*Situation 9*
Student records	You are a high school teacher who has decided to stay after school and review your students' records. You believe that learning more about your students will make you a more effective teacher. As you finish reviewing some of the folders, Brenda, a 16-year-old student of yours, walks in and asks to see her folder. You refuse. Within the hour, the student's parents call and ask if they can see the folder. At this point, you

_____ Explain that the information is confidential and sensitive and cannot be shared with nonprofessional personnel.

_____ Explain that parents can see the folder and describe the procedure for doing so.

Federal Law The Family Rights and Privacy Act, commonly referred to as the **Buckley Amendment,** allows parents and guardians access to their children's educational records. The amendment also requires that school districts inform parents of this right and establish a procedure for providing educational records on request. Moreover, written parental permission is needed before these records can be shared with anyone other than professionals connected with either the school the student attends or another school in which the student seeks to enroll, health or safety officials, or persons reviewing the student's financial aid applications. If the student has reached 18 years of age, he or she must be allowed to see the folder and is responsible for granting permission for others to review the folder. The Buckley Amendment was recently tested by the common teacher practice of asking students to exchange and grade others' papers. In *Owasso Independent School District v. Falvo*, the Supreme Court ruled that students can grade their peers' academic work and even announce the results in class without violating the privacy act. The Court determined that under the Buckley Amendment grades do not become private and part of students' educational records until they are recorded in a teacher's grade book.[17]

Under this law, you should have chosen the second option.

Issue	Situation 10
Suspension and discipline	You are teaching a difficult class, and one student is the primary source of trouble. After a string of disorderly episodes on this student's part, the iPods for the entire class mysteriously disappear. You suspect the student and send her to the principal's office to be suspended. The principal backs you up, and the student is told not to return to school for a week. This action is

_____ Legal and appropriate (and probably long overdue!).

_____ Illegal.

Legal Decision Although troublesome and disorderly students can be disciplined, suspension from school represents a serious penalty. In such cases, the Supreme Court has ruled (**Goss v. Lopez**) that teachers and administrators are required to follow certain procedures in order to guarantee the student's **due process** rights granted by the *Fourteenth Amendment.* In this case, the student must be informed of the rule that has been broken and of the evidence. The student is also entitled to tell his or her side of the story in self-defense. For suspensions in excess of 10 days, the school must initiate more formal procedures. School officials can be held personally liable for damages if they violate a student's clearly established constitutional rights (*Wood v. Strickland*).

If you look back at this vignette, you will notice that you do not know for sure that this student is responsible for the missing iPods, nor is the student given the opportunity for self-defense. If you selected "illegal," you chose the correct response.

Many schools have adopted zero-tolerance policies in an attempt to create safe schools. A **zero-tolerance policy** typically sets out predetermined consequences or punishment for specific offenses, regardless of the circumstances or disciplinary history of the student involved. Nine out of ten schools report zero-tolerance policies for firearms. Many schools have zero-tolerance policies covering possession of alcohol, drugs, and tobacco, as well as incidents of violence and sexual harassment. Courts have generally ruled that students' constitutional right to due process is not violated by zero-tolerance policies. However, opponents point out that zero-tolerance policies are too often taken to extremes. For example, one six-year-old was expelled for bringing a weapon into school. His grandmother had placed a "weapon" in his

IS CORPORAL PUNISHMENT LEGAL?

Corporal punishment, the physical discipline of students, is legal in 20 states.

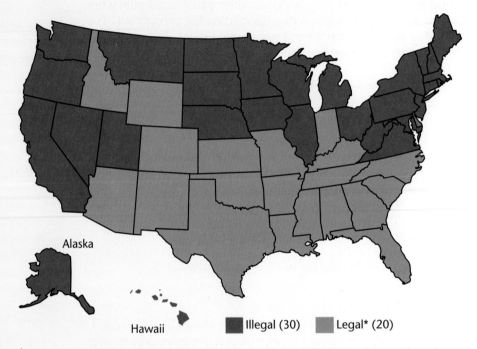

Alaska

Hawaii

■ Illegal (30) ■ Legal* (20)

* In states where corporal punishment is legal, not all school districts implement the policy.

SOURCE: Center for Effective Discipline, "States Banning Corporal Punishment," July 2010, www.stophitting.com.

REFLECTION: Knowing whether corporal punishment is legal in your school is only part of the issue; sorting out your philosophy on this issue is more to the point. As a teacher, would you use physical punishment against a student? Explain your reasoning.

lunch sack—a plastic knife for spreading peanut butter. Furthermore, zero-tolerance practices resulting in suspension often result in troubling patterns of discrimination. A recent study of 9,000 schools revealed that black boys are nearly three times as likely to be suspended as white boys for the same behaviors, and black girls are suspended four times more often than white girls. Hispanic and Native American students are also more likely to be suspended than white students, though not at such disproportionate rates as for black children.[18] Gay, lesbian, and bisexual youth are also far more likely to be harshly punished than their straight peers.[19]

While considering discipline, let us look at the legality of **corporal punishment.** In *Ingraham v. Wright,* the Supreme Court ruled that physical punishment may be authorized by the states. The Court ruled that the corporal punishment should be "reasonable and not excessive," and such factors as the seriousness of the student offense, the age and physical condition of the student, and the force and attitude of the person administering the punishment should be considered. Although the courts have legalized corporal punishment, many states and school districts do not believe in it and have prohibited the physical punishment of students; other districts and states provide very specific guidelines for its practice. You should be familiar with the procedures and norms in your district before you even consider this disciplinary strategy.[20] (See A Closer Look: Is Corporal Punishment Legal?)

Issue	*Situation 11*
Freedom of speech	During your homeroom period, you notice that several of your more politically active students are wearing T-shirts with a red line drawn through a cell phone. You call them to your desk and ask them about it. They explain that they are protesting the new school board policy that prohibits cell phone use and texting during regular school hours. You tell them that you share their concern but that wearing the T-shirts is specifically forbidden by school rules. You explain that you will let it go this time, since they are not disturbing the class routine, but that if they wear them again, they will be suspended.
	Sure enough, the next day the same students arrive at school wearing the T-shirts, and you send them to the principal's office. The students tell the principal that, although they understand the rule, they refuse to obey it. The principal, explaining that school rules are made to be followed, suspends them. The principal's action is

_____ Legally justified, since the students were given every opportunity to understand and obey the school rule.

_____ Illegal, since the students have the right to wear T-shirts if they so desire.

Legal Decision In December 1965, three students in Des Moines, Iowa, demonstrated their opposition to the Vietnam War by wearing black armbands to school. The principal informed them that they were breaking a school rule and asked that they remove the armbands. They refused and were suspended.

The students' parents sued the school system, and the case finally reached the Supreme Court. In the landmark *Tinker* case, the Court ruled that the students were entitled to wear the armbands, as long as the students did not substantially disrupt the operation of the school or deny other students the opportunity to learn. Because there was no disruption, the Court ruled that the school system could not prohibit students from wearing the armbands or engaging in other forms of free speech.[21] The school

Courts have upheld students' freedom of speech in a number of cases, so long as the protests were not disruptive of other students' right to learn and were not obscene.

system in this vignette acted illegally; it cannot prevent students from wearing the protest T-shirts.

Hate speech is another matter. For example, a California high school prevented a student from wearing a T-shirt with the slogan "Homosexuals are shameful." The student argued that such a dress code policy violated his First Amendment right to free speech. But a federal court ruled that "demeaning of young gay and lesbian students in a school environment is detrimental not only to their psychological health and well-being, but also to their educational development" and that students should feel safe from attacks based on sexual orientation, race, religion, and gender while at school.[22]

In *Morse v. Frederick,* limits were again placed on student speech, this time when the message might promote drug use. What does "Bong Hits 4 Jesus" mean to you? Is it offensive, or nonsensical? An Alaskan high schooler, Joseph Frederick, crossed the street and displayed the banner with the phrase as the Olympic torch passed by his school. Frederick explained: "I wasn't trying to say anything about religion. I wasn't trying to say anything about drugs. I was just trying to say *something.* I wanted to use my right to free speech." The school principal, concerned about the potentially offensive message, confiscated the banner. Although the student was not on school property, the Supreme Court supported the principal's action and opined that though the student was not disruptive, his speech was promoting an illegal activity.[23]

Does *Tinker* apply in cyberspace? Maybe.

Although the courts have not definitely resolved the issue, early "cyber-Tinker" decisions supported First Amendment rights. One of the first lawsuits arose after a Missouri high school suspended a student for creating a web page that criticized his school administration. The student created the web page outside of school on his home computer. The web page caused no documented disturbance at this school, and a federal district court reversed the suspension, citing the principal's simple dislike of the content as "unreasonable justification for limiting it."[24]

Yet tech-savvy students are increasingly paying a price, including criminal arrest, for parodying their teachers on the Internet. A study by the National School Boards Association found that more than one in four teachers have been targeted in online pranks by their students. Tired of jokes and false accusations, teachers and schools are fighting back against digital ridicule by their students, often with lawsuits and long-term suspensions or permanent expulsions.[25]

The issue of allegedly "obscene" speech has been considered by the Supreme Court. In *Bethel School District v. Fraser,* the Court evaluated the First Amendment rights of a high school senior, Matthew Fraser. Fraser presented a speech at a school assembly that contained numerous sexual innuendoes, though no explicit, profane language. After Fraser was suspended for his speech and told that he was no longer eligible to speak at his class's graduation, his father sued the school district. The Court upheld the suspension on the grounds that the language in the speech was indecent and offensive and that minors should not be exposed to such language.[26] (See Contemporary Issues: A View from the Field for another perspective on students' freedom of speech.)

A VIEW FROM THE FIELD: FIRST AMENDMENT RIGHTS

Max and Templeton were in real trouble. The school board had decided that they were to be expelled. But their school friends rallied behind them, evidence that Kate Lyman's lessons were taking root.

Kate Lyman is a Madison, Wisconsin, teacher and her students were second and third graders—and in case you are wondering, Max and Templeton were the pet rats kept in their classroom. The school board ruled that no animals could be kept in school, so Max and Templeton had to go. But the board had not counted on the commitment and tenacity of Kate's students.

Kate encouraged her students to speak out. She discussed persuasion and let students know they could write letters or send e-mails to the school board. As Kate writes in the journal *Rethinking Schools,* "The students practiced a lot of writing skills in those few days. They edited their

letters, typed them on the computer, and learned how to send them via e-mail to the school board members and superintendent." One student suggested sending the letters to a local newspaper; four were printed. Six of Kate's second- and third-grade students took their advocacy beyond letter writing and spoke at a school board meeting. "I was proud of them for speaking out in that daunting setting, in front of at least a hundred people, including school board members, the superintendent, and the school district lawyer." The school board decided to allow animals to return to the schools. Alas, it was too late for Max and Templeton. They had already been adopted by the local humane society.

To read more about Kate's work with her students, please visit http://rethinkingschools.org.

Issue	Situation 12
School prayer	A student in your class objects to the daily prayer recitation. You are sensitive to the student's feelings, and you make certain that the prayer is nondenominational. Moreover, you tell the student that he may stand or sit silently without reciting the prayer. If the student likes, he may even leave the classroom while the prayer is being recited. As a teacher, you have

_____ Broken the law.

_____ Demonstrated sensitivity to individual needs and not violated the law.

Legal Decision You were sensitive but not sensitive enough—you violated the law. As a result of leaving the classroom, the student might be subjected to embarrassment, ostracism, or some other form of social stigma. The Supreme Court has ruled that educators must be completely neutral with regard to religion and may neither encourage nor discourage prayer.

Although the First Amendment prevents educators from promoting religious activities, the issue varies for students. For example, students may engage in private prayer and religious discussion during school and form religious clubs on school property if other, nonreligious clubs are also given school space. Although "official" prayers given by school personnel are not permitted at graduation ceremonies (where they frequently are heard despite the law), state laws vary on whether a student can give a graduation speech when the speech includes prayer. However, the Court has declared that student-led public prayers at athletic events constitute school sponsorship of religion, a violation of the First Amendment.

PROFILE IN EDUCATION:

Morris Dees

 For most of his life, Morris Dees has been fighting inequality. One of his first fights was to desegregate the YMCA. Today, through the Teaching Tolerance organization that his Southern Poverty Law Center (SPLC) cofounded with teachers across the country, he fights inequity online through the site Tolerance.org. To read a full profile of Morris Dees, go to the Chapter 8 Profile in Education at www.mhhe.com/sadkerbrief3e.

The Pledge of Allegiance also sparks controversy in public schools. Though many state and local school districts often champion the need for patriotism when requiring students to recite the pledge, students cannot be compelled to salute the flag. Finally, a moment of silence can be observed in schools as long as it does not encourage prayer over any other quiet, contemplative activity. Students can, however, voluntarily choose to pray during this time.

Issue	Situation 13
Search and seizure	The drug problem in your school is spreading, and it is clear that strong action is needed. School authorities order a search of all student lockers, which lasts for several hours. Trained police dogs are brought in, and each classroom is searched for drugs. The dogs sniff suspiciously at several students, who are taken to the locker rooms and strip-searched.

_____ School authorities are within their rights to conduct these searches.

_____ Searching the lockers is legal, but strip-searching is inappropriate and illegal.

_____ No searches are called for, and all of these activities present illegal and unconstitutional violation of student rights.

Legal Decision Courts have ruled that school authorities have fewer restrictions than do the police in search-and-seizure activities. Moreover, the school has a parent-like responsibility (termed ***in loco parentis***) to protect children and to respond to reasonable concerns about their health and safety. Courts have indicated that school property, such as lockers or cars parked in the school lot, are actually the responsibility of the school. A student's locker may be searched by a school official if there is *reasonable suspicion* to suspect that the locker contains something illegal or dangerous. At the same time, courts have determined that randomly conducting strip-searches or spot-checking lockers for drugs, weapons, or other illicit materials violates students' rights under the *Fourth Amendment*. (The *Fourth Amendment* protects basic individual privacy and ensures due process.)

In this situation, the locker search is legal because they were not randomly searched, and the increased drug problem at the school gave the school principal *reasonable suspicion*. However, the strip-search is illegal because students were randomly selected with no grounds for suspicion.

The second choice is the correct response. Although school personnel have great latitude in conducting school search and seizures, educators should be familiar with proper legal procedures and should think carefully about the related ethical issues.[27]

Issue	Situation 14
Freedom of the press	*The Argus* is the official student newspaper, written by students as part of a journalism course, but it has run afoul of school administrators. First, the student newspaper ran a story critical of the school administration. In the next edition, the paper included a supplement on contraception and abortion. With their patience worn thin, school administrators closed the publication for the remainder of the school year.

_____ Closing the student newspaper is a legal action.

_____ Closing the student newspaper is an illegal action.

Legal Decision The Supreme Court ruled in the *Hazelwood* case that student newspapers may be censored under certain circumstances. The Court held that student newspapers written as part of a school journalism course should be viewed as part of the official school curriculum. School administrators, according to the Court, can readily censor such a paper. In situation 14, because the publication is part of a journalism course, closing the school newspaper would be legal. Additional grounds for censoring a school newspaper include obscenity, psychological harm, and disruption of school activities.[28] On the other hand, if the newspaper were financed by the students or not associated with an official school course, the students would enjoy a greater degree of freedom.

Issue	*Situation 15*
HIV-infected students	As you enter school one morning, you are met by a group of angry parents. They have found out that Randy, one of your students, is HIV positive. There is no compromise in the voices of the parents confronting you. Either Randy goes, or they will keep their children at home. You listen sympathetically, but find your mind wandering to your own contact with Randy. You worry that you, too, may be at risk. In this case, you decide

_____ It's better to be safe than sorry, so you ask Randy to return home while you arrange a meeting with the principal to discuss Randy's case. There is no cure for AIDS and no reason to put every child's life in jeopardy.

_____ AIDs treatments have greatly improved. It's probably okay for Randy to attend school, so you check with your principal and try to calm the parents down.

Legal Decision In *Bragdon v. Abbott,* the Supreme Court determined that HIV-infected students are protected under the Individuals with Disabilities Education Act and cannot be denied a public education. The Court determined that the loss of a student's loss of education is more harmful than the remote chance of other students contracting AIDS. If some AIDS children present more of a public risk (for example, because of biting behavior, open sores, or fighting), more restrictive school environments may be required. To date, however, HIV-infected students and teachers are not viewed as a significant risk to the health of the rest of the population and cannot be denied their educational rights.[29]

Issue	*Situation 16*
Sexual harassment	Christina, an eleventh-grader, confided in her guidance counselor: "I didn't do too well on a pop quiz in Mr. Armando's algebra class. Mr. Armando suggested I repeat the quiz after school in his office. I thanked him for the second chance, especially since I want to make highest honors this

year. But before I began the quiz, he started stroking my hair and whispering that I'd have to be nice to him if I really wanted to bring up my grade. I felt really uncomfortable." Sexual harassment?

_____ This is a clear example of an unwanted sexual request.

_____ While the teacher's behavior is suggestive, sexual harassment cannot be proven based on a student's uncomfortable feelings. Without witnesses or evidence, this is a classic "he said-she said" scenario.

Legal Decisions Educators wrestle every day with helping students feel safe in schools and have both a legal and ethical responsibility to prevent and respond to harassment. What is **sexual harassment?** Is it what happens if a male student or teacher accidentally bumps into a girl in the hallway? Does it mean teachers can't hug students? That hand-holding between students is wrong? Absolutely not! These are popular misconceptions. Sexual harassment *is not* an accidental jostle on the way to class, an encouraging hug, or a show of affection. Sexual harassment *is* unwelcome behavior of a sexual nature that interferes with students' and teachers' abilities to learn, study, work, achieve, or participate in school activities. It includes insults, name calling, offensive jokes, unwanted touching, imitation by words or actions, pressure for sexual activity, and rape or sexual assault.

Sadly, sexual harassment is a pervasive, harrowing part of everyday school life for both males and females (see Figure 8.1). Four out of five students report being harassed at school. The consequences are troubling. Students fear attending school, withdraw from friends and activities, and suffer difficulties with sleeping and eating.

Title IX is the federal law that prohibits sex discrimination, including sexual harassment, in schools. The law recognizes two broad categories of sexual harassment: *quid pro quo* and *hostile environment*.[30] *Quid pro quo* is a Latin phrase meaning "this for that." This type of sexual harassment occurs

FIGURE 8.1

Who harasses whom?

SOURCE: Harris Interactive, Hostile Hallways: Bullying, Teasing and Sexual Harassment in School. (Washington, DC: American Association of University Women, 2008)

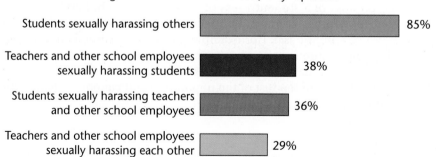

When students were asked for their perceptions of who is harassing whom in their own schools, they reported:

Students sexually harassing others — 85%

Teachers and other school employees sexually harassing students — 38%

Students sexually harassing teachers and other school employees — 36%

Teachers and other school employees sexually harassing each other — 29%

REFLECTION: As a teacher, if you observed each of these four kinds of harassment, how would you respond?

when a person with authority, like Mr. Amando above, abuses that authority to get sexual favors. *Hostile environment* consists of unwelcome sexual behavior so severe or widespread that it creates an abusive environment. This hostile behavior can be inappropriate spoken or written comments or physical conduct. Here's an example of a hostile environment:

> Albert is slender and not athletically inclined. In the locker room before gym class, his male peers tease him about his weight and clumsiness. They call him "fag," "sissy," and "girl," and snap their wet towels on his butt. Several times when Albert opened his locker, he found a bra and girls' panties with his name written on them. Albert now tries to skip gym class.

In *Franklin v. Gwinnett* (1992), the Supreme Court extended the reach of Title IX, allowing students to sue a school district for monetary damages in cases of sexual harassment. The Gwinnett County case involved a Georgia high school student who was sexually harassed and abused by a teacher. The school district was instructed to pay monetary damages to the student—establishing a precedent.[31]

Two relatively recent Court decisions make collecting personal damages from school districts more difficult, although an individual accused of sexual harassment can still be sued for personal damages. In *Gebser v. Lago Independent School District* (1998) and *Davis v. Monroe County Board of Education* (1999), a more conservative Supreme Court ruled that a school district must show "deliberate indifference" to complaints about teacher and peer sexual harassment before a district would be forced to pay damages. That means that complaining to a teacher or even a principal is now not enough; the complaint has to go higher.[32]

Sexual harassment complaints against teachers have been increasing. Teachers need to realize that sexual harassment laws prohibit not only overt actions but also offensive words and inappropriate touching. While a teacher's intention might be pure and caring, a student's perception can be quite different. The threat of the legal broadside that can result from this gap between teacher intentions and student perceptions has sent a chill through many school faculties. Teachers now openly express their fears about the dangers of reaching out to students, and some teachers are vowing never to touch a student or be alone in a room with a student, no matter how honorable the intention. Many teachers lament the current situation, recalling earlier times when a teacher's kindness and closeness fostered a caring educational climate, rather than a legal case.[33]

Scoring   To determine your RQ (Rights Quotient), the following scoring guide may be useful:

13 to 16 correct: Legal eagle

11 or 12 correct: Lawyer-in-training

9 or 10 correct: Paralegal

7 or 8 correct: Law student

6 or fewer correct: Could benefit from an LSAT prep course

This brief review of the legal realities that surround today's classroom is not meant to be definitive. These situations are intended to highlight the

www.mhhe.com/
sadkerbrief3e
INTERACTIVE ACTIVITY
Practice with court
cases. Match names of
court cases with their
description.

TEACHERS' AND STUDENTS' RIGHTS

The following summaries highlight some critical Supreme Court cases that define the boundaries of civil rights in American schools.

TEACHERS' RIGHTS

FREEDOM OF SPEECH

Pickering v. Board of Education (1968)

A teacher retains the First Amendment's freedom of speech. This includes the same right as all other citizens to comment on issues of legitimate public concern, even if those comments are critical of school policies and practices. (See Situation 6.)

SEPARATION OF CHURCH AND STATE

Engel v. Vitale (1962)

A local school board instructed that a prayer be recited aloud every day during the first class of the day. The prayer was nondenominational and voluntary. Students who did not want to recite the prayer were permitted to remain silent or leave the classroom while the prayer was said. The Supreme Court held that authorizing prayer in school violated the First Amendment's prohibition of government establishment of religion and that official, organized prayer in school is not permitted. (See Situation 12.)

Wallace v. Jaffree (1985)
Lee v. Weisman (1992)

Alabama enacted a law that authorized a 1-minute period of silence in all public schools for meditation or voluntary prayer. The Supreme Court held that the Alabama law amounted to government establishment of religion, which is prohibited under the First Amendment. To determine whether the Alabama law was constitutional, the Court applied the three-part test established in *Lemon v. Kurtzman,* (1971): did the policy (1) have a secular purpose, (2) have a primarily secular effect, and (3) avoid excessive government entanglement with religion? In *Wallace,* the Alabama statute was found to have a religious rather than a secular purpose and was thus ruled unconstitutional. A moment of silence may be observed when its purpose is secular and does not require or encourage prayer over other contemplative activities. In *Weisman,* the court declared prayer led by school personnel at public school graduation to violate the establishment clause. (See Situation 12.)

Stone V. Graham (1980)

A Kentucky statute required the posting of a copy of the Ten Commandments, purchased with private contributions, on the wall of each public classroom in the state. Despite the fact that the copies of the Ten Commandments were purchased with private funds and had a notation describing them as secular, the statute requiring that they be posted in every public school classroom was declared unconstitutional. Under the three-part *Lemon* test, the Court concluded that posting the Ten Commandments failed under part 1 of the test in that it lacked a secular purpose. Merely stating that the Ten Commandments are secular does not make them so.

ACADEMIC FREEDOM AND TEACHING EVOLUTION

Epperson v. Arkansas (1968)
Edwards v. Aquillard (1987)

In *Epperson,* the Court ruled that the teaching of evolution does not violate the First Amendment's call for separation of church and state. During the 1980s, religious fundamentalists won state "balanced" rulings that required science teachers to give equal instructional time to Biblical creationism and evolution. But the Supreme Court did not agree. In *Edwards,* the Court declared that policies *requiring* instruction in creationism violate the First Amendment's establishment clause.

STUDENTS' RIGHTS

FREEDOM OF SPEECH (SYMBOLIC)

Tinker v. Des Moines Independent Community School District (1969)

Unless there is substantial disruption in a school, a school board cannot deprive students of their First Amendment right to freedom of speech. Students do not shed their constitutional rights at the school door, though they can be limited. (See Situation 11.)

West Virginia State Board of Education v. Barnette (1943)

A compulsory flag-salute statute in the public school regulations required all students and teachers to salute the U.S. flag every day. Two Jehovah's Witness students refused to salute the flag because doing so would be contrary to their religious beliefs, and they were not permitted to attend the public schools. The Court determined that students cannot be compelled to pledge allegiance to the flag in public schools, a right protected by the First Amendment.

FREEDOM OF SPEECH (VERBAL)

Bethel School District v. Fraser (1986)

The Supreme Court, balancing the student's freedom to advocate controversial ideas with the school's interests in setting the boundaries of socially appropriate behavior, found that the First Amendment does not prevent school authorities from disciplining students for speech that is lewd and offensive. (See Situation 11.)

FREEDOM OF THE PRESS

Hazelwood School District v. Kuhlmeir (1988)
Two controversial articles written in the student paper were deleted by a principal. The Supreme Court held that because the student paper was school-sponsored and school-funded and was part of the school's journalism class, the school principal had the right to control its content. On the other hand, the courts have ruled that school authorities may not censor student newspapers produced at the students' own expense and those produced off school property, papers not part of any school's curriculum. (See Situation 14.)

FREEDOM OF ACCESS TO THE PRINTED WORD

Board of Education, Island Trees Union Free School District No. 26 v. Pico (1982)
A school board decided to remove nine books from the school library because the board members felt the books were objectionable and improper for students. The court ruled that school boards may not suppress ideas by removing books from a school library based on their feelings that the material contains controversial or unpopular viewpoints.

RIGHT TO DUE PROCESS

Goss v. Lopez (1975)
New Jersey v. T.L.O. (1985)
In *Goss,* several high school students were suspended from school for 10 days. The Supreme Court held that before a principal can suspend a student, he or she must present the student with the charges and provide the student with a hearing or opportunity to defend against the charges. The Fourteenth Amendment's due process procedures mandated as a result of this decision can be compared to the *"Miranda* rights" required in criminal cases. In *T.L.O.* the Court determined that school officials are not necessarily bound by the Fourth Amendment but by reasonable cause when engaged in a search. (See Situation 10.)
Ingraham v. Wright (1977)
Florida statute allowed corporal punishment. Two students were punished by being hit with a flat wooden paddle and later sued the schools. The Supreme Court held that corporal punishment, such as the paddling, is not cruel and unusual punishment and does not necessarily deprive the student of his or her rights. (See Situation 10.)

SEPARATION OF CHURCH AND STATE

Santa Fe Independent School District v. Doe (2000)
In a 6–3 ruling, the Supreme Court held that student-led prayer at football games violated the U.S. Constitution's prohibition against a government establishment of religion. The majority said the Texas school district's authorization of a student vote on whether to have an invocation before games and the election of a student speaker amounted to government sponsorship of prayer. (See Situation 12.)

SCHOOL ATTENDANCE AND CHOICE

Pierce v. Society of Sisters of the Holy Names of Jesus & Mary (1925)
Plyer v. Doe (1982)
Zelman v. Simmons-Harris (2002)
Most of us take school for granted, yet the right to an education and freedom to choose a school often spark legal debate. School choice appeared on the legal landscape with *Pierce.* The Court deemed unconstitutional an Oregon law requiring parents to send their children to public schools. Such a law denied parents the right to control their children's education. *Plyer* extended the reach of public education. The Court ruled that Texas could not withhold free public education from illegal immigrants because "education provides the basic tools by which individuals might lead economically productive lives to the benefit of us all." *Zelman* ushered in a new era of school choice as the Court affirmed that parents could use public vouchers to send their children to private religious schools.

SEXUAL HARASSMENT

Franklin v. Gwinnett County Public Schools (1992)
The *Franklin* case involved a Georgia high school student who alleged that a teacher-coach engaged in behavior toward her ranging from unwelcome verbal advances to pressured sexual intercourse on school grounds. The Court ruled that "victims of sexual harassment and other forms of sex discrimination in schools may sue for monetary damages" under Title IX.
Gebser v. Lago Vista Independent School District (1998)
The Court limited the circumstances under which a school district can be held liable for monetary damages for a teacher's sexual harassment of a student. A district cannot be held liable under Title IX unless a district official with the authority to take corrective action had actual knowledge of *teacher* misconduct and was deliberately indifferent to it.
Davis v. Monroe County Board of Education (1999)
The Court held that districts may be found liable under Title IX only when they are "deliberately indifferent" to information about *student* harassment at school and when the harassment is so "severe, pervasive, and objectively offensive" that it bars the victim's access to an educational program or benefit. (See Situation 16.)

REFLECTION: Recall a time when you believe your rights as a student (or the rights of a classmate) were denied. What court cases and parts of the U.S. Constitution would apply to the situation?

rapid growth and changing nature of school law and the importance of this law to teachers. It will be your responsibility to become informed and stay current on legal decisions that influence your actions inside and outside the classroom. Ignorance of the law, to paraphrase a popular saying, is no defense. More positively, knowledge of fundamental legal principles allows you to practice "preventive law"—that is, to avoid or resolve potential legal conflicts so that you can attend to your major responsibility: teaching.

Teaching and Ethics

Focus Question 3

What are the ethical responsibilities of teachers and students?

Some citizens believe that the most important issues facing U.S. schools are ethical. Beyond simply following the law, students need to understand right from wrong. Cheating, for example, is not only against the rules, it is morally wrong, and students know this. An overwhelming majority say: "It's not worth it to lie or cheat because it hurts your character." The problem is that 90 percent of teens admit they cheat[34] (see Figure 8.2). Why this troubling disconnect? Students blame pressure to perform, the competitive college-admissions process, and apathy toward school work.[35] People always seem to find good reasons to do not-so-good things. Adults, the role models for the young, are caught in similar hypocrisies. From politicians to salespeople, from professional athletes to media stars, students are immersed in a less-than-honest culture. This does not mean cheating is OK; it means we need to look in and beyond schools to remedy the problem.

Cheating in school has become easier. Forget the traditional crib sheet tucked away under a sleeve; students today have discovered more high-tech forms of cheating. Invisible-ink pens, cell phones, and other palm-size gadgets are the new crib sheets at school, while the Internet has become a powerful temptation at home. The Internet has made it easy for students to cut and paste their way to a term paper, downloading a few sentences or even

FIGURE 8.2
The dishonor roll.

SOURCE: Josephson Institute for Youth Ethics: The Ethics of American Youth (2008).

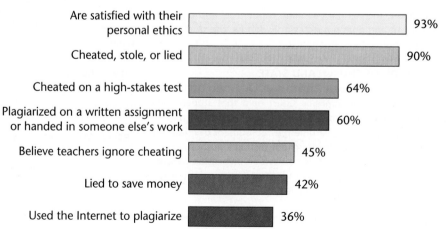

Percentage of students polled admitted they:

Are satisfied with their personal ethics	93%
Cheated, stole, or lied	90%
Cheated on a high-stakes test	64%
Plagiarized on a written assignment or handed in someone else's work	60%
Believe teachers ignore cheating	45%
Lied to save money	42%
Used the Internet to plagiarize	36%

REFLECTION: This is from a recent study of 30,000 high school students. Is cheating an acceptable norm in American schools? Why or why not? As a teacher, how will you address cheating?

Classroom Observation

15. Students and a Teacher Discuss Cheating

As a teacher you will be faced with difficult decisions that will test your ethics. In this two-part observation you will observe a scenario in which students cheat during an exam. In part one, when the teacher is called out of class during an exam, some students take to cheating. When the teacher returns, some students tell him what happened, and he must decide how to deal with the cheating. In part two, the students and teacher discuss the incident during an interview.

Classroom Observation Videos are available on the CD Reader and at the Online Learning Center.

www.mhhe.com/
sadkerbrief3e

entire essays and then weaving them into their papers, without crediting the original sources. Such practice constitutes plagiarism, grounds for suspension from many schools. Yet more than half of high school students admit to this "cut-and-paste" method to complete assignments. One-fifth of students do not even cut and paste; they buy ready-made term papers from commercial websites.[36]

Just how easy is it to plagiarize online? Type "*Scarlet Letter* essay" into a search engine such as Google, and dozens of websites pop up, offering hundreds of essays on topics from symbolism to adultery. Fortunately, online companies, such as Turnitin.com, offer schools plagiarism-detection programs. Students submit their completed work online, and the detection program then produces a report for teachers that highlights material copied from other sources. Teachers can also type a suspicious sentence or two from a student essay into a search engine such as Google to identify plagiarized material.

Perhaps most important, teachers can be proactive and work with students to promote honesty over deceit. Not only is plagiarism dishonest, it may also be a sign that students lack certain academic skills. Develop those skills, and plagiarism will decrease. For example, some students are unable to synthesize and then summarize information. Unable to do these intellectual tasks, they resort to plagiarizing. If teachers can help students learn these skills, summarize information, use citations properly, and develop their own insights, plagiarism may well decrease.[37] Finally, when teachers help students to explore values related to cheating, such as integrity and honesty, and when a consistent no-cheating policy or honor code is applied, students get the message and cheating is less likely.[38]

Cheating is only one of a myriad of ethical issues teachers and students will confront in and beyond the classroom; the digital world is also proving to be a tricky ethical challenge. Half of all teens send and receive at least 50

TEACHING TIP

SOCIAL NETWORKING GUIDELINES

Teachers are held to a high standard of professional conduct. Think before you post, text, or e-mail. Anything that is publicly available online could be seen by your students, their parents, or school administrators. Before you post any information or images, consider whether it could cause you embarrassment or potentially damage your reputation or career. Here are some tips to consider when using Facebook, MySpace, or Twitter accounts:

- Inform parents that you might text message students or communicate with them through MySpace, Twitter, or Facebook about school-related issues. Establish an opt-out opportunity if parents are uncomfortable.
- Establish clear rules for connecting with students via cell phones, texting, or the Internet.
- Communicate only about classroom and school matters.

- Do not accept students as friends on personal social networking sites.
- Limit personal information made available to students.
- Create separate professional and personal sites.
- Do not discuss students or co-workers or publicly criticize school policies or personnel.
- Do not post images that include students.
- Check personal sites regularly if the public has access to them. Even if you don't post inappropriate material, that doesn't mean your "friends" won't.

REFLECTION: Do you think these guidelines are fair? Why or why not? What additional social networking suggestions would you offer to teachers, or to anyone?

text messages a day; one-third more than 100. More than half of students ages 9 to 17 use social networking tools, such as Facebook, MySpace, or Twitter, at least once a day.[39] With such rocketing popularity, some teachers have started using these new tools to build rapport, answer questions about class assignments, and keep students informed about school activities. Teachers report that by connecting with students on networking sites, they often discover interests or hobbies that help them engage kids in the classroom, positively affecting academic performance. But potential pitfalls loom. Because most e-communication lacks facial or voice clues, even the most well-intentioned interactions can be misinterpreted. Boundaries can quickly blur when teachers "friend" their students. Some students worry about looking like the "teacher's favorite." Others say it would be "creepy" to have a teacher as a social networking friend. And sometimes "friending" has turned criminal. A small, but increasing, number of teacher-student cyber interactions have led to sexual encounters.[40]

Finding what role, if any, social networking, texting, and other cyber-inspired communications play in schools can be challenging. Some schools prohibit any teacher-student interaction via texting and social networking sites. Others are trying to find a balance and allow cyber-communications for educational purposes only. (See the Teaching Tip: Social Networking Guidelines for specific suggestions on how to safely and ethically navigate this online world.)

As a teacher, you will be called to follow your ethical compass to protect the physical and emotional well-being of your students and to guide students' own ethical development.

Here is an idea to help you along this ethical path. Do some Googling for "teacher code of ethics." Both the National Education Association (NEA) and the American Federation of Teachers (AFT) have teacher codes of ethics. Read them to get an idea about what they believe is important. Also, it might be interesting to read the ethical codes of other careers to see how they are similar and different. Ethics is too little talked about in our culture, but it is the heart of leading an honorable personal and professional life.

Protecting Your Students

Sam, the new student, seems so awkward in school, and he is often late. You have asked him more than once why he can't get to class on time, but he is barely audible as he mumbles, "I dunno." What's more, his behavior is strange. He seems to have an aversion to chairs, and, whenever possible, he prefers to stand in the back of the room alone. You have never seen Sam laugh or even smile. Every day, even on the hot ones, he wears a long-sleeve shirt. What is that all about? What a puzzle.

Then, one day, Sam arrives in class with some bruises on his face, and you begin to suspect that there is more to this story. You ask Sam, who shrugs it off and says that he fell and bruised his face. But you are not so sure. You arrive at a frightening thought: Could Sam be an abused child? How horrible! Now, what do you do?

In this case, you are confronting both an ethical dilemma and a legal challenge. Maybe you should speak to Sam's parents. Or should you press Sam for more information? Checking with other teachers makes sense, to see how they would handle the problem. Or perhaps it is time to go to the administration and let them find out what is going on.

Wait a second. What if you are wrong? Sam says he fell down and bruised himself. Maybe that is all it is. You should not go around accusing people without real evidence. Are you responsible for Sam's family situation? Is that a private concern rather than your business? Maybe the prudent course of action would be to monitor the situation for now and keep your suspicions to yourself. What would you do?

The ethical issue is pressing. If Sam is being injured, if his safety is in jeopardy, then waiting could be costly. Many would find that the most ethical course to follow is to share your concerns with an appropriate person in your school—perhaps a school psychologist, counselor, or administrator—or to notify Child Protective Services, a report that can be confidential. The potential for injury is simply too great to remain silent. Sharing your concern is not the same as making an accusation of child abuse, which may be false. By bringing the situation to the school's attention, you start the wheels in motion to uncover facts.

Child abuse and neglect include a range of mistreatments, including physical, emotional, and sexual harm. (See A Closer Look: Child Abuse Warning Signs.) The American Humane Institute documents that very few child abuse reports come from educators. Yet, it is the ethical responsibility of teachers to report the abusive treatment of children. As far as suspicion of child abuse is concerned, this ethical responsibility is reinforced by the law. Every state requires that teachers report "suspected" cases of abuse, and failure to report such cases can result in the loss of a teacher's license. Most of these laws also protect teachers from any legal liability for reporting such cases.[41]

CHILD ABUSE: WARNING SIGNS

Children who suffer physical, emotional, or sexual abuse and neglect may

- Exhibit signs of injury—burns, black eyes, welts, or bite marks
- Wear long sleeves even in very warm weather
- Be dirty or unbathed
- Not show emotion—no joy, pain, or anger
- Be apathetic toward school and friends
- Be frequently absent or tardy
- Be unusually eager to please
- Demonstrate hostility or distress
- Show signs of an eating disorder or extreme hunger
- Exhibit unusually sophisticated knowledge of sexual behavior
- Create stories or drawings of an unusually sexual nature
- Have difficulty sitting or walking
- Be frequently absent or tardy
- Show signs of depression
- Lack concentration
- Fear adults

SOURCE: Childhelp USA, Signs of Child Abuse (2010). www.childhelpusa.org

REFLECTION: If one of your students showed warning signs of abuse, whom in your school would you inform? How would you phrase your concern?

Moral Education: Programs that Teach Right from Wrong

During the American colonial experience, schools transmitted a common set of values. Back then (and in many places today), the teacher inculcated ideas of diligence, hard work, punctuality, neatness, honesty, conformity, and respect for authority, both civil and religious. It was thought that inculcating these values in children would produce virtuous adults. This approach continued in college where the most important course was moral philosophy, required of all students and often taught by the college president. But not everyone agrees that preaching such values is the only or the best way to produce moral citizens. Today, schools choose from different approaches, and four of the most widely known are (1) character education, (2) values clarification, (3) moral stages of development, and (4) comprehensive values education.

Character Education **Character education** programs assume that there are core attributes of a moral individual that children should be directly taught in school. Most states either are recipients of federal character education grants or require character education through legislation. What values are promoted? Core values include trustworthiness, respect, responsibility, fairness, caring, and good citizenship and are encouraged through the school culture, conduct codes, curriculum, and community service. Younger students may be asked to find examples of these qualities in literature and history, while older students may consider these values through ethical reasoning exercises. Along with developing core values, character education programs can challenge students to act on these values. For example, students may debate how best to implement a school's honor code, organize a food drive, or plan a ceremony honoring local military veterans.

Not everyone is enamored with character education. Critics view this approach as superficial, forcing a diverse student population into a simplistic and narrow set of unexamined values that does not really alter behaviors. Others believe that character education is little more than an old-fashioned "fix-the-kids" approach, a return to a traditional or religious agenda that simply rewards students who do what adults desire.[42] A nationwide study of more than 6,000 students at 84 schools that have implemented character education programs in all classes and activities found no improvement in student behavior or academic performance. The federal government, however, continues to distribute millions of dollars for character education programs despite the lack of proven effectiveness.[43]

Values Clarification The controversial **values clarification** program is designed to help students develop and eventually act on their values. Students might explore questions such as: What qualities do you value in a friend? When is lying acceptable? Would you be willing to donate your body to science when you die? How do you feel about competition? Would you welcome a person of a different race into your neighborhood? Throughout such values clarification exercises, students begin to bring their private values into a public light, where they can be analyzed, evaluated, and eventually put into action. This allows students to respond to each other's beliefs, to consider different points of view, and to analyze their own values. Many believe that values, like plants, need light and thoughtful nurturing to be healthy.

Critics charge that values clarification is itself valueless. In this approach, all values are treated equally, and there is no guarantee that good and constructive values will be promoted or that negative ones will be condemned. If, for example, a student decides that anti-Semitism or fascism is a preferred value, values clarification might do little to contradict this view. This "value neutral" stance is troubling to some and has led to the barring of values clarification in some school districts.

Moral Stages of Development Based on the work of Jean Piaget, the psychologist who identified stages of intellectual development (see "The Hall of Fame" in Chapter 5), a schema proposed by **Lawrence Kohlberg** identifies **moral stages of development.** The earliest stages focus on simple rewards and punishments. Young children are taught "right" and "wrong" by learning to avoid physical punishment and to strive for rewards. Most adults function at a middle, or conventional, stage, in which they obey society's laws, even laws that may be unjust. At the highest level, individuals act on principles, such as civil rights or pacifism, that may violate conventional laws. Kohlberg believes that teachers can facilitate student growth to higher stages of morality. In Kohlberg's curriculum, students are encouraged to analyze moral dilemmas presented in brief scenarios. For example, one such scenario might tell the story of someone breaking into a store and stealing, and the question is posed: Is stealing always wrong, or can it be justified? What if the person was stealing medicine needed to save a life; would that justify the theft? The teacher's role in this curriculum is to help students move to higher stages of moral development.

Critics point out that Kohlberg's theory was developed on an all-male population and that females may go through different stages of moral reasoning. Harvard professor Carol Gilligan, for example, found that women and men react differently when responding to moral dilemmas. While males seem to strongly

Moral Education and Ethical Lessons

ARE BEST TAUGHT BY INSTILLING AMERICAN VALUES THROUGH CHARACTER EDUCATION BECAUSE . . .

SHOULD HELP STUDENTS DEVELOP THEIR OWN VALUES BECAUSE . . .

OUR YOUTH ARE BEING CORRUPTED BY THE MEDIA

Television, music, and videos bombard children with commercialism, violence, and sex. Schools must be proactive in helping families instill the moral attitudes and values needed to counteract our lax social mores.

SOCIETAL INDIFFERENCE IS CORRUPTING OUR YOUTH

Traditional character education adopts a "blame the media" approach while neglecting real social issues. By ignoring poverty, racism, and sexism, traditionalists inculcate their own rosy picture of America, overlooking genuine if unattractive social injustices.

CHILDREN ARE UNABLE TO MAKE THEIR OWN MORAL CHOICES

Throughout history, educators have recognized that children have "impressionable" minds. Without moral training at a young age, as Theodore Roosevelt once noted, they can quickly become "a menace to society."

CHILDREN MUST LEARN TO MAKE MEANINGFUL MORAL CHOICES

Through character education, students are manipulated to adopt a narrow set of values. Far better is for teachers to help students become reflective thinkers, active citizens ready to work for social justice.

SHARED VALUES AFFIRM A NATIONAL IDENTITY

Americans believe in a common code of values to teach our children: respect, patriotism, tolerance, and responsibility. Our national fabric is built on such values, and our nation's future depends on them.

INDIVIDUAL VALUES HONOR DIVERSITY

In a nation of people with diverse cultural backgrounds, indoctrinating one set of fixed values is undemocratic and unwise. Respect for different cultural values will help create a safe and fair society marked by tolerance.

www.mhhe.com/sadkerbrief3e **YOU DECIDE . . .**

What role should character education play in public schools? Examine textbooks and curriculum used in a local school to determine the major values being taught to students. Are students expected to accept the values or to critically examine them? Which strategy do you support?

value those who follow the rules and laws, females tend to value relationships and caring. Kohlberg rated males as reaching a higher level of moral development than females because the scales he developed were male oriented.

Comprehensive Values Education Now that we have reviewed three approaches to teaching about values and ethics, it is worth noting that some teachers "mix and match," creating what might be considered a hybrid or fourth approach. Howard Kirschenbaum suggests that both values clarification and character education have important lessons for children. In his approach, **comprehensive values education,** traditional values such as honesty, caring, and responsibility are taught and demonstrated directly. However, because other values are less straightforward, such as favoring or rejecting the death penalty, students are taught analytical skills and engage in dialogues that will help them make wise decisions. There is an appropriate place in the school curriculum for each approach, Kirschenbaum insists, and many teachers instinctively apply multiple approaches.[44]

Classrooms that Explore Ethical Issues

For many educators and parents, concerns about values are daily events, too important to be left solely to a specific program or curriculum. How should teachers handle matters of ethics that appear on a daily basis? Consider that as a teacher, you might find

A student complains that her Vietnamese culture is being demeaned by the Christian and Western classroom activities.

A student with learning disabilities is ignored by classmates at lunchtime. Rather than sitting alone in the cafeteria, he hides in the bathroom.

A gifted student with advanced verbal skills is frequently bullied by a classmate in the locker room before gym class. Other students remain bystanders and do not stop or report the bullying.

Your best student, the one you just recommended for a special award, stored exam answers on her cell phone.

How are teachers to navigate this tricky moral minefield? Educators have offered several recommendations, summarized below:

The Setting

- *Climate.* Create an environment that respects and encourages diverse points of view and that promotes the sharing of diverse opinions, by both the teachers and the students.

- *School and class rules.* Requiring that students unquestioningly follow rules does not lead to democratic values. School and class rules need to be explained to students, and the reasons behind them understood. Many teachers go further and ask students to participate in formulating the rules they will live by.

- *Parents and community.* Citizens and community leaders should participate with the school in developing mission statements and ethical codes of responsibility. One way to encourage such cooperation is to plan joint efforts that tie the family and civic organizations into school-sponsored programs. The key is to reinforce ethical lessons in the school, the home, and the community.

The Teacher

- *Model.* You need to demonstrate the ethical lessons you teach. Teacher behavior should reflect such values as tolerance, compassion, forgiveness, and open-mindedness. (Values are often caught, not taught.)

- *Interpersonal skills.* You need effective communication skills to encourage students to share their concerns. A critical component of interpersonal skills is empathy—the ability to see problems from more than one point of view, including through the eyes of students.

- *Commitment.* It takes determination and courage on your part to confront ethical dilemmas, rather than to take the easier path of indifference or even inattention.

- *Reflection skills.* To unravel moral questions, you must know how to analyze a dilemma objectively and how to evaluate its essential components. Teachers with effective and deliberate reasoning skills are best suited for this challenge.

- *Personal opinions.* You should not promote or indoctrinate students with your personal points of view, nor should you shy away from showing students that you have strong beliefs. The key is to create a classroom in which individuals can freely agree or disagree, as they see fit.[45]

While laws direct us to what we can and cannot do, moral guidelines direct us in what we should and should not do. Moral issues will continue to be a major concern in the years ahead, in many ways a measure of the quality of our culture. Indeed, even as our society grows in wealth and makes great scientific strides and technological breakthroughs, the final measure of our worth may not be our materialistic accomplishments but, rather, the way we treat each other.

SUMMARY

CHAPTER REVIEW

Go the Online Learning Center to take a quiz, practice with key terms, and review concepts from the chapter.

www.mhhe.com/
sadkerbrief3e

1. **What are your legal rights and responsibilities as a teacher?**

   Teachers enjoy job security as long as their behavior and personal life do not disrupt or interfere with teaching effectiveness. Teachers have academic freedom, but cannot promote religious practices, such as prayer, in school. Teachers are also protected from racial or sexual discrimination.

2. **What legal rights do students enjoy (and do they have legal responsibilities)?**

   Parents and guardians have the right to see their child's educational record. Title IX prohibits many forms of sex discrimination. Students have constitutionally protected rights to due process before they can be disciplined or suspended from school. As long as students do not disrupt the operation of the school or deny other students the opportunity to learn, they have the right to freedom of speech within the schools. The school's *in loco parentis* responsibility allows it to search school lockers and cars in school parking lots and submit student athletes to random drug testing. Student publications can be censored if they are an integral part of the school curriculum, or if they are obscene, psychologically damaging, or disruptive.

3. **What are the ethical responsibilities of teachers and students?**

   Beyond simply following the law, students need to understand right from wrong. Cheating and social networking are two of a myriad of ethical challenges encountered at school. Teachers are also ethically responsible for providing a safe learning space for students as well as responding to issues of child abuse or neglect. To promote values and ethics, schools are incorporating moral education into the curriculum. Values clarification curriculum promotes values through personal reflection and individual analysis. Character education teaches a core set of values, including respect, responsibility, citizenship, caring, and fairness. What teachers do and say provides a model for students, serving as an "informal" curriculum on ethical behavior.

KEY TERMS AND PEOPLE

academic freedom, 247

Buckley Amendment, 252

character education, 268

child abuse, 267

comprehensive values
   education, 270

Copyright Act, 250

corporal punishment, 254

due process, 253

educational malpractice, 249

fair use, 250

First Amendment, 249

DISCUSSION QUESTIONS AND ACTIVITIES

1. If you were to suggest a law to improve education, what would that law be? Would you make it federal, state, or local? Why?

2. The role of religion and prayer in schools has always been controversial, and teachers are advised to neither *encourage* nor *discourage* religious observances. As a teacher, what religious celebrations or practices might you encounter in your class? How would you respond to these issues while maintaining your neutrality?

3. Construct an argument to support the principle that students and their property should not be searched without students' consent.

4. Which of the paths to moral education (values clarification, moral development, character education, or comprehensive values education) appeals to you most? Why?

5. Describe some steps you might explore to promote ethical student behavior in your classroom.

WEB-*TIVITIES*

Go to the Online Learning Center to do the following activities:

1. Teachers' and Students' Rights and Responsibilities
2. Students' Rights: Title IX and Sexual Harassment
3. Values Clarification
4. Character Education
5. Classrooms That Explore Ethical Issues

YOUR CD-ROM: THE *TEACHERS, SCHOOLS, AND SOCIETY* READER WITH CLASSROOM OBSERVATION VIDEO CLIPS

Articles, Case Studies, and Videos correspond to chapter content and are not always in numeric order. Go to your Teachers, Schools, and Society Reader CD-ROM to:

Read Current and Historical Articles

37. "Teaching about Religion," Susan Black, *American School Board Journal,* April 2003.

38. "Seven Worlds of Moral Education," Pamela Bolotin Joseph and Sara Efron, *Phi Delta Kappan,* March 2005.

39. "Promoting Altruism in the Classroom," E. H. Mike Robinson III and Jennifer R. Curry, *Childhood Education,* Winter 2005/2006.

40. "Please Help Me Learn Who I Am," Barry Boyce, *Shambhala Sun,* January 2007.

Analyze Case Studies

18. **Amanda Jackson:** A teacher discovers that her principal has a drinking problem, which is well known but never discussed among the staff. She faces a dilemma when she realizes that the principal is planning to drive a student home during a snowstorm.

19. **Ellen Norton:** A teacher, whose concern for a shy, underachieving student has led to the student becoming her "shadow," learns that another student may be the victim of child abuse at home. The teacher has to decide if she should become involved.

Observe Teachers, Students, and Classrooms In Action

15. **Classroom Observation: Students and a Teacher Discuss Cheating**
See page 265 of this text for a description of this video. You'll find the video on the CD Reader and at the Online Learning Center.

www.mhhe.com/
sadkerbrief3e

REFORMING AMERICA'S SCHOOLS

chapter 9

Focus Questions

1. What are the goals of America's schools?
2. What school goals are important to you?
3. Why has school reform become a top national priority?
4. What new school options are replacing the traditional neighborhood public school?
5. What is the role of teachers and students in reforming our schools?
6. What are the characteristics of effective schools?

WHAT DO YOU THINK? What do you think schools and students are like today? Check off what you think and see how others respond.

www.mhhe.com/ sadkerbrief3e

Chapter Preview

Although most of us take school for granted, the proper role of this institution continues to evoke heated debate. Are schools to prepare students for college, for a vocation, or to achieve high scores on standardized tests? Should schools help students develop good interpersonal relationships, patriotism, simply adjust to society or, more ambitiously, change and improve society?

In this chapter, you will have the opportunity to examine the major purposes assigned to schools and some of the major criticisms that have been leveled at them. The recent emphasis on standards and tests once again raises the crucial question: What's a school for? Some believe that poor test scores mean that America's schools are failing, and reform efforts have led to the creation of new schools, quite different from the old neighborhood school that you may have attended. The creation of virtual schools that teach via the Internet has made even a physical school building unnecessary. Some concerned parents are giving up on schools entirely, choosing to educate their children at home. The call for educational reform is not new, but today it is a national issue. Defining the place and the purpose of schools has never been more challenging. And sorting out what makes one school effective and another ineffective broadens the question from What is a school for? to What does it take to make a school work well? As we close this chapter, we will look at the factors associated with effective schools.

What Is the Purpose of School?

It sounds like a complaint many of us have uttered after a bad day at school, but it is more than that: It is a deceptively complex question. Although we all agree that students go to school to learn things, we do not agree on just what those things are. Quite popular today is the idea that the nation's financial well-being depends on an educated workforce, one that can compete in the global economy. On a personal level, you have heard this purpose targeted to you: "If you want to get a good job, you better get a good education!" Politicians and businesspeople are on the same page but with even more focus: They want schools to emphasize science, math, and technology so we can compete with countries such as India and China. Some people believe the purpose of schools is to post high scores on international tests, expecting American students to rank number one (instead of lower down the list, where we actually score). But not everyone is interested in worldly competitions or the workforce. Traditionalists focus on the basics, the "three Rs": reading, 'riting, and 'rithmatic (although spelling might be a good addition). Then there are those who say that given all the corruption in business, the improper conduct of politicians, the cheating in school, white-collar crime, and society's ethical dilemmas, perhaps schools should focus on making us all better people, more honest, kinder, and compassionate. Some schools call this character development, and many Americans believe that is the most important goal any school can have. There is always a group, small but energized, that believes schools should promote creativity in the arts and develop the hidden skills and talents within each of us. New York City's High School of Performing Arts does just that, and became famous in the movie *Fame.* Who wouldn't want to go to a school like that? How about patriotism? Many believe that schools must focus on graduating loyal Americans. Others believe that patriotic Americans are those who question and even challenge their government. How would you define a good citizen?

Focus Question 1
What are the goals of America's schools?

We will stop here, but you get the idea. This simple question is not so simple. Our views of what schools should be doing are diverse, sometimes superficial, and even contradictory. Let's spotlight what many see as the two fundamental, yet somewhat antithetical, purposes of all schools.

Purpose 1: To Transmit Society's Knowledge and Values (Passing the Cultural Baton)

Society has a vital interest in what schools do and how they do it. Schools reflect and promote society's values. A world of knowledge exists out there, more than any school can possibly hope to teach, so one of the first tasks confronting the school is to *select* what to teach. This selection creates a cultural message. Each country chooses the curriculum to match and advance its own view of history, its own values, its self-interests, and its own culture. In the United States, we learn about U.S. history, often in elementary, middle, and high school, but we learn little about the history, geography, and culture of other countries—or of America's own cultural diversity, for that matter. Even individual states and communities require schools to teach their own state or local history, to advance the dominant "culture" of Illinois or of New York City. By selecting what to teach—and what to omit—schools are making clear decisions as to what is valued, what is worth preserving and passing on.

Literature is a good example of this selection process. American children read works mainly by U.S. and British writers, and only occasionally works by Asian, Latin American, and African authors. This is not because literary genius is confined to the British and U.S. populations; it is because of a selection process, a decision by the keepers of the culture and creators of the curriculum that certain authors are to be taught, talked about, and emulated, and others are to be omitted. Similar decisions are made concerning which music should be played, which art viewed, which dances performed, and which historical figures and world events studied. As each nation makes these cultural value decisions, it is the role of the school to transmit these decisions to the next generation.

As society transmits its culture, it also transmits a view of the world. Being American means valuing certain things and judging countries and cultures from that set of values. Democratic countries that practice religious tolerance and respect individual rights are generally viewed more positively by Americans than are societies characterized by opposing norms, standards, and actions—that is, characteristics that do not fit our "American values." That Afghani women were denied access to schools, hospitals, and jobs by the Taliban conflicted with our cultural and political standards and was repulsive to most Americans. Repression of religious, racial, and ethnic groups usually engenders similar negative feelings. By transmitting culture, schools breathe cultural eternity into a new generation and mold its view of the world.

But this process is limiting as well. In transmitting culture, schools are teaching students to view the world from the wrong end of a telescope, yielding a constricted view that does not allow much deviation or perspective. Cultural transmission may contribute to feelings of cultural superiority, a belief that "we are the best, number one!" Such nationalistic views may decrease tolerance and respect for other cultures and peoples.

WHAT'S IN A NAME?

Ever wonder how schools get their names—and which names are the most popular? The National Education Resource Center researched the most popular proper names for U.S. high schools: Washington, Lincoln, Kennedy, Jefferson, Roosevelt (both Franklin and Teddy), and Wilson. (Presidents do well.) Lee, Edison, and Madison round out the top ten names. But proper names are not the most common high school names. Directions dominate: Northeastern, South, and Central High School are right up there. Creativity obviously is not a criterion, but politics is. Citizens fight over whether schools should be named after George Washington or Thomas Jefferson—who, after all, were slaveholders—and over why so few African Americans, Hispanics, and people of non-European ancestry are honored by having a school named after them. And, considering how many women are educators, it is amazing that so few schools are named to honor women—Eleanor Roosevelt, Amelia Earhart, Christa McAuliffe, and Jacqueline Kennedy are exceptions. Some schools have honored writers (Bret Harte, Walt Whitman, and Mark Twain) or reflect local leaders and culture. (In Las Vegas, you will find schools named Durango, Silverado, and Bonanza, which some complain sound more like casinos than western culture.)

REFLECTION: What choices do you think educators might make if they were responsible for school names? If students were in charge, would schools be named after sports figures or music and media stars? How do our school names reflect the power and culture in a society? What's in a name?

Purpose 2: Reconstructing Society (Schools as Tools for Change)

If society were perfect, transmitting the culture from one generation to the next would be all that is required of schools. But our world, our nation, and our communities are far from ideal. Poverty, hunger, injustice, pollution, overpopulation, racism, sexism, and ethical challenges—and, of course, the dark clouds of terrorism, economic turmoil, global warming, nuclear, chemical, and biological weapons—are societal problems on a depressingly long list. To **reconstructionists,** society is broken; it needs to be fixed, and the school is a perfect tool for making the needed repairs. Reconstructionists see successful students as citizens ready to make change by transforming injustices.

To prepare students for such engagement, *social democratic reconstructionists* believe that civic learning—educating students for democracy—needs to be on par with other academic subjects. Yet knowing how to achieve this goal is not easy. Some believe that students should be made aware of the ills of society; study these critical, if controversial, areas; and equip themselves to confront these issues as they become adults.[1] Other reconstructionists are more action-oriented and believe that schools and students shouldn't wait until students reach adulthood. They call for a *social action curriculum,* in which students actively involve themselves in eliminating social ills. For example, to gain public and government support for increased school construction and repairs, high school students in Baltimore, Maryland, organized a photo exhibit of their decaying school buildings. State legislators received a guided tour of the photos, which showed broken heaters, moldy walls, library shelves with no books, cockroaches, a stairwell filled with garbage, and broken windows.[2] As another example, students of all ages can learn about poverty and hunger in their communities and then organize a food drive or work in a soup kitchen.

This idea of students contributing to society is not unique. The Carnegie Foundation for the Advancement of Teaching recommends that every student be required to earn a **service credit,** which might include volunteer work with the poor, the elderly, or the homeless. The idea behind a service credit is not only to reduce social ills but also to provide students with a connection to the larger community, to develop a sense of personal responsibility for improving the social condition.[3] Service learning became more popular nationwide throughout the 1990s, and Maryland became the first state to require service learning for high school graduation.[4] More than half of students in grades 6 through 12 participate in service learning, although who participates and what they do to gain service credits is somewhat erratic. Girls are more likely to participate than are boys, and whites outnumber students of color. Participation increases when schools take an active role in setting up the service opportunities and when they require it for graduation. And student participation increases with the educational level of their parents.[5]

Social democratic reconstructionists are reform minded, but *economic reconstructionists* hold a darker view of society's ills and advocate more drastic, even revolutionary, action. They believe that schools generally teach the poorer classes to accept their lowly stations in life, to be subservient to authority, to unquestioningly follow rules while laboring for the economic benefit of the rich. To economic reconstructionists, schools are currently tools of oppression, not institutions of learning. They believe that students must be introduced to curricula that analyze and reform economic realities. For example, one such curriculum project targets a popular and highly visible athletic company, one that produces incredibly expensive sport shoes. This company manufactures its products in developing nations, maintaining horrid working conditions. Children in these poor countries are sold into labor bondage by their impoverished families. As young as age 6, they work 12 or more hours a day, enduring cruelty and even beatings as they earn only pennies an hour. Although the companies defend themselves by saying that they cannot change local conditions, economic reconstructionists believe that companies intentionally select locations because of their cheap labor costs. Economic reconstructionists point out that American children play with products made through the agonizing toil of other children. All the while, the companies profit. Educators who focus on economic reform have developed materials, websites, and social action projects that not only teach children about such exploitation but also provide them with strategies to pressure companies into creating more humane and equitable working conditions.[6]

Is the purpose of schools just academic learning, or might the goals include fostering an awareness of the benefits of community service, such as volunteering to tutor others?

Perhaps the most noted contemporary economic reconstructionist was **Paulo Freire,** author of *The Pedagogy of the Oppressed,* a book about his efforts to educate and liberate poor, illiterate peasants in Brazil.[7] In his book, Freire describes how he taught these workers to read in order to identify problems that were keeping them poor and powerless. From this new awareness, they began to analyze their problems—such as how the lack of sanitation

causes illness—and what they could do to solve specific problems and liberate themselves from their oppressive conditions. Freire highlighted the distinction between schools and education. Schools often miseducate and oppress. But true education liberates. Through education, the dispossessed learned to read, to act collectively, to improve their living conditions, and to reconstruct their lives. (See the education *Hall of Fame* in Chapter 5 for more about Freire.)

Public Demands for Schools

Preserving the status quo and promoting social change represent two fundamental directions available to schools, but they are not the only possible expectations. When you think about it, the public holds our schools to a bewildering assortment of tasks and expectations.

John Goodlad, in his massive study, *A Place Called School,* examined a wide range of documents that tried to define the purposes of schooling over 300 years of history. He and his colleague found four broad goals:

1. *Academic,* including a broad array of knowledge and intellectual skills
2. *Vocational,* aimed at readiness for the world of work and economic responsibilities
3. *Social and civic,* including skills and behavior for participating in a complex democratic society
4. *Personal,* including the development of individual talent and self-expression[8]

Goodlad included these four goal areas in questionnaires distributed to parents, and he asked them to rate their importance (see Figure 9.1). Parents gave "very important" ratings to all four. When Goodlad asked students and teachers to rate the four goal areas, they rated all of them as "very important." When pushed to select one of these four as having top priority, approximately half the teachers and parents selected the intellectual area, while students spread their preferences fairly evenly among all four categories, with high school students giving a slight edge to vocational goals. When it comes to selecting the purpose of schools, both those who are their clients and those who provide their services resist interpreting the purpose of schools narrowly.

What do Americans want from their schools? Evidently, they want it all! As early as 1953, Arthur Bestor wrote, "The idea that the school must undertake to meet every need that some other agency is failing to meet, regardless of

FIGURE 9.1
Goals of schools.

REFLECTION: Under each goal, list specific efforts a school could make to reach the goal. How would you prioritize these goals? Explain.

the suitability of the schoolroom to the task, is a preposterous delusion that in the end can wreck the educational system."[9]

Then, in the 1980s, Ernest Boyer conducted a major study of secondary education and concluded:

> Since the English classical school was founded over 150 years ago, high schools have accumulated purposes like barnacles on a weathered ship. As school population expanded from a tiny urban minority to almost all youth, a coherent purpose was hard to find. The nation piled social policy upon educational policy and all of them on top of the delusion that a single institution can do it all.[10]

Three decades later, the public continues to hold schools to a myriad of high expectations: More than two-thirds of Americans believe that schools are responsible for the academic as well as behavioral, social, and emotional needs of all students.[11]

Where Do You Stand?

Identifying school goals seems to be everyone's business—parents, teachers, all levels of government, and various professional groups. Over the years, dozens of lists have been published in different reform reports, each enumerating goals for schools. The problem arises when schools cannot fulfill all these goals, either because there are too many goals or because the purposes conflict with one another. It is these smaller pieces that often dominate discussion. Should schools focus on preparing students for college? Should they try to inhibit drug use, or lessen the threat of AIDS? Perhaps schools ought to focus on the economy and train students to compete in the world marketplace.

Look at the following list of school goals. Drawn from a variety of sources, these goals have been advocated singly and in combination by different groups at different times and have been adopted by different schools. In each case, register your own judgment on the values and worth of each goal. When you have completed your responses, we shall discuss the significance of these goals, and you can see how your responses fit into the bigger picture.

Circle the number that best reflects how important you think each school goal is.

1 Very unimportant

2 Unimportant

3 Moderately important

4 Important

5 Very important

Focus Question 2
What school goals are important to you?

	Very Unimportant				Very Important
1. To transmit the nation's cultural heritage, preserving past accomplishments and insights	1	2	3	4	5
2. To encourage students to question current practices and institutions; to promote social change	1	2	3	4	5
3. To prepare competent workers to compete successfully in a technological world economy	1	2	3	4	5

	Very Unimportant				Very Important
4. To develop healthy citizens aware of nutrition, exercise, and good health habits	1	2	3	4	5
5. To lead the world in creating a peaceful global society, stressing an understanding of other cultures and languages	1	2	3	4	5
6. To provide a challenging education for America's brightest students	1	2	3	4	5
7. To develop strong self-concept and self-esteem in students	1	2	3	4	5
8. To nurture creative students in developing art, music, and writing	1	2	3	4	5
9. To prevent unwanted pregnancy, AIDS, drugs, addiction, alcoholism	1	2	3	4	5
10. To unite citizens from diverse backgrounds (national origin, race, ethnicity) as a single nation with a unified culture	1	2	3	4	5
11. To provide support to families through after-school child care, nutritional supplements, medical treatment, and so on	1	2	3	4	5
12. To encourage loyal students committed to the United States; to instill patriotism	1	2	3	4	5
13. To teach students our nation's work ethic: punctuality, responsibility, cooperation, self-control, neatness, and so on	1	2	3	4	5
14. To demonstrate academic proficiency through high standardized test scores	1	2	3	4	5
15. To provide a dynamic vehicle for social and economic mobility, a way for the poor to reach their full potential	1	2	3	4	5
16. To prepare educated citizens who can undertake actions that spark change	1	2	3	4	5
17. To ensure the cultural richness and diversity of the United States	1	2	3	4	5
18. To eliminate racism, sexism, homophobia, anti-Semitism, and all forms of discrimination from society	1	2	3	4	5
19. To prepare as many students as possible for college and/or well-paid careers	1	2	3	4	5
20. To provide child care for the nation's children and to free parents to work and/or pursue their interests and activities	1	2	3	4	5

Now, think about your three most valued goals for school and write those goals below:

Three valued goals:

_____, _____, _____

Purpose of Schools

Transmitting Culture		Reconstructing Society	
Focused Item		*Focused Item*	
1	_____	2	_____
3	_____	5	_____
10	_____	9	_____
12	_____	15	_____
13	_____	16	_____
19	_____	18	_____
Total	_____	*Total*	_____

REFLECTION: Do your responses reflect the school experiences you had, or the ones you had hoped for? Which camp are you in: transmitting culture or reconstructing society?

Do your responses to these items and your three priority goal selections cast you as transmitter of culture or as change agent for restructuring society? To help you determine where your beliefs take you, record your scores on the following selected items:

Let's investigate how your choices reflect your values. The current emphasis on standards, tests, and academic performance is reflected in items 1, 13, and especially 14. Are you in agreement with this contemporary educational priority? If you scored high on items 1 and 10, you value the role schools serve in preparing Americans to adhere to a common set of principles and values. This has been a recurrent theme in schools as each new group of immigrants arrives. Some people called this the melting pot, more formally termed **acculturation,** or **Americanization** (replacing the old culture with the new American one). Others believe that it is a mistake to try to forge a singular definition of an American. Given our nation's diversity, they want schools to honor cultural pluralism, to learn and honor our different cultural and ethnic traditions, and to gain different insights on our world. Look at how you responded to item 17 to see the degree of your support for cultural pluralism. Item 17, along with items 2 and 18, also suggests a commitment to civil rights and student empowerment, hallmarks of the 1960s and 1970s, and since history often runs in cycles, perhaps those goals will resurface in the not-too-distant future. Do you like the Horatio Alger folklore: hard work and a little elbow grease, and the poor become wealthy? Agree with this folklore and you probably rated items 15 and 19 pretty high. Take a little time and see where you stand on the other items. And while you look them over, consider item 20, which may seem a bit odd. After all, few people see schools as babysitters, but without this "service," most parents would be overwhelmed. And consider the impact that millions of adolescents would have on the job market. Unemployment would skyrocket and wages would tumble. By minding the children, schools provide parents with time and keep our workforce down to a manageable size.

What did your ratings teach you about your values and your view of schools? Were your goals popular during particular periods of our past, or are you more future-oriented? You may want to compare your goals for education here with your philosophical preferences as identified in Chapter 6.

www.mhhe.com/
sadkerbrief3e

INTERACTIVE ACTIVITY
**How Important Are
These School Goals?** Do
this exercise online. See
how others responded to
each statement.

A History of Educational Reform

Focus Question 3

Why has school reform become a national priority?

This is an exciting time to be an educator. Education reform is front and center in the debate about America's future. But reforming America's schools is not new. The 1983 report titled *A Nation at Risk: The Imperative for Educational Reform* began this way:

> Our Nation is at risk. Our once unchallenged prominence in commerce, industry, science, and technological innovation is being overtaken by competitors throughout the world. . . . If an unfriendly foreign power had attempted to impose on America the mediocre educational performance that exists today, we might well have viewed it as an act of war. . . . We have, in effect, been committing an act of unthinking, unilateral educational disarmament.[12]

The report cited declining test scores, the weak performance of U.S. students compared with students in other industrialized nations, the fear that the United States is losing ground economically to other countries, and the high number of functionally illiterate Americans.[13] It sounds like it could have been written today, but even this effort was far from the first.

At the end of the nineteenth century, the United States was undergoing profound changes. New industries and giant corporations were being formed, massive numbers of immigrants were arriving, factory labor was being exploited, cities were growing and farms were disappearing. How should schools respond? In 1892, the National Education Association (NEA) established the *Committee of Ten* to develop a national policy for high schools.[14] The committee, composed for the most part of college presidents and professors, wanted consistency and order in the high school curriculum for an easier transition into college. The committee report required that high schools teach certain required courses four or five times a week for one year, and that student progress be measured by *Carnegie Units.* Now it became easier for colleges to decide which students were prepared to do college-level work.

The NEA repeated the process in 1918, but this time committee members focused not on transition to college but on preparing adults for their life roles. The truth is, very few Americans went to college at that time; most went on to work and family. The committee wanted to know: What can high school do to improve the daily lives of citizens in an industrial democracy? This committee's report, *Cardinal Principles of Secondary Education*, identified seven goals for high school: (1) health, (2) worthy home membership, (3) command of fundamental academic skills, (4) vocation, (5) citizenship, (6) worthy use of leisure time, and (7) ethical character. The high school was seen as a socializing agency, an opportunity to improve all aspects of a citizen's life. (Almost a century later, those 1918 goals still sound balanced and useful.) Nevertheless, today's reform movement, focused on academics and test scores, echoes the narrower academic spotlight of the 1893 Committee of Ten.

At the turn of this century, No Child Left Behind, with its huge testing culture,

A by-product of recent calls for educational reform has been an explosion of student (and teacher) testing to ensure that revised school goals are being met.

became law, and a school's success was measured by student test scores. (We will discuss this at greater length in Chapter 10, "Curriculum, Standards, and Testing.") If students scored well, the school was seen as successful. When students did poorly, the school was considered a failing school. But what could be done with a failing school?

School Choice

The idea to actually shut down a poor performing neighborhood school could be traced back to the 1950s and economist **Milton Friedman,** who believed that local public schools were often weak because they functioned as a monopoly. Neighborhood families were a "trapped" clientele, and so the local school had no incentive to improve. He believed that public schools would be more effective if they functioned in a free market, competing against one another so that the public would send their children to the better schools and the weak schools would lose their students and be forced to close. Friedman noted that not every family was trapped, because wealthy parents could bail out of a weak neighborhood school by moving to a different community or choosing a private school. His voucher plan, which we will discuss shortly, would give every family the same choice that the wealthy enjoyed. For Friedman, choice and competition were needed to improve schools.

In a 1981 study, *James Coleman* found that private schools were doing a better job of educating students than were the neighborhood public schools. Private school students were better behaved and scored higher on tests. In 1993, another study found that Catholic schools were particularly effective for inner-city students of color and were less costly and more racially integrated than the neighboring public schools.[15] So now we had two arguments for giving parents a choice in school selection. One was Friedman's marketplace idea—competition creates better schools—and the other that private schools were doing better than public schools.

By the late 1980s, a third, even more persuasive, argument emerged: Many public schools, especially inner-city schools, were disasters. In these under-resourced schools, teacher turnover was high, the buildings were in disrepair (and often rodent-infested), test scores were abysmal, and dropout rates high. Rather than finding open doors to promising futures, many students in these schools did not even make it to graduation. To require parents, typically poor parents, to send their children to such troubled neighborhood public schools seemed both cruel and unfair. The neighborhood public school, once sacrosanct, was now vulnerable.

By the early 2000s, national figures such as Bill Gates were telling the nation that if we were to compete on the world stage, more than the neighborhood elementary schools needed to be fixed; high schools were also failing. Gates argued that our high schools were "obsolete," designed to prepare students for a world that has not existed for decades. "Only one-third of our students graduate from high school ready for college, work and citizenship . . . In 2001, India graduated almost a million more students from college than did the United States; China graduates twice as many students with bachelor's degrees as the United States, and they have six times as many graduates majoring in engineering."[16] The Bill and Melinda Gates Foundation committed several billion dollars to strengthening America's high schools.

The prestigious consulting firm McKinsey & Company voiced a similar concern in a 2009 report titled *The Economic Impact of the Achievement Gap in America's Schools.* This report examined the dimensions of four distinct achievement gaps in education: (1) between the United States and other nations, (2) between black and Latino students and white students, (3) between students of different income levels, and (4) between similar students schooled in different systems or regions. The report actually put a monetary cost on these gaps. It concluded that the nation's Gross Domestic Product, or GDP (that is, the total value of all goods and services produced each year), would be $1.3–2.3 trillion higher if these achievement gaps did not exist. If educational reform had been successful after *A Nation at Risk* was initially published in 1983, our nation's economy today would be far stronger. The slow pace of educational reform has led to the economic equivalent of a permanent national recession, with lower earnings, poorer health, and higher rates of incarceration. One author of the report put it this way: "We waste 3 to 5 billion dollars a day by not closing these achievement gaps. This is not simply an issue about poor kids in poor schools; it's about most kids in most schools." To underscore our international performance gap, 15-year-old American students ranked 25th out of 30 industrialized nations in math problem-solving skills, and 24th out of 30 in science problem-solving skills. U.S. students scored on a par with Portugal and the Slovak Republic, but well behind our economic competitors, such as Canada, Korea, and Australia. Our lagging education system is costing us all.[17]

By the time President Obama took office in 2009, reforming schools was a top national priority. Offering parents a choice of schools was central. Students and parents (and often teachers) can choose from a variety of schooling options. As we describe each of these options, consider which sound attractive to you, perhaps places where you would like to teach. Perhaps the option that most impacted public education is the charter school movement. (See Figure 9.2.)

FIGURE 9.2
Do you favor or oppose the idea of charter schools?

SOURCE: Highlights of the 2010 Phi Delta Kappa/Gallup Poll: "What Americans Said About the Public Schools," http://www.pdkintl.org/kappan/docs/2010_Poll_Report.pdf.

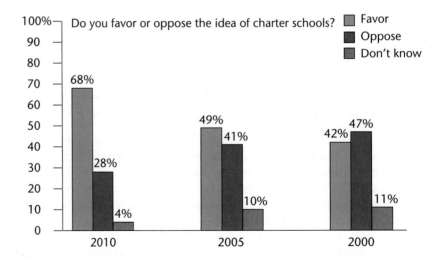

REFLECTION: Given the evaluations that many charter schools are weak, what do you attribute the public's attraction to this option?

Charter Schools

In the early 1990s, Minnesota created the first charter school, launching an idea that has mushroomed into almost 5,000 charter schools operating in 40 states and the District of Columbia, creating new competition for neighborhood public schools. While Arizona, California, Texas, and Florida have created the most charter schools, other states have been more cautious. (To check on the charter schools in your state, visit www.uscharterschools.org.)

Focus Question 4
What new school options are replacing the traditional neighborhood public school?

What are these charter schools? The concept is simple. A **charter school** is a tax-supported public school that has legal permission (called a charter or a contract) from a local or state school board to operate a school, usually for a fixed period of time with the right to renew the charter if the school is successful. So if you and a group of your friends wanted to create a school, you would apply for a charter. If the school board accepted your plan, you could begin your school. You would look for a building to rent, or perhaps discover an unused school building, or if you were really stuck, find a benefactor to help finance your school. (Charter schools have drawn some very wealthy benefactors.) You would create your budget, develop your curriculum, hire your teachers and staff, and recruit students. For each student who enrolled in the school, you would receive a certain amount of money from the state. Enroll enough students, and you will have the money you need to fund your school. Your charter school curriculum could be as creative or as traditional as you like because it is your school. You would be exempt from most state and local regulations, although you would have to follow health, safety, and civil rights rules. In effect, charter schools "swap" regulations for greater freedom and the promise that they will be effective and their students will do well. After a certain period of time, perhaps five years, your school would be evaluated to make certain that students were performing well.

A charter school typically

- Allows for the creation of a new school or the conversion of an existing public school
- Prohibits admission tests
- Is nonsectarian
- Requires a demonstrable improvement in performance
- Can be closed if it does not meet expectations
- Does not need to conform to most state rules and regulations
- Receives public funding based on the number of students enrolled (with additional private funding possible and not uncommon)

Okay, because you are taking what might be your first education class, perhaps it is a bit premature for you to open a charter school, but you might be wondering who would take on such a task. Tom Watkins, director of the Detroit Center for Charter Schools, describes three types of charter advocates: reformers, zealots, and entrepreneurs. *Reformers* are those who want to expand public school options, create a positive option for parents and children, and perhaps promote a specific approach, such as a more student-centered institution. Reformers engender positive reports in the press. Watkins also describes *zealots,* who want to promote more conservative schools and who typically do not like teacher unions. Often, these charters model private schools and emphasize traditional curricular ideas and teacher-centered class-rooms. The final group consists of *entrepreneurs,* businesspeople who believe that efficiency can convert schools into untapped profit centers. This last group believes that you can have effective charter schools that teach students well and make a profit for investors. We will take a closer look at these educational entrepreneurs a bit later.[18]

Some charter schools can offer you, as a new teacher, more freedom than the traditional neighborhood school, allowing you to create your own standards and curriculum, establish rules for discipline, plan programs with your colleagues, and even make budget decisions. That is what Casey Mason, a social studies teacher at the Amy Biehl High School (ABHS) in New Mexico, likes about her charter school experience. (See the Contemporary Issues feature.) But other charters offer you less teacher freedom. KIPP schools (which stands for Knowledge Is Power Program) were begun by two graduates of Teach for America who had some very firm ideas about what it takes to make inner-city schools work. Unlike Casey's experience at Amy Biehl High School, KIPP teachers follow specific rules and lessons and are far more strictly controlled than most public school teachers. KIPP charter schools follow five principles:

1. *More time.* KIPP schools have longer school days and a longer school year. For example, school days may run 7:30–5:00 Mondays through Fridays, and 9:30–1:30 several Saturdays a month. School also continues for several weeks in the summer. Teachers earn a higher salary (typically 15–20 per-cent more than a typical teacher's salary) to compensate for this additional time. This longer school day and year is a KIPP practice that is gaining popularity in other schools as well.

2. *High expectations.* Students, parents, teachers, and staff work to create a culture of achievement and support. Parents sign contracts guaranteeing their involvement in monitoring their children's work and participating in school activities.

3. *Choice and commitment.* Everyone in a KIPP school chooses to be there and to put in the time and the effort required to succeed.

4. *Power to lead.* The principals of KIPP schools have control over their school budget and personnel and are held accountable for learning. There is no central bureaucracy. Principals are expected to achieve results, or the KIPP organization replaces them.

5. *Focus on results.* What are those results? Certainly, high student scores on standardized tests are a KIPP priority. Students are expected to achieve a level of academic performance that will enable them to graduate and go on to the nation's best high schools and colleges.

There are more than 100 KIPP schools, usually grades 5–8 but expanding to other grades as well, in major cities across the nation, and these schools have a lot of fans. Most of KIPP students are African American or Hispanic, and the majority go on to college-preparatory high schools; test scores for KIPP students are stronger than the scores in the local public schools. KIPP charter schools are successful, but there is a catch: KIPP, like so many inner-city schools, loses many students before they graduate. The urban environ-ment has many distractions, and when a KIPP student cannot keep up with the academics, he leaves the school. So although KIPP students and graduates

A VIEW FROM THE FIELD: TEACHING AT A CHARTER SCHOOL

Casey Mason, 28, teaches ninth grade social studies at Amy Biehl High School (ABHS), a charter school in New Mexico. Casey is also one of two certified special education teachers at the school. Her interests in social justice and special education led to her current position teaching inclusive classes at the small school of 250 students.

Casey is intensely collaborative with her fellow teachers.

I have not once planned a class in isolation. Our curriculum is planned with our colleagues; we decide what is enduring and important about New Mexico history, the quadratic equation, and biology. We have academic discussions where we explore what we will teach our students. At times I feel as though I'm still in college. It's wonderful. I chose ABHS because I knew creative lessons that value critical thinking and differentiation would be expected here.

After teaching in a more traditional middle school for two years, Casey finds that she enjoys a different kind of school. "Through the luxury of a small learning community, I am able to build more personal relationships with my students and really get to know their learning needs. At traditional public schools I would teach 150 students per day, with up to 35 students in each class. At ABHS, I have no more than 20 students in a class." ABHS is a public high school and any student can attend; because of the limited enrollment, students are picked by lottery. How do students chosen by lottery become so special? Casey's answer: being part of an intimate community.

There are no prerequisites for attending ABHS, it is a public school. I have wonderful students not because they are the highest achievers, the most talented, or the best behaved. At our small school, my students get to be who they are without fear of being the other. The size of ABHS allows for and mandates this. You can't hide in a small school. The same goes for the teachers. The power of small personal communities is what makes my school magical.

Casey Mason has a BA in women's studies and African American studies and an MA in special education from the University of New Mexico.

do well, the challenge is keeping students in school long enough to learn and graduate.[19]

A wide variety of charter schools exist, but let's conclude by returning to the idea that opened this section: You can start your own school. In fact, that is what teachers are doing, even new teachers. In 2010, after three years in the classroom, a group of six young teachers in Newark, New Jersey, were frustrated with seeing so much failure, so they asked for and received their own K-8 charter school. They became the teacher-leaders who decided what to teach and how long the school day or school year should be. In teacher-led schools from Los Angeles to New York, studies show that there is higher morale, less turnover, and greater motivation.[20] So your teaching in and running a charter school may not be so farfetched after all.

But managing an effective charter school, that is the challenge. Despite all their cultural cachet and acclaim, the majority of the 5,000 or so charter schools nationwide do not appear to be any better than local public schools, and a number of them are weaker. A Stanford University study found that fewer than one-fifth of charter schools offered a better education than local schools, almost half offered a similar level of education, and more than a third, 37 percent, were "significantly worse."[21] Many charters struggle even to find an appropriate building, qualified teachers, funds needed for computers or library books, and have a high teacher turnover.[22] Another problem is that charter school enrollments are more racially isolated than traditional public schools in virtually every state and large metropolitan area in the nation.[23] Not unlike neighborhood public schools, some charter schools do well, while others struggle; more time is needed before the final verdict is in. What is

Classroom Observation

9. Tour of a Boston Charter School

You may one day want to explore teaching in a charter school. In this observation you will observe the faculty and administrators of the Match charter school who provide insights into daily life and teaching in a charter school. A number of comparisons with typical public schools are made.

Classroom Observation videos are available on the CD Reader and at the Online Learning Center.

www.mhhe.com/
    sadkerbrief3e

exciting about charter schools is that they offer an opportunity to experiment, to try new schooling options and approaches. Will the charter school movement eventually improve American education? Time will tell.

Full Service Schools for the Whole Child

When Mayor Michael Bloomberg was asked to identify the most important person living in New York City, he did not name a famous New York actor, billionaire, renowned artist, or scientist; he named Geoffrey Canada. Geoffrey Canada, educator and community advocate, created the Harlem Children's Zone, a nearly 100-block area in the Harlem section of New York City where his community based organization and charter schools serve 17,000 children. If you visit one of his schools, you would encounter more than teachers and principals working with children; you would find dentists, nutritionists, drivers to help with transportation, and counselors helping both the parents and the children create productive lives. Canada explains, "In communities where kids are failing in record numbers, you can't just do one thing. . . We start with children at birth and stay with them until they graduate from college. . . . In the end, you have to create a series of supports that really meet all of their needs." Like KIPP schools, his are open most of the day and 11 months a year, recognizing that children cannot learn when they come to school tired, hungry, or abused, or if their families are in distress.[24] Such schools are rare. Called **full service schools,** they can be public or charter, and both types are often impressive.

Vouchers

Although the charter school movement has greatly impacted public education, this not at all what Milton Friedman had in mind when he promoted school choice over half a century ago. Friedman was promoting competition through vouchers, not charters. What's a voucher? You might think of an educational **voucher** as an admission ticket to any school, public or private. The

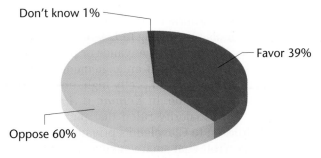

Do you favor or oppose allowing students and parents to choose private schools at public expense?

Don't know 1%

Favor 39%

Oppose 60%

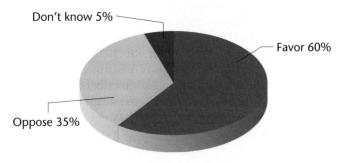

Do you favor or oppose charter schools?

Don't know 5%

Favor 60%

Oppose 35%

FIGURE 9.3

Americans view vouchers and charter schools.

SOURCE: *The 2007 Phi Delta Kappa/Gallup Poll of the Public's Attitudes toward the Public Schools*

REFLECTION: Using these pie charts, explain why the public is more reticent to support vouchers than charter schools.

government gives parents an educational voucher, a ticket for each child, and then the family would go "shopping" for the best school. After a school was chosen, the parent would give the voucher to the school administrator, the school would turn it over to the local or state government, and the government would pay the school a fixed sum for each voucher. In Friedman's mind, good schools would collect many vouchers, convert them into cash, and thrive, perhaps even expand, while weak schools would find it difficult to attract "customers" and would go out of business. Competition would do the work of reforming schools by simply eliminating weak schools and expanding the good ones.

In 1990, Milwaukee became the site of the first publicly financed voucher program. Wisconsin lawmakers approved a plan for Milwaukee students to receive about $3,000 each to attend nonsectarian private schools and then, in 1995, amended the law to allow students to attend religious schools as well. The inclusion of religious schools, first in the Milwaukee voucher plan, then in a similar plan in Cleveland, sparked a heated controversy and a round of lawsuits. The reason that religious schools are so closely involved in the voucher dispute is that they are the prime beneficiaries, receiving upward of 90 percent of the students using such vouchers. Why is this? Two reasons: First, most private schools are religious schools, and second, most religious schools have low tuition rates. Voucher plans offer only modest financial support, too little for elite private schools but adequate to cover the cost of many parochial schools.[25] So perhaps you might be thinking: How can vouchers—public taxpayer money—be used to send children for religious instruction? Doesn't the First Amendment of the Constitution ensure the separation of church and state—or has all that changed?

In fact, the legal picture is in flux. Back in 1971 in **Lemon v. Kurtzman** and in 1973 in the *Nyquist* case, the Supreme Court constructed clear walls limiting the use of public funds to support religious education. What became known as the *Lemon* test provided three criteria to determine the legality of government funds used in religious schools. According to *Lemon,* the funds (1) must have a secular purpose, (2) must not primarily advance or prohibit religion, and (3) must not result in excessive government entanglement with religion. So the wall separating church and state seemed pretty high, until 2002, when a more conservative court revisited the issue. In **Zelman v. Simmons-Harris** (2002), a narrow 5–4 Supreme Court majority ruled that publicly funded vouchers could be used to send children to Cleveland's private religious schools. Chief Justice William Rehnquist wrote that such vouchers permit a "genuine choice among options public and private, secular and religious." Justice John Paul Stevens dissented, writing, "Whenever we remove a brick from the wall that was designed to separate religion and government, we increase the risk of religious strife and weaken the foundation of our democracy."[26] Even though this Supreme Court decision allowed the use of vouchers, some state constitutions restrict public aid to private and religious institutions.[27] Many Americans oppose public funds going to promote religious doctrine.[28] Moreover, evaluations of the few voucher programs that do exist indicate that they have not been particularly effective.[29] Little surprise that vouchers are used in just a handful of states, while charter schools remain popular in many parts of the country.

Magnet Schools

Although few people thought of it as a "choice" option more than 70 years ago, for talented students, magnet schools were just that. You may have heard of magnet schools, or perhaps you even attended one. A **magnet school** offers one or more special programs, perhaps in math or science or the arts. These programs are so highly regarded that, like a magnet, they draw students from near and far. In large school districts such as New York City, some very fine magnet schools have been serving students for a very long time. In 1936, New York City Mayor Fiorello H. LaGuardia founded the High School of Music & Art for students gifted in the arts. Today, it is the LaGuardia School of Arts, a public magnet school open to students who pass a rigorous audition. Among its hundreds of well-known graduates are Jennifer Aniston, Ellen Barkin, and Al Pacino. Stuyvesant High School, also in New York, is a magnet school for mathematics, science, and technology. As many as 20,000 students each year are tested for admission to Stuyvesant, but only 800 or so are accepted. Stuyvesant proudly announces on its website that four of its graduates went on to become Nobel Laureates.

Although magnets like these were created to offer high-quality programs for talented students in metropolitan areas, the magnet idea gained additional momentum in the 1960s and 1970s as a method to voluntarily racially desegregate schools. A magnet school with a strong specialized program would be established in a school in a predominantly African American community. White students would voluntarily travel to attend these special programs, and the result would be an integrated school. But it is important to remember that although the school was integrated, many of the classrooms were not. Most of the African American students in the school attended the regular high school classes, whereas most of the white students attended the special magnet classes. About half of today's magnet schools have helped racial desegregation, but as today's cities and communities become ever more racially segregated, the ability of magnet schools to desegregate communities is diminished.

More than 2 million students attend magnet schools today. Unlike charter schools, magnet schools are not in the spotlight, and many suffer from underfunding, especially when it comes to paying for transportation costs, but that is not to say they are not doing an effective job. Often, magnet schools are more effective and racially integrated than public neighborhood or charter schools.[30]

Open Enrollment

In 1988, Minnesota instituted **open enrollment,** which eliminated the requirement that students must attend the closest public school. Like the magnet schools, open enrollment encouraged parents to choose a school, but it greatly increased the number of schools to choose from. Any public school with available space became eligible. Arkansas, Iowa, Nebraska, and other states soon followed Minnesota's lead and introduced open enrollment legislation. Today, more than 40 states allow open enrollment within school districts. However, even more radical proposals are available that may redefine, if not eliminate, the neighborhood school.[31]

Schools.com

One of the most unusual schools we shall look at (well, perhaps not exactly "look at" because you cannot really see it) is a school that has no building and no parking lot, and no one actually goes there. (Some might call it a "dream school.") But before you get carried away, **virtual schools** provide a wealth of learning, usually through technology. Actually, a virtual school is a form of **distance learning,** or learning provided over long distances by means of television, the Internet, and other technologies. The first virtual high schools (VHS) began in Utah, Florida, and Massachusetts in the 1990s. Today, K–12 online learning programs exist in about half of the states, with more than 700,000 students enrolled in over 1 million courses. Recognizing the importance of online literacy, in 2006 Michigan became the first state to require high school students to complete one online course to graduate.[32] Rather than taking cars or buses to school, more students now ride the Internet to class, attending class when they want with students from their own community, or from across the country or even around the world. Although many virtual high schools offer specific courses for students, some have been organized as full-time charter high schools, offering an entire high school curriculum online. Whether students attend full- or part-time, virtual high schools

PROFILE IN EDUCATION

Jonathan Kozol

For almost four decades, Kozol has given voice to the poor. In his bestselling book, *Savage Inequalities* (1991), he describes life in destitute schools from East St. Louis to the Bronx. To read a full profile of Jonathan Kozol, go to the Chapter 9 Profile in Education at www.mhhe. com/sadkerbrief3e.

How would you feel about teaching in a virtual school? What are the advantages and disadvantages?

provide expanded opportunities for students who prefer virtual learning, or are homebound with special needs, as well as students who want specialized or advanced courses not offered at their school. (For more information, visit "Welcome to the Virtual High School" at www.govhs.org.)

Critics of virtual schools argue that they isolate students and deprive them of important social interactions (one reason why there are so few virtual schools at the elementary level). But some students report that learning online can be quite personal, interactive, and individualized. Other supporters point out that virtual schools may hold the answer to a growing teacher shortage.[33] Whatever your take, virtual schools and courses are now part of our educational landscape.

Schools for Profit

Did you ever think of school as a business? Private companies have, and the growth of charter has opened wide this door. Many businesses have provided lunches and bus transportation for years, but in the 1990s business involvement took a great leap forward as **privatization** took hold, the belief that private profit-making businesses can run schools more efficiently than public employees. The Edison Schools Inc., started in 1992, was an early example of this trend; it is a private company claiming that it could do three things: run public schools for less, improve student achievement, and do all this while making a profit for its shareholders. Edison's plan was to develop teaching strategies and curriculum, be paid to implement its plan in the schools, and make a profit in the process. To school boards in a number of cities, including Philadelphia and Baltimore, this sounded like a dream come true—school costs going down as test scores go up. Actually, it was closer to a dream than to reality. Edison schools did not do well, and by 2003, the company lost the confidence of its stockholders. Studies by the American Federation of Teachers, National Education Association, and RAND Corporation found Edison students doing no better than regular public school students, and sometimes worse.[34] Edison still exists, but now it is called Edison Learning and focuses only on managing charter schools, moving away from teaching, curriculum development, or being responsible for student test scores.[35]

Privatization is growing, with an increase in the number of charter schools managed by for-profit companies. Advantage Schools, a Boston-based company, focuses on urban school districts, hires nonunion teachers, and promotes intense and frequent teacher-student interactions. Sylvan Learning Systems provides after-school instruction for students who are performing below expectations. While some applaud the role of business in education, others worry that the profit motive will shortchange students' academic and social needs, and some private firms, like Imagine Schools, are attracting increased scrutiny.[36] (See "You Be the Judge: For-Profit Schools")

Home Schools

Thirteen-year-old Taylor is working at the kitchen table, sorting out mathematical exponents. At 10, Travis is absorbed in *The Story of Jackie Robinson,* while his brother Henry is practicing Beethoven's Minuet in G on his acoustic guitar. The week before, the brothers had attended a local performance of a musical comedy, attended a seminar on marine life, and participated in a lively debate

For-Profit Schools

ARE A GOOD IDEA BECAUSE . . .

COMPETITION LEADS TO BETTER SCHOOLS

For-profit schools will break down the public school monopoly by creating competition and choice. As schools compete, parents (particularly poor parents) will finally have a choice and not be forced to place their children in the neighborhood school. Just as in business, the weak schools will lose students and declare "bankruptcy." The stronger schools will survive and prosper.

SCHOOLS WILL BE ABLE TO REWARD GOOD TEACHERS AND REMOVE WEAK ONES

The current public school bureaucracy protects too many incompetent teachers through the tenure system, and does not recognize teaching excellence. Using sound business practices, for-profit schools will reward superior teachers through profit-sharing incentives, retain competent teachers, and terminate ineffective teachers.

BUSINESS EFFICIENCY WILL IMPROVE SCHOOL PERFORMANCE

Education needs the skills and know-how of the business community. For-profit schools will implement the most effective educational strategies in a business culture. The top-heavy management of today's schools will be replaced by only a handful of administrators, and teachers will be driven to greater productivity through the profit incentives.

FOCUSED PROGRAMS AND INVESTOR OVERSIGHT LEAD TO ACADEMIC SUCCESS

For-profit schools will do a better educational job because they provide a focused and proven instructional plan. These schools avoid the public school pitfall of trying to offer "something-for-everyone." And if they falter and profits disappear, investor pressure will put them back on track.

ARE A BAD IDEA BECAUSE . . .

COMPETITION LEADS TO WEAKER SCHOOLS

Transplanting businesslike competition into the education arena would be a disaster. Competition is not all that business brings: false advertising, "special" promotions, a "feel-good" education—all the hucksterism of the marketplace to mislead students and their parents. Worse yet, the local public school, which holds a community together, will be lost.

TEACHERS WILL LOSE THEIR INFLUENCE AND ACADEMIC FREEDOM

Teachers who speak out against the company, or teach a controversial or politically sensitive topic, will have a brief career. The business community is quite vocal about teachers sharing in the profits but strangely silent about what will happen during economic hard times.

PROFITS AND EDUCATION DO NOT MIX

For-profit schools are exactly that, "for profit," and when the interests of children and investors clash, investor interests will prevail. If investors demand better returns, if the stock market drops, if the economy enters hard times, the corporate executives will sacrifice educational resources. After all, while students enjoy little leverage, stockholders can fire business executives.

FOCUSED PROGRAMS MEANS KEEPING SOME STUDENTS OUT

Their one-size-fits-all approach practiced by these schools might be good for efficiency, but it is bad for students. The more challenging students, those with special needs, nonnative speakers of English, or those who need special counseling, will be left to the underfunded public schools to educate.

www.mhhe.com/
sadkerbrief3e **YOU DECIDE . . .**

Do you believe that business and schools are a good or a bad match? Explain. Do you believe that profits can be made in schooling the nation's children? As a teacher, would you want to work for a for-profit school?

Now here is your chance to be the author! What additional advantages and disadvantages of for-profit schools can you add to the above lists?

about news reports concerning corporal punishment in Singapore. What makes their homeschooling story somewhat unusual is that their father is unable to fully participate, since he spends much of his time teaching other children at a local public high school.[37]

Homeschooling is also a choice—a decision not to send a child to the neighborhood school, or any school, but to educate the child at home. Only a few decades ago, a mere 12,500 students were homeschooled; today close to 2 million children are taught at home.[38] Why the huge increase?

Although concerns about the school environment, such as safety, drugs and peer pressure, motivate some families to homeschool, most parents opt for homeschooling to ensure specific religious and moral instruction, usually evangelical Christian beliefs. Researcher Van Galen divides parents who homeschool as ideologues or pedagogues. *Ideologues* focus on imparting certain values. They create a homeschool where they choose the curriculum, create the rules, enforce a schedule, and promote their beliefs, usually religious beliefs. *Pedagogues* are motivated to offer a more effective education than what is available in a public school (like the opening description of Taylor, Travis, and Henry homeschooling).[39] States vary in how tightly they monitor and support homeschooling, and today, technology can provide a big boost for homeschools. (You can visit www.hslda.org/laws/default.asp for specific state information.)

Here is a snapshot of homeschool families:[40]

- The median annual income is between $75,000 and $80,000.
- The majority of homeschooling parents have a college degree.
- Homeschool families typically have three or more children.
- More than 91 percent of homeschooling children are white and non-Hispanic.
- More than 80 percent of homeschool mothers do not work outside the home.

Is homeschooling effective? In fact, homeschooled children do quite well on school achievement tests and earn higher GPAs in college than conventionally schooled students. Professors describe them as more self-directed and willing to take risks than the traditional student.[41] But critics express concern about what homeschoolers are taught. Science and history subjects are often heavily influenced by religious doctrine, and concepts like evolution are disparaged. Most homeschooling families want a Bible version of the earth's creation, and not a scientific one.[42] Other critics are concerned about homeschool isolation, learning in an environment where diverse beliefs and backgrounds are absent. Because public schools were intended to meld a single nation from people with differing backgrounds, critics fear the impact of disparate homeschools on the nation's cohesion.[43]

Green Schools

Today, public and charter schools, magnet schools—in fact, all kinds of schools—are being affected by a movement initiated decades ago by Wisconsin Senator Gaylord Nelson. Worried about the impact of population growth on the earth's resources, Senator Nelson announced the first Earth Day: April 22, 1970. Coast-to-coast "teach-ins" and rallies protested oil spills, raw sewage, polluting factories and power plants, pesticides, freeways, toxic dumps, the loss of wilderness, and the extinction of wildlife. What was happening to the planet was not a pretty picture, and a green consciousness was born.

Schools have become a focal point of the green movement; the very health of teachers and students depends upon the school environment. The problem is that about half of all schools have unsatisfactory indoor environmental conditions. One in five schools has unhealthy air quality, and about a third of all school buildings are in need of extensive repair. Many of the 60 million students, teachers, administrators, and staff spend their days in these unhealthy school buildings. **Green schools,** on the other hand, offer

healthier environments with clean air and water, nourishing and natural foods, nontoxic cleaners, and more outdoor activities. As you might have guessed, when schools become green, incidences of illness and teacher and student sick days decrease.

Green schools also promote energy efficiency and sustainability through recycling, the use of solar and wind energy sources, alternative means of transportation, and teaching children how to promote sustainability in their own lives. The Earth Day Network has the goal of greening all America's schools within a generation. (For more information, visit www .earthday.net/education.)[44]

It does not take much to start greening a school. Incandescent bulbs can be exchanged for more energy-efficient ones, recycling drives or a school garden can be started, or energy-efficient power strips can be used for computers. With bigger budgets, solar water heaters and solar electricity can be installed. Then there are schools like Sidwell Friends Middle School in Washington, DC, truly living up to its Quaker value of environmental stewardship. The school itself is built with recycled materials, including reclaimed cedar wine casks, and every part of the building was constructed with an eye toward sustainability. Photovoltaic roof panels provide energy to the computer lab, and another part of the roof is home to a garden growing herbs and vegetables for school lunches. Sloping grasslands in front of the building set the urban school in a picturesque natural setting, but there is more at work than appearances. The school's wastewater actually flows beneath the grasses and plants, where it is filtered and recycled into the school's toilets. Skylights and windows directing natural light mean that Sidwell can light its classrooms at a small fraction of the cost of a nongreen school. Windows with light-filtering shades also save on heating costs in the winter and air-conditioning costs in the summer. In a typical school, utility costs (fuel, water, wastewater, and trash disposal) average $140 per student per year. A green school such as Sidwell can save many of these utility costs and redirect those funds to teaching and learning activities.

Fossil Ridge High School in Fort Collins, Colorado, despite its name, depends less on fossil fuels, and more on renewable energy. The sustainability of such schools is certified by LEED® (Leadership in Energy and Environmental Design), a national benchmark for the design, construction, and operations of high-performance green buildings. To learn more, visit the U.S. Green Building Council's website at www.usgbc.org.

Academics are enhanced by green practices. Teacher retention is higher in green schools, and some studies report that schools with natural daylight post higher test scores. A green school also uses its "greenness" to provide relevant learning opportunities. Here are a few examples:[45]

- At Robins Elementary School in Tucson, Arizona, students have designed and built a desert habitat. Selecting and caring for plants while providing desert animals with shelter, food, and water resources have earned the school a National Wildlife certification. The gardens also provide science lessons in identifying native plants and monitoring rainfall, as well as natural subjects for drawings and journaling.

- At Whitmore Lake High School in Michigan, students design shoebox-size cars that work on solar power, and investigate wind power as part of their "Green Tech" program.

- The Chesapeake Bay Foundation feared the unintended consequences of No Child Left Behind, a testing culture that contributed to students spending 90 percent of their time indoors. The No Child Left Inside program was created to help children be more active in the outdoors and overcome "nature deficit disorder."[46] The foundation sponsors canoeing trips on the Chesapeake Bay, Rhode Island camps for endangered butterflies, and a Texas nature center to show kids live bison. No Child Left Inside works with schools to develop a green curriculum and to promote environmental education and more active learning.

Most students (and teachers) embrace the green movement, and it is likely that the school you teach in will have some level of climate consciousness, some commitment to greening the planet.

Teachers, Students, and Reform

Focus Question 5

What is the role of teachers and students in reforming our schools?

In the mid- and late 1980s, leading educators such as Theodore Sizer, John Goodlad, and Ernest Boyer called for teachers to assume a greater role in educational reform. Alarmed at the loss of teacher autonomy in what too often felt like oppressive school climates, they believed that teachers should be given more responsibility to reshape their schools, a process called *empowering teachers*. These educators believed that schools managed by teachers would reduce bureaucracy, create a better-trained and better-paid teacher faculty, practice local decision making, and be able to study subjects in greater depth. They saw teachers as the focal point of reforming America's schools. Today, many in the public and the media view teachers as quite the opposite, as an obstacle to school reform. This has been a monumental turnaround.

The rise of charter schools is one indicator of public dissatisfaction with neighborhood public schools, especially poor-performing inner-city schools. Rightly or wrongly, many attribute ineffective schools to ineffective teachers. Because public schools are mostly staffed by tenured teachers, replacing any teacher is difficult.[47] Beyond tenure, salaries are typically determined by years of teaching experience, advanced degrees attained, and classroom observations, not teaching effectiveness. Seniority has its limits. Both the Obama and Bush administrations sponsored school reforms that challenged teacher seniority, and with it teacher unions. "To say that we're under attack is an understatement," explained a Los Angeles union leader.[48]

The focus of teacher evaluation became less about the quality of a teacher's background and more about teacher performance. The 2009–10 federal program called Race to the Top rewarded states with extra money if they reformed their education practices, including teacher evaluations. States began assessing each teacher by how much their student test scores improved—or did not improve—over the year.[49] This approach is called **value added;** i.e., how much value did each teacher add to the student's education? Value added would determine which teachers would be rewarded and which teachers would be replaced.

Despite its popularity, using only student test scores to measure teachers is not problem-free. After all, teachers are not the only factor influencing student scores, and not everyone considers test scores to be the best or only measure of a good education. So teacher associations, administrators, researchers, and politicians began working together to develop a more comprehensive and equitable system, possibly including the use of more classroom videotaping.[50] Today, a growing number of school districts has accepted student performance data as at least part of a teacher's evaluation.

Blaming teachers is a new and discomforting part of the reform movement, and while few actually ask teachers for their opinions,[51] the non-profit Education Sector did. They surveyed more than 1,000 teachers on how they view the reform movement.[52] The survey found that most teachers want change and are interested in reform but are skeptical about what really will happen. Many teachers do not trust administrators or politicians and find trading away their job protections frightening. Let's take tenure as an example, a job protection you may already know a bit about. Historically, if you teach well for your first three years or so, you will earn **tenure,** an expectancy of continued employment. Tenure protects teachers from arbitrary dismissal because they are teaching an inconvenient fact or an unpopular idea, a job protection we call academic freedom. But tenure also has been used to protect teachers who are incompetent. (Perhaps you have had such a teacher, which is not a pleasant experience.) Teachers in the survey reported that they do not feel comfortable in a system that rewards longevity rather than competence, and this is especially true for younger teachers. Older teachers or teachers with more college credits are not necessarily the most skilled. Many teachers report that they know at least one colleague who should be fired, but they fear that firing an incompetent teacher might put all teachers at risk. Tenure is a roadblock to change, but no tenure sets fear in motion.

To bring more accountability to teaching, many advocate **merit pay,** a system that bases a teacher's pay on performance. Merit pay certainly sounds fairer than seniority, but basing salary solely on student test scores does not sit well with many teachers. So how can we determine which teachers deserve merit pay?[53] Let's listen in on a hypothetical (but incredibly realistic) faculty meeting to get a sense of teachers' concerns:

PRINCIPAL MOORE: "As you may have heard, our school board is now promoting a merit plan for our district. I have outlined four different approaches to merit pay, and I'd like to hear your reactions to them."[54] Dr. Moore turns to her PowerPoint presentation:

- *Teacher performance.* This plan sends observers into your classroom to measure your teaching effectiveness, and merit is determined by these observations.

- *Individualized productivity.* Do you remember the professional goals each of you wrote for this school year? This plan would ask you to write more detailed goals for what you would like to accomplish this year, including new skills you will be working on and any additional assignments you agree to take on. You would receive financial bonuses based on how much of your plan school administrators believe you have accomplished.

- *Teaching assignment.* With this plan, compensation is related to market demands. Our math, science, and special education teachers would probably receive the greatest bonuses if we were to adopt this plan.

- *Student performance—Value added.* This plan is the one supported by President Obama, and if made into law, it will be the one we need to follow. Teacher salary raises will be tied to student gains on standardized tests. As you know, test scores are very important to the school board and to our parents. So if your students score well, you will get merit pay. If they do not, you will not.

As the PowerPoint shuts down, the teachers jump in:

"This sounds great! I can finally get that bonus I deserve for all my extra hours."

"Does only the teacher with all the smart kids get merit when they do well on tests?"

"I don't think I'd feel comfortable if other people found out that I was getting extra money. Teaching is supposed to mean working as a team, not competing for bonuses."

"Dr. Moore, you try to be fair, but not everyone does. What about supervisors who give merit pay to their friends? Or don't know how to evaluate teachers?"

"What if I teach well and the students bomb the test? There is not a lot of research backing this 'value added' model."

"Kids' scores are influenced by their home situation, their stresses, their health; why should I be the only one held accountable?"

"I teach special ed kids how to take a bus, dress for work, and hold a job. I think that is incredibly valuable, but nobody tests that. What happens to me?"

"I'm in the same boat. I teach art."

"In my grade, students have nine teachers. How do you tell which teacher is most responsible for a good—or bad—test score? And what if they all contribute to strong student test performance?"

"Why can't we all get merit pay? We all do a tough job."

"I don't think we all deserve merit pay. I think some of us are stronger teachers than others, and it is well past time that we recognize that. When kids don't learn, we need to bear at least some of the responsibility."

As you can hear from these comments, merit pay can strain relationships among teachers, raise serious questions about measuring classroom success, fan the fear of "playing politics," and create a sense of being manipulated by outside forces. But many teachers, particularly young ones, are excited about the possibility of a higher salary and feel that too many weak teachers are paid the same as stronger ones. The Education Sector survey reported that almost 80 percent of teachers express a desire for a stronger teacher evaluation system, as well as financial incentives for superior teachers, but they want one that is fair. Influential teacher organizations are also supportive, but cautious, and more likely to support a merit plan if it is not based solely on test scores, if local teachers are involved in planning, and if the plan does not penalize teachers who work in under-resourced schools.[55]

History suggests that teachers may be right, and that linking teacher pay to student performance may not be a successful long-term strategy. When merit pay was first tried, back in 1710 in England, teacher salaries were tied to student test scores. You can probably predict the results: Schools became all about test preparation.[56] Historians David Tyack and Larry Cuban write: "The history of merit performance-based salary plans has been a merry-go-round" as districts initially embrace such plans, only to drop them after a brief trial. But in spite of these failures, school officials keep "proposing merit pay again and again."[57] Will merit pay work this time? Will tenure become a thing of the past? Will skeptical teachers join the reform movement? It may all depend on something too few talk about: trust.

The Importance of Trust

After almost a decade of research, interviews, and observations in the Chicago public schools, researchers came to a conclusion that was both startling and obvious: Meaningful school improvement and reform depend on trust.[58] Teachers in schools without trust naturally cling to tenure for protection and are unlikely to feel comfortable trying new strategies. If teachers are expected to reform their schools, they need to feel safe and to be part of the process. A school built on trust, one that involves teachers in the decision-making process and reduces teacher vulnerability, is what teachers need to be willing to try new approaches. Teachers in trusting schools thrive, and so do their students. The researchers uncovered that when trust is present in a school, student academic performance improves.

What does a trusting school look like? You probably intuitively know the answer. People respect one another, even when they disagree, and rude behavior is not tolerated. Teachers and parents listen carefully to each other, and they keep their word. Tenure is not used to protect weak teachers, and competent teachers are recognized for their talents. Educators are willing to reach out to students, parents, and one another, and nothing is more important than the welfare and education of the students. We hear a great deal about school reform but too little about creating trust in schools. Clearly, if reform is going to work, teachers need to be a central part of the effort—trusted partners. To date, their voices are not heard.

Students and School Reform

If teachers feel left out of decision making in school reform, just imagine how students feel. Their opinions are rarely sought; their voices rarely heard. Elementary students, asked to draw pictures of typical learning situations, sketch teachers and chalkboards and books in their drawings, but not themselves.

Many college students feel disengaged from classroom instruction. Visit "A Vision of Students Today" on YouTube to get a sense of their alienation.

Source: http://mediatedcultures.net/ksudigg/?p=188

Their drawings show how disengaged elementary students feel from traditional classroom instruction. But when asked to draw learning activities they like, they draw themselves as central in those activities.[59] When they enjoy learning, they are not drawing teachers and classrooms.

Nor do things improve at the high school level, where one in four students frequently arrives at school without paper, pencil, or homework.[60] Some call this "pretend attend," a situation where student bodies are in school but their minds and their interests are elsewhere. Many college students also are disengaged. A YouTube video titled *A Vision of Students Today* is based on a survey of 200 college students. The video depicts the survey results by showing students sitting in a large lecture hall taking turns holding up signs: "My average class size is 115." "18% of my teachers know my name." "My neighbor paid for this class, but never comes." "I spend two hours a day on my cell phone." "I spend 3½ hours a day online." "I Facebook through most of my classes." "I do 49 percent of the reading assigned." And then a close-up of a question written on the back of a chair: "If students learn what they do, what are they learning sitting here?" The video, made by students and their professor in an anthropology class at Kansas State University, is a stunning example of college student alienation. (Ironically, the students who made the tape were probably very engaged in their activity.)

While many talk about reform in terms of improving student test scores, too few discuss it in terms of engaging students in their own learning and in preparing for their own futures. Statistics suggest that students drop out of school more from boredom than from academic failure.[61] If teachers need a basis of trust to become part of the reform movement, then students need to feel ownership of their own learning.

If students had a voice in educational reform, what changes would they envision? Middle and high school students throughout the United States and Canada were asked that question, and here are some of their suggestions:[62]

- Take me seriously.
- Point me toward my goal.
- Challenge me to think.
- Make me feel important.
- Nurture my self-respect.
- Build on my interests.
- Show me I can make a difference.
- Tap my creativity.
- Let me do it my way.
- Bring out my best self.

Teachers and students agree that school should be more than test scores, and students clearly desire more relevance and meaning in their education. Some schools do listen to students.[63] In these schools, students participate in textbook selection, in writing school behavior policies, and even in designing new school buildings. In Washington State, many high school students are encouraged to research their dream careers along with the state's graduation requirements and, on the basis of that research, plan their coursework. In other high schools, students participate in hiring the principal, teaching others how to use technology, and organizing school forums. Unfortunately, these schools are far too few.

Although most reform reports focus on academics, a few recognize that students' *affective needs,* their social, emotional, and psychological development, are also important. The Carnegie Council on Adolescent Development report, *Turning Points: Preparing American Youth for the 21st Century,* looks beyond test scores and warns that one in four adolescents does not have caring relationships with adults, guidance in facing sometimes overwhelming biological and psychological changes, the security of belonging to constructive peer groups, and the perception of future opportunity. Students report that when they are feeling sad or depressed, overwhelmingly they turn for help to friends (77 percent) or family (63 percent); far less frequently do they seek out educators (33 percent).[64] Educational researcher Sara Lawrence Lightfoot describes the following incident, which took place in an elite school in a wealthy suburb in the Midwest:

> A student with a history of depression . . . had been seeing a local psychiatrist for several years. For the last few months, however, she had discontinued her psychotherapy and seemed to be showing steady improvement. Since September, her life had been invigorated by her work on *Godspell*—a student production that consumed her energies and provided her with an instant group of friends.
>
> After *Godspell,* her spirits and enthusiasm declined noticeably. After a visit to her psychiatrist, she killed herself.
>
> The day after, the school buzzed with rumors as students passed on the gruesome news—their faces showing fear and intrigue. . . . But I heard only one teacher speak of it openly and explicitly in class—the drama teacher who had produced *Godspell.* Her words brought tears and looks of terror in the eyes of her students. "We've lost a student today who was with us yesterday. We've got to decide where our priorities are. How important are your gold chains, your pretty clothes, your cars? . . . Where were we when she needed us? Foolish old woman that I am, I ask you this because I respect you. . . . While you still feel, damn it, feel . . . reach out to each other."[65]

The nation listens to the speeches of politicians and educational administrators about educational reform, but perhaps the unheard voices of teachers and students would be more useful.

This chapter has explored a deceptively simple question: What's a school for? The many approaches to schooling offer us a variety of insights into the purposes of schools, but there is one critical question that we have left unasked (until now): What makes a school effective? So let's close this chapter with a look at what we know (and don't know) about effective schools.

What Makes a School Effective?

Consider the following situation: Two schools are located in the same neighborhood and are considered "sister schools." They are approximately the same size and serve the same community, and the student populations are

Focus Question 6
What are the characteristics of effective schools?

www.mhhe.com/
sadkerbrief3e

**INTERACTIVE ACTIVITY
What Makes Schools
Effective?** Rate what
you think makes schools
effective. Compare your
responses with those of
your colleagues.

identical. However, in one school, state test scores are low and half the students drop out. In the other school, student test scores exceed the state average and almost all students graduate. Why the difference?

Puzzled by such situations, researchers attempted to determine what factors create successful schools. Several studies have revealed a common set of characteristics, a **five-factor theory of effective schools.**[66] Researchers say that effective schools are able, through these five factors, to promote student achievement. Let's take a look at these classic five factors, and then move on to some more-recent studies.

Factor 1: Strong Leadership

In her book *The Good High School,* Sara Lawrence Lightfoot drew portraits of six effective schools.[67] Two, George Washington Carver High School in Atlanta and John F. Kennedy High School in the Bronx, were inner-city schools. Highland Park High School near Chicago and Brookline High School in Brookline, Massachusetts, were upper-middle-class and suburban. St. Paul's High School in Concord, New Hampshire, and Milton Academy near Boston were elite preparatory schools. Despite the tremendous difference in the styles and textures of these six schools, ranging from the pastoral setting of St. Paul's to inner-city Atlanta, they all were characterized by strong, inspired leaders, such as Robert Mastruzzi, principal of John F. Kennedy High School.

When Robert Mastruzzi started working at Kennedy, the building was not yet completed. Walls were being built around him as he sat in his unfinished office and contemplated the challenge of not only his first principalship but also the opening of a new school. During his years as principal of John F. Kennedy, his leadership style has been collaborative, actively seeking faculty participation. Not only does he want his staff to participate in decision making, but he also gives them the opportunity to try new things—and even the right to fail. For example, one teacher made an error about the precautions necessary for holding a rock concert (800 adolescents had shown up, many high or inebriated). Mastruzzi realized that the teacher had learned a great deal from the experience, and he let her try again. The second concert was a great success. "He sees failure as an opportunity for change," the teacher said. Still other teachers describe him with superlatives, such as "he is the lifeblood of this organism" and "the greatest human being I have ever known."[68]

Mastruzzi seems to embody the characteristics of effective leaders in good schools. Researchers say that students make significant achievement gains in schools in which principals

- Articulate a clear school mission
- Are a visible presence in classrooms and hallways
- Hold high expectations for teachers and students
- Spend a major portion of the day working with teachers to improve instruction
- Are actively involved in diagnosing instructional problems
- Create a positive school climate[69]

Factor 2: A Clear School Mission

A day in the life of a principal can be spent trying to keep small incidents from becoming major crises. But the research is clear: In effective schools, good principals somehow find time to develop a vision of what that school should be and to share that vision with all members of the educational community. Successful principals can articulate a specific school mission, and they stress innovation and improvement. In contrast, less effective principals are vague about their goals and focus on maintaining the status quo. They make such comments as, "We have a good school and a good faculty, and I want to keep it that way."[70]

A positive, energizing school atmosphere characterized by accepting relationships between students and faculty often begins and ends with the principal.

It is essential that the principal share his or her vision so that teachers understand the school's goals and all work together for achievement. Unfortunately, when teachers are polled, more than 75 percent say that they have either no contact or infrequent contact with one another during the school day. In less effective schools, teachers lack a common understanding of the school's mission, and they function as individuals charting their own separate courses.

The need for the principal to share his or her vision extends not only to teachers but to parents as well. When teachers work cooperatively and parents are connected with the school's mission, the children are more likely to achieve academic success.

Factor 3: A Safe and Orderly Climate

Certainly, before students can learn or teachers can teach, schools must be safe. An unsafe school is, by definition, ineffective. Despite those horrific headlines reporting student shootings, today's schools in fact are safer than they have been in years.[71] (See Figure 9.5.) The vast majority of teachers (96 percent) and students (93 percent) report feeling safe in school (thank goodness).[72] LGBT students represent an exception to this general rule; they are three times more likely to feel unsafe in school than their peers.[73]

Good schools have safe environments.

The vast majority of schools provide safe learning environments. This is accomplished by more than metal detectors and school guards. Safe schools focus on academic achievement, the school mission, involving families and communities in school activities, and creating an environment where teachers, students, and staff are treated with respect. Student problems are identified early, before they deteriorate into violence. School psychologists, special education programs, family social workers, and schoolwide programs increase communication and reduce school tension.

FIGURE 9.4
School-related violence:
On the decrease.

SOURCE: National Center for
Education Statistics, Indica-
tors of School Crime and
Safety, 2010.

REFLECTION: How do
you explain the popular
perception of a more
violent society contrasted
with these statistics
reflecting a decrease in
school violence?

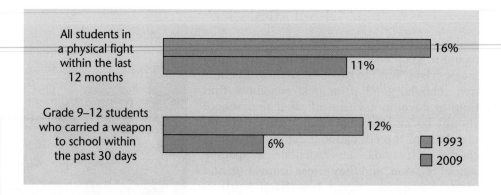

In some of America's most distressed neighborhoods, safe schools provide a much needed neighborhood refuge. Sara Lawrence Lightfoot tells of
the long distances that urban students travel to reach John F. Kennedy High
School in the Bronx. One girl, who did not have money to buy a winter coat
or glasses to see the chalkboard, rode the subway 1 hour and 40 minutes each
way to get to school. She never missed a day, because for her school was a
refuge—a place of hope where she could learn in safety.[74]

Factor 4: Monitoring Student Progress

As the researcher walked through the halls of a school we will call Clearview
Elementary School, she noted attractive displays of student work mounted
on bulletin boards and walls. Also posted were profiles clearly documenting
class and school progress toward meeting academic goals. Students had a clear
sense of how they were doing in their studies; they kept progress charts in their
notebooks. During teacher interviews, the faculty talked about the individual
strengths and weaknesses of their students. Teachers referred to student fold-
ers that contained thorough records of student scores on standardized tests, as
well as samples of classwork, homework, and performance on weekly tests.

A visit to Foggy Bottom Elementary, another fictitious school with a reveal-
ing name, disclosed striking differences. Bulletin boards and walls were attractive, but few student papers were posted, and there was no charting of progress
toward academic goals. Interviews with students showed that they had only
a vague idea of how they were doing and of ways to improve their academic
performance. Teachers also seemed unclear about individual student progress. When pressed for more information, one teacher sent the researcher to
the guidance office, saying, "I think they keep some records like the California
Achievement Tests. Maybe they can give you what you're looking for."

Following the visit, the researcher wrote her report: "A very likely reason
that Clearview students achieve more than Foggy Bottom students is that one
school carefully monitors student progress and communicates this information to students and parents. The other school does not."

Effective schools carefully monitor and assess student progress in a variety of ways:

• **Norm-referenced tests** compare individual students with others in a nationwide norm group (e.g., the Stanford, the Iowa Test of Basic Skills, or the
SAT).

- **Objective-referenced tests** measure whether a student has mastered a designated body of knowledge (e.g., state assessment tests used to determine who has "mastered" the material).

Other measures may be less formal. Teacher-made tests are an important (and often overlooked) measure of student progress. Some teachers ask students to track their own progress in reaching course objectives as a way of helping them assume more responsibility for their own learning.[75] Homework is another strategy to monitor students. Researcher Herbert Walberg and colleagues found that homework increases student achievement scores from the 50th to the 60th percentile. When homework is graded and commented on, achievement is increased from the 50th to nearly the 80th percentile. Although these findings suggest that graded homework is an important ingredient in student achievement,[76] how much homework to assign and what kinds of homework tasks are most effective continue to be points of contention.

Factor 5: High Expectations

The teachers were excited. A group of their students had received extraordinary scores on a test that predicted intellectual achievement during the coming year. Just as the teachers had expected, these children attained outstanding academic gains that year.

Now for the rest of the story: The teachers had been duped. The students identified as gifted had been selected at random. However, eight months later, these randomly selected children did show significantly greater gains in total IQ than did another group of children, the control group.

In their highly influential 1969 publication, **Pygmalion in the Classroom,** researchers Robert Rosenthal and Lenore Jacobson discussed this experiment and the power of teacher expectations in shaping student achievement. They popularized the term *self-fulfilling prophecy* and revealed that students may learn as much—or as little—as teachers expect.[77] Although methodological criticisms of the original Rosenthal and Jacobson study abound, those who report on effective schools say that there is now extensive evidence showing that high teacher expectations do, in fact, produce high student achievement, and low expectations produce low achievement.[78] Too often, teacher expectations have a negative impact. An inaccurate judgment about a student can be made because of error, unconscious prejudice, or stereotype. For example, good-looking, well-dressed students are frequently thought to be smarter than their less attractive peers. Often, male students are thought to be brighter in math, science, and technology, and girls are given the edge in language skills. Students of color are sometimes perceived as less capable or intelligent. A poor performance on a single standardized test (perhaps due to illness or an "off" day) can cause teachers to hold an inaccurate assessment of a student's ability for months and even years. Even a casual comment in the teachers' lounge can shape the expectations of other teachers. When teachers hold low expectations for certain students, their treatment of these students often differs in unconscious and subtle ways. Typically, they offer such students

- Fewer opportunities to respond
- Less praise
- Less challenging work
- Fewer nonverbal signs (eye contact, smiles, positive regard)

In effective schools, teachers hold high expectations that students can learn, and they translate those expectations into teaching behaviors. They set objectives, work toward mastery of those objectives, spend more time on instruction, and actively monitor student progress. They are convinced that students can succeed.

Do high expectations work if students do not believe they exist? Probably not, and that is too often the case. Whereas a majority of secondary school principals believe that their schools hold such expectations for their students, only 39 percent of teachers believe this to be true, and, even more discouraging, only one in four students believes their school holds high expectations for them.[79] We need to do a better job of communicating these expectations to students and making certain that these expectations truly challenge students.

It is not only students who benefit from high expectations. In *The Good High School,* Sara Lawrence Lightfoot reported that when teachers hold high expectations for their own performance, the entire school benefits. At Brookline High School, "star" teachers were viewed as models to be emulated. Always striving for excellence, these teachers felt that no matter how well a class was taught, next time it could be taught better.

A Note of Caution on Effective Schools Research

Although the research on what makes schools effective has had a direct impact on national reform movements, it has limitations.[80] First, there is disagreement over the definition of an effective school. Researchers use varying descriptions, ranging from "schools with high academic achievement" to schools that foster "personal growth, creativity, and positive self-concept." Although the five factors we have described are helpful, they do not really provide a prescription for developing successful schools.

Another problem is that much of the research has been conducted in elementary schools. Although some researchers suggest applicability to secondary and even higher education, caution must be used in carrying the effective-schools findings to higher levels of education. The generalizability of the research is also limited, because several of the studies were conducted in inner-city schools and tied closely to the achievement of lower-order skills in math and science. If one wanted to develop a school that nurtures creativity rather than basic skills, another set of characteristics might be more appropriate.

Beyond the Five Factors

New effective-schools findings offer us insights beyond these original five factors of effective schooling:[81]

- *Early start.* The concept that there is a particular age for children to begin school needs to be rethought. The earlier schools start working with children, the better children do. High-quality programs during the first three years of life include parent training, special screening services, and appropriate learning opportunities for children. Such programs are rare, but

A WORLD WITHOUT SCHOOLS

In *Deschooling Society,* Ivan Illich compared schools to a medieval church, performing more a political than an educational role. The diplomas and degrees issued by schools provide society's "stamp of approval," announcing who shall succeed, who shall be awarded status, and who shall remain in poverty. By compelling students to attend, by judging and labeling them, by confining them, and by discriminating among them, Illich believed that schools harm children. He would replace schools with learning "networks," lifelong and compulsory. To Illich, the notion of waking up to a world without schools would be a dream fulfilled.

Education reformer John Holt agreed, and coined the term "un-schooling" to describe an education where kids, not parents or teachers, decide what they will learn. Holt believed that children do not need to be coerced into learning; they will do so naturally if given the freedom to follow their own interests and a rich assortment of resources. For un-schooled kids, there are no mandatory books, no curriculum, no tests, and no grades. Children are given complete freedom to learn and explore whatever they choose—from Chinese to aesthetic mathematics to tuba lessons to the Burmese struggle for civil rights.

SOURCE: Ivan Illich, *Deschooling Society* (New York: Harper & Row, 1973); John Holt, *Instead of Education* (New York: Dutton, 1976).

REFLECTION: How are schools more a political than an educational institution? What would your community be like if it were de-schooled?

those that are in operation have significantly raised IQ points and have enhanced language skills. It is estimated that $1 spent in an early intervention program saves school districts $7 in special programs and services later in life.

- *Focus on reading and math.* Children not reading at grade level by the end of the first grade face a one-in-eight chance of ever catching up. In math, students who do not master basic concepts find themselves playing catch-up throughout their school years. Effective schools identify and correct such deficiencies early, before student performance deteriorates.

- *School size.* Some studies find that students in small schools learn more, are more likely to pass their courses, are less prone to resort to violence, and are more likely to attend college than those attending large schools. Studies also show that disadvantaged students in small schools outperform their peers in larger schools, and many large schools have responded to these findings by reorganizing themselves into smaller units, into schools within schools. But this may be a bit simplistic, because students in some very large schools do very well also. More research is needed to clarify the importance of school size.

- *Smaller classes.* Although the research on class size is less powerful than the research on school size, studies indicate that smaller classes are associated with increased student learning, especially in the earlier grades. Children in classes of 15 outperform students in classes of 25, even when the larger classes have a teacher's aide present.

- *Increased learning time.* Though not an amazing insight, research tells us what we already suspect: More study results in more learning. Longer school days, longer school years, more efficient use of school time, and

10. Classroom Observation: Family-to-School Connection

Positive relationships between families and teachers help build connections that enrich students' performance and create a home and school bond. In this video, an elementary school principal, a middle school principal, and a middle school guidance counselor discuss various successful strategies they have used to involve parents in their children's education.

Classroom Observation videos are available on the CD Reader and at the Online Learning Center.

www.mhhe.com/ sadkerbrief3e

more graded homework are all proven methods of enhancing academic learning time and student performance.

- *Teacher training.* Researcher Linda Darling-Hammond reports that the best way to improve school effectiveness is by investing in teacher training. Stronger teacher skills and qualifications lead to greater student learning. Conversely, students pay an academic price when they are taught by unqualified and uncertified teachers.

- *Trust.* Trusting relationships among parents, students, principals, and teachers are a necessary ingredient to govern, improve, and reform schools. As trust levels increase, so does academic performance.

- *Parental involvement.* Learning is a cooperative venture, and a strong school-home partnership creates a more positive attitude toward learning, and improves academic achievement and social well-being. Not surprisingly, teachers' expectations for student success also rise as parents become more engaged in school life.

Research and experience will continue to offer answers to that pressing question, "What makes a school effective?" Are there factors that you believe might someday be added to this list? Perhaps we could expand the notion of "effective school" to venture beyond academics. Some schools are already doing this, adopting a broader view of an educated American. Such schools create a climate of kindness, teaching students to serve their community and to treat the earth and all its inhabitants with compassion. Perhaps one day soon more schools will see that students are so much more than test scores.

CONNECTING TEACHERS AND FAMILIES

Research shows that when families and teachers work together, students do better academically and socially. Families may need specific information on how to help and what to do. Here are a few ideas to consider:

1. *Create a listserv to send messages to families.* You can fill them in on assignments and projects, current and future activities, test dates, and other reminders. If you are more tech savvy, develop a class web page with similar information. If your families are not online, send home a brief newsletter, an informational outline of the week's objectives and activities.

2. *Encourage participation.* Send a questionnaire home to families asking if they can contribute to the class. Is someone artistic? Can someone help in class or on a field trip? Perhaps there is a special interest or expertise, and a family member can be a guest speaker.

3. *Homework help.* In the earlier grades especially, you can help monitor homework by asking parents to sign the homework assignment sheet each day.

4. *Share good news.* A message from the teacher need not be a negative sign. Make positive phone calls about student progress and insights.

5. *Assessment understanding.* Share test results with families, explaining both the purpose and the results of the assessment, as well as how they can help their child in future assessments. Be specific. Provide parents with the materials and insights to assist their child.

6. *Visit homes and get to know families.* A good source of information for this is the parent-teacher home visit project at www.pthvp.org/.

SUMMARY

1. What are the goals of America's schools?

Since their inception, public schools have been the focus of conflict as they work to meet society's academic, vocational, social, civic, and personal goals. Two fundamental, often opposing, purposes of schools are (1) to transmit society's knowledge and values, passing on the cultural baton, and (2) to reconstruct society, empowering students to promote social reform.

2. What school goals are important to you?

This chapter also gave you the opportunity to consider your own school priorities. How strongly should schools emphasize test scores, skills for the future, focus on eliminating hatred and distrust in society, or promote cultural diversity? These are just a few of the myriad goals confronting American schools—and perhaps you as a classroom teacher.

3. Why has school reform become a top national priority?

Over a century of reform efforts have preceded the current reform movement. In 1983, *A Nation at Risk* triggered increased testing and a back-to-basics school curriculum, an emphasis that echoes in today's schools. Other reform efforts followed, including No Child Left Behind, Race to the Top legislation, and a growing and exciting diversity of school choices. Poor scores by American students on international tests, media attention, persistent high dropout rates in urban schools, an increase in private funding for educational initiatives, and the growth of alternative teacher licensing programs helped to fuel the reform movement.

CHAPTER REVIEW

Go to the Online Learning Center to take a chapter self-quiz, practice with key terms, and review concepts from the chapter.

www.mhhe.com/
sadkerbrief3e

4. **What new school options are replacing the traditional neighborhood public school?**

   These different schools offer parents choices, and free-market economists like Milton Friedman believed that such choices lead to more competitive and successful schools. As an example, the charter school movement, which started in the early 1990s, encourages groups to contract with school boards and open their own public school, home schools are growing, aided by the development of virtual schools that allow students to take classes via the Internet.

5. **What is the role of teachers and students in reforming our schools?**

   While some see teachers as the critical element in any successful reform effort; others blame union protectionism and teachers as obstacles to change. Neither teachers nor students have been successfully included in shaping educational reform, and until trust can be established among teachers, students, and reformers, tension will persist.

6. **What are the characteristics of effective schools?**

   The five-factor theory of effective schools includes: (1) strong administrative leadership, (2) clear school goals shared by faculty and administration, (3) a safe and orderly school climate, (4) frequent monitoring and assessment of student progress, and (5) high expectations for student performance. Newer research connects effective schools with early intervention programs, an emphasis on reading and math, smaller schools, smaller classes, increased learning time, assessment of student progress, and expanded teacher training.

KEY TERMS AND PEOPLE

acculturation, 283
Americanization, 283
charter school, 287
distance learning, 293
five-factor theory of
   effective schools, 304
Paulo Freire, 279
Milton Friedman, 285
full service school, 290
John Goodlad, 280

green schools, 297
homeschooling, 296
Jonathan Kozol, 293
Lemon v. Kurtzman, 292
magnet school, 292
merit pay, 299
A Nation at Risk, 284
norm-referenced tests, 306
objective-referenced tests, 307
open enrollment, 293

privatization, 294
Pygmalion in the Classroom,
   307
reconstructionists, 278
service credit, 279
tenure, 299
value added, 299
virtual schools, 293
voucher, 290
Zelman v. Simmons-Harris, 292

DISCUSSION QUESTIONS AND ACTIVITIES

WEB-*TIVITIES*

Go to the Online Learning Center to do the following activities:

1. The Purposes of Schools
2. Paulo Freire and Reconstructionism

1. Discuss your list of school goals that you recorded with your classmates. Which goals seem to be most important to your peers? To your instructor? Which do you consider most important? Give reasons for your priorities.

2. Congratulations! You have been put in charge of designing the next charter school in your district. Describe the charter school that you would design. Be sure to include the research on effective schools in your description. Going beyond the current research, what unique factor(s) would you make part of your school because you believe they would contribute to an effective school?

3. Reform movements are not new, but the current one has been under way for a quarter of a century and still has a great deal of momentum. How would you describe the strengths and the weaknesses of this movement? Explain whether you believe it will succeed and strengthen America's schools—or come up short.

4. What do you think of private businesses contracting to run schools? What factors would cause you to seek or avoid teaching for a corporation? Would you feel secure in your job, even without tenure?

5. Does your local public school district have an official (or unofficial) policy concerning home-schooling? Do homeschooled students participate in any school activities or receive any school resources? How do you feel about these (un)official policies?

YOUR CD-ROM: THE *TEACHERS, SCHOOLS, AND SOCIETY READER* WITH CLASSROOM OBSERVATION VIDEO CLIPS

Articles, Case Studies, and Videos correspond to chapter content and are not always in numeric order. Go to your *Teachers, Schools, and Society Reader* CD-ROM to:

Read Current and Historical Articles

17. "Questionable Assumptions about Schooling," Elliot Eisner, *Phi Delta Kappan,* 2003.

18. "Teaching against Idiocy," Walter Parker, *Phi Delta Kappan,* January 2005.

19. "Charting a New Course for Schools," Marc Tucker, *Educational Leadership,* April 2007.

20. "International Education: What's in a Name?" Walter Parker, *Phi Delta Kappan,* November 2008.

Analyze Case Studies

9. **Amy Rothman:** A high school resource room teacher is confronted by a parent during a staffing meeting about a gifted, autistic student in her resource room for whom the parent wants a service not provided by the school district.

10. **Chris Kettering:** A teacher finds to his dismay that his white, middle-class students are not interested in social activism and that he is unable to promote awareness and openmindedness in them.

Observe Teachers, Students, and Classrooms In Action

9. **Classroom Observation: Tour of a Boston Charter School**

10. **Classroom Observation: Family-to-School Connection**

See pages 290 and 310 of this text for a description of these videos. You'll find the videos on the CD Reader and at the Online Learning Center.

www.mhhe.com/ sadkerbrief3e

chapter

10

CURRICULUM, STANDARDS, AND TESTING

Focus Questions

1. What is the formal curriculum taught in schools?
2. How does the invisible curriculum influence learning?
3. What is the place of the extracurriculum in school life?
4. What forces shape the school curriculum?
5. How do textbook publishers and state adoption committees "drive" the curriculum?
6. What is standards-based education?
7. How has No Child Left Behind influenced America's schools?
8. What problems are created by high-stakes testing, and what are the testing alternatives?
9. How are cultural and political conflicts reflected in the school curriculum?
10. How has technology affected the curriculum?
11. What are new directions for the curriculum?
12. How can we rethink tomorrow's curriculum?

www.mhhe.com/
sadkerbrief3e

WHAT DO YOU THINK? What books did you read in high school English? Compare what you read with what others read for a larger view of the high school canon.

Chapter Preview

"We shape our buildings and afterwards our buildings shape us," said Winston Churchill. Had the noted statesman been a noted educator, he might have rephrased this epigram, substituting curriculum for buildings, for what children learn in school today will affect the kind of adults they will become and the kind of society they will eventually create. In fact, it is the power of curriculum to shape students, and ultimately society, that takes curriculum development out of the realms of philosophy and education and into the political arena. Children learn through the formal curriculum, made up of objectives and textbook assignments, and through the more subtle lessons of the hidden, null, and extracurriculum. This chapter will provide a brief overview of what has been taught and how curricular decisions are reached.

Several trends are pushing schools toward a similar curriculum: the indomitable textbook, technology in schools, and the recent emphasis on national standards and testing. Protests (perhaps better titled "antitests") have been growing against the increasing influence of standardized tests in general, and the legacy of No Child Left Behind in particular. The benefits of standards and the many problems with high-stakes tests are explored in this chapter, as are more positive and creative ways of looking at curriculum and testing.

The Saber-Tooth Curriculum*

New-Fist was a brilliant educator and thinker of prehistoric times. He watched the children of his tribe playing with bones, sticks, and brightly colored pebbles, and he speculated on what these youngsters might learn that would help the tribe derive more food, shelter, clothing, security, and, in short, a better life. Eventually, he determined that to obtain food and shelter, the people of his tribe must learn to fish with their bare hands and to club and skin little woolly horses; and to live in safety, they must learn to drive away the saber-tooth tigers with fire. So New-Fist developed the first curriculum. It consisted of three basic subjects: (1) "Fish-Grabbing-with-the-Bare-Hands," (2) "Woolly-Horse-Clubbing," and (3) "Saber-Tooth-Tiger-Scaring-with-Fire."

New-Fist taught the children these subjects, and they enjoyed these purposeful activities more than playing with colored pebbles. The years went by, and by the time New-Fist was called by the Great Mystery to the Land of the Setting Sun, all the tribe's children had been systematically schooled in these three skills. The tribe was prosperous and secure.

All would have been well and the story might have ended here had it not been for an unforeseen change—the beginning of the New Ice Age, which sent a great glacier sliding down upon the tribe. The glacier so muddied the waters of the creeks that it was impossible for people to catch fish with their bare hands. Also, the melted water of the glacier made the ground marshy, and the little woolly horses left for higher and drier land. They were replaced by shy and speedy antelopes with such a scent for danger that no one could get close enough to club them. And finally, as if these disruptions were not enough, the increasing dampness of the air caused

*Summary of and excerpt from The Saber-Tooth Curriculum by J. Abner Peddiwill. Copyright © 1939 The McGraw-Hill Companies, Inc. Reprinted with permission of The McGraw-Hill Companies, Inc.

the saber-tooth tigers to contract pneumonia and die. The tigers, however, were replaced by an even greater danger: ferocious glacial bears, who showed no fear of fire. Prosperity and security became distant memories for the suffering tribe.

Fortunately, a new breed of brilliant educators emerged. One tribesman, his stomach rumbling with hunger, grew frustrated with fruitless fish-grabbing in cloudy waters. He fashioned a crude net and in one hour caught more fish than the whole tribe could have caught had they fish-grabbed for an entire day. Another tribesman fashioned a snare with which he could trap the swift antelope, and a third dug a pit that captured and secured the ferocious bears.

As a result of these new inventions, the tribe again became happy and prosperous.

Some radicals even began to criticize the school's curriculum and urged that netmaking, snare-setting, and pit-digging were indispensable to modern life and should be taught in the schools. But the wise old men who controlled the schools objected:

With all the intricate details of fish-grabbing, horse-clubbing, and tiger-scaring—the standard cultural subjects—the school curriculum is too crowded now. We can't add these fads and frills of net-making, antelope-snaring, and—of all things—bear-killing. Why, at the very thought, the body of the great New-Fist, founder of our Paleolithic educational system, would turn over in its burial cairn. What we need to do is to give our young people a more thorough grounding in the fundamentals. . . . The essence of true education is timelessness. It is something that endures through changing conditions like a solid rock standing squarely and firmly in the middle of a raging torrent. You must know that there are some eternal verities, and the saber-tooth curriculum is one of them.[1]

The Saber-Tooth Curriculum was written in 1939, but it still resonates. How do educators avoid a curriculum programmed for obsolescence? What in today's curriculum is "Saber-Tooth-Tiger-Scaring-with-Fire," and what skills are we not teaching that we should be? Those are just some of the questions that you should be thinking as you read this chapter.

Focus Question 1

What is the formal curriculum taught in schools?

The Visible Curriculum

If you ask a teacher for a copy of the curriculum, you will likely be handed a curriculum guide, a description of courses offered, or perhaps some syllabi describing what the students are supposed to be learning at each grade level and in each subject. Ask for more detailed information, and a teacher might share some specific lesson plans, classroom activities that will enable students to meet those objectives. Educator Hilda Taba emphasized the importance of a school curriculum: "Learning in school differs from learning in life in that it is formally organized. It is the special function of the school to arrange the experiences of children and youth so that desirable learning takes place."[2] While many would call arranging classroom experiences for learning, like creating a lesson plan, the *curriculum*, it is more accurately called the **formal or explicit curriculum.** And if you could go back in time (and in this text, you can!), you soon realize that the formal curriculum is not a fixed course of study but changes to reflect the values of the time. If you were a student in colonial America in the 1660s, your formal curriculum would focus on religion and reading, the "two *Rs*." If you were a student in the 1960s, you would explore exciting new electives like Multicultural Education, Peace Studies, Ecology, and Women's Studies. But by the 1980s, schools were eliminating many of these electives and increasing the number of required basic courses, sometimes referred to as a **core curriculum.** Support for clear academic standards and frequent testing increased, topics we will explore later in this chapter.

The Invisible Curriculum

Let's face it, some of the most powerful curricular lessons taught in school are not to be found in the formal curriculum at all. This "invisible curriculum" has two parts, and by describing each we hope to make it more visible for you. Let's start with what educators sometimes call the **implicit or hidden curriculum**—learnings that are not always intended but emerge as students are shaped by the school culture, including the attitudes and behaviors of teachers. Here is an example offered by Jules Henry, an anthropologist who has analyzed the hidden curriculum of the elementary school. Henry described a fourth-grade spelling bee. Team members were chosen by two team captains. When a student spelled a word correctly on the board, a "hit" was scored. When three spelling errors were made, the team was "out." Students cheered or groaned, depending on the outcome for their team. Did you see the hidden curriculum?

According to Henry, these students were learning powerful lessons: the importance of winning, the pain of losing, how competition can turn a friend into an adversary, the joy of being chosen early for a team, and the embarrassment and rejection when you are not. Some of the more thoughtful students may have seen the absurdity of a spelling lesson being taught as a baseball game.[3] Schools teach many powerful but hidden lessons, from the importance of punctuality to following the rules, from social conformity to respecting authority. Although some hidden lessons are useful, others can be destructive. The first step in evaluating the appropriateness of the hidden curriculum is to actually see it.

Let's remove the veil from another part of the invisible curriculum, all the material that you do not learn in school. When someone or some group decides that a topic is unimportant or too controversial, inappropriate or not worth the time, that topic is never taught and becomes part of the **null curriculum.** If your American History class never went beyond World War II, your null curriculum included the Korean and Vietnam Wars; the fall of communism; the Civil Rights and Women's Rights movements; an assassination and an impeachment; the disaster in Somalia; widespread corporate corruption; the technology revolution; the September 11, 2001, attack; and the abuses at Abu Ghraib prison in Iraq. When a school board decides not to teach about the theory of evolution or sex education, they have made a decision that these topics will become part of the null curriculum. The null curriculum is rich but invisible. (It would be fascinating to witness what students would learn if some enterprising educators created a charter school to focus on the null curriculum.)

Focus Question 2
How does the invisible curriculum influence learning?

Focus Question 3
What is the place of the extracurriculum in school life?

The Extracurriculum

Now let's look at one last curriculum, a vibrant ingredient of school life but often not thought of as a curriculum at all. The **extracurriculum** teaches the lessons students learn in school activities such as sports, clubs, governance, and the student newspaper, places where a great deal of learning occurs, without tests or grades. A majority of students participate in at least one extracurricular activity, with students from smaller schools and with stronger academic records the most likely to be involved.[4] In high school, varsity sports attract more than half of the boys and about 40 percent of the girls, reducing behavior problems and increasing positive attitudes toward school while teaching lessons in leadership, teamwork, persistence, diligence, and fair play.[5] Though it may surprise some, the fastest-growing high school sport for both girls and boys is bowling, defying the perception that it is a sport of a bygone era.[6] About one student in four participates in music and drama, and about the same percentage joins academic clubs in science, languages, computers, debate, and the like—clubs that enhance not only academic learning but social skills as well. Nationwide programs such as Odyssey of the Mind, National Forensics Study, and Scholars Bowl promote cross-curricular interests and creative problem-solving skills. Advocates see these activities as so important that they refer to them not as the extracurriculum but as the *co-curriculum,* and believe that their value goes far beyond the high school years. Participation in the extracurricular activities has been connected with:

- Enriched student life and learning
- Higher student self-esteem, school completion, and civic participation
- Improved race relations
- Higher SAT scores and grades
- Better health and less conformity to gender stereotypes
- Higher career aspirations, especially for boys from poor backgrounds[7]

But the extracurriculum is not without problems. The underrepresentation of low-socioeconomic students is evident in many programs, as are gender differences in participation in performing arts, athletics, school government, and

Extracurricular activities enrich student life and learning.

A VIEW FROM THE FIELD: HEAR THE MUSIC

While schools across the country eliminate many extracurricular activities, Eric Schopmeyer, 36, an elementary school music teacher in Portland, Oregon, is fighting back. Despite the lack of any financial support from his school, Eric developed an extracurricular program that touches the lives of children.

Eric's discovery was marimba, music from an instrument in the percussion family. He created a Zimbabwean-style marimba program for fourth to seventh graders at Marysville School. Though marimbas may not seem to be the intuitive choice for students just learning to play an instrument and read music, Eric explains that they have been a part of music education for years, albeit not in the United States. "This style of contemporary Zimbabwean marimba actually began as an educational tool in that country's schools about 50 years ago. Now, as more schools in the region incorporate marimba into their music curriculum, it is once again serving its original purpose."

Eric began the program in his second year of teaching. Like many music teachers, Eric uses the Orff approach to music education. Not a strict methodology, the Orff approach attempts to engage a child's intrinsic creativity and playfulness. Observing a colleague playing his own marimba for a group of kids, Eric says that he "immediately recognized a strong resonance between the Orff ideas and marimba. The accessibility of the music to children may be the strongest advantage that a marimba band has."

The program has been wildly successful with the students. A recent look at test scores showed that almost all of the children making the most significant academic improvements over the course of a year participated in the marimba band. Twice the number of students than the program has room for sign up, and being in the band has social significance among the students. "It's a dose of self-esteem," Eric says, "even for kids struggling academically. It's one place in school where they are excited and engaged. Seeing the way marimba ignites kids' creativity is one of the most amazing parts of teaching. There is great beauty in giving children the power to get their communities dancing."

Eric Schopmeyer graduated from Portland State University with a BA in music and a master's in education.

---

literary activities.[8] Skeptics suggest that the best we can say "is that the effects of extracurricular participation on secondary school students' personal development and academic achievement are probably positive, but very modest, and are definitely different among students with different social or intellectual backgrounds."[9] Given the current emphasis on test scores and academic standards, the extracurriculum is sometimes viewed as little more than a distraction.[10] In Texas and other states, "no pass, no play" rules deny students in poor academic standing the right to participate in varsity sports. In other communities, budget tightening has led to "pay to play" rules, in which a fee is required for sports participation, posing a serious problem for low-income families and students. Such policies raise puzzling questions and issues. Should academic performance and financial constraints be factors in deciding who participates in extracurricular activities? Since the top academic students, more likely to be wealthy and white, already dominate the extracurriculum, will "pay to play" and "pass to play" regulations make this curriculum even more exclusive, driving deeper divisions between the haves and the have-nots and further segregating racial and ethnic groups?

Who and What Shape the Curriculum?

Although all three curriculums are powerful forces, the public and the press typically focus on the most visible—the formal or official curriculum—when evaluating schools. Given the current emphasis on standards and testing, and the recurrent controversies over the teaching of evolution or the place of

Focus Question 4
What forces shape the school curriculum?

FIGURE 10.1

A pressure cooker of groups shapes the curriculum.

REFLECTION: What groups today exert the most influence on the curriculum? Do you see all these groups as a mark of democratic participation, or as an inappropriate intrusion in curricular decision making?

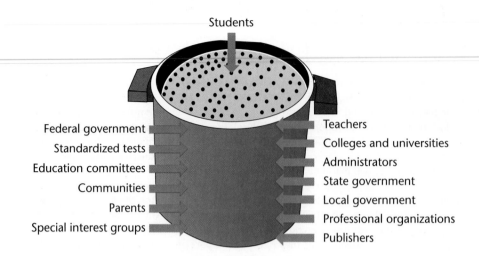

Students

Federal government
Standardized tests
Education committees
Communities
Parents
Special interest groups

Teachers
Colleges and universities
Administrators
State government
Local government
Professional organizations
Publishers

religion in the curriculum, the formal curriculum is constantly in the news. It makes a lot of sense for you, as a future teacher, to begin thinking about who decides what you should teach. In fact, what you teach is decided by competing interest groups, and the product sometimes feels as though it was created in a pressure cooker. (See Figure 10.1.) Anyone, from the president of the United States to a single parent, can have an impact on what is taught in your classroom. Let's take a brief tour of the chefs at work on the curricular pressure cooker.

Teachers

Teachers develop curriculum both formally and informally. They may serve on textbook selection committees that determine what texts the school will purchase, or they may actually work on writing a district's curriculum. In a less formal but no less powerful way, classroom teachers interpret and adapt whatever official text, standards, or curriculum guide has been assigned, stressing certain points in a text while giving scant attention to others; supplementing with teacher-made materials or directing students to the Internet.

Parental and Community Groups

Parents can be quite forceful in influencing the curriculum. They might advocate for more rigorous academic courses, they might be concerned about poor student performance on standardized tests, or they may desire more practical vocational training, such as an increase in computer science courses. Banning certain books or videos from the curriculum is also not unusual. In conservative communities, religious fundamentalists have objected to the absence of Christian values, and liberal communities have objected to books that use racial, ethnic, or gender slurs and stereotypes.

Students

During the 1960s and 1970s, students demanded curricular relevance. Although students have not seemed particularly interested in influencing curriculum policy recently, they have been active in protests against standardized testing.

Typically, students are given some freedom to select topics for independent projects, research papers, book reviews, and even authentic learning.

Administrators

Principals, in their role as instructional leaders, can wield substantial influence in shaping the curriculum. For example, a principal announces at a faculty meeting that the school's scores on the state standardized test in mathematics were disappointing, and this year's priority is to raise those scores. The result might well be a math curriculum that "teaches to the test." Sometimes central-office personnel, such as a language arts coordinator or a social studies supervisor, might create a new or revised school or district curriculum.

State Government

States are now assuming a larger role in education, and their interest in curriculum matters has sharpened through state standards and tests, curriculum guides, and frameworks for all schools to follow. In some states, religion and evolution are hot-button issues. In other states, instructional materials are expected to include, or exclude, cultural diversity.

Local Government

Local school boards make a variety of curriculum decisions, requiring courses from sex education to financial literacy to technology. Supporters feel that local school boards should have a strong voice in the curriculum because they are closest to the needs of the local community and the interests of the students. Others feel that school board members lack training to make curricular decisions.

Colleges and Universities

Institutions of higher learning influence curricula through their entrance requirements, which spell out courses high school students must take to gain admittance. As A. Bartlett Giamatti noted when he was president of Yale University:

> The high schools in this country are always at the mercy of the colleges. The colleges change their requirements and their admissions criteria and the high schools . . . are constantly trying to catch up with what the colleges are thinking. When the colleges don't seem to know what they think over a period of time, it's no wonder that this oscillation takes place all the way through the system.[11]

Standardized Tests

The results of state and national tests—from the state subject-matter tests needed for graduation to the SATs—influence what is taught in the school. If students perform poorly in one or more areas of these standardized tests, the government or public pressure pushes school officials to strengthen the curriculum in these weak spots.

Schools of education are not immune from the current focus on test performance. Because an increasing number of states are requiring new teachers to take qualifying tests, such as the Praxis Series, these tests influence what is covered in teacher education programs. For example, if Benjamin Bloom's Taxonomy of Educational Objectives is emphasized on such tests, teacher education colleges will teach more about Bloom in their own programs.

Education Commissions and Committees

From time to time in the history of U.S. education, various committees, usually on a national level, have been called upon to study an aspect of education. Their reports often draw national attention and influence elementary and secondary curricula. In 2010, for example, the Council of Chief State School Officers and the National Governors Association developed common core state standards, identifying the skills and content students should master at each grade level in math and English from kindergarten to grade 12. More than 40 states adopted these standards.

Professional Organizations

Professional organizations publish journals and hold conferences that emphasize curriculum developments. Their programs and materials help teachers in a number of areas, from technology to authentic learning. Teachers receive these curricular updates from the National Education Association (NEA), the American Federation of Teachers (AFT), the National Association for the Education of Young Children (NAEYC), and numerous subject area associations (teacher groups in English, math, science, and the like).

Special Interest Groups

Today's students are tomorrow's customers, so it is not surprising that businesses and interest groups offer teachers free (and attractive) curricular materials promoting their view of the world. A student-friendly magazine on protecting the environment looks wonderful at first glance, but how do you handle Company X's self-promoting distortion of its own environmental policies that may be part of the narrative? A month's supply of free newspapers for all students is appealing, but does acceptance mean that you are endorsing the editorial opinions of the paper? Teachers need to examine materials and products carefully to present a fair and accurate view.

Publishers

The major goal of textbook publishers is—not surprisingly—to sell books. That is why textbooks are attractively packaged and chock full of terms and names deemed important at the time (including this text!). Unfortunately, most elementary and secondary texts rarely provide in-depth coverage of topics, and they avoid unpopular points of view (unlike this text). Teachers need to remember that textbooks are published to meet market demands, and not necessarily objective or complex viewpoints.

Federal Government

The federal government influences the curriculum through judicial decisions, financial incentives, and legislation. In 2001, No Child Left Behind was a major piece of legislation that significantly altered the curricular landscape. (We will look closer at this law a little later in this chapter.)

Focus Question 5

How do textbook publishers and state adoption committees "drive" the curriculum?

The Reign of the Textbook

The textbook may be our *de facto* national curriculum. Students around the nation study from the same books, do the same exercises, and are expected to master the same material. Studies reveal that students spend as much as 95 percent of classroom time using textbooks. Teachers base more than 70 percent of their instructional decisions and as much as 90 percent of homework assignments on the text.[12] No wonder some believe that textbooks rule.

Before 1850, there were no textbooks. Instructional materials consisted of what teachers and their students could bring to class. Picture yourself trying to teach a class with random materials children had in their homes. Despairing teachers appealed for common texts so that all students could be on the same page (literally). Local legislators responded by requiring schools to choose specific books, and then requiring parents to buy them. Today, this process continues with school districts buying the textbooks, but the quality of those textbooks has come under increasing criticism:

> Imagine a public policy system that is perfectly designed to produce textbooks that confuse, mislead, and profoundly bore students, while at the same time making all the adults in the process look good, not only in their own eyes, but in the eyes of others. Although there are some good textbooks on the market, publishers and editors are virtually compelled by public policies and practices to create textbooks that confuse students with non sequiturs, that mislead them with misinformation, and that profoundly bore them with pointedly arid writing.
>
> None of the adults in this very complex system intends this outcome. To the contrary, each of them wants to produce good effects, and each public policy regulation or conventional practice was intended to make some improvement or prevent some abuse. But the cumulative effects of well-intentioned and seemingly reasonable state and local regulations are textbooks that squander the intellectual capital of our youth.[13]

Why are so many people frustrated with the quality of textbooks? The story starts with textbook adoption states. About half the states, located mainly in the South and the West, are **textbook adoption states.** (These states are indicated in Figure 10.2.) Local school districts in these states must select their texts from an official, state-approved list. This system creates a common, statewide curriculum, and because of the large numbers of books purchased, the hope is that the per-book cost is kept relatively low. The other states do not provide a state approved list of texts to their schools, so teachers in these states can select whatever text they want.

So far so good. The problem begins with the power that a few of the textbook adoption states have to shape the content of the nation's texts. Here's how it works: Four states (Texas, California, North Carolina, and Florida) because of their large student populations, exert an enormous influence on what is included in—or omitted from—these textbooks. Publishers view them as critical markets where profits are made or lost. When these states adopt standards for what they would like to see in a textbook, publishers listen. In a typical year, American schools spend upward of 7 billion dollars on

FIGURE 10.2

Textbook adoption states. Although some school districts are free to choose any text, others are limited to state-approved textbooks.

SOURCE: American Association of Publishers, School Division, Washington, DC, 2011.

REFLECTION: What patterns do you notice in the states that require texts to be selected from an approved list? Would such state adoption procedures be a factor in deciding where you might teach? Visit the site for updates at www.publishers.org.

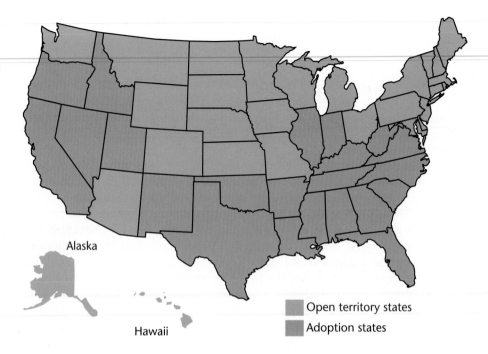

Open territory states

Adoption states

textbooks, and the lure of such profits has created a corporate feeding frenzy among the four publishing giants. Powerful adoption states, such as these four, have reduced the choices further by dictating to these companies what content to include, and sometimes what topics, words, or names to exclude. The remaining publishers cannot afford to lose the sales of these major adoption states, and so they comply, too. As a result, there is little competition about what should be included in the textbook, and all textbooks become quite similar. School districts in other states find themselves selecting from the texts that these four states prefer, especially the largest adopters, Texas and California. So if you are thinking that pre-K through grade 12 textbook authors, experts, and publishers decide what should be in these books, you need to rethink that idea.

In some of these textbook adoption states, deciding on what should be taught becomes more political than educational. In recent years, Texas has required very fundamental changes in its texts and has exerted a great deal of influence on publishers. In 2009, Texas voters elected a very politically conservative board of education that decided that the science curriculum should accept neither evolution nor global warming. In 2010, the social studies standards were up for review, and the Texas State Board of Education approved more controversial changes. The new Texas guidelines required publishers to write texts that included Phyllis Schlafly, the Contract with America, the Heritage Foundation, the Moral Majority, and the National Rifle Association. The standards also required teachers to describe the Judeo-Christian influences of the nation's Founding Fathers, but avoid emphasis on the rationale for the separation of church and state. Publishers were to alter references to American "imperialism" in favor of American "expansionism." Margaret Sanger, the birth-control pioneer, would be omitted because she "and her followers promoted eugenics." Also dropped from the Texas standards were Ralph Nader,

Edward Kennedy, and Ross Perot (and for a time, Thomas Jefferson, before the board reconsidered). Stonewall Jackson, the Confederate general, was to be described as a role model for effective leadership, and the ideas in Jefferson Davis's inaugural address were to be presented alongside Abraham Lincoln's speeches. The board also tweaked the history of the civil rights movement and removed references to race, sex, or religion in talking about how different groups have contributed to the national identity.[14]

Will the Texas version of history be the national version of history, as it so often was in the past? It is not clear. At least one publisher claims that with the arrival of digital publication technology, Texas social studies texts will be restricted to Texas. (However, it is interesting to speculate if other school districts may want the Texas version of American history.) As we go to press, so do the new texts in Texas.[15]

When those selecting a text have a choice, they can be influenced not only by the content, but by superficial qualities such as the cover, the graphics, and the design. Although visual attractiveness can enhance learning, it is no substitute for well-written and accurate content, and texts are increasingly criticized for their lack of originality or accuracy.[16] (This textbook, of course, is an exception!)

Because some states will buy texts only if they have a specified reading level, publishers are under pressure to develop books that meet this criterion. Often, authors avoid difficult words and long sentences so that, for example, esophagus becomes food tube and protoplasm becomes stuff. The result is the *dumbing down* of the textbook. Ironically, dumbing down can make books harder, not easier, to read. When authors simplify vocabulary, they replace precise and clear terminology with less precise, even ambiguous words. Shorter sentences often leave out the connective tissue—and, but, therefore— words that clarify the relationships between events and ideas. Shortening sentences to make reading simple can make understanding challenging ideas even more difficult.

Critics also are frustrated by the *mentioning phenomenon,* the attempt of publishers to include as many topics and names as possible to show how comprehensive their texts are, and why schools should buy them. But the result is so superficial that students do not really understand what is going on.[17] Nor are publishers alone to blame. State adoption committees, as we have just seen in Texas, sometimes delineate in minute detail all the names, dates, and places they want included, and what skills they want students to attain. In-depth analysis and clarifying examples are lost in favor of mentioning all the required names, places, and dates. Researchers have also found that basal readers and other texts, in attempting to be inoffensive to potential purchasers, include only a limited range of story types, often devoid of interpersonal and internal conflict.[18]

Textbooks offer an inviting target, but before we banish them from schools, let's consider some of their strengths and some ways that teachers can use them effectively. With a clear narrative, informative graphics, and exercises that develop skills, students can learn a great deal from a textbook. And if a teacher is fortunate to be working with a well-crafted text, research suggests that the text can actually motivate the teacher to try new ideas in the classroom.[19] At its best, a good text is a catalyst for change. Even when a text is less well crafted and floods the reader with too much information, the teacher

SEVEN FORMS OF BIAS

Although yesterday's stark racist and sexist texts are thankfully gone, subtle bias persists. Here are descriptions of seven forms of bias that emerge in today's texts. These categories can identify bias toward racial and ethnic groups, the elderly, English language learners, females, and gays and lesbians (and others). By teaching your students about the forms of bias, you can help them to become critical readers, an important skill they can take into adulthood.

Invisibility: Before the 1960s, African Americans, Latinos, Asian Americans, women, and Native Americans were largely invisible; that is, not even included in texts. Today, those with disabilities or gays and lesbians are often invisible.

Stereotyping: When rigid roles or traits are assigned to all members of a group, a stereotype is born. Examples include portraying all African Americans as athletes, Mexican Americans as laborers, and women only in their family roles.

Imbalance and Selectivity: Texts can perpetuate bias by presenting only one side of an issue, such as describing how women were "given" the vote. In fact, women endured physical abuse and other sacrifices in their struggle to gain their civil rights.

Unreality: Curricular materials often paint a Pollyanna picture of the nation. (And that goes for any nation!) Our history texts often ignore class differences, the lack of basic health care for tens of millions, as well as ongoing racism, classism, and sexism.

Fragmentation and Isolation: Have you ever seen a chapter or a section focusing on one group, perhaps titled "Ten Famous Asian Americans"? When texts isolate groups in this way, they are subtly suggesting that those groups are not part of society's mainstream.

Linguistic Bias: Using words such as "roaming" and "wandering" to describe Native Americans suggests nondirected behavior and relationships, language that implicitly justifies the seizure of native lands by white Americans who "settled" the lands. Other examples are word choices that place men in primary roles and women in family roles: "men and their wives."

Cosmetic Bias: Cosmetic bias offers the "illusion of equity" to lure educators into purchasing books that appear current, diverse, and balanced. A science textbook brandishes a female scientist on the cover, but alas, there is almost no content on female scientists in the text content.

SOURCE: The forms of bias were developed by Myra Sadker and David Sadker for Title IX equity workshops.

REFLECTION: These forms of bias emerge in more than just textbooks. Choose a television program, a website, a movie, or a news show, and see how many of these biases you can identify.

can make critical choices on how best to use it. One simple idea is to be selective: Choose certain chapters while skipping others; assign a few of the better exercises in the book rather than require that all be done. Even a weak text can be used effectively. Texts can be supplemented, either online or with other books, to provide more depth or other points of view. Here's one final idea: although blatant stereotypes of the past are rarely found in today's texts, subtle bias persists. Rather than ignore this bias, teach your students how to see the inequity, offer examples of how bias appears in texts, and then ask your students to evaluate their own books. This approach empowers students to become critical readers. (For more on this, see "A Closer Look: Seven Forms of Bias.")

The Standards Movement

Focus Question 6
What is standards-based education?

For as long as anyone can remember, free public schools have been the nation's pride, and a sore spot. In recent times, the poor performance of American students on international test scores has led to headlines announcing "America's Students Fall Further Behind." This pressure to "fix" the nation's schools

COMMON CORE STANDARDS

What do these mathematics and English standards look like? They can be quite broad, allowing room for teachers, publishers, and school districts to develop a curriculum to meet them. Here's a sample:

MATHEMATICS:

- Make sense of problems and persevere in solving them.
- Reason abstractly and quantitatively.
- Construct viable arguments and critique the reasoning of others.
- Attend to precision.
- Use appropriate tools strategically.
- Look for and make use of reasoning.

ENGLISH AND LANGUAGE ARTS

- Read and comprehend why complex individuals, events, and ideas develop and interact over the course of a text.

- Read and comprehend complex literary and informational texts independently and proficiently.
- Integrate and evaluate content presented in diverse formats and media, including visually and quantitatively, as well as in words.
- Develop and strengthen writing as needed by planning, revising, editing, rewriting, or trying a new approach.
- Use technology, including the Internet, to produce and publish writing and to interact and collaborate with others.

REFLECTION: How do you feel about the idea of teaching to national standards? What is lost, and what is gained? For more information, visit www.corestandards.org

---

fueled standards-based education. **Standards-based education** specifies precisely what students should learn, focuses the curriculum and instruction on meeting these standards, and provides continual testing to see if the standards are achieved. Standard-based education has become the driving force behind curricular reform at the national, state, and local levels. Standards lay out clear academic goals, and hold not only students to those goals, but schools and teachers as well.

When states have revised their standards, teachers report higher student expectations and a more demanding curriculum.[34] States' standards differed in the past; some states created demanding ones, and others not so much. The federal government wanted standards that were uniform and rigorous, in a sense, quality control for all American students. While some states, Texas and Alaska among them, rejected these math and English standards, by 2010, with federal encouragement, more than 40 states accepted a common set of standards in mathematics and English. These **Common Core State Standards** identify the skills and content a student should master at each grade level from kindergarten to grade 12, providing "a consistent, clear understanding of what students are expected to learn." [20] (See www.corestandards.org for more information.) The curriculum, historically and constitutionally a state responsibility, is more and more being shaped by a national approach. Some believe that rigorous, uniform, national standards are the first step in improving the performance of American students on international tests. Others view this approach as simplistic at best, and potentially damaging.

Stanford University professor Linda Darling-Hammond points out that students from Finland do strikingly well on international tests without any such detailed national standards. To the contrary, Finland improved its students' test scores by doing quite the opposite, shifting "to a more localized

www.mhhe.com/
sadkerbrief3e

INTERACTIVE ACTIVITY
What Is the Bias? Match scenarios with the bias being displayed.

system in which highly trained teachers design curriculum around very lean national standards."[21] Others note that students from countries with national standards scored at the bottom as well as the top on international tests in math and science. So standards by themselves do not lead to higher student test scores, and the current standards movement, although quite popular among many, may be the wrong approach.

Critics like Alfie Kohn (see Profiles in Education) wonder if requiring all students—from different states, different backgrounds, and with different skills and talents—to meet the same standards is a wise move. He fears that common standards will not lead to quality education, but simply to standardization. "If standards comprise narrowly defined facts and skills, then education consists of transmitting vast quantities of material to students, material that even the most successful may not remember, care about, or be able to use."[22] And he wonders if education should be viewed as a sports competition, focused on outscoring students from other countries. Are standards more about winning more test points than learning, more about gaining an economic advantage internationally than gaining an education? Many of Kohn's fears emerged in No Child Left Behind, the law that preceded and in many ways planted the seeds for the common core state standards.

The Long Shadow of No Child Left Behind

No Child Left Behind (NCLB) was a law supported by both Democrats and Republicans and described as "the most significant change in federal regulation of public schools in three decades."[23] In the decade that followed, NCLB changed the face of American education, creating a high-stakes testing culture and labeling thousands of schools as underperforming. By 2011, both President Obama and the Congress began making changes to the law, but the influence of NCLB can still be felt, both in the creation of national standards and in the emphasis on testing. Here is a snapshot of NCLB:

- *Annual testing in reading, math, and science in grades 3–8 and once in high school.* Schools needed to report not only individual student test scores but also student scores by race, ethnicity, disability, social class, and limited English proficiency. States created their own tests and their own passing grades, some easy, and some more demanding. By 2013–14, all students were supposed to be proficient in reading and mathematics, a goal that is not being reached.

- *States and school districts received "report cards" and underperforming schools were closed.* School test results would be made public, a kind of report card, and if the school did not do well on the state exams for five years, the school would be closed and either reconstituted by the state or reopened as a charter school.

- *All teachers had to be "highly qualified," licensed with an academic major in the field they taught.* Paraprofessionals were to have at least two years of college or pass a rigorous test, and parents were to be informed if their child's teacher was not "highly qualified." While this sounded pretty reasonable, small rural schools could not afford to enlarge their faculties to include specialists in each subject area, and urban areas struggled even to attract teachers not categorized as "highly qualified."[24]

Although these aspects of NCLB were often in the news, other requirements were less well known but caused considerable consternation. For example, NCLB emphasized reading, but only the *phonics approach.* (Phonics associates letters with their sounds, and at times provided scripted lessons for teachers.) While this reading approach was popular with supporters of basic education, it was less so with progressive educators and with teachers who used multiple approaches in their teaching. This phonics requirement seemed based more on politics than education, a criticism that was confirmed in 2008 when a government report found that "students enrolled in a $6 billion federal (phonics) reading program that is at the heart of the No Child Left Behind law are not reading any better than those who don't participate."[25] NCLB also had requirements that seemed more political than educational. All school officials had to certify in writing that every student has the right to pray and to submit this certification to the federal government every two years. Detractors charge that such provisions do nothing to improve the nation's schools.[26]

Both teachers and students often find that a testing culture diminishes education to test score.

The "do-or-die" NCLB testing culture generated much of the criticism against NCLB. Critics argued that deciding if a school is successful or not based on a single test is fundamentally unsound, especially when there are huge resource differences in wealthy and poor schools. Worse yet, even schools that improve on most measures were likely to find themselves labeled "underperforming." This was possible because schools were rated not only on schoolwide test scores, but also on the performance of particular groups. For example, if African Americans did poorly one year and improved the second year, but another group, let's say students with disabilities, did poorly the second year, even if most student scores improved every year, that school would be labeled "underperforming." Some schools were accused of underreporting minority group scores, and some states simply lowered the passing score so fewer schools would be labeled "underperforming."[27]

A decade after No Child Left Behind became law, a growing number of parents, politicians, and many educators voiced their concerns that the law was, in fact, doing just the opposite, leaving many children behind. In fact, one of the law's original and well-known supporters had changed her mind, too. Diane Ravitch, a former undersecretary of education in the first Bush administration, became an outspoken critic. She calls NCLB and current reform efforts "corporate reform," funneling money from public schools to private companies that sell tests or run charter schools, without any research evidence that this will improve education. She believes the emphasis should be not on creating students who are master test-takers, but on improving early childhood and parent education, requiring higher standards for new teachers and incentives for those who stay in teaching, hiring experienced educators as superintendents, and including more arts, physical education, foreign language, and history in the curriculum. She, like many others, does not believe that high-stakes testing worked in the past, or will work in the future.[28]

If No Child Left Behind continued unchanged, in 2012, 80 percent of America's schools would be failing. But we know better: four out of five American schools are not failing. The law was failing, and an overhaul was needed. Many educators, parents, and politicians are committed to improving standards and assessments, giving high-performing schools more flexibility and providing the lowest-performing schools more resources. And many believe that recruiting better teachers and rewarding them for how effectively they improve student performance is also needed.[29] But will these "fixes" be made? Will the testing culture still pervade schools? And with Congress preoccupied with budget reductions and interested in diminishing the federal influence in education, what changes will they seek? In 2011, the federal government announced that it would loosen its testing accountability and give more of that responsibility to the states. As we go to press, the future of the federal role in education is far from clear.

The Problem with Standardized Tests

Focus Question 8

What problems are created by high-stakes testing, and what are the testing alternatives?

Although it may sound as if we believe that all tests are bad, this is not the case. Tests can be extremely useful. Standardized tests can help educators analyze the curriculum and teaching methods to see what's working—or what's not. When the scores are in, problems can be fixed. Yet as educational researchers Sharon Nichols and David Berliner point out, although standardized tests can be very useful, *high-stakes* standardized tests—the kind used in NCLB—create many problems. When people's careers, salaries, and futures rely on a test score, on a single test score, havoc and hurt can be the results.[30]

In a New York City middle school, the principal asked teachers to spend fifteen minutes a day with students practicing how to answer multiple-choice math questions in preparation for the state-mandated test. One teacher protested, explaining she taught Italian and English, not math. But the principal insisted, and she followed his directive. As you might suspect, the plan failed, and in the end, fewer than one in four New York City middle schoolers passed the exam. While the importance of the test dominated the formal curriculum, the lessons learned through the hidden curriculum were no less powerful. Students learned that test scores mattered more than English or Italian, and that teachers did not make the key instructional decisions. In fact, once the test was over, one-third of the students in her class stopped attending school, skipping the last five weeks of the school year.[31]

Inner-city schools aren't the only ones experiencing testing woes; rural communities and wealthy suburbs have their own complaints. In Scarsdale, New York, an upscale, college-oriented community, parents organized a boycott of the eighth-grade standardized tests. Of 290 eighth-graders, only 95 showed up for the exam.[32] In Massachusetts, some local school boards defied the state and issued their own diplomas to students they believed were being unfairly denied graduation because of the state-mandated test.[33] Why are teachers, students, and parents protesting? What's wrong with measuring academic progress through such tests? Here are some reasons why high-stake tests are problematic:

1. *At-risk students placed at greater risk.* Using the same tests for all students, those in well-funded posh schools along with students trying to learn in underfunded, ill-equipped schools, is grossly unfair, and the

NATIONAL STANDARDS AND TESTS

ARE DESIRABLE BECAUSE . . .

SCHOOLS AND EDUCATORS ARE NOT BEING HELD ACCOUNTABLE FOR STUDENT FAILURE

"If they don't want to learn, we can't make them" has been the modus operandi of educators. As a result, we have high school graduates who cannot read or write, and college graduates who do little better. Standards and tests will finally hold educators accountable. We will be able to see what students know and how well they know it. We can reward successful schools, help troubled schools, and finally close failing schools.

THEY MAKE US EDUCATIONALLY AND ECONOMICALLY COMPETITIVE

Many of today's high school graduates must be retrained in basic literacy skills by the corporations that hire them, because they are unable to do the work that is required. This is a sign that schools are failing. This sort of educational inefficiency leads to technically incompetent workers and weakens our ability to compete in world markets. We must have standards and tests to educate a first-class labor force and maintain our standard of living.

TEACHERS WORK COLLABORATIVELY RATHER THAN IN ISOLATION

A common set of standards promotes cooperation. Teachers and principals will work together to identify problems, develop instructional solutions, and collaborate as a professional team working to ensure that all the standards are met.

THEY WILL BIND THE NATION

National standards offer a unifying experience, as children learn about our common heritage. Without such standards, we become dangerously pluralistic and suffer the risk of becoming not one nation but several. There are already examples of countries that have lost this common thread and whose cultures have disintegrated.

LOCAL PAROCHIALISM WILL BE ELIMINATED

National standards will bring new insights and diverse points of view to the nation's children. Rather than being held hostage to the desires and views of local school boards, students will be able to consider broader perspectives. National standards can end debilitating local parochialism and broaden students' horizons.

ARE A MISTAKE BECAUSE . . .

HIGH-STAKES TESTS REPRESENT A TERRIBLE ACCOUNTABILITY

Taking time from studies to prepare for a high-stakes test is not an effective demonstration of educational progress or school accountability. In fact, schools simply replace real learning with test preparation programs. One test is a terribly unreliable way to assess a person's knowledge and flies in the face of all that we have learned about multiple intelligences, individual differences, and authentic assessment.

NATIONAL STANDARDS AND TESTS ARE A STEP BACKWARD FOR MANY STUDENTS AND SCHOOLS

National standards represent a step down for the nation's strongest school districts. The nation's best schools are well beyond such standards yet must invest time and resources preparing for the state tests. Our schools prepare very competent scientists and engineers, many of whom are the first to be "downsized" by the same business executives who complain about educational quality. In fact, given our service economy, we may be overeducating our workforce.

TEACHERS WORK IN ISOLATION RATHER THAN COLLABORATIVELY

The pressure of tests and standards will drive teachers away from cooperative planning on educational goals and into the trap of drilling their students to ensure that their class does well. Teachers will become competitors in a survival of the fittest scenario.

NATIONAL STANDARDS WILL DIVIDE THE NATION

We simply cannot agree on a single set of standards, on which facts to remember (and which to forget). What is important to one group of Americans may be unimportant or offensive to another. The effort to create unifying standards and tests will divide our people.

CENTRAL CONTROL OF OUR LIVES WILL GROW

The authors of the Constitution had it right: local communities and individuals know their children best, and they hold the practical wisdom that made this nation great. All we need is faith in the common sense of Americans, because they do know what's best for their children.

NATIONAL TESTS WILL GIVE US CRITICAL INFORMATION AND DIRECTION

Standardized tests will enable us to compare student performance and to understand what it takes to earn an "A" in one school, versus an "A" in another. We will discover who is really learning, and who is not. Finally, we will be able to make sense out of what is going on in almost 100,000 school buildings.

NATIONAL TESTS WILL HURT EDUCATION

High-stakes tests hurt students who are bright but simply don't test well. Such standardized tests encourage a school curriculum based on test preparation, drive away talented teachers, increase pressure to cheat, and create the kind of boring, predictable, "one-size-fits-all" curriculum that is a disservice to a true democracy.

www.mhhe.com/
sadkerbrief3e **YOU DECIDE . . .**

Where do you stand on the standards and the testing issue? Can you separate standards from testing? How might you determine if standards are being met—without using a standardized test? Some educators assert that test development should precede standards development. Do you agree or disagree? Why?

As national, state, and district decision makers require more testing, many teachers have protested or boycotted these exams.

outcome is quite predictable. Since students do not receive equal educations, holding identical expectations for all students places the poorer ones at a disadvantage. State data confirm that African Americans and Hispanics, females, students from poverty, and those with disabilities are disproportionately failing high-stakes standardized tests. For example, one year in Georgia, two out of every three low-income students failed the math, English, and reading sections of the state's competency tests. No students from well-to-do counties failed any of the tests, and more than half exceeded standards. Even moderate income differences could result in major test score differences.

Wealthy students grow up with the intellectual abundance, such as books and educational videos, and learning opportunities at home that poor students often lack. These resources may not make wealthier children smarter, but such students often arrive at school with the academic competencies measured on standardized tests. Because the students are already prepared for the high-stakes tests, the schools can move on to teach higher-level thinking skills. Poor and minority children do not learn many of these basic skills at home, so schools must focus on drilling them for the tests. As a result, these students miss out on higher-level thinking skills, and the assets they do bring to school—other languages, knowledge of other cultures, oral storytelling, unique music and artistic experiences—are not honored or developed, much less tested.[34]

In No Child Left Behind, there was a standard that received little attention: opportunity-to-learn. *Opportunity-to-learn standards* were created to help at-risk students by ensuring a level playing field by providing all students with appropriate educational resources, competent teachers, and modern technology. Differences in student learning styles were to be accommodated and additional time provided for students to relearn material if they failed the test. Teachers were to be given quality in-service training. Yet most states did not allocate enough resources to remedy dramatic educational differences between school districts, and real barriers to achievement— racism, poverty, sexism, low teacher salaries, language differences, inadequate facilities—were lost in the sea of testing and inadequate funding. Although the rhetoric of the standards movement is that a rising tide raises all ships, in fact, without the adequate resources, some ships do not rise. In the current standards and testing movement, opportunity-to-learn is the forgotten standard.[35]

2. *Lower graduation rates.* Grade-by-grade testing and graduation tests actually increase school dropouts. A Harvard University study found that students in the bottom 10 percent of achievement were 33 percent more likely to drop out of school in states that required graduation tests. The National Research Council found that low-performing elementary and secondary school students who are held back do less well academically, are much worse off socially, and are far likelier to drop out than equally weak students who are promoted. Retention in grade is the strongest predictor of which students will drop out—stronger even than parental income or mother's education level. When a weak student drops out, the school's average score actually rises, giving a picture of success when the real picture is failure.[36]

   With limited resources, schools create a triage. The strong students do not need special attention to pass the tests. They might be excellent students, but the tests are geared to measure minimal skills, not excellence. The weakest students can also be ignored, since they need more time and resources than most schools have. The students who do get the attention are called "bubble kids," because they are closest to a passing grade. A Texas teacher poignantly captures this dilemma:

   Ana's got a 25 percent. What's the point in trying to get her to grade level? It would take two years to get her to pass the test, so there's really no hope for her. I feel like we might as well focus on the ones there's hope for.[37]

3. *Higher test scores do not mean more learning.* Evidence is mounting that for a growing number of schools, teaching is being redefined as test preparation. Seventy-nine percent of teachers surveyed by *Education Week* said they spent "a great deal" or "somewhat" of their time instructing students in test-taking skills, and 53 percent said they used state practice tests a great deal or somewhat. In Texas, James V. Hoffman and his colleagues asked reading teachers and supervisors to rate how often they engaged in test preparation. The study used a scale of 1 to 4, in which 1 stood for never, 2 for sometimes, 3 for often, and 4 for always. Most of those surveyed said that teachers engaged in the following activities "often" or "always":

   • Teaching test-taking skills—3.5
   • Having students practice with tests from prior years—3.4
   • Using commercial test preparation materials—3.4
   • Giving general tips on how to take tests—3.4
   • Demonstrating how to mark an answer sheet correctly—3.2

BETTER TO GUESS THAN LEAVE IT BLANK (OR IS IT?)

Knowing that they will not get any credit for not answering a question, students would rather guess or fudge their responses and hope for the best. Here are some actual student answers that are more than a little off base, though they do offer a humorous insight into student thinking:

1. Solomon had three hundred wives and seven hundred porcupines.

2. Actually, Homer was not written by Homer but by another man of that name.

3. Socrates was a famous Greek teacher who went around giving people advice. They killed him. Socrates died from an overdose of wedlock. After his death his career suffered a dramatic decline.

4. The greatest writer of the Renaissance was William Shakespeare. He was born in the year 1564, supposedly on his birthday. He never made much money and is famous only because of his plays. He wrote tragedies, comedies, and hysterectomies, all in Islamic pentameter. Romeo and Juliet are an example of a heroic couplet.

5. Writing at the same time as Shakespeare was Miguel Cervantes. He wrote Donkey Hote. The next great author was John Milton. Milton wrote *Paradise Lost.* Then his wife died and he wrote *Paradise Regained.*

6. One of the causes of the revolutionary war was the English put tacks in their tea . . . Ben Franklin died in 1790 and is still dead.

7. The nineteenth century was a time of a great many thoughts and inventions. People stopped reproducing by hand and started reproducing by machine. The invention of the steam boat caused a network of rivers to spring up.

8. Ancient Egypt was inhabited by mummies and they all wrote in Hydraulics. They lived in the Sarah Dessert and traveled by Camelot. The climate of the Sarah is such that the inhabitants have to live elsewhere.

SOURCE: Teachers First, www.teachersfirst.com/humor.shtml.

In one school, for example, students were taught to cheer "Three in a row? No, No, No!" The cheer was a reminder that if students answered "c" three times in a row, probably at least one of those answers is wrong, since the test maker is unlikely to construct three questions in a row with the same answer letter.[38]

Although this kind of test preparation may boost scores, it does not necessarily produce real gains in understanding that show up on other tests or performance measures or that students can apply in a nontesting situation. Consider these findings:

- A study of eighteen states compared trends in state test scores with long-term trends on national standardized tests. When state tests were given, performance went down on the ACT, the SAT, and the math test of the National Assessment of Educational Progress (NAEP). The study concluded that higher state test scores were most likely due to direct test preparation rather than increased student learning.[39]

- Three-quarters of fourth-grade teachers surveyed by RAND in Washington State, and the majority of principals, believed that better test preparation (rather than increased learning) was responsible for most of the score gains.[40]

- To score well on standardized tests, students are expected to master a wide range of topics, but often superficially. This "breadth over depth" approach to learning has serious consequences. A study of 8,310 students conducted by the University of Virginia found that high school students who studied fewer topics in math and science, but studied them in greater depth, earned higher grades in college than their peers who studied more topics but in less depth.[41] These findings suggest that "learning just to pass a standardized test" may give students only a superficial understanding of the curriculum and jeopardize future success.

4. *Standardized testing shrinks the curriculum.* Educator Alfie Kohn advises parents to ask an unusual question when a school's test scores increase: "What did you have to sacrifice about my child's education to raise those scores?"[42] Many teachers believe that their schools give less attention to subjects that are not on the state test. One teacher had this to say about how the timing of state tests drives teaching: "At our school, third- and fourth-grade teachers are told not to teach social studies and science until March."[43] Indeed, a study by the Center on Education Policy found that about 62 percent of school districts increased the amount of time spent in elementary schools on English/language arts or math, and 44 percent of districts cut time on science, social studies, art and music, physical education, lunch, or recess.[44] Such a narrow view of the curriculum is self-defeating. In schools where the arts are part of the core curriculum, one finds self-motivated students, improved social and emotional development, greater parental involvement, intensified student and teacher engagement, stronger collegiate aspirations, greater civic engagement, and respect for cultural differences. While the global economy demands innovation, schools view the world through a traditional and narrow perspective.[45]

5. *When tests fail.* Tests themselves are often flawed, and high-stakes errors become high-stakes disasters. Stories continue to mount as the crush of millions of new tests overwhelms the handful of testing companies. In Massachusetts, a senior spotted an alternative answer to a math question, and the scores of 449 students were suddenly propelled over the passing mark. A flawed answer key incorrectly lowered multiple-choice scores for 12,000 Arizona students, erred in adding up scores of essay tests for students in Michigan, and forced the re-scoring of 204,000 essay tests in Washington. Another error resulted in nearly 9,000 students in New York City being mistakenly assigned to summer school, and $2 million in achievement awards being denied to deserving students in Kentucky.[46] The National Board on Educational Testing and Public Policy reported that 50 high-profile testing mistakes had occurred in 20 states from 1999 through 2002; and in 2006, rain fell on some SAT answer sheets, affecting the test scores of 4,000 college hopefuls, most in a negative direction.[47] Many question the wisdom of rewarding and punishing students, teachers, and schools on the basis of the flawed history of the testing industry.[48]

6. *Teacher stress.* Although teachers support high standards, they object to learning being measured by a single test.[49] Not surprisingly, in a national study, nearly 7 in 10 teachers reported feeling test stress, and 2 out of 3 believed that preparing for the test took time from teaching important but nontested topics.[50] Fourth-grade veteran teachers were requesting transfers, saying that they could not stand the pressure of administering the high-stakes elementary exams, and teachers recognized for excellence were leaving public schools, feeling their talents were better utilized in private schools where test preparation did not rule the curriculum.[51] When

FIGURE 10.3

A teacher's impression of the testing movement.

SOURCE: http://ganesh.ed.asu.edu/aims/view_image.php?image_id=72&grade_range_id=3. See also Tirupalavanam Ganesh, "Held Hostage by High-Stakes Testing: Drawing as Symbolic Resistance," *Teacher Education Quarterly* (2002).

REFLECTION: *Try your own hand at drawing an image of how you feel when you are about to take a high-stakes test.*

80 Arizona teachers and teacher educators were asked to visually depict the impact of standardized tests, their drawings indicated test-driven classrooms where boredom, fear, and isolation dominate. Teachers feel that they are shortchanging schoolchildren from a love for learning. Figure 10.3 presents one of those drawings.

7. *What's worth knowing?* The fact that history, drama, the arts, and a host of subjects are given less attention in the current testing movement raises intriguing curricular questions: What is really important to teach? What is worth knowing? Although it may sound obvious, thinking beyond the obvious is often a good idea. Much of what is taught in schools is tradition and conventional wisdom, curricular inertia rather than careful thought. To see how society's notion of what is important can change, try your hand at the test questions on the next page that were used to make certain that eighth-graders in Kansas knew "important information." We have shortened the exam, but all these questions are from the original. (Hint: Brush up on your orthography.) See if you would qualify to graduate from elementary school in 1895.[52]

How did you do? Well, if you bombed it, don't feel too badly; few of today's PhDs would pass. So what does this teach us? Are today's schools far weaker than earlier ones? If we failed, are we not truly educated? Or perhaps what we consider "important knowledge" is less enduring than we believe. How much of today's "critical" information will be a curious and unimportant footnote in the years ahead?

8TH GRADE EXAMINATION GRADUATION QUESTIONS
SALINE COUNTY, KANSAS
APRIL 13, 1895

Reading and Penmanship—The Examination will be oral and the Penmanship of Applicants will be graded from the manuscripts.

Grammar

1. Give nine rules for the use of Capital Letters.
2. Define Verse, Stanza, and Paragraph.
3. What are the Principal Parts of a verb? Give Principal Parts of do, lie, lay, and run.

Arithmetic

1. District No. 33 has a valuation of $35,000. What is the necessary levy to carry on a school seven months at $50 per month, and have $104 for incidentals?
2. What is the cost of a square farm at $15 per acre, the distance around which is 640 rods?
3. Write a Bank Check, a Promissory Note, and a Receipt.

U.S. History

1. Give the epochs into which U.S. History is divided.
2. Tell what you can of the history of Kansas.
3. Describe three of the most prominent battles of the Rebellion.

Orthography

1. What are the following, and give examples of each: Trigraph, subvocals, diphthong, cognate letters, linguals?
2. Give four substitutes for caret "u."
3. Mark diacritically and divide into syllables the following, and name the sign that indicates the sound: card, ball, mercy, sir, odd, cell, rise, blood, fare, last.

Geography

1. Name and describe the following: Monrovia, Odessa, Denver, Manitoba, Heela, Yukon, St. Helena, Juan Fernandez, Aspinwall, and Orinoco.
2. Name all the republics of Europe and give capital of each.
3. Describe the movements of the earth. Give inclination of the earth.

Physiology

1. How does nutrition reach the circulation?
2. What is the function of the liver? Of the kidneys?
3. Give some general directions that you think would be beneficial to preserve the human body in a state of health.

Alternatives to High-Stakes Testing

Standardized tests are popular because they are relatively inexpensive compared with other assessments, offer clear results, and can be rapidly implemented. But, as we have seen, high-stakes standardized tests are plagued with problems. In fact, testing guidelines issued by the American Psychological Association specifically prohibit basing any consequential decisions about individuals on a single test score.[53] Most educational organizations and measurement experts agree that a better gauge of student performance is multiple

11. High-Stakes Testing

As a teacher, part of your job will be to be able to explain your students' assessment to their parents. In this observation you will observe a teacher discuss a student's test scores, and the meaning behind the norm-referenced scores, to his mother.

Classroom Observation videos are available on the CD Reader and at the Online Learning Center.

www.mhhe.com/
sadkerbrief3e

assessments: tests, portfolios, formal exhibitions, independent student projects, and teacher evaluations. **Authentic assessment** (also called alternative or performance-based assessment) captures actual student performance, encourages students to reflect on their own work, and is integrated into the student's whole learning process. Such tests usually require students to synthesize knowledge from different areas and actively use that knowledge. The student might demonstrate what has been learned through a portfolio (like the ones we encourage you to develop in the RAPs found in this text), or a journal, or by undergoing an interview, conducting an experiment, or giving a presentation. Authentic assessment offers a focused and intense insight into what the student has learned, and requires evidence quite different from what is required by responding to questions on a typical high-stakes test.[54] Comparisons are often made to sports, in which participants are expected to demonstrate in a game what they have learned in practice. A tennis player works on her backhand so that she can demonstrate mastery in a game; similarly, when students know that they will be called on to demonstrate and use their knowledge, they are more motivated to practice their academic skills. Many states are exploring authentic methods of assessment.[55]

Authentic assessment is used in the Coalition of Essential Schools, founded by prominent educator Theodore Sizer. The coalition encourages schools to define their own model for successful reform, guided by nine basic principles that emphasize the personalization of learning. These principles include the requirement that students complete "exhibitions," tasks that call on them to exhibit their knowledge concretely. The high school curriculum is structured around these demanding, creative tasks, which may include:

- Completing a federal Internal Revenue Service Form 1040 for a family whose records you receive, working with other students in a group to ensure that everyone's IRS forms are correct, and auditing a return filed by a student in a different group

- Designing a nutritious and attractive lunch menu for the cafeteria within a specified budget and defending your definitions of nutritious and attractive

- Designing and building a wind instrument from metal pipes, then composing and performing a piece of music for that instrument

- Defining one human emotion in an essay, through examples from literature and history, and in at least three other ways (through drawing, painting, or sculpture; through film, photographs, or video; through music; through pantomime or dance; or through a story or play that you create)[56]

An increase in authentic assessment may contribute to a greater classroom focus on critical thinking and personal development. Authentic assessments may help us go beyond the current dependence on high-stakes standardized tests in determining the competence of students and the success of schools.

Tension Points

You can read a curriculum the way you read the day's newspaper, for in it you can see the fractures and tensions in our society. Often, the curriculum becomes a battleground for competing political and cultural ideas. Here are some examples.

Focus Question 9

How are cultural and political conflicts reflected in the school curriculum?

Intelligent Design versus Evolution

In colonial New England, the Bible was the major text, and religious instruction was the center of the curriculum. But the new nation's constitution changed all that. Or did it? From prayer in school to sex education, courts continually debate the role of religion in school. Here are two examples of too much religious influence.

The following questions were assigned to students in a public school in Virginia:

1. List six proofs that the Bible is God's word.

2. God is supreme ruler and has given man free choice. This shows that God is:
   A. Omniscient
   B. Good
   C. Sovereign
   D. Merciful[57]

A California public school system was using textbooks that taught that God helped Columbus discover America, that Native American accomplishments were "worthless" since they had no knowledge of the "true" God, described non-Christian religions as "cults," and asked students to punctuate a sentence that read: "The Hebrew people often grumbled and complained."[58]

These examples were clearly religious instruction and illegal, since the First Amendment does not allow schools to promote or denigrate any religion. (See Chapter 8, "School Law and Ethics," for a detailed discussion on the role of religion in schools.) According to the Supreme Court, also illegal is the teaching of **creationism,** the position that God created the universe in six 24-hour periods as described in the Bible. But does that mean that the theory of evolution should be taught as the only explanation of life's origin?

FIGURE 10.4

Do you believe in evolution?

SOURCE: "Trend Lines: Acceptance of Evolution," *Washington Post*, January 16, 2007.

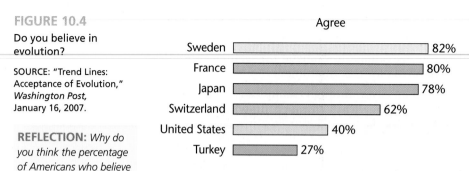

Agree

Sweden	82%
France	80%
Japan	78%
Switzerland	62%
United States	40%
Turkey	27%

REFLECTION: *Why do you think the percentage of Americans who believe in evolution is so much lower than many other countries?*

Evolution, as put forth by Charles Darwin, is a keystone of modern biological theory and postulates that animals and plants have their origin in other preexisting types and that there are modifications in successive generations. Christian fundamentalists (also referred to as religious fundamentalists or the religious right) do not believe that this explains the origin of human life, and they are not alone. They support the teaching of **intelligent design,** which credits an unnamed intelligence or designer for aspects of nature's complexity still unexplained by science, and that evolution is simply a theory, not a fact. While civil rights attorneys and many scientists argue that intelligent design is religious and unscientific, polls indicate that a large segment of the public is comfortable with this notion that students deserve to hear "competing theories."[59] More than a dozen states (a number likely to grow) are either considering passing or have already passed legislation requiring that when evolution is taught, criticism be included, or alternative explanations of the origins of humans, including the supernatural, be taught as well. Some states and school districts have actually removed the word "evolution" from the curriculum. Compared with people in other countries, Americans are far less likely to believe in evolution.[60] (See Figure 10.4.)

The subtlety of language is partially responsible for this tension point, because "theory" has two separate meanings. In common language, "theory" means an idea or a hunch. In science, a theory is a thoroughly tested belief unlikely to change, such as the theory of gravitation or cell theory or evolutionary theory.[61] Scientific theories are the results of decades or centuries of insights drawn on many interconnected observations and ideas. The theory of evolution is more than a hunch and needs to be understood as a well-founded scientific explanation. But that does not mean that evolution exists in a vacuum. Science refutes a literal interpretation of the Bible as a measure of the age of the earth, but it does not refute a spiritual or higher intelligence at work. Perhaps intelligent design works through evolution. The bottom line is that we still have much to learn. It is unfortunate that such debates create pro- and anti-science camps.

A warning sticker placed in science textbooks in Cobb County, Georgia, saying evolution is "a theory, not a fact" was removed by court order.

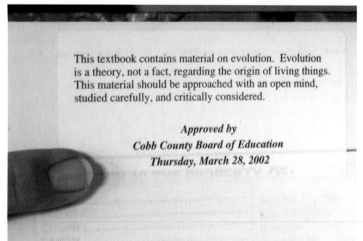

This textbook contains material on evolution. Evolution is a theory, not a fact, regarding the origin of living things. This material should be approached with an open mind, studied carefully, and critically considered.

Approved by
Cobb County Board of Education
Thursday, March 28, 2002

These controversies frighten some teachers, and this is unfortunate. Teaching should be about opening minds, not indoctrination. Teaching the theory of evolution is important; teaching *about* different religions is important. Promoting or disparaging religious or scientific beliefs is inappropriate. Unfortunately, many teachers, fearful of the consequences, avoid teaching about religion or evolution.[62] Teaching spirituality is even more rare. *Spirituality,* a personal and pluralistic view of life's meaning, is broader than any particular religion. Spirituality encompasses many ideas common to all religions; activities that renew, lift up, comfort, heal, and inspire both ourselves and others. Religion, science, and spirituality need not be in conflict. Religious intolerance, scientific hostility, and spiritual ignorance do not move the world forward; instead, they limit learning.

Censorship and the Curriculum

Ruth Sherman lived just outside New York City, in a Long Island neighborhood known for its Italian community and its easy commute to the city. Although she traveled only a short distance to P.S. 75, where she taught third grade, she might as well have been teaching in another country. P.S. 75 was in the Bushwick section of Brooklyn, a graffiti-filled neighborhood populated by poor black and Hispanic families living in the midst of a rampant drug culture. "Why there?" her friends asked her. "Because I want to turn things around," she responded. She was that kind of teacher. But, in just three months, it was Ruth Sherman, and not her students, who was turned around.

Her problems started in September, although she did not learn about it until later, when she assigned a book called *Nappy Hair,* by African American author Carolivia Herron. Her students loved the book, about a little black girl with "the nappiest, fuzziest, the most screwed up, squeezed up, knotted hair," and clamored for copies to take with them. By Thanksgiving, the parents in Ruth Sherman's class had also discovered the book, which they considered racially insulting. At a parents' meeting, she was confronted by 50 parents (most of them parents of children not in her class), who shouted racial epithets and eventually threatened her. The superintendent sent Ruth home for her own protection. A review of the book followed. The review brought only praise for a book that promoted positive images for children and presented stories that appealed to them. Within a few days, the superintendent wrote her a letter, commending her performance, inviting her back to the school, and promising security escorts to protect her. But, by then, it was too late. Ruth Sherman, the teacher who wanted to make a difference, did not want to work in a climate that required "escorts" to ensure her safety. She transferred to another school.[63]

This incident occurred in New York, but it could occur anywhere at anytime. Nearly everyone—teachers, parents, the general public, and various special interest groups—wants some say as to what is and is not in the school curriculum. No matter what content is found in a particular textbook or course of study, someone is likely to consider it too conservative or too liberal, too traditional or too avant-garde, racist, sexist, anti-Semitic, violent, un-Christian, or pornographic.[64] When this happens, pressure to censor the offending materials soon follows.

There is no such thing as a totally safe, acceptable, uncontroversial book or curriculum. Each of the following has been subjected to censorship at one time or another:

- Mary Rodgers's *Freaky Friday:* "Makes fun of parents and parental responsibility"
- Plato's *Republic:* "This book is un-Christian"
- Jules Verne's *Around the World in Eighty Days:* "Very unfavorable to Mormons"
- William Shakespeare's *Macbeth:* "Too violent for children"
- Fyodor Dostoyevsky's *Crime and Punishment:* "Serves as a poor model for young people"
- Herman Melville's *Moby Dick:* "Contains homosexuality"
- Anne Frank's *Diary of a Young Girl:* "Obscene and blasphemous"
- E. B. White's *Charlotte's Web:* "Morbid picture of death"
- J. R. R. Tolkien's *The Hobbit:* "Subversive elements"
- Roald Dahl's *Charlie and the Chocolate Factory:* "Racist"
- Mark Twain's *The Adventures of Huckleberry Finn:* "Racism, insensitivity, and offensive language"
- *Webster's Dictionary:* "Contains sexually explicit definitions"[65]

According to the American Library Association, more than 500 books are challenged in a typical year.[66] But the incidences of **self-censorship,** which some term **stealth censorship,** are considered much higher. Stealth censorship occurs when educators or parents quietly remove a book from a library shelf or a course of study in response to an informal complaint—or to avoid controversy. Teachers practice the same sort of self-censorship when they choose not to teach a topic or not to discuss a difficult issue. Numbers on the frequency of self-censorship are impossible to obtain. Tallying up the number of books that were officially removed or placed on restricted-access shelves in libraries is far easier. Frequently challenged authors include J. K. Rowling, John Steinbeck, Judy Blume, Robert Cormier, Mark Twain, Phyllis Reynolds Naylor, Stephen King, Lois Duncan, Maya Angelou, J. D. Salinger, and Toni Morrison. On today's list of challenged books, you will find:

- *To Kill A Mockingbird* by Harper Lee for offensive language, racism, and being unsuited to age group
- *Twilight* (series) by Stephenie Meyer for religious viewpoint, sexually explicit, and being unsuited to age group
- *It's Perfectly Normal* by Robie H. Harris for homosexuality, nudity, sex education, religious viewpoint, and abortion
- *Forever* by Judy Blume for sexual content and offensive language
- *The Catcher in the Rye* by J. D. Salinger for sexual content and offensive language
- *The Chocolate War* by Robert Cormier for sexual content and offensive language
- *And Tango Makes Three* by Justin Richardson and Peter Parnell for anti-ethnic, antifamily, homosexuality, religious viewpoint, and being unsuited to age group

- *His Dark Materials* trilogy by Philip Pullman for political viewpoint, religious viewpoint, and violence
- *Scary Stories* by Alvin Schwartz for occult/satanism, religious viewpoint, and violence
- *It's So Amazing! A Book about Eggs, Sperm, Birth, Babies, and Families* by Robie H. Harris for sex education and sexual content[67]

At the heart of the case against censorship is the First Amendment, which guarantees freedom of speech and of the press. Those who oppose censorship say that our purpose as educators is not to indoctrinate children but to expose them to a variety of views and perspectives. The case for censorship (or, perhaps in a more politically correct phrase, *mature judgment and selection*) is that adults have the right and obligation to protect children from harmful influences. But "harmful influences" are in the eye of the beholder. For instance, challenges to books that include homosexuality have become commonplace. Critics say that these books promote homosexuality, and that is not acceptable in school. Others believe that such books teach tolerance of sexual differences and serve a positive purpose for both heterosexual and homosexual students. Moreover, they argue, reading about different sexual orientations is a far cry from promoting any particular sexual outlook.[68] The censorship controversy is symbolic of how politicized the curriculum debate has become.

Cultural Literacy or Cultural Imperialism?

Both George Orwell and Aldous Huxley were pessimists about the future. "What Orwell feared were those who would ban books," writes author Neil Postman. "What Huxley feared was that there would be no one who wanted to read one."[69] Perhaps neither of them imagined that the great debate would revolve around neither fear nor apathy but, rather, deciding which books are most worth reading.

Proponents of **core knowledge,** also called **cultural literacy,** argue for a common course of study for all students, one that ensures that an educated person knows the basics of our society. Allan Bloom's *The Closing of the American Mind* (1987) was one of several books that sounded the call for a curricular canon. *Canon* is a term with religious roots, referring to a list of books officially accepted by the church or a religious hierarchy. A curricular canon applies this notion to schools by defining the most useful and valued books in our culture. Those who support a curricular canon believe that all students should share a common knowledge of our history and the central figures of our culture, an appreciation of the great works of art and music and, particularly, the great works of literature. A shared understanding of our civilization is a way to bind our diverse people.

Allan Bloom, professor of social thought at the University of Chicago, took aim at the university curriculum as a series of often unrelated courses lacking a vision of what an educated individual should know, a canonless curriculum. He claimed that his university students were ignorant of music and literature, and charged that too many students graduate with a degree but without an education.[70] One of the criticisms of Bloom's vision was that his canon consisted almost exclusively of white, male, European culture.

www.mhhe.com/
sadkerbrief3e

INTERACTIVE ACTIVITY
**Do You Know the
"Basics"?** See how you
do on this hypothetical
quiz created to test your
cultural literacy. Get a
firsthand feel for the
testing issue.

E. D. Hirsch, Jr., in his book *Cultural Literacy,* was more successful than Bloom in including the contributions of various ethnic and racial groups, as well as women. This is a rarity among core curriculum proponents. In fact, Hirsch believes children from poverty and children of color will benefit most from a cultural literacy curriculum. According to Hirsch, a core curriculum will teach them the names, dates, places, events, and quotes that every literate American needs to know to succeed. In 1991, Hirsch published the first volume of the core knowledge series, *What Your First Grader Needs to Know.* Other grades followed in these mass-marketed books directed not only at educators but at parents as well.[11]

Not everyone is enamored with the core curriculum idea. A number of educators wonder who gets included in this core and, just as interesting, who gets to choose? Are Hirsch, Bloom, and others to be members of a very select committee, perhaps a blue-ribbon committee of "Very Smart People"? Why are so many of these curricular canons so white, so male, so Eurocentric, and so exclusionary?

Many call for a more inclusive telling of the American story, one that weaves the contributions of many groups and of women as well as of white males into the textbook tapestry of the American experience. Those who support **multicultural education** say that students of color and females will achieve more, will like learning better, and will have higher self-esteem if they are reflected in the pages of their textbooks. (In Chapter 3, "Teaching Your Diverse Students" we discuss multicultural education in depth.) And let's not forget white male students. When they read about people other than themselves in the curriculum, they are more likely to honor and appreciate their diverse peers. Educator and author James Banks calls for increased cultural pluralism:

> People of color, women, and other marginalized groups are demanding that their voices, visions, and perspectives be included in the curriculum. They ask that the debt Western civilization owes to Africa, Asia, and indigenous America be acknowledged. . . . However, these groups must acknowledge that they do not want to eliminate Aristotle and Shakespeare, or Western civilization, from the school curriculum. To reject the West would be to reject important aspects of their own cultural heritages, experiences, and identities.[72]

New Directions for the Curriculum

Focus Question 10
How has technology affected the curriculum?

The tremendous knowledge explosion has created more information than schools can teach. Many believe that the answer to the knowledge explosion is using technology more effectively. Let's take a look at how technology has impacted schools.

The Technology Revolution

In the twentieth century, education was forever changed. Human beings serving as teachers, the core of schooling for centuries if not millennia, were made technologically obsolete. The new invention was used at home and then in the more affluent schools. Eventually, all schools were connected. Slowly but surely, the classroom teacher was replaced. These new machines took students where they had never been before, did things no human could do, and shared an unlimited reservoir of information. Clearly, this technological breakthrough had potential to teach more effectively at a far lower cost than human teachers. Predictions varied from the replacement of all teachers to the replacement of most teachers. Some even predicted the replacement of schools themselves.

Sound familiar? Although today's computer revolution has sparked those sorts of predictions, the developments just described had nothing to do with computers or the Internet, or even the twenty-first century. Those predictions were made in the 1950s about television. The popular perception back then was that educational television would reshape the classroom and revolutionize schools, and perhaps put a few million teachers out of work. That never happened. Although television has reshaped much of the cultural landscape (and not all for the good), predictions about its impact on schools were greatly exaggerated. Americans are quick to see a brave new world with each new invention. Consider the following soothsayers:

> "The motion picture is destined to revolutionize our educational system, and . . . in a few years it will supplant largely, if not entirely, the use of textbooks."
>
> **—Thomas Edison**

> "The time may come when a portable radio receiver will be as common in the classroom as is a blackboard."
>
> **—William Levenson**,
> **director of Cleveland Public School's radio station**[73]

So it should not be surprising that the large investments in computer-based technologies have not been matched by significant gains in student achievement. In fact, researchers are divided on the academic benefits brought by computers. Evidence suggests that drills and tutorials in science, social science, and math may be effective in helping students show increased performance on standard multiple choice tests, but more advanced simulations, such as virtual dissections, are not. While most educators have moved beyond the expectation that a simple application of technology will improve student achievement, there is still a diversity of opinion on the educational benefits of technology. Perhaps with more sophisticated uses of technology in the future, more effective learning will occur—or perhaps not.[74] Some believe that certain technologies actually can hamper learning. Students who become too dependent on calculators before understanding mathematical concepts can see their mathematics test scores tumble.[75] Word processing has produced longer, higher-quality writing by students, but teachers complain about the spelling and grammatical shortcuts that characterize students' e-texting.[76] Technology has created

Technology brings students instant information, but educators wonder about its ultimate impact on learning.

some ethical dilemmas as well. Nearly 40 percent of college students use the cut-and-paste function on their computers to lift text from the Internet. Text-messaging on cell phones has been used to share information during exams. High-tech cheating is rarely reported by students.[77]

Ways Technology Is Used in the Classroom   Although computers have not proved to be the silver bullet that magically improves student achievement, most adults believe that computers offer essential workplace skills. The public sees computers in the classroom as a sign of educational progress, and increasingly, teachers view technology as a central part of classroom life. What technology? When asked to rank their needs, teachers listed a computer station with access to e-mail at the top of the list, followed by the Internet, a telephone (yes, a telephone!), an encyclopedia and other reference materials on CD, and at least one computer for every four students. Presentation and multimedia authoring programs were also mentioned.[78] The interactive whiteboard is a technology in about 15 percent of classrooms in 2010, and growing rapidly.

In the curriculum, teachers use technology in some exciting ways:

- *Simulations* re-create events, such as elections, cross-cultural meetings, and historical events, with amazing realism that pulls students into another time or place. Science simulations allow modeling of natural concepts like molecular activity to help students understand concepts that would otherwise remain abstract.

- *Data sensors* allow students to use scientific tools to collect data measurements in real time on phenomena they are studying. The use of real data helps move student understanding from abstract to concrete.

- *Virtual field trips* transport students to the ocean depths, to outer space on NASA's shuttle site, and to the National Zoo, where zookeepers share their knowledge of the animals and students can talk with the experts. The technology can also create reverse field trips where the expert is brought into the class electronically to serve as a guest speaker.

Expanding the classroom is now commonplace with the Internet resources available to teachers:

- First People's Project provides a site, in Spanish and English, for students from indigenous cultures. The goal is for students to learn about different cultures and perhaps become involved in humanitarian efforts (see www.iearn.org.au/fp/). More than 6,000 schools in Mexico, the United States, and Canada participate in wildlife migration studies in the Western Hemisphere by recording sightings in their areas.

- "Journey North: A Global Study of Wildlife Migration" teaches students to care for wildlife by creating or protecting habitats (see www.learner.org/jnorth).

- At the Holocaust/Genocide Project, students produce a magazine called *An End to Intolerance* (see www.iearn.org/hgp/).

- World Wise Schools is a Peace Corps project where classrooms can partner with Peace Corps volunteers and follow them as they do their work during the course of a year (see www.peacecorps.gov/wws).

- Podcasting lectures and discussions is a way of teaching students even when they are not in class. Although teachers now podcast information to students, schools also are encouraging students to produce their own podcasts in various subjects.

Distance learning, the technology-enabled outgrowth of correspondence courses, provides opportunities for students to experience courses and earn credits and degrees without a brick-and-mortar building. Estimates range between one and two million such learners are already enrolled online. While Michigan became the first state to require an "online learning experience" before high school graduation back in 2006, today more than half of the states provide a state virtual education program.[79] Virtual education opens new opportunities for homebound students, homeschooling families, student athletes with rigorous practice schedules, students who have problems in traditional schools, or students wanting to access courses not available in their schools, such as Advanced Placement courses. For older adults, virtual education offers opportunities to those working unusual or unpredictable hours, commuters who would rather travel the Internet than the interstate, and individuals who simply like learning on their own time and in their own place. (What kinds of distance learning experience have you had?)

The next big growth area for technology enabled education is the hybrid course. Hybrid or blended courses are delivered neither entirely online nor entirely face-to-face in the classroom. Many teachers already use podcasting lectures and discussions, and as they learn more about virtual possibilities, their courses are likely to become more clearly hybrid, blending the best of both worlds.[80]

The federal government's National Educational Technology Plan calls for a "revolutionary transformation" of the educational system and a twenty-first century model of learning powered by technology.[81] They view technology as the lever for real educational change, eventually increasing the percentage of both high school and college graduates.

But Stanford University professor Larry Cuban, looking beyond even these positive signs, sees problems on the horizon. When academic advances do not follow technological advances, we often blame teachers for not adequately embracing new technology. If teachers are not to blame, we place our criticism on the doorstep of an unresponsive school bureaucracy unable to manage change. If that does not work, then we attribute failure to insufficient resources, a public unwilling to fund costly technology. Rarely do Americans question the technology itself. Cuban points out that we know little about using technology to enhance instruction, that the problem may not be teachers, administrators, or funding; it may be America's unbridled faith in technology.[82] How do you view technology's potential?

The Digital Divide Technology offers hope to many, but it does not always offer opportunity to everyone. The gap between technology haves and have-nots has been termed a **digital divide.** For years, African American, Hispanic, and female students had fewer computers and less access to or interest in the Internet, a technology gap with educational implications.[83] But in recent years, this gap has been closing because of the falling price of laptops, new cell phone technology, and the increasing number

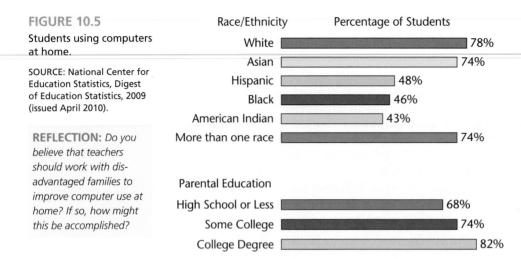

FIGURE 10.5
Students using computers at home.

SOURCE: National Center for Education Statistics, Digest of Education Statistics, 2009 (issued April 2010).

REFLECTION: *Do you believe that teachers should work with disadvantaged families to improve computer use at home? If so, how might this be accomplished?*

of school computers (although at the college level, whites, Asians, and males continue to constitute the majority of computer science majors and professionals).[84]

Although nearly all public schools have Internet access, the digital divide has not disappeared. For instance, every classroom in wealthier communities is more likely to have sufficient up-to-date technology with high-speed broadband Internet connections than are poorer communities. And although most students can be e-connected at school, differences emerge at home.[85] (See Figure 10.5.) Geography matters, because running fiber-optic cables to rural communities is often an expense that telecommunications companies avoid. The Internet connections are left to acoustic modems that are slow, making it almost impossible for students participating in online classes. Even in schools with high-speed Internet access to the building, an inadequate school network may create a digital divide that has its own title: the **last mile problem**.[86]

Finally, let's focus on a more subtle digital divide: *how* technology is used.[87] You probably have some friends who struggle with technology and others who are wizards. There is more to technology than simply access. Some schools use technology to promote drill and practice, whereas other schools use technology to challenge students. Professor Henry Jay Becker warns, "Efforts to ensure equal access to computer-related learning opportunities at school must move beyond a concern with the numbers of computers in different schools toward an emphasis on how well those computers are being used to help children develop intellectual competencies and technical skills".[88] Although technology can awe us, in the end it is how well we use the technology that matters.

It is unlikely that education will be redefined completely in the near future, yet it is also clear that technology's influence is growing. Consider technology mastery as part of your professional development. Attend relevant courses and workshops and observe colleagues applying technology, but do not lose your skepticism. Be wary of "magic bullets"—simple solutions to complex educational problems.

Skills Making Their Way into the Curriculum

Technology offers a new thinking tool, but many looking at the curriculum believe that we should focus more on our own operating systems—i.e., our brains. They argue that schools need to emphasize different content and stronger skills. What skills? Here are a few being explored by schools today:

Critical thinking skills—Have you noticed that students seem to do a lot of memorizing in school, but far less comparing, interpreting, observing, summarizing, classifying, decision making, creating, and criticizing? Using more of these critical thinking skills in subjects from mathematics to history increases higher order thinking as well as content knowledge.[89]

Metacognition—Another thinking focus, this one advocated by Robert Marzano and his colleagues, stresses the importance of teaching students how to think about their own thinking, called metacognition. Metacognition teaches students how to plan for a given learning task, monitor their own understanding, and evaluate their own learning.

Critical pedagogy—Some schools (although far too few in our opinion) focus on helping students develop a social conscience. Critical pedagogy teaches students how to identify and then work to remediate social challenges, from pollution to inadequate housing. Critical pedagogy puts students on the path to becoming thoughtful and involved citizens.[90]

Financial literacy—Today's economic challenges remind us that passing algebra, geometry, and calculus is one thing, but balancing a checkbook or keeping a credit card under control is quite another. According to the National Endowment for Financial Education, fewer than half of U.S. high school and college students have a regular savings plan, only a fourth of those students stick to a budget, and more than one-third don't keep track of their spending at all. But with as little as 10 hours of classroom instruction, students can improve their spending and saving habits. Nearly 20 states have added financial literacy to school curriculums in an effort to reach children and young adults before debt and credit-card companies do.[91]

Physical fitness—Too many of our children confront obesity, diabetes, and coronary disease in their lifetimes. Lifelong fitness activities—yoga and Pilates, how to climb a rock wall or kickbox, ice skate, dance, or golf—can be enjoyed today and promote health for years to come. While team sports are fun and exciting, not everyone is so skilled. But everyone can prepare for a more active and healthy adulthood. As one student explained: "I love it [lifelong fitness activities] because it's fun. I'm not an athlete, so I used to dread p.e. Now I am learning new activities that I enjoy and keep me healthy and I am not embarrassed about my body."[92]

Content and Skills Rarely Emphasized in the Curriculum

Now let's take a moment and do some critical thinking of our own. Imagine that you are in charge of taking the schools down an educational path. What path would you trailblaze? What content or skills do you see as most critical?

Tough question, and it's not fair to ask you such a question if we are not ready to answer it ourselves. So here's our response: We see a world marked by misunderstanding and anger, cultural, class, and religious warfare,

Focus Question 11
What are new directions for the curriculum?

Focus Question 12
How can we rethink tomorrow's curriculum?

widespread poverty, physical deprivation, and interpersonal and international conflicts. These issues scream for the attention of not only political leaders but of educators and students, yet schools rarely attend to these social tribulations. How can schools develop a curriculum that enables students to focus on improving the world, a curriculum that will always be timely and important? Here is a sample of what we would teach.

Enduring Lesson Number 1: Understand Ourselves There is a fundamental, even driving need to more deeply understand ourselves both as individuals and as part of the wider community. Often we learn only a few salient aspects of our backgrounds, such as personal and family history, cultural and religious beliefs, gender challenges, and a single view of our national heritage. But these are incomplete lessons. We lack a healthy appreciation of how our backgrounds have shaped lives and our worldview. Only through greater self-insight can we begin to understand our perceptions and motivations, our strengths and weaknesses, our limits and strengths, and why we behave and think as we do. This is the first enduring lesson: "Know yourself."

Enduring Lesson Number 2: Celebrate Others After we understand ourselves, we can seek insights from other peoples and cultures. Although some have called this *teaching tolerance,* we do not believe that diversity should be *tolerated.* Today, we tolerate things from sleazy politics to poor service when dining out. Tolerance falls woefully short, for we believe that diversity should be celebrated. Cultural, racial and ethnic, and religious differences offer us wondrous insights into the human experience. We can learn so much from one another. Our challenge is to learn from our differences, not fear them.

Enduring Lesson Number 3: Encourage Individual Talents and Contributions High test scores predict high test scores, but not much else: not problem-solving skills, not good work habits, not honesty, not dependability, not loyalty, not any cherished virtue.

Schools should prepare students to live purposeful and satisfying lives. To do this, students need to learn and develop their own unique interests and abilities, skills, and talents. By measuring all students against the same yardsticks of literacy and numeracy, individual creativity and differences are lost or denigrated. Contrary to the current testing wave, we support less standardization and more individualization.

Enduring Lesson Number 4: Promote Purposeful Lives At the Antioch College commencement in 1859, Horace Mann advised the graduates, "Be ashamed to die until you have won some victory for humanity." The real measure of an education is not what a student receives as a test grade or even does while in school; the real measure is what people do after graduation. Are students living higher lessons and working for noble purposes, or have they succumbed to baser temptations? Are adults honest and caring with one another, treating their children, families, colleagues, and even strangers with love, compassion, and forgiveness? The way we choose to live our lives as adults, and not our test scores, will be the true measure of our schooling.

Those are some of the keystones to our curriculum. What are the keystones to yours?

STUDENTS ON MY MIND

One of the things that has been most important to me in my daily work is to remember that I am not teaching a subject, but that I am teaching students. In these days of standards, clearly defined and often prescribed teaching objectives, it is hard to remember sometimes that the most important thing isn't the "standard"—it is the student. When I remember this, it calls me to use skills that aren't always written in my lesson plan. I have to be open-minded in my approach to students, remembering that their knowledge, experiences, and concerns are not what I might expect or predict. Remembering to teach to the student, I also call on the gifts of humor, patience, and creativity. While these are not written into any of my daily lesson plans, they are critical to reaching the students that I teach in authentic and transforming ways.

Diane Petteway is the International Baccalaureate Middle Years Program coordinator at East Millbrook Magnet Middle School in Raleigh, North Carolina.

REFLECTION: Can you construct a different kind of standard for your own teaching? Build your standard not around content, but on your connection with your students.

SUMMARY

1. **What is the formal curriculum taught in schools?**

   The Saber-Tooth Curriculum teaches us that a curriculum should preserve the past, but not be limited by it. The formal or visible curriculum is the school's official curriculum, but it is far from static. In colonial America, reading and religion were central. Spurred by poor international test scores, we now have a curriculum that emphasizes standards and high-stakes testing.

2. **How does the invisible curriculum influence learning?**

   Schools teach an invisible curriculum that has two components. The hidden or implicit curriculum offers lessons that are not always intended, but emerge as students are shaped by the school culture, including the attitudes and behaviors of teachers. Topics considered unimportant or too controversial, inappropriate or not worth the time, and therefore not taught constitute the null curriculum.

3. **What is the place of the extracurriculum in school life?**

   Most students participate in the extracurriculum, a voluntary curriculum that includes sports, clubs, student government, and school publications. Although some see these activities as part of a rich co-curriculum, others discount their value.

4. **What forces shape the school curriculum?**

   Many groups influence the content of the curriculum. In recent years, the federal government and specially appointed education commissions have been two groups promoting a standards-based, high-stakes testing curriculum.

5. **How do textbook publishers and state adoption committees "drive" the curriculum?**

   More than 20 states, mainly located in the South and West, are textbook adoption states. Local school districts in these states must select their texts from an official, state-approved list. The most populous of these states exert considerable influence in the development of textbooks.

CHAPTER REVIEW

Go to the Online Learning Center to take a chapter self-quiz, practice with key terms, and review concepts from the chapter.

www.mhhe.com/
sadkerbrief3e

6. **What is standards-based education?**

The pressure to improve test scores led to standards-based education, a process of focusing the curriculum on specified topics and skills, followed by continuous testing to see if these standards have been learned. Most states have signed on to Common Core State Standards outlining the skills and content in math and English.

7. **How has No Child Left Behind influenced America's schools?**

One of the most far-reaching federal education plans, No Child Left Behind, included annual testing, identification of underperforming schools, and employing only "highly qualified" teachers. Lack of funding and reliance on a single test to measure learning are just two of the criticisms leveled at the law, but standards and testing are part of its legacy.

8. **What problems are created by high-stakes testing, and what are the testing alternatives?**

High-stakes tests are believed to contribute to increases in the number of dropouts and the increase in teacher and student stress. High scores on such tests do not necessarily reflect greater learning, and teachers who teach to the test eliminate other important topics from the curriculum. One testing alternative, authentic assessment, evaluates students by asking them to synthesize what they have learned in a final product or "exhibit."

9. **How are cultural and political conflicts reflected in the school curriculum?**

Opposing the theory of evolution, some support intelligent design, an alternative explanation for the origin of humans. Cultural and political differences over what should be taught have led to book banning and censorship. Proponents of a core curriculum and cultural literacy argue with multiculturalists who advocate the greater inclusion of the roles, experiences, and contributions of women and people of color.

10. **How has technology impacted the curriculum?**

Americans have a history of utopian predictions when new technology is introduced. Despite exciting virtual field trips that take students around the world or the online activities that create fascinating learning communities, computers and the Internet have had only a limited impact on what students learn.

11. **What are new directions for the curriculum?**

As technology makes its way into schools, so does an increased emphasis on our own thinking skills. Critical thinking and metacognition put the focus on how are brains are thinking, bringing our thought processes to a more intentional and conscious level. Analyzing some of society's current social and medical challenges, advocates also call for more financial and physical fitness education in the curriculum.

12. **How can we rethink tomorrow's curriculum?**

Because of the knowledge explosion, some educators believe that we should focus less on content and more on process, including critical thinking skills, metacognition, and critical pedagogy. The reader is invited to consider a new approach to the current curriculum, and the authors suggest a four-tier curriculum that promotes self-understanding, human relations, and greater individualization.

authentic assessment, 338

Common Core State
 Standards, 327

core curriculum, 317

core knowledge, 343

creationism, 339

cultural literacy, 343

digital divide, 347

evolution, 340

extracurriculum, 318

formal or explicit curriculum,
 316

implicit or hidden
 curriculum, 317

intelligent design, 340

last mile problem, 348

multicultural education, 344

No Child Left Behind (NCLB),
 328

null curriculum, 317

standards-based education,
 327

stealth or self-censorship, 342

textbook adoption states, 323

DISCUSSION QUESTIONS AND ACTIVITIES

1. For some students, the hidden curriculum and the extracurriculum are most central to their school experience. Define the roles of these unofficial curricular experiences in your own education. If you were placed in charge of a school today, how would you change these hidden and extracurricular experiences? How might your changes be evident in elementary, middle, and high schools? Why?

2. What subject areas spark the greatest debate and controversy over creating a single, national curriculum? Are there strategies to help reach a consensus on these issues? How might a national history curriculum written today differ from one written a century from now? A century ago? Why?

3. Collect textbooks from your local elementary and secondary schools and analyze them according to the following criteria:

   • Do they include instructional objectives? Do these require students to use both recall of factual information and analytical and creative thinking skills?

   • Were readability formulas used in the preparation of the textbooks? If so, did this appear to have a negative or a positive impact on the quality of the writing?

   • Are under-represented group members included in the textbooks' narrative and illustrations? Are individuals with disabilities included?

   • When various individuals are included, are they portrayed in a balanced or a stereotyped manner?

4. If you were given the job of developing a standards-based curriculum with assessment tools, where would you go to identify standards? What kinds of tests would you use? What kinds of tests would you avoid? What subjects and skills do you consider crucial? Why?

5. Do you believe that children's educational materials should be censored? Are there any benefits to censorship? Any dangers? What kinds of materials would you refuse to let elementary school students read? Middle or high school students? Postsecondary students?

WEB-*TIVITIES*

Go to the Online Learning Center to do the following activities:

1. The Formal or Explicit Curriculum
2. The Curriculum Time Machine
3. New Directions for the Curriculum
4. Censorship and the Curriculum
5. The Textbook Shapes the Curriculum
6. Is the United States Going Test Crazy?
7. The Teacher as the Curriculum Developer
8. Computers in the Classroom, Virtual Field Trips, and Global Education

Articles, Case Studies, and Videos correspond to chapter content and are not always in numeric order. Go to your *Teachers, Schools, and Society Reader* CD-ROM to:

Read Current and Historical Articles

21. "The Authentic Standards Movement and Its Evil Twin," Scott Thompson, *Phi Delta Kappan,* January 2001.

22. "The Essential Cognitive Backpack," Mel Levine, *Educational Leadership,* April 2007.

23. "All Our Students Thinking," Nel Noddings, *Educational Leadership,* February 2008.

24. "Why Has High-Stakes Testing So Easily Slipped into Contemporary American Life?" Sharon Nichols and David Berliner, *Phi Delta Kappan,* May 2008.

Analyze Case Studies

11. **Elaine Adams:** A student teacher near the end of her assignment observes her cooperating teacher giving the students help while administering the district-mandated standardized tests. She finds herself unsure how to deal with the situation.

12. **Melinda Grant:** A teacher who has developed an innovative curriculum is concerned because another teacher continually warns her that she will be held responsible for her students' end-of-year standardized test scores.

Observe Teachers, Students, and Classrooms in Action

11. **Classroom Observation: High-Stakes Testing**
See page 338 of this text for a description of this video. You'll find the video on the CD Reader and at the Online Learning Center.

www.mhhe.com/
sadkerbrief3e

NEED HELP?
GOT QUESTIONS?
WE HAVE ANSWERS

Location: Learning
Resources Building

Hours
Mon.-Thurs.
8:30 am – 7:00 pm
Friday
8:30–12:30

Phone: 816.604.2205

Free Tutoring

...NG AN
...E TEACHER

7. How can teachers best tap into different student learning styles?
8. How can teachers use technology to
   support effective instruction?
9. What are several salient models of
   instruction?
10. What are the stages of teacher
    development?

WHAT DO YOU THINK? Qualities of a good teacher. Rate the qualities of a
good teacher, and see how other students rated these qualities.

www.mhhe.com/
sadkerbrief3e

Chapter Preview

Albert Einstein believed that they awakened the "joy in creative expression and knowledge." Ralph Waldo Emerson believed that they could "make hard things easy." About whom are these talented geniuses talking? You guessed it: teachers.

Some individuals seem to take to teaching quite naturally. With little or no preparation, they come to school with a talent to teach and touch the lives of students. Others bring fewer natural talents to the classroom yet, with preparation and practice, become master teachers, models others try to emulate. Most of us fall in the middle, bringing some skills to teaching but also ready to benefit and grow from teacher preparation and practice teaching.

In this chapter, we present recent research findings on effective instruction, focusing on a core set of skills that comprise good teaching. We also detail approaches to classroom management along with prevailing models of instruction, such as cooperative learning, problem-based learning, differentiated instruction and computer-supported learning.

Are Teachers Born or Made?

Focus Question 1
Are teachers born or made?

Think about the best teacher you ever had: Try to evoke a clear mental image of what this teacher was like. How do your memories compare with what some of today's teachers say about their favorite teachers from the past:

- The teacher I remember was charismatic. Going to his class was like attending a Broadway show. But it wasn't just entertainment. He made me understand things. We went step-by-step in such a clear way that I never seemed to get confused—even when we discussed the most difficult subject matter.

- I never watched the clock in my English teacher's class. I never counted how many times she said uh-huh or okay or paused—as I did in some other classes. She made literature come alive—I was always surprised—and sorry—when the bell rang.

- When I had a problem, I felt like I could talk about it with Mrs. Garcia. She was my fifth-grade teacher, and she never made me feel dumb or stupid—even when I had so much trouble with math. After I finished talking to her, I felt as if I could do anything.

- For most of my life, I hated history—endlessly memorizing those facts, figures, dates. I forgot them as soon as the test was over. One year I even threw my history book in the river. But Mr. Cohen taught history in such a way that I could understand the big picture. He asked such interesting, provocative questions—about our past and the lessons it gave for our future.

The debate has been raging for decades: Are teachers born, or made? What do you think?

If you think it is a combination of both, you are in agreement with most people who have seriously considered this question. Some individuals—a rare few—are naturally gifted teachers. Their classrooms are dazzlingly alive. Students are motivated and excited, and their enthusiasm translates into academic achievement. For these truly talented educators, teaching seems to be pure art or magic.

But behind even the most brilliant teaching performance, there is usually well-practiced skill at work. Look again at those brief descriptions of favorite teachers: Each of them used proven skills—structure, motivation, clarity, high expectations, and effective questioning.

- "We went step-by-step in such a clear way that I never seemed to get confused—even when we discussed the most difficult subject matter." *(structure and clarity)*
- "She made literature come alive." *(motivation)*
- "After I finished talking to her, I felt as if I could do anything." *(high expectations)*
- "He asked such interesting, provocative questions—about our past and the lessons it gave for our future." *(questioning)*

Although there is ample room for natural talent, most teaching is based on "tried and true" practices. Research helps us distinguish between what we "think" will work and what really works. In this chapter, we describe what research tells us about teaching skills and models of instruction that raise student achievement. If you decide to teach, it will be your responsibility to keep up with the burgeoning and sometimes shifting teacher effectiveness research through conferences, course work, and education journals.[1] For now, let's explore together the current findings supporting teacher effectiveness.

Academic Learning Time

Research shows that students who spend more time pursuing academic content achieve more. That's the commonsense part, and it's hardly surprising. What is startling is how differently teachers use their classroom time. For example, the classic Beginning Teacher Evaluation Study[2] showed that one teacher in the Los Angeles school system spent 68 minutes a day on reading, whereas another spent 137 minutes; one elementary school teacher spent only 16 minutes per day on mathematics, whereas another spent more than three times that amount. Similarly, John Goodlad's comprehensive research study, *A Place Called School,* found that some schools devote approximately 65 percent of their time to instruction, whereas others devote almost 90 percent.[3] The variation is enormous.

Although allocating adequate time to academic content is obviously important, making time on the schedule is not enough. How this allocated time is used in the classroom is the real key to student achievement. To analyze the use of classroom time, researchers have developed the following terms: allocated time, engaged time, and academic learning time.

Allocated time is the time a teacher schedules for a subject—for example, 30 minutes a day for math. The more time allocated for a subject, the higher student achievement in that subject is likely to be.

Engaged time is that part of allocated time in which students are actively involved with academic subject matter (intently listening to a lecture, participating in a class discussion, writing an essay, solving math problems). When students daydream, doodle, write notes to each other, talk with their peers about nonacademic topics, or simply wait for instructions, they are not involved in engaged time. When there is more engaged time within allocated time, student achievement increases.[4] As with allocated time, the amount of time students are engaged with the subject matter varies enormously from teacher to teacher and school to school. In some classes, engaged time is 50 percent; in others, it is more than 90 percent.

Academic learning time is engaged time with a high success rate. Many researchers suggest that students should get 70 to 80 percent of the answers right when

Focus Question 2

How is class time organized and what is academic learning time?

Academic learning time is engaged learning time during which students have a high success rate. When they are working independently, as here, the success rate should be particularly high.

working with a teacher. When working independently, and without a teacher available to make corrections, the success rate should be even higher if students are to learn effectively. Some teachers are skeptical when they hear these percentages; they think that experiencing difficulty challenges students and helps them achieve. However, studies indicate that a high success rate is positively related to student achievement.[5]

In the following sections, you will learn about research-based teaching skills that you can use to increase academic learning time and student achievement. Because much time can be frittered away on organizational details and minor student disruptions (see Figure 11.1), we will look first at effective strategies for classroom management. Then we will consider the instructional skills that seem consistently to produce higher academic achievement in students.

Classroom Management

The observer walked to the back of the room and sat down. It seemed to him that the classroom was a beehive of activity. A reading group was in progress in the front of the room, while the other children were working with partners on math examples. The classroom was filled with a hum of children working

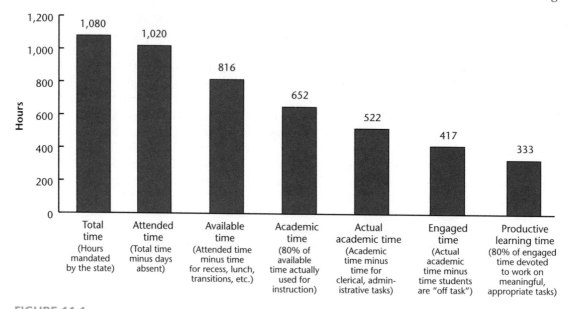

FIGURE 11.1

Estimated time available for academic learning.

SOURCE: Carol Simon Weinstein and Andrew Migano, Jr., *Elementary Classroom Management: Lessons from Research and Practice* 5th ed., New York: McGraw-Hill, 2010.

REFLECTION: Identify three classroom practices that you can implement to recapture productive learning time available to your students.

together, and in several languages—but the activity and the noise were organized and not chaotic.

The observer had been in enough schools over the past 20 years to know that this well-managed classroom did not result from magic, but that carefully established and maintained procedures were at work. The observer scrutinized the classroom, searching for the procedures that allowed 26 students and one teacher to work together so industriously, harmoniously, and effectively.

First he examined the reading group, where the teacher was leading a discussion about the meaning of a story. "Why was Tony worried about the trip he was going to take?" the teacher asked (a few seconds' pause, all the children with eyes on the teacher, several hands raised). "Sean?"

As Sean began his response, the observer's eyes wandered around the rest of the room, where most of the children were busy at work. Two girls, however, were passing notes surreptitiously in the corner of the room.

During a quick sweep of the room, the teacher spotted the misbehavior. The two girls watched the teacher frown and put her finger over her lips. They quickly returned to their work. The exchange had been so rapid and so quiet that the reading group was not interrupted for even a second.

Another student in the math group had his hand raised. The teacher motioned Omar to come to her side.

"Look for the paragraph in your story that tells how Tony felt after his visit to his grandmother," the teacher instructed the reading group. "When you have found it, raise your hands."

While the reading group looked for the appropriate passage, the teacher quietly assisted Omar. In less than a minute, Omar was back at his seat, and the teacher was once again discussing the story with her reading group.

At 10:15, the teacher sent the reading group back to their seats and quietly counted down from ten to one. As she approached one, the room became quiet and the students' attention was focused on her. "It is now time for social studies. Before you do anything, listen carefully to *all* my instructions. When I tap the bell on my desk, those working on math should put their papers in their cubbies for now. You may have a chance to finish them later. Then all students should take out their social studies books and turn to page 67. When you hear the sound of the bell, I want you to follow those instructions." After a second's pause, the teacher tapped the bell, and the class was once again a sea of motion, but it was motion that the teacher had organized while the students were now taking responsibility for their own learning.

The observer made some notes. There was nothing particularly flashy or dramatic about what he had seen. But he was satisfied, because he knew he had been witnessing a well-managed classroom.

Can you remember from your childhood those activity books in which you had to find the five things wrong in a picture? Let us reverse the game: Try rereading this classroom vignette and look for all the things that are *right* with the picture. Underline four or five examples of what the teacher did well.

The teacher in this vignette used several strategies to avoid interruptions and to keep instruction proceeding smoothly and keep students on task.[6] Did you notice that

1. The teacher used a questioning technique known as *group alerting* to keep the reading group involved. By asking questions first and then naming the student to respond, she kept all the students awake and on their toes. If she had said, "Sean, why did Tony feel concerned about his trip?" the other

Focus Question 3
What classroom management skills foster academic achievement?

students in the group would have been less concerned about paying attention and answering the question. Instead, she asked her question first and then called on a student to respond.

2. The teacher seemed to have "eyes in the back of her head." Termed *withitness* by researcher Jacob Kounin, this quality characterizes teachers who are aware of student behavior in all parts of the room at all times. While the teacher was conducting the reading group, she was aware of the students passing notes and the one who needed assistance.

3. The teacher was able to attend to interruptions or behavior problems while continuing the lesson. Kounin calls the ability to do several things at once *overlapping*. The teacher reprimanded the students passing notes and helped another child with a math problem without interrupting the flow of her reading lesson.

4. The teacher managed routine misbehavior using the principle of *least intervention*. Because research shows the time spent disciplining students is negatively related to achievement, teachers should use the simplest intervention that will work. In this case, the teacher intervened quietly and quickly to stop students from passing notes. Her nonverbal cue was all that was necessary, and did not disrupt the students working on math and reading. She could have praised the students who were attending to their math ("I'm glad to see so many partners working well on their math assignments"). If it had been necessary to say more to the girls passing notes, she should have alerted them to what they *should* be doing, rather than emphasize their misbehavior ("Deanne and U-Mei, please attend to your own work," *not* "Deanne and U-Mei, stop passing notes").

5. The teacher managed the transition from one lesson to the next smoothly and effectively, avoiding a bumpy transition, which Kounin termed *fragmentation*. When students must move from one activity to another, a gap is created in the fabric of instruction. Chaos can result when transitions are not handled competently by the instructor. Did you notice that the teacher gave a clear transition signal, either the countdown or the bell; gave thorough instructions so her students would know exactly what to do next; and made the transition all at once for the entire class? These may seem simple, commonsense behaviors, but countless classes have come apart at the seams because transitions were not handled effectively.

Management Models

When done well, classroom management goes unnoticed. When done poorly, it is about the only thing that is noticed. If you teach, you will develop your own style and techniques to manage a classroom. The style you select will reflect much about your own teaching philosophy. Why do you believe students misbehave? Should the focus of management be teacher control or the development of student self-control? Can misbehavior be avoided by exciting lessons and a class that feels a sense of community, or is there an overriding need for a firm set of rules and consequences? What kind of classroom climate can make both teacher and students comfortable?

Teachers disagree on the answers to those questions, and there is no single best strategy for classroom management. You might want to begin thinking

TIMES OF TRANSITION

Teachers must manage more than 30 major transitions every day. During these transitions, discipline problems occur twice as often as in regular classroom instruction. Classroom management expert Jacob Kounin identified five common patterns that can derail classroom management during times of transition:

- *Flip-flops.* In this negative pattern, the teacher terminates one activity, begins a new one, and then flops back to the original activity. For example, in making a transition from math to spelling, the teacher says, "Please open your spelling books to page 29. By the way, how many of you got all the math problems right?"

- *Overdwelling.* This bad habit includes preaching, nagging, and spending more time than necessary to correct an infraction of classroom rules. "Anna, I told you to stop talking. If I've told you once, I've told you 100 times. I told you yesterday and the day before that. The way things are going, I'll be telling it to you all year, and, believe me, I'm getting pretty tired of it. And another thing, young lady . . ."

- *Fragmentation.* In this bumpy transition, the teacher breaks directions into several choppy steps instead of accomplishing the instructions in one fluid unit—for example, "Put away your reading books. You shouldn't have any math books on your desk, either. All notes should be off your desk," instead of the simpler and more effective "Clear your desk of all books and papers."

- *Thrusts.* Classroom momentum is interrupted by *non sequiturs* and random thoughts that just seem to pop into the teacher's head—for example, the class is busily engaged in independent reading when their quiet concentration is broken by the teacher, who says, "Where's Roberto? Wasn't he here earlier this morning?"

- *Dangles.* Similar to the thrust, this move involves starting something, only to leave it hanging or dangling—for example, "Kate, would you please read the first paragraph on page 94. Oh, class, did I tell you about the guest speaker we're having today? How could I have forgotten about that?"

SOURCE: Charles H. Wolfgang, *Solving Discipline and Classroom Management Problems*, (New York: John Wiley & Sons, 2001).

REFLECTION: Because each of the above patterns represents a problem, can you reword the dialogue to produce a more effective transition?

---

about what approach appeals to you; to help you on this journey, we describe briefly several of the best-known models for classroom management. (See Table 11.1.) If any of these models speak to your heart, we invite you to research and read more about it.

Preventing Problems

The approach you choose will require planning, and research underscores that good managers are good planners.[7] They are waiting at the door when the children arrive, rather than entering a room late, after noise and disruption have had a chance to build. Starting from the very first day of school, they teach standards or norms of appropriate student behavior, actively and directly. Often they model procedures for getting assistance, leaving the room, going to the pencil sharpener, and the like. The more important rules of classroom behavior are posted, as are the consequences of not following them.[8]

In traditional teacher-centered schools, rules usually mean obeying the teacher, being quiet, and not misbehaving. When schools move away from autocratic teaching styles, student responsibility and ownership of rules (or as one teacher calls them "Habits of Goodness") are embraced. Some teachers like to develop the list of rules together with their students; other teachers prefer to present a list of established practices and ask students to give specific examples or to provide reasons for having such rules. The bottom line:

when rules are easily understood and convey a sense of moral fairness, most students will comply. We can create a productive learning community when rules are (1) few in number, (2) fair and reasonable, and (3) appropriate for student maturation.

TABLE 11.1 Models of Classroom Management

SOURCE: Carol M. Charles, *Building Classroom Discipline* (Upper Saddler River, N.J. Prentice Hall, 2010).

Advocate	Main Focus	Belief System
Lee and Marlene Canter	Assertive Discipline	Students deserve a safe and productive learning climate, and it is the teacher's job to provide it. Each student is taught how to behave responsibly through clear rules and consequences. When expectations are not met, students know that the teacher will mete out consequences.
Richard Curwin and Allen Mendler	Discipline with Dignity	Students should always be treated with dignity, even when they misbehave. Interesting learning activities, positive reinforcement, and opportunities for student success keep students on track, especially students with a history of misbehavior.
Barbara Coloroso	Developing Inner Control and Discipline	Students need to take responsibility for their actions to develop their inner discipline. If students are messy, they need to learn to clean up after themselves. If they are too noisy, they need to develop strategies to allow others to do their work.
Rudolf Dreikurs	Collaborative Decision Making and Belonging	The key in this approach is to identify the motivation behind misbehavior and, within a classroom community, to help students redirect their behavior in a positive way.
Haim Ginott	Communications	You speak to students as you, the teacher, would want to be spoken to. Model desirable behaviors and maintain your calm as a teacher. Focus on what needs to be done rather than on what was done wrong.
William Glasser	Student Satisfaction	The teacher meets with the class to discuss not only behavior rules but also the curriculum being taught. The teacher plans meaningful work for the students and holds them to high standards. Students feel a part of the school, possessing a sense of fun, power, and independence.
Thomas Gordon	Discipline as Control	Students are involved in making the rules about classroom life and procedures, and problem owners are identified—that is, those who are bothered by certain behaviors. The class as a group works to resolve those issues.
Jacob Kounin	Engagement and Supervision	Student misbehavior is reduced by engaging lessons, and the teacher's watchful monitoring skills keep students on track.
Fritz Redl and William Wattenberg	Group Dynamics	Group dynamics, insights, and peer influence are used to control misbehavior. The causes of any misbehavior are diagnosed, and appropriate consequences are applied.
B. F. Skinner	Behavior Modification	Desired behaviors are encouraged by immediately awarding positive reinforcement. Undesirable behaviors are ignored.

REFLECTION: Are there elements even in these brief descriptions that you find appealing? What are they, and what do they teach you about your own teaching philosophy?

Even the best rules need to be tied to consequences or the class can quickly deteriorate into chaos. Each consequence needs to be thoughtfully considered. A weak consequence might encourage rather than discourage a behavior, and a too-tough consequence might reflect an angry teacher's overreaction. Unfair consequences alienate a class and earn a teacher the reputation of being unfair. Never doubt the ability of students to detect injustices. Teachers rarely notice that they tend to penalize boys more harshly than girls for the same misbehavior. Students pick that up quickly. Subtle gender and race favoritism is alive and well in today's classrooms. Many teachers find it helpful to post a description of class rules and consequences, and to send

Good classroom management requires constant monitoring of student behavior.

that list home to parents to forge a consistent home–school partnership on appropriate behavior.

Now is a good time to consider a question too few ask: Is the purpose of consequences to punish inappropriate behavior? More and more educators believe that we should move beyond punishment and use consequences to solve behavior issues.[9] For example, let's say a student, we'll call him Jimmy, is not paying attention in class. (We know, this is a highly improbable situation in your class, but let's just pretend for the moment.) Rather than the teacher imposing a punitive consequence (reprimand, time-out, no recess, detention, call to parents, etc.), the teacher can invite the class to brainstorm useful suggestions to help Jimmy stay on task. For example, Jimmy's desk could be moved closer to the teacher's desk, discouraging off-task behaviors. Jimmy could be paired with a student who can model on-task behavior, perhaps even work with Jimmy sharing ways to stay on task. Students might suggest something as obvious as a vision or hearing exam to make certain Jimmy is getting the instructions. If we had a real class of students brainstorming constructive interventions right now, they could offer us many other potential solutions to help Jimmy. The point to remember is that consequences can be constructive rather than negative.

Good managers also carefully arrange their classrooms to minimize disturbances, provide students with a sense of confidence and security, and make sure that instruction can proceed efficiently. They set up their rooms according to the following principles:

- *Teaching eye to eye.* Teachers should be able to see all students at all times. Research shows that students who are seated far away from the teacher or the instructional activity are less likely to be involved in class discussions. As teachers intentionally move about the room, they can short-circuit off-task student behavior. Placing instructional materials (video monitor, overhead projector, demonstration activity, flip chart, lab station, and the like) in various parts of the room also gives each student "the best seat in the house" for at least part of the teaching day.

- *Teaching materials and supplies should be readily available.* Arranging a "self-help" area so that students have direct access to supplies encourages

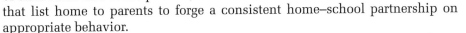

individual responsibility while freeing up the teacher to focus on instructional activities.

- *High-traffic areas should be free of congestion.* Place student desks away from supply cabinets, pencil sharpeners, and so on. Minor disturbances ripple out, distracting other students from their tasks.

- *Procedures and routines should be actively taught in the same way that academic content is taught.* Initial planning for classroom management is often rewarded with fewer discipline problems and smooth transitions to classroom routines and procedures.[10] For students who come from chaotic home environments, these routines offer a sense of stability. Once established, they allow teachers and all students more time for academic learning.

A child's misbehavior—from minor classroom disruptions to emotional outbursts to violence—is often rooted in trauma, feelings of powerlessness, or even "normal" daily events beyond a teacher's control. Yet, teachers must understand and manage student anger and aggression. Several classroom strategies can help:

- *Choice.* Constantly taking away privileges and threatening punishment can cause students to feel intimidated and victimized. Teachers can provide appropriate options to give a student a sense of some control and freedom. Encouraging a student to select a lunch mate or to choose a project topic offers a reasonable decision-making opportunity and can help avoid minor disruptions as well as aggressive acts.

- *Responsibility.* Rechanneling student energy and interest into constructive activities and responsibilities can reduce misbehavior. When instruction is meaningful and worthwhile, boredom and fooling around are less likely to occur.[11] When students are empowered, they are less likely to act out.

- *Voice.* Listening to young people is one of the most respectful skills a teacher can model. Students who feel they are not heard feel disrespected. Hearing and honoring students' words (and feelings) reduce the likelihood of misbehavior.[12]

Listening to students was exactly what Kathleen Cushman did when she wrote *Fires in the Mind.* Adolescents from around the nation were asked to tell teachers what they would like to see in their classrooms. Students advised teachers to: share your plans with me and tell me how I will be evaluated, be excited about what you teach, be firm when rules are broken, treat me fairly but remember I am an individual, give me feedback and encouragement, don't say "please" too much, and don't push yourself into my personal life.[13]

Although we can't always detect the signs of danger, we can be on the lookout and can create management plans to handle small distractions as well as major incidents. As researcher David Berliner says, "In short, from the opening bell to the end of the day, the better classroom managers are thinking ahead. While maintaining a pleasant classroom atmosphere, these teachers keep planning how to organize, manage, and control activities to facilitate instruction."[14] Berliner makes an important connection between management and instruction. Effective teachers, in addition to being good classroom managers, must also be good organizers of academic content and instruction.

The Pedagogical Cycle

How does one organize classroom life? Researcher *Arno Bellack* analyzed verbal exchanges between teachers and students and offers a fascinating insight into classroom organization, likening these interactions to a pedagogical game.[15] The game is so cyclical and occurs so frequently that many teachers and students do not even know that they are playing. There are four moves:

1. *Structure.* The teacher provides information, provides direction, and introduces the topics.
2. *Question.* The teacher asks a question.
3. *Respond.* The student answers the question, or tries to.
4. *React.* The teacher reacts to the student's answer and provides feedback.

These four steps make up a **pedagogical cycle,** diagrammed in Figure 11.2. Teachers initiate about 85 percent of the cycles, which are used over and over again in classroom interaction. When teachers learn to consciously enhance and refine each of the cycle's moves, student achievement is increased.[16]

Clarity and Academic Structure

Have you ever been to a class where the teacher is bombarded with questions? "What are we supposed to do?" "Can you explain it again?" "What do you mean?" When such questions are constant, it is a sure sign that the teacher is not setting the stage for instruction. Students need a clear understanding of what they are expected to learn, and they need motivation to learn it.[17] Effective *academic structure* sets the stage for learning and occurs mainly at the beginning of the lesson. Although the specific structure will vary depending on the students' backgrounds and the difficulty of the subject matter, an effective academic structure usually consists of the following:[18]

- *Objectives.* Let the students know the objectives (or purpose) of each lesson. Students, like the teacher, need a road map of where they are going and why.

- *Review.* Help students review prior learning before presenting new information. If there is confusion, reteach.

- *Motivation.* Create an "anticipatory set" that motivates students to attend to the lesson. Consider throwing out an intriguing question, an anecdote, a joke, or a challenging riddle.

- *Transition.* Provide connections to help students integrate old and new information.

- *Clarification.* Break down a large body of information. (This is sometimes

Focus Question 4
What are the roles of teachers and students in the pedagogical cycle?

www.mhhe.com/
sadkerbrief3e
INTERACTIVE ACTIVITY
Pedagogical Cycle Identify the moves in a sample classroom dialogue.

Focus Question 5
How can teachers set a stage for learning?

FIGURE 11.2
Pedagogical cycle and sample classroom dialogue.

REFLECTION: Continue the classroom dialogue around the cycle again. What might the teacher and the student(s) say?

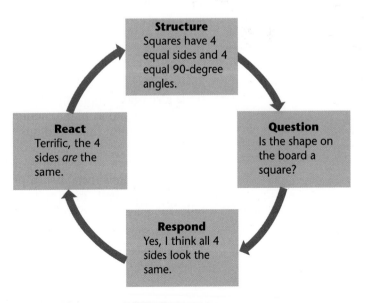

Structure
Squares have 4 equal sides and 4 equal 90-degree angles.

Question
Is the shape on the board a square?

Respond
Yes, I think all 4 sides look the same.

React
Terrific, the 4 sides *are* the same.

called "chunking.") Do not inundate students with too much too fast. This is particularly true for young children, English language learners, and slower learners.

- *Scaffolding.* Step-by-step practice and well-crafted questions support and encourage student understanding.
- *Examples.* Give several examples and illustrations to explain main points and ideas.
- *Directions.* Give directions distinctly and slowly. If students are confused about what they are supposed to do, repeat or break information into small segments.
- *Enthusiasm.* Demonstrate personal enthusiasm for the academic content. Make it clear why the information is interesting and important.
- *Closure.* Close the lesson with a brief review or summary. If students are able to provide the summary, so much the better, for it shows that they have really understood the lesson.

Through effective and clear structure, the stage is set for the remaining steps of the pedagogical cycle.

Questioning

Focus Question 6
What questioning strategies increase student achievement?

www.mhhe.com/
sadkerbrief3e

INTERACTIVE ACTIVITY
Questioning Levels
Match questions to the different questioning levels.

Good questioning is at the very core of good teaching. As John Dewey said,

> To question well is to teach well. In the skillful use of the question more than anything else lies the fine art of teaching; for in it we have the guide to clear and vivid ideas, and the quick spur to imagination, the stimulus to thought, the incentive to action.[19]

Because questioning is key in guiding learning, all students should have equal access to classroom questions and academic interaction. Yet sitting in the same classroom taught by the same teacher, students experience significant differences in the number of questions they are asked. Research shows that male students are asked more questions than female students, and white students are asked more questions than nonwhite students. One of the reasons boys get to answer questions as well as to talk more is that they are assertive in grabbing teacher attention. Boys are more likely than girls to call out the answers to the questions. In addition, when boys call out the answers to questions, teachers are likely to accept their responses. When girls call out the answers, teachers often remind them to raise their hands. Teacher expectations also play a role and are frequently cited as one of the reasons white students (perceived as higher achievers) receive more questions and more active teacher attention than students who are members of other racial and ethnic groups.[20]

If you want all students, not just the quickest and most assertive, to answer questions, establish a protocol for participation. For example, make a rule that students must raise their hands and be called on before they may talk. Too many classes offer variations of the following scene:

TEACHER: How much is 60 + 4 + 12? *(Many students raise their hands—both girls and boys.)*

TONY: *(Shouts out)* 76!

TEACHER: Okay. How much is 50 + 9 + 8?

This scene, repeated again and again in classes across the country, is a typical example of the squeaky wheel—not necessarily the most needy or most deserving student—getting the educational oil. Once you make the rule that students should raise their hands before participating, *hold to that rule.*

Many teachers are well-intentioned about having students raise their hands, but, in the rapid pace of classroom interaction, they sometimes forget their own rule. If you hold to that "wait to be recognized" rule, you can make professional decisions about who should answer which questions and why. If you give away this key to classroom participation, you are abandoning an important part of your professional decision making in the classroom.

There is more to managing classroom questions than taking the role of a traffic cop. For instance, you might assign pairs of students to work together (sometimes called "Think-Pair-Share") to develop and record answers and then present them to the class as a whole. Or perhaps teams of four or five students can be established to tackle academic questions on a regular basis. When students are actively involved in either of these approaches, the teacher can move around the room as a facilitator, answering questions, motivating student groups, and assessing how the groups are doing. More important, the students take ownership of the questions, asking sincere questions reflecting their genuine interests.

While the distribution and ownership of questions are important, the type of question asked is also meaningful. Many educators differentiate between factual, lower-order questions and thought-provoking, higher-order questions. Perhaps the most widely used system for determining the intellectual level of questions is Benjamin **Bloom's taxonomy,** which proceeds from the lowest level of questions, knowledge, to the highest levels, evaluation and creation.[21]

A **lower-order question** can be answered through memory and recall. For example, "What is the name of the largest Native American nation?" is a lower-order question. Without consulting outside references, one could respond with the correct answer only by remembering previously learned information. (Cherokee is the answer.) Students either know the answer or they don't. Research indicates that 70 to 95 percent of a teacher's questions are lower-order.

A **higher-order question** demands more thought and usually more time before students reach a response. These questions may ask for evaluations, comparisons, causal relationships, problem solving, or divergent, open-ended thinking. Following are examples of higher-order questions:

1. Do you think that William Clinton was an effective president? Why or why not?

2. What similarities in theme emerge in the three Coen movies: *True Grit, Fargo,* and *No Country for Old Men?*

3. Create your own pledge of allegiance to a cause or organization.

4. What could happen if our shadows came to life?

www.mhhe.com/
sadkerbrief3e

INTERACTIVE ACTIVITY
The Question Master
Game Test your knowledge
of Bloom's taxonomy.

BLOOM'S TAXONOMY APPLIED TO QUESTIONING LEVELS

LEVEL I: KNOWLEDGE

Requires student to recall or recognize information. Student must rely on memory or senses to provide the answer.

SAMPLE QUESTIONS

What does "quixotic" mean?

List the first 10 presidents of the United States.

LEVEL II: COMPREHENSION

Requires student to go beyond simple recall and demonstrate the ability to mentally arrange and organize information. Student must use previously learned information by putting it in his or her own words and rephrasing it.

SAMPLE QUESTION

In our story, the author discusses why the family left Oklahoma. Can you summarize why in your own words?

LEVEL III: APPLICATION

Requires student to apply previously learned information to answer a problem. At this level the student uses a rule, a definition, a classification system, or directions in solving a problem with specific correct 'answer.

SAMPLE QUESTIONS

Identify the proper noun in the following sentences. *(applying a definition)*

Solve the quadratic equation. *(applying a rule)*

LEVEL IV: ANALYSIS

Requires student to use three kinds of cognitive processes: (1) To identify causes, reasons, or motives (when these have not been provided to the student previously), (2) To analyze information to reach a generalization or conclusion, (3) To find evidence to support a specific opinion, event, or situation.

SAMPLE QUESTIONS

Why do you think King Lear misjudged his daughter? *(identifying motives)*

What generalizations can you make about the climate of Egypt near the Nile River basin? *(analyzing information to reach a conclusion)*

Many historians think that Abraham Lincoln was our finest president. What evidence can you find to support this statement? *(finding evidence to support a specific opinion)*

LEVEL V OR VI: SYNTHESIS/CREATION*

Requires student to use original and creative thinking: (1) To develop original communications, (2) To make predictions, and (3) To solve problems for which there is no single right answer.

SAMPLE QUESTIONS

Write a short story about life on another planet. *(developing an original communication)*

What do you think life would be like if Germany had won World War II? *(making predictions)*

How can our class raise money for the dance festival? *(solving problems for which there is no single right solution)*

LEVEL VI OR V: EVALUATION*

Requires student to judge the merits of an aesthetic work, an idea, or the solution to a problem.

SAMPLE QUESTION

Do you think that schools are too hard or not hard enough? Explain your answer.

REFLECTION: *Some educators have recently revised Bloom's original taxonomy, putting "creation" as the highest level. They believe that creating is a more demanding intellectual activity than evaluating. What do you think?

Although higher-order questions have been shown to produce increased student achievement, most teachers ask very few of them.[22]

Many educators think that different questioning levels stimulate different levels of thought. If you ask a fifth-grade student to define an adjective, you are working on lower-level basic skills. If you ask a fifth-grade student to write a short story, making effective use of adjectives, you are working on a higher level of student achievement. Both lower-order and higher-order questions are important and should be matched to appropriate instructional goals:

Ask lower-order questions when students are

- Being introduced to new information
- Working on drill and practice
- Reviewing previously learned information

Ask higher-order questions when students are

- Working on problem-solving skills
- Involved in a creative or affective discussion
- Asked to make judgments about quality, aesthetics, or ethics
- Challenged to manipulate already established information in more sophisticated ways

Student Response

If you were to spend a few minutes in a high school English class, you might hear a classroom discussion go something like this:

> TEACHER: Who wrote the poem "Stopping by Woods on a Snowy Evening"? Tomàs?
>
> TOMÀS: Robert Frost.
>
> TEACHER: Good. What action takes place in the poem? Kenisha?
>
> KENISHA: A man stops his sleigh to watch the woods get filled with snow.
>
> TEACHER: Yes. Michael, what thoughts go through the man's mind?
>
> MICHAEL: He thinks how beautiful the woods are, and how he would like to stay and watch. *(Pauses for a second)*
>
> TEACHER: Yes—and what else? Rita? *(Waits half a second))* Well, why does he feel he can't stay there indefinitely and watch the woods and the snow?
>
> RITA: He's got too many things to do to stay there for so long.
>
> TEACHER: Good. In the poem's last line, the man says that he has miles to go before he sleeps. What might sleep be a symbol for? Krista?
>
> KRISTA: Well, I think it might be . . . *(Pauses for a second)*
>
> TEACHER: Think, Krista. *(Waits for half a second)* All right then— Eugene? *(Waits again for half a second)* Dustin? *(Waits half a second)* What's the matter with everyone today? Didn't you do the reading?[23]

The teacher is using several instructional skills effectively. His is a well-managed classroom. The students are on task and engaged in a discussion appropriate to the academic content. By asking a series of lower-order questions ("Who wrote the poem?" "What action takes place in the poem?"), the teacher works with the students to establish an information base. Then the teacher builds to higher-order questions about the poem's theme and meaning.

If you were to give this teacher suggestions on how to improve his questioning techniques, you might point out the difficulty students have in answering the more complex questions. You might also note the lightning pace at which this lesson proceeds. The teacher fires questions so rapidly that the students barely have time to think. This is not so troublesome when they are answering factual questions that require a brief memorized response. However, students begin to flounder when they are required to answer more complex questions with equal speed.

Although it is important to keep classroom discussion moving at a brisk pace, sometimes teachers push forward too rapidly. Slowing down at two key places during classroom discussion can usually improve the effectiveness and equity of classroom responses. In the research on classroom interaction, this slowing down is called **wait time.**[24]

Mary Budd Rowe's research on wait time shows that, after asking a question, teachers typically wait only one second or less for a student response (wait time 1). If the response is not forthcoming in that time, teachers rephrase the question, ask another student to answer it, or answer it themselves. If teachers can learn to increase their wait time from one second to three to five seconds, significant improvements in the quantity and quality of student response usually take place.

There is another point in classroom discussion when wait time can be increased. After students complete an answer, teachers often begin their reaction or their next question before a second has passed (wait time 2). Again, it is important for teachers to increase their wait time from one second to three to five seconds. Based on her research, Mary Budd Rowe has determined that increasing the pause after a student gives an answer is equally as important as increasing wait time 1, the pause after the teacher asks a question. When wait time 1 and wait time 2 are increased, classroom interaction is changed in several positive ways.

Changes in Student Behavior

- More students participate in discussion.
- Fewer discipline problems disrupt the class.
- The length of student response increases dramatically.
- Students are more likely to support their statements with evidence.
- Speculative thinking increases.
- There are more student questions and fewer failures to respond.
- Student achievement increases on written tests that measure more complex levels of thinking.

Changes in Teacher Behavior

- Teacher comments are less disjointed and more fluent. Classroom discussion becomes more logical, thoughtful, and coherent.
- Teachers ask more sophisticated, higher-order questions.
- Teachers begin to hold higher expectations for all students.

Research indicates that teachers give more wait time to students for whom they hold higher expectations. A high-achieving student is more likely to get time to think than is a low-achieving student. If we do not expect much from our students, we will not get much. High expectations and longer wait times are positively related to achievement. Researchers suggest that white male students, particularly high achievers, are more likely to be given adequate wait time than are females, English language learners, quiet students, and students of color. Students who are quiet and reserved or who think more slowly may obtain special benefit from increased wait time. In fact, a key benefit of extended wait time is an increase in the quality of student participation, even from students who were previously silent.

Usually when teachers learn that they are giving students less than a second to think, they are surprised and have every intention of waiting longer, but that is easier said than done! In the hectic arena of the classroom, it is all too easy to slip into split-second question-and-answer patterns.

Teachers can adopt self-monitoring cues to slow themselves down at the two key wait-time points. For example, one teacher says that he puts his hand behind his back and counts on his fingers for three seconds to slow himself down. Another teacher says that she covers her mouth with her hand (in a thoughtful pose) to keep herself from talking and thereby destroying "the pause that lets them think."

As mentioned previously, wait time is more important in some cases than in others. If you are asking students to repeat previously memorized math facts and you are interested in developing speed, a three- to five-second wait time may be counterproductive. However, if you have asked a higher-order question that calls for a complicated answer, be sure that wait times 1 and 2 are ample. Simply put, students, like the rest of us, need time to think, and some students may need more wait time than others. For example, when a student speaks English as a newly acquired language, additional wait time could help that student accurately translate and respond to the question. And many of us could profit by less impulsive, more thoughtful responses, the kind that can be engendered by a five-second wait time.

When teachers allow more wait time, the results can be surprising. As one teacher told us, "I never thought Andrea had anything to say. She just used to sit there like a bump on a log. Then I tried calling on her and giving her time to answer. What a difference! Not only does she answer, she asks questions that no one else has thought of."

Reaction or Productive Feedback

"Today," the student teacher said, "we are going to hear the story of *The Three Billy Goats Gruff*." A murmur of anticipation rippled through the kindergarten children comfortably seated on the carpet around the flannel board. This student teacher was a favorite, and the children were particularly happy when she told them flannel-board stories.

"Before we begin the story, I want to make sure we know what all the words mean. Who can tell me what a troll is?"

A 5-year-old nicknamed B.J. raised his hand. "A troll is someone who walks you home from school."

"Okay," the teacher responded, a slightly puzzled look flickering over her face. "Who else can tell me what a troll is?"

Another student chimed in, "A troll is someone with white hair sticking out of his head."

"Okay," the teacher said.

Another student volunteered, "It hides under bridges and waits for you and scares you."

"Uh-huh," said the teacher.

Warming to the topic, another student gleefully recounted, "I saw a green troll named Shrek who lives in the woods."

"Okay," the teacher said.

Wide-eyed, B.J. raised his hand again, "I'm sure glad we had this talk about trolls," he said. "I'm not going home with them from school anymore."

"Okay," the teacher said.

This is a classroom in which several good teaching strategies are in operation. The teacher uses effective academic structure, and the students are on task, interested, and involved in the learning activity. The teacher is asking lower-order questions appropriately, to make sure the students know key vocabulary words before the flannel-board story is told. The problem with this classroom lies in the fourth stage of the pedagogical cycle: This teacher does not provide specific reactions and adequate feedback. Did you notice that the teacher reacted with "uh-huh" or "OK," no matter what kind of answer the students gave? Because of this vague feedback and "OK" teaching style, B.J. was left confused about the difference between a troll and a patrol. This real-life incident may seem amusing, but there was nothing funny to B.J., who was genuinely afraid to leave school with the patrol.

Researchers have looked at not only at how teachers ask questions but also at how they respond to student answers. When Myra and David Sadker analyzed classroom interaction in more than 100 classrooms in five states, they found that teachers generally use four types of reactions:

1. *Praise.* Positive comments about student work, such as "Excellent, good job."

2. *Acceptance.* Comments such as "Uh-huh" and "OK," which acknowledge that student answers are acceptable. These are not as strong as praise.

3. *Remediation.* Comments that encourage a more accurate student response or encourage students to think more clearly, creatively, or logically. Sample remediation comments include "Try again," "Sharpen your answer," and "Check your addition."

4. *Criticism.* A clear statement that an answer is inaccurate or a behavior is inappropriate. This category includes harsh criticism ("This is a terrible paper"), as well as milder comments that simply indicate an answer is not correct ("Your answer to the third question is wrong.")[25]

Which of these reactions do you think teachers use most frequently? Did you notice that the kindergarten teacher relied heavily on the acceptance, or "okay," reaction? The Sadkers' study found that from elementary through graduate school, acceptance is the most frequent response, accounting for more than half of all teacher reactions. The second most frequent teacher response was remediation, accounting for one-third of teacher reactions. Used infrequently, praise comprised only 11 percent of reactions. The rarest response was criticism. In two-thirds of the classrooms observed, teachers never told a student that an answer was incorrect. In the classrooms where criticism did occur, it accounted for only 5 percent of interaction (see Figure 11.3).

In *A Place Called School,* John Goodlad writes that "learning is enhanced when students understand what is expected of them, get recognition for their work, learn about their errors, and receive guidance in improving their performances."[26] But many students claim that they are not informed or corrected when they make mistakes.[27] Perhaps this is caused by overreliance on the acceptance response, which is the vaguest kind of feedback that teachers can offer. Since there is more acceptance than praise, criticism, and remediation combined, some educators are beginning to wonder: "Is the 'OK' classroom OK?"

Because achievement is likely to increase when students get clear, specific, productive feedback about their answers, it is important for teachers to reduce the "OK" reaction and to be more varied and specific in the feedback they provide. Researcher Jere Brophy has done an analysis of praise and student achievement. He found that praise may be particularly important for low-achieving students and those from low socioeconomic backgrounds. Brophy found that it is best when

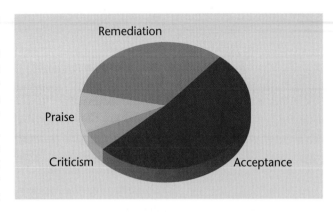

FIGURE 11.3
Teacher reactions.

REFLECTION: Most teacher reactions fall in the acceptance category. Suggest three reasons why this might occur.

1. *Praise is contingent upon student performance.* Praise should closely follow student behavior the teacher wants to recognize.

2. *Praise is specific.* When teachers praise, they should clearly indicate what aspect of the student behavior is noteworthy (for instance, creative problem solving or good use of evidence to support an argument).

3. *Praise is sincere.* Praise should reflect the experiences, growth, and development of the individual student. Otherwise, it may be dismissed as being disingenuous.

4. *Praise lets students know about their competence and the importance of their accomplishments*—for instance, "The well-documented review of studies on your website and the connection you made between the two tobacco filters may eventually impact the industry."

5. *Praise attributes success to ability or effort*—for example, "Your analysis of the paintings of the Impressionists is excellent. I'll bet you spent a long time studying their work in the museum" *(attribution to effort).* Or "This story is fantastic. You've got a real flair for creative writing" *(attribution to ability).* When praise is attributed to abilities or effort, students know that successful performance is under their own control.

6. *Praise uses past performance as a context for describing present performance*—for example, "Last week you were really having trouble with your breast stroke kick. Now you've got it together—you've learned to push the water behind you and increase your speed."[28]

Just as students need to know when they are performing well, they need to know when their efforts are inadequate or incorrect. If students do not have information about their weak areas, they will find it difficult to improve. Here are some types of effective feedback.

1. *Constructive feedback is specific and contingent on student performance.* The teacher's comments should closely follow the student behavior the teacher wants to improve.

2. *Critical comments focus on student performance and are not of a personal nature.* All of us find it easier to accept constructive criticism when it is detached from our worth as a person, when it is not personal, hostile, or sarcastic.

3. *Feedback provides a clear blueprint for improvement.* If you merely tell a student that an answer is wrong and nothing more, the student has clear feedback on level of performance but no strategies for improvement. Effective feedback suggests an approach for attaining success, such as "Check your addition," "Use the bold headings as a reading guide when you study for the exams," or "Let's conjugate this verb in both French and English to see where the error is."

4. *An environment is established that lets the student know it is acceptable to make mistakes.* "We learn from our errors. Hardly any inventions are perfected on the first try."

5. *Constructive feedback relates eventual success to effort.* "Now you have demonstrated the correct sequence in class. Give yourself a solid half-hour tonight working on this, and I bet that you will get most of it correct. I'll check with you tomorrow."

6. *Constructive feedback recognizes when students have made improvements in their performance.* "Last week you were having trouble identifying which of Newton's Laws are applicable in each of these time-motion studies. Now you've mastered the skill. You've done a good job."

An "okay classroom" allows student error and misunderstanding to go uncorrected; it lets B.J. think that the patrol will eat him up after school. In classrooms where there is appropriate use of remediation and constructive criticism, students know not only when they have made mistakes but also how to correct them. They also recognize that this process leads to growth and achievement.

Variety in Process and Content

Focus Question 7
How can teachers best tap into different student learning styles?

www.mhhe.com/
sadkerbrief3e

INTERACTIVE ACTIVITY
Create a Course Schedule
What do you think your students' week should consist of?

Variety is the spice of life, the saying goes—the spice of lessons also, because variety can enhance both teaching effectiveness and student achievement. Have you ever listened to a lecture for an hour and found your initial interest lapsing into daydreams? Have you ever watched a class begin a seat-work assignment with active concentration and found, after 30 minutes, that involvement had turned into passing notes and throwing paper airplanes? Students learn more when joy and excitement are part of classroom life (but we bet you knew that).[29]

As any savvy teacher knows, student interest can be maintained by moving from one activity to another during a single lesson. For example, a 60-minute lesson on the American Revolution might begin with a 10-minute overview providing the structure for the class, then move into a 15-minute question-and-answer session, then change to a 25-minute video, and conclude with a 10-minute discussion and closure. Another motivation to vary content and process in teaching is to accommodate different student learning styles. Some students might miss what is said in a lecture (not being auditory learners), but easily get it when the teacher shows pictures (because the visual connection is clear). Howard Gardner's growing inventory of intelligences offers another strong argument for instructional variety. (See Chapter 2 for a detailed discussion of multiple intelligences) Following is a sampler of activities teachers can use to maintain student interest by varying the pattern of the lesson.

discussions	tests	tutoring
lectures	silent reading	spot quizzes
films, videos, DVDs, PowerPoint	games	computer work
	contests	panel discussions
role plays	creative writing	brainstorming sessions
simulations	theater and drama	students tutoring one another
small-group activities	field trips	
guest speakers	boardwork	cooperative learning activities
independent seatwork	learning centers	
guided practice	music activities	debates
student presentations	art activities	

Many of these activities can be described as "hands-on" or active learning and can be captivating for students, but more is needed. Variety alone will not produce achievement: Connections with content must be made, or variety will be reduced to mere activity. Teachers must consider individual students and tailor activities based on their interests, learning styles, and abilities. This is no easy task. Consider an elementary student happily pasting animal pictures on charts, yet unable to explain what (if anything) he is learning about animal families. Students in a middle school may be dressing up for an evening on the Titanic, and from the lower to the upper decks, their clothing and accents reflect different social classes. Yet, if students have not connected their dress with social class and deck classifications, then they may miss learning about the relationship between social class and survival rate. Challenging students with engaging activities is admirable, but the effort must clearly connect the activity to both the content and the student.[30]

Technology as a Tool for Effective Teaching

Today's technology transports students around the world via virtual field trips, provides individualized tutorials and drill-and-practice of certain skills, and instantly and inexpensively adds millions of pages of new content to a teacher's curriculum. Many believe that technology will profoundly reshape education; currently, 40 states and the District of Columbia require formal teacher training in technology.[31] Educators today use technology to[32]

- *Motivate students* through the use and student creation of multimedia materials that capture their interest.
- *Increase basic skills* in math, reading, and writing, as well as content areas, through sample quizzes, drill-and-practice, and additional course-related information. This becomes particularly attractive in this time of standardized testing.

Focus Question 8
How can teachers use technology to support effective instruction?

Computers can be used for basic skills or for more demanding and creative activities.

- *Promote higher-order thinking and increased content understanding* by introducing simulations, modeling, problem-based learning, Internet research, collaborative work, and student authoring programs.
- *Increase academic resources* by bringing the unlimited written and multi-media assets of the Internet into local schools.
- *Increase responsiveness to different learning styles,* including children with special needs or students for whom the typical classroom culture means academic and/or social distress.
- *Improve workplace preparation* as students learn keyboarding, software, online learning, increased global awareness, and technological operations common to future employment.
- *Save work for teachers* by creating a class website. Homework assignments, worksheets, notes, and exam dates can be posted on the Web, and parent communication can be accomplished through text and e-mail. In fact, grading software can track attendance, average grades, and chart the results while even more cutting-edge programs use artificial intelligence, such as the Intelligent Essay Assessor (IEA), to grade essays.
- *Strengthen student learning* by adding resources, such as a presentation or a video clip, to create more dramatic and effective teacher instruction.
- *Make testing easier for teachers* by using computer applications that create and grade tests and maintain student records.
- *Modernize the school culture* by reshaping American education for the twenty-first century, moving beyond pencil and paper, whiteboards and overhead projectors to the world's digital resources.

Doesn't all this sound exciting? We Americans love our technology, and cool computers are high on our gadget love list. Unfortunately, in all this tech-glitz, student learning can get lost. Software developer and educator George Brackett reminds us, "Thoughtful, caring, capable people change schools, sometimes with the help of technology, sometimes not, and sometimes even despite it. Too often we focus on the technology rather than the reform."[33] Technology should be seen as a teacher's tool, and not the other way around. The first step is deciding how best to use that tool to enhance student learning.

Models for Effective Instruction

Focus Question 9
What are several salient models of instruction?

Part of the challenge for teachers is knowing which model of instruction to choose for particular educational purposes. The following four models differ dramatically from one another, yet each may find a productive use in your classroom.

Direct Teaching

Also called *systematic, active,* or *explicit teaching,* the **direct teaching** model emphasizes the importance of a structured lesson in which presentation of new information is followed by student practice and teacher feedback. In this model, which has emerged from extensive research, the role of the teacher is that of a strong leader, one who structures the classroom and sequences subject matter to reflect a clear academic focus.

Technology—Educational Marvel or Menace?

TECHNOLOGY IS A *MARVEL* BECAUSE IT. . .

TEACHES MORE EFFECTIVELY

With technology we can individualize instruction, grant students autonomy, and empower students to learn at their own pace, rather than wait for the teacher's personal attention. Each learner benefits from having an omnipresent tutor to individually tailor schoolwork, and the focus is on effective learning more than effective teaching.

REACHES MORE STUDENTS

Computers, the Internet, smart phones, and the like expand the educational horizons of children not only in isolated rural communities but also for children with limited resources, or who are homebound because of disability or illness. Even students who are fearful of going to school because of bullying or violence can use technology for distance learning.

OFFERS STUDENTS A WEALTH OF RESOURCES

Through technology, students have so much more than a school or local library, for they can use technology to tap into resources around the world. Students now can access limitless books, articles, pictures, sound clips, and newspapers; follow links to experts or virtual field trips; and participate in real-time communications across the globe.

PREPARES STUDENTS FOR THE FUTURE

Technology encourages interdisciplinary and collaborative efforts, facilitates problem-based learning, and encourages student creativity, the skills many believe will be in high demand in the future economy. Students at ease with technology will be assets to future employers.

TECHNOLOGY IS A *MENACE* BECAUSE. . .

EFFECTIVE TEACHING IS COMPROMISED

Technology often competes with teachers. Too many students become distracted from academic pursuits by cell phones, computers, and iPods. Even in school, students may be sidetracked by technology, texting in class (and even during exams!). When this happens, focus is lost and even the most effective teachers are compromised.

IT MAY LEAVE EVEN MORE STUDENTS OUT OF THE LOOP

Technology does not equalize many disparities, and in some cases amplifies economic inequalities. Children from families with means and resources, children with high-tech homes attending well-resourced schools have technological advantages not available to poorer students. Poor students and poor schools may be left even further behind in the technology revolution.

STUDENTS ARE FLOODED WITH MISINFORMATION

Too many of today's youngsters can surf the Internet but are unable to sort truth from fiction. The Internet is home to countless narrow-interest groups that promote political and other causes by disseminating misinformation. While some books and periodicals might have done this in the past, technology has made all kinds of misinformation accessible to children who are ill-equipped to sort fact from fiction.

WE MAY BE BUILDING A NOT-SO-WONDERFUL FUTURE

Americans may be too enthralled by new technology. Computer use is associated with increased eyestrain, repetitive motion injury, and the obesity that comes from a more sedentary life style. What are the other dangers lurk in a more technological world?

www.mhhe.com/sadkerbrief3e **YOU DECIDE . . .**

Do you believe that computers are an educational marvel or menace? In what ways has your education been enriched—or diminished—by technology?

PROFILE IN EDUCATION

Larry Cuban

Having assumed various roles in education over the past 50 years—from classroom teacher to professor to superintendent—Larry Cuban has had a first-hand view of how education has changed. Interestingly, he argues that, save for some minor reforms, it has not. To read a full profile of Larry Cuban and how he has viewed teaching to be relatively unchanged over the past five decades, go to the Chapter 11 Profile in Education at www.mhhe.com/sadkerbrie3e.

Researchers put forward seven principles of effective direct teaching:

1. *Daily review.* At the beginning of the lesson, teachers review prior learning. Frequently, teachers focus on assigned homework, clarify points of confusion, and provide extra practice for facts and skills that need more attention.

2. *Anticipatory set.* This is also known as a "grabber" and is a way to get students' attention and interest. This could be a teacher demonstration, a video, a story, a puzzle, or a handout before the actual lesson. The anticipatory set builds a bridge from previous knowledge to new information. If successful, the anticipatory set will get students mentally or physically ready for the lesson.

3. *New material.* Teachers begin by letting students know the objectives to be attained. New information is broken down into smaller bits and is covered at a brisk pace. Teachers illustrate main points with concrete examples. Teachers ask questions frequently to check for student understanding and to make sure that students are ready for independent work using new skills and knowledge.

4. *Guided practice.* Students use new skills and knowledge under direct teacher supervision. During guided practice, teachers ask many content questions ("What is the definition of a paragraph?") and many process questions ("How do you locate the topic sentence in a paragraph?"). Teachers check student responses for understanding, offering prompts and providing corrective feedback. Guided practice continues until students answer with approximately 70 to 80 percent accuracy.

5. *Specific feedback.* Correct answers to questions are acknowledged clearly, so that students will understand when their work is accurate. When student answers are hesitant, the teacher provides process feedback ("Yes, Juanita, that's correct because . . ."). Teachers correct inaccurate responses immediately, before errors become habitual. Frequent errors are a sign that students are not ready for independent work, and guided practice should continue.

6. *Independent practice.* Similar to guided practice, except that students work by themselves at their seats or at home. Independent practice continues until responses are assured, quick, and at a level of approximately 95 percent accuracy. Cooperative learning (see the next section) and student tutoring of one another are effective strategies during independent practice.

7. *Weekly and monthly reviews.* Regular reviews offer students the opportunity for more practice, a strategy related to high achievement. Barak Rosenshine, a pioneering researcher in developing the principles of direct teaching, recommends a weekly review every Monday, with a monthly review every fourth Monday.[34]

One of the best-known supporters of direct teaching was *Madeline Hunter.* Her ideas on direct teaching have become the foundation for writing lesson plans. Direct teaching works well when you are teaching skill subjects, such as grammar or mathematics, or helping students master factual material. The direct teaching model is particularly helpful during the first stages of learning new and complex information, but it is less helpful when imaginative responses and student creativity are called for.

Technology: Presentation software, such as PowerPoint or Prezi, are some of the more ubiquitous technologies to enhance direct teaching. Such software can help organize and add energy to student or teacher presentations. Savvy teachers also use these presentation tools with more esoteric technology, such as digital microscopes, or can bring an expert speaker into the classroom through a webcam.

Direct teaching can sometimes make it difficult for teachers to engage all students in class discussions. Technology encourages student participation. For example, students can use a handheld computer, or "clicker," to answer instructor-initiated questions. Teachers using such devices report that along with increasing participation, students are more attentive and better prepared.

Cooperative Learning

In a classroom using **cooperative learning,** students work on activities in small, heterogeneous groups, and they often receive rewards or recognition based on the overall group performance. Although cooperative learning can be traced back to the 1920s, it seems startling or new because the typical classroom environment is frequently competitive. For example, when grading is done on a curve, one student's success is often detrimental to others. This competitive structure produces clear winners and losers, and only a limited number of *As* are possible. But a cooperative learning structure differs from competitive practices because students depend on one another and work together to reach shared goals.

With direct teaching, teachers explain what students must do to accomplish a task, then present a carefully structured lesson that is usually broken down into small, manageable steps.

According to researchers, cooperative learning groups work best when they meet the following criteria.[35] Groups should be *heterogeneous* and, at least at the beginning, should be *small,* perhaps limited to two to six members. Because face-to-face interaction is important, the groups should be *circular* to permit easy conversation. Positive *interdependence* among group members can be fostered by a *shared group goal, shared division of labor,* and *shared materials,* all contributing to a sense that the group sinks or swims together.

Robert Slavin, a pioneer in cooperative learning techniques, developed student team learning methods in which a team's work is not completed until all students on the team understand the material being studied.[36] Rewards are earned only when the entire team achieves the goals set by the teacher. Students tutor one another, so that everyone can succeed on individual quizzes, and each member of the group is accountable for learning. Because students contribute to their teams by improving prior scores, it does not matter whether the student is a high, average, or low achiever. Increased achievement by an individual student at any level contributes to the overall performance of the group, resulting in equal opportunity for success.

Research shows that cooperative learning promotes both intellectual and emotional growth:

- Students make higher achievement gains; this is especially true for math in the elementary grades.
- Students have higher levels of self-esteem and greater motivation to learn.

In cooperative learning, students work together to gain new understanding.

- Students have a stronger sense that classmates have positive regard for one another.
- Understanding and cooperation among students from different racial and ethnic backgrounds are enhanced.[37]

Yet the practical realities of cooperative learning are not all commendable. Some students, accustomed to starring roles in full class instruction, continue to dominate the small groups. Accurate grading requires an analysis of both the individual and group performance. And, even the most committed practitioners acknowledge that cooperative learning may take more time than direct teaching. Still, as ability grouping becomes more controversial, educators are growing increasingly interested in cooperative learning as a strategy for working successfully with mixed-ability groups and diverse classroom populations.

Technology: Sometimes technology can isolate students, so some technology products are specifically designed to encourage student cooperation and collaboration. TakingITGlobal (www.tigweb.org/), for example, provides the tools for students from around the world to communicate and discuss various political, environmental, and social issues from a wide range of perspectives.

Mastery Learning

Mastery learning programs are committed to the credo that, given the right tools, all children can learn. Stemming from an individualized reward structure, these programs are in use from early childhood to graduate school. For example, after years of dismal test scores and lack of student motivation, the Chugach School District in Alaska adopted a student-centered, mastery learning approach. Unlike the standard grade-level system where students worry about passing into the next grade, with schoolwide mastery learning, each student moves at an individual pace and focuses on becoming proficient in 10 specific academic areas, like reading, mathematics, and service learning, as well as nonacademic subjects such as cultural awareness and career development. Some students achieve proficiency and graduate at age 14; some do not get there until 21. Not only have test scores and attendance greatly improved, but students report feeling motivated to learn.[38]

Mastery learning programs require specific and carefully sequenced learning objectives. The first step is to identify a **behavioral objective,** a specific skill or academic task to be mastered. Students are taught the skill or material in the objective; then they are tested to determine if the objective has been reached. Students who complete the test successfully go on for acceleration or enrichment, while the students who fail to demonstrate mastery of the objective receive corrective instruction and are retested. The success of mastery learning rests on the *instructional alignment,* which is a close match between what is taught and what is tested.

In mastery learning, students typically work at their own pace, perhaps at a computer or with individualized written materials. The teacher provides assistance and facilitates student efforts, but mastery still remains a student responsibility. Because studies have shown that many students, particularly younger ones, find it hard to take charge of their own instruction, mastery learning programs highlight the role of the teacher as instructional leader, motivator, and guide. Mastery learning is often geared for large groups, and it can benefit from technology, since computers and appropriate software can be particularly effective in self-paced mastery of skills and knowledge.

Studies suggest that mastery learning can be beneficial across grade levels and subject areas. In mastery learning:

- Teachers have more positive attitudes toward teaching and higher expectations for their students.

- In general, students have more positive attitudes about learning and their ability to learn.

- Students achieve more and remember what they have learned longer.[39]

Technology: In Metrotech High School in Phoenix, Arizona, students prepare for careers in areas as disparate as auto mechanics and television production, but what happens outside of class makes this school special. The school uses software that diagnoses a student's academic proficiency in areas like math and reading, and then offers individualized programs designed to improve the student's mastery of these skills. All this is done outside of class, saving valuable class time to focus on other learning.

Problem-Based Learning

Focusing on authentic or real-life problems that often go beyond traditional subject areas is at the heart of **problem-based learning (PBL).** As you might imagine, real problems are not bound by a single subject field or even by the school building. This emphasis is apparent in the other terms used to describe PBL: *experience-based education, project-based instruction,* and *anchored instruction* (because it is "anchored" in the real world). In this instructional model, a crucial aspect of the teacher's role is to identify activities that fuel students' interest, such as

- Design a plan for protecting a specific endangered species.

- Formulate solutions that might have kept the United States from plunging into a Civil War.

- How can we stop bullying and harassment in this school?

- How can pollution in a local river or bay or the ocean be checked, or even reversed?

- Develop a set of urban policies to halt the deterioration of a central city.

Finding scintillating questions and projects to excite and motivate students is critical, but it is only one aspect of PBL. Other characteristics include:

- *Learner cooperation.* Similar to cooperative learning, PBL depends on small groups or pairs of students collaborating as they explore and investigate various issues. This approach de-emphasizes competition. For teachers, the goal is to guide and challenge a dozen such small groups simultaneously.

- *Higher-order thinking.* Exploring real and complex issues requires students to analyze, synthesize, and evaluate material.

- *Cross-disciplinary work.* PBL encourages students to investigate how different academic subjects shed light on each other. In exploring ecological issues, for example, students touch not only on biology and chemistry but also on economics, history, sociology, and political science.

- *Artifacts and exhibits.* Students involved in PBL demonstrate what they learn in a very tangible way. Students may produce a traditional report or create a video, a physical model, a computer program, a portfolio of artifacts, or even a presentation, such as a play or a debate. Teachers might organize a class or schoolwide exhibit to share the progress made by PBL students.
- *Authentic learning.* Students pursue an actual unresolved issue. They are expected to define the problem, develop a hypothesis, collect information, analyze that information, and suggest a conclusion, one that might work in the real world.[40]

Technology: At John McDonough High School in New Orleans, teachers helped students write digital stories about their lives and their neighborhood. The Neighborhood Story Project collected nonfiction stories, in-depth interviews, and digital photographs. The project produced five best-selling books, and when Hurricane Katrina devastated the city, some of the area's rich cultural history was preserved by the work these students and teachers had done. (Visit www.neighborhoodstoryproject.org.)

Differentiated Instruction

It would make a teacher's life easier if all students learned the same way, but they do not. Student needs, learning styles, life experiences, and readiness to learn differ. To connect effectively with all your students, you will need to abandon the notion that all students fit comfortably into a particular teaching or testing style. **Differentiated instruction** responds to student differences by offering multiple options for instruction and assessment. Carol Ann Tomlinson, a pioneer in the field, defines differentiated instruction very broadly as "doing whatever it takes to ensure that struggling and advanced learners, students with varied cultural heritages, and children with different background experiences all grow as much as they possibly can."[41]

Differentiated instruction organizes instructional activities around student needs rather than content. At first glance, this may seem to be in conflict with the current emphasis on standards-based instruction, but Tomlinson sees it as quite complementary. As she describes it, standards-based curriculum tells us *what* curriculum to teach; differentiation tells us *how* to teach any curriculum well. Notes Tomlinson:

> Typically, what we're being asked to teach kids are facts and skills, but you can wrap them in understanding. You give kids a sense of how this makes sense in the world, how it all fits together, and what they can do with it as people. . . . No one would ask teachers not to teach what they feel responsible for. But you can teach those things in ways that are more meaningful and richer.[42]

Differentiation can show us how to teach the same standards to diverse learners by using different teaching and learning approaches, so teaching becomes a blend of whole-class, group, and individual instruction. Differentiated instruction creates a classroom climate where all students—from the gifted to special needs—can learn together. To help you see how this works, compare the following differentiated instructional approaches with traditional instructional practices:[43]

Traditional/Standardized Instruction	Differentiated Instruction
Literature is not Ethan's favorite class. Class discussions focus on analyzing the themes, characters, symbols, and writing styles of classic novels. Ethan struggles to see how these novels relate to his life, and his interest wanes.	Ethan's teacher works hard to link literacy concepts and skills with student interests. For example, students examine how the rules of writing vary in novels, journalism, music, science, and so on. They also explore how the concept of interdependence is exhibited in athletics, the arts, science, families, governments, and literature, their primary content area.
Latisha has a learning disability. She understands ideas well but has difficulty reading quickly and writing clearly. Nearly all assessments in Latisha's class are written. Most tests and papers have strict time limits. Latisha struggles	Latisha and her teacher work together to establish timetables for her written assignments. This flexibility enables her to write

Argument of over-educated citizens.

Schools were in really bad condition

Mann founded Normal schools preparing teachers in Pedagogy

Opposed corporal Punishment

↳ committed reformer as well as educator.

1828 - Andrew Jackson became President. Heard Pleas from Poor & blacks about Education.

Horace Mann established common School (Elementary) Public School

Private Schools protested Public schools.

Religion more & more a ...zite.

...ould it be in school?

Te...
lends i...
ended ...
them. T...
students,...
online qu...
the class t...
cussions, ...
style. (To e...
webquests/...
org/index.p...   ...und at http://webquest.

A Few More Thoughts on Effective Teaching

Teaching is hard. Teaching well is fiercely so. Often confronted by too many students, a schedule without breaks, a pile of papers that regenerates daily, and incessant demands from every educational stakeholder, teachers can become predictable and mundane in their practices. Nevertheless, innovative, engaged, and reflective teaching is the path to student achievement. Here are some ideas for you to consider:

"Less is more," is an aphorism attributed to education reformer Ted Sizer. According to Sizer, today's schools are misguided in their emphasis on "covering" material. The goal seems to be teaching and learning a vast body of information in order to have a sense of accomplishment or to score well on the ever-growing number of standardized tests. But international tests in science, for example, show that, although U.S. students have studied more science topics than have students in other countries, they have not studied them in depth, and their lower test scores reflect this superficiality. In Sizer's vision

16. Teachers Discuss Their Methods for Effective Teaching

Part of being an effective teacher is creating a positive learning community. In this observation you will observe classroom teachers explaining how they use different strategies to create exciting learning communities.

Classroom Observation Videos are available on the CD Reader and at the Online Learning Center

www.mhhe.com/
sadkerbrief3e

Have High Expectations

of effective instruction, good teachers limit the amount of content they introduce but develop it sufficiently for students to gain in-depth understanding.

This direction for teaching and schooling marks a radical departure from the current emphasis on uniform standards, test performance, and competition. In marked contrast to the superficial nature of such a test-centered curriculum, Sizer advocates deep teaching. In *deep teaching,* teachers work to organize their content around a limited set of key principles and powerful ideas and then engage students in discussing these concepts. The emphasis is on problem solving and critical thinking, rather than on memorizing.[44]

As the builder of a classroom **learning community,** the teacher is called on to be a guide or facilitator, skillful in conducting discussions, group work, debates, and dialogues. In this way, the teacher empowers the students to talk with one another and to rehearse the terminology and concepts involved in each discipline. Learning becomes a community effort, not an individual competition.[45] This learning environment highlights the social nature of learning and of the classroom.

It is not surprising, therefore, that educators are reconceptualizing schools to create more nurturing learning communities. When learning communities work well, students and teachers get to know each other well, and they can develop shared academic goals. Learning communities can be encouraged through several strategies, including looping and block scheduling. In **looping,** schools "promote" teachers along with their students, a process that allows the teacher an extra year or more to get to know students in depth, to diagnose and meet their learning needs, and to develop more meaningful communication with their parents and families. Looping offers students an increased sense of stability and community. Similarly, **block scheduling** increases teacher–student contact by increasing the length of class periods. The longer periods allow teachers to get to know these students better, while the students benefit from an uninterrupted and in-depth academic study. If you were to teach in a school with block scheduling, you might have 75 students on any given day or in a particular semester, instead of 150.

This notion of a learning community encourages a more thoughtful classroom, one in which the teacher is a reflective practitioner. **Reflective teachers** continually and intensely analyze their own practices to improve performance. Reflective teachers ask themselves:

- What teaching strategies did I use today? How effective were they? What changes might I make next time?
- Were all my students engaged with the material? What seemed to motivate them? If I were to reteach today's class, how could I get even more students involved?
- What did I do to help my students think more deeply during today's lesson? How can I further develop their critical thinking skills?
- What values and attitudes did my students cultivate from today's learning?
- How did I assess my students' learning today? Would there have been a better way to measure their learning? What evidence do I have that the students grasp the main points of today's lesson or do I need to reteach some of these concepts?
- What did I learn today? What did my students teach me?
- Can I fine-tune tomorrow's or next week's lessons based on what I learned today?

Such questions are designed to raise consciousness, encourage self-scrutiny, and move you toward more effective teaching. Becoming a reflective teacher involves growing beyond your current concerns with instructional and management techniques, the "how to" questions (where many beginning teachers naturally start) and moving toward "what" and "why" questions, the questions and answers that transform teachers into insightful and gifted instructors.

Reflection has many paths. A teaching journal is one way to record each day's reactions and insights. Reviewing the journal over time will hopefully provide a record of your professional growth. Asking a colleague to observe your teaching and share his or her insights can initiate a useful professional dialogue. Returning the favor and observing your colleagues can provide ideas not only for your colleagues, but for you as well.[46] Of course, you can be your own observer through the magic of technology. Video record your teaching behaviors and do your own analysis. As you see, there are many valuable routes to reflection.

You don't have to wait until student teaching to start being a reflective teacher. You can start right now by asking yourself:

- What roles, official and unofficial, does a teacher have?
- What roles, official and unofficial, does a student have?
- What qualities do good teachers have?
- What teaching strategies do I prefer?
- What is the purpose of school?
- How will I motivate myself to be a reflective teacher in the years ahead?

Your First Year and Beyond

Focus Question 10

What are the stages of
teacher development?

Will I be able to manage this class? Can I get through the curriculum? Do I know my
subject well enough? Will the other teachers like me? Will my students like me? Will
the administrators rehire me? Am I going to be a good teacher? Will I like teaching?

In your first year of teaching, you are likely to be concerned with managing your class, getting good evaluations from your supervisors, and connecting with your colleagues. By the second year, you will be more experienced
(and confident), and focus more on improving your skills and student performance. Your questions will mature as well. (How can I help this shy child?
Why is this student encountering learning problems?) You will be exploring
new approaches, so if you hear of a colleague achieving success using a new
teaching strategy, you may chose to observe and perhaps adapt that strategy.
With passing years, as your talent grows, your interests and vision might as
well, extending beyond your classroom to focus on developing programs
that could benefit large numbers of students. Figure 11.4 suggests stages that
teachers pass through as they become more skilled in their craft.[47]

Attempts to improve student achievement are dependent on our ability
to move teachers through these developmental stages. Every dollar spent to
improve teacher qualifications (as measured by teacher test scores, number of
graduate degrees, professional training, etc.) advances students' academic performance more than investments in most other areas. The most effective teachers not only demonstrate mastery of the subjects they teach, but also are adept
in the methods of teaching and understand student development. Although
efforts to reduce class size or provide schools with more resources are important, research reveals that *investments in teacher qualifications and skills are
among the MOST important factors in improving student performance.*[48]

Induction into the Profession

We wish we could relive the excitement and intensity of our first year in the
classroom. Okay, it was not always wonderful, and yes, it was often tough, but
truth is, it was magical. Your first year could also be a magical time of learning and growing—or it could be quite the opposite. The quality of support you
receive once you begin teaching may be the difference. Many schools understand
this challenge and have created supportive climates to not only recruit but retain
teachers. A growing number of educators believe that there is no "teacher shortage" in America; rather, there is a teacher retention problem. **Induction programs**
"provide some systematic and sustained assistance to beginning teachers for at
least one school year," in the hope that such support will create the first of many
magical years.[49] While some teachers are "naturals," gifted classroom instructors
from the first day they step foot in a classroom, most of us benefit from a support system that helps us refine our teaching skills. Induction programs typically
match new teachers with an experienced instructor, usually called a mentor.

Mentors are experienced teachers selected to guide new teachers through
the school culture and norms, shedding light on the *official* and the *hidden*
school culture (which memos need a quick response, which do not; who
keeps the key to the supply room; where the best DVD players are hidden) and
offering a shoulder to lean on during those very difficult days. Mentors offer
insights on how best to use curricular materials, hints on teaching strategies,
advice on scheduling problems, and suggestions on smoothing out stressful

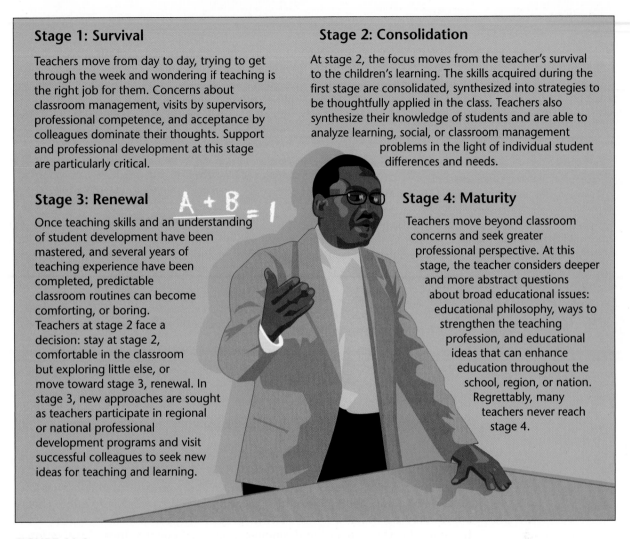

Stage 1: Survival

Teachers move from day to day, trying to get through the week and wondering if teaching is the right job for them. Concerns about classroom management, visits by supervisors, professional competence, and acceptance by colleagues dominate their thoughts. Support and professional development at this stage are particularly critical.

Stage 2: Consolidation

At stage 2, the focus moves from the teacher's survival to the children's learning. The skills acquired during the first stage are consolidated, synthesized into strategies to be thoughtfully applied in the class. Teachers also synthesize their knowledge of students and are able to analyze learning, social, or classroom management problems in the light of individual student differences and needs.

Stage 3: Renewal

Once teaching skills and an understanding of student development have been mastered, and several years of teaching experience have been completed, predictable classroom routines can become comforting, or boring. Teachers at stage 2 face a decision: stay at stage 2, comfortable in the classroom but exploring little else, or move toward stage 3, renewal. In stage 3, new approaches are sought as teachers participate in regional or national professional development programs and visit successful colleagues to seek new ideas for teaching and learning.

$$A + B = 1$$

Stage 4: Maturity

Teachers move beyond classroom concerns and seek greater professional perspective. At this stage, the teacher considers deeper and more abstract questions about broad educational issues: educational philosophy, ways to strengthen the teaching profession, and educational ideas that can enhance education throughout the school, region, or nation. Regrettably, many teachers never reach stage 4.

FIGURE 11.4
Stages of teacher development.

SOURCE: Based on the work of Lillian Katz.

REFLECTION: Have you been taught by teachers representing each of these four developmental stages? Describe behaviors at each of the four levels. If you were to build in strategies to take you from Stage 1 to Stage 4, what might they be?

communication with a student, a parent, an administrator, or a colleague. They can observe a class to analyze how you might improve your teaching or actually teach a class to model a skill for you to use.[50] Effective mentors offer a bridge for new teachers to become skilled professionals.

Your First Day: Creating a Productive Classroom Climate

The way you organize your classroom on that very first day sends a powerful message about who you are as a teacher. If that first day is done well, you are on your way to a smoother teaching year. On the other hand, any mistakes made early in

ADVICE FOR YOUR FIRST YEAR

Education World asked second-year teachers to reflect on their first year in the classroom, their successes and failures, and offer advice for new teachers:

- *Take charge.* Have a clear management plan, with well-defined rewards and consequences. Explain it to the students, send it home to the parents, and ask for signatures on the plan.
- *Keep students busy and engaged.* Have a number of potential class activities available. Bored kids get into trouble; busy kids stay out of trouble.
- *Get peer support.* If you are not assigned an official mentor, find an unofficial one.
- *Get parental support.* From extra supplies to celebration plans, parents are a hidden teacher resource, but only if they are pulled into class activities.
- *Organize yourself.* Develop a system that will keep you organized. There is a lot going on in teaching, grading, and monitoring dozens of children for hours each day.

- *Organize your students.* Teach students how to organize their homework, notebooks, desks, etc.
- *Write and reflect.* Keep a journal to help you reflect on your first year, and become a stronger teacher your second year.
- *Have fun.* Teaching is not only stressful; it is joyful. Get into it and have fun!
- *Renew.* Enjoy an interest outside of teaching.

SOURCE: *Education World* (www.educationworld.com).

REFLECTION: Compare this advice with the more formal areas of teacher effectiveness cited in the research and by the National Board for Professional Teacher Standards described in Chapter 1. What are the similarities and differences?

---

the year enter an echo chamber—they keep returning until June arrives. Earlier in the chapter we discussed setting clear classroom rules and consequences. Here are some additional suggestions for creating a productive class climate.

Physical Considerations Look around your classroom and ask yourself: "What do I want my room to say to the students?" Some of the physical features, such as doors, windows, and built-ins, are beyond your control. But there is still much you can do. Did you ever hear the phrase "If the walls could talk"? Guess what—they do. What do you want displayed on your classroom walls? Multicultural images of males and females, images of creative ideas, motivational statements, and fascinating facts can send powerful messages. (Blank walls convey their own messages, don't they?) When students walk into a thoughtfully prepared room, they appreciate the effort. But there are times when even a blank area of the wall can be positive—if it is designated as a student display area, postings that students will manage in the future. Walls do talk.

Do you want student desks all facing the front, or arranged for students to work in groups, or in a circle around the room for children to introduce themselves, or changing as activities change? You will also need a space for your instructional materials, a place easy to get to so there are no long delays as you move from one class activity to another. Where will you be positioned? You should select a place where you can see the entire class, a place with no blind spots so you can spot a student who needs help—or who is causing a disturbance. Some teachers plan to teach from different areas of the room, placing their desk in one place, audiovisual equipment in another, the day's agenda in yet another area, and even their water, tea, or coffee in yet another place. This ensures that they will be visiting different areas, be near different students, and not be locked in the front of the room. Have you thought about

A VIEW FROM THE FIELD

YOUR FUTURE CLASSROOM

We hope that these *Contemporary Issues* features inspire you to do amazing things in the classroom. For this last one, let's think about tomorrow's schools, the ones you may be working in.

Daniel Pink's book, *A Whole New Mind: Why Right-Brainers Will Rule the Future,* describes major changes he believes will reshape America in the years ahead. Pink contends that low-cost Asian workers will take over many of the math, technology, and science careers, and that the courses we think are so important—science, technology, math—will be less central in the future. To compete in the twenty-first century, he believes our schools should focus more on right-brain skills, the skills we often neglect. Here are some examples:

Boundary crossers: These are creative people who are comfortable working in different disciplines, cultures, and languages. A physician using both western and eastern medicine to heal patients, a businessperson helping American companies work more effectively with Indian computer experts, and a teacher working with students to improve the environment are all boundary crossers.

Design: We have lots of products that work well, so we now choose products that appeal to us. We buy a car or a laptop in part because we enjoy how it looks. We will need people with fine arts skills to design attractive and pleasing products, and perhaps they too can be boundary crossers by working with sustainable materials that honor the earth.

Joy: "People rarely succeed at anything unless they are having fun," is a Southwest Airline motto. More and more companies are realizing that happiness, yes happiness, is an important goal. Incorporating games, humor, laughing, and play into our businesses (and schools!) may increase productivity, satisfaction, and health.

Materialism vs. Meaning: Americans have acquired much material wealth, but many are still unhappy. People have confused material wealth with happiness. Pink believes that in the future, Americans will seek more meaningful lives. He cites the increase in meditation, yoga, public service, and spirituality as examples of our search for meaningful lives.

Intuition: Perhaps our greatest scientist, Albert Einstein, had it right when he wrote: "The intuitive mind is a sacred gift; the rational mind, its servant." Why do schools honor the servant (rational thinking) and disregard the sacred gift (intuition)? How can schools help people develop and honor their intuition?

In fact, how might we teach all of these topics? How will these new priorities change our world, our schools, and your classrooms?

any special touches that you want to bring in? Plants, carpet, pillows, posters? It is your room, and you get to create the ambience for you and your students.

Know Your Students Do you remember how it felt when the teacher called you by the wrong name, or no name at all—almost as if you did not exist? Don't forget that feeling, and dedicate yourself to learning your students' names. This is an easier assignment for teachers with one class of students than it is for a teacher with five classes a day, but the sooner all teachers learn the names of their students the smoother the class will run. And here is a special reminder: If a student is from another culture and has an unfamiliar-sounding name, work to learn the correct pronunciation. It will be much appreciated by the student and will help you grow as well.

Prepare for a Strong First Day This first class creates a first impression, and first impressions happen only once. Take the time to plan some exciting and meaningful activities for that first day. You may also want to share your vision and goals for the entire year with the class: what students will be learning and why that is important. An exciting and thoughtful beginning to the school year can create the tone for the weeks and months that follow.

Although you've reached the end of this text (congratulations!), your learning will continue. (See Contemporary Issues: A View from the Field.)

And we wish you and your students a fruitful future.

SUMMARY

CHAPTER REVIEW

Go to the Online Learning Center to take a chapter self-quiz, practice with key terms, and review concepts from the chapter.

www.mhhe.com/
sadkerbrief3e

1. Are teachers born, or made?

While the debate is decades old, most people agree that effective teaching can result from natural artistry as well as focused training.

2. How is class time organized and what is academic learning time?

Teachers vary dramatically in the efficient use of time. Wise distribution of classroom time—defined as allocated, engaged, and academic learning time—is a predictor of student achievement.

3. What classroom management skills foster academic achievement?

Student achievement is also associated with effective classroom management. A well-managed classroom includes reasonable rules for students to follow and teachers who can keep students on task through group alerting, smooth transitions, and similar skills.

4. What are the roles of teachers and students in the pedagogical cycle?

The pedagogical cycle consists of four stages: (1) structure, (2) question, (3) respond, and (4) react. The student's role is typically limited to responding, while teachers usually direct classroom discourse through structure, question, and reaction.

5. How can teachers set a stage for learning?

Most cycles of instruction begin by connecting prior learning to current objectives. Effective teachers motivate students, offer meaningful examples, give accurate directions, display enthusiasm, and present a brief closure to the lesson.

6. What questioning strategies increase student achievement?

Questioning is at the very foundation of effective teaching. Although teachers rely most heavily on lower-order questions, higher-order questions are associated with critical thinking and should be an important part of classroom instruction. Effective teachers use proper wait time to allocate questions fairly among all students. When providing feedback, teachers typically use neutral acceptance, but praise, remediation, and criticism are more precise and helpful reactions.

7. How can teachers best tap into different student learning styles?

Effective teachers provide variety. From discussions and debates to simulations and spot quizzes, teachers increase academic success by responding to the different learning styles in the class.

8. How can teachers use technology to support effective instruction?

Hardware, software, and websites can tie into effective teaching strategies. Technology raises some serious concerns for teachers, including monitoring the accuracy and biases of Internet material.

9. What are several salient models of instruction?

Five models of instruction are direct teaching, cooperative learning, mastery learning, problem-based learning, and differentiated instruction. Direct teaching includes teacher presentation, guided practice, teacher feedback, independent practice, and regular reviews. In a cooperative learning classroom, students work in small groups, and appraisals often reflect the entire group's performance. In mastery learning, students work at their own pace to reach specific objectives. Problem-based learning stimulates students to explore authentic issues. Differentiated instruction responds to student differences by offering multiple options for instruction and assessment.

10. **What are the stages of teacher development?**

Teachers provided with sufficient support can move through a series of stages: survival, consolidation, renewal, and maturity, growing from personal concerns (such as classroom management) to broader educational issues (school strategies that could enhance student learning). Studies underscore that investments in teacher qualifications and training translate into improved student achievement.

KEY TERMS AND PEOPLE

academic learning time, 357

allocated time, 357

behavioral objective, 380

block scheduling, 384

Bloom's taxonomy, 367

cooperative learning, 379

differentiated instruction, 382

direct teaching, 376

engaged time, 357

higher-order questions, 367

induction programs, 386

learning community, 384

looping, 384

lower-order questions, 367

mastery learning, 380

mentors, 386

pedagogical cycle, 365

problem-based learning, 381

reflective teaching, 385

Mary Budd Rowe, 370

Robert Slavin, 379

wait time, 370

DISCUSSION QUESTIONS AND ACTIVITIES

1. Do you think teachers are born, or made? Debate a classmate who holds the opposite point of view. Interview elementary and secondary teachers and ask them what they think about this question. Do some of them say that it is a combination of both? If so, why? Which part is art, which part skill?

2. Why do you think there is so much variation in how different teachers and schools use time for learning? Observe in your own college classrooms to determine how much time is wasted. For each class observed, keep a fairly detailed record of how time is lost (students 6 minutes late, class ends 15 minutes early, PowerPoint presentation takes 4 minutes to set up, and so on).

3. Research suggests that in order to achieve, students should be functioning at a very high success rate. Do you agree that this is likely to lead to higher achievement? Or do you think that students need to cope with failure and be "stretched" in order to achieve? Defend your position.

4. Analyze teacher reactions to student answers in elementary and secondary classrooms where you are an observer and in the college classrooms where you are a student. Are most of these classrooms "okay" classrooms? Why do you think some teacher reactions are vague and diffuse? What observations can you make about the use of praise, remediation, and criticism?

5. What do you look for in a mentor? What strategies can you use to recruit such a mentor in your first teaching job?

WEB-*TIVITIES*

Go to the Online Learning Center to do the following activities:

1. Cooperative Learning
2. Problem-Based Learning
3. Becoming Informed about the Job Market
4. Developing a Portfolio
5. Practice Teaching
6. Wiring Up Schools, Charging Up Teachers

Articles, Case Studies, and Videos correspond to chapter content and are not always in numeric order. Go to your *Teachers, Schools, and Society Reader* CD-ROM to:

Read Current and Historical Articles

41. "Mapping a Route Toward Differentiated Instruction," Carol Ann Tomlinson, *Educational Leadership*, September 1999.

42. "Learning to Love Assessment," Carol Ann Tomlinson, *Educational Leadership*, December 2007.

43. "Losing the Fear of Sharing Control," Lesley Roessing, *Middle School Journal*, January 2007.

44. "Discipline: Responding to Socioeconomic and Racial Differences," Doris Walker-Dalhouse; *Childhood Education*, Fall 2005.

45. "Lessons of a First-Year Teacher," Molly Ness, *Phi Delta Kappan*, May 2001.

Analyze Case Studies

20. **Ken Kelly:** A teacher having trouble with questioning and with discussion teaching visits a teacher who is holding a Socratic discussion with a fourth-grade class. He questions the applicability of her methods to his situation.

21. **Judith Kent:** A teacher engages her students in whole-class discussion, and then the students work with partners on an assignment. She explains the planning process she went through to reteach the lesson after it had not worked in the previous class.

22. **Christie Raymond:** A mature woman in the first month of her first full-time position teaching music in an elementary school loves the work as long as the children are singing, but dislikes the school's emphasis on and her part in disciplining the students. The case describes Christie's classroom teaching in detail as well as her after-school bus duty.

Observe Teachers, Students, and Classrooms In Action

16. **Classroom Observation: Teachers Discuss Their Methods for Effective Teaching**
See page 384 of this text for a description of these videos. You'll find the video on the CD Reader and at the Online Learning Center

www.mhhe.com/
sadkerbrief3e

APPENDICES

Text Appendices

1. Reflective Activities and Your Portfolio (RAPs)
2. Teacher Competency Exams and Praxis™ Sample Test Questions

Online Appendices

www.mhhe.com/
sadkerbrief3e

Online Appendix A: State Departments of Education

Online Appendix B: Classroom Observation Guidelines

Online Appendix C: Q And A Guide to Entering the Teaching Profession

APPENDIX 1

INTASC

Reflective Activities and Your Portfolio (RAPs)

INTASC Reflective Activities and Your Portfolio, what we like to refer to as RAPs, give you a chance to explore your role as an educator by carefully considering what you have just read and tying it to your own experiences. RAPs are intended to help you decide if teaching is right for you. If it is right, these very same RAPs can give you direction as you prepare for a career in teaching and can be used as an artifact in your professional portfolio. Each RAP includes the following sections:

Purpose—explains why this activity is useful, and what it is intended to accomplish.

Activity—allows you to apply your readings through observations, interviews, teaching, and action research.

Artifact—challenges you to collect and manage the items you will find useful for developing your portfolio.

Reflection—helps you think deeply and realistically about education and your place in it.

www.mhhe.com/sadkerbrief3e

The RAPs, accompanied by an introduction to portfolios, are located in the Course-wide Content section of the Student Online Learning Center. www.mhhe.com/sadkerbrief3e

INTASC Principle 1: Knowledge of Subject Matter

The teacher understands the central concepts, tools of inquiry, and structures of the discipline(s) he or she teaches and can create learning experiences that make these aspects of subject matter meaningful to students.

1.1: Nontraditional Hero

1.2: Self-Fulfilling Prophecy

INTASC Principle 2: Human Development and Learning

The teacher understands how children learn and develop and can provide learning opportunities that support children's intellectual, social, and personal development.

2.1: Scoping School Culture

2.2: Money Matters

INTASC Principle 3: Diversity in Learning

The teacher understands how students differ in their approaches to learning and creates instructional opportunities that are adapted to diverse learners.

3.1: Philosophy on the Big Screen

3.2: Curriculum Bias Detectors

INTASC Principle 4: Variety of Instructional Strategies

The teacher understands and uses a variety of instructional strategies to encourage students' development of critical thinking, problem solving, and performance skills.

4.1: Memories of a Teacher

4.2: If These Walls Could Talk

INTASC Principle 5: Motivation and Management

The teacher uses understanding of individual and group motivation and behavior to create a learning environment that encourages positive and social interaction, active engagement in learning, and self-motivation.

5.1: Write a Letter to Yourself

5.2: Rules, Rituals, and Routines

INTASC Principle 6: Communication Skills

The teacher uses knowledge of effective verbal, nonverbal, and media communication techniques to foster active inquiry, collaboration, and supportive interaction in the classroom.

6.1: Putting Your Philosophy into the Classroom

6.2: Public Service Announcement

INTASC Principle 7: Instructional Planning Skills

The teacher plans instruction based upon knowledge of subject matter, students, the community, and curriculum goals.

7.1:   Students' Bill of Rights

7.2:   A Real In-Service Program

INTASC Principle 8: Assessment

The teacher understands and uses formal and informal assessment strategies to evaluate and ensure continuous intellectual, social, and physical development of the learner.

8.1:   A Novel Read

8.2:   Memoirs of a Time-Tested Student

INTASC Principle 9: Reflection and Responsibility

The teacher is a reflective practitioner who continually evaluates the effects of her or his choices and actions of others (students, parents, and other professionals in the learning community) and who actively seeks out opportunities to grow professionally.

9.1:   Reflections of a High School Yearbook

9.2:   Website of the Month

INTASC Principle 10: Relationships and Partnerships

The teacher fosters relationships with school colleagues, parents, and agencies in the larger community to support students' learning and well-being.

10.1:   Special Education Services

10.2:   Support Staff Interview

SOURCE: Adopted from *Model Standards for Beginning Teacher Licensing and Development: A Resource for State Dialogue* developed by the Interstate New Teacher Assessment and Support Consortium (INTASC). Each principle includes knowledge, dispositions, and performance expectations for beginning teachers. INTASC updates can also be accessed online at www.ccsso.org.

APPENDIX 2

Teacher Competency Exams and Praxis™ Sample Test Questions

Evaluation Systems and Educational Testing Service (ETS)—developers of Praxis™—are two of the largest companies that provide tests and other services for states to use as part of their teacher licensure process. Some colleges and universities use these assessments to qualify individuals for entry into teacher education programs. Because more and more states are choosing to develop their own teacher competency exams, be sure to check with your specific teacher education program or state department of education for information on your particular testing requirements.

National Evaluation Systems

Although the Praxis™ assessments from ETS have received a great deal of attention, assessing more than half a million aspiring teachers, Evaluation Systems assesses as many prospective teachers, but is less well known. The reason is that Evaluation Systems customizes its exams for individual states. Some states use both Evaluation Systems and Praxis™ exams to assess their teachers. Specific information about Evaluation Systems–created tests is available directly from teacher licensure departments in the following states:

Arizona

California

Colorado

Connecticut

Florida

Georgia

Illinois

Massachusetts

Michigan

New Mexico

New York

Oklahoma

Oregon

Texas

Virginia

Washington

Praxis™

Each teacher college and state licensing organization that uses Praxis™ determines its own certification and Praxis™ passing score requirements. You will take The Praxis Series™ if you want to teach public school in one of these states or if you want to enter a teacher education program at a college or university that uses Praxis I:™ Academic Skills Assessments. Different states and institutions require different tests in The Praxis Series™, so be sure you know which tests you need before you register.

There are current two categories of assessments in The Praxis Series™:

Praxis I:™ Academic Skills Assessment. This assessment measures reading, writing, and mathematics skills and includes multiple-choice questions and an essay. The tests are designed to evaluate whether you have the academic skills needed to prepare for a career in education. In addition to licensure, these tests are often used to qualify candidates for entry into a teacher education program.

Praxis II:™ Principles of Learning and Teaching and Subject Assessments. Consists of three tests.

1. The Principles of Learning and Teaching exam assesses aspiring teachers' general pedagogy-related knowledge and skills at four grade levels: Early Childhood, Grades K–6, Grades 5–9, and Grades 7–12.

2. The Teaching Foundations Tests measure pedagogy in 5 areas: multisubject (elementary), English, Language Arts, Mathematics, Science and Social Science. *Praxis II:™* tests include multiple-choice questions and essay and constructed-response questions.

3. The Subject Assessments measure candidates' knowledge of the content areas they will teach, as well as how much they know about teaching that subject.

If you are planning to take one or more of these tests, you need a copy of *The Praxis Series:™ Professional Assessments for Beginning Teachers, Registration Bulletin.* The bulletin is free and provides complete test information plus test registration instructions. It's available online at www.ets.org/praxis. *Tests at a Glance* and *Praxis™ Study Guides* are other Praxis™ "must have" resources. These booklets include detailed descriptions of topics covered, test-taking strategies, sample tests, and scoring guides.

The states and territories listed next use The Praxis Series™ tests as part of their teacher licensure process. You should check with each state to find out which tests are required, what passing scores are, and other information.

Alabama	New Hampshire
Alaska	New Jersey
Arkansas	New Mexico
California	New York
Colorado	North Carolina
Connecticut	North Dakota
Delaware	Ohio
District of Columbia	Oklahoma
Georgia	Oregon
Guam	Pennsylvania
Hawaii	Rhode Island
Idaho	South Carolina
Indiana	South Dakota
Iowa	Tennessee
Kansas	Texas
Kentucky	U.S. Virgin Islands
Louisiana	Utah
Maine	Vermont
Maryland	Virginia
Mississippi	Washington
Missouri	West Virginia
Montana	Wisconsin
Nebraska	Wyoming
Nevada	

Praxis™ Sample Test Questions

The following sample test questions are from *Praxis II:™ Principles of Learning and Teaching*. For additional items visit the Praxis™ website at www.ets.org/praxis and download *Tests at a Glance*. Good luck!

Principles of Learning and Teaching: Grades 7–12

The sample questions that follow illustrate the kinds of questions in the test. They are not, however, representative of the entire scope of the test in either content or difficulty. Answers with explanations follow the questions.

CASE HISTORY: 7–12

<u>Directions:</u> The case history is followed by two short-answer questions.

Mr. Payton

Scenario

Mr. Payton teaches world history to a class of 30 heterogeneously grouped students ages 14 to 16. He is working with his supervisor, planning for his self-evaluation to be completed in the spring. At the beginning of the third week of school, he begins gathering material that might be helpful for the self-evaluation. He has selected one class and three students from this class to focus on.

Mr. Payton's first impression of the three students

Jimmy has attended school in the district for 10 years. He repeated fifth and seventh grades. Two years older than most of the other students in class and having failed twice, Jimmy is neither dejected nor hostile. He is an outgoing boy who, on the first day of class, offered to help me with "the young kids" in the class. He said, "Don't worry about me remembering a lot of dates and stuff. I know it's going to be hard, and I'll probably flunk again anyway, so don't spend your time thinking about me."

Burns is a highly motivated student who comes from a family of world travelers. He has been to Europe and Asia. These experiences have influenced his career choice, international law. He appears quiet and serious. He has done extremely well on written assignments and appears to prefer to work alone or with one or two equally bright, motivated students. He has a childhood friend, one of the slowest students in the class.

Pauline is a withdrawn student whose grades for the previous two years have been mostly C's and D's. Although Pauline displays no behavior problems when left alone, she appears not to be popular with the other students. She often stares out the window when she should be working. When I speak to Pauline about completing assignments, she becomes hostile. She has completed few of the assignments so far with any success. When I spoke to her counselor, Pauline yelled at me, "Now I'm in trouble with my counselor too, all because you couldn't keep your mouth shut!"

Mr. Payton's initial self-analysis, written for his supervisor

I attend workshops whenever I can and consider myself a creative teacher. I often divide the students into groups for cooperative projects, but they fall apart and are far from "cooperative." The better-performing students, like Burns, complain about the groups, claiming that small-group work is boring and that they learn more working alone or with students like themselves. I try to stimulate all the students' interest through class discussions. In these discussions, the high-achieving students seem more interested in impressing me than in listening and responding to what other students have to say. The low-achieving students seem content to be silent. Although I try most of the strategies I learn in workshops, I usually find myself returning to a modified lecture and the textbook as my instructional mainstays.

Background information on lesson to be observed by supervisor
Goals:

- To introduce students to important facts and theories about Catherine the Great
- To link students' textbook reading to other sources of information
- To give students practice in combining information from written and oral material
- To give students experience in note taking

I assigned a chapter on Catherine the Great in the textbook as homework on Tuesday. Students are to take notes on their reading. I gave Jimmy a book on Catherine the Great with a narrative treatment rather than the factual approach taken by the textbook. I told him the only important date is the date Catherine began her reign. The book has more pictures and somewhat larger print than the textbook.

I made no adaptation for Burns, since he's doing fine. I offered to create a study guide for Pauline, but she angrily said not to bother. I hope that Wednesday's lecture will make up for any difficulties she might experience in reading the textbook.

Supervisor's notes on Wednesday's lesson
Mr. Payton gives a lecture on Catherine the Great. First he says, "It is important that you take careful notes because

I will be including information that is not contained in the chapter you read as homework last night. The test I will give on Friday will include both the lecture and the textbook information."

He tape records the lecture to supplement Pauline's notes but does not tell Pauline about the tape until the period is over because he wants her to do the best note taking she can manage. During the lecture, he speaks slowly, watching the class as they take notes. In addition, he walks about the classroom and glances at the students' notes.

Mr. Payton's follow-up and reflection
Tomorrow the students will use the class period to study for the test. I will offer Pauline earphones to listen to the tape-recorded lecture. On Friday, we will have a short-answer and essay test covering the week's work.

Class notes seem incomplete and inaccurate, and I'm not satisfied with this test as an assessment of student performance. Is that a fair measure of all they do?

Sample Questions

This section presents two short-answer questions and sample responses along with the standards used in scoring these responses. When you read these sample responses, keep in mind that they are less polished than if they had been developed at home, edited, and carefully presented. Examinees do not know what questions will be asked and must decide, on the spot, how to respond. Readers assign scores based on the following scoring guide.

GENERAL SCORING GUIDE

A response that receives a score of 2:

- Demonstrates a thorough understanding of the aspects of the case that are relevant to the question
- Responds appropriately to all parts of the question
- If an explanation is required, provides a strong explanation that is well supported by relevant evidence
- Demonstrates a strong knowledge of pedagogical concepts, theories, facts, procedures, or methodologies relevant to the question

A response that receives a score of 1:

- Demonstrates a basic understanding of the aspects of the case that are relevant to the question
- Responds appropriately to one portion of the question

- If an explanation is required, provides a weak explanation that is supported by relevant evidence
- Demonstrates some knowledge of pedagogical concepts, theories, facts, procedures, or methodologies relevant to the question

A response that receives a score of 0:

- Demonstrates misunderstanding of the aspects of the case that are relevant to the question
- Fails to respond appropriately to the question
- Is not supported by relevant evidence
- Demonstrates little knowledge of pedagogical concepts, theories, facts, procedures, or methodologies relevant to the question

No credit is given for a blank or off-topic response.

Directions: Questions 1 and 2 require you to write short answers. You are not expected to cite specific theories or texts in your answers; however, your responses to the questions will be evaluated with respect to professionally accepted principles and practices in teaching and learning. Be sure to answer all parts of the questions. Write your answers in the spaces indicated in the response book.

Question 1

In his self-analysis, Mr. Payton says that the better-performing students say small-group work is boring and that they learn more working alone or only with students like themselves. Assume that Mr. Payton wants to continue using cooperative learning groups because he believes they have value for all students.

- Describe TWO strategies he could use to address the concerns of the students who have complained.
- Explain how each strategy suggested could provide an opportunity to improve the functioning of cooperative learning groups. Base your response on principles of effective instructional strategies.

Sample response that received a score of 2:

Mr. Payton has to be creative to find strategies that will address the concerns of the students who have complained and still support the strengths of cooperative learning.

One way he can do that is to assign these students a variety of roles in which they can share their insights and knowledge with others in a way that will provide them recognition and will help other students. He can also build specific requirements that provide for individual

work into the cooperative work, either before the groups meet or as the groups are working. This individual work provides the more able or motivated students with an opportunity to demonstrate their insights and knowledge and be given appropriate credit for them. The individual work can also serve as a basis for the group work.

Sample response that received a score of 1:

I understand why these students are concerned. But Mr. Payton shouldn't just give up on cooperative learning groups. I had a situation like this, when four really bright and eager kids just didn't want to work with students who were less able or less motivated. One thing he could do would be to assign his groups very carefully, so that one of the complaining kids is in each group. He could then use a system where he begins the cooperative work by regrouping, numbering the kids in each group 1, 2, 3, 4. First, all the "1's" work together, all the "2's" work together, and so forth. All the kids who complained would have the same number. After they have had the opportunity to work together on an advanced level, the groups would reform. The "1's" could go back to their own groups and share with them what the "1" group came up with. In this way, they have the intellectual stimulation of working together first, and then the status of sharing with other kids.

Sample response that received a score of 0:

Probably the best thing he can do is to let the complaining kids work individually. They are only going to resent the less able kids and will probably end up insulting them. The kids who are complaining will learn more if they work individually and can push themselves to their limits. The other kids can work at a level more appropriate to their ability.

Question 2

In the introduction to the lesson to be observed, Mr. Payton briefly mentions the modification he has or has not made for some students. Review his comments about modifications for Jimmy and Burns.

- For each of these two students, describe ONE different way Mr. Payton might have provided a modification to offer a better learning situation for each.
- Explain how each modification could offer a better learning situation. Base your explanation on principles of varied instruction for different kinds of learners.

Sample response that received a score of 2:

For Burns, who is a bright, independent learner, providing him the opportunity to take extra responsibility for mastering challenging material and figuring out how to help his classmates understand it might help him to be more open and positive in his classroom behavior. For example, he might use more complex materials to access information, or might create a program using technology to share his knowledge and insights with others. For Jimmy, Mr. Payton might have a conference with him to find out how he was expected to learn social studies in the past and why he is so accepting of failing social studies. This conference may lead to a strategy such as the use of information presented visually or orally, or the use of graphic organizers to access information, or an alternate means of demonstrating his understanding if written assessments are part of the problem.

Sample response that received a score of 1:

Jimmy is a very interesting student to consider. He has a history of failure and seems to accept the fact that he may fail again. However, he seems quite outgoing, so he might be willing to try if approached right. I think the first thing Mr. Payton could do would be to sit down and talk with him. He needs to try to figure out why Jimmy failed in the past. He might ask him if he has any ideas about how he learns best—and things teachers have had him do that don't help him. Then, with this information, Mr. Payton might be able to come up with some approaches based on Jimmy's learning style. If Jimmy says he hates to read, Mr. Payton needs to find a way for him to access the information other than reading! Another thing Mr. Payton might do is adjust what he expects Jimmy to learn. Jimmy says he has problems with "a lot of dates and stuff." But he may be interested in other aspects of history—why people did the things they did, for example. By tailoring the study of history to aspects that might be more appropriate for Jimmy, Mr. Payton might have a better chance of helping Jimmy succeed.

Sample response that received a score of 0:

I think the modification he should make for both students is to be much clearer about what the expectations of the course are. Sometimes students are tuned out or bored because they just don't know what is expected of them. Maybe Mr. Payton needs to post his expectations prominently in the room so that both of these students can see what is expected. The expectations also need to indicate what is required for passing, so that Jimmy and Burns will know what the limits are.

Discrete Multiple-Choice Questions

Directions: Questions 3–5 are not related to the previous case. For each question, select the best answer and mark the corresponding space on your answer sheet.

3. A teacher gives his students a list of terms to use in an essay and intends the list to serve as a kind of learning support called a scaffold. If the students use the list effectively, which of the following would be an appropriate next step for the teacher to take when assigning the students their next essay?
   (A) Asking the students to come up with their own list of terms to use in the new assignment
   (B) Giving the students a longer list of terms to use in the new assignment
   (C) Giving the students a list of terms and asking them to write down a definition of each before beginning the new assignment
   (D) Asking the students to use the same terms in the new assignment

4. The concept of the placement of students in the "least restrictive" educational environment developed as a result of efforts to
   (A) Equalize educational opportunities for females and minorities
   (B) Normalize the lives of those children with disabilities who were being educated in isolation from their peers
   (C) Obtain increased federal funding for the noneducational support of children living in poverty
   (D) Reduce the overall costs of educating students with special needs

5. A teacher would get better information from a criterion-referenced test than from a norm-referenced test about which of the following?
   (A) How much each individual student has learned about a particular aspect of the curriculum
   (B) How each individual student's knowledge of a particular aspect of the curriculum compares to that of students across the school district and state
   (C) How each individual student's knowledge of a particular aspect of the curriculum compares to that of a national sample of students at the same age level
   (D) How much of what each student knows about a particular aspect of the curriculum is based on prior knowledge

Questions 6–7 are based on the following passages.
The following passages are taken from a debate about the advantages and disadvantages of a constructivist approach to teaching.

Why constructivist approaches are effective
The point of constructivist instruction is to have students reflect on their questions about new concepts in order to uncover their misconceptions. If a student cannot reason

out the answer, this indicates a conceptual problem that the teacher needs to address. It takes more than content-related professional expertise to be a "guide on the side" in this process. Constructivist teaching focuses not on what the teacher knows, but on what and how the student learns. Expertise is focused on teaching students how to derive answers, not on giving them the answers. This means that a constructivist approach to teaching must respond to multiple different learning methods and use multiple approaches to content. It is a myth that constructivist teaching never requires students to memorize, to drill, to listen to a teacher explain, or to watch a teacher model problem-solving of various kinds. Constructivist approaches take advantage of a basic truth about human cognition: we all make sense of new information in terms of what we already know or think we know. And each of us must process new information in our own context and experience to make it part of what we really know.

Why constructivist approaches are misguided
The theory of constructivism is appealing for a variety of reasons—especially for its emphasis on direct student engagement in learning. However, as they are implemented, constructivist approaches to teaching often treat memorization, direct instruction, or even open expression of teacher expertise as forbidden. This demotion of the teacher to some sort of friendly facilitator is dangerous, especially in an era in which an unprecedented number of teachers are teaching out of their fields of expertise. The focus of attention needs to be on how much teachers know about the content being taught.

Students need someone to lead them through the quagmire of propaganda and misinformation that they confront daily. Students need a teacher who loves the subject and has enough knowledge to act as an intellectual authority when a little direction is needed. Students need a teacher who does not settle for minimal effort but encourages original thinking and provides substantive intellectual challenge.

6. The first passage suggests that reflection on which of the following after a lesson is an essential element in constructivist teaching?
   (A) The extent to which the teacher's knowledge of the content of the lesson was adequate to meet students' curiosity about the topic
   (B) The differences between what actually took place and what the teacher planned
   (C) The variety of misconceptions and barriers to understanding revealed by students' responses to the lesson

   (D) The range of cognitive processes activated by the activities included in the lesson design and implementation

7. The author of the second passage would regard which of the following teacher behaviors as essential for supporting student learning?
   (A) Avoiding lecture and memorization
   (B) Allowing students to figure out complex problems without the teacher's intervention
   (C) Emphasizing process rather than content knowledge
   (D) Directly guiding students' thinking on particular topics

ANSWERS

1. See sample responses on page A–4.
2. See sample responses on page A–5.
3. The best answer is A. A scaffold is a temporary learning aid, designed to help the student to grow in independence as a learner; thus, once the skill the scaffold is intended to help teach has been mastered, the scaffold should be withdrawn. Asking the students to come up with their own list of terms to use in the new assignment in effect withdraws the scaffold and encourages independence. None of the actions described in the other answer choices does these things.
4. The best answer is B. The concept of "least restrictive" stems from P.L. 94-142 and subsequent legislation regarding the education of students with disabilities and implies that special students are not to be classified by disability and given permanent special placement on the basis of these classifications. Rather, they are to be moved to special settings only if necessary and only for as long as necessary.
5. The best answer is A. Criterion-referenced tests are developed to assess knowledge and understanding of specified standards for learning particular content. They are designed to enable individual students or groups of students who have studied the same material to assess how much they have learned as compared to the criterion, or standard. A norm-group performance is not required for a criterion-referenced test, because the goal is to measure knowledge against a predefined knowledge standard. Whether a person passes a criterion-referenced test is not judged in relation to how other applicants performed (which would be norm-referenced) but in relation to an established standard for minimum number correct.
6. The best answer is C. Constructivist teaching depends on the connection of new information to already

learned information or understandings, whether or not they are accurate. The passage says, "The point of constructivist instruction is to have students reflect on their questions about new concepts in order to uncover their misconceptions. If a student cannot reason out the answer, this indicates a conceptual problem that the teacher needs to address." Thus, a consideration of barriers and/or misconceptions in response to the presentation of new material is an essential follow-up to a constructivist lesson.

7. The best answer is D. The second author maintains that students require teacher guidance and a direct expression of the teacher's expert content knowledge in order to learn most effectively. Choices A (avoiding lecturing), B (learning without teacher intervention), and C (de-emphasis on content knowledge) are not consistent with this approach to teaching. Direct guidance of students' thinking is consistent with the second author's approach.

GLOSSARY

A

ability grouping   The assignment of pupils to homogeneous groups according to intellectual ability or level for instructional purposes.

academic freedom   The opportunity for teachers and students to learn, teach, study, research, and question without censorship, coercion, or external political and other restrictive influences.

academic learning time   The time a student is actively engaged with the subject matter and experiencing a high success rate.

academy   A classical secondary school in colonial America that emphasized elements of Latin and English grammar schools and by the nineteenth century became more of a college preparatory school. Also the name of the ancient Greek school founded by Plato.

accelerated program   The more rapid promotion of gifted students through school.

accountability   Holding schools and teachers responsible for student performance.

accreditation   Certification of an education program or a school that has met professional standards of an outside agency.

acculturation   The acquisition of the dominant culture's norms by a member of the nondominant culture. The nondominant culture typically loses its own culture, language, and sometimes religion in this process.

achievement tests   Examinations of the knowledge and skills acquired, usually as a result of specific instruction.

adequate education   Provides a legal approach for ensuring educational opportunities for poorer students based on state constitution guarantees for an efficient, thorough, or uniform education. Calls for adequate education have replaced previous calls for equal educational expenditures.

advanced placement   Courses and programs in which younger students can earn college credit.

aesthetics   The branch of philosophy that examines the nature of beauty and judgments about it.

affective domain   The area of learning that involves attitudes, values, and emotions.

affirmative action   A plan by which personnel policies and hiring practices reflect positive steps in the recruiting and hiring of women and people of color.

allocated time   The amount of time a school or an individual teacher schedules for a subject.

alternative families   Viewed from a traditional perspective, any family lifestyle other than a married male and female living with their children. The concept of family is evolving and becoming more inclusive.

American Federation of Teachers (AFT)   A national organization of teachers that is primarily concerned with improving educational conditions and protecting teachers' rights.

Americanization   The acculturation of American norms and values.

American Spelling Book   An early elementary textbook written by Noah Webster that focused on the alphabet, grammar, and moral lessons.

A Nation at Risk: The Imperative for Education Reform   A 1983 federal report that characterized U.S. schools as mediocre, putting the nation at risk of losing economic and technological ground to other countries. The report called for renewed emphasis on core academic subjects and ushered in the era of "back to basics" education.

Appropriate Education   As part of Public Law 94-142, the principle protects the right of students with disabilities to an education that reflects an accurate diagnosis.

assertive discipline   A behavior modification program developed by Lee and Marlene Canter designed to "catch" and reward students being good, while discouraging off-task and inappropriate behavior.

assimilation   (See enculturation.)

assistive (adaptive) technology   Devices that help the disabled to perform and learn more effectively, from voice-activated keyboards and mechanical wheelchairs to laptops for class note taking and personal scheduling.

authentic assessment   A type of evaluation that represents actual performance, encourages students to reflect on their own work, and is integrated into the student's whole learning process. Such tests usually require that students synthesize knowledge from different areas and use that knowledge actively.

B

back to basics   During the 1980s, a revival of the back-to-basics movement evolved out of concern for declining test scores in math, science, reading, and other areas. Although there is not a precise definition of back to basics, many consider it to include increased emphasis on reading, writing, and arithmetic; fewer electives; and more rigorous grading.

behavioral objective   A specific statement of what a learner must accomplish to demonstrate mastery.

behaviorism   A psychological theory that interprets human behavior in terms of stimuli–response.

behavior modification   A strategy to alter behavior in a desired direction through the use of rewards.

bilingual education   Educational programs in which students of limited or no English-speaking ability attend classes taught in English as well as in their native language. There is great variability in these programs in terms of goals, instructional opportunity, and balance between English and a student's native language.

block grants   Federal dollars provided to the states, with limited federal restrictions, for educational aid and program funding.

block scheduling   Using longer "blocks" of time to schedule classes results in fewer but longer periods given to each subject. It is designed to promote greater in-depth study.

Bloom's taxonomy   A classification system in which each lower level is subsumed in the next higher level. Bloom's taxonomy describes simple to more complex mental processes, and usually is used to classify educational objectives or classroom questions.

board certification   Recognition of advanced teaching competence, awarded to teachers who demonstrate high levels of knowledge, commitment, and professionalism through a competitive review process administered by the National Board for Professional Teaching Standards.

board of education   Constituted at the state and local levels, this agency is responsible for formulating educational policy. Members are sometimes appointed but, more frequently, are elected at the local level.

bond   A certificate of debt issued by a government guaranteeing payment of the original investment plus interest by a specified future date. Bonds are used by local communities to raise the funds they need to build or repair schools.

Brown v. Board of Education of Topeka   U.S. Supreme Court ruling that reversed an earlier "separate but equal" ruling and declared that segrated schooling was inherently unequal and therefore unlawful.

Buckley Amendment   The 1974 Family Educational Rights and Privacy Act granting parents of students under 18 and students 18 or over the right to examine their school records.

busing   A method for remedying segregation by transporting students to create more ethnically or racially balanced schools. Before busing and desegregation were linked, busing was not a controversial issue, and, in fact, the vast majority of students riding school buses are not involved in desegregation programs.

C

career ladder   A system designed to create different status levels for teachers by developing steps one can climb to receive increased pay through increased responsibility or experience.

career technical education   A program to teach elementary and secondary students about the world of work by integrating career awareness and exploration across the school curriculum.

Carnegie unit   A credit awarded to a student for successfully completing a high school course. It is used in determining graduation requirements and college admissions.

Cartesian dualism   The belief that reality is composed of both materialism and idealism, body and mind.

categorical grant   Financial aid to local school districts from state or federal agencies for specific purposes.

certification   State government or professional association's evaluation and approval of an applicant's competencies.

character education   A model composed of various strategies that promote a defined set of core values to students.

charter school   A group of teachers, parents, and even businesses may petition a local school board, or state government, to form a charter school that is exempt from many state and local regulations. Designed to promote creative new schools, the charter represents legal permission to try new approaches to educate students. First charter legislation was passed in Minnesota in 1991.

chief state school officer   The executive head of a state department of education. The chief state school officer is responsible for carrying out the mandates of the state board of education and enforcing educational laws and regulations. This position is also referred to as *state superintendent*.

child abuse   Physical, sexual, or emotional violation of a child's health and well-being.

child-centered instruction (individual instruction)   Teaching that is designed to meet the interests and needs of individual students.

classroom climate   The physical, emotional, and aesthetic characteristics, as well as the learning resources, of a school classroom.

Coalition of Essential Schools (CES)   This was founded by Theodore Sizer and is a reform effort that creates smaller schools, learning communities, and more in-depth study of the curriculum.

cognitive domain   The area of learning that involves knowledge, information, and intellectual skills.

Coleman Report   A study commissioned by President Johnson (1964) to analyze the factors that influence the academic achievement of students. One of the major findings of James Coleman's report was that schools in general have relatively little impact on learning. Family and peers were found to have more impact on a child's education than the school itself did.

collaborative action research   Connects teaching and professional growth through the use of research relevant to classroom responsibilities.

collaborative decision-making   Teachers share power with the school principal and actively participate in curricular, budgetary, and other school policy decisions.

collective bargaining   A negotiating procedure between employer and employees for resolving disagreements on salaries, work schedules, and other conditions of employment. In collective bargaining, all teachers in a school system bargain as one group through chosen representatives.

Comer model   James Comer of Yale has created and disseminated a program that incorporates a team of educational and mental health professionals to assist children at risk by working with their parents and attending to social, educational, and psychological needs.

Common Core State Standards   Identifies the skills and content a student should master at each grade level from kindergarten to grade 12.

common school   A public, tax-supported school. First established in Massachusetts, the school's purpose was to create a common basis of knowledge for children. It usually refers to a public elementary school.

community schools   Schools connected with a local community to provide for the educational needs of that community.

compensatory education   Educational experiences and opportunities designed to overcome or compensate for difficulties associated with a student's disadvantaged background.

comprehensive high school   A public secondary school that offers a variety of curricula, including vocational, academic, and general education programs.

comprehensive values education   An approach to moral education that integrates traditional and progressive strategies for teaching values.

compulsory attendance   A state law requiring that children and adolescents attend school until reaching a specified age.

conditional teacher's license   Sometimes called an emergency license, a substandard license that is issued on a temporary basis to meet a pressing need.

consolidation   The trend toward combining small or rural school districts into larger ones.

constructivism   With roots in cognitive psychology, this educational approach is built on the idea that people construct their understanding of the world. Constructivist teachers gauge a student's prior knowledge, then carefully orchestrate cues, classroom activities, and penetrating questions to push students to higher levels of understanding.

content standards   The knowledge, skills, and dispositions that students should master in each subject. These standards are often linked to broader themes and sometimes to testing programs.

cooperative learning   In classrooms using cooperative learning, students work on activities in small groups, and they receive rewards based on the overall group performance.

Copyright Act   A federal law that protects intellectual property, including copyrighted material. Teachers can use such material in classrooms only with permission, or under specific guidelines.

core curriculum   A central body of knowledge that schools require all students to study.

core knowledge   Awareness of the central ideas, beliefs, personalities, writings, events, etc. of a culture. Also termed *cultural literacy*.

corporal punishment   Disciplining students through physical punishment by a school employee.

covert power   (See hidden government.)

Creationism   The position that God created the universe, the earth, and living things on the earth in precisely the manner described in the Old Testament, in six 24-hour periods.

critical pedagogy   An education philosophy that unites the theory of critical thinking with actual practice in real-world settings. The purpose is to eliminate the cultural and educational control of the dominant group, to have students apply critical thinking skills to the real world and become agents for social change.

critical thinking skills   Higher-order intellectual skills such as comparing, interpreting, observing, summarizing, classifying, creating, and criticizing.

cultural difference theory   This theory asserts that academic problems can be overcome if educators study and mediate the cultural gap separating school and home.

cultural literacy   Knowledge of the people, places, events, and concepts central to the standard literate culture.

culturally responsive teaching   Recognizes that students learn in different ways, and that effective teachers respond to these differences. This approach focuses on the learning strengths of students, as well as mediates the frequent mismatch between home and school cultures.

cultural pluralism   Acceptance and encouragement of cultural diversity.

culture   A set of learned beliefs, values, and behaviors; a way of life shared by members of a society.

curriculum (formal, explicit)   Planned content of instruction that enables the school to meet its aims.

curriculum development   The processes of assessing needs, formulating objectives, and developing instructional opportunities and evaluation.

D

dame schools   Primary schools in colonial and other early periods in which students were taught by untrained women in the women's own homes.

decentralization   The trend of dividing large school districts into smaller and, it is hoped, more responsive units.

deductive reasoning   Working from a general rule to identify particular examples and applications to that rule.

de facto segregation   The segregation of racial or other groups resulting from circumstances, such as housing patterns, rather than from official policy or law.

deficit theory   A theory that asserts that the values, language patterns, and behaviors that children from certain racial and ethnic groups bring to school put them at an educational disadvantage.

de jure segregation   The segregation of racial or other groups on the basis of law, policy, or a practice designed to accomplish such separation.

delegate representative   Form of representative government in which the interests of a particular geographic region are represented through an individual or "delegate." Some school boards are organized so that members act as delegates of a neighborhood or region.

descriptive data   Information that provides an objective depiction of various aspects of school or classroom life.

desegregation   The process of correcting past practices of racial or other illegal segregation.

detrack   The movement to eliminate school tracking practices, which often have racial, ethnic, and class implications.

differentiated instruction   Instructional activities are organized in response to individual differences rather than content standards. Teachers are asked to carefully consider each student's needs, learning style, life experience, and readiness to learn.

digital divide   A term used to describe the technological gap between the "haves" and the "have-nots." Race, gender, class, and geography are some of the demographic factors influencing technological access and achievement.

direct teaching   A model of instruction in which the teacher is a strong leader who structures the classroom and sequences subject matter to reflect a clear academic focus. This model emphasizes the importance of a structured lesson in which presentation of new information is followed by student practice and teacher feedback.

disability A learning or physical condition, a behavior, or an emotional problem that impedes education. Educators now prefer to speak of "students with disabilities," not "handicapped students," emphasizing the person, not the disability.

distance learning Courses, programs, and training provided to students over long distances through television, the Internet, and other technologies.

dual language instruction (See maintenance approach.)

due process The procedural requirements that must be followed in such areas as student and teacher discipline and placement in special education programs. Due process exists to safeguard individuals from arbitrary, capricious, or unreasonable policies, practices, or actions. The essential elements of due process are (1) a notice of the charge or actions to be taken, (2) the opportunity to be heard, and (3) the right to a defense that reflects the particular circumstances and nature of the case.

E

early childhood education Learning undertaken by young children in the home, in nursery schools, in preschools, and in kindergartens.

eclecticism In this text, the drawing on of elements from several educational philosophies or methods.

educable child A developmentally disabled child who is capable of achieving only limited basic learning and usually must be instructed in a special class.

educational malpractice A new experimental line of litigation similar to the concept of medical malpractice. Educational malpractice is concerned with assessing liability for students who graduate from school without fundamental skills. Unlike medical malpractice, many courts have rejected the notion that schools or educators be held liable for this problem.

educational partnership A business relationship between schools and corporations through which companies offer schools services and products and often have their corporate name used in the school.

Eight-Year Study Educator Ralph Tyler's study in the 1930s that indicated the effectiveness of progressive education.

elementary school An educational institution for children in grades 1 through 5, 6, or 8, often including kindergarten.

emergency license A substandard license that recognizes teachers who have not met all the requirements for licensure. It is issued on a temporary basis to meet the needs of communities that do not have licensed teachers available.

emotional intelligence (EQ) Personality characteristics, such as persistence, can be measured as part of a new human dimension referred to as EQ. Some believe that EQ scores may be better predictors of future success than IQ scores.

empiricism The philosophy that maintains that sensory experiences, such as seeing, hearing, and touching, are the ultimate sources of all human knowledge. Empiricists believe that we experience the external world by sensory perception; then, through reflection, we conceptualize ideas that help us interpret the world.

enculturation The process of acquiring a culture; a child's acquisition of the cultural heritage through both formal and informal educational means.

endorsement Having a license extended through additional work to include a second teaching field.

engaged time The part of time that a teacher schedules for a subject in which the students are actively involved with academic subject matter. Listening to a lecture, participating in a class discussion, and working on math problems all constitute engaged time.

English as a Second Language [ESL] An immersion approach to bilingual education that removes students from the regular classroom to provide instruction in English.

English Classical School The first free public high school, established in Boston in 1821. The school initially enrolled only boys.

English grammar school The demand for a more practical education in eighteenth-century America led to the creation of these private schools that taught commerce, navigation, engineering, and other vocational skills.

English language learners (ELL) (Also referred to as *limited English proficiency* or *LEP.*) Students whose native language is not English and who are learning to speak and write English.

English only movement Advocates that English should be the only language used or spoken in public, and that the purpose of bilingual education should be to quickly teach English to ELL students.

environmental education The study and analysis of the conditions and causes of pollution, overpopulation, and waste of natural resources, and of the ways to preserve Earth's intricate ecology.

epistemology The branch of philosophy that examines the nature of knowledge and learning.

equal educational opportunity Refers to giving every student the educational opportunity to develop fully whatever talents, interests, and abilities he or she may have, without regard to race, color, national origin, sex, disability, or economic status.

equity Educational policy and practice that are just, fair, and free from bias and discrimination.

essentialism An educational philosophy that emphasizes basic skills of reading, writing, mathematics, science, history, geography, and language.

establishment clause A section of the First Amendment of the U.S. Constitution that says that Congress shall make no law respecting the establishment of religion. This clause prohibits nonparochial schools from teaching religion.

ethics The branch of philosophy that examines questions of right and wrong, good and bad.

ethnic group A group of people with a distinctive culture and history.

ethnicity Shared common cultural traits such as language, religion, and dress. A Latino or Hispanic, for example, belongs to an ethnic group, but might belong to the Negro, Caucasian, or Asian race.

ethnocentrism   The tendency to view one's own culture as superior to others, or to fail to consider other cultures in a fair or equitable manner.

evaluation   Assessment of learning and instruction.

evolution   As put forth by Charles Darwin, a keystone of modern biological theory that postulates that animals and plants have their origin in other preexisting types and that there are modifications in successive generations.

exceptional learners   Students who require special education and related services to realize their full potential. Categories of exceptionality include developmentally disabled, gifted, learning disabled, emotionally disturbed, and physically disabled.

existentialism   A philosophy that emphasizes the ability of an individual to determine the course and nature of his or her life and the importance of personal decision making.

expectation theory   First made popular by Rosenthal and Jacobson, this theory holds that a student's academic performance can be improved if a teacher's attitudes and beliefs about that student's academic potential are modified.

expulsion   Dismissal of a student from school for a lengthy period, ranging from one semester to permanently.

extracurriculum   The part of school life that comprises activities, such as sports, academic and social clubs, band, chorus, orchestra, and theater. Many educators think that the extracurriculum develops important skills and values, including leadership, teamwork, creativity, and diligence.

F

failing school   The term given to a school when a large proportion of its students do not do well on standardized tests or other academic measures. Critics charge that students attending such schools are not receiving their constitutionally guaranteed adequate education.

fair use   A legal principle allowing limited use of copyrighted materials. Teachers must observe three criteria: brevity, spontaneity, and cumulative effect.

First Amendment   This constitutional amendment protects freedom of religion and speech. An important part of this amendment is the establishment clause, which prohibits schools and the government from promoting or inhibiting religion in schools.

five factor theory   School effectiveness research emphasizes five factors, including effective leadership, monitoring student progress, safety, a clear vision, and high expectations.

Flanders Interaction Analysis   An instrument developed by Ned Flanders for categorizing student and teacher verbal behavior. It is used to interpret the nature of classroom verbal interaction.

formal or explicit curriculum   A school's official curriculum that is reflected in academic courses and requirements.

Franklin Academy   A colonial high school founded by Benjamin Franklin that accepted females as students and promoted a less classical, more practical curriculum.

full service school   These schools provide a network of social services from nutrition and health care to parental education and transportation, all designed to support the comprehensive educational needs of children.

G

gatekeeping   An aspect of classroom interaction in which the teachers determines who will talk, when, and for how long.

gender bias (see sex discrimination)   The degree to which an individual's beliefs and behavior are unduly influenced on the basis of gender.

gender similarities hypothesis   A theory suggesting that males and females are more alike than different on most psychological and intellectual variables and therefore do not demonstrate gender-specific learning styles that require unique teaching approaches.

gendered career   A term applied to the gender stereotyping of career and occupational fields. Teaching, for example, was initially gendered male, and today is gendered female, particularly at the elementary school level.

generalization   A broad statement about a group that offers information, clues, and insights that can help you as a teacher plan more effectively. Generalizations are a good starting point, but as the teacher learns more about the students, individual differences become more educationally significant.

giftedness   A term describing individuals with exceptional ability. The National Association for Gifted Children defines five elements of giftedness: artistic and creative talents, intellectual and academic abilities, and leadership skills. There, however, continues to be great variance in definitions of the "gifted."

global education   Because economics, politics, scientific innovation, and societal developments in different countries have an enormous impact on children in the United States, the goals of global education include increased knowledge about the peoples of the world, resolution of global problems, increased fluency in foreign languages, and the development of more tolerant attitudes toward other cultures and peoples.

Great Books   The heart of the perennialists' curriculum that includes great works of the past in literature, philosophy, science, and other areas.

green schools   Schools that offer healthier learning environments with clean air and water, nourishing and natural foods, nontoxic cleaners, and more outdoor activities. Academic performance often improves in green schools, and absenteeism decreases.

Gun-Free Schools Act   Enacted in Congress in 1994, schools can lose federal funds if they do not have a zero-tolerance policy mandating one-year expulsions for students bringing firearms to schools. The vast majority of schools report zero-tolerance policies for firearms.

H

Head Start   Federally funded pre-elementary school program to provide learning opportunities for disadvantaged students.

heterogeneous grouping   A group or class consisting of students who show normal variation in ability or performance. It differs from homogeneous grouping, in which criteria, such as grades or scores on standardized tests, are used to group students similar in ability or achievement.

hidden (implicit) curriculum   What students learn, other than academic content, from what they do or are expected to do in school; incidental learnings.

hidden government   The unofficial power structure within a school. It cannot be identified by the official title, position, or functions of individuals. For example, it reflects the potential influence of a school secretary or custodian.

higher-order questions   Questions that require students to go beyond memory in formulating a response. These questions require students to analyze, synthesize, evaluate, and so on.

homeschooling   A growing trend (but a longtime practice) of parents educating their children at home, for religious or philosophical reasons.

homogeneous grouping   The classification of pupils for the purpose of forming instructional groups having a relatively high degree of intellectual similarity.

hornbook   A single sheet of parchment containing the Lord's Prayer and letters of the alphabet. It was protected by a thin sheath from the flattened horn of a cow and fastened to a wooden board—hence, the name. It was used during the colonial era in primary schools.

humanistic education   A curriculum that stresses personal student growth; self-actualizing, moral, and aesthetic issues are explored.

I

idealism   A doctrine holding that knowledge is derived from ideas and emphasizing moral and spiritual reality as a preeminent source of explanation.

ideologues   Home school advocates focused on avoiding public schools in order to impart their own set of values.

immersion   This bilingual education model teaches students with limited English by using a "sheltered" or simplified English vocabulary, but teaching in English and not in the other language.

inclusion   The practice of educating and integrating children with disabilities into regular classroom settings.

independent school   A nonpublic school unaffiliated with any church or other agency.

individualized education program (IEP)   The mechanism through which a disabled child's special needs are identified, objectives and services are described, and evaluation is designed.

individualized instruction   Curriculum content and instructional materials, media, and activities designed for individual learning. The pace, interests, and abilities of the learner determine the curriculum.

Individuals with Disabilities Education Act (IDEA)   Federal law passed in 1990, which extends full education services and provisions to people identified with disabilities.

induction programs   A formal program assisting new teachers to successfully adjust to their role in the classroom.

inductive reasoning   Drawing generalizations based on the observation of specific examples.

informal education   In many cultures, augments or takes the place of formal schooling as children learn adult roles through observation, conversation, assisting, and imitating.

infrastructure   The basic installations and facilities on which the continuance and growth of a community depend.

in loco parentis   Latin term meaning "in place of the parents"; that is, a teacher or school administrator assumes the duties and responsibilities of the parents during the hours the child attends school.

instruction   The process of implementing a curriculum.

INTASC   The Interstate New Teachers Assessment and Support Consortium, an organization that has identified competency standards for new teachers.

integrated curriculum (interdisciplinary curriculum)   Subject matter from two or more areas combined into thematic units (i.e., literature and history resources to study civil rights laws).

integration   The process of educating different racial and ethnic groups together, and developing positive interracial contacts.

Intelligent Design   The argument that instances in nature cannot be explained by Darwinian evolution, but instead are consistent with the notion of an intelligent involvement in the design of life.

interest centers   Usually associated with an open classroom, such centers provide independent student activities related to a specific subject.

Internet   The worldwide computer network that rapidly facilitates information dissemination.

J

junior high school   A two- or three-year school between elementary and high school for students in their early adolescent years, commonly grades 7 and 8 or 7 through 9.

K

Kalamazoo **case**   An 1874 U.S. Supreme Court decision that upheld the right of states to tax citizens in order to provide public secondary education.

kindergarten   A preschool, early childhood educational environment first designed by Froebel in the mid-nineteenth century.

L

labeling   Categorizing or classifying students for the purposes of educational placement. One unfortunate consequence may be that of stigmatizing students and inhibiting them from reaching their full potential.

laboratory schools   Schools often associated with a teacher preparation institution for practice teaching, demonstration, research, or innovation.

land grant colleges   State colleges or universities offering agricultural and mechanical curricula, funded originally by the Morrill Act of 1862.

Land Ordinance Act   This nineteenth-century federal law required newly settled territories to reserve a section of land for schools.

language submersion   This bilingual education model teaches students in classes where only English is spoken, the teacher does not know the language of the student, and the student either learns English as the academic work progresses or pays the consequences. This has been called a "sink or swim" approach.

last mile problem   Geography contributes to a digital divide, in part because running fiber optic cables to rural schools is often an expense that telecommunications companies avoid.

latchkey (self-care) kids   A term used to describe children who go home after school to an empty house; their parents or guardians are usually working and not home.

Latin grammar school   A classical secondary school with a Latin and Greek curriculum preparing students for college.

learning community   The creation of more personal collaboration between teachers and students to promote similar academic goals and values.

learning disability   An educationally significant language and/or learning deficit.

learning styles   Students learn in different ways and have different preferences, ranging from preferred light and noise levels to independent or group learning formats.

least-restrictive environment   The program best suited to meeting a disabled student's special needs without segregating the student from the regular educational program.

locus of control   Learners may attribute success or failure to external or internal factors. "The teacher didn't review the material well" is an example of attribution to an external factor and represents an external locus of control. In this case, the learner avoids responsibility for behavior. When students have an internal locus of control, they believe that they control their fate and take responsibility for events.

logic   The branch of philosophy that deals with reasoning. Logic defines the rules of reasoning, focuses on how to move from one set of assumptions to valid conclusions, and examines the rules of inference that enable us to frame our propositions and arguments.

looping   The practice of teaching the same class for several years, over two or even more grades. The purpose is to build stronger teacher-student connections.

lower-order questions   Questions that require the retrieval of memorized information and do not require more complex intellectual processes.

M

magnet school   A specialized school open to all students in a district on a competitive or lottery basis. It provides a method of drawing children away from segregated neighborhood schools while affording unique educational specialties, such as science, math, and the performing arts.

mainstreaming   The inclusion of special education students in the regular education program. The nature and extent of this inclusion should be based on meeting the special needs of the child.

maintenance approach (or developmental approach)   A bilingual model that emphasizes the importance of acquiring English while maintaining competence in the native language.

malfeasance   Deliberately acting improperly and causing harm to someone.

materialism   A philosophy focused on scientific observation and the belief that existence is only experienced in the physical realm.

mastery learning   An educational practice in which an individual demonstrates mastery of one task before moving on to the next.

McGuffey Reader   For almost 100 years, this reading series promoted moral and patriotic messages and set the practice of reading levels leading toward graded elementary schools.

McKinney Vento Homeless Assistance Act   The primary piece of federal legislation dealing with the education of homeless children in public schools.

mentor   A guide or an adviser, and a component of some first-year school induction programs designed to assist new teachers.

merit pay   A salary system that bases a teacher's pay on performance.

metaphysics   The area of philosophy that examines the nature of reality.

microteaching   A clinical approach to teacher training in which the teacher candidate teaches a small group of students for a brief time while concentrating on a specific teaching skill.

middle schools   Two- to four-year schools of the middle grades, often grades 6 through 8, between elementary school and high school.

misfeasance   Failure to act in a proper manner to prevent harm.

moral stages of development   Promoted by Lawrence Kohlberg as a model of moral development in which individuals progress from simple moral concerns, such as avoiding punishment, to more sophisticated ethical beliefs and actions.

Morrill Act   Federal legislation (1862) granting federal lands to states to establish colleges to promote more effective and efficient agriculture and industry. A second Morrill Act, passed in 1890, provided federal support for "separate but equal" colleges for African Americans.

multicultural education   Educational policies and practices that not only recognize but also affirm human differences and similarities associated with gender, race, ethnicity, nationality, disability, and class.

multiple intelligences   A theory developed by Howard Gardner to expand the concept of human intelligence to include such areas as logical-mathematical, linguistic, bodily-kinesthetic, musical, spatial, interpersonal, intrapersonal, and naturalist.

multiracial   A term that refers to people whose ancestry consists of more than one race. This is the fastest-growing student demographic in the United States.

N

National Assessment of Educational Progress (NAEP)   Program to ascertain the effectiveness of U.S. schools and student achievement.

National Board for Professional Teaching Standards (NBPTS)   A professional organization charged with establishing voluntary standards for recognizing superior teachers as board certified.

National Council for the Accreditation of Teacher Education (NCATE)   An organization that evaluates teacher education programs in many colleges and universities. Graduates of programs approved by the NCATE receive licenses in over half the states, pending the successful completion of required state exams.

national curricular standards   Nationally prescribed or recommended standards, content skills, and testing.

National Defense Education Act   Federally sponsored programs (1958) to improve science, math, and foreign language instruction in schools.

National Education Association (NEA)   The largest organization of educators, the NEA is concerned with the overall improvement of education and of the conditions of educators. It is organized at the national, state, and local levels.

networking   The term used to describe the intentional effort to develop personal connections with individuals who could be helpful in finding positions or gaining professional advancement.

neuroplasticity   The ability of our brain to change itself and create new neural pathways.

New England Primer   One of the first textbooks in colonial America, teaching reading and moral messages.

No Child Left Behind (NCLB)   A federal law passed in 2001 that emphasizes high-stakes standardized testing by requiring schools to annually assess students' achievement in reading, math, and science. Schools report not only individual test scores, but also scores by race, ethnicity, disability, social class, and limited English proficiency.

nondiscriminatory education   The principle of nondiscriminatory education, based on the Fifth and Fourteenth Amendments of the U.S. Constitution, mandates that children with disabilities be fairly assessed so that they can be protected from inappropriate classification and tracking.

nonfeasance   Failure to exercise appropriate responsibility that results in someone's being harmed.

nongraded school   A school organization in which grade levels are eliminated for two or more years.

nonverbal communication   The act of transmitting and/or receiving messages through means not having to do with oral or written language, such as eye contact, facial expressions, and body language.

normal school   A two-year teacher education institution popular in the nineteenth century, many of which were expanded to become today's state colleges and universities.

norm-referenced tests   Tests that compare individual students with others in a designated norm group.

Northwest Ordinance (1785, 1787)   Provided for the sale of federal lands in the Northwest territory to support public schools.

null curriculum   The curriculum that is not taught in schools.

O

objective   The purpose of a lesson expressed in a statement.

objective-referenced tests   Tests that measure whether students have mastered a designated body of knowledge rather than how they compare with other students in a norm group.

observation techniques   Structured methods for observing various aspects of school or classroom activities.

Old Deluder Satan Law (1647)   Massachusetts colony law requiring teachers in towns of 50 families or more and that schools be built in towns of 100 families or more. Communities must teach children to read so that they can read the Bible and thwart Satan.

open classroom   Based on the British model, it refers not only to an informal classroom environment but also to a philosophy of education. Students pursue individual interests with the guidance and support of the teacher; interest centers are created to promote this individualized instruction. Students may also have a significant influence in determining the nature and sequence of the curriculum. It is sometimes referred to as *open education.*

open enrollment   The practice of permitting students to attend the school of their choice within their school system. It is sometimes associated with magnet schools and desegregation efforts.

open-space school   A school building without interior walls. Although it may be designed to promote the concept of the open classroom, the open-space school is an architectural concept rather than an educational one.

oral tradition   Spoken language is the primary method for instruction in several cultures around the world. Word problems are used to teach reasoning, proverbs to instill wisdom, and stories to teach lessons about nature, history, religion, and social customs.

outcome based education (OBE)   An educational approach that emphasizes setting learning outcomes and assessing student progress toward attaining those goals, rather than focusing on curricular topics.

P

paraprofessional   A lay person who serves as an aide, assisting the teacher in the classroom.

parochial school   An institution operated and controlled by a religious denomination.

pay-for-performance   A salary method that attempts to make teaching more accountable by linking teacher and student performance to teacher salary (see also **merit pay**).

peace studies   The study and analysis of the conditions of and need for peace, the causes of war, and the mechanisms for the nonviolent resolution of conflict. It is also referred to as *peace education.*

pedagogical cycle   A system of teacher–student interaction that includes four steps: structure—teacher introduces the topic; question—teacher asks questions; respond—student answers or tries to answer questions; and react—teacher reacts to student's answers and provides feedback.

pedagogy   The science of teaching.

Pedagogy of the Oppressed   Pablo Freire's best known work illustrated how education could transform society, and challenged teachers to be agents for social change.

peer review   The practice of having colleagues observe and assess teaching, as opposed to administrators.

perennialism   The philosophy that emphasizes rationality as the major purpose of education. It asserts that there are universal truths and these ideas are best taught through the Great Books.

permanent license   Although some variation exists from state to state, a permanent license is issued after a candidate has completed all the requirements for full recognition as a teacher. Requirements may include a specified number of courses beyond the bachelor's degree or a specified number of years of teaching.

philosophy   The love of or search for wisdom; the quest to understand the meaning of life.

phonics   An approach to reading instruction that emphasizes decoding words by sounding out letters and combinations of letters (as contrasted with the whole language approach).

Plessey v. Ferguson   An 1896 Supreme Court decision that upheld that "separate but equal" was legal and that the races could be segregated. It was overturned in 1954 by *Brown v. The Board of Education of Topeka.*

political philosophy   An approach to analyzing how past and present societies are arranged and governed and how better societies may be created in the future.

portfolio   Compilations of work (such as papers, projects, videotapes) assembled to demonstrate growth, creativity, and competence. Often advocated as a more comprehensive assessment than test scores.

pragmatism   A philosophical belief that asserts truth is what works and rejects other views of reality.

Praxis series of tests   Developed by ETS to assess teachers' competence in various areas: reading, writing, math, professional and subject area knowledge. Praxis test requirements differ among states (see Appendix 2).

primary school   A separately organized and administered elementary school for students in the lower elementary grades, usually grades 1 through 3, and sometimes including preprimary years.

private school   A school controlled by an individual or agency other than the government, usually supported by other than public funds. Most private schools are parochial.

privatization   The movement toward increased private sector, for-profit involvement in the management of public agencies, including schools.

probationary teaching period   A specified period of time in which a newly hired teacher must demonstrate teaching competence. This period is usually three years for public school teachers and six years for college professors. Generally, on satisfactory completion of the probationary period, a teacher is granted tenure.

problem-based learning   An approach that builds a curriculum around intriguing real-life problems and asks students to work cooperatively to develop and demonstrate their solutions.

procedural due process   The right of children with disabilities and their parents to be notified of school actions and decisions; to challenge those decisions before an impartial tribunal, using counsel and expert witnesses; to examine the school records on which a decision is based; and to appeal whatever decision is reached.

professional development   School district efforts to improve the knowledge, skills, and performance of its professional staff.

progressivism   An educational philosophy that organizes schools around the concerns, curiosity, and real-world experiences of students.

progressive education (progressivism)   An educational philosophy emphasizing democracy, student needs, practical activities, and school-community relationships.

property tax   Local real estate taxes (also cars and personal property) historically used to fund local schools.

provisional license   Also referred to as a *probationary license,* a provisional license is frequently issued to beginning teachers. It may mean that a person has completed most, but not all, of the state requirements for permanent licensure. Or it may mean that the state requires several years of teaching experience before it will qualify the teacher for permanent licensure.

Public Law 94-142   Passed in 1975, this was the first law to require schools to provide free and appropriate public education to every child with special needs. This law evolved into today's Individuals with Disabilities Education Act (IDEA).

R

race   A group of individuals sharing common genetic attributes, physical appearance, and ancestry.

racial discrimination   Actions that limit or deny a person or group any privileges, roles, or rewards on the basis of race.

racism   Attitudes, beliefs, and behavior based on the notion that one race is superior to other races.

rationalism   The philosophy that emphasizes the power of reason and the principles of logic to derive statements about the world. Rationalists encourage schools to emphasize teaching mathematics, because mathematics involves reason and logic.

readability formulas   Formulas that use objective, quantitative measures to determine the reading level of textbooks.

reciprocity   States recognize and honor another state's actions, such as recognizing a teacher's license in one state as valid in another.

reconstructionism (reconstructionist)   Also called social reconstructionism, this is a view of education as a way to improve the quality of life, to reduce the chances of conflict, and to create a more humane world.

reflective teaching   Thoughtfully analyzing one's own teaching practices and classroom.

regular education initiative   The attempt to reduce the complications and expense of segregated special education efforts by teaching special needs students in the standard educational program through collaborative consultation, curricular modifications, and environment adaptations.

relational aggression   Subtle, unhealthy peer dynamics used to gain social power (examples include spreading rumors and gossip, excluding peers, teasing, and covert bullying).

résumé   A summary of a person's education and experiences, often used for application to school or employment.

revenue sharing   The distribution of federal money to state and local governments to use as they decide.

Robin Hood laws   As a result of court actions, many states are redistributing revenue from wealthier to poorer communities to equalize educational funding, a process not unlike the efforts of the hero of Sherwood Forest.

romantic critics   Critics such as Paul Goodman, Herbert Kohl, and John Holt, who believed that schools were stifling the cognitive and affective development of children. Individual critics stressed different problems or solutions, but they all agreed that schools were producing alienated, uncreative, and unfulfilled students.

rubric   A scoring guide that describes what must be done, and often describes performance levels ranging from novice to expert, or from a failing grade to excellence.

S

sabbatical   A leave usually granted with full or partial pay after a teacher has taught for a specified period of time (for example, six years). Typically, it is to encourage research and professional development. While common at the university level, it is rare for K–12 teachers.

scaffolding   Taking from the construction field, scaffolding provides support to help a student build understanding. The teacher might use cues or encouragement or well-formulated questions to assist a student in solving a problem or mastering a concept.

school boards   Elected or appointed officials who determine educational policies for school systems.

school-based management   The recent trend in education reform that stresses decision making on the school level. In the past, school policies were set by the state and the districts. Now the trend is for individual schools to make their own decisions and policies.

school choice   The name given to several programs in which parents choose what school their child will attend.

school financing   Refers to the ways in which monies are raised and allocated to schools. The methods differ widely from state to state, and many challenges are being made in courts today because of the unequal distribution of funds within a state or among states.

school infrastructure   The basic facilities and structures that underpin a school plant, such as plumbing, sewage, heat, electricity, roof, masonry, and carpentry.

school superintendent   The chief administrator of a school system, responsible for implementing and enforcing the school board's policies, rules, and regulations, as well as state and federal requirements. The superintendent is directly responsible to the school board and is the formal representative of the school community to outside individuals and agencies.

School to Work Opportunities Act   Programs that link school learning to job settings, often developed in partnerships between school and industry.

schools without walls   An alternative education program that involves the total community as a learning resource.

secondary school   A program of study that follows elementary school and includes junior, middle, and high school.

second-generation segregation   When a school's multiracial populations are separated through tracking, extracurricular activities, and even informal social events, the school is considered to be in second-generation segregation.

secular humanism   The belief that people can live ethically without faith in a supernatural or supreme being. Some critics have alleged that secular humanism is a form of religion and that publishers are promoting secular humanism in their books.

self-censorship   (Also called *stealth censorship*.) To avoid possible problems and parental complaints, some educators quietly remove a book from a library shelf or a course of study. Teachers practice the same sort of self-censorship when they choose not to teach a topic or not to discuss a difficult issue.

separate but equal   A legal doctrine that holds that equality of treatment is accorded when the races are provided substantially equal facilities, even though those facilities are separate. This doctrine was ruled unconstitutional in regard to race.

service credit   By volunteering in a variety of community settings, such as organizations serving the poor, the elderly, or the homeless, students meet what is now a high school graduation requirement in many states.

sex discrimination   Any action that limits or denies a person or group of persons opportunities, privileges, roles, or rewards on the basis of sex.

sexism   The collection of attitudes, beliefs, and behavior that results from the assumption that one sex is superior to the other.

sex-role stereotyping   Attributing behavior, abilities, interests, values, and roles to a person or group of persons on the basis of sex. This process ignores individual differences.

sexual harassment   Unwanted, repeated, and unreturned sexual words, behaviors, or gestures prohibited by federal and some state laws.

simulation   A role-playing technique in which students take part in re-created, lifelike situations.

site-based (school-based) management   A school governance method that shifts decision making from the central district office to individual schools.

Social Darwinism   Similar to Darwin's notion of "survival of the fittest," this idea contends that society is a sorting system, one in which the more talented rise to the top, while those less deserving find themselves at the bottom of the social and economic pecking order.

social reconstructionism   (See Reconstructionism.)

sociogram   A diagram that is constructed to record social interactions, such as which children interact frequently and which are isolates.

Socratic method   An educational strategy attributed to Socrates in which a teacher encourages a student's discovery of truth by questions.

special education   Programs and instruction for children with physical, mental, emotional, or learning disabilities or gifted students who need special educational services in order to achieve at their ability level.

special license   A nonteaching license that is designed for specialized educational careers, such as counseling, library science, and administration.

standards-based education   Education that specifies precisely what students should learn, focuses the curriculum and instruction (and perhaps much more) on meeting these standards, and provides continual testing to see if the standards are achieved.

state adoption   The process by which members of a textbook adoption committee review and select the books used throughout a state. Advocates of this process say that it results in a common statewide curriculum that unites educators on similar issues and makes school life easier for students who move within the state. Critics charge that it gives too much influence to large states and results in a "dumbed down" curriculum.

state board of education   The state education agency that regulates policies necessary to implement legislative acts related to education.

state department of education   An agency that operates under the direction of the state board of education, accrediting schools, certifying teachers, appropriating state school funds, and so on.

stereotypes   Absolute statements applied to all members of a group, suggesting that members of a group have a fixed, often inherited set of characteristics.

stereotype threat   A measure of how social context, such as self-image, trust in others, and a sense of belonging, can influence academic performance.

street academies   Alternative schools designed to bring dropouts and potential dropouts, often inner-city youths, back into the educational mainstream.

student-initiated questions   These are content-related questions originating from the student, yet comprising only a small percentage of the questions asked in class.

superintendent of schools   The executive officer of the local school district.

T

taxonomy   A classification system of organizing information and translating aims into instructional objectives.

Teach for America   A program that places unlicensed college graduates in districts with critical teacher shortages as they work toward attaining a teacher license.

teacher's license   A teaching credential issued by a state government that grants the legal right to teach, not unlike a driver's license, which grants the legal right to drive.

Tenth Amendment   This constitutional amendment establishes that areas not specifically mentioned in the Constitution as federal responsibilities are left to state authority. Since education is not mentioned, each state is free to create its own school system.

tenure   A system of employment in which teachers, having served a probationary period, acquire an expectancy of continued employment. The majority of states have tenure laws.

textbook adoption states   States, most often those in the South and West, that have a formal process for assessing, choosing, and approving textbooks for school use.

Title I   Section of the Elementary and Secondary Education Act that provides federal funds to supplement local education resources for students from low-income families.

Title VII of the Civil Rights Act (1964)   A federal law that prohibits employment discrimination based on race, color, religion, sex, or national origin.

Title IX   A provision of the 1972 Educational Amendments that prohibits sex discrimination in any educational program receiving federal financial assistance.

tracking   The method of placing students according to their ability level in homogeneous classes or learning experiences. Once a student is placed, it may be very difficult to move up from one track to another. The placements may reflect racism, classism, or sexism.

transitional bilingual education (transitional approach)   A bilingual education program in which students are taught for a limited time in their own language as well as English. The goal is to move students into English-only–speaking classrooms.

trustee representatives   This conception of a school board member's role differs from the delegate approach, as members are viewed as representatives of the entire community, rather than representing the narrower interests of a particular group or neighborhood.

tuition tax credits   Tax reductions for parents or guardians of children attending public or private schools.

U

United States Department of Education   Federal cabinet-level agency responsible for establishing national education policies, prohibiting discrimination in education, and collecting data on student achievement and other educational issues.

unobtrusive measurement   A method of observing a situation without altering it.

V

value-added   A statistical measure showing the contribution of teachers and schools toward growth in student achievement. Value-added measures are increasingly used to determine which teachers are rewarded and which teachers are replaced.

values clarification   A model, comprising various strategies, that encourages students to express and clarify their values on different topics.

virtual field trip   Visiting distant sites and events via the computer and the Internet.

virtual school   A type of distance education offered through the Internet. Virtual schools provide asynchronous learning and may offer specialized courses not typically found in traditional schools.

vouchers   A voucher is like a coupon, and it represents money targeted for schools. In a voucher system, parents use educational vouchers to "shop" for a school. Schools receive part or all of their per-pupil funding from these vouchers. In theory, good schools would thrive and poor ones would close for lack of students.

W

wait time   The amount of time a teacher waits for a student's response after a question is asked and the amount of time following a student's response before the teacher reacts.

whole language approach   Teaching reading through an integration of language arts skills and knowledge, with a heavy emphasis on literature (as contrasted with a phonics approach).

women's studies   Originally created during the 1970s to study the history, literature, psychology, and experiences of women, topics typically missing from the traditional curriculum.

Z

zero reject   The principle that no child with disabilities may be denied a free and appropriate public education.

zero-tolerance policies   Such rigorous rules offer schools little or no flexibility in responding to student infractions related to alcohol, drugs, tobacco, violence, and weapons. These policies have been developed by both local school districts and a number of state legislatures, and in most cases, students who violate such policies must be expelled.

zone of proximal development   The area where students can move from what they know to new learning, a zone where real learning is possible.

NOTES

CHAPTER 1: THE TEACHING PROFESSION AND YOU

1. National Education Association, *Status of the American Public School Teacher, 2000–2001* (Washington, DC: NEA, 2003); see also *The Metlife Survey of the American Teacher: Past, Present and Future* (New York: Metropolitan Life Insurance Company, October, 2008), http://www.metlife.com/assets/cao/contributions/citizenship/teacher-survey-25th-anniv-2008.pdf; Mathew DiCarlo, Nate Johnson, Pat Cochran, *Survey and Analysis of Teacher Salary Trends 2007* (Washington, DC: American Federation of Teachers, 2008).

2. Andrew L. Yarrow, "State of Mind," *Education Week* 29, no. 8 (October 21, 2009), pp. 21–23.

3. Kim Marshall, "Is Merit Pay the Answer?" *Education Week* 29, no. 15 (December 15, 2009), pp. 22, 28; Justin Snider, "Tying Teacher Tenure to Student Scores Doesn't Fly," *Education Week*, http://www.edweek.org (retrieved February 9, 2010), in print February 10, 2010, as *The Cult of Statistical Pyrotechnics*; Stephen Sawchuk, "New Teacher-Evaluation Systems Face Obstacles: Stimulus Funds Require Districts to Revamp Teacher Yardsticks," *Education Week* 29, no. 14 (December 11, 2009), http://www.edweek.org; Michele Kerr, "The Right Way to Assess Teachers' Performance," *Washington Post*, June 18, 2010, p. A27; Bryan Toporek, "Poll: Americans in Favor of Teacher Merit Pay," http://www.teachermagazine.org (retrieved September 16, 2010).

4. Amy DePaul, *What to Expect Your First Year of Teaching* (Washington, DC: U.S. Department of Education, September 1998), p. 28. There are also some worthwhile contemporary teaching experiences and insights described on the Internet. See, for example, "10 Things to Expect & Not Expect Your First Year of Teaching," at http://specialedandme.wordpress.com/2009/08/31/10-things-to-expect-not-expect-your-first-year-of-teaching-easier/.

5. Quoted in Ann Lieberman and Lynn Miller, *Teachers, Their World and Their Work* (Alexandria, VA: Association for Supervision and Curriculum Development, 1984), p. 22.

6. Lowell C. Rose and Alec M. Gallup, "The 39th Annual Phi Delta Kappa/Gallup Poll of the Public's Attitudes toward the Public Schools," *Phi Delta Kappan* (September 2007), Table 27, p. 40.

7. Lieberman and Miller, *Teachers, Their World and Their Work*, p. 47.

8. William Lyon Phelps, quoted in Oliver Ikenberry, *American Education Foundations* (Columbus, OH: Merrill, 1974), p. 389.

9. Quoted in Myron Brenton, *What's Happened to Teacher?* (New York: Coward, McCann & Geoghegan, 1970), p. 164.

10. Stephen Gordon quoted in "What Keeps Teachers Going?" *Educational Leadership* 60, no. 8 (May 2003), p. 18.

11. Steve Twomey and Richard Morin, "Teachers: Besieged, Delighted," *Washington Post*, July 4, 1999, pp. A1, A12.

12. Shane Lopez and Sangeeta Agrawal, "Teachers Score Higher than Other Professionals in Well-Being," Gallup Poll, December 23, 2009, http://www.gallup.com/poll/124778/teachers-score-higher-professionals.aspx.

13. Quoted in Brenton, *What's Happened to Teacher?* p. 97.

14. Ibid., p. 94.

15. Trip Gabriel and Sam Dillon, "G.O.P. Governors Take Aim at Teacher Tenure," *New York Times*, February 1, 2011, pp. A1, A3; Jeremy P. Meyer, "Colorado Renews Teacher-Tenure Debate," *Denver Post*, April 13, 2010; Jason Felch, Jessica Garrison, and Jason Song, "Bar Set Low for Lifetime Job in L.A. Schools," *Los Angeles Times*, December 20, 2009, http://latimes.com/news/local/education/la-me-teacher-tenure20-2009dec20,0,2529590.story (retrieved January 3, 2010); Julie Bykowicz, "O'Malley to Push Teacher Changes Proposal that Would Add Year to Tenure Track Might Better Position Md. for Federal Funds," *Baltimore Sun*, February 14, 2010, http://www.baltimoresun.com/news/education/bal-md.race-14feb14,0,1490150.story (retrieved April 7, 2010).

16. Thomas Newkirk, "Stress, Control, and the Deprofessionalizing of Teaching," *Education Week*, October 21, 2009; Jillian N. Lederhouse, "Show Me the Power," *Education Week*, June 13, 2001; National Education Association, *Status of the American Public School Teacher, 2000–2001*.

17. Ron Brandt, "On Teacher Empowerment: A Conversation with Ann Lieberman," *Educational Leadership* 46, no. 8 (May 1989), pp. 23–24; *The MetLife Survey of the American Teacher: Expectations and Experience: A Survey of Teachers, Principals, and Leaders of College Education Programs* (September 26, 2006), http://www.metlife.com/WPSAssets/81821402701160505871V1F2006MetLifeTeacherSurvey.pdf (retrieved January 31, 2008).

18. Adopted from Robert Howsam et al., *Educating a Profession, Report on the Bicentennial Commission of Education for Profession of Teaching* (Washington, DC: American Association of Colleges for Teacher Education, 1976), pp. 6–7.

19. *Tomorrow's Teachers: A Report of the Holmes Group* (East Lansing, MI: Holmes Group, 1986).

20. Carnegie Forum on Education and the Economy, Task Force on Teaching as a Profession, *A Nation Prepared: Teachers for the Twenty-First Century* (New York: Forum, 1986).

21. Scott Stephens and Edith Starzyk, "Colleges Use Programs as Cash Cows, with Few Standards, Critics Say," *Cleveland Plain Dealer*, May 25, 2008, http://groups.google.com/group/oregon-arts-education/msg/a764bcd3a00d2bb7 (retrieved February 20, 2009); Jay Mathews, "Breaking Down the Ivy Tower: Study Finds Schools of Ed in Poor Shape," *Washington Post*, October 31, 2006, p. A8; Doug Selwyn, "Teacher Quality: Teacher Education Left Behind," *Rethinking Schools* 20, no. 2 (Winter 2005/2006), http://www.rethinkingschools.

org/archive/20_02/left202.shtml (retrieved May 10, 2008); George K. Cunningham, *Can Education Schools Be Saved?* speech at the American Enterprise Institute (AEI) in Washington, DC, June 9, 2003, http://www.aei.org/publications/pubID.17804,filter.all/pub_detail.asp (retrieved May 10, 2008); Ellen Condliffe Lagemann, "Whither Schools of Education? Whither Education Research?" *Journal of Teacher Education* 50, no. 5 (November/December 1999), pp. 373–376.

22. National Board for Professional Teaching Standards website, http://www.nbpts.org; "National Certification Picks Up Steam," *American Teacher* 76, no. 6 (May/June 1992), p. 3.

23. Retrieved on February 16, 2009, from http://www.nbpts.org/.

24. Debra Viadero and Vaishali Honawar, "National Board Teachers Found to Be Effective," *Education Week* 27, no. 42 (June 11, 2008), http://www.tasb.org/services/hr_services/hrexchange/2008/sept08/research_confirms_nb.asp (retrieved February 20, 2009).

25. Michael Winerip, "Chosen Few Are Teaching for America," *New York Times,* July 11, 2010; Lisa W. Foderaro, "Alternate Path for Teachers Gains Ground," *NY Times*, April 18, 2010; Paul F. Peterson and Daniel Nadler, "What Happens When States Have Genuine Alternative Certification?" *Education Next* 9, no. 1, Winter 2009, http://www.hoover.org/publications/ednext/34564684.html (retrieved February 12, 2009); National Center for Education Information, "Alternative Routes Are Attracting Talented Individuals from Other Careers Who Otherwise Would Not Become Teachers," http://www.ncei.com/part.html (retrieved February 12, 2009). See also Wendy Kopp, "Ten Years of Teach for America" in *Education Week on the Web,* June 21, 2000, and Wendy Kopp, *One Day All Children Will Triumph: The Unlikely Story of Teach for America and What I Learned along the Way* (New York: Public Affairs, 2003).

26. Michael Birnbaum, "With Limited Training, Teach for America Recruits Play Expanding Role in Schools," *Washington Post,* August 23, 2010; Megan Greenwell, "Applicants Flock to Teacher Corps for Needy Areas," *Washington Post,* December 6, 2008, p. A1.

27. Megan Hopkins, "Training the Next Generation for America: A Proposal for Reconceptualizing Teach for America," *Phi Delta Kappan* 89, no. 10 (June 2008), pp. 721–725.

28. Quoted in Linda Darling-Hammond, "A Future Worthy of Teaching for America," *Phi Delta Kappan* 89, no. 10 (June 2008), p. 733.

29. Debra Viadero, "Panel Finds No Favorite in Teacher-Prep Pathways," *Education Week* 29, no. 31 (April 29, 2010); Jill Constantine, Daniel Player, Tim Silva, Kristin Hallgren, Mary Grider, and John Deke, *An Evaluation of Teachers Trained through Different Routes to Certification* (Washington, DC: U.S. Department of Education, February 2009).

30. Charlotte Danielson, "A Framework for Learning to Teach," *Education Leadership* 66, June 2009, http://www.ascd.org/publications/educational-leadership.aspx (retrieved May 2010); Susan Moore Johnson and Sarah Birkeland, "Fast-Track Certification: Can We Prepare Teachers Both Quickly and Well?" *Education Week* 25, no. 23 (February 15, 2006), pp. 37, 48; "Research-Based Characteristics of High-Quality Teacher Preparation," *ASCD SmartBrief* 1, no. 4 (February 19, 2003); Linda Darling-Hammond, Deborah J. Holtzman, Su Jin Gatlin, and Julian Vasquez Heilig, *Does Teacher Preparation Matter? Evidence about Teacher Certification, Teach for America, and Teacher Effectiveness,* paper presented at the American Educational Association Annual Meeting, Montreal, April 2005, http://www.schoolredesign.net/srn/binaries/teachercert.pdf (retrieved July 19, 2005); Marilyn Cochran-Smith and Kenneth Zeichner, eds., *Studying Teacher Education: The Report of the AERA Panel on Research and Teacher Education* (Mahwah, NJ: Lawrence Erlbaum, 2005).

31. *Different Drummers: How Teachers of Teachers View Public Education* (New York: Public Agenda, 1997).

32. Peter D. Hart and Robert M. Teeter, *A National Priority: Americans Speak on Teacher Quality* (Princeton, NJ: Educational Testing Service, 2002); Leslie Kaplan and William Owning, "No Child Left Behind: The Politics of Teacher Quality," *Phi Delta Kappan* 84, no. 9 (2003), pp. 687–692.

33. Linda Darling-Hammond, "Keeping Good Teachers: Why It Matters What Leaders Can Do," *Educational Leadership* 60, no. 8 (May 2003), pp. 7–13.

34. David C. Berliner, "A Personal Response to Those Who Bash Teacher Education," *Journal of Teacher Education* 51, no. 5 (November/December 2000), pp. 358–71; Suzanne M. Wilson, Robert E. Floden, and Joan Ferrini-Mundy, "Teacher Preparation Research: An Insider's View from the Outside," *Journal of Teacher Education* 53, no. 3 (May/June 2002), pp. 190–204.

35. Berliner, "A Personal Response," p. 363. See also College Board, "2005 College-Bound Seniors," http://www.collegeboard.com/prod_downloads/about/news_info/cbsenior/yr2005/2005-college-bound-seniors.pdf (retrieved February 11, 2006).

36. Lowell Rose and Alec Gallup, "The 33rd Phi Delta Kappa Poll of the Public's Attitudes toward the Public Schools," http://www.pdkintl.org/kappan/kimages/kpoll83.pdf (retrieved February 12, 2006). For other public reaction to education issues, follow the annual Phi Delta Kappa/Gallup Poll Report on the Public's Attitudes toward the Public Schools at http://www.pdkintl.org/kappan/kpollpdf.htm.

37. Arthur E. Wise, "What's Wrong with Teacher Certification?" *Education Week* 22, no. 30 (April 9, 2003), pp. 56, 42; Susan Moore Johnson and Sarah Birkeland, "Fast-Track Certification: Can We Prepare Teachers Both Quickly and Well?" *Education Week* 25, no. 23, (February 15, 2006), pp. 37, 48.

38. Andy Baumgartner, "A Teacher Speaks Out: Insights from the National Teacher of the Year," *Washington Post,* March 26, 2000, p. B4.

39. Albert Shanker, "Where We Stand: Is It Time for National Standards and Exams?" *American Teacher* 76, no. 6 (May/June 1992), p. 5.

40. LaPointe quoted in Gerald W. Bracey, "The Second Bracey Report on the Condition of Public Education," *Phi Delta Kappan* (October 1992), pp. 104–117, cited in David C. Berliner and Bruce J. Biddle, *The Manufactured Crisis* (Reading, MA: Addison Wesley, 1995), p. 54.

41. Fair Test, *2007 College Bound Seniors Average SAT Scores,* http://fairtest.org/sites/default/files/SATScores 2007Chart.pdf (November 12, 2007); Nation's Report Card, *Reading Scores,* http://nces.ed.gov/nationsreport card/reading (February 2, 2008); Dianne Reed and others, "Gender Equity in Testing and Assessment," in Susan S. Klein, ed., *Handbook for Achieving Gender Equity through Education,* 2nd ed. (New York: Lawrence Erlbaum Associates, Taylor & Francis Group, 2007), pp. 155–169.

42. Berliner and Biddle, *The Manufactured Crisis*, p. 146; see also Sara Mead, *The Evidence Suggests Otherwise; The Truth About Boys and Girls* (Washington, DC: Education Sector, 2006), pp. 14–16; and Richard Rothstein, *The Way We Were? The Myths and Realities of America's Students Achievement* (Washington, DC: Century Fund, 1998).

CHAPTER 2: DIFFERENT WAYS OF LEARNING

1. Heather Wolpert-Gawron, "The Bunk of Debunking Learning Styles," *Teacher Magazine,* February 17, 2010, http://www.teachermagazine.com; Kenneth Dunn and Rita Dunn, "Dispelling Outmoded Beliefs About Student Learning," *Educational Leadership* 45, no. 7 (March 1987), pp. 55–63.

2. Marge Scher, "Celebrate Strengths, Nurture Affinities: A Conversation with Mel Levine," *Educational Leadership* 64, no. 1 (September 2006), pp. 8–15.

3. Wolpert-Gawron, "The Bunk of Debunking Learning Styles"; James Keefe, *Learning Style Theory and Practice* (Reston, VA: National Association of Secondary School Principals, 1987); Tamara Henry, "Open Up Schools, Let Sun Shine In: Creature Comforts Can Aid Learning," *USA Today,* March 22, 2001, p. 8D.

4. Wolpert-Gawron, "The Bunk of Debunking Learning Styles"; Dunn and Dunn, "Dispelling Outmoded Beliefs About Student Learning"; see also G. Price, "Which Learning Style Elements Are Stable and Which Tend to Change?" *Learning Styles Network Newsletter* 4, no. 2 (1980), pp. 38–40; J. Vitrostko, *An Analysis of the Relationship Among Academic Achievement in Mathematics and Reading, Assigned Instructional Schedules and the Learning Style Time Preferences of Third-, Fourth-, Fifth-, and Sixth-Grade Students,* unpublished doctoral dissertation, St. John's University, Jamaica, New York, 1983.

5. Janet Hyde, "New Directions in the Study of Gender Similarities and Differences," *Current Directions in Psychological Science* 16 (2007), pp. 259–263; Janet Hyde, "The Gender Similarities Hypothesis," *American Psychologist* 60 (2005), pp. 581–592.

6. Pamela Davis-Kean, "Dads Influence Daughters' Interest in Mathematics," paper presented at Educating a STEM Workforce: New Strategies for U-M and the State of Michigan, Ann Arbor, MI, 2007.

7. Norman Doidge, *The Brain that Changes Itself* (New York: Viking Press, 2007); Andrea Miller, "The Mindful Society," *Shambhala Sun* (September 2008), pp. 58–59.

8. Howard Gardner and Thomas Hatch, "Multiple Intelligences Go to School: Educational Implications of the Theory of Multiple Intelligences," *Educational Researcher* 18, no. 8 (November 1989), p. 5; Seana Moran, Mindy Kornhaber, and Howard Gardner, "Orchestrating Multiple Intelligences," *Educational Leadership* 64, no. 1 (September 2006), pp. 22–27.

9. Kathy Checkley, "The First Seven . . . and the Eighth: A Conversation with Howard Gardner," *Educational Leadership* 55, no. 1 (September 1997), pp. 8–13; Moran, Kornhaber, and Gardner, "Orchestrating Multiple Intelligences."

10. Richard Louv, *Last Child in the Woods: Saving Our Children from Nature-Deficit Disorder* (New York: Algonquin Books, 2005).

11. Moran, Kornhaber, and Gardner, "Orchestrating Multiple Intelligences"; Thomas Armstrong, "Multiple Intelligences: Seven Ways to Approach Curriculum," *Educational Leadership* 52 (November 1994), pp. 26–28; see also Howard Gardner, *Intelligence Reframed: Multiple Intelligences for the 21st Century* (New York: Basic Books, 1999).

12. Howard Gardner, "Can Technology Exploit the Many Ways of Knowing?" in David T. Gordon, ed., *The Digital Classroom* (Cambridge: Harvard College, 2000), pp. 32–35.

13. Howard Gardner, "Reflections on Multiple Intelligences: Myths and Messages," *Phi Delta Kappan* 77, no. 3 (November 1995), pp. 200–209; Veronica Borruso Emig, "A Multiple Intelligence Inventory," *Educational Leadership* 55, no. 1 (September 1997), pp. 47–50.

14. Thomas R. Hoerr, "How the New City School Applies the Multiple Intelligences," *Educational Leadership* 52 (November 1994), pp. 29–33.

15. Howard Gardner, *Five Minds for the Future* (Cambridge, MA: Harvard Business School Press, 2006).

16. Nancy Gibbs, "The E.Q. Factor," *Time* 146, no. 14 (October 2, 1995), pp. 60–68.

17. Ibid.; see also Daniel Goleman, *Working with Emotional Intelligence* (New York: Bantam Books, 2000), and Kevin R. Kelly and Sidney M. Moon, "Personal and Social Talents," *Phi Delta Kappan* 79, no. 10 (June 1998), pp. 743–746.

18. Daniel Goleman, "The Socially Intelligent Leader," *Educational Leadership* 64, no. 1 (September 2006), pp. 76–81; Daniel Goleman, "Emotional Intelligence: Why It Can Matter More than IQ," *Learning,* May/June 1996, pp. 49–50; see a sample application of EQ in Emily Wax, "Educating More than the Mind," *Washington Post,* October 4, 2000, p. B3.

19. These categories build on the ones described by William Heward, Sara Ernsbarger Bicard, and Rodney A. Cavanaugh, "Educational Equality for Students with Disabilities," in James Banks and Cherry Banks, eds., *Multicultural Education,* 7th ed. (San Francisco: Jossey Bass, 2010), pp. 329–367.

20. Michael Janofsky, "Some New Help for the Extremely Gifted," *New York Times,* October 26, 2005.

21. Walt Gardner, "Gifted Children Are Stepchildren in School Reform," *Education Week*, May 7, 2010, http://www.edweek.org; Christina A. Samuels, "'Gifted' Label Said to Miss Dynamic Nature of Talent," *Education Week* 28, no. 8 (October 15, 2008), pp. 1, 18.

22. Valerie Strauss, "Looking for a Few Wise Children," *Washington Post,* September 17, 2002, p. A11.

23. National Association for Gifted Children, Frequently Asked Questions, http://www.nagc.org/index.aspx?id=548 (August 7, 2010).

24. Tamara Fisher, "I Don't Want to Be a Smarty Anymore," *Education Week* online (June 30, 2010); Dona J. Matthews and Joanne F. Foster, "Refinements, Bridges, and Themes in Our Conceptual Foundations: Mystery to Mastery: Shifting Paradigms in Gifted Education," *Roeper Review* 28, no. 2 (Winter 2006), pp. 64–69; Tracy L. Cross, Jerrell C. Cassady, and Kimberly A. Miller, "Suicide Ideation and Personality Characteristics Among Gifted Adolescents," *Gifted Child Quarterly* 50, no. 4 (Fall 2006), pp. 295–306.

25. Fisher, "I Don't Want to Be a Smarty Anymore."

26. National Association for Gifted Children, Frequently Asked Questions; Cross, Cassady, and Miller, "Suicide Ideation and Personality Characteristics Among Gifted Adolescents."

27. Gardner, "Gifted Children Are Stepchildren in School Reform"; Diana Jean Schemo, "Schools, Facing Tight Budgets, Leave Gifted Students Behind," *New York Times,* March 2, 2004.

28. Gardner, "Gifted Children Are Stepchildren in School Reform"; Dona J. Matthews and Joanne F. Foster, "Mystery to Mastery: Shifting Paradigms in Gifted Education," *Roeper Review* 28, no. 2 (Winter 2006), pp. 64–69; Matthews and Foster, "Refinements, Bridges, and Themes in Our Conceptual Foundations"; Susan Winebrenner, "Gifted Students Need an Education, Too," *Educational Leadership* 58, no. 1 (September 2000), pp. 52–56.

29. National Association for Gifted Education, *Critical Issues and Practices in Gifted Education: What the Research Says* (New York: Prufrock Press, 2007); Matthews and Foster, "Refinements, Bridges, and Themes in Our Conceptual Foundations."

30. National Association for Gifted Education, *Critical Issues and Practices in Gifted Education: What the Research Says.*

31. Tamara Fisher, "On the Up-Side," *Education Week* online (July 7, 2010).

32. Ibid.

33. Marie Killilea, *Karen* (New York: Dell, 1952), p. 171.

34. Ed Martin, quoted in "PL 94–142," *Instructor* 87, no. 9 (1978), p. 63; Heward, Bicard, and Cavanaugh, "Educational Equality for Students with Disabilities," in Banks and Banks (eds.), *Multicultural Education.*

35. Heward, Bicard, and Cavanaugh, "Educational Equality for Students with Disabilities"; Linda Greenhouse, "Parents Now Have the Burden of Proof in School Cases, Court Rules," *New York Times,* November 15, 2005.

36. U.S. Department of Education, National Center for Education Statistics, "Children and Youth with Disabilities, Indicator 6," Table A-6-1, *Condition of Education 2010*, http://nces.ed.gov/programs/coe/2010/section1/indicator06.asp.

37. Ibid.

38. Heward, Bicard, and Cavanaugh, "Educational Equality for Students with Disabilities"; United States Department of Education, Office of Special Education Programs, *Twenty-Ninth Annual Report to Congress on the Implementation of the Individuals with Disabilities Education Act*, Washington, DC (2007), http://www2.ed.gov/about/reports/annual/osep/ (retrieved August 16, 2010).

39. Howard Witt, "Discipline Tougher on African Americans," *Chicago Tribune,* September 25, 2007, http://www.chicagotribune.com/services/newspaper/eedition/chi-070924discipline,0,7975055.story (retrieved August 16, 2010); Council for Exceptional Children, *New Study Verifies the Disproportionate Number of Diverse Students in Special Education* (Arlington, VA: CEC, 2008), http://www.cec.sped.org/AM/Template.cfm?Section5Search&template=/CM/HTMLDisplay.cfm&ContentID=2052 (retrieved August 16, 2010); "Special Report/Racial Inequities in Special Education," *Education Leadership* 60, no. 4 (December 2002/January 2003), p. 91.

40. National Women's Law Center, *When Girls Don't Graduate We All Fail: A Call to Improve the Graduation Rates of Girls* (Washington, DC: National Women's Law Center, 2007), http://www.nwlc.org (retrieved August 17, 2010); Heward, Bicard, and Cavanaugh, "Educational Equality for Students with Disabilities."

41. Heward, Bicard, and Cavanaugh, "Educational Equality for Students with Disabilities"; Suzy Ruder, "We Teach All," *Educational Leadership* 58, no. 1 (September 2000), pp. 49–51; Mary Beth Doyle, "Transition Plans for Students with Disabilities," *Educational Leadership* 58, no. 1 (September 2000), pp. 46–48.

42. Heward, Bicard, and Cavanaugh, "Educational Equality for Students with Disabilities"; United States Department of Education, Office of Special Education Programs, *Twenty-Ninth Annual Report to Congress on the Implementation of the Individuals with Disabilities Education Act.*

43. Quoted in David Milofsky, "Schooling the Kid No One Wants," *New York Times Magazine,* January 2, 1977, pp. 24–29.

44. Nancy Trejos, "Handheld PCs Put to the Test," *Washington Post,* September 4, 2001, pp. B1, B2; Jennifer Medina, "Technology Eases the Way for the Visually Impaired," *New York Times,* July 3, 2002; Michael P. Bruno, "High-Tech Help for Disabled Children," Washtech.com, May 10, 2002, p. 5. For more information about special education services and adaptive technology, visit the United States Department of Education Office of Special Education website at http://www.ed.gov/about/offices/list/osers/osep/.

45. Solomon Moore, "Special Ed Joins the Mainstream," *Los Angeles Times,* October 25, 2002.

CHAPTER 3: TEACHING YOUR DIVERSE STUDENTS

1. National Center for Educational Statistics, U.S. Department of Education, *Status and Trends in the Education of Racial and Ethnic Groups,* Susan Aud, National Center for Education Statistics, and Mary Ann Fox and Angelina Kewal Ramani, Education Statistics Services Institute–American Institutes for Research, July 2010, http://nces.ed.gov/pubs2010/2010015.pdf; the Center for Public Education, *At a Glance: Changing Demographics* (Washington, DC: The Center for Public Education, 2007), http://www.centerforpubliceducation.org/Main-Menu/Staffingstudents/Changing-Demographics-At-a-glance- (retrieved August 22, 2011).
2. James A. Banks, "Multicultural Education: Characteristics and Goals," in James Banks and Cherry Banks, eds., *Multicultural Education,* 6th ed. (San Francisco: Jossey Bass, 2007), pp. 3–30.
3. The demographic information is based on the following: Debra Viadero, "Multiracial Children Attracting Interest as Visibility Increases," *Education Week* 28, no. 18 (January 21, 2009), pp. 1, 14–15; National Center for Educational Statistics, U.S. Department of Education, *Status and Trends in the Education of Racial and Ethnic Groups*; "Overview of Race and Hispanic Origin," *Census 2000 Brief* (Washington, DC: U.S. Census Bureau, March 2001); "Projections of the Resident Population by Race, Hispanic Origin, and Nativity: 2025 to 2045," *Census 2000 Brief.*
4. National Center for Educational Statistics, U.S. Department of Education, *Status and Trends in the Education of Racial and Ethnic Groups*; College Board, *2010 College Bound Seniors,* 2008, http://www.collegeboard.com/press/releases/213182.html (retrieved September 13, 2010); Sara Mead, *The Evidence Suggests Otherwise; The Truth About Boys and Girls* (Washington, DC: Education Sector, 2006), pp. 14–16; Christopher B. Swanson, *The Real Truth about Low Graduation Rates, An Evidence Based Commentary* (Washington, DC: The Urban Institute, 2004); Debra Viadero and Robert Johnson, "Lifting Minority Achievement: Complex Answers," *Education Week* 19, no. 30 (April 5, 2000), pp. 14–16; U.S. Department of Education, National Center for Educational Statistics, *The Nation's Report Card,* http://nationsreportcard.gov (retrieved February 24, 2009).
5. Lowell C. Rose and Alec M. Gallup, "The 38th Annual Phi Delta Kappa/Gallup Poll of the Public's Attitude Toward the Public Schools," *Phi Delta Kappan* 88, no. 1 (September 2006), Table 20, pp. 42–53.
6. Robert Evans, "Reframing the Achievement Gap," *Phi Delta Kappan* 86, no. 8 (April 2005), pp. 582–589.
7. Gay, Lesbian, and Straight Education Network, http://www.glsen.com; Ian K. Macgillivray, *Gay-Straight Alliances: A Handbook for Students, Educators, and Parents* (Binghampton, NY: Haworth Press, 2007).
8. Benoit Denzet-Lewis, "Coming Out in Junior High School," *New York Times Magazine*, September 27, 2009, pp.36–41, 52, 54–55; Jason Cianciotto and Sean Cahill, *Education Policy: Issues Affecting Lesbian, Gay, Bisexual and Transgender Youth* (New York: The National Gay and Lesbian Task Force Policy Institute, 2003).
9. Gay, Lesbian, and Straight Education Network, *Number of Gay-Straight Alliance Registrations Passes 3,500,* http://www.glsen.org (retrieved February 13, 2008).
10. Andrew Hacker, *Two Nations: Black, White, Separate, Hostile, Unequal* (New York: Charles Scribner's, 1992), pp. 31–32.
11. Jennifer Holliday, "The ABC's of Whiteness and Anti-Racism," *Teaching Tolerance,* http://www.tolerance.org/teach/activities/activity.jsp?ar=713 (retrieved March 2, 2009).
12. Ana Maria Villegas, *Culturally Responsive Pedagogy for the 1990s and Beyond* (Washington, DC: ERIC Clearinghouse on Teacher Education, American Association of Colleges for Teacher Education, 1991).
13. Israel Zangwill, *The Melting Pot* (play), 1909, cited in Pamela Tiedt and Iris Tiedt, *Multicultural Education* (Needham Heights, MA: Allyn & Bacon, 1999), p. 2.
14. James Crawford, ed., *Language Loyalties: A Source Book on the Official English Controversy* (Chicago: University of Chicago Press, 1992); see also Jonathon Zimmerman, "A Babel of Tongues," *U.S. News & World Report,* November 24, 1997, p. 39.
15. Richard Rothstein, "Bilingual Education: The Controversy," in James W. Noll ed., *Taking Sides* (Dubuque, IA: McGraw-Hill/Dushkin, 2005), pp. 290–301.
16. James Lyon, *Legal Responsibilities of Education Agencies Serving National Origin Language Minority Students* (Chevy Chase, MD: Mid-Atlantic Equity Center, 1992), http://www.maec.org/lyons/contents.html (retrieved May 9, 2008).
17. The National Clearinghouse for English Language Acquisition, *The Growing Number of Limited English Proficient Students* (Washington, DC: NCELA, November 2007), http://www.ncela.gwu.edu/policy/states/reports/statedata/2005LEP/GrowingLEP_0506.pdf; U.S. Department of Education, *The Condition of Education, 2007,* Indicator 6.
18. Tom Stritikis and Manka M. Varghese, "Language Diversity and Schooling," in Banks and Banks, eds., *Multicultural Education,* pp. 297–325.
19. Christine Bennett, *Comprehensive Multicultural Education: Theory and Practice,* 6th ed. (Boston: Allyn & Bacon, 2006).
20. Yilu Zhao, "Wave of Pupils Lacking English Strains Schools," *New York Times,* August 5, 2002, http://query.nytimes.com/gst/fullpage.html?res=9A01EFD9133BF936A3575BC0A9649C8B63 (retrieved May 10, 2008).
21. James Crawford, *Hold Your Tongue: Bilingualism and the Politics of "English Only"* (New York: Addison-Wesley, 1992), pp. 111–112.
22. Gary A. Cziko, "The Evaluation of Bilingual Education: From Necessity and Probability to Possibility," *Educational Researcher* 21, no. 2 (March 1992), p. 24; J. David Ramirez, "Executive Summary," *Bilingual Research Journal* 16 (Winter/Spring, 1992), pp. 1–245; Lisa Kocian, "Some Educators Say Pushing Immersion Before Bilingual Classes May Do More Harm than Good, *Boston*

Globe, September 25, 2008, http://www.boston.com/news/local/articles/2008/09/25/english_period/ (retrieved February 27, 2009); Stritikis and Varghese, "Language Diversity and Schooling," pp. 297–325.

23. Bennett, *Comprehensive Multicultural Education: Theory and Practice;* Stritikis and Varghese, "Language Diversity and Schooling," pp. 297–325.

24. Peter Schmidt, "Three Types of Bilingual Education Effective, E.D. Study Concludes," *Education Week,* February 20, 1991, pp. 1, 23.

25. Wayne Thomas and Virginia Collier, "Two Languages Are Better than One," *Educational Leadership* 55, no. 4 (December 1997/January 1998), pp. 23–26; Kenneth J. Cooper, "Riley Endorses Two-Way Bilingual Education," *Washington Post,* March 26, 2000, p. A2; Cara Simmon, "School Puts New Accent on Learning Two Languages," *Seattle Times,* April 1, 2003; Wayne Thomas and Virginia Collier, *A National Study of School Effectiveness for Language Minority Students' Long-Term Academic Achievement, Final Report 1.1,* Center for Research on Education, Diversity, and Excellence, U.S. Department of Education, Office of Educational Research and Improvement, 2008; Brian Cobb, Diego Vega, and Cindy Kronauge, "Effects of an Elementary Dual Language Immersion School Program on Junior High School Achievement, *Middle Grades Research Journal* 1 no. 1 (2006), pp. 27–47.

26. Frederick M. Hess, "Schools of Reeducation," *Washington Post,* February 5, 2006, p. B7.

27. Education Research Center, *Cities in Crisis Education Week,* April 2008; Christopher B. Swanson, *The Real Truth about Low Graduation Rates, An Evidenced-Based Commentary* (Washington, DC: The Urban Institute, 2004); U.S. Department of Education, *The Condition of Education 2007* (Washington, DC: National Center for Education Statistics, 2007), (NCES 2007-064), Indicator 23, 2007; Gary Orfield and Chungmei Lee, *Racial Transformation and the Changing Nature of Segregation* (Cambridge, MA: The Civil Rights Project, Harvard University, 2006); Erica Frankenberg and Gary Orfield, *Lessons in Integration: Realizing the Promise of Racial Diversity in America* (Charlottesville, VA: University of Virginia Press, 2007).

28. Christine Sleeter, "Curriculum Controversies in Multicultural Education," in Margaret Early and Kenneth Rehage, eds., *Issues in the Curriculum: A Selection of Chapters from Past NSSE Yearbooks, Ninety-Eighth Yearbook of the National Society for the Study of Education* (Chicago: University of Chicago Press, 1999), p. 261; Banks, "Multicultural Education: Characteristics and Goals," in Banks and Banks, *Multicultural Education: Issues and Perspectives*, pp. 3–30.

29. Banks, "Multicultural Education: Characteristics and Goals."

30. James Banks, "Approaches to Multicultural Curriculum Reform," in Banks and Banks, *Multicultural Education: Issues and Perspectives*, pp. 247–269.

31. Justin Britt-Gibson, "What's Wrong with this Picture?" *Washington Post,* March 18, 2007, p. B01; Peter Schmidt, "New Survey Discerns Deep Divisions Among U.S.

Youths on Race Relations," *Education Week,* March 25, 1992, p. 5.

32. Cristina Fernandez-Pereda, "Media Falls Flat in Covering Race Relations, New Survey Says," *New America Media,* February 19, 2009, http://news.newamericamedia.org/news/view_article.html?article_id=fa22894b6bee1753da1e89c189126106.

33. Mathew Bigg, "U.S. School Segregation on the Rise: Report," Reuters, January 14, 2009.

34. Christine I. Bennett, *Comprehensive Multicultural Education: Theory and Practice,* 6th ed. (Boston: Allyn & Bacon, 2006); Gloria Ladson-Billings, *Crossing Over to Canaan: The Journey of New Teachers in Diverse Classrooms* (San Francisco: Jossey Bass, 2001); Gloria Ladson-Billings, "But That's Just Good Teaching," *Theory into Practice* 34, no. 3 (Summer 1995), pp. 159–165.

35. Geneva Gay, "Achieving Educational Equality Through Curriculum Desegregation," *Phi Delta Kappan* 72, no. 1 (September 1990), pp. 56–62.

36. Carol Gilligan, *In a Different Voice: Psychological Theory and Women's Development* (Cambridge, MA: Harvard University Press, 1982); David Sadker, Myra Sadker, and Karen Zittleman, *Still Failing at Fairness: How Gender Bias Cheats Girls and Boys in School and What We Can Do about It* (New York: Charles Scribner's, 2009). See also Mary Field Belenky, Blythe McVicker Clinchy, Nancy Rule Goldberger, and Jill Mattuck Tarule, *Women's Ways of Knowing: The Development of Self, Voice, and Mind* (New York: Basic Books, 1986).

37. Julie Chlebo, "There Is No Rose Garden: A Second Generation Rural Head Start Program," unpublished doctoral dissertation, 1999, quoted in Christine I. Bennett, *Comprehensive Multicultural Education: Theory and Practice,* 4th ed. (Needham Heights, MA: Allyn & Bacon, 1999), p. 259.

38. Joshua Aronson, "The Threat of Stereotype," *Educational Leadership* 62, no. 3 (November 2004), pp. 14–19.

39. Joshua Aronson, "The Effects of Conceiving Ability as Fixed or Improvable on Responses to Stereotype Threat," unpublished manuscript, New York University, 2004.

40. Aronson, "The Threat of Stereotype"; Carol Dweck, *Self Theories: Their Role in Motivation, Personality and Development* (Philadelphia: Taylor & Francis, 1999).

41. Bennett, *Comprehensive Multicultural Education: Theory and Practice;* Carlos Cortes, *The Children Are Watching: How the Media Teach About Diversity* (New York: Teachers College Press, 2000), pp. 149–150; Barbara J. Shade, Cynthia Kelly, and Mary Oberg, *Creating Culturally Responsive Classrooms* (Washington, DC: American Psychological Association, 1997).

42. *Common Core Data, 2005–06* (Washington, DC: U.S. Department of Education, NCES), http://nces.ed.gov/ccd/ (retrieved February 27, 2008); Children's Defense Fund, http://www.childrensdefense.org (retrieved February 27, 2008).

43. The information about generalizations and different group learning styles is drawn from a variety of sources, including Bobby Ann Starnes, "What We Don't Know Can Hurt Them: White Teachers, Indian Children," *Phi*

Delta Kappan 87, no. 5 (January 2006), pp. 384–392; Banks and Banks, *Multicultural Education: Issues and Perspectives*; Bennett, *Comprehensive Multicultural Education: Theory and Practice*; Kenneth Cushner, *Human Diversity in Action: Developing Multicultural Competencies for the Classroom* (New York: McGraw-Hill, 2006); Gary A. Davis and Sylvia Rimm, *Cultural Diversity and Children from Low Socioeconomic Backgrounds* (Boston: Allyn & Bacon, 1997); K. M. Evenson Worthley, "Learning Style Factor of Field Dependence/Independence and Problem Solving Strategies of Hmong Refugee Students," master's thesis, University of Wisconsin–Stout, July 1987 (cited in Bennett, *Comprehensive Multicultural Education: Theory and Practice*); Norene Dresser, *Multicultural Manners: New Rules of Etiquette for a Changing Society* (New York: John Wiley & Sons, 1996); Education Alliance at Brown University, *The Diversity Kit: An Introductory Resource for Social Change in Education* (Providence, RI: Northeast and Islands Regional Educational Laboratory–LAB at Brown University, 2002); Rowena Fong and Sharlene B. Furuto, *Culturally Competent Practice: Skills, Interventions, and Evaluations* (Needham Heights, MA: Allyn & Bacon, 2001); Eleanor W. Lynch and Marci J. Hanson, eds., *Developing Cross-Cultural Competence: A Guide for Working with Children and Their Families* (Baltimore, MD: Paul H. Brookes, 2004); and Ian K. Macgillivray, *Sexual Orientation and School Policy: A Practical Guide for Teachers, Administrators, and Community Activists* (Lanham, MD: Rowman & Littlefield, 2004).

44. We thank Louise Wilkinson for this poignant quote. We couldn't have said it better.

45. Kent L. Koppelman with R. Lee Goodhart, *Understanding Human Differences: Multicultural Education for Diverse America* (Boston: Pearson Education, 2005), p. 344.

46. Nancy P. Gallavan, "I, Too, Am an American: Preservice Teachers Reflect upon National Identity," *Multicultural Teaching,* Spring 2002, pp. 8–12.

CHAPTER 4: STUDENT LIFE IN SCHOOL AND AT HOME

1. Philip W. Jackson, *Life in Classrooms* (New York: Holt, Rinehart & Winston, 1968).
2. Ibid.
3. Center for Public Education, *Class Size and Student Achievement,* http://www.centerforpubliceducation.org/ (retrieved March 1, 2008); Elena Silva, *On the Clock: Rethinking How Schools Use Time* (Washington, DC: Education Sector, January 2007), http://www.educationsector.org/; Manuel Justiz, "It's Time to Make Every Minute Count," *Phi Delta Kappan* 65, no. 7 (March 1984), pp. 483–485.
4. John Goodlad, *A Place Called School* (New York: McGraw-Hill, 1984/2004); American Association of School Librarians, *Making Every Moment Count: Maximizing Quality Instructional Time* (June 2007), http://www.reading.org/downloads/resources/memc_070620.pdf; Warren Kubitschek, Maureen Hallinan, Stephanie Arnett, and Kim Galipeau, "High School Schedule Changes and the Effect of Lost Instructional Time on Achievement," *High School Journal* 89, no.1 (October–November, 2005), pp. 63–71; Erik Gleibermann, "Teaching Even 100 Hours a Week Leaves Children Behind," *Phi Delta Kappan* 88, no. 6 (February 2007), pp. 455–459; Bill Metzker, *Time and Learning: ERIC Digest* (2003), http://www.ericdigests.org/ (retrieved March 1, 2008); BetsAnn Smith, "Quantity Matters: Annual Instruction Time in an Urban School System," *Educational Administration Quarterly* 36, no. 5 (December 2000), pp. 652–682.

5. Elena Silva, *On the Clock: Rethinking the Way Schools Use Time* (Washington, DC: Education Sector, January 2007), http://www.educationsector.org (retrieved March 1, 2008).

6. Quoted in Ernest L. Boyer, *High School* (New York: Harper & Row, 1983).

7. Gleibermann, "Teaching Even 100 Hours a Week Leaves Children Behind"; Metzker, *Time and Learning: ERIC Digest;* Smith, "Quantity Matters: Annual Instruction Time in an Urban School System"; G. Madaus et al., *School Effectiveness: A Reassessment of the Evidence* (New York: McGraw-Hill, 1980).

8. Jackson, *Life in Classrooms.*

9. Ned Flanders, "Intent, Action, and Feedback: A Preparation for Teaching," *Journal of Teacher Education* 14, no. 3 (September 1963), pp. 251–260; Jill Bourne and Caery Jewitt, "Orchestrating Debate: A Multimodal Analysis of Classroom Interaction," *Reading* 37, no. 2 (July 2003), pp. 64–72; Kristiina Kumpulainen, *Investigating Classroom Research* (Rotterdam, the Netherlands: Sense Publishers, 2009).

10. Arno Bellack, *The Language of the Classroom* (New York: Teachers College Press, 1965); K. Kumpulainen, *Investigating Classroom Research.*

11. Romiett Stevens, "The Question as a Measure of Classroom Practice," in *Teachers College Contributions to Education* (New York: Teachers College Press, 1912); David Sadker, Myra Sadker, and Karen Zittleman, "Questioning Skills," in James M. Cooper, ed., *Classroom Teaching Skills,* 9th ed. (Belmont, CA: Cengage, 2011), pp. 107–152.

12. W. D. Floyd, *An Analysis of the Oral Questioning Activity in Selected Colorado Primary Classrooms,* unpublished doctoral dissertation, Colorado State College, 1960; John M. Bridgeland, John J. DiIulio, Jr., and Karen Burke Morison, *The Silent Epidemic* (Seattle, WA: The Bill and Melinda Gates Foundation, 2006), http://www.civicenterprises.net/pdfs/thesilentepidemic3-06.pdf; K. Kumpulainen, *Investigating Classroom Research.*

13. Sadker, Sadker, and Zittleman, "Questioning Skills."

14. Mary Budd Rowe, "Wait Time: Slowing Down May Be a Way of Speeding Up!" *Journal of Teacher Education* 37 (1986), pp. 43–50; K. Kumpulainen, *Investigating Classroom Research.*

15. Goodlad, *A Place Called School;* Sadker, Sadker, and Zittleman "Questioning Skills"; K. Kumpulainen, *Investigating Classroom Research.*

16. Talcott Parsons, "The School as a Social System: Some of Its Functions in Society," in Robert Havinghurst and Bernice Neugarten, eds., *Society and Education* (Boston: Allyn & Bacon, 1967), pp. 191–214.

17. Robert Lynd and Helen Lynd, *Middletown: A Study in American Culture* (New York: Harcourt Brace Jovanovich, 1929).

18. W. Lloyd Warner, Robert Havinghurst, and Martin Loeb, *Who Shall Be Educated?* (New York: Harper & Row, 1944).

19. Jeannie Oakes, "Keeping Track: Structuring Equality and Inequality in an Era of Accountability," *Teachers College Record* 110, no. 3 (2008), pp. 12–13 (ID Number: 14610), http://www.tcrecord.org; Jeannie Oakes, "Two Cities' Tracking and Within-School Segregation," *Teachers College Record* 96, no. 4 (Summer 1995), pp. 681–690; Jeannie Oakes, *Keeping Track* (New Haven, CT: Yale University Press, 2005); Carol Corbett Burris and Kevin G. Welner, "Closing the Achievement Gap by Detracking," *Phi Delta Kappan* 86, no. 8 (April 2005), pp. 594–598.

20. Ray Rist, "Student Social Class and Teacher Expectations. The Self-Fulfilling Prophecy of Ghetto Education," *Harvard Education Review* 40, no. 3 (1970), pp. 411–451.

21. Oakes, *Keeping Track;* The Principals' Partnership, Research Brief: Tracking and Ability Grouping (2007), http://www.principalspartnership.com/tracking.pdf; Daphna Oyserman, Daniel Brickman, and Marjorie Rhodes, "School Success, Possible Selves, and Parent School Involvement," *Family Relations* 56, no. 5 (2007), pp. 479–489; Christopher Spera, "A Review of the Relationship Among Parenting Practices, Parenting Styles, and Adolescent School Achievement," *Educational Psychology Review* 17, no. 2 (2005), p. 125; Oakes, "Keeping Track: Structuring Equality and Inequality in an Era of Accountability."

22. James Rosenbaum, "If Tracking Is Bad, Is Detracking Better?" *American Educator* (Winter 1999–2000), pp. 24–29, 47; Oakes, "Keeping Track: Structuring Equality and Inequality in an Era of Accountability."

23. Oakes, *Keeping Track;* The Principals' Partnership, *Research Brief: Tracking and Ability Grouping.*

24. Carol Ascher, "Successful Detracking in Middle and Senior High Schools," *ERICICUE Digest* 82 (New York: ERIC Clearinghouse on Urban Education, October 10, 1992) (ED351426); Delia Garrity, "Detracking with Vigilance," *The School Administrator* online, August 2004, http://www.aasa.org/; Carol Ann Tomlinson, "Differentiating Instruction for Academic Diversity," in Cooper, *Classroom Teaching Skills*, pp. 154–187.

25. Quoted in "Tracking," *Education Week on the Web,* October 14, 1998; see also Robert E. Slavin, "Achievement Effects of Ability Grouping in Secondary Schools: A Best-Evidence Synthesis," *Review of Educational-Research* 60 (1990), pp. 471–499; Burris and Welner, "Closing the Achievement Gap by Detracking"; Samuel Lucas, *Tracking Inequality: Stratification and Mobility in American High Schools* (New York: Teachers College Press, 1999).

26. Raphaela Best, *We've All Got Scars* (Bloomington: Indiana University Press, 1983).

27. Ibid., p. 162.

28. "Unpopular Children," *Harvard Education Letter,* Harvard Graduate School of Education in association with Harvard University Press, January/February 1989, pp. 1–3; see also Lisa Wolcott, "Relationships: The Fourth 'R," *Teacher* (April 1991), pp. 26–27.

29. Quoted from a student letter in the *Arlingtonian,* May 13, 1993.

30. Jaana Juvonen et al., *Focus on the Wonder Years: Challenges Facing the American Middle School* (Santa Monica, CA: RAND Corporation, 2004), http://www.rand.org/pubs/monographs/2004/RAND_MG139.pdf.

31. Jay Matthews, "Traditional Social Focus Yielding to Academics," *Washington Post,* October 4, 2005, p. A04.

32. Karen R. Zittleman, "Gender Perceptions of Middle Schoolers: The Good and the Bad," *Middle Grades Research Journal* 2, no. 2 (Fall 2007), pp. 65–97.

33. Ibid.

34. Ibid.

35. Benoit Denzet-Lewis, "Coming Out in Junior High School," *New York Times Magazine*, September 27, 2009, pp. 36–41, 52, 54–55.

36. Karen R. Zittleman, "Gender Perceptions of Middle Schoolers: The Good and the Bad," *Middle Grades Research Journal* 2, no. 2 (Fall 2007), pp. 65–97.

37. Girls Inc., *The SuperGirl Dilemma: Girls Feel the Pressure to Be Perfect, Accomplished, Thin, and Accommodating* (New York: Girls Inc., 2006).

38. U.S. Department of Education, National Center for Education Statistics, "Enrollment in Educational Institutions, by Level and Control of Institution: Selected Years, Fall 1980 through Fall 2009," *Digest of Education Statistics,* 2009, Table 2, http://nces.ed.gov/pubs2010/2010013_1.pdf.

39. K. M. Pierce, "Posing, Pretending, Waiting for the Bell: Life in High School Classrooms," *High School Journal* 89, no. 2 (December 2005/January 2006), pp. 1–15.

40. Quoted in Boyer, *High School,* p. 202.

41. David Owen, *High School* (New York: Viking Press, 1981).

42. Lloyd Temme, quoted in Keyes, *Is There Life After High School?*

43. Patricia Hersch, *A Tribe Apart: A Journey into the Heart of American Adolescence* (New York: Random House, 1999).

44. *America's Children: Key National Indicators of Well-Being, 2010,* http://www.childstats.gov/americaschildren/.

45. Helena Holgeersson-Shorter, "Helping the Homeless in School and Out," *Teaching Tolerance* (Fall 2010, no. 38), pp. 47–50; Barry D. Ham, "The Effects of Divorce on the Academic Achievement of High School Seniors," *Journal of Divorce & Remarriage* 38 (2003), pp. 167–185.

46. "Study: Older, More Educated Moms on the Rise," *Arizona Daily Star,* May 6, 2010, p. A13.

47. *Statistics on Stepfamilies in the United States* (New York: The Stepfamily Foundation, 2010), http://www.stepfamily.org/statistics.html.

48. "Winding Road to Adulthood Taking Longer: Research Shows Marked Age Shifted for Marriage, Careers, Parenthood," *Arizona Daily Star,* June 13, 2010, p. A3; U.S.

Census Bureau, Statistical Abstracts of the United States, *Current Population Survey 2009.*

49. Maria Shriver and the Center for American Progress, *The Shriver Report: A Woman's Nation Changes Everything* (2009), http://www.shriverreport.com.

50. "Study Cites Dramatic Rise in Family Togetherness," *Arizona Daily Star,* April 6, 2010, p. A14.

51. Frances Kemper Alston, *Latch Key Children* (New York: NYU Child Study Center, 2007), http://www.about ourkids.org/articles/latch_key_children.

52. Childstats.gov, Federal Interagency Forum on Child and Family Statistics, *America's Children: Key National Indicators of Well-Being, 2010,* http://www.childstats.gov.

53. William Jeynes, *Divorce, Family Structure, and the Academic Success of Children* (New York: Routledge, 2002).

54. Quoted in John O'Neil, "A Generation Adrift?" *Educational Leadership* 49, no. 2 (September 1991), pp. 4–10.

55. U.S. Census Bureau, *Current Population Statistics: Income, Poverty, and Health Insurance Coverage in the United States, 2009* (issued September 2010), http://www.census.gov/prod/2010pubs/p60-238.pdf.

56. Richard Rothstein, "Whose Problem Is Poverty?" *Educational Research* 65, no. 7 (2008), pp. 8–13; Royal Van Horn, *Bridging the Chasm between Research and Practice: A Guide to Major Educational Research* (Lanham, MD: Rowman and Littlefield Education, 2008); Lisa Delpit, *Other People's Children: Cultural Conflict in the Classroom* (New York: Norton, 2006).

57. Rob Stein, "Research Links Poor Kids' Stress, Brain Development," *Washington Post,* April 6, 2009, p. A6.

58. Oscar Lewis, *La Vida: A Puerto Rican Family in the Culture of Poverty—San Juan and New York* (New York: Random House, 1966).

59. Shirley Brice Heath, *Ways with Words: Language, Life, and Work in Communities and Classrooms* (New York: Cambridge University Press, 1983).

60. Ibid.; Rothstein, "Whose Problem Is Poverty?"

61. This material is gathered from the Big Picture Longitudinal Study. The information was compiled and sent by the research team including Karen D. Arnold, Katherine Lynk Wartman, Shezwae Fleming, Mario A. DeAnda, Benjamin L. Castleman, and Carmen Perez. *The Summer Flood: The Gap between College Admission and Matriculation among Low-Income Students* (Draft of Findings, May 2009). Funding from the Lumina Foundation and the Irvine Foundation.

62. Ibid.

63. U.S. Census Bureau, *Current Population Statistics: Income, Poverty, and Health Insurance Coverage in the United States, 2009.*

64. National Association for the Education of Homeless Children and Youth, *Fact Sheet,* (September 2010), http://www.naehcy.org.

65. National Law Center on Homelessness and Poverty, *Fact Sheet* (September 2010), http://www.nlchp.org; John Holloway, "Research Link: Addressing the Needs of Homeless Students," *Educational Leadership* 60, no. 4 (December 2002/January 2003), pp. 89–90.

66. "Study: Fatalistic View Possibly Tied to Kids' Risky Behavior," *Arizona Daily Star,* June 29, 2009, p. A5.

67. Chris Swanson, "Diplomas Count: Graduation by the Numbers," *Education Week* 29, no. 34 (June 10, 2010), pp. 4–5; Gary Orfield, *Dropouts in America: Confronting the Graduation Rate Crisis* (Cambridge, MA: Harvard University Press, 2004).

68. Swanson, "Diplomas Count: Graduation by the Numbers," p. 5.

69. Ibid., pp. 4–5; Christopher Swanson, *Cities in Crisis: A Special Analytic Report on High Graduation Rates* (Washington, DC: Editorial Projects in Education Research Center, April 2008); National Women's Law Center, *When Girls Don't Graduate We All Fail: A Call to Improve the Graduation Rates of Girls* (Washington, DC: National Women's Law Center, 2007).

70. Ibid.

71. Laura Stepps, "Study Casts Doubt on Abstinence-Only Programs," *Washington Post*, April 14, 2007, p. A02.

72. Sexuality Information and Education Council of the United States, *Fact Sheet, 2007 & Policy Updates, January 2008,* http://www.siecus.org.

73. Childstats.gov, Federal Interagency Forum on Child and Family Statistics, "Sexual Activity," *America's Children: Key National Indicators of Well-Being, 2010,* http://www.childstats.gov/americaschildren/; Erik Robelin, "Program Promoting Sexual Abstinence Gets Resurrected," *Education Week* 29, no. 28 (April 7, 2010), pp. 6–7.

74. The National Center on Addiction and Substance Abuse at Columbia University, *CASA National Survey of American Attitudes on Substance Abuse XV: Teens and Parents* (August 2010), http://www.casacolumbia.org/.

75. Lloyd Johnston, Patrick O'Malley, Jerald Bachman, and John Schulenberg, *Monitoring the Future: National Results on Adolescent Drug Use: Overview of Key Findings, 2008* (Bethesda, MD: National Institute on Drug Abuse, 2009), http://www.monitoringthefuture.org.

76. Office of Applied Studies, *Results from the 2007 National Survey on Drug Use and Health: National Findings* (DHHS Publication No. SMA 08-4343, NSDUH Series H-34), (Rockville, MD: Substance Abuse and Mental Health Services Administration, March 2009), http://oas.samhsa.gov.

77. Ibid.

78. The National Center on Addiction and Substance Abuse at Columbia University, *CASA National Survey of American Attitudes on Substance Abuse XV: Teens and Parents.*

79. Ibid.

80. S. Schlozman, "The Shrink in the Classroom: Why 'Just Say No' Isn't Enough," *Educational Leadership* 59, no. 7 (2002), pp. 87–89; Matthew Rees, "Neither Safe nor Drug-Free," *New Directions: Federal Education Policy in the 21st Century* (Washington, DC: The Thomas B. Fordham Institute, 1999), http://www.edexcellence.net/institute/publication/publication.cfm?id538&pubsubid=610#610.

81. Centers for Disease Control and Prevention, *Overweight and Obesity Data and Statistics,* August 2010, http://www.cdc.gov/obesity/.

82. Valerie Strauss, "In Some PE Classes, Counting Small Steps to Achieve Fitness," *Washington Post*, May 21, 2008, p. B1.

83. Claudia Kalb, "Culture of Corpulence," *Newsweek*, March 22, 2010, pp. 42–44.

84. National Eating Disorders Coalition, *Stats About Eating Disorders: What the Research Shows*, http://www.eating disorderscoalition.org/ (retrieved September 29, 2010).

85. Lauren Greenfield and Joan Jacobs Brumberg, *Thin* (San Francisco: Chronicle Books, 2006); National Eating Disorders Coalition, *Statistics and Study Findings*; Margo Maine and Joe Kelly, *The Body Myth* (New York: Wiley, 2005).

86. National Institute on Drug Abuse, *Anabolic Steroid Abuse*, NIH Publication Number 06-3721, August 2006, http://www.nida.nih.gov/PDF/RRSteroids.pdf (retrieved March 7, 2008).

87. Centers for Disease Control and Prevention, National Center for Injury Prevention and Control, *Suicide: Facts at a Glance*, Summer 2007, http://www.cdc.gov/ncipc/dvp/suicide/SuicideDataSheet.pdf (retrieved March 7, 2008).

88. Jeanne Wright, "Treating the Depressed Child," *Washington Post*, December 2, 1996, p. C-5; Suicide and Mental Health Association International, *Suicide Prevention for Schools*, http://suicideandmentalhealthassociation international.org/preventionteachers.html (retrieved March 7, 2008).

89. Sarah Shulkind, "Reframing Bullying in Middle Schools," *Education Spotlight on Bullying*, (2010), p. 7.

90. Lesli A. Maxwell, "Principals' Views on Bullying," *Education Spotlight on Bullying* (2010), p. 4; KidsHealth, *What Kids Say about Bullying*, 2007, http://www.kidshealth.org/; Josephson Institute Center for Youth Ethics, *The Ethics of American Youth: 2010* (October 2010), http://charactercounts.org/programs/reportcard/2010/.

91. Jennifer Hollday, "Cyberbullying," *Teaching Tolerance*, Fall 2010, pp. 43–46.

92. Ibid., pp. 43–44.

93. Ibid., pp. 43–46.

94. Dakarai I. Aarons, "Efforts to End Bullying, A Challenge to Leaders, Gains Momentum," *Education Spotlight on Bullying*, 2010, pp. 1–3; Dan Olweis, "A Profile of Bullying at School," *Educational Leadership* 60, no. 6 (March 2003), pp. 12–17.

95. Hollday, "Cyberbullying," pp. 43–46.

96. Aarons, "Efforts to End Bullying, A Challenge to Leaders, Gains Momentum."

97. Dirk Johnson, "Dalai Lama Donates to Center in Wisconsin," *New York Times*, September 27, 2010, p. A10; Ian Shapira, "Peacemakers in Training," *Washington Post*, February 28, 2006, pp. B1, B4.

98. Lyn Mikel Brown, "Ten Ways to Move Beyond Bullying Prevention (and Why We Should Do It), *Education Spotlight on Bullying*, 2010, pp. 10–11.

CHAPTER 5: THE MULTICULTURAL HISTORY OF AMERICAN EDUCATION

1. Sheldon Cohen, *A History of Colonial Education, 1607–1776* (New York: Wiley, 1974); Joel Spring, *American Education*, 14th ed. (New York: McGraw-Hill, 2009).

2. Nathaniel Shurtlett, ed., *Records of the Governor and Company of the Massachusetts Bay in New England, II* (Boston: Order of the Legislature, 1853); see also H. Warren Button and Eugene F. Provenzo, Jr., *History of Education and Culture in America* (Englewood Cliffs, NJ: Prentice Hall, 1983); Wayne Urban and Kevin Wagoner, *American Education: A History*, 3rd ed. (New York: McGraw-Hill, 2003).

3. James Hendricks, "Be Still and Know! Quaker Silence and Dissenting Educational Ideals, 1740–1812," *Journal of the Midwest History of Education Society*, Annual Proceedings, 1975; R. Freeman Butts and Lawrence A. Cremin, *A History of Education in American Culture* (New York: Holt, 1953).

4. Lawrence A. Cremin, *American Education: The Colonial Experience, 1607–1783* (New York: Harper & Row, 1970); see also Spring, *American Education*.

5. James C. Klotter, "The Black South and White Appalachia," *Journal of American History*, March 1980, pp. 832–849; Urban and Wagoner, *American Education: A History*.

6. John H. Best, *Benjamin Franklin on Education* (New York: Teachers College Press, 1962); L. Dean Webb, *The History of American Education: A Great American Experiment* (Upper Saddle River, NJ: Prentice Hall, 2005).

7. Jonathon Messerli, *Horace Mann: A Biography* (New York: Alfred A. Knopf, 1972); Webb, *The History of American Education: A Great American Experiment*.

8. Lawrence Cremin, *The Transformation of the School: Progressivism in American Education, 1876–1957* (New York: Alfred A. Knopf, 1961).

9. Wilbur R. Jacobs, "The Tip of an Iceberg: Pre-Columbian Indian Demography and Some Implications for Revisionism," *William and Mary Quarterly*, 3rd ser., 31, no. 1 (January 1974), pp. 123–132.

10. Much of the early educational history discussion of Native Americans, African Americans, and Latinos is based on Meyer Weinberg, *A Chance to Learn: A History of Race and Education in the United States* (New York: Cambridge University Press, 1977); Joel Spring, *Deculturalization and the Struggle for Equality: A Brief History of the Education of Dominated Cultures in the United States*, 6th ed. (New York: McGraw-Hill, 2009).

11. Robert S. Catterill, *The Southern Indians: The Story of the Civilized Tribes Before Removal* (1954; reprinted, Norman: University of Oklahoma Press, 1966); Spring, *Deculturalization and the Struggle for Equality*.

12. Bobby Ann Starnes, "What We Don't Know Can Hurt Them: White Teachers, Indian Children," *Phi Delta Kappan* 87, no. 5 (January 2006), pp. 384–392; see also Spring, *Deculturalization and the Struggle for Equality*; Mary Ann Zehr, "Indian Tribes Decry Plan to Privatize BIA-Run Schools," *Education Week* 21, no. 30 (April 10, 2002), pp. 20, 23.

13. Starnes, "What We Don't Know Can Hurt Them: White Teachers, Indian Children"; Lee Little Soldier, "Is There an 'Indian' in Your Classroom?" *Phi Delta Kappan* 78, no. 8 (April 1997), pp. 650–653.

14. Jackie M. Blount, "Spinsters, Bachelors and Other Gender Transgressors in School Employment, 1850–1990,"

Review of Educational Research 70, no. 1 (Spring 2000), pp. 83–101.

15. E. Marcus, *Making History: The Struggle for Gay and Lesbian Equal Rights, 1945–1990, an Oral History* (New York: Harper Collins, 1992).

16. Blount, "Spinsters, Bachelors and Other Gender Transgressors in School Employment, 1850–1990," p. 94.

17. Edward A. Krug, *The Shaping of the American High School, 1880–1920,* I (New York: Harper & Row, 1964); see also Spring, *American Education.*

18. M. Lee Manning, "A Brief History of the Middle School," *The Clearing House 73,* no. 4 (March-April 2000), p. 192.

19. Susie King Taylor, *Reminiscences of My Life in Camp with the 33rd U.S. Colored Troop Late First S.C. Volunteers* (1902; reprinted, New York: Amo Press, 1968).

20. W. E. B. Du Bois, "The United States and the Negro," *Freedomways* (1971), quoted in Weinberg, *A Chance to Learn.*

21. Spring, *American Education.*

22. National Advisory Commission on Civil Disorders, *Report of the National Advisory Commission on Civil Disorders* (Washington, DC: U.S. Government Printing Office, 1968), p. 369; see also Andrew Hacker, *Two Nations Black and White, Separate, Hostile, Unequal* (New York: Charles Scribner's, 1992).

23. Louis Fischer, David Schimmel, and Leslie Stellman, *Teachers and the Law,* 7th ed. (Boston: Allyn & Bacon, 2006); "ACLU Expresses Mixed Feelings About Supreme Court Decision in School Desegregation Cases," June 29, 2007, http://www.commondreams.org/news2007/0629 02.htm; Gary Orfield, *Reviving the Goal of an Integrated Society: A 21st Century Challenge* (Los Angeles: The Civil Rights Project/Proyecto Derechos Civiles at UCLA, January 2009).

24. Orfield, *Reviving the Goal of An Integrated Society.*

25. Ibid.; Stephanie McCrummen and Michael Birnbaum, "Study of Montgomery County Schools Shows Benefits of Economic Integration," *Washington Post,* October 15, 2010.

26. Richard M. Merleman, "Dis-integrating American Public Schools," *Education Week,* May 19, 2002, p. 37.

27. U.S. Census Bureau, *Hispanic Americans by the Numbers,* www.census.gov, 2010.

28. Ibid.; U.S. Census Bureau, *2007 American Community Survey,* released April 28, 2009, http://www.census.gov/acs/www/.

29. National Women's Law Center, *When Girls Don't Graduate We All Fail: A Call to Improve the Graduation Rates of Girls* (Washington, DC: National Women's Law Center, 2007), http://www.nwlc.org; John Bridgeland, John J. Diluilo, Jr., and Karen Burke Morison, *The Silent Epidemic* (Seattle, WA: The Bill and Melinda Gates Foundation, March 2006), http://www.civicenterprises.net/pdfs/thesilentepidemic3-06.pdf.

30. Quoted in Weinberg, *A Chance to Learn.*

31. U.S. Census Bureau, *Hispanic Americans by the Numbers.*

32. Edna Costa-Belen and Carlos Santiago, *Puerto Ricans in the United States: A Contemporary Portrait* (Boulder, CO: Lynne Rienner Publishers, 2006).

33. U.S. Census Bureau, *Hispanic Americans by the Numbers.*

34. U.S. Census Bureau, *Facts for Features: Asian/Pacific American Heritage Month 2009,* http://www.census.gov/newsroom/releases/archives/facts_for_features_special_editions/cb10-ff07.html.

35. Much of the information on the history of Asian Americans is adapted from James Banks and Cherry Banks, eds., *Multicultural Education,* 7th ed. (San Francisco: Jossey Bass, 2009).

36. U.S. Department of Education, National Center for Educational Statistics, *National Assessment of Educational Progress (NAEP): Reading and Math Scores, 2009,* http://nces.ed.gov/nationsreportcard.

37. U.S. Census Bureau, *Facts for Features: Asian/Pacific American Heritage Month 2011,* http://www.census.gov/newsroom/releases/archives/facts_for_features_special_editions/cb11-ff06.html

38. Carlos Ovando, "Interrogating Stereotypes: The Case of the Asian 'Model Minority,'" *Newsletter of the Asian Culture Center* (Indiana University, Fall 2001), http://www.modelminority.com/academia/interrogating.htm.

39. Zhenchao Qian and Priyank Shah, "Educational Attainment and Intermarriage: Asian Indian and Filipino Americans Compared," paper presented at the annual meeting of *the American Sociological Association,* Philadelphia, PA, August 12, 2005, http://www.allacademic.com/meta/p22142_index.html.

40. Laurie Olsen, "Crossing the Schoolhouse Border: Immigrant Children in California," *Phi Delta Kappan* 70, no. 3 (November 1988), p. 213.

41. J. Shaheen, *The TV Arab* (Bowling Green, OH: Bowling Green State University, 1984); Arab American Institute, *American Views on Arab and Muslim Americans,* September 2010, http://www.aaiusa.org/page/-/Images/Polls/AAIPoll%20Report-Sept2010.pdf.

42. For more information about Arab Americans, visit the websites of the American-Arab Anti-Discrimination Committee at http://www.adc.org and the Arab American Institute at http://www.aaiusa.org.

43. Much of the information on Arab Americans is adapted from Banks and Banks, *Multicultural Education.*

44. Arab American Institute, *Demographics,* 2010, http://www.aaiusa.org.

45. David Sadker, Myra Sadker, and Karen R. Zittleman. *Still Failing at Fairness: How Gender Bias Cheats Girls and Boys in School and What We Can Do About It* (New York: Charles Scribner, 2009); Spring, *American Education.*

46. M. Carey Thomas, "Present Tendencies in Women's Education," *Education Review* 25 (1908), pp. 64–85, quoted in David Tyack and Elisabeth Hansot, *Learning Together: A History of Coeducation in American Schools* (New Haven: Yale University Press, 1990), p. 68.

47. Adapted from "Opening the Schoolhouse Door" and "Higher Education: Peeking Behind the Campus

Curtain," in Sadker, Sadker, and Zittleman, *Still Failing at Fairness.*

48. Special thanks to Kate Volker for developing the Crandall and Ashton-Warner biographies.

CHAPTER 6: PHILOSOPHY OF EDUCATION

1. William Bagley, "The Case for Essentialism in Education," *National Education Association Journal* 30, no. 7 (1941), pp. 202–220.

2. Andrew J. Rotherham, "Core Convictions: An Interview with E.D. Hirsch," *Education Sector,* September 26, 2006, http://www.coreknowledge.org/blog/2006/09/26/core-convictions-an-interview-with-ed-hirsch/.

3. Robert M. Hutchins, *The Higher Learning in America* (New Haven, CT: Yale University Press, 1962), p. 78.

4. Mortimer Adler, *Reforming Education* (Boulder, CO: Westview Press, 1977), pp. 84–85.

5. John Dewey, *Experience and Education* (New York: Macmillan, 1963).

6. Larry Cuban, *How Teachers Taught,* 2nd ed. (New York: Teachers College Press, 1993).

7. Paulo Freire, *Pedagogy of the Oppressed* (New York: Continuum Press, 1989).

8. Maxine Greene, *Landscapes of Learning* (New York: Teachers College Press, 1978); see also Maxine Greene, "Reflections on Teacher as Stranger" in C. Kridel, ed., *Books of the Century Catalog* (Columbia, SC: University of South Carolina, Museum of Education, 2000), and *Releasing the Imagination: Essays on Education, the Acts, and Social Change* (Hoboken, NJ: John Wiley & Sons, 2000).

9. Danna Harman, "This Is School?" *Christian Science Monitor,* May 18, 2004, p. 11; Nick Anderson, "Learning on Their Own Terms: Md. School with No Curriculum Challenges Conventions of Modern Education," *Washington Post,* April 24, 2006, p. A01.

10. Jay Mathews, "Educators Blend Divergent Schools of Thought," *Washington Post,* May 9, 2006, p. A12.

11. Timothy Reagan, *Non-Western Educational Traditions: Alternative Approaches to Educational Thought and Practice* (Mahwah, NJ: Lawrence Erlbaum Associates, 2000).

12. Aristotle, *The Politics,* trans. and intro. by T. A. Sinclair (Middlesex, England: Penguin, 1978).

CHAPTER 7: FINANCING AND GOVERNING AMERICA'S SCHOOLS

1. Heller Reports Virtual Round Table, *Teacher Buying Behavior,* 2007, http://www.qeddata.com/MarketKno/ResearchReports/TBB%20Roundtable%20Summary.pdf (retrieved March 18, 2008).

2. Mark G. Yudof, David L. Kip, and Betsy Levin, *Educational Policy and the Law,* 3rd edition (St. Paul, MN: West, 1992), p. 658; Betsy Levin, Thomas Muller, and Corazon Sandoval, *The High Cost of Education in Cities* (Washington, DC: The Urban Institute, 1973).

3. Barry Siegel, "Parents Get a Lesson in Equality," *Los Angeles Times* (Washington edition), April 13, 1992, pp. A-1, A-18, A-19.

4. *Robinson v. Cahill,* 69 N.J. 133 (1973); *Abbott v. Burke,* 119 N.J. 287 (1990) (known as *Abbott I); Abbott v. Burke,* 153 N.J. 480 (1998) (known as *Abbott V).*

5. Catherine Gerwitz, "Though N. J. Funding Formula Upheld, Abbott Intact," *Education Week* 8, no. 33 (June 10, 2009), p. 10; Peter Enrich, "Leaving Equality Behind: New Directions in School Finance Reform," *Vanderbilt Law Review* 48 (1995), pp. 101–194. For a description of this movement to adequacy arguments, visit http://nces.ed.gov/edfin/litigation/Contents.asp. For a discussion of the impact in Wisconsin, see Daniel W. Hildebrand, "2000 Significant Court Decisions," *Wisconsin Lawyer* 74, no. 6 (June 2001). Similar analyses are available in other such law updates.

6. "Financing Better Schools: Too Often, Traditional Methods of Paying for Schools Come Up Short," *Education Week* 24, no. 17 (January 6, 2005), p. 7.

7. Richard Rothstein, "Equalizing Education Resources on Behalf of Disadvantaged Children," in Richard D. Kahlenberg, ed., *A Nation at Risk: Preserving Public Education as an Engine for Social Mobility* (New York: Century Foundation Press, 2000), p. 74; Alan Odden and Lawrence O. Picus, *School Finance: A Policy Perspective,* 4th ed. (New York: McGraw-Hill, 2007).

8. W. E. Thro, "The Third Wave: The Impact of the Montana, Kentucky and Texas Decisions on the Future of Public School Finance Reform Litigation," *Journal of Law and Education* 199, no. 2 (Spring 1990), pp. 219–250; Robert F. McNergney and Joanne M. Herbert, *Foundations of Education: The Challenge of Professional Practice* (Boston: Allyn & Bacon, 1995), pp. 475–478; Chris Pipho, "Stateline: The Scent of the Future," *Phi Delta Kappan* 76 (September 1994), pp. 10–11; Greg Kocher, "Group Says Education Not Getting Enough Money Due It by Law," *Lexington Herald-Leader,* June 25, 2003, http://www.kentucky.com.

9. Cited in *Campaign for Fiscal Equality v. New York,* 86 N.Y. 2d 307 (1995). See also Bess Keller, "School Finance Case Draws to Close in N.Y.," *Education Week,* August 2, 2000.

10. Lori Montgomery, "Maryland Seeks 'Adequacy,' Recasting School Debate," *Washington Post,* April 22, 2002, p. A1.

11. Liz Bowie, "As State Increased Aid, Grades Went Up," *Baltimore Sun,* January 8, 2009, http://www.goodschoolspa.org/pdf/news_articles/Baltimore%20Sun%201-8-09.pdf (retrieved May 15, 2009).

12. Joshua Benton, "One District Reaps the Benefit of Another's Belt-Tightening," *Dallas Morning News,* December 12, 2002, http://www.dallasnews.com; David Mace, "Act 60 Reform Likely," *Rutland Herald,* January 6, 2003; "Tennessee's School Funding Declared Unconstitutional Again," *Associated Press,* October 9, 2002.

13. Alfred A. Lindseth, "A Reversal of Fortunes: Why Courts Have Cooled to Adequacy Lawsuits," *Education Week* 27, no. 3 (September 10, 2007).

14. Robert Slavin, "How Can Funding Equity Ensure Enhanced Achievement?" *Journal of Educational Finance* 24, no. 4 (Spring 1999), pp. 519–528.

15. Bruce J. Biddle and David C. Berliner, "Unequal School Funding in the United States," *Education Leadership* 59, no. 8 (May 2002), pp. 48–59; Diana Jean Schemo, "Neediest Schools Receive Less Money, Report Finds," *New York Times,* August 9, 2002; Odden and Picus, *School Finance: A Policy Perspective;* Carmen G. Arroyo, *The Funding Gap* (Washington, DC: Education Trust, January 17, 2008), http://www2.edtrust.org/NR/rdonlyres/5AF8F288-949D-4677-82CF-5A867A8E9153/0/FundingGap2007.pdf (retrieved March 19, 2008).

16. Stephen Sawchuk, "Out-of-Field Teaching Called Worse in Poor Schools," *Education Week* 28, no. 15 (November 25, 2008).

17. "SFFF Files Public School Lawsuit," *Topeka Capital-Journal*, November 2, 2010, http://cjonline.com/news/state/2010-11-02/sfff_files_public_school_lawsuit; Lesli A. Maxwell, "Funding Formula Aims at Equity," *Education Week* 29, no. 37 (July 19, 2010); *Is School Funding Fair? A National Report Card*, National Law Center, October 12, 2010, http://www.schoolfundingfairness.org/.

18. Amanda Paulson, "Does Money Transform Schools?" *Christian Science Monitor,* August 9, 2005, http://www.csmonitor.com/2005/0809/p01s03-ussc.html (retrieved March 19, 2008).

19. Arroyo, *The Funding Gap.*

20. Debra Viadero, "Rags to Riches in U.S. Largely a Myth, Scholars Write," *Education Week* 26, no. 9 (October 25, 2006), p. 8.

21. Thomas Toch, "Separate but Not Equal," *Agenda* 1 (Spring 1991), pp. 15–17; Odden and Picus, *School Finance: A Policy Perspective.*

22. Peter Keating, "How to Keep Your State and Local Taxes Down," *Money* 24, no. 1 (January 1995), pp. 86–92; Odden and Picus, *School Finance: A Policy Perspective.*

23. Bill Norris, "Losing Ticket in Lotteries," *Times Educational Supplement,* March 19, 1993, p. 17.

24. U.S. Department of Education, *The Federal Role in Education,* 2008, http://www.ed.gov/about/overview/fed/role.html (retrieved March 20, 2008).

25. Stephen Sawchuk and Erik Robelen, "Stimulus Guidance Spotlights Teacher Evaluations," *Education Week* 28, no. 28 (April 1, 2009); Valerie Strauss, "Schools Chief Returns Race to the Top Money—for His Teachers," *Washington Post,* November 24, 2010, http://voices.washingtonpost.com/answer-sheet/schools-chief-returns-race-to.html; Gerald Seib, "In Education, a Chance for Change," *Wall Street Journal,* March 27, 2009; "Obama Wants Stimulus to Transform Schools," *USA Today,* February 17, 2009, http://www.usatoday.com/news/education/2009-02-17-stimulus-schools_N.htm (retrieved May 18, 2009); Maria Glod, "Budget Outlines Funding for Teacher Merit Pay Programs," *Washington Post,* May 7, 2009, http://www.washingtonpost.com/wp-dyn/content/article/2009/05/07/AR2009050703786.html (retrieved May 21, 2009); "Obama Wants 5K Closed Schools to Rebound," *USA Today,* May 11, 2009, http://www.usatoday.com/news/education/2009-05-11-duncan-schools_N.htm (retrieved on May 18, 2009); Libby Quaid, "Plan to Fix Schools Could Help Students,"

Arizona Daily Star, January 1, 2009, p. A3; Sam Dillon, "U.S. Stimulus Plan Would Provide Flood of Aid to Education," *New York Times,* January 28, 2009, http://www.nytimes.com/2009/01/28/education/28educ.html (retrieved May 23, 2009).

26. Juliet Schor, *Born to Buy: The Commercialized Child and the New Consumer Culture* (New York: Charles Scribner's, 2004).

27. "FTC Report Sheds New Light on Food Marketing to Children and Adolescents," (Washington, DC: Federal Trade Commission, July 29, 2008), http://www.ftc.gov/opa/2008/07/foodmkting.shtm (retrieved May 30, 2009).

28. Many of the examples in this section are adapted from "Commercializing Childhood: The Corporate Takeover of Kids' Lives: An Interview with Susan Linn," *Multinational Monitor* 30, no. 1 (July/August 2008), http://www.multinationalmonitor.org/mm2008/072008/interviewlinn.html (retrieved May 22, 2009).

29. Ibid. See also Linda Matchan, "A Sober Look at Ads and Children," *Boston Globe,* May 17, 2009, http://www.boston.com/ae/movies/articles/2009/05/17/a_sober_look_at_ads_and_children (retrieved May 22, 2009).

30. *FTC Issues Report on Marketing Violent Entertainment to Children*, April 12, 2007 (Washington, DC), http://www.ftc.gov/opa/2007/04/marketingviolence.shtm (retrieved May 22, 2009).

31. Miriam H. Zoll, "Psychologists Challenge Ethics of Marketing to Children," American News Service, April 5, 2000, http://www.mediachannel.org/originals/kidsell.shtml (retrieved May 22, 2009).

32. Tamar Lewin, "In Public Schools, the Name Game as a Donor Lure," *New York Times*, January 26, 2006; Pam Belluck, "And for Perfect Attendance, Johnny Gets . . . a Car," *New York Times*, February 5, 2006; Alex Molnar and David Garia, "The Battle over Commercialized Schools," *Educational Leadership* 63, no. 7 (April 2006), pp. 78–82.

33. Neil Buckley, "Obesity Campaign Eyes School Drinks," *Financial Times,* June 23, 2003; Alex Molnar, "The Corporate Branding of Our Schools," *Educational Leadership* 60, no. 2 (October 2002), pp. 74–78.

34. "School Soda Ban Has Limited Effect," *Washington Post,* November 27, 2008, http://www.washingtonpost.com/wp-dyn/content/article/2008/11/27/AR2008112701843.html (retrieved July 12, 2009).

35. Alfie Kohn, "The 500–Pound Gorilla," *Phi Delta Kappan* 84, no. 2 (October 2002), p. 117; Molnar and Garia, "The Battle over Commercialized Schools."

36. Linda Lou, "Money Helps Pay for Printing Costs after Budget Cuts," *San Diego Union Tribune,* November 22, 2008, http://www.signonsandiego.com/news/metro/20081122-9999-1mc22rbteach.html (retrieved July 12, 2009).

37. Molnar, "The Corporate Branding of Our Schools," p. 76.

38. Bill Turque, "District Considers Longer School Day," *Washington Post,* November 8, 2010, p. B01.

39. Kris Axtman, "Schools Bend under Tight Budgets," *Christian Science Monitor,* November 20, 2002; "Schools Cut Costs with 4–Day Weeks," September 11, 2002, cnn

.com; Richard Rothstein, "Raising School Standards and Cutting Budget: Huh?" *New York Times,* July 10, 2002; Ann E. Marimow and Rosalind S. Helderman, "Taxing Times for County Budgets," *Washington Post,* March 18, 2008, p. A01; Maria Glod, "Strapped Schools May Boost Class Sizes," *Washington Post,* December 5, 2008, p. A1.

40. Jay Matthews, "More Public Schools Using Private Dollars," *Washington Post,* August 28, 1995, pp. A-1, A-8; Justin Blum, "PTAs Give Some D.C. Schools an Edge," *Washington Post,* April 17, 2000, p. B1; Nancy Trejos, "Schools Turning to No-Fuss Fundraising Online," *Washington Post,* May 23, 2000, p. A1; Peter Schworm, "Is It Good for Education Foundations to Fund What Taxes Don't Cover?" *Boston Globe,* February 25, 2007, http://www.boston.com/news/local/articles/2007/02/25/what_taxes_dont_cover/ (retrieved March 20, 2008); Jennifer Gonzalez, "Public School Endowments on the Rise," *Cleveland Plain Dealer,* June 2007, http://www.publiceducation.org/newsblast/June07/June15_text.htm (retrieved March 20, 2008).

41. "Educator's Wish List: Infrastructure Tops High-Tech," *Washington Post,* October 24, 2000, p. A-13; "Fast Response Survey System, Survey on the Conditions of Public School Facilities," U.S. Department of Education, National Center for Education Statistics, Washington, DC, 1999.

42. Bradford Chaney and Laurie Lewis, *Public School Principals Report on Their School Facilities: Fall 2005* (NCES 2007–007), (Washington, DC: U.S. Department of Education, National Center for Education Statistics; issued January 2007), http://nces.ed.gov/pubs2007/2007007.pdf (retrieved May 5, 2009).

43. Lowell C. Rose and Alec M. Gallup, "The 39th Annual Phi Delta Kappa/Gallup Poll on the Public's Attitude toward the Public School," *Phi Delta Kappan* (September 2007), pp. 33–48, http://www.pdkintl.org/kappan/kpollpdf.htm (retrieved May 5, 2009).

44. Frederick M. Hess, *School Boards at the Dawn of the 21st Century* (Arlington, VA.: National School Boards Association, 2002).

45. For an insightful discussion of school boards, see Joel Spring, *American Education* (New York: McGraw-Hill, 2002), pp. 178–182.

46. Chester Finn, "Reinventing Local Control," in Patricia First and Herbert Walberg, eds., *School Boards: Changing Local Control* (Berkeley: McCutchan, 1992); Emily Feistritzer, "A Profile of School Board Presidents," in *School Boards: Changing Local Control;* Neal Pierce, "School Boards Get Failing Grades, in Both the Cities and the Suburbs," *Philadelphia Inquirer,* April 27, 1992, p. 11; Mary Jordan, "School Boards Need Overhaul, Educators Say," *Washington Post,* April 5, 1992, p. A-51.

47. Jay Mathews, "Playing Politics in Urban City Schools," *Washington Post,* September 11, 2002; American Association of School Administrators, *The State of the American School Superintendency: A Mid-Decade Study* (September 2007), http://www.aasa.org/newsroom/pressdetail.cfm?ItemNumber=9401 (retrieved May 5, 2009); Catherine Gewertz, "Race, Gender, and the Superintendency," *Education Week* 26, no. 24 (February 17, 2006), pp. 1, 22, 24.

48. American Association of School Administrators, *The State of the American School Superintendency: A Mid-Decade Study;* Gewertz, "Race, Gender, and the Superintendency."

49. Cited in Spring, *American Education.*

50. Jay Mathews, "Nontraditional Thinking in Central Office," *The School Administrator* Web Edition, *Washington Post,* June 2001; Tamar Lewin, "Leaders from Other Professions Reshape America's Schools, from Top to Bottom," *New York Times,* June 8, 2000; Nancy Mitchell, "Nontraditional School Bosses," *Denver Rocky Mountain News,* April 16, 2001; Abby Goodnough, "Retired General Takes on New Mission: Schools," *New York Times,* November 6, 2002; Jennifer Steinhauer, "Bloomberg Picks a Lawyer to Run New York Schools," *New York Times,* July 30, 2002; Timothy Waters and Robert J. Marzano, "The Primacy of Superintendent Leadership," *The School Administrator,* March 2007, http://www.aasa.org/publications/saarticledetailtest.cfm?ItemNumber=8435 (retrieved May 28, 2009).

51. Valerie Strauss, "Rhee in D.C.: The Myth of the Heroic Leader," *Washington Post*, September 9, 2010, http://voices.washingtonpost.com/answer-sheet/guest-bloggers/rhee-in-dc-the-myth-of-the-her.html (retrieved November 3, 2010).

52. Joanna Richardson, "Contracts Put Superintendents to Performance Test," *Education Week,* September 14, 1994, pp. 1, 12.

53. Debra Viadero, "Turnover in Principalship Focus of Research," *Education Week,* 29, no. 9 (October 28, 2009), pp. 1, 14; Emily Wax, "A Tough Time at the Head of the Classes," *Washington Post,* June 18, 2002, p. A9.

54. Vincent L. Ferrandino, "Challenges for 21st-Century Elementary School Principals," *Phi Delta Kappan* 82, no. 6 (February 2001), pp. 440–442; Linda Borg, "The Principal Dilemma Facing Schools in R.I.," *Providence Journal,* http://www.projo.com/education (August 26, 2001); Jacques Steinberg, "One Principal's World (The Unscripted Version)," *New York Times,* January 1, 2003.

55. "Seeing the Big Picture" in Education Vital Signs, *American School Board Journal,* December 1999.

56. Ferrandino, "Challenges for 21st-Century Elementary School Principals."

57. Elissa Gootman and Robert Gebeloff, "Principals Younger and Freer, but Raise Doubts in the Schools," *New York Times,* May 26, 2009, pp. A1, A15.

58. Jenny Upchurch, "Custodians Keep Schools Running without a Hitch," Tennessean.com, December 30, 2007; Edmund Janko, "The Untouchables: There Are Some People You Don't Mess With, and Many of Them Work in Schools," *Teacher Magazine* 16, no. 6 (May 1, 2005), pp. 50–51.

59. James G. Cibula, "Two Eras of Urban Schooling: The Decline of Law and Order and the Emergence of New Organizational Forms," *Education and Urban Society,* 29, no. 3 (May 1997), pp. 317–341.

60. Quoted in "Building Better Business Alliances," *Instructor* (Winter 1986, special issue), p. 21. See also Brian

Dumaine, "Making Education Work," *Fortune* (Spring 1990, special issue), pp. 12–22.

61. For a good overview of school consolidation, see Karen Irmsher, "School Size," *ERIC Digest,* no. 113 (Eugene, OR: ERIC Clearinghouse on Educational Management, July 1997) (ED414615).

62. U.S. Department of Education, "Number of Public School Districts and Public and Private Elementary and Secondary Schools: Selected Years, 1869–70 through 2006–07," *Digest of Education Statistics, 2008* Table 87 (issued March 2009), http://nces.ed.gov/pubs2009/2009020_2a.pdf (retrieved May 5, 2009).

63. Catherine Gewertz, "The Breakup: Suburbs Try Smaller High Schools," *Education Week on the Web,* May 2, 2001; Craig Howley and Marty Strange and Robert Bickel, "Research about School Size and School Performance in Impoverished Communities" (Charleston, WV: ERIC Clearinghouse on Rural Education and Small Schools, December 2000); William Ayers, Gerald Bracey, and Greg Smith, "The Ultimate Education Reform? Make Schools Smaller" (Milwaukee: Center for Education Research, Analysis, and Innovation, University of Wisconsin–Milwaukee, December 14, 2000).

64. Elissa Gootman, "New York City Plans to Open Small Secondary Schools," *New York Times,* March 12, 2004.

65. See Marianne Perle and David Baker, *Job Satisfaction among America's Teachers: Effects of Workplace Conditions, Background Characteristics, and Teacher Compensation* (Washington, DC: National Center for Education Statistics, U.S. Department of Health, Education and Welfare, August 1997), pp. 41–42. See also John Lane and Edgar Epps, eds., *Restructuring the Schools: Problems and Prospects* (Berkeley: McCutchan, 1992); Jeff Archer, "New Roles Tap Expertise of Teachers," *Education Week,* May 30, 2001.

66. Fern Shen, "New Strategy for School Management," *Washington Post,* February 17, 1998, pp. B-1, B-7; Patrick McCloskey, "Vocal Arrangement," *Teacher Magazine* 17, no. 1 (September 1, 2005), pp. 30–35; Jeff Archer, "S.F. School Councils Help Chart Improvement Course," *Education Week* 25, no. 31 (April 12, 2006), p. 10.

CHAPTER 8: SCHOOL LAW AND ETHICS

1. Harris Interactive Poll for the Common Good, *Evaluating Attitudes Toward the Threat of Legal Challenges in Public Schools* (March 10, 2004). Available at http://commongood.org/assets/attachments/11.pdf.

2. Louis Fischer, David Schimmel, and Leslie Stellman, *Teachers and the Law,* 8th ed. (Boston: Prentice Hall, 2010); Karen Zittleman, "Title IX and Gender: A Study of the Knowledge, Perceptions, and Experiences of Middle and Junior High School Teachers and Students," *Dissertation Abstracts International* 66, no. 11 (2005) (UMI No. 3194815); Gerry Doyle, "Study: Americans Know Bart Better than 1st Amendment," *Chicago Tribune,* February 28, 2006, http://www.chicagotribune.com.

3. Louis Fischer and David Schimmel, *The Civil Rights of Teachers* (New York: Harper & Row, 1973).

4. The legal situations and interpretations included in this text are adapted from a variety of sources, including Myra Sadker and David Sadker, *Sex Equity Handbook for Schools* (New York: Longman, 1982); Fischer and Schimmel, *The Civil Rights of Teachers,* and *Your Legal Rights and Responsibilities: A Guide for Public School Students* (Washington, DC: U.S. Department of Health, Education and Welfare, n.d.); Fischer, Schimmel, and Stellman, *Teachers and the Law;* Michael LaMorte, *School Law: Cases and Concepts* 9th ed. (Boston, MA: Allyn and Bacon, 2007); Karen R. Zittleman, "Teachers, Students and Title IX: A Promise for Fairness" in David Sadker and Ellen Silber (eds.), *Gender in the Classroom: Foundations, Skills, Methods and Strategies across the Curriculum* (Mahwah, NJ: Lawrence Erlbaum, 2007), pp. 73–107.

5. Sadker and Sadker, *Sex Equity Handbook for Schools;* Zittleman, "Teachers, Students and Title IX: A Promise for Fairness."

6. *Gebser v. Lago Vista Independent School District* (96 U.S. 1866 (1998); Greg Henderson, "Court Says Compensatory Damages Available Under Title IX," UPI, February 26, 1992; *North Haven Board of Education v. Bell,* 456 U.S. 512 (1982); *Franklin v. Gwinnett County Schools,* 503 U.S. 60 (1992).

7. *Thompson v. Southwest School District,* 483 F. Supp. 1170 (W.D.M.W. 1980); see also Fischer, Schimmel, and Stellman, *Teachers and the Law;* Human Rights Campaign Foundation, "Discrimination in the Workplace" (August 7, 2003), http://www.hrc.org.

8. *Kingsville Independent School District v. Cooper,* 611 F. 2d 1109 (5th Cir. 1980); *Parducci v. Rutland,* 316 F. Supp. 352 (M.D. Ala. 1979); *Brubaker v. Board of Education, School District 149, Cook County, Illinois,* 502 F. 2d 973 (7th Cir. 1974); see also Michael LaMorte, *School Law: Cases and Concepts.*

9. Nathan L. Essex, *School Law and the Public Schools: A Practical Guide for School Leaders,* 4th ed. (Boston: Allyn & Bacon, 2007).

10. *Pickering v. Board of Education of Township High School District 205, Will County,* 391 U.S. 563 (1968); Nathan L. Essex, *School Law and the Public Schools: A Practical Guide for School Leaders.*

11. "California: Ruling Against Anti-Creationism Teacher," *New York Times,* May 5, 2009, p. A18.

12. Javier Hernandez, "Judge Says No to Teachers' Campaign Buttons, but Yes to Certain Politicking," *New York Times,* October 18, 2008, p. A20.

13. *Basic Books v. Kinko's Graphics Corp.,* 758 F. Supp. 1522 (S.D.N.Y.1991); Gary Becker, "Copyright in a Digital Age: How to Comply with the Law and Set a Good Example for Students," *American School Board Journal* 187, no. 6 (June 2000), pp. 26–27; Hall Davidson, "The Educators' Guide to Copyright and Fair Use," *Technology & Learning 23,* no. 3 (October 2002), pp. 26–32.

14. Essex, *School Law and the Public Schools: A Practical Guide for School Leaders.*

15. Ibid.

16. La Morte, *School Law: Cases and Concepts; Hortonville Joint School District No. 1 v. Hortonville Education Association,* 426 U.S. 482 (1976).

17. See Fischer, Schimmel, and Stellman, *Teachers and the Law; Owasso Independent School District v. Falvo* 534 U.S. 426 (2002).

18. Sam Dillion, "Racial Disparity in School Suspensions," *New York Times,* September 13, 2010, p. A16.

19. Tara Parker-Pope, "Schools and Legal System Mistreat Gays, Study Says," *The New York Times,* December 7, 2010, p. A22.

20. *Goss v. Lopez,* 419 U.S. 565 (1975); *Wood v. Strickland,* 420 U.S. 308 (1975); *Ingraham v. Wright,* 430 U.S. 651 (1977); Michael Martin, "Does Zero Mean Zero? Balancing Policy with Procedure in the Fight Against Weapons at School," *American School Board Journal* 187, no. 3 (March 2000), pp. 39–41; Stacy Teicher, "To Paddle or Not to Paddle? It's Still Not Clear in U.S. Schools," *Christian Science Monitor,* March 17, 2005; The Center for Effective Discipline, "States Banning Corporal Punishment," July 2010, http://www.stophitting.com.

21. *Tinker v. Des Moines Independent Community School District,* 393 U.S. 503 (1969).

22. Howard Fischer, "Court: Schools Can Ban Hurtful T-Shirt Slogans," *Arizona Daily Star,* April 21, 2006, http://www.azstarnet.com.

23. *Morse v. Frederick,* 127 S. Ct. 2618 (2007); Warren Richey, "Court Restricts Student Expression," *Christian Science Monitor,* June 26, 2007.

24. *Beussink v. Woodland R-IV School District,* 30 F. Supp. 2d 1175 (1998); Jamin Raskin, *We the Students: Supreme Court Cases for and about Students* (Washington, DC: CQ Press, 2000).

25. Patrik Jonsson, "Teachers Strike Back at Students' Online Pranks," *Christian Science Monitor,* February 25, 2008.

26. *Bethel School District No. 403 v. Fraser,* 478 U.S. 675 (1986); Kathleen Conn, "Offensive Student Web Sites: What Should Schools Do?" *Educational Leadership* 50, no. 5 (February 2001), pp. 74–77.

27. *Bellnier v. Lund,* 438 F. Supp. 47 (N.Y. 1977); *Doe v. Renfrou,* 635 F. 2d 582 (7th Cir. 1980), cert. denied, 101 S. Ct. 3015 (1981); *Veronia School District v. Acton,* 115 U.S. 2386 (1995); *New Jersey v. T.L.O.,* 105 U.S. 733 (1985); Jesse Holland, "Court Says Strip Search of Arizona Teenager Illegal," *Arizona Daily Star,* June 25, 2009, p. A1.

28. *Hazelwood School District v. Kuhlmeier,* 108 S. Ct. 562 (1988); *Shanley v. Northeast Independent School District,* 462 F. 2d 960 (5th Cir. 1972); Fischer, Schimmel, and Stellman, *Teachers and the Law.*

29. Fischer, Schimmel, and Stellman, *Teachers and the Law*

30. Ibid.; Zittleman, "Teachers, Students, and Title IX: A Promise for Fairness."

31. Zittleman, "Teachers, Students, and Title IX: A Promise for Fairness."

32. Ibid.

33. Harris Interactive Poll, *Hostile Hallways: Bullying, Teasing, and Sexual Harassment in School;* Zittleman, "Title IX and Gender: A Study of the Knowledge, Perceptions, and Experiences of Middle and Junior High School Teachers and Students"; Fischer, Schimmel, and Stellman, *Teachers and the Law.*

34. Susan Donaldson James, "Cheating Scandals Rock Three Top-Tier High Schools," ABCnews.com (February 29, 2008); *Ethics of American Youth: 2008* (Los Angeles, CA: The Josephson Institute, October 2008), http://charactercounts.org/programs/reportcard/2008/index.html.

35. James, "Cheating Scandals Rock Three Top-Tier High Schools"; Regan McMahon, "Everybody Does It," sfgate.com (September 9, 2007); *Ethics of American Youth: 2008.*

36. *Ethics of American Youth: 2008.*

37. Rebecca Moore Howard and Laura J. Davies, "Plagiarism in the Internet Age," *Educational Leadership* 66, no. 6 (March 2009), pp. 64–67.

38. McMahon, "Everybody Does It"; "Poll: Student Cheating Prevalent," *Detroit News,* April 30, 2004; *Ethics of American Youth: 2008.*

39. Amanda Lenhart, *Teens, Cellphones, and Texting,* Pew Research Center Publications (April 20, 2010), http://pewresearch.org/pubs/1572/teens-cell-phones-text-messages; Rhonda Bodfield, "Should Teachers, Kids Be 'Friends'?" *Arizona Daily Star,* May 24, 2009, p. A1.

40. Ibid.; Michelle Davis, "Social Networking Goes to School," *Education Week* 3, no. 3 (June 14, 2010), pp. 16, 18, 20, 22–23.

41. Administration on Children, Youth, and Families, U.S. Department of Health and Human Services, *Child Maltreatment: 2008,* http://www.acf.hhs.gov/programs/cb/pubs/cm08/.

42. Sarah Spark, "Character Education Found to Fall Short in Federal Study," *Education Week* online, 30, no. 9 (October 21, 2010); Joan F. Goodman, "Objections (and Responses) to Moral Education," *Education Week* 20, no. 38 (May 30, 2001), pp. 32, 35; Debra Viadero, "Nice Work," *Education Week* 22, no. 33 (April 30, 2003), pp. 38–41; Alfie Kohn, "How Not to Teach Values," *Phi Delta Kappan* 78, no. 8 (April 1997), pp. 428–437 (cited in James Noll, *Taking Sides,* 13th ed. (New York: McGraw-Hill, 2005), pp. 102–117.

43. Spark, "Character Education Found to Fall Short in Federal Study."

44. Howard Kirschenbaum, "A Comprehensive Model for Values Education and Moral Education," *Phi Delta Kappan* 73, no. 10 (June 1992), pp. 771–776; Nel Noddings, "Handle with Care," *Greater Good* (Spring/Summer 2006), pp. 18–21.

45. Charles Haynes, "Teaching Social Responsibility," *Education Leadership* 66, no. 8 (May 2009), pp. 6–13; Katherine Simon, "Making Room for Moral Questions in the Classroom," *Education Week* 21, no. 10 (November 7, 2001), pp. 51, 68.

CHAPTER 9: REFORMING AMERICA'S SCHOOLS

1. James Shaver and William Strong, *Facing Value Decisions: Rationale Building for Teachers* (Belmont, CA: Wadsworth, 1976); Barbara Slater Stern and Karen Lea Riley, "Reflecting on the Common Good: Harold

Rugg and the Social Reconstructionists," *Social Studies* 92 (2001); Michael E. James, *Social Reconstructionism through Education* (Stamford, CT: Ablex Publishing, 1995).

2. Sara Neufeld, "Photos Reveal Decrepit State of City Schools," *Baltimore Sun,* February 24, 2006, http://healthyschoolscampaign.org/news/media/environ/2006-0224_photos.php (retrieved April 17, 2009).

3. Ernest L. Boyer, *High School: A Report on Secondary Education in America* (New York: Harper & Row, 1983), pp. 209–210.

4. Linda Perlstein, "'Serving' the Community Without Leaving School," *Washington Post,* June 28, 1999, pp. A1, A6.

5. *The Condition of Education 2001,* U.S. Department of Education, NCES, Indicator 16: Social and Cultural Outcomes, Community Service Participation in Grades 6–12, p. 142, http://nces.ed.gov/pubs2001/2001072_2.pdf; Helen M. Marks and Susan Robb Jones, "Community Service in Transition: Shifts and Continuities in Participation from High School to College," *Journal of Higher Education* 75 (2004), pp. 307–339.

6. Bill Bigelow, "The Human Lives Behind the Labels: The Global Sweatshop, Nike, and the Race to the Bottom," *Phi Delta Kappan* 79, no. 2 (October 1997), pp. 112–119.

7. Paulo Freire, *Pedagogy of the Oppressed* (New York: Herder & Herder, 1970).

8. John Goodlad, *A Place Called School* (New York: McGraw-Hill, 1984), pp. 35–39.

9. Arthur Eugene Bestor, *Educational Wastelands: The Retreat from Learning in Our Public Schools* (Urbana: University of Illinois Press, 1953), p. 75.

10. Boyer, *High School,* p. 5.

11. Lowell C. Rose and Alec M. Gallup, "The 39th Annual Phi Delta Kappa/Gallup Poll of the Public's Attitude toward the Public Schools," *Phi Delta Kappan* 89, no. 1 (September 2007), Table 33, pp. 33–48.

12. National Commission on Excellence in Education, *A Nation at Risk: The Imperative for Educational Reform* (Washington, DC: U.S. Government Printing Office, 1983), p. 1.

13. Valerie Strauss, "Federal Report Fuels a Quarter-Century of Restructuring, and Controversy," *Washington Post,* April 7, 2008, p. B02; Sally Blake, "*A Nation at Risk* and the Blind Men," *Phi Delta Kappan* 89 (April 2008), pp. 601–602; Thomas W. Hewitt, "Speculations on *A Nation at Risk:* Illusions and Realities," *Phi Delta Kappan* 89 (April 2008), pp. 575–579.

14. National Education Association, *Report of the Committee on Secondary School Studies* (Washington, DC: U.S. Government Printing Office, 1893).

15. Debra Viadero, "Students Learn More in Magnets than Other Schools, Study Finds," *Education Week,* March 6, 1996, p. 6; Caroline Hendrie, "Magnets' Value in Desegregating Schools Is Found to Be Limited," *Education Week on the Web,* November 13, 1996; "Research Notes," *Education Week on the Web,* September 16, 1998.

16. Alicia Mundy, "Gates 'Appalled' by High Schools," *Seattle Times,* February 7, 2005, http://seattletimes .nwsource.com/html/localnews/2002191433_gates27m .html (retrieved April 20, 2009).

17. *The Economic Impact of Achievement Gaps in America's Schools,* McKinsey Group, Social Sector Office, 2009, http://www.mckinsey.com/clientservice/socialsector/achievementgap.asp (retrieved April 24, 2009).

18. Alex Molnar, "Charter Schools: The Smiling Face of Disinvestment," *Educational Leadership* 54, no. 2 (October 1996), pp. 9–15; Chuck Sudetic, "Reading, Writing, and Revenue," *Mother Jones,* May/June 2001, pp. 84–95.

19. Mary Ann Zehr, "KIPP Middle Schools Found to Spur Learning Gains," *Education Week* 36, no. 29 (June 22, 2010); Jay Mathews, "Inside the Bay Area KIPP Schools," *Washington Post,* September 19, 2008, http://www .washingtonpost.com/wp-dyn/content/article/2008/09/19/AR2008091900978.html (retrieved March 27, 2009); Mary Ann Zehr "Regular Public Schools Start to Mimic Charters," *Education Week* 30, no. 11 (November 8, 2010), pp. 1, 12, http://www.edweek.org/ew/articles/2010/11/10/11charter.h30.html.

20. Winnie Hu, "In a New Role, Teachers Are Given the Chance to Run Poorer Schools," *New York Times*, September 7, 2010, pp. A1, A20.

21. Lesli A. Maxwell, "Study Finds No Clear Edge for Charter Schools," *Education Week*, June 29, 2010, http://www .edweek.org/ew/articles/2010/06/29/36ies.h29.html; Lesli A. Maxwell, "Study Casts Doubt on Charter School Results," *Education Week*, June 15, 2009, http://www .edweek.org/ew/articles/2009/06/15/36charters.h28.html; Trip Gabriel, "Despite Push, Success at Charter Schools Is Mixed," *New York Times*, May 2, 2010, pp. 1, 22, 23.

22. Leah Fabel, "Charter School Teachers More Likely to Leave Teaching," *Washington Examiner,* July 6, 2010; Jack Buckley and Mark Schneider, *Charter Schools: Hope or Hype?* (Princeton, NJ: Princeton University Press, 2007); Robin J. Lake, ed., *Hopes, Fears, and Reality: A Balanced Look at Charter Schools in 2007* (The National Charter School Research Project, December 2007), http://www.ncsrp.org/cs/csr/view/csr_pubs/17 (retrieved April 9, 2008); Andrew Rotherham and Sara Mead, *A Sum Greater than the Parts: What States Can Teach Each Other about Charter Schooling* (Washington, DC: Education Sector, 2007), http://www.educationsector.org/usr_doc/CharterSchoolSummary.pdf (retrieved April 17, 2009); Patrik Jonsson, "As New Orleans Restarts Its Schools, Most Are Now Charter Schools," *Christian Science Monitor,* September 4, 2007, http://www.csmonitor.com/2007/0904/p01s08-ussc.html (retrieved April 17, 2009).

23. *Choice Without Equity: Charter School Segregation and the Need for Civil Rights Standards,* The Civil Rights Project, UCLA, February 4, 2010.

24. Alyson Klein, "Needs of 'Whole Child' May Factor in ESEA Renewal; Wide Range of Supports, Services, and Enrichment Seen as Vital but Costly," *Education Week* 29, no. 30, pp. 16, 21 (April 28, 2010); Sharon Otterman, "Despite Money and Attention, It's Not All A's at 2 Harlem Schools," *New York Times,* October 13, 2010, pp. A18–19; Javier C. Hernandez, "Harlem Educator Is Said to Have Rejected Schools Chancellor Job," *New*

York Times, December 10, 2010, p. 10; Klein, "Needs of 'Whole Child' May Factor in ESEA Renewal."

25. For more on the legal dispute, see *Jackson v. Benson* (1998), which held that vouchers used for religious school tuition did not violate the Wisconsin state constitution; Sam Dillon, "For Parents Seeking a Choice, Charter Schools Prove More Popular than Vouchers," *New York Times,* July 23, 2005, http://www.nytimes.com/2005/07/13/education/13voucher.html (retrieved April 7, 2008).

26. David Stout, "Public Money Can Pay Religious-School Tuition, Court Rules," *New York Times,* June 27, 2002.

27. Erin Richards, "New Data Shows Similar Academic Results Between Voucher and MPS Students," *Milwaukee Journal Sentinel*, April 7, 2010, http://www.jsonline.com/news/education/90169302.html; Kavan Peterson, "School Vouchers Slow to Spread," http://www.Stateline.org, May 5, 2005; National Education Association, "Florida High Court Rules Against Vouchers," http://www.nea.org/vouchers/flvouchers1-06.html (retrieved January 5, 2006); Maria Glod and Bill Turque, "Report Finds Little Gain from Vouchers," *Washington Post,* June 17, 2008, p. B6.

28. Jeremy P. Meyer, "Douglas County School District Considers Starting Voucher Program," *Denver Post,* November 5, 2010, http://www.denverpost.com/news/ci_16528490; Dillon, "For Parents Seeking a Choice, Charter Schools Prove More Popular than Vouchers"; U.S. Charter Schools, "Frequently Asked Questions," March 22, 2006, http://www.uscharterschools.org/pub/uscs_docs/o/faq.html; Center for Education Reform, "Charter Schools," March 22, 2006, http://www.edreform.com; "New CER Report Gives Evidence of Charters' Impact," *Charter Schools Today,* Washington, DC, May 5, 2004; National Education Association, *Vouchers* (2008), http://www.nea.org/vouchers/index.html (retrieved April 7, 2008).

29. Timothy McDonald, "The False Promise of Voucher," *Educational Leadership* 59, no. 7 (April 2002), pp. 33–37; Kaleem M. S. Caire, "The Truth about Vouchers," *Educational Leadership* 59, no. 7 (April 2002), pp. 38–42; Joseph P. Viteritti, "Coming Around on School Choice," *Educational Leadership* 59, no. 7 (April 2002), pp. 44–48; National Education Association, "Vouchers," March 22, 2006, http://www.nea.org/vouchers/index.html; Pat Kossan and Emily Gersema, "Arizona's High Court Bans School Vouchers," *Arizona Republic,* March 26, 2009, http://www.azcentral.com/arizonarepublic/news/articles/2009/03/26/20090326vouchers0326.html (retrieved March 29, 2009); National Education Association, "Florida High Court Rules Against Vouchers."

30. A. S. Byrk, Valerie Lee, and P. B. Holland, *Catholic Schools and the Common Good* (London: Harvard University Press, 1993); Public School Review, "What Is a Magnet School?" http://www.publicschoolreview.com/magnet-schools.php (retrieved March 22, 2006); Howard Blume, "Support for Magnet Schools Waning Despite Their Success," *Los Angeles Times,* November 26, 2008, http://articles.latimes.com/2008/nov/26/local/me magnets26 (retrieved April 1, 2009).

31. National Center of Education Statistics, *State Education Reforms. Table 4.1: Number and Types of Open Enrollment Policies, by State, 2005*, http://nces.ed.gov/programs/statereform/sssco_tab1.asp (retrieved April 7, 2008).

32. Amanda Paulson, "Virtual Schools, Real Concerns," *Christian Science Monitor,* May 4, 2004; U.S. Department of Education, National Center for Education Statistics, Fast Response Survey System (FRSS), "Distance Education Courses for Public School Elementary and Secondary School Students: 2002–03," Washington, DC; Kate Moser, "Online Courses Aren't Just for Home-Schoolers Anymore," *Christian Science Monitor,* March 30, 2006, http://www.csmonitor.com/2006/0330/p14s02-legn.html; Sean Cavanagh, "Survey Finds Interest in Blend of Tradition and Online Courses," *Education Week,* March 5, 2007.

33. Bill Tucker, *Laboratories of Reform: Virtual High Schools and Innovation in Public Education* (Washington, DC: Education Sector, June 2007), http://www.educationsector.org/research/research_show.htm?doc_id=502307 (retrieved April 10, 2008); Cavanagh, "Survey Finds Interest in Blend of Tradition and Online Courses," Moser, "Online Courses Aren't Just for Home-Schoolers Anymore"; Michelle Galley, "Despite Concerns, Online Elementary Schools Grow," *Education Week* 22, no. 16 (January 8, 2003), pp. 1, 12.

34. Diana B. Henriques, "Edison Schools' Founder to Take It Private," *New York Times,* July 15, 2003; Gerald Bracey, "The 12th Bracey Report on the Condition of Public Education," *Phi Delta Kappan* 84, no. 2 (October 2002), pp. 135–150; Chris Brennan, "Ex-Edison Official: Company Lacks Integrity," Philly.com, July 24, 2002; Michael Fletcher, "Private Enterprise, Public Woes in Phila. School," *Washington Post,* September 17, 2002, p. A1; Brian Gill, Laura S. Hamilton, J. R. Lockwood, Julie A. Marsh, Ron Zimmer, Deanna Hill, and Shana Pribesh, *Inspiration, Perspiration, and Time: Operations and Achievements in Edison Schools,* October 2005, RAND Corporation, http://www.rand.org/pubs/monographs/MG351.html (retrieved May 1, 2009).

35. Joel Spring, *American Education* (New York: McGraw-Hill, 1996), pp. 184–185.

36. Stephanie Strom, "For School Company, Issues of Money and Control," *New York Times,* April 23, 2010, p. A1; Katrina E. Bulkley, *Recentralizing Decentralization? Educational Management Organizations and Charter Schools' Educational Programs* (National Center for the Study of the Privatization of Education, Columbia Teachers College, 2003). For additional studies on the privatization of schools and school choice, see the National Center for the Study of the Privatization of Education, http://www.ncspe.org/. Bill Brubaker, "Sylvan Learning Systems Renamed Laureate to Focus on Universities," *Washington Post,* May 18, 2004, p. E04; Jamie Smith Hopkins, "Sylvan, LeapFrog Plan to Tutor Kids in Big Stores: Parents Might Soon Be Able to Shop While Their Children Are Being Tutored a Few Aisles Away," *Baltimore Sun,* December 22, 2004.

37. "Live and Learn," *Harper's Bazaar,* September 1994, pp. 268–270.

38. National Center for Education Statistics, "Homeschooling in the United States: 2003" (February 2006), http://nces.ed.gov/pubs2006/2006042.pdf (retrieved May 1, 2009).

39. J. A. Van Galen, "Schooling in Private: A Study of Home Education," doctoral dissertation, University of North Carolina, Chapel Hill, 1986; National Center for Education Statistics, "Homeschooled Students," *The Condition of Education* (May 2009), Indicator 6, http://nces.ed.gov/pubs2009/2009081.pdf.

40. Brian D. Ray, "Homeschooling Across America: Academic Achievement and Demographic Characteristics," August 10, 2009, http://www.nheri.org/Latest/Homeschooling-Across-America-Academic-Achievement-and-Demographic-Characteristics.html; Gregory J. Millman, "Home Is Where the School Is," *Washington Post,* March 23, 2008, p. B1; National Center for Education Statistics, "Homeschooling in the United States: 2003"; Moser, "Online Courses Aren't Just for Home-Schoolers Anymore." For examples of online homeschooling curricula, see HomeSchool.com at http://www.homeschool.com/onlinecourses/ and Online Learning Haven at http://www.learninghaven.com/. See also, Nancy Trejos, "Home Schooling's Net Effect," *The Washington Post,* July 16, 2000, pp. C1, C9.

41. Brian Ray, "Customization through Homeschooling," *Educational Leadership* 59, no. 7 (April 2002), p. 50.

42. "Top-Selling Home-School Texts Disparage Evolution," *Arizona Daily Star*, March 7, 2010, p. A14.

43. Rob Reich, "The Civic Perils of Home Schooling," *Educational Leadership* 59, no. 7 (April 2002), pp. 56–59.

44. Lucy Hood, "The Greening of Environmental Ed: Teachers Focus on Complexity, Evidence, and Letting Students Draw their Own Conclusions," *Harvard Graduate School of Education Newsletter* 27, no. 1 (January/February 2011); Gregory Kats, "Greening America's Schools: Costs and Benefits," October 2006, a Capital E Report, http://www.cape.com/ewebeditpro/items/O59F9819.pdf; "Daylighting in Schools: An Investigation into the Relationship between Daylighting and Human Performance," Heschong Mahone Group (August 1999), http://www.coe.uga.edu/sdpl/research/daylightingstudy.pdf; *Healthier, Wealthier, Wiser: A Report on National Green Schools,* a Report by Global Green USA, http://www.globalgreen.org/news/155 (retrieved April 2, 2009); Laurie Lewis, Kyle Snow, Elizabeth Farris, Becky Smerdon, Stephanie Cronen, and Jessica Kaplan, U.S. Department of Education, National Center for Education Statistics, *Condition of America's Public School Facilities: 1999,* NCES 2000-032, Bernie Greene, project officer (Washington, DC: 2000), http://nces.ed.gov/pubs2000/2000032.pdf.

45. Rhonda Bodfield, "Schoolchildren Aware of Environmental Woes," *Arizona Daily Star,* January 3, 2009, http://www.azstarnet.com/metro/274326 (retrieved April 3, 2009); Sean Cavanagh, "'Green' Classes Flourish in Schools," *Education Week,* 28, no. 20, p. 1, 13; Chelsy Killebrew, "Schoolchildren Go Green: Gardens Offer Science, Art and Enviro Lessons," *Arizona Daily Star,* September 26, 2008, pp. B1, B2; No Child Left Inside, http://www.cbf.org/site/PageServer?pagename=act_sub_actioncenter_federal_NCLB (retrieved April 3, 2009); James Daly, "School Retrofits Go Green" *Edutopia,* October 28, 2009, http://www.edutopia.org/green-schools-retrofitting-health-budget.

46. United States Environmental Protection Agency, Office of Radiation and Indoor Air, *The Inside Story: A Guide to Indoor Air Quality,* U.S. (6609J), Washington, DC, cosponsored with the Consumer Product Safety Commission, EPA 402-K-93-007, http://www.epa.gov/iaq/pubs/insidest.html.

47. Anna Phillips, "In State of the City, Mayor Calls for an End to Seniority Layoffs," GothamSchools.org, January 19, 2011; "Study Questions Seniority-Based Teacher Layoffs," *Daily Caller,* December 23, 2010, Center for Education Data and Research, http://www.cedr.us; Steven Greenhouse and Sam Dillon, "A Wholesale School Shake-Up Is Embraced by the President, and Divisions Follow," *New York Times,* March 7, 2010, p. 18; Jason Felch, Jason Song, and Sandra Poindexter "In Reforming Schools, Quality of Teaching Often Overlooked," *Los Angeles Times,* December 21, 2010.

48. Mitchell Landsberg, "Influence of Teachers Unions in Question," *Los Angeles Times*, November 7, 2010, http://articles.latimes.com/2010/nov/07/local/la-me-teachers-unions-20101107.

49. Dakarai I. Aarons, "Tennessee Targets Teaching with Race to Top Winnings: State Officials See Unique Chance for Big Change in Expectations for Schools," *Education Week* 29, no. 28 (April 2, 2010), p. 28; Catherine Gewertz, "Race to Top Rules Aim to Spur Shifts in Testing," *Education Week* 29, no. 29 (April 8, 2010), http://www.edweek.org/ew/articles/2010/04/07/29assessment_ep.h29.html.

50. Sam Dillon, "Teacher Ratings Get New Look, Pushed by a Very Rich Watcher," *New York Times,* December 4, 2010, pp. A1, A14; Nick Anderson, "Education Secretary Duncan and Teachers Unions Announce Summit," *Washington Post,* October 14, 2010, http://www.washingtonpost.com/wp-dyn/content/article/2010/10/14/AR2010101404094.html.

51. "Is America Listening to Its Teachers? Annual MetLife Teacher Survey Reveals Two-Thirds of Teachers Say Voices Unheard," *MetLife,* B2E News Alert, February 17, 2010; Steven Brill, "The Teachers' Union Last Stand," *New York Times Magazine,* May 23, 2010, pp. 32–39, 44, 46–47.

52. Ann Duffett, Steve Farkas, Andrew J. Rotherham, and Elena Silva, *Waiting to Be Won Over: Teachers Speak on the Profession, Unions, and Reform* (Washington, DC: Education Sector, May 2008).

53. Jocelyn Wiener, "Teachers Wary on Risk, Rewards of Merit Pay" *Sacramento Bee,* January 18, 2005; Briant Farnsworth, Jerry Debenham, and Gerald Smith, "Designing and Implementing a Successful Merit Pay Program for Teachers," *Phi Delta Kappan* 73, no. 4 (December 1991), pp. 320–325.

54. Circe Stumbo and Peter McWalters, "The Effective Educator Measuring Effectiveness: What Will It Take?" *Educational Leadership* 68, no. 4 (December 2010), pp. 10–15; Juan A. Lozano, "Houston to Link Teachers' Pay, Test Scores," *The Guardian,* January 11, 2006, http://www.guardian.co.uk; Holly K. Hatcher and Terrence Stutz, "Incentive Pay Enters Classroom; Other States Watching as Texas Ties Teacher Bonuses to Test Scores," *Dallas Morning News,* June 12, 2006, http://www.dallasnews.com.

55. Stumbo and McWalters, "The Effective Educator Measuring Effectiveness"; "Teachers Willing to Talk about Merit Pay," *Chicago Daily Herald,* June 7, 2006.

56. John Norton, "These Things We Believe," *Teacher Magazine* online, February 10, 2010; Vivian Truen and Katherine C. Boles, "How 'Merit Pay' Squelches Teaching," *Boston Globe,* September 28, 2005.

57. Kenneth J. Cooper, "Performance Pay for Teachers Catches On," *Washington Post,* February 26, 2000, p. A4; Alfie Kohn, "The Folly of Merit Pay," *Education Week* 23, no. 3 (September 17, 2003), pp. 44, 31.

58. Anthony S. Byrk and Barbara Schneider, "Trust in Schools: A Core Resource for School Reform," *Educational Leadership* 60, no. 6 (March 2003), pp. 40–44.

59. Penny A. Bishop and Susanna W. Pflaum, "Student Perceptions of Action, Relevance, and Pace," *Middle School Journal* 36, no. 4 (March 2005), pp. 1–12.

60. National Center for Educational Statistics, *The Condition of Education 2007* (Washington DC: U.S. Department of Education, 2007), Indicator 22: Student Preparedness.

61. Marge Scherer, "Perspectives/Learning: Whose Job Is It?" *Educational Leadership* 66, no. 3 (November 2008), p. 7.

62. "What Students Want from Teachers," *Educational Leadership* 66, no. 3 (November 2008), pp. 48–51.

63. Adam Fletcher, "Giving Students Ownership of Learning: The Architecture of Ownership," *Educational Leadership* 66, no. 3 (November 2008), http://www.ascd.org/publications/educational_leadership/nov08/vol66/num03/The_Architecture_of_Ownership.aspx (retrieved April 15, 2009).

64. *The Metropolitan Life Survey of the American Teacher 2000: Are We Preparing Students for the 21st Century?* (New York: Harris Interactive, Inc., 2000); *The MetLife Survey of the American Teacher: Expectations and Experiences,* Figure 3.9, p. 52 (issued September 26, 2006), http://www.metlife.com/Applications/Corporate/WPS/CDA/PageGenerator/0,4132,P2315,00.html (retrieved April 13, 2008).

65. Sara Lawrence Lightfoot, *The Good High School* (New York: Basic Books, 1983). See also Anthony Jackson and Gayle Davis, *Turning Points: Educating Adolescents in the 21st Century* (New York: Teachers College Press, 2000).

66. George Weber, *Inner-City Children Can Be Taught to Read: Four Successful Schools* (Washington, DC: D.C. Council for Basic Books, 1971); Ronald Edmonds, "Some Schools Work and More Can," *Social Policy* 9 (1979), pp. 28–32; Barbara Taylor and Daniel Levine, "Effective Schools Projects and School-Based Management," *Phi Delta Kappan* 72, no. 5 (January 1991), pp. 394–397. See also Herman Meyers, "Roots, Trees, and the Forest: An Effective Schools Development Sequence," paper delivered at the American Educational Research Association, San Francisco, April 1992.

67. Sara Lawrence Lightfoot, *The Good High School* (New York: Basic Books, 1983).

68. Ibid., p. 67.

69. David Clark, Linda Lotto, and Mary McCarthy, "Factors Associated with Success in Urban Elementary Schools," *Phi Delta Kappan* 61, no. 7 (March 1980), pp. 467–470; *The MetLife Survey of the American Teacher: Expectations and Experiences,* Figure 3.7, p. 50 (issued September 26, 2006), http://www.metlife.com/ (retrieved April 23, 2009). See also David Gordon, "The Symbolic Dimension of Administration for Effective Schools," paper delivered at the annual meeting of the American Educational Research Association, San Francisco, April 1992.

70. William Rutherford, "School Principals as Effective Leaders," *Phi Delta Kappan* 67, no. 1 (September 1985), pp. 31–34; Carl Glickman, "The Courage to Lead," *Educational Leadership* 59, no. 8 (2002), pp. 41–44. See also R. McClure, "Stages and Phases of School-Based Renewal Efforts," paper presented at the annual meeting of the American Educational Research Association, New Orleans, 1988.

71. Steven C. Schlozman, "The Shrink in the Classroom: Fighting School Violence," *Educational Leadership* 60, no. 2 (October 2002), pp. 89–90; Gay, Lesbian, and Straight Education Network, *2007 Climate Survey* (New York: GLSEN, 2008), http://www.glsen.org; National Center for Education Statistics, *Indicators of School Crime and Safety, 2008* (issued April 21, 2009), http://nces.ed.gov/pubs2008/2008021.pdf (retrieved April 30, 2009).

72. *The Metropolitan Life Survey of the American Teacher 1999* (New York: Harris Interactive, Inc., 2001), pp. 39, 42.

73. Lowell C. Rose and Alec M. Gallup, "The 39th Annual Gallup Poll of the Public's Attitudes toward the Public Schools," *Phi Delta Kappan* 89, no. 1 (September 2007), Table 43, pp. 33–48; *The MetLife Survey of the American Teacher: Expectations and Experiences,* Figure 3.7, p. 50.

74. Lightfoot, *The Good High School;* Kevin Dwyer and D. Osher, *Safeguarding Our Children: An Action Guide* (Washington, DC: U.S. Department of Education, August 2000).

75. Wilbur Brookover, Laurence Beamer, Helen Efthim, Douglas Hathaway, Lawrence Lezotte, Stephen Miller, Joseph Passalacqua, and Louis Tornatzky, *Creating Effective Schools* (Holmes Beach, FL: Learning Publications, 1982); Harris Cooper, Jorgianne Robinson, and Erika Patall, "Does Homework Improve Academic Achievement? A Synthesis of Research," *Review of Educational Research* 76 (2006), pp. 1–62.

76. Herbert Walberg, Rosanne Paschal, and Thomas Weinstein, "Homework's Powerful Effects on Learning," *Educational Leadership* 42 (1985), pp. 76–79.

77. Robert Rosenthal and Lenore Jacobson, *Pygmalion in the Classroom* (New York: Holt, Rinehart & Winston, 1968).

78. Patrick Proctor, "Teacher Expectations: A Model for School Improvement," *Elementary School Journal,* March 1984, pp. 469–81; Karin Spader, "The Effects of Teacher Expectations on Student Achievement," paper presented at the annual meeting of the American Sociological Association, Montreal, Canada, August 11, 2006; Robert Marzano, *What Works in Schools* (Alexandria, VA: Association for Supervision and Curriculum Development, 2003).

79. *The Metropolitan Life Survey of the American Teacher 2001* (New York: Harris Interactive, Inc., 2001), p. 61.

80. Daniel Levine, "Creating Effective Schools: Findings and Implications from Research and Practice," *Phi Delta Kappan* 72, no. 5 (January 1991), pp. 389–393; M. Donald Thomas and William L. Bainbridge, "The Contamination of the Effective Schools Movement," *School Administrator* 58, no. 3 (June 2001), p. 55.

81. Debra Viadero, "Study Finds Success in NYC's 'Small Schools,'" *Education Week* 29, no. 36 (June 23, 2010); Sam Dillon, "4,100 Students Prove 'Small Is Better' Rule Wrong," *New York Times,* September 27, 2010, p. A1; Lorna Jimerson, *The Hobbit Effect: Why Small Works in Public Schools* (2006), http://www.smallschoolsproject .org/PDFS/RSCT_hobbit-effect.pdf (retrieved April 23, 2009); Christina A. Samuels "Study: Effective Principals Embrace Collective Leadership," *Education Week* 29, no. 37 (July 23, 2010); Jay Feldman, Lisette Lopez, and Katherine Simon, *Choosing Small: The Essential Guide to Successful High School Conversion* (San Francisco: Jossey Bass, 2006). Douglas Ready, Valerie Lee, and Kevin Welner, "Educational Equity and School Structure: School Size, Overcrowding, and Schools-within-Schools," *Teachers College Record* 106 (2004), pp. 1989–2014; Barbara Taylor, Michael Pressley, and David Pearson, "Research-Supported Characteristics of Teachers and Schools that Promote Reading Achievement," in B. Taylor and D. Pearson, eds., *Teaching Reading: Effective Schools, Accomplished Teachers* (Mahwah, NJ: Erlbaum, 2002), pp. 361–374; Marzano, *What Works in Schools*; Anne T. Henderson, *A New Wave of Evidence: The Impact of School, Family, and Community Connections on Student Achievement* (Southwest Educational Development Laboratory, 2002), http://www.sedl.org/pubs/catalog/items/ fam33.html (retrieved April 23, 2009).

CHAPTER 10 CURRICULUM, STANDARDS, AND TESTING

1. Abner Peddiwell (Harold Benjamin), *The Saber-Tooth Curriculum* (New York: McGraw-Hill, 1939).

2. Hilda Taba, *Curriculum Development: Theory and Practice* (New York: Harcourt Brace Jovanovich, 1962).

3. Stephen Hamilton, "Synthesis of Research on the Social Side of Schooling," *Educational Leadership* 40, no. 5 (February 1983), pp. 65–72.

4. Women's Sports Foundation, *2008 Statistics—Gender Equity in High School and College Athletics: Most Recent Participation & Budget Statistics*, http://www .womenssportsfoundation.org/ (retrieved April 17, 2009).

5. Ibid.; National Federation High School Athletic Association, *The Case for High School Activities*, http:// www.nfhs.org (retrieved April 17, 2009).

6. National Federation High School Athletic Association, *LaCrosse, Bowling among Nation's Emerging High Sports*, http://www.nfhs.org (retrieved April 17, 2009); Staci Hupp, "As Fastest Growing High School Sport, Bowling a Hit," *Dallas Morning News,* October 23, 2007.

7. National Federation High School Athletic Association, *The Case for High School Activities*; Jennifer A. Fredericks and Jacquelynne S. Eccles, "Developmental Benefits of Extracurricular Involvement: Do Peer Characteristics Mediate the Link between Activities and Youth Outcomes?" *Journal of Youth and Adolescence* 34, no. 6 (December 2005), pp. 507–520; John Holloway, "Extracurricular Activities and Student Participation," *Educational Leadership* 60, no. 1 (September 2002), pp. 80–81.

8. National Center for Education Statistics, *Trends among High School Seniors, 1972–2004* (Washington, DC: U.S Department of Education, 2008); Women's Sports Foundation, *Go Out and Play: Youth Sports in America* (October 2008), http://www.womenssportsfoundation.org.

9. John Hoffman, "Extracurricular Activities, Athletic Participation, and Adolescent Alcohol Use: Gender-Differentiated and School-Contextual Effects," *Journal of Health and Social Behavior* 47 (September 2006), pp. 275–290; Fredericks and Eccles, "Developmental Benefits of Extracurricular Involvement."

10. Sean Cavanaugh, "Electives Getting the Boot? It Depends on Where and What," *Education Week* 35, no. 2 (April 19, 2006), p. 7.

11. Paul Barry, "Interview: A Talk with A. Bartlett Giamatti," *College Review Board* (Spring 1982), p. 48.

12. Bobbi Ann Starnes, "Textbooks, School Reform, and the Silver Lining," *Phi Delta Kappan* 86, no. 2 (2004), pp. 170–171; L. Fan and G. Kaeley, "The Influence of Textbooks on Teaching Strategies," *Mid-Western Educational Researcher* 13, no. 4 (2000), pp. 2–9; A. Woodward and D. L. Elliot, "Textbook Use and Teacher Professionalism," in D. L. Elliot and A. Woodward, eds., *Textbooks and Schooling in the United States,* 89th Yearbook of the National Society for the Study of Education (Chicago: University of Chicago Press, 1990), pp. 178–193.

13. Harriet Tyson Bernstein, *A Conspiracy of Good Intentions: America's Textbook Fiasco* (Washington, DC: The Council for Basic Education, 1988), p. 2.

14. Russell Shorto, "How Christian Were the Founders?" *New York Times Magazine,* February 14, 2010; James McKinley, Jr., "Texas Conservatives Seek Deeper Stamp on Texts," *New York Times*, March 10, 2010; Katherine Mangan, "Ignoring Experts' Pleas, Texas Board Approves Controversial Curriculum Standards," *Chronicle of Higher Ed*, May 23, 2010; "Educators Seek Delay of School Curriculum Vote," *Houston Chronicle,* April 15, 2010.

15. Paul Weber, "Experts: Texas Textbooks are Unlikely to Spread," ABC News (AP) San Antonio, May 31, 2010, http://abcnews.go.com/US/Media/ wireStory?id510790382 (retrieved June 21, 2010).

16. Gilbert Sewall, "Textbook Publishing," *Phi Delta Kappan* 48, no. 1 (March 2005), pp. 498–502; Diana Jean Schemo, "Schoolbooks Are Given F's in Originality," *New York Times,* July 13, 2006, http://www.nytimes.com/2006/07/13/books/13textbook.html (retrieved April 17, 2009).

17. Sewall, "Textbook Publishing."

18. Kate Walsh, "Basal Readers: The Lost Opportunity to Build the Knowledge that Propels Comprehension, *The American Educator,* Spring 2003, pp. 24–27, http://www.aft.org/pubs-reports/american_educator/spring2003/Basal_readers.pdf (retrieved April 18, 2009); Andrew Haslett, *Political Propaganda in Elementary Reading Texts* (Chicago: The Heartland Institute, 1999). See also Michael Apple, "Regulating the Text: The Social His-torical Roots of State Control," paper delivered at the annual meeting of the American Educational Research Association, San Francisco, April 1992.

19. M. Pittman and Jeff Frykholm, "Turning Points: Cur-riculum Materials as a Catalyst for Change," paper presented at the annual meeting of the American Educational Research Association, Seattle, April 2002; Starnes, "Textbooks, School Reform, and the Silver Lin-ing"; Fan and Kaeley, "The Influence of Textbooks on Teaching Strategies."

20. Common Core State Standards Initiative, http://www.corestandards.org/ (retrieved February 17, 2011). These standards were developed by the Council of Chief State School Officers and the National Governors Associa-tion; Catherine Gewertz, "Gates Awards 15 Grants for Common-Standards Work," *Education Week* 29, no. 22 (February 18, 2010), http://www.edweek.org/ew/articles/2010/02/18/22gates.h29.html (retrieved January 19, 2011).

21. Linda Darling-Hammond, *The Flat World and Education: How America's Commitment to Equity Will Determine Our Future* (New York: Teachers' College Press, 2010).

22. Alfie Kohn, "Debunking the Case for National Stan-dards," commentary in *Education Week* 29, no. 17 (January 14, 2010), pp. 28, 30.

23. L. Hardy, "A New Federal Role," *American School Board Journal* 189, no. 9 (September 2002), pp. 20–24.

24. Leslie S. Kaplan and William A. Owings, "The Politics of Teacher Quality," *Phi Delta Kappan* 84, no. 9 (May 2003), pp. 687–692; Michael Alison Chandler, "For Teachers Being 'Highly Qualified' Is a Subjective Mat-ter," *Washington Post,* January 13, 2007, p. A01.

25. Teresa Mendez, "Reading Choices Narrow for Schools with Federal Aid," *Christian Science Monitor,* January 22, 2004; Maria Glod, "Study Questions 'No Child' Act's Reading Plan," *Washington Post,* May 2, 2008, p. A01; Learning Point Associates, *Understanding the No Child Left Behind Act* (2007), http://www.learningpt.org/pdfs/qkey1.pdf (retrieved April 18, 2009).

26. O. L. Davis, "New Policies and New Directions: Be Aware of the Footprints! Notice to Nightmares!" *Journal of Curriculum and Supervision* 18, no. 2, (Winter 2003), pp. 103–109; David Sadker and Karen R. Zittleman, "Test Anxiety: Are Students Failing Tests—or Are Tests Failing Students?" *Phi Delta Kappan* 85, no. 10 (June 2004), pp. 740–744, 751.

27. David J. Hoff, "More Schools Facing Sanctions Under NCLB," *Education Week* 28, no. 16 (January 7, 2009), pp. 1, 14–15; Susan Saulny, "Meaning of 'Proficient' Varies for Schools Across Country," *New York Times,* January 19, 2005, http://www.nytimes.com/2005/01/19/education/19scores.html (retrieved September 1, 2009); Lynn Olson and Linda Jacobson, "Analysis Finds Minor-ity NCLB Scores Widely Excluded," *Education Week,* April 26, 2006; Tamar Lewin, "States Found to Vary Widely on Education," *New York Times,* June 8, 2007, http://www.nytimes.com/2007/06/08/education/08scores.html (retrieved April 19, 2009); Ledyard King, "Data Suggest States Satisfy No Child Law by Expecting Less of Students," *USA Today,* June 6, 2007, http://www.usatoday.com/news/education/2007-06-06-schools-main_N.htm (retrieved April 19, 2009); Pauline Vu, "Do State Tests Make the Grade," Stateline.org (Janu-ary 17, 2008), http://www.stateline.org/live/details/story?contentId=272382 (retrieved April 25, 2008); Daniel De Vise, "'Safe Harbor' Offers Shelter from Strict 'No Child' Targets," *Washington Post,* April 7, 2008, pp. B01, B02.

28. Diane Ravitch, *The Death and Life of the Great American School System: How Testing and Choice Are Undermining Education* (New York: Basic Books, 2010); Alexis Hulcochea, "Education Expert Knocks Reform in Schools, Standardized Testing," *Arizona Star,* February 19, 2011, p. A5.

29. Helen Cooper, "Obama Urges Education Law Overhaul," *New York Times,* March 15, 2011, p. A22; Gail Russell Chaddock, "No Child Left Behind: Why Congress will Struggle to Hit Obama Deadline," *Christian Science Monitor,* March 14, 2011.

30. Sharon Nichols and David Berliner, *Collateral Damage: How High-Stakes Testing Corrupts America's Schools* (Cambridge, MA: Harvard Education Press, 2007).

31. John Merrow, "Undermining Standards," *Phi Delta Kap-pan* 82, no. 9 (May 2009), p. 655.

32. Kate Zernike, "Scarsdale Mothers Succeed in First Boy-cott of 8th-Grade Test," *New York Times on the Web,* May 4, 2001, http://tv.nytimes.com/learning/general/spe-cials/testing/04SCAR.html (retrieved January 16, 2005).

33. Michael A. Fletcher, "High Stakes Rise, School Group Put Exam to Test," *Washington Post,* July 9, 2001, p. A1; Michele Kurtz, "Berkshire District to Flout MCAS Rule," *Boston Globe,* February 21, 2003, p. B5; David Hoff, "Teacher Probed for Role in Anti-Testing Activity," *Edu-cation Week* 21, no. 36 (May 15, 2002), p. 3.

34. David Keyes, "Classroom Caste System," *Washington Post,* April 9, 2007, p. A13.

35. Monty Neill, "The Dangers of Testing." *Educational Leadership* 60, no. 5 (February 2003), pp. 43–46; Nichols and Berliner, *Collateral Damage: How High-Stakes Test-ing Corrupts America's Schools.*

36. Alfie Kohn, *The Case Against Standardized Testing: Raising Scores and Ruining Schools* (Portsmouth, NH: Heinemann, 2000); Dalia Zabala, *State High School Exit*

Exams: Patterns in Gaps in Pass Rates (Center on Education Policy, February 2008), http://www.cep-dc.org/ (retrieved April 27, 2008); "Only '50-50' Chance of High School Graduation for U.S. Minority Students, Weak Accountability Rules Found" (Washington, DC: The Civil Rights Project at Harvard and the Urban Institute, February 25, 2004).

37. Jennifer Booher-Jennings, "Rationing Education," *Washington Post,* October 5, 2006, p. A33.

38. Linda McNeil, "Creating New Inequities: Contradictions of Reform," *Phi Delta Kappan* 81, no. 10 (June 2000), pp. 729–734.

39. Diane Rado, "New ISAT Lets Kids Pass with More Wrong Answers," *Chicago Tribune.* October 18, 2010, http://www.chicagotribune.com/news/education/ct-met-isat-answers-20101018,0,308277.story; Ben Feller, "Gaps Appear in State, Federal Test Scores," *Boston Globe,* March 3, 2006; Susan Saulny, "Meaning of 'Proficient' Varies for Schools Across Country," *New York Times,* January 19, 2005; Nichols and Berliner, *Collateral Damage: How High-Stakes Testing Corrupts America's Schools;* Sadker and Zittleman, "Test Anxiety: Are Students Failing Tests—or Are Tests Failing Students?"

40. Nichols and Berliner, *Collateral Damage;* Sadker and Zittleman, "Test Anxiety."

41. University of Virginia, "Students Benefit from Depth, Rather than Breadth, in High School Science Courses," *ScienceDaily,* March 10, 2009, http://www.sciencedaily.com/releases/2009/03/090305131814.htm (retrieved April 19, 2009); see also Kelly Gallagher, "Why I Will Not Teach to the Test: It's Time to Focus on In-Depth Learning, Not Shallow Answers," *Education Week* 30, no. 12 (November 17, 2010), pp. 29, 36.

42. Connie Langland, "Tests No Help to Learning," *Philadelphia Inquirer,* May 29, 2003.

43. James Hoffman, Assaf Czop, Lori Paris, and Scott Paris, "High-Stakes Testing in Reading: Today in Texas, Tomorrow?" *The Reading Teacher* 54, no. 5 (February 2001), pp. 482–492.

44. Alex Kingsbury, "Schools Cut Other Subjects to Teach Reading and Math," *U.S. News and World Report,* July 25, 2007, http://www.usnews.com/usnews/edu/articles/070725/25nclb.htm (retrieved April 19, 2009).

45. Fran Smith, "Why Arts Education Is Crucial and Who Is Doing It Best," *Edutopia,* February 18, 2009, http://www.edutopia.org/arts-music-curriculum-child-development; Stephanie Perrin, "Why Arts Education Matters," *Education Week* 27, no. 21 (January 30, 2008), pp. 26–27; Shirley Dang, "Schools Pile on English, Math Classes," *Contra Costa Times,* May 19, 2007.

46. Nancy Kober, "Teaching to the Test: The Good, the Bad, and Who's Responsible," *TestTalk for Leaders* (June 2002); Michele Kurtz and Anand Vaishnav, "Student's MCAS Answer Means 449 Others Pass," *Boston Globe,* December 5, 2002, p. A1.

47. Sam Dillon, "Before the Answer, the Question Must Be Correct," *New York Times,* July 16, 2003; Karen W. Arenson and Diana B. Henriques, "SAT Errors Raise New Questions about Testing," *New York Times,* March 10, 2006.

48. Diana B. Henriques and Jacques Steinberg, "Right Answer, Wrong Score: Test Flaws Take Toll," *New York Times on the Web,* May 20, 2001; Thomas M. Haladyna, "Perils of Standardized Achievement Testing," *Educational Horizons* 85, no. 1 (Fall 2006), pp. 30–43. See also the National Center for Fair and Open Testing, http://www.fairtest.org; Catherine Gewertz, "More Testing Seen for High School Students," *Education Week* 30, no. 15 (December 21, 2010).

49. Michele Kurtz, "Teachers' Views Mixed on Testing," *Boston Globe,* March 5, 2003, p. B5; Perrin, "Why Arts Education Matters"; Sarah M. Fine, "Consumed by Failure," *Education Week* 28, no. 25 (March 18, 2009), pp. 22–23.

50. Kathleen Kennedy Manzo, "Protests over State Testing Widespread," *Education Week on the Web,* May 16, 2001; Howard Blume, "L.A. Teachers' Union Calls for Boycott of Testing," Parajo Valley Federation of Teachers (January 18, 2009), http://www.pvft.net.

51. Abby Goodnough, "Strains of Fourth-Grade Tests Drive Off Veteran Teachers," *New York Times on the Web,* June 14, 2001; Liz Seymour, "SOL Tests Create New Dropouts," *Washington Post,* July 17, 2001, pp. A1, A8.

52. David Clouston, "1895 Saline County Exam Continues to Raise Interest," *Saline Journal,* February 2, 2008, http://www.saljournal.com/news/story/1895-Eighth-grade-test-SE1-0123082008-02-22T16-03-32 (retrieved January 10, 2009). The test can be retrieved at http://www.salina.com/www/1895test/test_1895.pdf.

53. Richard Elmore, "Testing Trap," adapted from *Education Next* 105 (September/October 2002), p. 35; Barbara Gleason, "ASCD Adopts Positions in High-Stakes Testing and the Achievement Gap," *ASCD Conference News,* March 20–22, 2004.

54. Grant Wiggins, "Healthier Testing Made Easier," EDU-TOPIQ George Lucas Educational Foundation, April 6, 2006, http://www.edutopia.org/magazine/.

55. Sonja Steptoe, "How Nebraska Leaves No Child Behind," *Time,* May 30, 2007; Winnie Hu, "Schools Move toward Following Students' Yearly Progress on Tests," *New York Times,* July 6, 2007, http://www.nytimes.com/2007/07/06/education/06test.html (retrieved May 21, 2008).

56. Theodore Sizer, *Horace's School: Redesigning the American High School* (New York: Houghton Mifflin, 1992).

57. Craig Timberg, "Bible's Second Coming," *Washington Post,* June 4, 2000, p. A1.

58. "Public School Drops Christian Textbooks," *Washington Post,* September 17, 1999, p. 2.

59. Mark Sappenfield and Mary Beth McCauley, "God or Science?" *Christian Science Monitor,* November 23, 2004; Lisa Anderson, "Darwin's Theory Evolves into Culture War Kansas Curriculum Is Focal Point of Wider Struggle Across Nation," *Chicago Tribune,* May 22, 2005, http://www.religionnewsblog.com/11267/darwins-theory-evolves-into-culture-war (retrieved March 5, 2008); Scott Stephens, "Panel OKs Disputed 10th-grade Biology Plan," *Cleveland Plain Dealer,* March 10, 2004, http://www.cleveland.com/debate/index.ssf?/debate/more/1078914742102330.html (retrieved July 18, 2007).

60. "Frank Newport "Four in 10 Americans Believe in Strict Creationism," December 17, 2010, http://www.gallup.com/poll/145286/Four-Americans-Believe-Strict-Creationism.aspx (retrieved January 12, 2011); "Why Evolution Is True," http://whyevolutionistrue.wordpress.com/2010/12/20/new-gallup-poll-america-still-creationist-surprise/ (retrieved January 16, 2007).

61. Steve Olson, "An Argument's Mutating Terms," *Washington Post,* March 20, 2005, p. B01.

62. David Van Biema, "The Case for Teaching the Bible," *Time,* March 22, 2007, http://www.time.com/time/magazine/article/0,9171,1601845,00.html; G. Jeffrey MacDonald, "Now Evolving in Biology Classes: A Testier Climate," *Christian Science Monitor,* May 3, 2005, http://www.csmonitor.com/2005/0503/p01s04-legn.html.

63. Liz Leyden, "Story Hour Didn't Have a Happy Ending," *Washington Post,* December 3, 1998, p. A3.

64. Michael Alison Chandler, "Two Guys and a Chick Set Off Tiff over School Library Policy," *Washington Post,* February 17, 2008, p. C06. For an extensive discussion on censorship and intellectual freedom, see the American Library Association at http://www.ala.org/ala/aboutala/offices/oif/bannedbooksweek/bbwlinks/fightcensorship.cfm.

65. American Library Association, "Frequently Challenged Books," http://www.ala.org/.

66. Ibid.

67. Ibid.

68. Chandler, "Two Guys and a Chick Set Off Tiff over School Library Policy."

69. Quoted in Lynne Cheney, *Humanities in America: A Report to the President, Congress and the American People* (Washington, DC: National Endowment for the Humanities, 1988), p. 17.

70. Allan Bloom, *The Closing of the American Mind* (New York: Simon & Schuster, 1987), p. 63.

71. E. D. Hirsch, Jr., *What Your First Grader Needs to Know and What Your Second Grader Needs to Know* (New York: Doubleday, 1991).

72. James Banks, "Multicultural Education: For Freedom's Sake," *Educational Leadership* 49, no. 4 (December 1991/January 1992), pp. 32–36.

73. Todd Oppenheimer, "The Computer Delusion," *Atlantic Monthly,* July 1997, pp. 45–48, 50–56, 61–62.

74. Andrew Trotter, "Major Study on Software Stirs Debate," *Education Week,* April 4, 2007; Greg Toppo, "Computers May Not Boost Student Achievement," *USA Today,* April 11, 2006; North Central Regional Educational Laboratory, *Critical Issue: Using Technology to Improve Student Achievement* (2005), http://www.ncrel.org/sdrs/areas/issues/methods/technlgy/te800.htm (retrieved April 17, 2008).

75. Andrew Trotter, "Major Study on Software Stirs Debate."

76. "The Effects of Computers on Student Writing: What the Research Tells Us," *ASCD SmartBrief* 1, no. 7 (April 1, 2003), http://www.ascd.org; Jennifer Lee, "Nu Shortcuts in School R 2 Much 4 Teachers," *New York Times,* September 19, 2002; Victoria Irwin, "Hop, Skip . . . and Software?" *Christian Science Monitor,* March 11, 2003.

77. Regan McMahon, "Everybody Does It," SFGate.com, September 9, 2007 (retrieved April 17, 2009); Don McCabe, "Levels of Cheating and Plagiarism Remain High," *Center for Academic Integrity* (June 2005), http://www.academicintegrity.org.

78. *Computer Technology in the Public School Classroom: Teacher Perspectives,* U.S. Department of Education, Institute of Educational Science, March 2005.

79. *Staying the Course: Online Education in the United States,* the Sloan Consortium, 2008; Public Act 123 and 124 of 2006, http://www.michigan.gov/documents/PA_123_and124_159920_7.pdf (retrieved July 8, 2009); John Watson, Butch Gemin, Jennifer Ryan, and Mathew Wicks, *Keeping Pace with K-12 Online Learning 2009,* http://www.inacol.org/research/docs/KeepingPace07color.pdf.

80. *Synthesis of New Research on K-12 Online Learning,* 2005, North Central Regional Education Laboratory/Learning Point Associates, http://www.ncrel.org/tech/synthesis/.

81. National Educational Technology Plan 2010, executive summary, http://www.ed.gov/sites/default/files/NETP-2010-exec-summary.pdf (retrieved September 2, 2010).

82. Larry Cuban, *Oversold and Underused: Computers in the Classroom* (Cambridge, MA: Harvard University Press, 2003).

83. Andrew Trotter, "Closing the Digital Divide," *Education Week* 20, no. 35 (2001), pp. 37–38, 40; Maisie McAdoo, "The Real Digital Divide: Quality Not Quantity," in David T. Gordon, ed., *The Digital Classroom* (Cambridge: Harvard College, 2000), pp. 143–151; U.S. Department of Education, National Center for Education Statistics, "Computers and Technology," *Digest of Educational Statistics, 2008,* Tables 427–432 (issued March 2009), http://nces.ed.gov.

84. Ellen McCarthy, "Where Girls and Tech Make a Match," *Washington Post,* March 20, 2003, p. E1; Trotter, "Closing the Digital Divide," pp. 37–38, 40; Andrew Trotter, "Minorities Still Face Digital Divide," *Education Week* 26, no. 3, (2006), p. 14.

85. U.S. Department of Education, National Center for Education Statistics, "Computers and Technology"; Chris Rother, "Teachers Talk Tech," *Technological Horizons in Education* 33, no. 3, (2005), pp. 34–36; Trotter, "Minorities Still Face Digital Divide," p. 14.

86. Glen Bull and Joe Garofalo, "Internet Access: The Last Mile," *Learning and Leading with Technology* 32, no. 1 (September 2004), pp. 16–18, 21.

87. Larry Cuban, *Growing Instructional Technology in U.S. Classrooms* (J. George Jones and Velma Rife Jones Lecture: University of Utah, Salt Lake City, 2005).

88. Tamar Lewin, "Children's Computer Use Grows, but Gaps Persist, Study Says," *New York Times,* January 22, 2001, p. A11.

89. Selma Wasserman, "Teaching for Thinking: Louis E. Raths Revisited," *Phi Delta Kappan* 68, no. 6 (February 1987), pp. 460–666; Valerie Strauss, "Relentless Questioning Paves a Deeper Path," *Washington Post,* February 18, 2008, p. B2.

90. J. Wink, *Critical Pedagogy: Notes from the Real World* (New York: Addison Wesley Longman, 1999), pp. 28–45.

91. Amy Green, "Push for Financial Literacy Spreads to Schools," *Christian Science Monitor,* March 9, 2009, http://www.csmonitor.com/2009/0309/p13s01-wmgn.html.

92. Scott Melville, "Implications of the Physical Educators' Wellness Role," *Journal of Physical Education, Recreation, and Dance* 80, no. 2 (February 2009), p. 58.

CHAPTER 11: BECOMING AN EFFECTIVE TEACHER

1. Among the resources on teacher effectiveness that you may want to consult are the *Journal of Teacher Education, Instructor,* and *Educational Leadership.*

2. N. Filby Fisher, E. Marleave, L. Cahen, M. Dishaw, M. Moore, and D. Berliner, *Teaching Behaviors, Academic Learning Time, and Student Achievement: Final Report of Beginning Teacher Evaluation Study* (San Francisco: Far West Laboratory, 1978).

3. John Goodlad, *A Place Called School,* 2nd ed. (New York: McGraw-Hill, 2004).

4. Robert Shostak, "Involving Students in Learning," in James M. Cooper, ed., *Classroom Teaching Skills,* 9th ed. (Belmont, CA: Cengage, 2011), pp. 82–106; Sam Intrator, "The Engaged Classroom," *Educational Leadership* 20, no. 1 (September 2004), pp. 20–25; Susan Black, "Time for Learning," *American School Board Journal* 189, no. 9 (September 2002), pp. 58, 60, 62; Chip Wood, "Changing the Pace of School: Slowing Down the Day to Improve the Quality of Learning," *Phi Delta Kappan* 83, no. 7 (March 2002), pp. 545–550; WestEd, "Making Time Count," *Policy Brief,* 2001, http://web.wested.org/online_pubs/making_time_count.pdf.

5. Robert Shostak, "Involving Students in Learning"; Marge Scherer, "Meeting Students Where They Are?" *Educational Leadership* 67, no. 5 (February 2010), p. 5; Intrator, "The Engaged Classroom"; Herbert Walberg, Richard Niemiec, and Wayne Frederick, "Productive Curriculum Time," *Peabody Journal of Education* 69, no. 3 (1994), pp. 86–100; Geoffrey Borman, "Academic Resilience in Mathematics Among Poor and Minority Students," *Elementary School Journal* 104, no. 3 (2004), pp. 177–195; WestEd, "Making Time Count."

6. Jacob Kounin, *Discipline and Group Management in Classrooms* (New York: Holt, Rinehart & Winston, 1970); Carol Weinstein and Andrew Migano, Jr., *Elementary Classroom Management,* 5th ed. (New York: McGraw-Hill, 2010).

7. Carol Weinstein and Wilford Weber, "Classroom Management," in Cooper, *Classroom Teaching Skills,* pp. 215–251; C. M. Evertson, E. T. Emmer, and M. E. Worsham, *Classroom Management for Elementary Teachers,* 8th ed. (Boston: Allyn & Bacon, 2008); see also Carolyn Evertson and Alene Harris, "What We Know About Managing Classrooms," *Educational Leadership* 49, no. 7 (April 1992), pp. 74–78.

8. Weinstein and Weber, "Classroom Management"; Robert Slavin, "Classroom Management and Discipline," in *Educational Psychology: Theory into Practice* (Englewood Cliffs, NJ: Prentice Hall, 1986); Vernon F. Jones and Louise S. Jones, *Comprehensive Classroom Management: Creating Communities of Support and Solving Problems,* 8th ed. (Boston, MA: Allyn & Bacon, 2007).

9. Weinstein and Weber, "Classroom Management"; Jane Nelson, Lynn Lott, and H. Stephen Glenn, *Positive Discipline in the Classroom: Developing Mutual Respect, Cooperation, and Responsibility in Your Classroom* (Roseville, CA: Prima, 2000).

10. Emmer, Evertson, and Worsham, *Classroom Management for Secondary Teachers.*

11. Thomas L. Good and Jere E. Brophy, *Looking in Classrooms,* 10th ed. (Boston: Allyn & Bacon, 2008).

12. Carol Frederick Steele, "Inspired Responses," *Educational Leadership* 68, no. 4 (December 2010/January 2011), pp. 64–68; Marilyn E. Gootman, *The Caring Teacher's Guide to Discipline: Helping Young Students Learn Self-Control, Responsibility, and Respect* (Thousand Oaks, CA: Corwin Press, 1997).

13. Kathleen Cushman, *Fires in the Mind* (New York: The New Press, 2010).

14. Steele, "Inspired Responses"; David Berliner, "What Do We Know About Well-Managed Classrooms? Putting Research to Work," *Instructor* 94, no. 6 (February 1985), p. 15; Carol Cummings, *Winning Strategies for Classroom Management* (Alexandria, VA: Association for Supervision and Curriculum Development, 2000).

15. Arno Bellack, *The Language of the Classroom* (New York: Teachers College Press, 1966).

16. Several of the sections on the pedagogical cycle are adopted from David Sadker, Myra Sadker, and Karen R. Zittleman, "Questioning Skills" in Cooper, *Classroom Teaching Skills,* pp. 107–152.

17. Donald Cruickshank, "Applying Research on Teacher Clarity," *Journal of Teacher Education* 36 (1985), pp. 44–48.

18. Sadker, Sadker, and Zittleman, "Questioning Skills"; P. Smagoinsky, "The Social Construction of Data: Methodological Problems of Investigation Learning in the Zone of Proximal Development," *Review of Educational Research* 65, no. 3 (1995), pp. 191–212.

19. John Dewey, *How We Think,* rev. ed. (Boston: D.C. Health, 1933), p. 266.

20. Myra Sadker and David Sadker, "Sexism in the Schoolroom of the '80s," *Psychology Today* 19 (March 1985), pp. 54–57.

21. Benjamin Bloom, ed., *Taxonomy of Educational Objectives, Handbook I: Cognitive Domain* (New York: David McKay, 1956); Lorin Anderson and David Krathwohl, *A Taxonomy for Learning, Teaching, and Assessing: A Revision of Bloom's Taxonomy of Educational Objectives* (Boston: Allyn & Bacon, 2000).

22. Sadker, Sadker, and Zittleman "Questioning Skills"; Arthur C. Grassier and Natalie K. Person, "Question Asking During Tutoring," *American Educational Research Journal* 31 (1994), pp. 104–137; William S. Carlsen, "Questioning in Classrooms: A Sociolinguistic Perspective," *Review of Educational Research* 61 (1991),

pp. 157–178; David Berliner, "The Half-Full Glass: A Review of Research on Teaching," in Philip L. Hosford, ed., *Using What We Know About Teaching,* pp. 51–84; L. M. Barden, "Effective Questions and the Ever-Elusive Higher-Order Question," *American Biology Teacher* 57, no. 7 (1995), pp. 423–426; Meredith D. Gall and T. Rhody, "Review of Research on Questioning Techniques," in William W. Wilen, ed., *Questions, Questioning Techniques, and Effective Teaching* (Washington, DC: National Education Association, 1987), pp. 23–48.

23. Adapted from Sadker, Sadker, and Zittleman, "Questioning Skills."

24. Mary Budd Rowe, "Wait Time: Slowing Down May Be a Way of Speeding Up!" *Journal of Teacher Education* 37 (January/February 1986), pp. 43–50; Mary Budd Rowe, "Science, Silence, and Sanctions," *Science and Children* 34 (September 1996), pp. 35–37; Sadker, Sadker, and Zittleman, "Questioning Skills."

25. Myra Sadker, David Sadker, and Susan Klein, "The Issue of Gender in Elementary and Secondary Education," *Review of Research in Education* 17 (1991), pp. 269–334.

26. Goodlad, *A Place Called School.*

27. Intrator, "The Engaged Classroom"; Martha McCarthy, *High School Survey of Student Engagement* (Bloomington: University of Indiana Press, 2005).

28. Thomas L. Good and Jere E. Brophy, *Looking in Classrooms,* 10th ed. (Boston: Allyn & Bacon, 2008); Jere E. Brophy, "Teacher Praise: A Functional Analysis," *Review of Educational Research* 51 (1981), pp. 5–32; Dan Laitsch, "Student Behaviors and Teacher Use of Approval versus Disapproval," *ASCD Research Brief* 4, no. 3 (March 27, 2006), http://www.ascd.org.

29. Judy Willis, "The Neuroscience of Joyful Education," *Educational Leadership* 4, no. 9 (Summer 2007); Intrator, "The Engaged Classroom."

30. Metropolitan Life, *The American Teacher* (New York: Metropolitan Life Company, 2001), pp. 13–15; Willis, "The Neuroscience of Joyful Education."

31. "Technology Counts 2009: Breaking Away from Tradition: E-Education Expands Opportunities for Raising Achievement," *Education Week* 28, no. 26 (March 26, 2009).

32. Margaret Roblyer, *Integrating Educational Technology into Teaching,* 5th ed. (Boston, MA: Allyn & Bacon, 2009).

33. George Brackett, "Technologies Don't Change Schools—Caring, Capable People Do," in David T. Gordon, ed., *The Digital Classroom* (Cambridge: Harvard College, 2000), pp. 29–30.

34. Cathy Watkins and Timothy Slocum, "The Components of Direct Instruction," in Nancy E. Marchand-Martella, Timothy A. Slocum, and Ronald Martella, eds., *Introduction to Direct Instruction* (Boston: Allyn & Bacon, 2004), pp. 28–65; Gary R. Morrions, *Designing Effective Instruction,* 6th ed. (Hobokon, NJ: Wiley, 2010); Bruce R. Joyce and Emily F. Calhoun, *Learning Experiences: The Role of Instructional Theory and Research* (Alexandria, VA: Association for Curriculum and Supervision, 1996); Barak Rosenshine, "Synthesis of Research on Explicit

Teaching," *Educational Leadership* 43, no. 4 (May 1986), pp. 60–69.

35. Mary Leighton, "Cooperative Learning," in Cooper, *Classroom Teaching Skills,* pp. 252–295; R. Bruce Williams, *Cooperative Learning: A Standard for High Achievement* (Thousand Oaks, CA: Corwin Press, 2007); Robyn M. Gilles, *Cooperative Learning: Integrating Theory into Practice* (Thousand Oaks, CA: Sage Publications, 2007); David Johnson and Roger Johnson, *Learning Together and Alone: Cooperative, Competitive, and Individualistic Learning,* 5th ed. (Boston: Allyn & Bacon, 1999).

36. Williams, *Cooperative Learning: A Standard for High Achievement*; Gilles, *Cooperative Learning: Integrating Theory into Practice*; Robert E. Slavin, "Cooperative Learning in Middle and Secondary Schools," *Clearinghouse* 69, no. 4 (March–April 1996), pp. 200–204.

37. Leighton, "Cooperative Learning,"; Williams, *Cooperative Learning: A Standard for High Achievement*; Gilles, *Cooperative Learning: Integrating Theory into Practice*; Robert E. Slavin, *Cooperative Learning: Theory, Research, and Practice* (Boston: Allyn & Bacon, 1995).

38. Jay Matthews, "Students Move at Own Pace Toward Proficiency," *Washington Post,* June 13, 2006, p. A8.

39. Glenn Hymel, "Harnessing the Mastery Learning Literature: Past Efforts, Current Status, and Future Directions," paper presented at the annual meeting of the American Educational Research Association, Boston, MA, 1990; Ronald Gentile and J. P. Lalley, *Standards and Mastery Learning: Aligning Teaching and Assessment so All Children Can Learn* (Thousand Oaks, CA: Corwin, 2003); J. Ronald Gentile, "Assessing Fundamentals in Every Course through Mastery Learning," *New Directions in Teaching and Learning* 100 (December 2004), pp. 15–20; Jenifer M. Fox, *Your Child's Strengths: Discover Them, Develop Them, Use Them* (Toronto: Penguin Group, 2008).

40. Diane Curtis, "The Power of Projects," *Educational Leadership* 60, no. 1 (September 2002), pp. 50–53; John Barell, *Problem-Based Learning: An Inquiry Approach,* 2nd ed. (Thousand Oaks, CA: Sage Publications, 2006); Diane Ronis, *Problem-Based Learning for Math and Science,* 2nd ed. (Thousand Oaks, CA: Sage Publications, 2008); Vicki Shuster, "Camelot Teachers, Staff, Implement New Learning Techniques," *Brookings Register Online* (February 23, 2010).

41. Anthony Rebora, "Making a Difference: Carol Ann Tomlinson Explains How Differentiated Instruction Works and Why We Need It Now," *Teacher Magazine* 2, no. 1 (September 10, 2008), pp. 26, 28–31.

42. Ibid., p. 28.

43. Carol Ann Tomlinson, "Differentiated Instruction for Academic Diversity," in Cooper, *Classroom Teaching Skills,* pp. 153–187.

44. Kenneth Leithwood, *Teaching for Deep Understanding: What Every Educator Should Know,* (Thousand Oaks, CA: Corwin Press, 2006); Jay McTighe, Elliott Seif, and Grant Wiggins, "You Can Teach for Meaning," *Educational Leadership* 62, no. 1 (September 2004), pp. 26–30.

45. Jonathan Supovitz and Jolley Bruce Christman, "Small Learning Communities that Actually Learn: Lessons for School Leaders," *Phi Delta Kappan* 86, no. 9 (May 2005), pp. 649–651; Robert Blum, "A Case for Connectedness," *Educational Leadership* 62, no. 7 (April 2005), pp. 16–20.

46. James Cooper, "The Effective Teacher," in Cooper, *Classroom Teaching Skills*, pp. 1–20; Melody J. Shank, "Common Space, Common Time, Common Work," *Educational Leadership* 62, no. 8 (May 2005), pp. 16–19; John Ward and Suzanne McCotter, "Reflection as a Visible Outcome for Preservice Teachers," *Teaching and Teacher Education* 20, no. 3 (April 2004), pp. 243–258; Carol Rodgers, "Seeing Student Learning: Teacher Changes and the Role of Reflection," *Harvard Educational Review* 72 (2002), pp. 230–253.

47. Lilian Katz, "The Development of Preschool Teachers," *Elementary School Journal* 73, no. 1 (October 1972), pp. 50–54; John L. Watzke, "Longitudinal Study of Stages of Beginning Teacher Development in a Field-Based Teacher Education Program," *Teacher Educator* 38, no. 3 (Winter 2003), pp. 209–229.

48. Linda Darling-Hammond, "Keeping Good Teachers: Why It Matters, What Leaders Can Do," *Educational Leadership,* May 2003, pp. 6–13; Linda Darling-Hammond and John Bransford, eds., *Preparing Teachers for a Changing World: What Teachers Should Learn and Be Able to Do* (San Francisco: Jossey Bass, 2007).

49. Harry Wong, "Induction Programs that Keep New Teachers Improving and Growing," *NASSP Bulletin* 88, no. 638 (March 2004); Andrew J. Wayne, Peter Youngs, and Steve Fleischman, "Improving Teacher Induction," *Educational Leadership* 62, no. 8 (May 2005), pp. 76–77; Mary C. Clement, "My Mother's Teaching Career—What It Can Tell Us about Teachers Who Are Not Certified," *Phi Delta Kappan* 87, no. 10 (June 2006), pp. 772–776.

50. Donna Niday, Jean Boreen, Joe Potts, and Mary K. Johnson, *Mentoring Beginning Teachers: Guiding, Reflecting, Coaching,* 2nd ed. (Portland, ME: Stenhouse Publishers, 2009); Hal Portner, *Mentoring New Teachers,* 3rd ed. (Thousand Oaks, CA: Corwin Press, 2008).

CREDITS

Text Credits

CHAPTER 1

Fig. 1.2: From *Teachers, Schools and Society,* 9th Edition by David M. Sadker, et al. Copyright © 2010 The McGraw-Hill Companies, Inc. Reprinted by permission of The McGraw-Hill Companies, Inc. **p. 15:** "What Teachers Should Know and Be Able to Do" from *Five Core Propositions* reprinted with permission from the National Board for Professional Teaching Standards, www.nbpts.org. All rights reserved.**Fig. 1.3:** From *The 2006 Lemelson-MIT Invention Index*, http://mit.edu/invent/n-pressreleases/n-press-06index.html. Used with permission.

CHAPTER 2

Fig. 2.3: Adapted from Heward, William L., *Exceptional Children: An Introduction to Special Education*, 8th Edition, Copyright © 2006. Reproduced by permission of Pearson Education, Inc., Upper Saddle River, New Jersey.

CHAPTER 3

Fig. 3.3: From U.S. English, Inc. (2002). Reprinted with permission. **Fig. 3.4:** Banks, James A. "Levels of Integration of Ethnic Content" from *Teaching Strategies for Ethnic Studies, 8th Edition* by James A. Banks. (Boston: Allyn & Bacon, 2009) p.19. Reprinted with permission of James A. Banks.
pp. 95–96: "I, Too, Am an American," reprinted courtesy of Lacey Rosenbaum. **p. 96:** "I, Too, Am an Original American," reprinted by permission of Mandie Rainwater.

CHAPTER 4

pp. 110–111:"Letter to The Arlington school newspaper". Reprinted with permission.

CHAPTER 7

p. 214: Excerpts from http://www.adoptaclassroom.com. Reprinted with permission. **Fig. 7.5:**"Salaries and Wages for Professional and Support Personnel in Public Schools" used by permission of Educational Research Service.

CHAPTER 10

Fig. 10.2: From Association of American Publishers web site, http://www.publishers.org/school/schoolarticle.cfm?SchoolArticleID=32. Reprinted with permission from the Association of American Publishers. **Fig. 10.3:** From the collection of Tirupalavanam G. Ganesh (2002), "Educators = images of high-stakes testing: An exploratory analysis of the value of visual methods."Paper presented at the Annual Meeting of the American Educational Research Association, April 1–5, 2002, New Orleans, LA. Reprinted by permission.

APPENDIX

PRAXIS materials from The Praxis Series: Test at a Glance—Principles of Learning and Teaching: Grades 7-12. Reprinted by permission of Educational Testing Service. Permission to reprint PRAXIS materials does not constitute review or endorsement by Educational Testing Service of this publication as a whole or of any other testing information it may contain.TRADEMARK NOTICE: ETS(R), PRAXIS™, PRAXIS I™, PRAXIS II™, PRAXIS III™, and THE PRAXIS SERIES™, are registered trademarks of Educational Testing Service (ETS). This publication is not endorsed or approved by ETS.

Photo Credits

CHAPTER 1

p. 1: Big Cheese Photo/age fotostock; p. 3: Comstock/PictureQuest; p. 10: Bonnie Kamin Photography; p. 12: Library of Congress Prints and Photographs; p. 16: BananaStock/age fotostock; p. 17: Dynamic Graphics/Jupiter Images; p. 19: Heather Harris; p. 21: AP Wide World Photo/Marcio Jose Sanchez.

CHAPTER 2

p. 31: Superstock; p. 34: Photodisc/Getty Images; p. 37: Mary Kate Denny; p. 40: BananaStock/Punchstock; p. 49: Courtesy of Sally Smith; p. 50: Photodisc/Getty Images; p. 55: Bob Daemmrich/PhotoEdit Inc.

CHAPTER 3

p. 60: Comstock Images/PictureQuest; p. 64: Robin Samper Image Services; p. 71: Thinkstock/PictureQuest; p. 72: Woodfin Camp/Woodfin Camp & Associates; p. 73: Florida State Archives; p. 86t: Charles Gupton Photography; p. 86b: Erin Patrice O'Brien/Getty Images Inc.; p. 87: Comstock/PictureQuest; p. 88t: Dynamic Graphics Group/Creatas/Alamy; p. 88b: Michael Newman/PhotoEdit; p. 89t: David Young-Wolff/PhotoEdit; p. 89b: Bruce Ando/Index Stock Imagery; p. 90t: David Young-Wolff/PhotoEdit; p. 90b: Digital Vision/PunchStock.

CHAPTER 4

p. 99: Photodisc/Getty Images; p. 103: Ellen B. Senisi/The Image Works Inc.; p. 106: Jeannie Oakes/UCLA/GSE; p. 107: Image 100; p. 110: BananaStock/Punch-Stock; p. 114: Digital Vision/Getty Images Inc.; p. 128: Aude GUERRUCCI/AFP/Getty Images.

CHAPTER 5

p. 135: Dorothea Lange/Library of Congress; p. 137: Culver Pictures; p. 139: BananaStock/AGE Fotostock; p. 140: Bettmann/Corbis; p. 154: Library of Congress; p. 155: AP Wide World Photos; p. 156: Time Life Pictures/Getty Images Inc.; p. 159: Bonnie Kamin/PhotoEdit; p. 164: Brown Brothers; p. 168t: New York Public Library Picture Collection; p. 168b: AP Wide World Photos; p. 169: Syndicated Features Limited/The Image Works; p. 170t: Bettmann/Corbis; p. 170b: Wallace Britton/Black Star; p. 171: Raimondo Borea & Associates; p. 172: Jeremy Bigwood; p.173 top to bottom: (Comenius) Stock Montage; p. 173: (Rousseau) Culver Pictures; p. 173: (Pestalozzi) Johann Heinrich Pestalozzi © New York Public Picture Library Collection; p. 173: (Herbart) New York Public Library Picture Collection; p. 173: (Willard) Culver Pictures; p. 173: (Mann) Culver Pictures; p. 173: (Dewey) Bettmann/Corbis; p. 173: (Piaget) Bettmann/Corbis; p. 173: (Skinner) Katherine Bendo, NYC.

CHAPTER 6

p. 178: Royalty Free/Corbis; p. 185: Ariel Skelley/Corbis; p. 187: Michael Newman/PhotoEdit Inc.; p. 191: Andy Sacks/Getty Images Inc.; 192: Kevin Radford/SuperStock; p. 193: Courtesy of Jane Roland Martin; p. 198 left top to bottom: (Bagley) Columbia University Teacher's College; p. 198: (Hutchins)University of Chicago-News & Information Office; p. 198: (Dewey) Special Collections, Morris Library, Southern Illinois University, Carbondale, IL/Morris Library Special Collections; P. 198: (Counts) AP Wide World Photos; p. 198: (Neill)Courtesy of A.S. Neill; P. 198 right from top to Bottom: (Hirsch) The Core Knowledge Foundation; p. 198: (Adler) Bettmann/Corbis; p. 198: (Noddings) Nel Noddings; p. 198: (Hooks) John Pinderhughes; p. 198: (Greene) Special Collections, Milbank Memorial Library, Teachers College/Columbia University.

CHAPTER 7

p. 211: Comstock/PictureQuest; p. 213: Bob Daemmrich/The Image Works; p. 215: AP Wide World Photos; p. 222: Quittani Producciones/Getty Images Inc.; 224: Tim Boyle/Getty Images Inc.; p. 227: Yvonne Hemsey/Liason/Getty Images; p. 236: Jacobs Stock Photography/BananaStock/Jupiter Images/Getty Images Inc.; p. 237t: AP Wide World Photos; p. 237b: Ingram Publishing.

CHAPTER 8

p. 241: Spencer Platt/Getty Images Inc.; p. 246: Creatas/Jupiter Images; p. 248: Bob Daemmrich Photography/The Image Works; p. 251: R. Holz/Zefa/Corbis; p. 255: AP Wide World Photos; p. 257: Acey Harper/TimePix/Getty Images Inc.

CHAPTER 9

p. 275: Photo by Linda Davidson/ The Washington Post via Getty Images; p. 279: Tony Freeman/PhotoEdit Inc.; p. 284: Digital Stock/Corbis; p. 293t: James Wilson/ Woodfin Camp & Associates; p. 293b: Rick Gomez/Corbis; p. 297 both: Courtesy of Al Herbel; p. 302: Courtesy of Dr. Michael Wesch and the Digital Ethnography Working Group, Kansas State University; p. 305t: Photodisc/Punchstock; p. 305b: Photodisc/Getty Images.

CHAPTER 10

p. 314: Ingram Publishing; p. 319l: Brand X Pictures/Getty Images Inc.; p. 319r: Image Source/Punchstock; p. 329: David M. Jennings/The Image Works; p. 332: Published with the permission pf Globe Newspaper company Inc/The Boston Globe; p. 336: Alfie Kohn; p. 340: Todd R. McQueen; p. 345: PunchStock.

CHAPTER 11

p. 355: BananaStock/Picture Quest; p. 358: Corbis RF; p. 363: BananaStock/age fotostock; p. 371: Stanford University; p. 375: Blend Images/Getty Images; p. 379: Royalty-Free/Corbis; p. 380: Royalty-Free/Corbis.

INDEX